CONSTITUTIONAL TRIUMPHS, CONSTITUTIONAL DISAPPOINTMENTS

The 1996 South African Constitution was promulgated on December 18, 1996 and came into effect on February 4, 1997. Its aspirational provisions promised to transform South Africa's economy and society along non-racial and egalitarian lines. Following the twentieth anniversary of its enactment, this book co-edited by Rosalind Dixon and Theunis Roux examines the triumphs and disappointments of the Constitution. It explains the arguments in favor of the Constitution's being replaced with a more authentically African document, untainted by the necessity to compromise with ruling interests predominant at the end of apartheid. Others believe it remains a landmark attempt to create a society based on social, economic, and political rights for all citizens, and that its true implementation has yet to be achieved. This book considers whether the problems South Africa now faces are of Constitutional design or implementation, and analyzes the Constitution's external influence on constitutionalism in other parts of the world.

Rosalind Dixon is Professor of Law at University of New South Wales, Sydney, and co-president of the International Society of Public Law. Dixon's research focuses on a broad range of comparative constitutional law topics, including questions of constitutional design, amendment, socio-economic rights, law and gender, and constitutional courts and judicial review. Dixon was born in South Africa, and has written extensively about the South African Constitution.

Theunis Roux is Professor of Law at University of New South Wales, Sydney. Before moving to Australia in 2009, he was the founding director of the South African Institute of Advanced Constitutional, Public, Human Rights and International Law and Secretary General of the International Association of Constitutional Law. His book on the first South African Constitutional Court was published by Cambridge University Press in 2013. His current research interest is comparative historical analysis of the evolution of judicial review regimes – clusters of legitimating ideas about the law/politics relationship in societies that have adopted a system of judicial review.

Constitutional Triumphs, Constitutional Disappointments

A CRITICAL ASSESSMENT OF THE 1996 SOUTH AFRICAN CONSTITUTION'S LOCAL AND INTERNATIONAL INFLUENCE

Edited by

ROSALIND DIXON
University of New South Wales

THEUNIS ROUX
University of New South Wales

CAMBRIDGE
UNIVERSITY PRESS

CAMBRIDGE
UNIVERSITY PRESS

University Printing House, Cambridge CB2 8BS, United Kingdom

One Liberty Plaza, 20th Floor, New York, NY 10006, USA

477 Williamstown Road, Port Melbourne, VIC 3207, Australia

314-321, 3rd Floor, Plot 3, Splendor Forum, Jasola District Centre, New Delhi - 110025, India

79 Anson Road, #06-04/06, Singapore 079906

Cambridge University Press is part of the University of Cambridge.

It furthers the University's mission by disseminating knowledge in the pursuit of education, learning and research at the highest international levels of excellence.

www.cambridge.org
Information on this title: www.cambridge.org/9781108401180
DOI: 10.1017/9781108233231

First published 2018
First paperback edition 2019

A catalogue record for this publication is available from the British Library

Library of Congress Cataloging in Publication data
Names: Dixon, Rosalind, editor. | Roux, Theunis, editor.
Title: Constitutional triumphs, constitutional disappointments : a critical assessment of the 1996 South African Constitution's local and international influence / edited by Rosalind Dixon, Theunis Roux.
Description: Cambridge [UK] ; New York, NY : Cambridge University Press, 2018. | Includes bibliographical references and index.
Identifiers: LCCN 2017059345 | ISBN 9781108415330 (hardback)
Subjects: LCSH: South Africa. Constitution of the Republic of South Africa, 1996. | Constitutional law—South Africa. | Equality before the law—South Africa. | Civil rights—South Africa. | South Africa—Economic policy. | South Africa—Politics and government.
Classification: LCC KTL2064.51996 .D59 2018 | DDC 342.68—dc23 LC record available at https://lccn.loc.gov/2017059345

ISBN 978-1-108-41533-0 Hardback
ISBN 978-1-108-40118-0 Paperback

Contents

Contributors

Penelope Andrews
Professor and Dean, Faculty of Law, University of Cape Town

David Bilchitz
Professor, Faculty of Law, University of Johannesburg; Director, South African Institute for Advanced Constitutional, Public, Human Rights and International Law; Secretary-General, International Association of Constitutional Law

Jill Cottrell Ghai
Katiba Institute, Kenya

Joel Colón-Ríos
Senior Lecturer, Faculty of Law, Victoria University of Wellington

Rosalind Dixon
Professor, Faculty of Law, University of New South Wales

Andrea Durbach
Professor and Director, Australian Human Rights Centre, Faculty of Law, University of New South Wales

Charles Fombad
Professor of Law and Head of the Constitutional Law Unit, Institute for International and Comparative Law in Africa, Faculty of Law, University of Pretoria

Steven Friedman
Research Professor, Faculty of Humanities, University of Johannesburg

Yash Ghai
Emeritus Professor, Faculty of Law, University of Hong Kong; Katiba Institute, Kenya

Beth Goldblatt
Associate Professor, Faculty of Law, University of Technology Sydney; Visiting Fellow, Faculty of Law, University of New South Wales; Visiting Associate Professor, School of Law, University of the Witwatersrand

Aziz Z. Huq
Professor, University of Chicago Law School

Coel Kirkby
Smuts Visiting Fellow in Commonwealth Studies at the University of Cambridge

Heinz Klug
Evjue-Bascom Professor in Law, University of Wisconsin; Honorary Senior Research Fellow, University of the Witwatersrand

David Landau
Mason Ladd Professor and Associate Dean for International Programs, College of Law, Florida State University

Catherine O'Regan
Former Judge of the Constitutional Court of South Africa; Director of the Bonavero Institute of Human Rights, Faculty of Law, University of Oxford

Theunis Roux
Professor, Faculty of Law, University of New South Wales

Richard Stacey
Assistant Professor, Faculty of Law, University of Toronto

Julie C. Suk
Professor, Benjamin N. Cardozo School of Law, Yeshiva University

Foreword

That the South African Constitution is a compromise document located within the context of the triumphalist ascendancy of a global liberal legal ideology at the end of the twentieth century does not detract from its transformative potential. To discount this possibility and what it has meant for South Africans is almost to ignore the potency of rights and dignity.

Penelope Andrews (Chapter 9, p. 246)

These words from Penelope Andrews' contribution to the collection that follows are ones that sound, to my ear, a keynote for the whole. Dean Andrews' clear-eyed placement of the Constitution in suspense between the ideological and the universal, combined with her refusal even then to let go the liberal hope of transformation-through-constitution, are hallmarks, as I see them, of this book.

A "constitution," as that term figures throughout the collection, is a *basic, legal, scriptural* production. "Scripture" means the constitution is a publicly identified corpus of canonically worded prescriptive sentences, laid down in advance and fixed until duly amended. "Legal" means these sentences carry the status and force of law within an institutional complex where specialized authorities decide on questions of application and compliance and hand out declarative and other sanctions for noncompliance. "Basic" means these scriptural legal sentences set institutional and procedural protocols and conditions for the generation and validity of any further law for the country whose constitution they compose, and for the conduct of legal administration therein.

Now, it is not strictly necessary that any society at any time has in place a "constitution" of the basic legal scriptural type. Modes of social ordering we call customary, which apparently can succeed under favorable conditions, do not. The idea of any well-ordered society's need for a basic legal scripture, upon which to found and conduct a lawful and regular process of government, is not itself a human universal but rather belongs to an historically particular body of ideas, that of modern liberal constitutionalism. Every reference in this book to South Africa's "Constitution" enters into that tradition, at least to the point of assuming a space in that country's affairs for a basic legal scripture and perceiving the Constitution in the light of a text designed to fill that space.

There can be no doubting the accuracy or aptness of that perception. It was perhaps overdetermined, by sundry causes, that South Africa should have put into place a constitution of that type at the time of transition away from the apartheid regime. First, the old order had had in force its own basic-legal-scriptural constitution, and any effective displacement of that order by a successor may have seemed more or less inevitably to involve a displacement and replacement of *its* constitution by a new one. Second, aims for a mainly peaceful succession of regimes required some space or platform for a negotiation of terms, which a constitution of that type would have seemed perfectly designed to supply. Third, the transition took place within that very ascendancy of liberal legal ideology to which Dean Andrews adverts, at a historical high-water moment of widespread enthusiasm for (these words from the editors) "liberal constitutionalism as the internationally preferred political system," and of course the leaders of the transition could not have proceeded without due regard to the opinions of mankind.

Fourth, it seems that prevailing forces within the ANC itself may have formed (as suggested below by Jill Cottrell Ghai and Yash Ghai) their own considered, value-based preference for a "liberal-democratic constitution." But then please note that "liberal-democratic" carries us beyond the broad idea of a government chartered by a scriptural basic law. That term takes us into the more detailed structural space of institutional checks and balances, and furthermore into the substantive-value space – as the new South African Constitution announces right off the bat – of the redemption of human dignity, "the achievement of equality," "non-racialism," "non-sexism," and in general "the advancement of human rights and freedoms." However notably "post"-liberal and transformative the South African instrument doubtless also is, that instrument is instantly and easily – and very noticeably so by the authors here – placed safely within bounds of the broadly speaking liberal tradition of constitutional democracy.

Expressly or tacitly, every contributing author to this book accepts and embraces this very salient fact about the Constitution of the Republic of

South Africa 1996. None shows inclination to regard it as possibly a historic misstep for the country. Elsewhere one reads doubts or denials that any possible practice of liberal constitutionalism, no matter how relatively or professedly left-leaning, could possibly have led a country under the conditions of South Africa toward the transformative ends declared by the South African version. Sceptics worry that transformative ends are already at the start defeated by a constitutionalistic instinct to limit and contain – as opposed to empower and obligate – the state; or that they are blocked by a liberal priority to insulate from social responsibility a "private sphere," or a liberal propensity to fall back on proceduralistic (hence inevitably compromised) responses to intractable social conflicts; or that an African cultural *milieu* is out of joint with liberal elevations of subjective entitlement over associative obligation and of contestation over consensus as the medium of joint decision, or even with the very notion of a "law" distinct from other social norms and segregated therefrom into specialized institutional authorities and discourses.

Some of the work here reports with concern such dim views of the prospects in South Africa for what the editors call a "constitutionally led" transformation of society. None that I could see finally buys into them. Taken as a group or taken one by one, these chapters report a mix of achievements and shortfalls, and so also a mix of signs both attractive and aversive for onlookers in countries seeking to learn from South African trailblazing. The lesson-topics range through stages of a constitution's life history, from the processes of its birthing, to its main structural components, to the wordings of its clauses, to the applicative works of courts engaged in value-filling, doctrinal construction on the footprint laid by the text, to the manner of engagement with the constitution by state officials and agencies, and the responses of civil-society actors, educators, and sectors of the populace at large.

The proportions of commendation and critique vary from chapter to chapter, but they all, so far as one can read, share with Justice O'Regan a reluctance to conclude that grievous shortfalls in achievement to date of the Constitution's social-transformative aims are rightly attributable to the "constitutional framework" itself. Rather, these papers conduct their critical appraisals against – as the editors say – the backdrop of a "universal" set of "understandings of a constitution's role in promoting democracy, the rule of law, and substantive equality, security, and freedom for all citizens." The authors engage in a kind mid-course stock-taking, in a search they all apparently continue to support, for apt and workable specifications, in South African conditions, of that set of understandings. They look for corrections of course accomplishable within the bounds of the broadly liberal constitutionalist idea and without upsetting the South African transformative constitutional applecart. So far as appears in these pages, their faith remains (I draw here on again on words of Penelope Andrews with which I began) in the transformative potential of a pursuit of "rights and dignity" by the means of law, which the Constitution, under stress, continues in their view – and in mine – to represent.

Professor Frank I. Michelman
Robert Walmsley University Professor
Emeritus at Harvard Law School

1

Introduction

Rosalind Dixon and Theunis Roux

The 1990s were a time of great global optimism about the possibilities of constitutionally limited democratic government. The dominant belief among Western commentators at the time was that the end of the Cold War presented a unique opportunity to entrench liberal constitutionalism as the internationally preferred political system. By learning from past experience, it was thought, constitutions could be designed not only to persuade reluctant authoritarian rulers to hand over power, but also to institutionalize democratic government in the countries concerned. If the 1990s represented the high point of the third wave of democracy, liberal constitutionalism was seen as its principal vehicle.[1]

The 1996 South African Constitution was in many ways at the center of this enterprise. Following the contribution made by South Africa's liberation struggle to the global human rights movement, there was extensive international involvement in the drafting and conceptualization of the constitutional text.[2] On its enactment, the Constitution was hailed as a remarkable document, with numerous state-of-the-art provisions. While addressed to the uniquely South African situation, the Constitution was also looked on as an experiment of sorts in translating lessons learned from past experience, through the medium of constitutional design, into social and political practice. The African National Congress (ANC), with its proud tradition of democratic

[1] On the wave of liberal-democratic constitution-making after the end of the Cold War and the optimism attached to constitutional courts as democratic stabilizers, see S. Issacharoff, *Fragile Democracies: Contested Power in the Era of Constitutional Courts* (Cambridge: Cambridge University Press, 2015).

[2] The seminal study of this phenomenon remains H. Klug, *Constituting Democracy: Law, Globalism and South Africa's Political Reconstruction* (Cambridge: Cambridge University Press, 2000).

struggle and stated commitment to human rights,[3] was seen as the ideal custodian of this project. The Constitutional Court in turn, with its widely admired judges, seemed ideally placed to breathe life into the constitutional text and in so doing contribute to international understanding of the transformative possibilities of judicially enforced constitutional rights.

Twenty years later, many of these hopes have been realized, but others have not. The Constitutional Court, for its part, has arguably surpassed expectations. Its decisions on the right to housing,[4] same-sex marriage,[5] and HIV/AIDS treatment[6] have demonstrated how a sympathetic group of judges, backed by a well-crafted constitution, can assist civil society groups in driving meaningful social change, even in the face of a reluctant ruling elite. At the same time, the 1996 Constitution has served as a model for constitutional revival on the African continent and beyond. In countries as diverse as Kenya, Tunisia, and Nepal, there has been a renewed commitment to constitutionalism, in part because of the demonstration effect of the South African experience.

The picture is not uniformly rosy, however. To the extent that poverty, gender violence, and political corruption remain deeply entrenched, the South African experience also points to the limits of judicially enforced constitutional rights. While a peaceful fifth democratic election has been held, significant problems of corruption and clientelism have emerged.[7] Within South Africa, the Constitutional Court has been criticized for failing to do enough to realize the transformative possibilities of the 1996 Constitution.[8] A separate line of criticism concerns the Court's democratic rights jurisprudence, and its alleged failure to check the pathologies attendant on the ANC's political

[3] On the ANC's human rights tradition, see T. Roux, *The Politics of Principle: The First South African Constitutional Court, 1995–2005* (Cambridge: Cambridge University Press, 2013) 152–61. For a more pessimistic account of the ANC's paradoxical emancipatory and authoritarian tendencies, see R. Southall, *Liberation Movements in Power: Party and State in Southern Africa* (Woodbridge: James Currey, 2013).

[4] *Government of the Republic of South Africa* v. *Grootboom* (2001) 1 SA 46 (CC) (*Grootboom*).

[5] *Minister of Home Affairs* v. *Fourie* (2006) 1 SA 524 (CC).

[6] *Minister of Health* v. *Treatment Action Campaign (No 2)* (2002) 5 SA 721 (CC).

[7] For an early study of the link between corruption and democratization, see T. Lodge, "Political corruption in South Africa" (1998) 97 *African Affairs* 157. For a coruscating account of the present situation, see R. W. Johnson, *How Long Will South Africa Survive? The Crisis Continues* (Johannesburg: Jonathan Ball, 2015).

[8] The seminal text here is K. E. Klare, "Legal culture and transformative constitutionalism" (1998) 12 *South African Journal on Human Rights* 146–88. For an updated version of the same critique, see D. M. Davis and K. E. Klare, "Transformative constitutionalism and the common and customary law" (2010) 26 *South African Journal on Human Rights* 403–509.

dominance.[9] While the Court could not have been expected to build a thriving multi-party democracy all on its own, it might have done more, the argument goes, to open out South Africa's democracy to greater political competition.

All of this makes it an opportune time to reflect on South Africa's post-1996 constitutionalist experience and the lessons it has to teach. According to Zachary Elkins and his coauthors, the average lifespan of a constitution is roughly nineteen years.[10] This, as Justice O'Regan notes in Chapter 2, also makes the twenty-year mark of a constitution a natural time to reflect on its achievements, and limitations: if it has endured, this fact itself may be considered a mark of relative success. Yet the degree to which it has endured in substance, or realized its substantive goals, remains open to evaluation. Two decades, one might also suggest, is roughly the minimum time necessary to assess substantive compliance or implementation of this kind. What, then at the local level, are some of the explanations for South Africa's successes and failures? To the extent that the 1996 Constitution has not delivered on its promises, how much of this is down to constitutional-design features and how much to the way the Constitution has been used, both by the judiciary and by civil society groups? And what, reflecting on these issues, does the South African experience have to teach about what liberal constitutionalism has to offer in the current global climate? For democrats in other countries, is the central lesson that constitutionally led social change is powerless in the face of larger global forces? Or is it that concessions made to drive democratization forward in the course of constitutional negotiations exact a heavy price on social transformation possibilities thereafter?

These questions are all the more pressing in the current global climate. In the twenty years since 1996, much of the shine has come off the global democratization movement. The third wave appears, if not to have been turned back, at least to have halted. On the one hand, the failure of the Arab Spring has revealed some of the perils of democratization in circumstances of deeply entrenched ethnic or religious/secular division. On the other hand, the economic crisis in the West has seen other models of governance emerging and proving attractive, from China's one-party-state capitalist model to Russia's socially conservative nationalism. Consequently, countries democratizing now, like Myanmar, do not have just one model from which to choose. Rather, the triumphalism of the immediate post-Cold War period has been

9 See S. Issacharoff, "The democratic risk to democratic constitutions" (2014) 5 *Constitutional Court Review* 1.

10 Z. Elkins, T. Ginsburg, and J. Melton, *The Endurance of National Constitutions* (Cambridge: Cambridge University Press, 2009) 2.

replaced by a choice between rival options. While there has been no returning to the starkly opposed ideologies and political models of the Cold War, there is a sense in which liberal constitutionalism is now not the only game in town: other models of governance are available and provide potentially more viable routes to national economic growth and social stability.

1.1. CRITERIA FOR ASSESSING PERFORMANCE

The success of the South African constitutional project, this discussion suggests, may be assessed from two broad perspectives. First, the question is whether the goal of rights-based social transformation has been achieved: to the extent that the 1996 South African Constitution imagined a constitutionally led transformation "toward a more democratic and caring society,"[11] has that situation come to pass? Second, the question is whether the South African constitutional project has in turn contributed to international understanding of, and support for, liberal constitutionalism as a political system and mode of governance: to what extent have other countries drawn on the South African experience, either as a positive or as a negative model, and does that experience as things now stand give cause for confidence in the transformative possibilities of liberal constitutionalism?

Both of these perspectives obviously have multiple dimensions and pose several methodological challenges. As to the first broad perspective, the initial distinction to make is between issues of constitutional design and implementation. To the extent that there are doubts about whether the 1996 Constitution's transformative vision is being realized, is the underlying problem one of design, in the sense that insufficient thought at the time of constitution-making was given to the context within which, and the institutions through which, the Constitution would be implemented? Or is the underlying problem one of practice – of a failure on the part of those charged with the Constitution's implementation to do their jobs properly? If design is at least part of problem, was it really a case of insufficient thought or was it rather a problem of political constraint – of the compromises that needed to be made to drive the transition to democracy forward detracting from the purity of the design process? Or perhaps it was neither a lack of adequate thinking nor a function of political constraint, but simply the fact that constitutional design is an imperfect science?

[11] Klare, "Legal culture and transformative constitutionalism" 149.

On the side of implementation, what institutions were chiefly responsible for the realization of the 1996 Constitution's vision? The purpose-built Constitutional Court was clearly a leading player, but how much power did it really wield and what sort of relationship was it appropriate for it to forge with the political branches? To what extent have the African National Congress's internal ructions contributed to deficiencies in implementation and might the Constitutional Court and other institutions protecting constitutional democracy have done more to prevent this from happening? Outside the formal institutions of state, have civil society organizations, public impact litigators, and public intellectuals (including legal academics) done enough to assist constitutional institutions in performing their functions?

Turning to the second broad perspective – the contribution the South African constitutional project has made to international understanding of the possibilities of liberal constitutionalism – what evidence is there of positive or negative learning, and how enduring, sustained and mutually beneficial has that learning been? Clearly, it is one thing to point to instances where South African constitutional institutions have been copied or doctrinal approaches followed, and another to discern a real shift in international understanding. In an early contribution to the debate, for example, Cass Sunstein wrote that, through its decision in *Grootboom*,[12] the South African Constitutional Court "has provided the most convincing rebuttal yet to those who have claimed ... that judicial protection of socio-economic rights could not possibly be a good idea."[13] That comment suggests, not just that the decision was right as a matter of South African constitutional law, but also that it had a demonstration effect – that in fulfilling, to a certain extent, the 1996 Constitution's promise of meaningful socio-economic rights enforcement the *Grootboom* decision at the same time taught the Court's international audience something about the transformative possibilities of this set of rights.

Beyond building international understanding, what substantive contribution has the South African constitutional experience made to constitutional design and practice in other countries, and has this made a discernible difference to the quality of life in those countries? Here, the lines of causal influence may be difficult to follow. Constitutional text and institutional arrangements are clearly copied across borders for a variety of reasons. Some of those reasons say very little if anything about the *merits* of the South African constitutional model: some forms of borrowing are extremely "shallow" or isomorphic. They

12 *Government of the Republic of South Africa* v. *Grootboom*.

13 C. Sunstein, "Social and Economic Rights? Lessons from South Africa" (1999) 11 *Constitutional Forum* 123–32 at 132.

take the form of reflex impulses toward the borrowing of ideas from certain countries, within certain constitutional communities, without proper attention to how those choices have operated in a particular jurisdiction, and why, and thus how those lessons might actually translate to a different constitutional context.[14] Or they may reflect the immediate needs of constitutional drafters, faced with time and resource constraints, to find some kind of plausible model for borrowing or adaptation, and little serious engagement with the actual history, meaning or impact of foreign constitutional models.

Other forms of borrowing, however, may be more considered and deliberate, and reflect more detailed engagement with, and thought about, the actual advantages or experiences of a foreign constitutional system. This may be true, for instance, of certain forms of borrowing by foreign constitutional judges, or even by drafters – where there is some mechanism (such as an individual drafter with knowledge or experience in multiple jurisdictions, or credible international organization) for informing drafters about the actual practice and impact, not just form, of various foreign constitutional choices. "Deep" borrowing of this kind is also itself a potential source of validation of the success of a country's constitutional arrangements: it reflects the judgment of many foreign minds (i.e., foreign judges, legislators or constitution drafters) about the merits of a particular set of foreign constitutional arrangements. There is, as Posner and Sunstein point out,[15] also clearly independent epistemic value to this kind of judgment of "many minds." In the South African context, it may also provide a useful additional means of assessing the relative success, or failure, of the South African constitutional model – based on the degree to which it has, or has not, been emulated elsewhere.

It is, of course, important to note an asymmetry in the degree to which "borrowing" and "non-borrowing" of the South African model is informative in this context. Providing it is sufficiently deep, borrowing of the South African constitutional model will almost always provide some *prima facie* evidence of both local and foreign judgments about the relative success of the model. (If the internal assessment is negative, this will generally also affect how the model is perceived by *informed* outsiders.) Nonborrowing, however, need not reflect any negative judgment about the relative success of the South African model, on its own terms. Often, it may simply reflect that constitutional

[14] See, e.g., L. Pritchett, M. Woolcock, and M. Andrews (2010) "Capability Traps? The Mechanisms of Persistent Implementation Failure" (*CGD Working Article* 234, Washington, DC: Center for Global Development) 2 (available at www.cgdev.org/content/publications/detail/1424651) (accessed date November 20, 2017).

[15] See, e.g., E. A. Posner and C. R. Sunstein, "The law of other states" (2006) 59 *Stanford Law Review* 131–79.

decision-makers in other countries do not have sufficient knowledge of the South African model to allow meaningful borrowing. Or it may reflect an internal battle, within a country, about how best to define its new relationship with a former colonial or occupying power – in some cases, there might still be a pragmatic desire to retain links and benefit from technical and legal assistance from such a power, but in others, there may be a desire to affirm a more distinctive independent identity. In other cases, the nonborrowing of the South African model by a foreign constitutional actor may reflect a considered judgment by foreign decision-makers that their own social, economic, and political conditions or challenges are quite different to those facing South African constitutionalists, and thus ones that demand a quite different constitutional response. By itself, such a conclusion also does little to suggest that the South African constitutional model has been a failure, for South Africa, or a country facing similar social, political, and economic challenges.

A final interesting and important complication to this picture is the way in which foreign ideas have continued to travel to South Africa, beyond the initial drafting of the 1996 Constitution, in ways that have shaped its constitutional jurisprudence and broader constitutional discourse. Penny Andrews, for instance, in her contribution to this book on race and the transformation of higher education under the Constitution, notes the challenges posed by the ongoing influence of US discourses on race: whatever its relevance for the United States, she suggests that the "Black Lives Matter" campaign has a quite different resonance in South Africa, where there is a black majority grappling with how best to guide the transformation of institutions within its own political control. Indeed, at times, she suggests, the ongoing influence of US discourse can be damaging to the sense of possibility and agency South Africans have in seeking to create a path toward greater racial and economic transformation.

In addressing these questions, this book contributes to a growing literature on assessing constitutional performance, but does so in a way that makes a distinctive contribution to that literature – one that focuses less on producing measurable indicators of performance and more on assessing the value of comparative constitutional law as a repository for knowledge on how to improve constitutional performance. In their introduction to a recent collection, for example, Tom Ginsburg and Aziz Huq developed the idea of "external" and "internal" criteria for assessing constitutional performance – i.e., criteria that are general or universalizable across some or all countries, and those which are more specific to particular constitutional settings. They further offer four distinct criteria for assessing external constitutional performance: first, the idea of constitutions as sources of "legitimacy"; second, the idea of constitutions as mechanisms for channeling political conflict; third, the idea of constitutions as mechanisms for reducing principal-agent problems, or limiting agency costs, in a representative democracy, by increasing the responsiveness of government actors to citizen preferences, or self-serving political behavior; and fourth, the idea of constitutions being used to create structures to address the provision of public goods which cannot be provided by citizens alone, or to solve "collective action" problems.[16]

Two important qualifications, however, should be made to this framework. First, while clearly offering a valuable list of criteria for judging constitutional performance, Ginsburg and Huq do not purport to offer a *complete* or exhaustive set of external criteria. Rather, they identify four important criteria that they believe almost all constitutional scholars could endorse, regardless of their particular legal or political philosophy, which can thus provide a useful starting point for ongoing debates and scholarship on the question of constitutional performance. Second, the notion of "internal" and "external" criteria for judgment offered by Ginsburg and Huq should be understood in an appropriately interrelated, interdependent way.

Of course, at its broadest, the idea of "legitimacy" that Ginsburg and Huq endorse *could* potentially be understood to encompass almost all aspects of democratic constitutional performance – i.e., whether or not a constitution creates the conditions for democratic decision-making, respects and promotes substantive freedom, and equality for all citizens, including via the provision of certain minimum goods to all citizens, and creates a state capable of ensuring the individual and collective security of citizens. One of the difficulties with criteria of this kind, however, is that they are extremely difficult to apply in any kind of "objective" way, or in a way that lends itself to agreement among observers about the relevant criteria for judgment. Their application also clearly depends on quite thick, detailed engagement with facts on the ground in a particular jurisdiction, in ways that make it difficult for any outside observer to assess performance.[17] Indeed, this is one reason why John Rawls, in *Political Liberalism*, argued that our criteria for assessing the legitimacy of a liberal political order should be somewhat thinner, and more focused on criteria that allow for "transparent" judgments by outsiders.[18]

[16] T. Ginsburg and A. Huq, "What can constitutions do? The Afghan case" (2014) 24 *Journal of Democracy* 116–30. See also discussion in T. Ginsburg and A. Huq, *Assessing the Performance of South Africa's Constitution* (International IDEA, 2016).

[17] On outsider interpretation compare R. Dixon and V. Jackson, "Constitutions inside out: outsider interventions in domestic constitutional contests" (2013) 38 *Wake Forest Law Review* 149–209.

[18] J. Rawls, *Political Liberalism* (New York, NY: Columbia University Press, 1993).

Ginsburg, in particular, has also been a lead contributor to attempts to assess constitutional performance from this kind of external viewpoint. This itself suggests that the idea of legitimacy in the Ginsburg and Huq framework should be understood in a more limited, sociological way – i.e., whether a constitution is in fact accepted by a democratic population, or national citizenry, as legitimate, not whether it can be judged substantively legitimate based on some more freestanding conceptual criteria.[19]

The contributions to this book seek to grapple with ideas about constitutional performance that are at once both narrower and broader than those identified by Ginsburg and Huq. Together, the contributions to the book address four broad themes: (i) questions of democratic constitutionalism and constitution-making; (ii) the rule of law, corruption, and accountability; (iii) gender justice; and (iv) race, poverty, and social and economic transformation. In this sense, the focus of this book is distinctly narrower than the contributions to Ginsburg and Huq's volume on *Assessing Constitutional Performance*. It covers a narrower range of themes, while still deploying some of the same external criteria for assessment. The process by which constitutions are enacted, for instance, can clearly affect their sociological legitimacy. How constitutions address questions of corruption and accountability will also be integrally bound up with their ability to address agency costs, or prevent self-dealing by political actors. Addressing gender violence, through adequate policing, prosecution, situational crime prevention, and historical redress, also necessarily involves the creation of public goods, in ways that constitutions may help realize. The same goes for social rights: often, social rights involve the delivery of basic services, which are quintessential public goods.

The focus of the book, however, is also in important ways broader than the framework provided by Ginsburg and Huq. How constitutions are adopted can affect their substantive democratic legitimacy, not just their sociological legitimacy. Whether or not constitutions meet the basic needs of citizens is also a question of fundamental equality and distributive justice, not just the provision of "public goods." Constitutions – and constitutional judicial review by courts – can also play an important role in ensuring that democratic political processes are in fact responsive to these kinds of needs, not simply to majoritarian preferences, or the ideas of democratic responsiveness captured by the principal-agent metaphor.[20] By focusing on questions of this kind, this

19 Compare R. H. Fallon, "Legitimacy and the Constitution" (2005) 118 *Harvard Law Review* 1787–853.

20 Compare R. Dixon, "The Core Case for Weak-form Review" (Working Paper, April 2016).

book hopes to contribute to the project of *broadening*, as well as employing, the range of external criteria for assessment offered by Ginsburg and Huq.

Implicit in almost all the contributions to this book is an understanding that it is important to approach the idea of "internal" and "external" criteria for assessment in an appropriately nuanced and interdependent way. Internal criteria for assessment will themselves be notoriously difficult to identify in any meaningful or objective way: as US critics of both "originalism" and "purposive" interpretation have long argued, there is often profound disagreement among the drafters of a democratic constitutional document about underlying purposes or objectives, in ways that make it difficult to identify any truly shared purposes beyond the compromise reflected in the constitutional text itself.[21] Where such purposes are identified, they are inevitably shaped by certain external interpretive practices, which make it impossible to identify a meaningful shared legislative "purpose" in some more objective sense.[22]

Moreover, there is a clear danger to viewing any such "internal" purposes in isolation, without attention to their broader global or external context. Take an extreme hypothetical example: if a constitution seeks to achieve *no* meaningful change in social, economic, and political arrangements, it will almost certainly be judged a "success" on purely internal criteria. Because the constitution does not seek to create social, economic, or political change, even the total absence of such change in a society plagued by social and economic equality cannot be counted as a sign of failure. Similarly, if change does occur, even without direct constitutional pressure, this will also be fully consistent with the idea of constitutional "success" – because the constitution does not purport to *prevent* such change, only to avoid mandating it. But to judge such a constitution as truly "successful," in such circumstances, is clearly to make a judgment that deprives the concept of any meaningful content. Rather, for internal criteria for judgment to be useful or meaningful, those criteria must themselves be reasonable when viewed from an external standpoint: if a constitution, for instance, is enacted against a backdrop of relatively stable democratic traditions, and meaningful protections for liberty and equality for all, it will be reasonable for it to have quite modest "reactive" or preservation-oriented goals.[23]

21 See, e.g., F. H. Easterbrook, "Pragmatism's role in interpretation" (2008) 31 *Harvard Journal of Law and Public Policy* 901–6. Compare T. Ginsburg and R. Dixon, "The South African Constitutional Court and socio-economic rights as insurance swaps" (2011) 4 *Constitutional Court Review* 1–9.

22 Compare, e.g., S. Breyer, *Active Liberty: Interpreting Our Democratic Constitution* (New York, NY: Knopf Doubleday, 2007).

23 See, e.g., B. Ackerman, *We the People: Foundations* (Cambridge, MA: Belknap Press, 1991). See also Klare, "Legal culture and transformative constitutionalism" and M. Hailbronner,

Conversely, if a constitution is enacted in conditions of massive violence, inequality or persecution by government actors, it will be patently *unreasonable* for the constitution to fail even to *attempt* to address such problems, or create some minimum degree of political and social "transformation."[24] Existing international legal understandings, and global political commitments, suggest that there are at least some minimum conditions for "constitutionalism" in terms of the rule of law, and freedom and security for citizens, and thus that one of the key requirements of any truly "constitutional" order is that it at least attempt to realize such conditions.

Equally, the way in which we construct our understanding of "external" constitutional purposes is often deeply informed by the scope and practices – or internal goals – of actual constitutional systems. Our understanding of the "goals" of constitutions is, in large part, the product of a complex dialogue between the national, international, and transnational legal spheres. As Klug noted, national constitutional goals are often picked up in international human rights norms, as a form of global best practice, and those international norms then inform the scope and drafting of new constitutions.[25] Similarly, when it comes to drafting and interpreting a national constitution, courts may often look both explicitly and implicitly to transnational practices in order to interpret its key provisions, and their *objective* "purpose."[26]

Ultimately, various contributors therefore suggest that the best way of understanding constitutional performance is to start with general or universal ("external") understandings of a constitution's role – in promoting democracy, the rule of law, and substantive equality, security and freedom for all citizens – and then give more concrete content to those understandings in the particular context in which they operate. In South Africa, for instance, it is impossible to understand the goal of establishing a true multi-party democracy based on respect for the rule of law without connecting that goal to the

Traditions and Transformations: The Rise of German Constitutionalism (Oxford: Oxford University Press, 2015).

[24] Compare Klare, "Legal culture and transformative constitutionalism"; Ackerman, *We the People*.

[25] See H. Klug, *Constituting Democracy: Law, Globalism and South Africa's Political Reconstruction* (Cambridge: Cambridge University Press, 2000).

[26] Compare, e.g., the use of notions of dignity in the jurisprudence of the Hungarian Constitutional in the first 15 years: see L. Sólyom and G. Brunner, *Constitutional Judiciary in a New Democracy: The Hungarian Constitutional Court* (Ann Arbor, MI: University of Michigan Press, 2000); K. L. Scheppele, "The new Hungarian Constitutional Court" (1999) 8 *Eastern European Constitutional Review* 81–7. Compare also R. Dixon and D. Landau, "Transnational constitutionalism and a limited doctrine of unconstitutional constitutional amendment" (2015) 13 *International Journal of Constitutional Law* 606–38.

history and repudiation of apartheid. As Bilchitz notes in his contribution to this book, the Constitution's commitment to racial and economic transformation reflects *both* a general commitment to substantive equality, and human dignity and flourishing (or capabilities) for all those living in South African *and* a more historically specific commitment to ensuring that poor, black South Africans identify with the Constitution, as one that speaks directly to their needs – and not simply "a Charter of Luxuries."[27] Similarly, the South African Constitution's commitment to eradicating sexual and domestic violence should be understood as reflecting both universal goals of nonsexism and nonracism in democratic societies and more contextual commitments to overcoming the specifically apartheid-era history (and indeed even longer colonial history) of institutionalized sexual violence and brutalization of black South African men. The same can be said of the Constitution's commitment to the right to education: the right to education, as Andrews notes in her chapter (Chapter 9), is both a reflection of an understanding of universal international law and of more contextually specific commitments in South Africa to social and economic transformation.

This, we suggest, is also the kind of dual understanding of "external" and "internal" criteria for assessment that informs almost all the contributions to this book, and all of the best work to date on constitutional performance.

1.2. APPLYING THE CRITERIA: QUESTIONS OF CAUSATION

Another complex set of challenges in assessing constitutional performance relates to *causal* questions, and how we go about identifying the role played by various formal constitutional-design choices, or subsequent institutional choices surrounding the implementation of that design, in creating subsequent patterns of apparent "success" or "failure." Untangling causal questions of this kind is notoriously difficult. In the case of constitutional "success," there is always the possibility that what is being observed is in fact a product of other, ongoing social trends or political and economic dynamics, rather than the exogenous influence of the Constitution or constitutional actors.[28] It is also

[27] Compare E. Mureinik, "Beyond a charter of luxuries: economic rights in the Constitution" (1992) 8 *South African Journal on Human Rights* 464–74; D. M. Davis, "The case against inclusion of socio-economic demands in a Bill of Rights except as directive principles" (1992) 8 *South African Journal on Human Rights* 475–90. See also discussion in D. Bilchitz, *Poverty and Fundamental Rights: The Justification and Enforcement of Socio-economic Rights* (Oxford: Oxford University Press, 2008).

[28] In social science, e.g., this problem is often referred to as the problem of an ongoing trend.

possible that, even though we observe a clear pattern of improvement, more could have been achieved in South Africa with a different set of constitutional-design or doctrinal choices.

Equally, for cases of apparent constitutional failure, it is difficult for any legal or constitutional scholar to account – or appropriately control – for the relevant external pressures or conditions facing a country, which may make it difficult fully to realize a constitution's aims. There is also a further question of how far it is reasonable to ascribe to the drafters responsibility for having foreseen, or provided for, these external factors or eventualities. In South Africa in the last twenty years, for instance, there have been a number of major challenges to the achievement of full substantive freedom and equality for all citizens under ss. 1, 9, 12, and 26–8 of the Constitution: a significant increase in migration from the rest of Africa; a worsening of the HIV/AIDS epidemic; a fall in global resource prices; the progressive depreciation of the rand; and a worsening of the trade, and thus the budgetary, position of the government.[29] All of these factors have made it much more difficult for the government to ensure adequate food, water, housing and health-care, and security for all citizens. There is an open question as to the extent to which ss. 9, 26–8, and the Constitutional Court's decisions enforcing these rights, have failed to make a difference to this situation, and how much this should be judged a true "failure" of the Constitution rather than a set of developments that ought realistically to be regarded as beyond the scope of ordinary democratic constitutional control.

None of the contributions to the book purport to provide definitive answers to these questions. Rather, they attempt to make progress in providing answers by following three basic logical steps. First, they identify the available social evidence as to the "ultimate" performance of the South African social and political system as a whole, across given domains. In the context of corruption, for instance, both Klug and Fombad note the available evidence of corrupt and noncorrupt behavior, as well as public perceptions regarding corruption. In the domain of gender justice, Goldblatt and Durbach note the very high rates of sexual and domestic violence in South Africa both in absolute and comparative terms, but also the rates of complaint, prosecution,

[29] See, e.g., M. A. Collinson, S. M. Tollman, and K. Kahn, "Migration, settlement change and health in post-apartheid South Africa: triangulating health and demographic surveillance with national census data" (2007) 35 *Scandinavian Journal of Public Health* 77–84; A. Segatti and L. B. Landau (eds.), *Contemporary Migration to South Africa: A Regional Development Issue* (Washington, DC: World Bank, 2011); M. Nowak and L. A. Ricci (eds.), *Post-Apartheid South Africa: The First Ten Years* (IMF, 2006); H. Marais, *Limits to Change: The Political Economy of Transition* (Cape Town: University of Cape Town Press, 2001).

and conviction for such crimes within South Africa over time. In the domain of education, Penny Andrews refers to evidence relating to the number of black South Africans tenured at various elite universities,[30] and Julie Suk notes the level of educational attainment for black and white school students, and students in wealthy and poor school districts.

Second, having noted this evidence, contributors offer an individual judgment as to whether this level of performance can be considered more or less successful. Judgments of this kind also inevitably vary based on the particular subject-matter and perspective of contributors: no country is likely to be perfect in achieving the rule of law, gender justice, or racial and economic transformation, and so inevitably scholars reach different judgments about what level of achievement can be counted as "good enough," a success or at least a partial success in these areas.

Third, contributors consistently take a distinctly qualitative approach to assessing the plausible constitutional *mechanisms* that explain these findings of ultimate success, or failure. Thus, where various contributors identify evidence of success, they focus on identifying the particular formal constitutional-design choices, subsequent legislative choices, judicial decisions, or other institutional practices, that plausibly underpin that success. Several contributors also consider the role of social movements, individual leaders, and institution builders, and the interaction between different institutions as important mechanisms underpinning patterns of apparent success.[31] Conversely, where contributors reach a more pessimistic view of ultimate performance, they focus on untangling the role played by formal constitutional design choices versus the way the Constitution has been used, both by the judiciary and by civil society groups.

A fourth important dimension to several contributions is their focus on questions of constitutional change, or adaption. The 1996 South African Constitution, like most modern constitutions, provides mechanisms for its own updating and improvement – both by way of formal constitutional amendment, and the delegation of various constitutional-design choices to courts and legislatures, in ways that allow for the updating or adaption of

[30] See P. Andrews, Chapter 9 in this book, n. 108.

[31] Cf M. McCann, *Rights at Work: Pay Equity Reform and the Politics of Legal Mobilization* (Chicago, IL: University of Chicago Press, 1994); C. R. Epp, *The Rights Revolution: Lawyers, Activists, and Supreme Courts in Comparative Perspective* (Chicago, IL: University of Chicago Press, 1998); S. Gloppen, Roberto Gargarella, and Elin Skaar (eds.), *Democratization and the Judiciary: The Accountability Function of Courts in New Democracies* (London: Frank Cass Publishers, 2004).

the constitutional system by way of ordinary legislation or judicial decision.[32] Where contributors observe success, one of the questions this therefore raises is whether this is due to specific initial choices about constitutional design, or rather more general choices about the scope for constitutional adaption – and the subsequent willingness of legislators and judges to deploy that adaptive potential (see, e.g., Chapter 5 by Heinz Klug in this book). Conversely, where various contributors observe failure, an important question they address is whether this failure is hard-baked into the South African constitutional model, or likely to be self-perpetuating, or can still in some way be addressed by appropriate legislative change or doctrinal development (see, e.g., Chapter 7 by Andrea Durbach).

This, in many ways, is also the crux of the book in terms of its contribution to debates over *constitutional* performance. As constitutional scholars, our greatest potential contribution is not to judging ultimate performance, but rather, to assessing *intermediate mechanisms* that can drive performance of different kinds.

1.3. COMPARATIVE ASSESSMENT?

A further set of questions relates to how judgments about constitutional performance intersect with broader comparative constitutional experiences. International and comparative constitutional influences were, as Heinz Klug noted sixteen years ago,[33] a major force in shaping the adoption of the 1993 Interim Constitution in South Africa and in shaping the actual form of the final 1996 Constitution. To the extent that comparative learning went into the design of the postapartheid Constitutions, what light does the performance of those Constitutions cast on the value of such comparative knowledge? Conversely, to the extent that the South African experience may now be relied on elsewhere as an opportunity for learning, what does a decision to draw on the South African experience say (or not say) about the success of the South African constitutional project?

One potential value to a comparative approach to the South African constitutional experience is that it provides a benchmark for *realistic* constitutional performance ("a benchmark for realistic assessment"). There will obviously be significant challenges to identifying appropriate countries for comparison in this context: is South Africa, for example, best understood as a form of

[32] Compare R. Dixon and T. Ginsburg, "Deciding not to decide: deferral in constitutional design" (2011) 9 *International Journal of Constitutional Law* 636–72.

[33] See Klug, *Constituting Democracy*.

white-settler society grappling with a history of colonialism, a country in the global South grappling with the challenges of democracy and development, or a more distinctly "Afropolitan" nation, with its own distinctive place in Africa and the world and set of postapartheid challenges? But, however we answer these questions, the process of comparison can offer useful insights as to how to judge South Africa's constitutional performance in *relative* terms. By focusing on countries that have quite different constitutional structures, but similar social, economic and political challenges, we can potentially gain a better sense of the actual role played by South Africa's constitutional system in addressing those same social, political, and economic challenges. An assessment of this kind is clearly not precise or truly social scientific in nature.[34] But it captures the basic insights of what Ran Hirschl has called a "most similar cases" approach to case study selection – i.e., the ability to draw plausible causal inferences based on a limited set of qualitative case-studies.[35]

A second potential value to comparative inquiry in this context is its ability to allow us to see the contours of the South African "constitutional system" in a clearer light ("a definitional benchmark"). The constitutional system of any country is more than the sum of the formal legal text, or even court decisions interpreting the text. It also comprises a vast array of other institutional practices. By assessing the South African experience in a comparative light, we can also more clearly identify the *key* dimensions of that vast array of institutional practices – i.e., see what is at their core or what is defining about them. This is arguably the form of comparative "engagement" that leading US scholars, such as Vicki Jackson and Frank Michelman, have labeled "reflective" in nature.[36]

The comparative dimension to the collection is ultimately quite select, and focused. At its core, the aim is to invite comparison from scholars working on other constitutional democracies facing similar challenges to that of South Africa – i.e., constitutional scholars in Africa, the Pacific, and Latin America – where there have been similar attempts to create a transition to true multiparty democracy over the last few decades, and severe ongoing challenges in terms of corruption, violence, gender justice, poverty, and economic inequality. One of the chapters, by Julie Suk, also draws on the US experience of

34 Such an analysis would require a controlled randomized experiment or at least what econometricians call a "difference in difference" analysis.

35 R. Hirschl, "The question of case selection in comparative constitutional law" (2005) 53 *American Journal of Comparative Law* 125–55; R. Hirschl, *Comparative Matters: The Renaissance of Comparative Constitutional Law* (Oxford: Oxford University Press, 2014).

36 See also S. Choudhry, "Globalization in search of justification: toward a theory of comparative constitutional interpretation" (1999) 74 *Indiana Law Journal* 819–92.

racial and economic inequality, and segregation, as an important comparator for South Africa (and indeed other constitutional systems) in assessing questions of constitutional performance in the domain of education rights.

Other regions in the global South, and particularly parts of Asia, could also offer an equally useful source of comparison in this context, but the coverage of the volume is necessarily select. In many parts of Asia and South-East Asia, our impression is that there is relatively little knowledge, or at least little deep knowledge, of the South African constitutional model. German and American constitutional ideas have travelled extensively to Asia, in part due to a well-funded and organized effort to share those ideas within the region.[37] The South African constitutional experience, in contrast, remains relatively understudied. We thus hope that, in the future, this book itself may contribute to a deeper understanding of the South African experience within Asia as well as elsewhere, and thus also increase the two-way traffic of ideas between that region of the world and Africa.[38]

1.4. SUMMARY OF CONTRIBUTIONS

The chapters that follow bring together the knowledge and expertise of leading South African scholars working inside and outside South Africa, and comparative constitutional scholars. Some chapters focus largely on a "domestic" or inward-focused form of assessment, while others are more directly comparative, and others still attempt to combine a domestic and comparative approach to assessing performance.

In assessing the record of the Constitution in the domain of socio-economic rights, David Bilchitz (Chapter 3) concludes that the Constitution has "had a significant effect on law and policy," and in this sense played an important role in addressing poverty. But he also notes the limits to what has been achieved in this context: while there has generally been a high rate of "thin" or formal compliance with the decisions of the Constitutional Court of South Africa (CCSA)

[37] See, e.g., R. Dixon and T. Ginsburg, "Introduction" in R. Dixon and T. Ginsburg (eds.), *Comparative Constitutional Law in Asia* (Cheltenham: Edward Elgar, 2014) 1, 5; Y. Okudaira, "Forty years of the Constitution and its various influences: Japanese, American, and European" (1990) 53 *Law and Contemporary Problems* 17–49; T. Ginsburg, "Constitutional Courts in East Asia: understanding variation" (2008) 3 *Journal of Comparative Law* 80–99.

[38] On the idea of Asian-African exchange, and its potential virtues and dark sides, see, e.g., S. S. Tan and A. Acharya (eds.), *Bandung Revisited: The Legacy of the 1995 Asian-African Conference for International Order* (Singapore: NUS Press, 2008); D. Brautigam, "Close encounters: Chinese business networks as industrial catalysts in Sub-Saharan Africa" (2003) 102 *African Affairs* 447–67; C. Alden, D. Large, and R. Soares de Oliveira (eds.), *China Returns to Africa: A Rising Power and a Continent Embrace* (New York, NY: Columbia University Press, 2008).

in this context, thicker or more substantive compliance has been far more mixed. On the one hand, by some estimates, decisions such as the *TAC Case* have saved more than two million lives, but on the other hand, median life-expectancy has fallen from 52 to 43 since the adoption of the Constitution. He further attributes this to various decisions by the Constitutional Court to adopt a relatively "weak" approach to the enforcement of these rights, rather than to the design of the Constitution itself. In support of this, he points to the comparative experience of countries such as India and Colombia as demonstrating the alternative paths the Constitutional Court might have taken in interpreting and enforcing the Constitution's guarantee of socio-economic rights.

In assessing the CCSA's property rights jurisprudence, Justice Kate O'Regan takes a similarly sanguine view of the overall record of the CCSA in this context: the CCSA, she suggests, has achieved an important balance between private property rights and informal housing rights, and thus between respecting the role of markets and addressing "the apartheid and colonial legacy that has left so many Black South Africans without security of tenure or access to homes or land" (p. 41). It has, in this context, thus been "supportive of the constitutional goal of addressing the legality of inequality in South Africa, not destructive of it" (p. 44). At the same time, like Bilchitz, she notes the degree to which the South African constitutional framework as a whole has failed to deliver on the promise of major socio-economic transformation, or improving the day-to-day to quality of life of many poor, predominantly black South Africans. This, she notes, also helps highlight the degree to which fulfilment of the promise of the Constitution remains a goal that requires political, not just legal or judicial, action (p. 34). She likewise notes the key interplay between law and politics in the way in which the role of the provinces has played out under the Constitution.

Steven Friedman (Chapter 4), in contrast, defends this relatively weak, procedural approach to the enforcement of social rights by the CCSA, suggesting that it has an important capacity to "enhance democratization" (p. 89). Democratization was clearly both an external and internal goal of the 1996 Constitution, or "deeply rooted in the Constitution's ethos, as well as the struggle against apartheid." Among other things, Friedman argues, it also clearly entails a commitment to "citizen agency." If courts take too strong or substantive an approach to social rights enforcement, they also substantially undermine both the scope and incentive for this kind of agency. A weaker, more procedural approach, such as seen in cases such as *Grootboom* or *Joe Slovo*, Friedman argues, is thus critical to avoiding the danger of democratic "debilitation" identified by scholars such as Mark Tushnet[39] – or, as Friedman suggests, to promoting democracy itself.

David Landau (Chapter 16) takes a more complex view of how we should judge the success, or failure, of the CCSA's jurisprudence in this context. In one view, which in some ways echoes Friedman's, the Court's combination of deferential and indirect enforcement, with a pro-poor focus, has provided an "ideal answer to a theoretical puzzle: how to square the enforcement of social rights with the particularly heavy strain that those rights put on judicial legitimacy and capacity." But Landau suggests another, revisionist view of the CCSA "not as a universalist solution to a theoretical problem, but as a response to a high-capacity court working in a formalist legal context, with a limited constitutional text, and most important, a dominant party system" (p. 407). A third, and Landau suggests even more useful, perspective is to see the CCSA's approach through a more dialogic lens – one that is neither purely universalist, nor contextual, but "part of a dialogue with other courts around the world that are seriously engaged in the enforcement of social rights" (p. 407). Following this point of view, Landau argues, the CCSA's jurisprudence can be understood as "successful" in a quite different way to that envisaged by Bilchitz – i.e., as contributing to a "broadened set of potential tools," and judicial and scholarly imagination, about how best to respond to the common challenge of courts "prodding recalcitrant or low-capacity bureaucracies into action" (p. 407).

Penny Andrews, in contrast, suggests that South Africa is at a cross-roads in fulfilling the promise of the 1996 Constitution in respect of social rights, such as the right to education: with sufficient grass-roots political activism and change, she still sees the potential for meaningful social and economic transformation in South Africa, but reminds us of the limited progress to date in achieving economic transformation in the lives of many black South Africans. She notes that: "[a]s the markers of affluence in South Africa become more multi-racial, the face of poverty continues to be black" (p. 237). There is also a close connection between this and the state of education, in particular legal education, in South Africa. Apartheid left a legacy of historically white universities that were prestigious and well-resourced, and black universities that were under-resourced, and thus a major challenge for achieving economic transformation along racial lines (p. 225). A formalist legal culture, and approach to legal education, also made it more difficult to achieve true legal and economic transformation, given the connection between private law and markets.

[39] See M. V. Tushnet, "Alternative Forms of Judicial Review" (2003) 101 *Michigan Law Review* 2781–802.

Part of the test of transformation, Andrews thus suggests, will lie in ongoing calls for, and attempts at, more comprehensive transformation in the domain of legal education. The Constitution, she suggests in this context, is also both a potential impetus and obstacle to transformation: it sets out the values that can shape and inform further transformation in legal education, but also risks creating a form of "Constitution worship" that obscures the need for broader, more radical forms of transformation. Her argument is, in this sense, an analysis directly inspired by US-style critical race theoretic traditions: it embraces the rights and values of the Constitution as potentially transformational, but also highlights their potential downside.

Julie Suk (Chapter 8) likewise focuses on education, and the Constitution's goals of both educational adequacy (s. 29) and racial equality (s. 9). She suggests that, assessed against the backdrop of the US experience of attempts at school desegregation and equalization of the racial achievement gap in schools, South Africa's record looks distinctly more favorable or "successful." Further, she suggests that one reason for this is that, unlike the US Supreme Court, the CCSA has seemingly been mindful of the danger of resistance or backlash against attempts "to do away with incumbent privilege" in education (p. 200): the CCSA, she suggests, "has sustained a transformative vision of postapartheid constitutional education rights by employing weak remedies accompanied by strong norm articulation" (p. 202).

In assessing the Constitution's impact on gender and sexual justice, Beth Goldblatt (Chapter 6) and Andrea Durbach (Chapter 7) reach more mixed conclusions as to the "success" of the 1996 constitutional framework. Goldblatt acknowledges the significant ongoing problems of gender and sexual violence, and their complex causes, but suggests that the Constitution has contributed to significant progress in this context: the Constitution recognizes commitments to nonsexism and gender equality, and also bodily integrity, and freedom and security of the person. The Preamble also contains references to patriarchy, and at a structural level, the Constitution creates a Commission on Gender Equality. In implementing these provisions, the National Assembly has passed a range of laws, including the Domestic Violence Act, the Prevention of Family Violence Act, and the Sexual Offences Act, which give broad recognition to gender crimes. And the CCSA, Goldblatt concludes, has "improved substantive and procedural law, and to some extent, [the] administration of justice" in this context, including by "defending women's rights to freedom and security and affirm[ing] the state's obligations to protect them" (p. 162). There is, of course, a great deal more work to be done in this context, but Goldblatt suggests that the constitutional framework provides an important resource for those advocating for social, economic and legal change.

Durbach, in contrast, notes the degree to which the Constitution itself addressed questions of gender justice, but at the same time authorized a truth and reconciliation process that almost entirely overlooked gendered harms and crimes. This failure to connect the Truth and Reconciliation Commission (TRC) process to questions of gender harm, she argues, also continues to reverberate in South African society today, contributing to levels of sexual violence that rank among some of the highest in the world (p. 195). In this sense, the Constitution itself can also be understood as having failed to achieve a key form of gender justice: while it had the structural potential to deliver justice of this kind, it did not sufficiently put pressure on key-decision makers, after 1996, to focus on issues of sex and gender.

Linked to this evidence of ongoing gender violence is the evidence, presented by Aziz Huq in Chapter 15 on "Constitutionalism, legitimacy and public order," about a broader failure on the part of the police in South Africa to maintain public order. This failure, Huq argues, is despite the significant formal promise of the 1996 Constitution in this context: significant reform in the structure of the police force in South Africa preceded the adoption of the 1996 Constitution, and the Constitution itself sought to address police reform via a range of measures including various accountability structures (e.g., ss. 221 and 222) (p. 391) (compare also Chapter 13 by Richard Stacey). It also represents a significant threat to public trust in the state generally in South Africa. This, Huq suggests, is itself also a phenomenon that merits greater attention from comparative constitutional scholars: police, as street-level bureaucrats who routinely interact with the public, may be a critical channel for establishing the sociological legitimacy of a new constitutional order. Absent this channel for establishing legitimacy, in South Africa, the question is thus what other factors have served to contribute to the relatively stable constitutional order, to date. Huq also suggests some interesting answers to these questions, but leaves the task of providing a more definitive answer to another day.

Heinz Klug, in writing about the independent institutions found in Chapter 9 of the South African Constitution, suggests that these institutions must be considered equally – along with more rights-focused norms – as part of the key architecture of the Constitution. "The revolutionary nature of the Constitution," he suggests, "lies not only in the expansive network of rights it guarantees ... But also in the constitutionalizing of a set of independent institutions whose role it is to uphold the progressive vision of the Constitution in the face of ordinary pressures of political horse-trading and interest group politics" (p. 140); and the "integrity institutions" found in Chapter 9 are key to achieving this accountability function. The relative success, or otherwise, of such institutions is thus also key to assessing the Constitution's performance overall. To date, Klug suggests, such institutions have a mixed record: they have built the capacity to deliver and enforce decisions involving the highest levels of government (as in the *Nkandla Case*) (pp. 134–39), but equally failed to prevent the diversion of approximately $US50b in government resources since the adoption of the Constitution (p. 109).

In assessing the South African Constitution's influence on the drafting, or interpretation, of other constitutions, the contributors reach a similarly rich and varied set of conclusions – both about outcomes, and the various channels of potential influence. Joel Colón-Ríos (Chapter 11), in writing about the South African constitution-making process as a potential global model, notes the South African Constitution as exemplifying a model of two-stage constitution-making. This model, he suggests, has clear normative advantages: like Andrew Arato, he suggests it has the power to challenge mythologized notions of constituent power, which in Latin America in particular have often served to support antidemocratic processes of constitutional change, or the abuse of democratic constitution-making process. It is also a model that has been actively debated in recent processes of constitutional reform, in countries such as Chile, in ways that suggest that at least some global observers see broader relevance in the South African model.

Charles Fombad (Chapter 14), in writing about the diffusion of South African-style integrity institutions in the rest of Africa, notes evidence of both constitutional "success" and "failure." The chapter 9 institutions in the Constitution, he suggests, have been "consciously or unconsciously copied" in various ways across the continent (p. 370), to an unusual degree within inter-African constitutionalism (pp. 366–70). The constitutions of Angola, Burundi, Morocco, and Tunisia all have institutions that in some way resemble South Africa's chapter 9 institutions. Tanzania and Zambia have sought partially to transplant these institutions, while Kenya and Zimbabwe have recently engaged in deeper, more full-scale borrowing of these institutions. Yet Fombad also suggests that the *performance* of such institutions, in other parts of Africa, provides a more mixed record of success and failure. The broad preconditions exist for the success of such institutions – independent personnel, and effective implementation of their recommendations – and there is a mixed record in this context. This, in turn, suggests that both South African and other African institutions could further be strengthened and reformed, as countries in Africa seek to create "much-needed bulwark(s) against the looming resurgence of authoritarianism" (p. 387).

Jill Cotterell Ghai and Yash Ghai (Chapter 10), examining the influence of the South African Constitution on the 2010 Kenyan Constitution, notice multiple linguistic similarities between the two constitutions, and also other influences of the South African Constitution. This, they suggest, is not surprising given the role of Ghai himself, and Philip Knight as a legal drafter, in both countries, and the degree to which the Kenyans actively sought out information and advice from key South African constitutional figures. But it should also not be confused, they argue, with a deeper more structural influence: while there was important borrowing in the design of the Bill of Rights, the National Assembly, and the model for the devolution of power, the two countries were ultimately facing very different legal and political challenges, and thus adopted quite different constitutional structures or solutions in response to these challenges. The apparent failures or limitations of the Kenyan Constitution in various contexts, therefore, should not be seen as reflecting negatively on the South African constitutional model. If anything, Cotterell Ghai and Ghai are quick to praise the South African experience as highly successful when judged against the Kenyan experience.

Richard Stacey, in his chapter on South Africa and Kenya, focuses on policing, and the degree to which, in designing the 2010 Kenyan Constitution, constitutional designers both borrowed from South Africa and "benefited from several years of South African experience, identifying flaws in the South African model of police oversight and adapting it to avoid those mistakes in Kenya" (p. 343). Implicitly, the South African influence he traces on the Kenyan Constitution is thus simultaneously evidence of success and failure on the part of the South African model: success, in that the South African model was the template for drafting in Kenya, but also failure, in that South African experiences were a negative model for drafting in Kenya. Stacey also notes further complexity to this process of transnational "borrowing," to the extent that, when refined and transplanted to Kenya, the South African model of police accountability did not succeed in preventing police violence and brutality. This may be more directly traceable to the failure in Kenya to reform the underlying institutional structures, rather than flaws in the model itself.

Finally, Coel Kirkby (Chapter 12), in writing about the influence of the South African Constitution on Fijian constitutionalism, notes the influence of the South African Constitution as a model for "transformative liberal constitutionalism" in Fiji. Despite notable differences, Kirkby argues, the South African and Fijian constitution share important historical commonalities: a British colonial history involving governance based on principles of communalism and racial segregation, as well as authoritarianism. Thus, while constitution-makers in Fiji drew on a range of global sources in processes of constitution-making, "the South African experience proved especially important when considering how to cure their shared colonial legacies" (p. 313). Kirkby also notes the multiple pathways of influence between South Africa and Fiji in this context, and in particular the role of Christina Murray (as a drafter of the South African Constitution[40]) and Yash Ghai (as advisor on the South African Constitution[41]), as members of the 2012 Fijian Constitutional commission, in transmitting South African and Kenyan constitutional ideas and experiences. In this sense, he also notes modest evidence of a perception of South African constitutional success. Yet Kirkby also notes the complicated ultimate relationship between South Africa and Fiji in this context. While borrowing the form of liberal constitutionalism from South Africa, Fiji has ended up creating something far closer to liberal authoritarianism.

As these brief summaries indiçate, all the chapters in this book adopt their own particular approach to the task of assessing the South African Constitution's internal and external performance. All of the chapters, too, point to the significant interpretive and methodological difficulties in teasing out the Constitution's local and international influence. Nevertheless, collectively, they do point to the ongoing relevance of the liberal constitutionalist model and the role of the South African constitution in keeping alive the ideal of democratic government under law. Where the constitution has failed to deliver on its local transformation promises, none of the contributors suggests that this was attributable to inherent problems with the liberal constitutionalist model or with the specifically South African version of it. Rather, they point to problems of implementation, political commitment and extra-national pressures. Similarly, those chapters that focus on foreign borrowing of the South African model do not attribute either the reluctance to borrow in some cases or postborrowing failure in others to inherent weaknesses in the model itself. While these conclusions do not amount to a conclusive vindication of the South African constitutional experiment, they do indicate that the strength of the liberal constitutional model may precisely be its capacity to act as a repository for comparative knowledge about the conditions for human freedom.

40 See Coel Kirkby, Chapter 12.
41 See Cottrell Ghai and Ghai, Chapter 10.

2

Mission in Progress: Toward an Assessment of South Africa's Constitution at Twenty

Catherine O'Regan

2.1. INTRODUCTION

Given that the South African Constitution is now nineteen years old, it is timely to be assessing its strengths and weaknesses. The median survival time for constitutions (the age at which one-half of constitutions are expected to have died) is just nineteen years.[1] So on this analysis, South Africa's Constitution has just exceeded its likely lifespan, for it came into force on February 4, 1997, just over nineteen years ago. The coincidence between the predicted lifespan of modern constitutions and Thomas Jefferson's view that a constitution should be replaced every nineteen years is striking.[2] Jefferson's comment was based on the proposition that each generation should determine its own fundamental rules, to ensure that the citizenry remains engaged in the process of self-governance. A constitution, Jefferson seems to suggest, requires the commitment of each new generation.

It makes sense to me that a constitution requires the commitment of each new generation, for a constitution, after all, forms the basis for a system of democratic government. And when a generation questions the legitimacy or vision of a constitution, both the constitution and the political system it constitutes, may be – at least partly – at risk. South Africa seems to be in the midst of just such a generational questioning of our constitutional framework. In the last year we have seen attacks on South Africa's constitutional project, either generally or in relation to a specific issue. Questions have been raised by different groups, including students, some politicians and also some within the

[1] See Z. Elkins, T. Ginsburg, and J. Melton, *The Endurance of National Constitutions* (Cambridge: Cambridge University Press, 2009) 2, 129; see also T. Ginsburg, "Constitutional endurance" in T. Ginsburg and R. Dixon (eds.), *Comparative Constitutional Law* (Cheltenham: Edward Elgar, 2011) 112.

[2] See Ginsburg "Constitutional endurance" 113.

union movement.[3] An example is the following statement issued on April 20, 2016 by Irwin Jim, general secretary of the National Union of Metalworkers of South Africa (NUMSA), the union that has broken away from the Congress of South African Trade Unions (COSATU):

> We reject with the contempt it deserves the understanding that in 1994 South Africans, all South Africans of all classes, surrendered their struggle for sovereignty to the compromise liberal capitalist Constitution which ushered in the newly repackaged but old racist and colonial capitalist "constitutional democratic order." Only a fool would think that a compromise is a permanent solution.[4]

Of course, just as there are those questioning the Constitution's value, there are many too who see its worth. And sometimes, the same person may disparage the Constitution on one occasion and praise it on another. One of the memorable images of the television coverage that followed the Constitutional Court's recent decision in *Economic Freedom Fighters* v. *Speaker of the National Assembly*,[5] was Julius Malema at a press conference holding up a copy of the Constitution and saying "[t]his is a victory of our Constitution."[6]

Questions about the value of the Constitution are legitimate and important questions. Indeed, each generation needs to ask and answer such questions in the process of forming a commitment to the Constitution. So, the questions need to be considered with a seriousness of purpose. If a constitution is to attract each generation's commitment, it must be the subject of robust review.

Yet assessing how a constitution actually works is a task of great complexity. By what standards should we assess a constitution? Longevity is often employed as a measure of assessment, and indeed it is interesting to know that a constitution has remained in force for, say, twenty years, or even 200 years,

[3] See, e.g., Julius Malema's recent reported statements: News24Wire, "Zuma is not our enemy" (April 18, 2016) *Polity* (available at http://polity.org.za/print-version/zuma-is-not-our-enemy-malema-2016-04-18) (accessed date November 20, 2017).

[4] The statement may be found here: I. Jim, "On the ANC's crisis of leadership – NUMSA" (April 20, 2016) *Politicsweb* (available at www.politicsweb.co.za/opinion/on-the-ancs-crisis-of-leadership–numsa) (accessed date November 20, 2017).

[5] *Economic Freedom Fighters* v. *Speaker of the National Assembly*; *Democratic Alliance* v. *Speaker of the National Assembly* [2016] ZACC 11 (2016) 3 SA 580 (CC).

[6] See the image on the Daily Maverick: R. Poplak, "Trainspotter: king con court – Malema emerges victorious" (March 31, 2016) *Daily Maverick* (available at www.dailymaverick.co.za/article/2016-03-31-trainspotter-king-con-court-malema-emerges-victorious/) (accessed date November 20, 2017).

after its adoption.[7] But longevity tells us little about the actual workings and influence of a constitution in practice.

Another way of assessing the Constitution might be to determine whether it has achieved its own explicit or implicit goals or missions. Not all constitutions are explicit about their goals, but the South African Constitution is. In its Preamble, it declares that the Constitution has been adopted to "heal the divisions of the past and establish a society based on democratic values, social justice and fundamental human rights; [to] lay the foundations for a democratic and open society in which government is based on the will of the people and every citizen is equally protected by law; [and to] improve the quality of life of all citizens and free the potential of each person … "[8]

For ease, I am going to propose that there are at least two broad goals identified in the Preamble of our Constitution. The first is the institutional or democratic goal of establishing an open, accountable and responsive democracy. The second is the substantive goal of establishing a society based on social justice in which the quality of life of all citizens is improved and the potential of each individual is freed. I do not wish to suggest that these are the only goals set in the South African Constitution, but I do suggest that they are two of its most important goals.

An assessment of our Constitution thus might ask whether the Constitution has achieved these goals, or at least made progress toward their achievement. In general terms it might be said that we have made good progress in relation to the achievement of the Constitution's institutional or democratic goal. South Africa is a vibrant democracy. But the dynamic nature of a democracy means that its character inevitably changes as political, social and economic circumstances change. An analysis of any constitution must consider whether the constitutional framework is capable of both enabling and constraining the changing character of a democratic society. For the establishment of a democracy is a task that never ends: new challenges arise and must be addressed. South Africa's democracy will be no different. The test of our Constitution will be whether it continues to provide a framework and institutions to protect and deepen democracy.

Progress on the second goal has been less encouraging. Although some steps have been taken to undo the legacy of apartheid and colonialism, deep social and economic inequality continues to disfigure our society. In considering the

7 See the interesting recent study by Elkins, Ginsburg, and Melton, *The Endurance of National Constitutions*.

8 See Constitution of the Republic of South Africa Act 1996, Preamble.

challenges that we still face in this regard, it is important to ask whether the text of the Constitution has been a help or a hindrance.

I intend to assess our Constitution at the age of twenty by measuring it against the goals set out in its Preamble, the goals the Constitution itself sets. I have chosen two particular issues regulated by the Constitution for examination. In choosing them, I recognized that the South African Constitution, like most constitutions, performs two central functions. First, it establishes the structures of government, at the national, provincial and local levels, as well as the institutions that both exercise and monitor the exercise of public power. In a sense, one can see this aspect of the Constitution as being engaged with the institutional or democratic goal of the Constitution. Secondly, the Constitution contains a generous and justiciable Bill of Rights, with a full array of rights including both civil and political rights and social and economic rights. These aspects of the Constitution are, it seems to me, related both to the institutional goal of the Constitution and to the substantive goal of the Constitution, the improvement of the quality of life of all South Africans.

In order to undertake an assessment of our Constitution, I thought it would be useful to analyze one aspect of the Constitution drawn from each of the two key areas of our Constitution's design; that is, the structures of government and the Bill of Rights. In addition, I have chosen to identify aspects of the Constitution that were highly politically contested at the time the Constitution was drafted, in order to examine how these aspects of the Constitution have fared in the last two decades.

First, I discuss the constitutional powers of the provinces, which are set out in chapter 6 of the Constitution. This issue was arguably the most intensely politically contested issue of constitutional structure during the constitutional negotiations, as I shall describe more fully in a moment.

My discussion of provincial powers will illustrate that this question, once the subject of intense political disagreement, is now less politically sensitive. However, I shall also show that new questions have arisen relating to provincial powers. The most important of these concerns the sharp variation in the bureaucratic capacity of the different provinces, which has the consequence that the delivery of social services is uneven across provinces. It is not surprising then that perceived differences in the level of provincial service delivery have been a cause of intense political conflict in response to proposals to shift provincial boundaries.

A second issue relating to provinces has arisen in recent years. It concerns the manner in which political parties, and particularly the African National Congress (ANC), have organized their internal party structures along provincial lines. It is quite possible that the emergence of provincially based political leaders will have the effect of embedding the constitutional framework as it relates to provincial powers. These developments illustrate that not only do changing political circumstances affect how a constitutional framework functions, but also the constitutional framework may influence how political institutions develop. The following discussion of provinces in our constitutional framework thus demonstrates a reciprocal relationship between constitutional text and political institutions and practice.

In relation to the Bill of Rights, again, many issues would warrant close consideration, but I have elected to talk about two related clauses, the property clause and the right of access to housing, as set out in ss. 25 and 26 of the Constitution, respectively. These two clauses lie at the heart of arguably the greatest challenge for South Africa's constitutional democracy, the need to address the unjust legacy of colonial and apartheid dispossession. I shall argue that the manner in which the Court has approached these questions is very sensitive to that need, but it is a sensitivity that appears to have gone unnoticed, or at least rarely acknowledged in the political debate generated by these issues.

More importantly, my discussion of ss. 25 and 26 will show that the text of the Constitution cannot provide the solutions to complex social problems. That remains the task of politics and of government. The corollary is that regardless of the text of the Constitution, these problems will remain without solutions if government does not act decisively to address them.

2.2. CONSTITUTIONAL STRUCTURE: THE POWERS OF PROVINCES

I start with arguably the most contentious issue of the constitutional negotiations in the 1990s: provincial powers. Provincial powers were contentious then because of political disagreement about the nature and scope of the powers that should be conferred on provinces. Today, political contestation about the scope of provincial powers has waned. Nevertheless, provinces remain in the spotlight for different reasons. Under the constitutional framework, provinces are central to the delivery of important social services, including education, health and housing. Significant variation across the bureaucratic capacity of provinces has resulted in marked differences in the quality of service delivery. This shift in focus in relation to provincial issues over the first twenty years is representative of shifts that inevitably occur in constitutional democracies over time. It is interesting to consider how a constitutional framework shapes, and is shaped by, such shifts in focus.

At the time of drafting the interim Constitution in the early 1990s, the political controversy centered on the question of how to assign power to the provinces within a unitary constitutional framework in a manner that would gain adequate support, particularly from the Inkatha Freedom Party (IFP) whose main electoral base lay in KwaZulu-Natal. The IFP was keen for a federal constitutional framework to be adopted, in which the provinces would be given extensive powers, but the ANC was opposed to this proposal.[9] Initially the IFP intended to boycott the first democratic elections but in the end, it decided to contest the elections just days before the elections were held, causing a major headache for the Independent Electoral Commission.

The process of constitution-making was split into two stages. In the first stage, which was completed before the first democratic elections were held in April 1994, the leaders of the liberation movements, the National Party government and other political parties convened to draft and agree the text of an interim Constitution. That interim Constitution included a schedule that listed thirty-four constitutional principles with which the final Constitution had to comply.[10] This stage was completed before the first democratic elections in 1994.

The final Constitution was then negotiated and agreed by democratically elected Members of Parliament who convened also as the Constitutional Assembly. The text drafted by the Constitutional Assembly was put before the Constitutional Court for it to certify whether it did indeed comply with the thirty-four constitutional principles. Of the 485 paragraphs in the certification judgment,[11] which traversed dozens of issues, 175 paragraphs (well more than a third) were concerned with the single question: were the powers of provinces as provided in the text "substantially less than or substantially inferior to" the powers of provinces as provided for in the interim Constitution? The Court answered affirmatively with the result that the text relating to the powers of the provinces was one of the nine issues in relation to which the Court held that the constitutional text did not comply with the Constitutional Principles set out in the interim Constitution. The text was referred back to the Constitutional Assembly for revision, and the text was then once again presented to the Court for certification.[12] This time, the Court held that the powers of provinces under the new text were still less than or inferior to the

9 Hassen Ebrahim *The Soul of a Nation: Constitution-making in South Africa* (Cape Town: Oxford University Press, 1999) 230.

10 See Constitution of the Republic of South Africa Act 1993.

11 See *Certification of the Constitution of the Republic of South Africa* (1996) 4 SA 744 (CC).

12 *Certification of the Amended Text of the Constitution of the Republic of South Africa* (1997) 2 SA 97 (CC).

powers of provinces in the interim Constitution, but the difference was not substantial, and accordingly the Court concluded on this issue that the revised constitutional text was in compliance with the constitutional principles.[13]

Given the intense political contestation about provincial powers in the period between 1990 and 1997, it is surprising that only approximately twenty-five cases (of the 600 or so cases that have been heard by the Constitutional Court since 1994) have concerned the constitutional allocation of powers between the three spheres of government (national, provincial and municipal) and none of these cases has been highly contentious. Section 146 of the Constitution provides a deadlock-breaking mechanism that has hardly ever been called upon in court. Moreover, the number of cases concerned with provincial powers has been declining. Indeed, since 2010 the Court has heard only three key cases concerning provincial powers (although in the same period it has dealt with five cases on the distribution of power between provincial and local government).[14]

The paucity of cases that have come before the Constitutional Court suggests that the issue of provincial powers, while not entirely dormant, is markedly less divisive than it was in the early 1990s. There are at least two possible reasons for this. The first is that in 1994 only two of the provinces established had previously been provinces (the Free State and Kwa-Zulu Natal). The remaining seven provinces were carved out of other provinces and the former homeland states of Transkei, Bophuthatswana, Ciskei and Venda. Arguably, then, there was little sense of strong provincial identity within the newly established provinces, an identity that takes time to develop. A second, perhaps more influential, reason is that in the first twenty years of democracy in South Africa, the ANC has been the governing party in the national government and the governing party in most of the provinces.

There has been disagreement between the provincial government of the Western Cape (where the Democratic Alliance has held political control for some years) and the national government over the scope of provincial powers. This disagreement was evident when the Western Cape, following insistent demands by nongovernmental organizations, appointed a commission of inquiry into policing in Khayelitsha. The authority of the Premier of the Western Cape to appoint such a commission, and to clothe it with powers of

13 Ibid. para. 198.

14 See *Premier, Limpopo Province* v. *Speaker: Limpopo Provincial Legislature* (2011) 6 SA 396 (CC); *Premier, Limpopo Province* v. *Speaker of Limpopo Provincial Legislature (No 2)* (2012) 40 SA 58 (CC); *Minister of Police* v. *Premier of the Western Cape* (2014) 1 SA 1 (CC).

subpoena, was challenged by the SAPS and the national government, initially in the High Court and then in the Constitutional Court.[15]

The issue of provincial oversight of policing had been one of the contentious issues in the certification process, and one in which the Constitutional Court had found the powers of the provinces to be wanting. The commission of inquiry power at issue in the case was one of the late amendments to the constitutional text.[16] In the Western Cape case, the Constitutional Court unanimously upheld the right of the province to appoint a Commission of Inquiry and to grant it subpoena powers. Deputy Chief Justice Moseneke reasoned that a province "has a legitimate interest that its residents are shielded from crime and that they enjoy the protection of effective, efficient and visible policing. That explains why the province has the authority and duty to raise its concerns on policing in the province with the Minister. Thus, the entitlements accord with the province's duty to respect, protect and promote fundamental rights of its residents."[17]

This case provides a clear example of how the Constitution provides a mechanism for the resolution of disputes over the powers of provinces when those disputes arise. It shows that the Constitution can accommodate, and at times, resolve conflict.

The fact that the issue of the powers of provinces is less controversial than it once was should not lead us to overlook the fact that provinces remain of central importance in our constitutional design. Not only do the provinces have significant powers in respect of their own geographical areas, but they also have a key role in Parliament.

The second house, the National Council of Provinces (the NCOP), is designed to represent the issues of provinces in Parliament "to ensure that provincial interests are taken into account in the national sphere of government."[18] It does this "by participating in the national legislative process and by providing a national forum for public consideration of issues affecting the provinces."[19] Where a Bill does not impact the provinces, the Bill may be passed without the support of the NCOP.[20] Where the Bill does affect the provinces, then the NCOP must pass the Bill for it to become law. If a deadlock

[15] See *Minister of Police* v. *Premier of the Western Cape* (2014) 1 SA 1 (CC).

[16] Constitution of the Republic of South Africa Act 1996, s. 206(5). See *Certification of the Amended Text of the Constitution of the Republic of South Africa* (1997) 2 SA 97 (CC), para. 168.

[17] Ibid. para. 37.

[18] Constitution of the Republic of South Africa 1996, s. 41(4).

[19] Ibid.

[20] See Constitution of the Republic of South Africa 1996, s. 74.

arises between the National Assembly and the NCOP then the Bill is referred to a constitutionally mandated Mediation Committee.

In its Joint Rules, Parliament has adopted a procedure for classifying or "tagging" bills as to whether they are bills that affect provinces or not.[21] The Constitutional Court has held that in "tagging" a bill the question to be asked is whether the bill's provisions "in substantial measure" affect the provinces.[22] If a bill is incorrectly tagged as not affecting provinces when it does, the subsequently enacted legislation will be invalid.[23]

To date the NCOP has rarely resisted legislation proposed by the National Assembly. Perhaps this is partly because a sense of provincial interests, as distinct from national interests, has not yet emerged; and perhaps it is partly because of the ANC's electoral dominance, both nationally and across eight of the nine provinces. I am not suggesting that this will not change; far from it. Should electoral politics shift, the contestation around provincial powers is likely to revive. Moreover, as time goes on, a sense of provincial identity appears to be emerging that might influence the impact of the Constitution in this area.

In the meantime, although the debate over the scope of provincial powers may have temporarily subsided, a different issue of urgent concern relating to the provinces has arisen. It relates to the unevenness in performance among provinces and, in particular, the weakness of many provinces in relation to crucial areas of service delivery. The constitutional structure makes provincial government the lynchpin for delivery of the key social services, including health, education and housing.[24] The exception is social grants. In this respect, interestingly, the Constitutional Court held, in a 2004 challenge, that the legislation that governs social assistance grants was not legislation that could be assigned to the provinces as it required to be regulated in terms of national uniform norms and standards.[25]

Because social service delivery is premised upon provinces that function well, the need to address the problem of weak provinces is an urgent question. Indeed, these issues surfaced in several cases before the Constitutional Court that related to the redrawing of provincial boundaries, where communities

[21] Joint Rules of Parliament pt 18.

[22] See *Tongoane* v. *National Minister for Agriculture and Land Affairs* (2010) 6 SA 214 (CC) paras. 58, 72.

[23] Ibid. para. 109.

[24] See Constitution of the Republic of South Africa 1996, sch. 4.

[25] See *Mashavha* v. *President of the RSA* 2005 (2) SA 476 (CC).

were resisting being shifted into provinces that were perceived to be poor at service delivery.[26]

Provinces are funded from allocations made from the National Revenue Fund.[27] Section 100 permits the national government to intervene when a province "cannot or does not fulfil an executive obligation."[28] The dismal failure of the Eastern Cape and Limpopo provinces in relation to education led national government to employ the s. 100 override. However, the recent school textbook litigation suggests that the exercise of the s. 100 intervention power has not been a great success, prompting questions as to how the failures of provincial governments may be addressed.[29]

An assessment of the role of provinces under our constitutional order twenty years on suggests that the high levels of contestation as to the constitutional powers of provinces have for the moment abated, but a greater concern as to the responsiveness and efficiency of provinces has arisen. What can be done to improve service delivery in the provinces remains uncertain. Extensive litigation relating to the functioning of schools, especially in the Eastern Cape, has demonstrated just how weak the province is in delivering quality education. How this will be improved is not clear.

Yet, simultaneously it is clear that provincial political interests have developed within political party structures, particularly the ANC. Although calls are heard from time to time for a reduction in the number of provinces, or the redrawing of provincial boundaries, it is far from certain that such a course would be politically feasible, given the vested interest the provinces have in the powers they enjoy. Time will tell.

There are two conclusions that we may draw from this analysis of provincial powers. First, democracies are not static. They shift over time as political forces change. The consequence is that the manner in which a constitutional framework operates will also change, even when the text does not. Secondly, there is a reciprocal relationship between constitutional text and political developments. Political developments may affect both the constitutional text and its framework, and the constitutional framework itself may influence political developments. The interplay between the constitutional framework and political institutions that we have seen over the past twenty years, demonstrates the dynamic nature of our constitutional democracy.

26 See *Matatiele Municipality* v. *President of the Republic of South Africa (No. 2)* (2007) 1 BCLR 47 (CC).

27 See Constitution of the Republic of South Africa Act 1996, s. 214.

28 See the discussion in *Minister of Basic Education* v. *Basic Education for All* (2016) 4 SA 63 (SCA).

29 Ibid.

2.3. THE BILL OF RIGHTS

2.3.1. *The Property Clause: Section 25*

In South Africa, the process of colonial dispossession culminated in the Natives Land Act, 27 of 1913, which together with subsequent legislation,[30] set aside 87 percent of rural land in South African for white ownership and occupation. The scheme envisaged by the Land Act was rigorously enforced and led to brutal forced removals under a variety of legislative provisions that continued over many decades. Its impact at the time was movingly described by a spokesperson for the Transvaal branch of the ANC to the Beaumont Commission: "The Act causes our people to be derelict and hopeless ... There is winter in the Natives Land Act. In winter the trees are stripped and leafless."[31]

The Surplus People's Project estimated that, between 1960 and 1982, 3.5 million people were removed from rural land in the decades following 1950.[32] Addressing this bitter legacy of dispossession, forced removals and insecure tenure was recognized to be one of the imperatives of our new constitutional order.

Given the injustices manifest in our history, it is not surprising that the property clause is one of the Constitution's most controversial provisions. The clause, with its nine subdivisions, is deeply sensitive to the historical injustices but is also clear in its protection of property rights. The clause has two halves.[33] The first half of the clause provides that arbitrary deprivation of property is impermissible and that expropriation may only take place for a public purpose in the public interest and subject to the payment of compensation.[34] The clause states explicitly that the public interest includes "the nation's commitment to land reform, and to reforms to bring about equitable access to all South Africa's natural resources."[35]

The second half of the clause imposes three positive obligations upon the state to address the legacy of landlessness. First, it requires the state to take reasonable legislative and other measures to foster conditions that enable citizens

[30] Natives Trust and Land Act 18 of 1936.

[31] Cited in C. Bundy, "Land, law and power: Forced removals in historical context" in C. Murray and C. O'Regan (eds.), *No Place to Rest: Forced Removals and The Law* (Cape Town: Oxford University Press, 1990) 6.

[32] L. Platzky and C. Walker, *The Surplus People: Forced Removals in South Africa* (Johannesburg: Ravan, 1985) 5.

[33] A. J. Van der Walt, *Constitutional Property Law*, 3rd ed. (Cape Town: Juta, 2011) 16.

[34] Constitution of the Republic of South Africa Act 1996, ss. 25(1)–(3).

[35] Ibid. s. 25(4)(a).

to gain access to land on an equitable basis.[36] Second, it imposes an obligation upon Parliament to enact legislation to provide people whose tenure of land is legally insecure as a result of past racially discriminatory laws to secure tenure or comparable redress.[37] And third, it provides that people whose land was taken from them as a result of racially discriminatory laws after June 19, 1913 (the day the Natives Land Act was promulgated) are entitled to restitution of that land or equitable redress in accordance with an Act of Parliament.[38]

These three obligations suggest that the Constitution requires at least three policy interventions by government: first, a land restitution program to provide those communities and individuals who were dispossessed of land or housing as a result of *apartheid* legislation during the twentieth century with restitution of their land or other redress; second, a process to provide secure tenure for those whose tenure was rendered insecure as a result of racially discriminatory laws; and third, a land reform program to change the racial pattern of land ownership in South Africa.

Initially, the property clause did not lead to significant litigation in the Constitutional Court. Of 260 judgments delivered by the Court in its first decade, only about five judgments considered the property clause. However, in the second decade that changed significantly. Since 2005, approximately thirty judgments out of a total of 340 judgments concerned s. 25. Accordingly, nearly 10 percent of all the Court's decisions related to the property clause in that decade, which constituted a dramatic increase over the previous decade.

The leading case on what constitutes "arbitrary deprivation" of property is the *First National Bank (FNB)* case.[39] There, the Court held that where a deprivation of property occurs, there must be "an appropriate relationship between means and ends, between the sacrifice the individual is asked to make and the public purpose this is intended to serve."[40] The test has been summarized in a later case to mean a deprivation will be arbitrary if it is without "sufficient reason" or is procedurally unfair.[41]

36 Ibid. s. 25(5).

37 Ibid. s. 25(6).

38 Ibid. s. 25(7).

39 *First National Bank of SA Ltd t/a Wesbank* v. *Commissioner for the South African Revenue Service; First National Bank of SA Ltd t/a Wesbank* v. *Minister of Finance* (2002) 4 SA 768 (CC) ("*First National Bank*").

40 Ibid. para. 98.

41 See *Mkontwana* v. *Nelson Mandela Metropolitan Municipality; Bissett* v. *Buffalo City Municipality; TRAC* v. *MEC, Local Government and Housing, Gauteng* (2005) 1 SA 530 (CC) para. 93.

In *FNB*, the Court was concerned with the constitutionality of s. 114 of the Customs and Excise Act, 91 of 1964, which provided that goods found on the premises of a customs debtor could be sold in execution without a prior order of court to satisfy any customs debts of the customs debtor. Vehicles belonging to FNB that were, in effect, being leased to customs debtors, had been attached by the tax authorities to satisfy the debts of the customs debtors. The Court held that there was no sufficient reason for the attachment (and sale) of property of noncustoms debtors to meet the debt of customs debtors.[42]

The Court has applied the *FNB* test for arbitrariness in at least fourteen subsequent cases. Four of these cases have concerned forfeitures under the Prevention of Organised Crime Act 121 of 1998. In all but one of these, the forfeiture was held not to constitute an arbitrary deprivation of property.[43] The approach adopted by the Court is that it should consider whether the forfeited property is closely associated with the commission of the crime, whether the forfeiture will prevent further wrongdoing, whether the owner of the property is innocent of the crime, and the nature and use of the property and the effect of forfeiture on the owner.[44]

The remaining arbitrary deprivation challenges have concerned a raft of different pieces of legislation including property rates regulations,[45] foreign exchange regulations[46] and the National Credit Act.[47] One of the most recent was a challenge by a supermarket to a new legislative scheme that removed supermarkets' licenses to sell liquor. The scheme was, by a majority, held not to be unconstitutional.[48] Six judges held that the liquor license did constitute property within the meaning of the Constitution, and four of those held that the scheme to end supermarket sales of liquor was not arbitrary. However, Deputy Chief Justice Moseneke supported by four other judges, held that the liquor license did not constitute property within the meaning of the Constitution.

In reaching this conclusion, Judge Moseneke noted in an interesting passage that "[a]dministrative law in this country provides ample redress against

42 Ibid. paras. 108–109.

43 See *Mohunram* v. *National Director of Public Prosecutions* 2007 (4) SA 222 (CC).

44 See also *Prophet* v. *NDPP* (2007) 6 SA 169 (CC).

45 See *Mkontwana* v. *Nelson Mandela Metropolitan Municipality*; *Bissett* v. *Buffalo City Municipality*; *TRAC* v. *MEC, Local Government and Housing, Gauteng* (2005) 1 SA 530 (CC).

46 See *Van der Merwe* v. *Taylor NO* (2008) 1 SA 1 (CC); *Armbruster* v. *Minister of Finance* (2007) 2 SA 550 (CC); *SARB* v. *Shuttleworth* (2015) 5 SA 146 (CC).

47 *National Credit Regulator* v. *Opperman* (2013) 6 SA 192 (CC).

48 See *Shoprite Checkers (Pty) Ltd* v. *MEC for Economic Development, Eastern Cape* (2015) 6 SA 125 (CC).

arbitrary executive decisions on whether to grant, renew, cancel or alter a liquor license. A prerequisite to these remedies is not whether a liquor license is property or not."[49] He added: "If the impugned statute had authorised a wanton and irrational termination of the liquor licences ... in a law that was not properly related to public good, it would have been constitutionally bad."[50] These passages are interesting because they point to the inherent rule of law protections that exist in other aspects of the Constitution against arbitrary actions by government, regardless of a specific constitutional protection of property.

Perhaps the most interesting property case of the last few years is *AgriSA* v. *Minister for Minerals and Energy*,[51] which concerned the question whether the Mineral and Petroleum Resources Development Act 28 of 2002 (the MPRDA) expropriated the coal-mining rights of a company when it came into force in 2004. The Act had the effect of freezing the ability to sell, lease or cede unused old-order mining rights until they were converted to prospecting or mining rights under the new Act. Holders of old-order mining rights who did not apply for new order mining rights lost their old-order rights. The appellants argued that the Act had the effect of expropriating old-order mining rights without compensation. Sixteen judges in three courts heard the case. Only one (Du Plessis J in the High Court) upheld the claim. Although five judgments in all were written in the Supreme Court of Appeal (SCA) and the Constitutional Court, not one of those judgments would have upheld the claim. Wallis JA held for the majority in the SCA that no expropriation had occurred because, properly construed, the State has always asserted that the right to mine vests in the State, and it either exercises or allocates that right.[52] Mogoeng CJ on behalf of a majority in the Constitutional Court held that the MPRDA had resulted in a deprivation of property, but not an expropriation. Whatever the merits of the different judgments, no reader of the decisions could conclude that the Courts had been blind to the economic and historical importance of mining rights in South Africa, or insensitive to the need for a democratic government to seek to establish a new statutory framework for mining rights.

In sum, of the fourteen or so challenges based on the question of whether there has been an arbitrary deprivation of property under s. 25, all but four have failed.[53] A quite different picture emerges when we look at the jurisprudence

49 Ibid. para. 128.

50 Ibid. para. 129.

51 2013 (4) SA 1 (CC).

52 See *Minister of Minerals and Energy* v. *AgriSA* (2012) 5 SA 1 (SCA) para. 84.

53 *First National Bank*; *Mohunram* v. *NDPP* 2007 (4) SA 222 (CC); *National Credit Regulator* v. *Opperman* (2013) 6 SA 192 (CC); *Chevron SA* v. *Wilson* (2015) 10 BCLR 1158 (CC).

under the Restitution of Land Rights Act 22 of 1994. The Restitution Act is the legislation contemplated in s. 25(7) of the Constitution, which provides that individuals or communities dispossessed of property after June 1913 are entitled to restitution or compensation for that dispossession.

Seven judgments of the Constitutional Court consider the interpretation and application of the Restitution Act. In an early case,[54] the Constitutional Court held that the proper interpretation of the Act raised a constitutional matter. In its judgments on the Act, the Court demonstrates an acute awareness of the painful history of racial dispossession, and has sought to ensure that it is attentive to that history in interpreting and applying the Act.

For example, the Court has held that the termination of labor tenancies by private famers entitled the labor tenants to restitution under the Act.[55] In the case *Department of Land Affairs v. Goedgelegen Tropical Fruits*, the Constitutional Court found that the ancestors of the applicants had lived on the land since the 1880s and transmitted their right to live on the land to their descendants. Their security of tenure was interrupted when the government of the Zuid Afrikaansche Republiek granted the land to white farmers in 1889. The new farmers forced the community into labor tenancy, an insecure form of tenancy, in terms of which the community were required to work for the new farmers in return for cropping and grazing rights on the land. In 1969, the farmer terminated the labor tenancy arrangements, and the community was required to sell their livestock and continue only as wage laborers on the farm. Many of them left, but some stayed on. When the Restitution Act was promulgated they sought restitution of their land rights under it. They did not succeed before the Land Claims court but the Constitutional Court upheld their claim.

It is striking that this is the result reached in most of the Constitutional Court judgments concerned with restitution. No doubt this is because of the Court's close attention to the purpose of the Restitution Act, and the history that lies behind that purpose. But this reflects quite a different pattern to the approach of the Court in relation to the question of arbitrary deprivation, set out above.

A reading of the judgments on s. 25 of the Constitution thus makes it clear that the property clause has been interpreted and applied by the courts in a manner that is respectful of legislative choices in the sphere of property. The Court has rarely struck down legislative programs that result in deprivation of property as arbitrary. On the other hand, the Court has been expansive in

[54] *Alexkor Ltd* v. *Richtersveld Community* (2004) 5 SA 460 (CC).

[55] See *Department of Land Affairs* v. *Goedgelegen Tropical Fruits (Pty) Ltd* (2007) 6 SA 199 (CC).

relation to the interpretation of the Restitution Act, and has generally sought to ensure that communities who were dispossessed of their land under *apartheid* land law receive either restitution or appropriate compensation.[56]

Very few cases concerning expropriation and compensation have come before the Court.[57] And none concerning land reform. It is interesting that the Expropriation Act 63 of 1975 has thus far remained in place throughout the first twenty years of our constitutional democracy, despite the express regulation of expropriation and compensation in s. 25 of the Constitution. However, the National Assembly has recently passed an Expropriation Bill, which will repeal the 1975 Act and fundamentally change the process of expropriation. This Bill will also redefine the factors relevant to the determination of compensation.

2.3.2. *The Right of Access to Housing Clause: Section 26*

The provisions of the property clause need to be read in conjunction with the very next provision of the constitution. Section 26 entrenches the right of everyone to have access to adequate housing, imposes positive obligations upon the state to take reasonable legislative and other measures within available resources to achieve the progressive realization of the right of access to housing, and prohibits arbitrary evictions and evictions without an order of court taken after a consideration of all relevant circumstances.

Like the property clause, there were very few judgments concerning s. 26 in the first decade: just three out of 280. But in the second decade, that jumped to twenty-four judgments concerning s. 26 out of a total of 340. Again, this is a remarkable increase. Seventeen of the twenty-four right-to-housing judgments since 2005 have involved the question of eviction in some form. Many of these cases have involved applications for eviction at the instance of a local authority.

What is clear from the jurisprudence is that the Court has been insistent that evictions should be a matter of last resort, that they may not be effected without attention to the interests of the occupiers, and in most circumstances without a process of meaningful engagement, especially where it is a local government that seeks to evict. Even applications for eviction at the instance of private individuals have been refused (or overturned) where the Court is

[56] Arguably *Florence* v. *Government of the Republic of South Africa* (2014) 6 SA 456 (CC) is an exception to the overall pattern.

[57] See *Du Toit* v. *Minister of Transport* (2006) 1 SA 297 (CC); *Haffeejee NO* v. *Ethekwini Municipality* (2011) 6 SA 134 (CC).

of the view that the interests of the occupiers being evicted have not been properly considered.[58] Moreover, the Court has imposed a duty upon local government to assist with alternative accommodation where occupiers are evicted at the instance of private landlords.[59] The balance that is being sought was formulated first by Justice Sachs in *Port Elizabeth Municipality*:

> In sum, the Constitution imposes new obligations on the courts concerning rights relating to property not previously recognized by the common law. It counterposes to the normal ownership rights of possession, use and occupation, a new and equally relevant right not arbitrarily to be deprived of a home. The expectations that ordinarily go with title could clash head-on with the genuine despair of people in dire need of accommodation. The judicial function in these circumstances is not to establish a hierarchical arrangement between the different interests involved, privileging in an abstract and mechanical way the rights of ownership over the right not to be dispossessed of a home, or vice versa. Rather it is to balance out and reconcile the opposed claims in as just a manner as possible, taking account of all the interests involved and the specific factors relevant in each particular case.[60]

This is not an easy balance. Nor is it one that admits of emphatic certainty. Yet it is a balance that needs to be sought in an acknowledgement of the injustices of South African history. Most cases are brought under the Prevention of Illegal Eviction from and Unlawful Occupation of Land Act, 19 of 1998 (PIE). In many senses, the legal developments relating to s. 26, and particularly in the eviction jurisprudence developed by the Constitutional Court has resulted in a fundamental shift in our law of eviction, so that a title deed is no longer automatically determinative of the outcome in an eviction case, where the case concerns the eviction from a home.

I hope that I have illustrated that the jurisprudence under both ss. 25 and 26 evinces a deep concern about the apartheid and colonial legacy that has left so many Black South Africans without security of tenure or access to homes or land at all. How the balance is struck in any case may be a matter upon which we can reasonably disagree, but that there is a balance to be struck in cases that concern homelessness or landlessness seems to be immanent within the text of s. 25 itself.

58 See, e.g., the recent judgment in *Pitje* v. *Shibambo* (2016) 4 BLCR 460 (CC).

59 See *City of Johannesburg Metropolitan Municipality* v. *Blue Moonlight Properties 39 (Pty) Ltd* (2012) 2 SA 104 (CC).

60 *Port Elizabeth Municipality* v. *Various Occupiers* (2005) 1 SA 217 (CC) para. 23.

2.3.3. *The Land Question*

And yet, of course, the land question remains. Simply put, South Africa has approximately 85 million hectares of viable agricultural land. The new government's plan was to transfer 30 percent of existing agricultural land to black farmers within twenty years. However, that target was not met. Just less than one-third of the target 25 million hectares has been redistributed so far.

According to the National Development Plan 2030 (the Plan), about 40 000 households had benefited from government's land reform program by 2009. A further 270 000 households had benefited from the government's land restitution program.[61] However, the vast majority of claims under the restitution program relate to urban property and many claims resulted in the payment of compensation rather than the return of the land.

The Plan also acknowledges that many of the beneficiaries of the land restitution program have been unable to work the land effectively, because they lacked infrastructure, inputs and technical support.[62] Land reform beneficiaries are also hampered by high debt burdens, and by the State's inability to provide postsettlement support. The Plan proposes a stepped financing program to resolve this problem.[63]

The Plan also proposes a model for land reform. It is proposed that each district municipality in South Africa in which there are commercial farms should establish a District Lands Committee, to be comprised of agricultural landowners, as well as private- and public-sector stakeholders. It proposes that each Committee identify 20 percent of the agricultural land in the district for transfer to black farmers. Land that might fall in this category would include deceased estates, land already on the market and land held by absentee landlords willing to exit. The Plan proposes that the State pay 50 percent of the market value in order to acquire the land[64] and that the shortfall be made up by cash or in kind contributions from farmers in the district, in return for a guarantee that they would keep their land, and black economic empowerment status.

But, disappointingly, the Plan has not been implemented. It was followed in 2011 by a Green Paper on Land Reform, which makes some broad outline

[61] See National Planning Commission, *National Development Plan 2030: Our Future – Make it Work*, 221 (available at https://nationalplanningcommission.files.wordpress.com/2015/02/ndp-2030-our-future-make-it-work_0.pdf) (accessed date November 20, 2017).

[62] Ibid.

[63] Ibid. 222.

[64] Ibid. 227.

proposals concerning land reform, but which has also not proceeded to legislation.

There are no doubt reasons for the failure to develop a major land program. Chief among them is that successful land reform is both costly and difficult. It requires far more than a change in land ownership: new farmers need extensive support in the form of infrastructural development; training and support; agricultural inputs such as seeds, fertilizers and equipment; as well as assistance with access to local and global markets.

Once government does develop and implement a land reform program, it is clear that a balance will need to be struck between the rights of existing landowners and the public interest in land reform. That balance will need to be similar to the balance already pursued by the Court in relation to ss. 25 and 26. It is probable that the Court will evince the same concern in seeking that balance as it has already demonstrated. But until the land reform program is designed and implemented how that balance will be struck remains uncertain.

2.4. CONCLUSION

Nineteen years on there are many measures by which we could choose to assess the South African Constitution. One of the most important measures can be found in the goals that the Constitution itself explicitly declares. The two most important of these goals, both identified in the Preamble, are the goal of laying the foundation for a democratic and open society, and the goal of establishing a society based on social justice – one in which the quality of life of all may be improved. Although challenges remain, I would suggest that South Africa has made good headway in establishing an open and democratic society. Like all democracies, ours is a dynamic democracy. The analysis of provincial powers in this chapter has demonstrated a reciprocal interplay between text and political practice, which we should expect in a healthy and vibrant democracy.

However, the second goal of our Constitution – a society in which the quality of life of all is improved – remains unaccomplished. In this regard, the analysis of the property and right of access to housing clauses show that the Constitutional Court has been sensitive to the history of land dispossession in South Africa. The case law does not suggest that either s. 25 or s. 26 have been interpreted in a manner that hampers the achievement of the substantive goal of the Constitution. However, the jurisprudence also suggests that courts cannot provide the policy direction required for achieving the Constitution's substantive goal. Finding this direction will require thoughtful and responsive engagement with politicians, government and citizens. The Constitution endorses a range of values and constructs a set of institutions that together enable the achievement of the substantive goal of the Constitution. However, the achievement of that goal remains in the first instance the task of politics rather than law.

To my mind, a generational review of our Constitution should conclude that we have made good progress in achieving the goal of establishing a democratic society; but unsatisfactory progress on establishing a society in which the potential of each person is freed. Yet the preceding analysis has found no evidence to suggest that our constitutional framework has been a cause of this worrying failure. We should be wary of those claiming otherwise. The jurisprudence of the Constitutional Court, at least in relation to ss. 25 and 26 (the property clause and the right of access to housing) has been supportive of the constitutional goal of addressing the legacy of inequality in South Africa, not destructive of it.

3

The Performance of Socio-economic Rights in the South African Constitution

David Bilchitz

3.1. EVALUATING PERFORMANCE AND METHODOLOGY

One of the features of the South African Constitution that is often referred to as "transformative" is the inclusion of fully justiciable socio-economic rights. Most Constitutions prior to the wave of constitution-making in the late 1980s did not include such rights, or if they did, they were included as directive principles which could not be adjudicated upon by courts. The South African Final Constitution was one of the first African constitutions to include such rights as fully justiciable and was unusual in the English-speaking world in that regard (constitutions in Latin America and Eastern Europe more frequently included such rights). As a result, the South African experience has attracted much attention internationally: could South Africa overcome the many objections that have been lodged against the inclusion of such rights as fully justiciable? Does South Africa provide a model for the inclusion of these rights and is there some way of determining whether their inclusion has been a success or not?

Some of these questions can be summarized in an enquiry into whether or not socio-economic rights have "performed." Answering that question is complex, as will be seen. This chapter on socio-economic rights in particular is based upon a larger project undertaken by the South African Institute for Advanced Constitutional, Public, Human Rights and International Law

This chapter is based upon a segment of a major project that the South African Institute for Advanced Constitutional, Public, Human Rights and International Law was commissioned to conduct on behalf of International IDEA. I revised it for publication as a chapter in this book. Linette Du Toit is thanked for her work on the section on the right to education.

(SAIFAC) that was commissioned by the International Institute for Democracy and Electoral Assistance (International IDEA). That wider project sought to evaluate the performance of the South African Constitution over the past twenty years.[1] The notion of the performance of a constitution or constitutional provisions is itself contested: what does it in fact mean for a constitution to perform? How can this be evaluated?

The methodology utilized to assess the performance of the South African Constitution was a modified version of that proposed by Professor Tom Ginsburg and Professor Aziz Huq.[2] Some of the complexities involved in answering these questions have been engaged already in the introductory chapter to this book. After outlining in brief the various steps of this methodology, and how it was modified, I turn to applying it to a particular area of analysis, namely, the performance of socio-economic rights. Since the nature of such a project is vast, the focus of this chapter will be on three rights, namely, the rights to housing, health care and education. I shall argue that the socio-economic rights in the South African constitution have had a significant effect on law and policy and, in this sense, can certainly be said to have "performed." At the same time, their potential impact on the lives of individuals has perhaps been lessened as a result of the weak approach adopted by the Constitutional Court to give effect to them. Comparative experience – only canvassed very briefly in this chapter – helps to highlight alternative trajectories that might have been followed. The South African experience thus provides a strong case for the constitutionalization of social rights more generally but also provides a fruitful space for analyzing the conditions and factors that play a role in ensuring that they make a qualitative difference in people's lives.

1 The full report is published on the website Constitutionnet (available at www.constitutionnet.org/vl/item/report-assessment-south-africa) (accessed date November 20, 2017).

2 T. Ginsburg and A. Huq, "What can constitutions do? Lessons from Afghanistan's experience?" (2014) 24 *Journal of Democracy* 116–30; T. Ginsburg and A. Huq, "Evaluating constitutional implementation," paper presented at the Chicago Conference on Constitutional Performance, University of Chicago Law School, 24–25 April (2015). A revised version of the conference paper has recently been published as follows: T. Ginsburg and A. Huq, "Assessing Constitutional Performance," in T. Ginsburg and A. Z. Huq (eds.), *Assessing Constitutional Performance* (New York, NY: Cambridge University Press, 2016) 3–11. This methodology has already been summarized in the introduction to this chapter. I do not engage with alternative methodologies in this chapter given the focus is on applying a particular approach to measuring performance. However, I also recognize the valuable contributions and methodologies that have been developed to measure the performance of socio-economic rights by the non-governmental organization, the Studies in Poverty and Inequality Institute (available at www.spii.org.za/index.php/ser-monitoring-tool/) (accessed date November 20, 2017).

3.2. METHODOLOGY

The guiding methodology outlines two perspectives from which the performance of a constitution can be engaged. The first perspective is an "internal" one that seeks to evaluate the performance of the constitution against its own self-declared goals. The second perspective is "external" and evaluates the constitution against a set of general standards and normative criteria about what any good constitution "should" seek to achieve. The methodology initially proposed sought to begin with an internal evaluation of a constitution against its own goals and thereafter to consider its performance against external criteria. In the South African context, this approach creates difficulty as the internal criteria themselves are extremely ambitious and often include some of the external criteria. The SAIFAC team consequently adapted the proposed methodology and adopted a five-step approach toward evaluating the performance of the South African constitution:

- The first step involves analyzing/interpreting the Constitution in order to determine its internal goals.
- The second step was to engage in an analysis of the relationship between internal and external goals.
- The third step considers possible design flaws in the constitutional architecture itself whereby institutions and particular provisions were not well-suited to achieving their ends.
- The fourth step involves evaluating the actual extent to which the goals of the Constitution have been achieved in particular areas and in an overarching manner.
- The last step involves recommendations for reform where clear underperformance of the Constitution was found.

I do not elaborate in detail on each of these steps as the approach adopted toward them will become evident below in the concrete application of socio-economic rights and has largely been outlined in the introductory chapter of this book. However, to understand the approach adopted below toward socio-economic rights a few comments need to be made on the fourth step above, namely, the evaluation of actual, empirically determined performance against the goals identified in the first two steps.

In approaching this question, the SAIFAC project considered how the South African Constitution has helped to address some of the key tensions and stress points that have arisen in the past twenty years within the South

African political community as a method of analyzing some of the key goals of the Constitution and whether they are met.[3] The focus was on goals where it is reasonable to expect that the Constitution can itself make a difference in a particular sphere.

The analysis of actual performance has also been split into two parts. The first involves *compliance in a "thin" sense* which involves considering whether or not branches of the government have responded to an express mandate in the Constitution to pass legislation, make policy or perform a specific action. Thus, for instance, this enquiry involves considering whether the government has passed access to information legislation in conformity with the requirements of section 32 of the Constitution; or whether national elections have been held every five years in conformity with section 49 of the Constitution. This enquiry is factual and quantitative in nature.

The second part considers whether the Constitution has *performed in a "thick" sense*, which necessitates a much more qualitative assessment. Questions here include, for example: has the Constitution created a stable system of legitimate government, and has the Constitution achieved its socio-economic goals? To address these questions, there is consideration of case law, reports by the government itself, nongovernmental organization reports and other empirical data. An empirical survey was also commissioned to provide an understanding of the attitudes of members of the public in the most populous province of South Africa, Gauteng, toward a number of key dimensions of the Constitution. This survey provided some empirical data which enabled this assessment to take place.[4]

3.3. THE INTERNAL AND EXTERNAL GOALS OF INCLUDING SOCIO-ECONOMIC RIGHTS IN THE SOUTH AFRICAN CONSTITUTION

The purpose of including socio-economic rights in a constitution is itself debated amongst scholars and, thus, it is not possible to identify goals that are free of controversy in doing so.[5]

3 In doing so, we drew upon an interesting paper by R. Gargarella, "When is a constitution doing well? The Alberdian test in the Americas," in T. Ginsburg and A. Z. Huq (eds.), *Assessing Constitutional Performance* (New York, NY: Cambridge University Press, 2016), 99–133.

4 The data can be seen online in Appendix A of the larger report at Constitutionnet.org.

5 F. I. Michelman, "Socio-economic rights in constitutional law: explaining America away" (2008) 6 *International Journal of Constitutional Law* 663–86 at 673–74; K. McLean, *Constitutional Deference, Courts and Socio-Economic Rights in South Africa* (Pretoria: Pretoria University Law Press, 2009) 14.

At the same time, the South African and global context point to two sets of reasons why these rights were included. First, the policy of apartheid had essentially sought to maintain black people as an economic under-class and source of labor for the advancement of white economic interests. One of the main architects of apartheid, Hendrik Verwoerd, had expressly indicated the racist view that black people did not need further education as they were to be physical laborers.[6] The Apartheid government deliberately instituted a policy of providing inferior education to black people (known as Bantu education), prevented most black people from going to university, and confined black people that were not needed for manual labor to areas that were economically under-developed through a permit system which prevented free movement across South Africa. The effect of these policies and others was to create a situation where the vast majority of black people had a limited education and were living in conditions of poverty. One important rationale for the inclusion of socio-economic rights was, therefore, what might be said to be a concern for "corrective justice":[7] the need to address this shocking legacy of the past. The inclusion of socio-economic entitlements would signal to black people that the government was committed to reversing the severe effects these policies had. A guarantee of access to housing would address those whose economic situation left them without a fixed abode; a basic social welfare net was envisaged by requirements to provide food, water and social assistance; the health care services would be expanded; and, the right to education guaranteed with a requirement continually to improve access to the education that people were afforded.[8]

6 D. Harrison, *The White Tribe of Africa: South Africa in Perspective* (Los Angeles: University of California Press, 1981) 191. During a debate in the Senate about the Bantu Education Act 1953, Verwoerd made the following statement:

> The school must equip the Bantu to meet the demands which the economic life in South Africa will impose on him ... There is no place for him in the European community above the level of certain forms of labour. Within his own community, however, all doors are open ... Until now he has been subject to a schools system which drew him from his own community and misled him by showing him the green pastures of European society in which he is not allowed to graze ... What is the use of teaching a Bantu child mathematics when it cannot use it in practice? ... That is absurd. Education is not, after all, something that hangs in the air. Education must train and teach people in accordance with their opportunities in life ... It is therefore necessary that the native education must be controlled in such a way that it should be in accordance with the policy of the state.

7 C. Mbazira, *Litigating Socio-Economic Rights in South Africa: A Choice Between Corrective and Distributive Justice* (Pretoria: Pretoria University Law Press, 2009) 103–11.

8 R. Dixon and T. Ginsburg point out that there may also have been political reasons for the inclusion of these rights. When it was accepted to include a right to property, socio-economic

The second rationale is more "universalistic" in nature. The South African Constitution was not created in a vacuum and, at the time it was drafted, a greater emphasis was being placed upon the realization of socio-economic rights with, for instance, the publication of General Comment No 3 of the United Nations Committee on Economic, Social and Cultural Rights in 1990 and the inclusion of these rights in many constitutions across Latin America and Eastern Europe. In these contexts, it would seem, such rights were regarded as necessary conditions for the very legitimacy of the basic structure of the society in question.[9] The international community recognized that guaranteeing a minimum level of resources was the hallmark of a decent society and that, failing to do so, could lead poor people to regard the social structures as not catering adequately for them. These rights could also create a more "balanced" constitution[10] where civil and political rights did not automatically trump socio-economic rights and allow for a proper weighing of their respective merits in the case of a normative conflict. Moreover, they could attempt to address the political problem that the interests of the poor are often not adequately addressed through representative structures and require concerted government attention to be focused upon their concerns.[11] In relation to each right, there are goals that relate specifically to its field of focus, such as housing or food.

The manner in which these rights were included in the South African Constitution also indicates an understanding of the scale and scope of the problems facing South African society and that the immediate realization of these rights would not be possible. The conditions in which these rights were to be realized were described by Chaskalson P in the judgment of *Soobramoney* v. *Minister of Health*[12] as follows:

> We live in a society in which there are great disparities in wealth. Millions of people are living in deplorable conditions and in great poverty. There is a high level of unemployment, inadequate social security, and many do not have access to clean water or to adequate health services. These conditions

rights may have been included to "help shield, or immunize, progressive legislation or policies against the potential for further constitutional attack": "The South African Constitutional Court and socio-economic rights as 'insurance swaps'" (2011) 4 *Constitutional Court Review* 1–29 at 8.

9 Michelman, "Explaining America away," 684–5.

10 K. D. Ewing, "Constitutional reform and human rights: unfinished business?" (2001) 5 *The Edinburgh Law Review* 297–324 at 323.

11 D. Bilchitz, "Are socio-economic rights a form of political rights?" (2015) 31 *South African Journal on Human Rights* 86–111 at 93, 97–101.

12 *Soobramoney* v. *Minister of Health* [1998] 1 SA 765 (CC) (*Soobramoney*).

> already existed when the Constitution was adopted and a commitment to address them, and to transform our society into one in which there will be human dignity, freedom and equality, lies at the heart of our new constitutional order.[13]

These conditions influenced how the provisions relating to socio-economic rights were structured. The first subsection outlines the general right such as in subsection 26(1), which states that "everyone has the right to have access to adequate housing." The second subsection, however, involves a number of internal limitations being placed on what can be claimed. Subsection 26(2) thus, for instance, requires the state to take "reasonable legislative and other measures, within its available resources, to achieve the progressive realization of this right." The Constitution thus creates three potential limitations on the right: (a) the government has the duty to take reasonable legislative and other measures; (b) it can only do so within its available resources; and (c) it must do so through progressive realization. These limitations have been the subject of Constitutional Court judgments and provoked much discussion in the literature around socio-economic rights in South Africa. It can be said, at a minimum, that the Constitution on its face recognizes the impossibility of fully realizing the socio-economic rights immediately and, as a result, imposes limitations on those obligations. There is also a commitment to incremental but steady change. Exactly what model the Constitution proposes for giving effect to these rights has been the subject of controversy and affects how we capture the goals of including such provisions in the Constitution.

The Constitutional Court signaled in the seminal case of *Grootboom*[14] that its analysis would largely focus on the notion of reasonableness. It held that the government has a duty to develop a program to realize the right and the Court would order the government to do so if it had not developed any such program. The court would then evaluate the program against the standard of "reasonableness."[15] That standard, the Court held, would involve considerations of the rationality of the program (were the means suited to the achievement of the ends?), whether it treats people equally, and whether it gives priority to the needs of those who are most vulnerable.[16] The underlying goal of the reasonableness enquiry seems to be that government programs must be justifiable and that the role of courts is essentially to expose weaknesses in policies, to require transparent justifications and thereby to improve existing

[13] *Soobramoney* para. 8.

[14] *Government of the Republic of South Africa* v. *Grootboom* [2001] 1 SA 46 (CC) (*Grootboom*).

[15] *Mazibuko* v. *City of Johannesburg* [2010] 4 SA 1 (CC) para. 60.

[16] *Grootboom*, paras. 39–44.

programs.[17] The focus here is on putting in place a justifiable process that will advance the access individuals have to socio-economic resources without any determinate substantive standards of what must be provided.[18]

Critics have argued that the reasonableness standard moves away from a substantive focus on rights and what they enable individuals specifically to claim. They have highlighted that the notion may itself be incoherent as an evaluative tool without committing to any determinate goals that must be achieved in terms of provision. Moreover, some assert that the reasonableness approach has failed to provide concrete guidance to courts and individuals, which severely weakens the effect of these rights.[19] Instead, it has been argued, the socio-economic rights in the South African Constitution should be recognized as providing certain concrete guarantees, such as the entitlement to be provided, as a matter of priority, with a minimum essential level of provision – referred to as a "minimum core" – that is to be determined by identifying the urgent interests each right seeks to cater for.[20] The duty on the government on this view is not simply, for instance, to increase the number of people with access to housing as the reasonableness approach allows. Instead, the government is required to provide everyone with basic shelter in the immediate future whilst increasing their access to a higher level of provision over time. The focus in this alternative approach is thus on determinate standards of provision: a universal minimum must be guaranteed and the quality of provision continuously improved for everyone in contrast with the gradual, quantitative increase in access required by the reasonableness approach.

We raise this controversy concerning the interpretation of socio-economic rights as, in some sense, it identifies some of the tensions in capturing the internal goals of these rights. Are they in the bill of rights simply to place the government under a duty to justify its programs on socio-economic questions and to initiate a process for increasing provision? Or do they require specific substantive goods to be provided to every individual? In a sense, the South African Constitution left open the answer to these questions. That openness could be defended and the ensuing debate around the minimum core could be seen as a success of these rights, in forcing a deeper articulation of the

17 D. Bilchitz, *Poverty and Fundamental Rights: The Justification and Enforcement of Socio-economic Rights* (Oxford: Oxford University Press, 2007) 9–10.

18 B. Ray, *Engaging with Social Rights* (Cambridge: Cambridge University Press, 2016) 42–3.

19 See, for instance, D. Brand, "The proceduralisation of South African socio-economic rights jurisprudence, or 'What are socio-economic rights for?'" in H. Botha et al. (eds.), *Rights and Democracy in a Transformative Constitution* (Stellenbosch: Sun Press, 2003) 33–56; Bilchitz, *Poverty and Fundamental Rights*.

20 Bilchitz, *Poverty and Fundamental Rights*, 14.

point of including them in the Constitution. The fact that they embrace the contested nature of economic policy and models for development could be regarded as a plus, too, in enabling decisions on these questions to be reached through the democratic process.

Yet, that very vagueness could also be regarded as a design flaw: if these rights were envisaged as providing specific goods for the deprived, the lack of clarity has led to courts avoiding doing so in many cases. The approach articulated by the court has rendered it difficult for the poor to run successful cases: large amounts of evidence need to be gathered to show the unreasonableness of a government program. For a country with the high level of poverty of South Africa, the number of cases that directly implicate socio-economic rights has also been relatively small.[21] This can be contrasted with the significant number of socio-economic rights cases in a jurisdiction like Colombia.[22] The socio-economic rights have thus not perhaps had the major impact in ensuring that a social minimum is provided for everyone that was predicted when they were first included in the Constitution. At the same time, as will become evident from an analysis of the specific rights engaged below, they have had some significant impacts.

3.3.1. *Relationship Between Internal and External Goals*

The discussion thus far has indicated how we might seek to capture the internal goals of including socio-economic rights in a constitution and the difficulties of doing so. There are also several important relationships that exist between the internal and external goals identified by Ginsburg and Huq in their methodology.

As has already been mentioned, one key reason for including these rights relates to the legitimacy of the constitutional order. Individuals who lack the most basic needs may have little reason to show fidelity to a constitutional order in which they are starving and homeless. By committing to addressing these forms of deprivation and by requiring the government to make concerted efforts to do so under the possible supervision of the courts, the Constitution itself proclaims its commitment to addressing the inadequate material conditions within which many people live. That, in turn, enhances

21 See, for instance, J. Dugard and S. Wilson, "Constitutional Jurisprudence: the first and second waves," in M. Langford et al. (eds.), *Socio-Economic Rights in South Africa: Symbols or Substance?* (Cambridge: Cambridge University Press, 2014) 36 (counting about 12 cases). The tally depends on what one classifies as a case concerning socio-economic rights.

22 D. Landau, "The reality of social rights enforcement" (2012) 53 *Harvard International Law Journal* 190–246 at 209–11.

its own legitimacy in the eyes of citizens. The approach of the Constitutional Court and its failure to connect with the real reasons people are interested in these rights (addressing their lack of resources) may be seen to reduce the effectiveness of these rights in this regard. In Colombia, for instance, where the courts have adopted a more stringent approach, the role of the Constitution in responding to people's needs has been enhanced and the legitimacy of the courts increased.[23]

The rights were also rendered justiciable in courts. This meant that they were enforceable through legal methods. In this way, instead of taking extra-legal approaches to addressing their interests, the poor were encouraged to channel their concerns through the legal system. This has led social movements and other civil society actors to adopt legal mobilization strategies whereby "a desire or want is translated into a demand as an assertion of rights."[24] The inclusion of these rights also plays a role in legitimizing claims made by the poor in the political space and thus also helps them to advance their interests through simply claiming that they are attempting to have existing rights enforced. The inclusion of these rights also ensures that the political space has to address these interests and helps channel conflict in this manner. People are thus encouraged to use "lawfare" rather than violence in giving expression to their socio-economic demands.[25]

The inclusion of these express rights in the Constitution entails that one of the key responsibilities of government agencies becomes the realization of those rights. There is a moral and legal imperative placed upon these agencies in that regard. Corruption has often been regarded as a violation of these rights through channeling much-needed resources away from the poor.[26] The imperative placed on state agencies has also helped create a moral disapproval of corrupt practices. Unfortunately, the realization of these rights has also created incentives for corrupt activities: desperate and law-abiding individuals may well lose out to those who are prepared to pay for some form of priority.

[23] R. Uprimny Yepes, "The enforcement of social rights by the Colombian Constitutional Court: cases and debates," in R. Gargarella, P. Domingo, and T. Roux (eds.), *Courts and Social Transformations in New Democracies: An Institutional Voice for the Poor* (Aldershot: Ashgate, 2006) 128.

[24] Zeemans quoted in T. Madlingozi, "Post-apartheid social movement and legal mobilisation," in M. Langford et al. (eds.), *Socio-economic Rights in South Africa: Symbols or Substance?* (Cambridge: Cambridge University Press, 2014) 92.

[25] J. Dugard, "Phiri: lawfare rather than warfare," *Mail and Guardian*, July 27, 2009 (available at www.mg.co.za/article/2009-07-27-phiri-lawfare-rather-than-warfare) (accessed date November 20, 2017).

[26] *Glenister* v. *President of the Republic of South Africa* [2011] 3 SA 347 (CC) [167].

Finally, socio-economic rights are centrally concerned with the provision of public goods. Ensuring individuals have access to decent health care and education systems is crucial for enabling individuals to develop their potential and access opportunities. Access to adequate housing improves the lives of people and communities whilst creating adequate social security and welfare systems relieves the worst levels of desperation in society.

3.4. EVALUATION OF THE PERFORMANCE OF SOCIO-ECONOMIC RIGHTS

In evaluating the performance of these rights, a large number of initiatives taken by the government as well as key failures are relevant. I cannot exhaustively analyze policy and legislation in these areas. The focus will be on the main issue as to whether the constitutionalization of these rights has made a difference to law, policy and people's lives. It will be easier to answer this question in relation to law and policy, though I will attempt to marshal evidence to provide some understanding of the impact on people's lives as well. In this evaluation, I will not be considering the performance of all the socio-economic rights protected in the Constitution, but focus on three key rights, namely the rights to have access to: adequate housing, adequate health care and education.[27] These are arguably amongst the core socio-economic rights that seek to ensure a basic set of needs that all people require and are entitled to.

3.4.1. *Right to Have Access to Adequate Housing*

The historical background to housing in South Africa is required to understand the "corrective" component involved. The Apartheid Government instituted a system of controlling the movement of black people through a pass system, which strictly sought to regulate the entry of black persons into urban areas (this was known as influx control). Since black people were not meant to be there (or in very limited numbers), no provision was made to house them. Thus, in the Cape Peninsula area (comprising the city of Cape Town), there was a freeze placed on the provision of family housing for African people from 1962.[28] Despite this, African people continued to move to urban areas due to

[27] Due to the time and space constraints of this chapter, it was decided that the focus should be on the socio-economic rights which have most often been the subject of court battles and civil society campaigns. Although the importance of the right to food, water and social security cannot be discounted, the performance of these rights is not included in the scope of this chapter.

[28] *Grootboom*, para. 6.

colonial dispossession and a rigidly enforced racial distribution of land which had disrupted the rural economy and rendered African farming precarious.[29] This led to the growth of informal settlements around urban areas in South Africa. As the Constitutional Court details in the *Grootboom* case, the "cycle of the apartheid era, therefore, was one of untenable restrictions on the movement of African people into urban areas, the inexorable tide of the rural poor to the cities, inadequate housing, resultant overcrowding, mushrooming squatter settlements, constant harassment by officials and intermittent forced removals."[30] This led to two key violations of rights. First, there was the ability to evict individuals rather easily through legislation such as the Prevention of Illegal Squatting Act 1951 (PISA). If occupation of property was found to be unlawful, individuals could be evicted and they were subject to criminal prosecution. Second, there was a failure to plan and provide housing for black people which led to a massive housing shortage. There was, for instance, a shortage of more than 100,000 housing units in the Cape Metropolitan areas upon the advent of democracy in 1994.[31] Housing is, of course, also important as a universally important human need: as Yacoob J recognizes in the *Grootboom* case, this raises questions of dignity and treating human beings "as human beings."[32]

It is in this light that section 26 of the Constitution needs to be seen. It provides that:

1. everyone has the right to have access to adequate housing;
2. the state must take reasonable legislative and other measures, within its available resources, to achieve the progressive realization of this right;
3. no one may be evicted from their home, or have their home demolished, without an order of court made after considering all the relevant circumstances. No legislation may permit arbitrary evictions.

The right to housing can be seen as an attempt to correct the twin problems of the past whilst recognizing a universal entitlement. On the one hand, it creates negative obligations not to interfere with people's housing and only to do so in a manner where the court has taken into account all relevant considerations and is "non-arbitrary." It also, in the first two subsections, envisages a range of positive obligations which are qualified by the notions of having to be "reasonable," having "available resources," and achieving "progressive realisation."

[29] Ibid.
[30] Ibid.
[31] Ibid.
[32] Ibid. para. 83.

3.4.1.1. Thin Compliance

The government has enacted a number of important measures to give effect to its constitutional obligations. In relation to evictions, the most important Act is the Prevention of Illegal Eviction from and Unlawful Occupation of Land Act 1998 (known as "PIE"). This Act creates procedural and substantive requirements that have to be met when the eviction of unlawful occupiers is being addressed. Several Constitutional Court judgments have elaborated upon the protections afforded by the Constitution and PIE. These will be considered in relation to thick compliance. PIE moves away from a criminal law framework for addressing unlawful occupation and attempts to create an equitable balance between the rights of those who lack a home and the rights of land-owners.[33] It clearly requires an order of court before any eviction can take place and creates requirements that are nonarbitrary and thus conforms to the terms of subsection 26(3).

In relation to the positive obligations of the government, the government adopted a series of measures post-1994 to give effect to housing policy. It issued several white papers and passed both the Housing Act 1997, which came into operation on April 1, 1998, and a Housing Code. The Housing Act seeks to facilitate sustainable housing development. It defines housing development to include two elements: "(a) permanent residential structures with secure tenure, ensuring internal and external privacy and providing adequate protection against the elements; and (b) potable water, adequate sanitary facilities and domestic energy supply."[34] The Act also outlines general principles for housing development, and outlines the responsibilities of different tiers of government (national, provincial and local) in relation to housing. It does not contain detailed policy and instead provides that the Minister must publish a Housing Code that contains the national housing policy.

In September 2004, the Minister published a policy known as "Breaking New Ground: A Comprehensive Plan for the Creation of Sustainable Human Settlements."[35] In 2009, a Revised Housing Code was published which now governs the sector. There have also been additional pieces of legislation such as the Social Housing Act 2008 and the Rental Housing Act 1999. The

33 *Port Elizabeth Municipality* v. *Various Occupiers* [2005] 1 SA 217 (CC) [33] (*Port Elizabeth Municipality*).

34 Housing Act 1997, s. 1.

35 National Department of Human Settlements, *Breaking new ground: a comprehensive plan for the development of sustainable human settlements* (2004) (available at www.thehda.co.za/uploads/files/BREAKING_NEW_GROUND_DOC_copy-2_1.pdf) (accessed date November 20, 2017).

government has clearly established a policy framework for housing and passed legislation in this regard. One possible area of concern, identified by McLean, is that the Constitution in subsection 26(2) mandates the taking of "reasonable *legislative* and other measures" in order to realize the right. Arguably, "[a] purposive interpretation of this injunction would mean that the most important principles and policy choices relating to housing delivery should be deliberated upon by Parliament."[36] Yet, the Housing Act is in a sense secondary to the Housing Code, which contains the most important policies relating to housing. The executive is thus placed in charge of housing policy and implementation with very limited legislative oversight. As McLean argues, "[t]his situation arguably amounts to the abdication by Parliament of its constitutionally mandated role, and may, in addition, violate the principle of legality and the rule of law."[37] Subject to the qualification mentioned by McLean, it does seem that there has been thin compliance with the constitutional provisions, at least, in the sense of developing a policy and legislative framework.

3.4.1.2. Thick Compliance: Negative Obligations and Evictions

In attempting to assess thick compliance, the obligations of the state need to be considered and the extent to which they have in fact been realized against the internal goals highlighted above. In terms of negative obligations, the key legislation as we have seen is PIE. The courts have elaborated upon PIE and developed a number of principles governing eviction: first, as per the Constitution, there must be a court order. Such an order allows the court to evaluate a number of elements of the situation before it with the central principle being to attempt to strike a balance between the rights of the landowner and the rights of the unlawful occupiers.[38] Striking such a balance means that evictions will not automatically be allowed even where there is a legal reason for them. For instance, in the case of an individual who is unable to pay their mortgage, the courts will engage in a proportionality enquiry to determine whether it is fair to evict the individual from his/her home: the Constitutional Court has indicated that, for a very small debt, it would not be just to do so.[39]

36 K. McLean, "Housing," in S. Woolman and M. Bishop (eds.), *Constitutional Law of South Africa*, 2nd edn (Cape Town: Juta, 2008, Vol 4) 55–5.

37 Ibid.

38 *Port Elizabeth Municipality*, para. 33.

39 *Jaftha* v. *Schoeman* [2005] 2 SA 140 (CC).

The courts have also recognized that in order to grant an order, they must be satisfied that there has been a process of engagement between local authorities and the individuals (or the community) concerned. The process of engagement can be considered to connect with the right to dignity as well as the right to political participation. As such, fundamental decisions cannot be taken about people's lives without engaging with them and this understanding embodies at least a minimal form of deliberative democracy. Often, that engagement leads to a solution without having to use the strong arm of the law as occurred in the case of *Occupiers of 51 Olivia Road, Berea Township and 197 Main Street Johannesburg* v. *City of Johannesburg*.[40] In that case, the city had wanted to vacate a number of unsafe buildings in which residents were living in terrible, unsanitary conditions. At the same time, the local government offered to move them far away from their places of income which would have rendered them even worse off. An agreement was reached between the parties whereby temporarily the residents would remain in the buildings and various safety and health measures would be taken to improve the conditions in which they lived. The residents then agreed to the eviction several months later after the city offered to provide accommodation to them in the inner city.[41]

Apart from engagement, a key element of the Constitutional Court's jurisprudence in this area has been the requirement that individuals who are evicted must be provided with alternative accommodation. The Court here recognizes that eviction from a particular property should not be allowed to result in homelessness which would constitute a further violation of the right of individuals to housing. The requirement for alternative accommodation was initially outlined in relation to evictions from public land; however, in the important *Blue Moonlight Properties* case,[42] it was also held to apply to evictions from private land. The government is required in such instances to step in and ensure individuals are provided with alternative accommodation. Private landowners have a duty to be patient with unlawful occupiers for an interim period pending their access to alternative accommodation which is an important implication flowing from the horizontal application of the right to have access to adequate housing.[43] The courts have also refused on occasion to remove occupiers from land where that would disrupt a community of 40,000

[40] [2008] 3 SA 208 (CC).

[41] For a detailed discussion on engagement, see B. Ray, *Engaging with Social Rights* (Cambridge: Cambridge University Press, 2016) 274–329.

[42] *City of Johannesburg Metropolitan Municipality* v. *Blue Moonlight Properties 39 (Pty) Ltd* [2012] 2 SA 104 (CC).

[43] Ibid. para. 40.

people and instead have ordered the state to provide compensation to the private land-owner of the land.[44]

The framework set out in PIE and articulated by the courts has the potential to change fundamentally the face of evictions in South Africa and prevent resulting homelessness. The Constitution can be said to have stimulated the development of standards which attempt to address the legacy of the past and exemplify a sense of equity concerning the conflicting interests at stake. Yet, unfortunately, despite these principles being laid down by the highest court, it is clear that evictions continue to take place in violation of these standards. An example of this took place in a complex of buildings known as Schubart Park, which housed between 3000 and 5000 people. After protests erupted around living conditions in these buildings, the city evicted large numbers of people and refused to allow them to return. The Constitutional Court had to intervene to enable them to return to their properties.[45] Evictions without court orders and in the absence of engagement and meaningful accommodation also continue unabated in places such as Hillbrow.[46]

One of the strange aspects of unlawful evictions is that the high courts have often appeared to disobey the very law laid down by the Constitutional Court. This is extremely concerning and poses a threat to the rule of law itself. Very few cases reach the Constitutional Court and thus, high court decisions can affect individuals in a negative way. A few examples are outlined below.[47] In the *Golden Thread* case,[48] the Constitutional Court dealt with the unlawful occupation of land in Tshwane Municipality and an application in the North Gauteng High Court for the eviction of the occupiers. The High Court ordered an eviction without the provision of alternative accommodation, effectively finding it was just and equitable to do so. The Constitutional Court criticized the High Court for not taking account of the local authority's obligation to provide reasonable alternative accommodation to the occupiers (even where the occupation had been less than six months as part of the "all relevant circumstances enquiry" as required by subsection 26(3) of the Constitution) and working with a conception of ownership rights as "virtually

[44] *President of the Republic of South Africa* v. *Modderklip Boerdery (Pty) Ltd* [2005] 5 SA 3 (CC).

[45] *Schubart Park Resident's Association* v. *City of Tshwane Metropolitan Municipality* [2013] 1 SA 323 (CC).

[46] N. Shange, "'Red' ants evict dozens in Hillbrow," *News 24*, August 12, 2015 (available at www.news24.com/SouthAfrica/News/Red-Ants-evict-dozens-in-Hillbrow-20150812) (accessed date November 20, 2017).

[47] This analysis is drawn from D. Bilchitz, "Avoidance remains avoidance: is it desirable in socio-economic rights cases?" (2013) 5 *Constitutional Court Review* 297–308.

[48] *JR* v. *Golden Thread (Ltd)* [2012] 2 SA 337 (*Golden Thread*).

unlimited."[49] In the *Occupiers of Skurweplaas* 353 case,[50] similarly, an eviction was granted by the North Gauteng High Court. Whilst the High Court did consider alternative accommodation, the judge preferred the land-owner's rights, allowing the people to be rendered homeless pending the provision of alternative accommodation by the city. The Constitutional Court ruled that this was "neither just nor equitable."[51]

The *Marlboro Crisis Committee* case saw the Constitutional Court approve a settlement in terms of which the City of Johannesburg was required to provide emergency housing to the occupiers of various properties in Marlboro and engage meaningfully with them pending their eviction. The unlawful occupiers were removed twice in June and August 2012, with their possessions being destroyed during the latter eviction. The city claimed that the Johannesburg Metropolitan Police Department (JMPD) acted pursuant to their law enforcement functions to prevent trespassing and that this was not an ordinary eviction. In a deeply troubling High Court judgment,[52] the judge upheld this argument, contending that when JMPD acted pursuant to its law enforcement powers, its actions did not constitute an eviction. The judge made it clear that in his view, "it must be instilled in the minds and consciences of potential land-grabbers and unlawful or illegal occupiers, that landowners and contractors of space too are bearers of constitutional rights and that conduct violating those rights tramples, not only on them but on all."[53] The framework developed by the Constitutional Court surrounding evictions clearly recognizes that unlawful occupiers are not to be treated as criminals.[54] Moreover, the judge in this case, also incorrectly used preconstitutional common law to avoid the application of the constitutional framework relating to evictions, of which the PIE is the central pillar. The balancing framework evident in this legislation and the need to consider the engagement between the municipality and the occupiers as well as the availability of alternative accommodation were all improperly applied.[55]

49 Ibid. para. 17.

50 *Occupiers of Skurweplaas 353 JR v. PPC Aggregate Quarries (Pty) Ltd* [2012] 4 BCLR 382 (CC) (*Skurweplaas*).

51 Ibid. para. 13.

52 *Marlboro Crisis Committee v. City of Johannesburg* (29978/12) [2012] ZAGPJHC 187 (September 7, 2012).

53 Ibid. para. 100.

54 *Port Elizabeth Municipality*, para. 12.

55 For a detailed engagement with the flaws in this judgment, see D. Bilchitz and D. Mackintosh, "PIE in the sky: where is the constitutional framework in high court eviction proceedings? Marlboro Crisis Committee & others v. City of Johannesburg" (2014) 131 *South African Law Journal* 521–37.

In *Johannesburg Housing Corporation* v. *Unlawful Occupiers of Newtown Village*,[56] Willis J was also concerned with an eviction application against the unlawful occupiers of a property in Newtown, Johannesburg. The judge raised an understandable concern relating to the need for "clear, certain, and implementable guidelines" as to how the Court should go about making its order.[57] The judge then raised a number of questions concerning how to interpret the notion of what is "just and equitable" as used in PIE and, disturbingly, articulated an approach to socio-economic rights which appeared to be at odds with the normative thrust of Constitutional Court decisions which require a balance to be achieved between the property rights of land-owners and the housing rights of occupiers.

These cases are not designed to create the impression that high court judges are all ignoring or bypassing the constitutional framework on evictions. Yet, the results in these cases suggest a problem in translation from the Constitutional Court's progressive jurisprudence to the manner in which high courts give effect to its rulings; and the experience of individuals on the ground with less than optimal results being obtained for the poor. Part of the problem perhaps relates to the fact that the Court has sought to allow every matter to be determined on its own facts and within its own context. In general, it has been unwilling to provide general principles as to how to make decisions. Whilst this sounds reasonable, this approach grants judges in the high courts significant discretion as to whether to grant an eviction order or not. Those not sharing the Constitutional Court's sensitivity to vulnerability and working with a more traditional conception of the common law, often tend to over-emphasize the rights of land-owners. This situation results in eviction orders which create much misery and hardship. The lack of clear guidelines and the failure to develop a more substantive framework allows the space to be filled by judges whose normative views are not in conformity with the new constitutional framework relating to evictions.[58] In this area, we thus see a development of the law that complies substantively with the requirements of the right to have access to adequate housing; at the same time, there is a serious failure in the implementation of these changes by other branches of government, security companies conducting evictions and even the courts tasked with giving effect to this framework.

56 [2013] 1 SA 583 (GSJ) (*Newtown Village*).

57 Ibid. para. 28.

58 See *Port Elizabeth Municipality*, which appears to be an exception in this regard; see also, the discussion of this case M. Dafel, "On the flexible procedure of housing eviction applications" (2014) 5 *Constitutional Court Review* 331–45.

3.4.1.3. Thick Compliance: Positive Obligations and the Provision of Housing

As we have seen, the Constitution imposes a series of positive obligations on the government in relation to housing. Only a brief analysis can be provided here of the fulfilment of these obligations. The Constitutional Court in the *Grootboom* case had an opportunity to consider the obligations of the government in relation to housing. The case concerned a group of people who landed up on a field in the driving rain of the Western Cape with only plastic sheeting to cover them. They claimed that the Constitution provided them with the right to have access at least to shelter from the elements. The case offered the opportunity for the Constitutional Court to outline its approach to socio-economic rights. As indicated above, it held that the government had a duty to develop a program in relation to the right to housing and that the program should be evaluated against the standard of reasonableness. The Court examined the government program in that case and found that whilst a lot had been done in relation to housing, there was no plan to address the short-term situation of those in desperate need. The Court found that the housing program was unconstitutional as it did not make provision for those "with no access to land, no roof over their heads, and who are living in intolerable conditions or crisis situations."[59] The Court thus clarified that the government could not simply focus on providing housing needs in the longer-term whilst ignoring the desperation of individuals in the shorter term.

The General Household Survey of 2014 conducted by Statistics South Africa provides a snapshot of some of the state's activities in relation to housing. The percentage of people receiving a government subsidy in relation to housing increased from 5.5 percent in 2002 to 15.3 percent in 2014. This would seem to indicate that the government was progressively increasing the number of South Africans with access to housing. Government housing policy can be broken down into those who receive actual homes (those earning below a threshold of R3,500/month) and those who receive a subsidy to assist them in being able to afford a home (those earning between R3,500 and R15,000).

The annual report of the Department of Human Settlements in 2015 claims that in the previous year, around 120,000 housing units were built and that around 75,000 units were upgraded from informal to formal housing.[60] By May 2013, the government had provided three million houses or housing

59 *Grootboom*, para. 99.

60 Department of Human Settlements, *Annual Report 2014/2015* (2015) (available at www.dhs.gov.za/sites/default/files/annual_reports/Annual%20report%202015_web.pdf) (accessed date November 20, 2017).

opportunities.[61] Since 1994, one study suggests that the government had provided more than 2.5 million houses and 1.2 million serviced sites.[62]

What is clear from these figures is that the government has been attempting to increase the amount of formal housing available to individuals. Unfortunately, there remains a major backlog, which is estimated by some NGOs to be in the region of 2.1 million units.[63] Around three million individuals in 2013 still lived in shacks.[64] Reasons for this relate to increased urbanization in South Africa as well as a strong influx of individuals from other parts of the African continent in particular. The government has, in response, revised its housing policy which now focuses particularly on the upgrading of informal settlements.[65]

There is some tension as well between providing housing to the greatest number of people (the breadth requirement) and attempting to provide better quality housing to fewer persons (the depth requirement). The initial approach was to provide a lesser standard of housing to more people rather than a higher standard to fewer people.[66] Yet, in practice, the policy has changed from breadth to depth with fewer people gaining access to housing and the backlog increasing.[67]

Whilst the quality of housing has improved over the years, the General Household survey of 2014 still indicates significant problems in that regard. Of households surveyed 14.5 percent complain of weak or very weak walls and 13.9 percent complain of weak or very weak roofs.[68] The results suggest wholesale mismanagement and lack of capacity to provide in provinces such as the Eastern Cape, where over 33 percent of individuals claimed

61 South African Government, *Housing* (available at www.gov.za/about-SA/housing) (accessed date November 20, 2017).

62 M. Tomlinson, "South Africa's housing conundrum" (2015) 20(4) *@Liberty*, 1–7, 11–14 (available at www.irr.org.za/reports-and-publications/atLiberty/files/liberty-2013-south-africas-housing-conundrum) (accessed date November 20, 2017).

63 SANGONET, *Addressing the housing backlog in South Africa* (2013) (available at www.ngopulse.org/article/addressing-housing-backlog-south-africa) (accessed date November 20, 2017). See also ibid.

64 Housing Development Agency, *South Africa: informal settlements status 2013* (2013) (available at www.thehda.co.za/uploads/files/had_South_Africa_Report_lr.pdf) (accessed date November 20, 2017).

65 Socio-Economic Rights Institute of South Africa (SERI), *A review of housing policy and development in South Africa since 1994* (2013) (available at www.spii.org.za/wp-content/uploads/2013/12/review-of-the-right-to-housing.pdf) (accessed date November 20, 2017).

66 Tomlinson, "South Africa's housing conundrum," 4.

67 Ibid.

68 Statistics South Africa, *General household survey: 2014* (2015) Figure 26 (available at www.statssa.gov.za/publications/P0318/P03182014.pdf) (accessed date November 20, 2017).

weak walls and roofs. The uneven quality of the provision of housing highlights areas of particularly weak governance within South Africa. Indeed, whilst initially, a strong centralized approach was envisaged, the federal elements of the South African Constitution led provinces to take a lead in this regard. The role of local government was unclear initially and, whilst its competences in this area have been bolstered in recent policy, it is often constrained by funding allocations and provincial decisions.[69] The overlapping competences contained in the Constitution thus could play some role in inefficient delivery.[70]

Moreover, in response to the *Grootboom* case, the government did pass Chapter 12 of the Housing Code which made provision for local governments to be able to access funding for emergency housing. As McLean writes, "[t]he programme, however, fails to provide adequate short-term relief for those in crisis situations, and relies on a cumbersome set of procedures which do not allow for the immediate accommodation of those in need."[71] In addition the policy has often not been put into practice and thousands of people remain homeless on the streets of the main cities in South Africa with limited attempts by the government to address their conditions.[72]

3.4.1.4. Performance of the Right to Housing

The inclusion of the right to have access to adequate housing in the South African Constitution has not solved the housing problems created by past policies or current conditions. Nevertheless, as one commentator puts it, the right to housing has been the "cornerstone of housing policy, and is likely to remain so."[73] One possible way of evaluating performance would be to consider what would have been the position in South African law without the right. It can almost certainly be asserted that the cases based on this right, relating to evictions, have fundamentally changed the law in that regard, which has the potential to affect the lives of thousands of individuals in a positive way. Including this right has been important for establishing a balance

69 Tomlinson, "South Africa's housing conundrum," 5–6.

70 More is said about this issue in the chapter of the full IDEA report on multi-level governance which is available at Constitutionnet.org.

71 McLean, Housing, 55–21.

72 This report, for instance, indicates that there were at least 2,500 homeless people living in Cape Town on the streets: see A. Lewis, "Homeless choose streets over shelter," *IOL News*, March 9, 2015 (available at www.iol.co.za/news/south-africa/western-cape/homeless-choose-streets-over-shelters-1.1829353#.Vi9PDdIrLIU) (accessed date November 20, 2017).

73 Tomlinson, "South Africa's housing conundrum," 13.

between the rights of landowners and those of occupiers.[74] It has also led to an emphasis being placed on participation and a recognition of the need to provide alternative accommodation. The choice to recognize the horizontal application of the Bill of Rights has also been important in placing a number of obligations on landowners to avoid evicting individuals by following the correct legal procedures and also to allow occupiers to remain on their land temporarily pending the provision of alternative accommodation by the government. Whilst there is no doubt that greater burdens have been placed upon landowners through this revised legal regime, the courts have attempted to focus on striking a balance between their interests and those of occupiers to avoid severe impacts upon the rental market.

As we have highlighted, there have been significant efforts taken to help realize this right positively, though the implementation of government initiatives and policy in this regard remains uneven. Similarly, the inclusion of positive obligations on the part of the government has not eliminated homelessness, the most extreme deprivation of this right, as some commentators have urged. The latter failing may, to some extent, result from the choice of the drafters to qualify the right to have access to adequate housing through the notions of "reasonableness," and "progressive realisation" without providing any specific guidelines as to how these notions were to be understood. Section 20(5) of the Kenyan Constitution suggests an alternative whereby the attention of courts can be directed specifically at the vulnerability of individuals. The approach adopted by the Constitutional Court to these vague provisions has not helped to provide a firmer commitment on the part of the government to eradicating homelessness. It has, though, led to the development of certain constitutional factors for evaluating a government program on housing and driven certain policy changes by the government, such as Chapter 12 of the Housing Code which, unfortunately, is a narrower response to the *Grootboom* judgment than could have been expected. The Constitutional Court's approach to adjudicating this right may, arguably, be blamed for the lack of more cases on the positive obligations flowing from it and, perhaps also, for the lack of more radical implications such as a concerted effort by government to eliminate homelessness. The inclusion of this right in the Constitution has nevertheless had an important effect on housing policy and can, to that extent, be considered a success. It can plausibly be contended though that the approach of the

[74] In a sense, this bears out the argument of R. Dixon and T. Ginsburg, that socio-economic rights help to counter-balance the effects of including the right to property in the South African Constitution: "The South African Constitutional Court and socio-economic rights as 'insurance swaps'" (2011) 4 *Constitutional Court Review* 1–29.

Constitutional Court to interpreting the right has limited the more extensive impact it may have had, by not focusing on ensuring provision for those with the most urgent needs and not providing a greater specification of what can be claimed.

3.4.2. *Right to Have Access to Health Care Services*

Apartheid had deliberately sought to create separate structures for providing services to black and white people. The field of health care was no different and the separation led to vast inequality. World-class facilities were developed for whites, whereas the provision of health care for black people was wholly inadequate. There are several reasons for the negative effect apartheid created for the health of black people in particular. First, there were a range of social conditions which led to disease. The migrant labor system, for example, drew African men away from their families to work in industry and in the mines. The pass laws prevented them from living in "white" areas and so they were confined to living in under-developed townships in unsanitary conditions. Many also lived in single-sex hostels which were a breeding ground for diseases such as tuberculosis (TB). The removal from their families created mental health problems and alcoholism. The sex work trade grew, and later on this would have an impact in the 1990s on the growth of HIV/AIDS in South Africa. Environmental conditions thus led black people to become more at risk of disease. For instance, in 1971, deaths from diarrhea were hundred times more likely in black children than white children and, in 1978, black people were 48 times more likely to contract typhoid fever than white people.

Black people were also less able to access health care services which were segregated according to race. The provinces and Bantustans had separate health departments. In 1987, the number of dentists for every white member of the population was 1:2,000 whereas the number of dentists for black people was 1:2,000,000. In 1990, the number of doctors in urban areas was 1:900 whereas in rural areas, it was 1:4,100. Black people were prevented from training as doctors at "white" universities and from seeing white patients. The apartheid government's spending was also unequal according to race: in 1987, it spent R137 on each black person whereas it spent R597 on each white person.[75]

[75] The statistics and analysis in this section are taken from the J. Berger, A. Hassim, and M. Heywood (eds.), *Health & Democracy: A Guide to Human Rights, Health Law and Policy in Post-Apartheid South Africa* (Cape Town: SiberInk, 2007) 11–3. See also Section 27, "Background to health and human rights in South Africa," (2010) (available at www.section27.org.za/wp-content/uploads/2010/04/Chapter1.pdf) (accessed date November 20, 2017).

In the face of these inequities, the postapartheid final Constitution included various provisions guaranteeing the right to health. Subsection 27(1)(a) provides an entitlement of everyone "to have access to health care services, including reproductive health care." Subsection 27(2) specifies the state's obligations in this regard, requiring, once again that the state must take reasonable legislative and other measures, within its available resources to achieve the progressive realization of this right. Subsection 27(3) provides that no-one may be refused emergency medical treatment. Subsection 24(a) also includes a requirement that everyone has a right to "an environment that is not harmful to their health or well-being." These constitutional rights can be seen, on the one hand, to have a corrective purpose: to address the inequities of the past. On the other hand, they attempt to achieve the distributive justice goal of ensuring all South Africans can gain access to a decent level of health care services. It must also be noted that there is a close relationship between these specific rights dealing with health and other rights – such as the right to have access to adequate housing and sufficient food and water – which have an impact on health.

3.4.2.1. Thin Compliance

Since 1994, the government has taken a range of measures to advance South Africans' rights to have access to health care. The primary piece of legislation in this area is the National Health Act 2003 which creates the framework for a unified health care system. The Act defines the rights and duties of users of the health care system as well as health care personnel. It also provides an understanding of the respective roles of national, provincial and local spheres of government in respect of health matters. The National Health Amendment Act 2013 established an office of health standards compliance which requires an inspection of public hospitals every four years and a complaint mechanism from members of the public. Legislation relating to the general functioning of the health care system, which has been updated since 1994, includes the Health Profession Act 1974 and the Medicines and Related Substances Act 1965.

There are many other pieces of legislation that have been passed which focus on particular areas. The Mental Health Care Act 2002 sought to change the approach to the care of those with psychosocial disabilities in South Africa with a focus on their rights. The Choice on Termination of Pregnancy Act 2004 provided for legal abortions up until three months and restricted access to abortion after twenty weeks of pregnancy. The Tobacco Product Controls Amendment Act 2000 banned smoking in public places.

Health is also impacted by other laws which are not directly focused upon it. For instance, the National Environmental Management Act 1998 and the

National Environmental Management Air Quality Act 2004 address wider questions of environmental impact and pollution; the Occupational Health and Safety Act 1993 addresses health at work; and the Water Services Act 1997 prescribes national norms and standards that must be met in the provision of water services.

The government has also adopted several policies to address issues around health care. For instance, between 2009 and 2014, it adopted a ten-point plan that sought amongst other things to improve the management of the health system as well as the quality of health care services. It also sought to improve human resources in the health care sector. It has passed a national strategic plan from 2012 to 2016 to address HIV/AIDS and TB which engages with questions of prevention and treatment. An ambitious plan for a National Health Insurance scheme has been outlined which is designed to ensure universal access to decent health care for all in South Africa. It has also embarked on a project to improve health infrastructure through refurbishing public health facilities.

It is clear, therefore, that the government has taken legislative and other measures to address issues in relation to the right to health. Perhaps the single biggest failure of health care policy in the past twenty years has been the approach of the government to HIV/AIDS, where its policies failed initially to include a program of treatment for those suffering from HIV/AIDS which had become a pandemic in South Africa. This situation could be seen as a failure of thin compliance in that there was a lack of any reasonable program to address HIV/AIDS in place. I will, however, consider this matter at length under the thick compliance section as it involves a range of issues which also highlight wider failures of government policy in this area.

3.4.2.2. Thick Compliance

It cannot be said that the government does not spend in the health care sector. In 2015, the government aimed to spend R157 billion on health care, which amounts to around 11 percent of the national budget. Yet, one of the major problems relating to funding involves where that money is spent, inefficiencies in allocation and detailed problems overall in the health care system. In 2009, an Integrated Support Team appointed by the Minister released a report in which it detailed many problems facing the public health care system.[76] The report found significant over-spending and a variety of unfunded

[76] P. Barron et al., "Rural Health Advocacy Project, Consolidated report of the integrated support team: review of health overspending and macro-assessment of the public health system in South Africa" (May 2009) (available at www.rhap.org.za/ist-reports-on-the-state-of-the-health-system-and-the-publics-right-to-know/) (accessed date November 20, 2017).

mandates: these included new policies such as new vaccinations, promises made by members of executive councils, such as the funding of new clinics, and even legislative requirements, such as the funding of the district health system.[77] The provision of a legislative scheme without a proper funding plan would violate the requirements laid out for a reasonable program in *Grootboom* (according to which appropriate resources must be allocated for a specific program).

The report also detailed the fact that there were ten health departments in South Africa without one coherent vision or strategy. There was also fragmentation between the national government policies and those developed at the provincial level. There is a lack of coordination and communication between these various layers.[78] The structure of cooperative governance and federalism created by the government clearly has impacted negatively upon the efficient delivery of services. There are inadequate systems to address the human resource needs in the system and to ensure the provision of decent care by nurses and there is a shortage of doctors in rural areas. Similarly, there is a lack of adequate information management systems. Medicines were also not treated as a major strategic issue and many provinces ran out of critical supplies as a result of over-expenditure.[79]

All these maladies facing the public health care system have a large impact upon access to health care services of the population in South Africa. In a study conducted by Harris et al.,[80] the authors found that "poor, uninsured, black Africans and rural groups have inequitable access" to health care services in South Africa.[81] The facts that transport was unaffordable and there was an expectation of disrespectful treatment, and the belief that care would be ineffective, played roles in hampering access for these groups. The poor can least afford to use private health care services, yet a fifth of them have done so to try and gain access to decent treatment. Many of the groups supposed to be exempted from paying service fees in the public hospitals still had to do so.[82] In the public sector, 37.5 percent of out-patients and 25.5 percent of in-patients surveyed complained about the timeliness of treatment. Over half (54.7 percent) of all respondents said that those who utilized public hospitals were not treated with respect and dignity.[83]

77 Ibid. 9.

78 Ibid. 11–12.

79 Ibid. 19.

80 B. Harris et al., "Inequities in access to health-care in South Africa" (2011) 32 *Journal of Public Health Policy* 102–23.

81 Ibid. 119.

82 Ibid. 118.

83 Ibid. 115.

These empirical facts suggest that the goal of reducing inequalities created by apartheid has largely not been achieved despite large amounts of government expenditure. Access to decent health care services is still the preserve largely of the rich who can afford to pay for private services (South Africa still has a strong division between public and private services). These inequities have a major impact on health outcomes. A study in 2000 found that 90 percent of premature deaths in South Africa are from four main causes: the HIV/AIDS pandemic (accounting for 75 percent of premature deaths), injuries from interpersonal violence and road traffic accidents (around 5 percent), diseases flowing from poverty (around 5 percent) and cardiovascular conditions (around 5 percent).[84] Diseases such as diabetes, kidney disease and prostate cancer have also grown.[85] Obesity rates are high, with roughly 10 percent of men and a quarter of women being obese; and a fifth of the South African population above fifteen suffers from hypertension.[86]

As can be seen from the above statistics, the major crisis facing health in South Africa from the 1990s onwards concerned the massive growth of the population who had HIV/AIDS. By 2008, it was estimated that over 5.5 million people lived with the disease.[87] The mortality rates that resulted provide an alarming picture. The number of deaths increased substantially in South Africa between 1994 and 2006, which seemed to be the peak. By 2009, it was estimated that over 2.6 million South Africans had died of HIV/AIDS, mainly children and young adults.[88] The number of deaths of children doubled over that time period, whilst the number of deaths of young adults trebled.[89] The median life expectancy in South Africa dropped from 52 in 1997 to 43 in 2007.[90]

The catastrophic health policy of the government was partly to blame for these figures together with the high-cost of antiretroviral drugs.[91] Initially, the government's response seemed promising as it passed legislation to allow for

84 D. Harrison, "An overview of health and health care in South Africa 1994–2010: priorities, progress and prospects for new gains" discussion document commissioned by the Henry J. Kaiser Family Foundation to help inform the national health leaders' retreat (2009) at 9 (available at www.ftp.bhfglobal.com/files/bhf/overview1994-2010.pdf) (accessed date November 20, 2017).

85 Ibid. 9.

86 Ibid. 12–3.

87 P. Chigwedere et al., "Estimating the lost benefits of antiretroviral drug use in South Africa" (2008) 49 *Journal of Acquired Immune Deficiency Syndromes* 410–15 at 410.

88 Harrison, "An overview of health," 6.

89 Ibid.

90 Ibid.

91 Other factors also existed such as the stigma of the disease and cultural beliefs surrounding its causes and treatment: see J. Steinberg, *Three-Letter Plague: A Young Man's Journey Through a Great Epidemic* (Johannesburg: Jonathan Ball Publishers, 2010).

the manufacture of these drugs in South Africa without the patent holder's authorization (compulsory licensing) and parallel importation of these drugs from places where they were sold for a cheaper price. These measures drew the ire of the pharmaceutical industry, which in 2001, took the government to court for infringement of their patents on these drugs.[92] Protests erupted around the world which had a highly negative effect on the image of these corporations and eventually they dropped the litigation. It seemed that South Africa would be able to drop the prices of the drugs finally and render them accessible to all.

Unfortunately, the President decided to involve himself directly with health care policy. Together with the pliant Health Minster, they aligned themselves with dissident views which denied that HIV caused AIDS. The President and Health Minister emphasized the toxicity of antiretroviral drugs without recognizing their benefits and essentially refused to make them accessible in the public health system throughout the country to treat those infected by the disease. They also obstructed the acquisition of Global Fund grants.[93]

This situation eventually led a civil society organization, the Treatment Action Campaign (TAC), to launch a challenge in the courts. The case it took related to a drug called nevirapine which had been shown to be effective in reducing the likelihood of transmission of HIV from mothers to their children at birth (this is known as mother-to-child transmission).[94] The manufacturer had offered to make the drug available for free to the government for five years. The government, however, insisted that it would make the drug available only at two health care facilities per province in order to test its efficacy and develop a program relating to it. The effect of the government's policy was to prevent thousands of people across the country from gaining access to the drug and allowing unnecessary HIV infections of children.

The TAC challenged the reasonableness of the government's policy of restricting access to these drugs to only two sites per province and also the failure of the government to develop a comprehensive program to roll out the drugs across the country. The organization won in the High Court[95] and the case went up to the Constitutional Court. The Court re-affirmed its view that the right required the development of a program which would be assessed on

92 L. Ferreira, "Access to affordable HIV/AIDS drugs: The human rights obligations of multinational pharmaceutical corporations" (2002) 71 *Fordham Law Review* 1133–79 at 1148–58.

93 Chigwedere et al., "Estimating the lost benefits," 413.

94 The case resulted in a Constitutional Court judgment reported as *Minister of Health* v. *Treatment Action Campaign* [2002] 5 SA 721 (CC).

95 The High Court judgment is reported as *Minister of Health* v. *Treatment Action Campaign* (2002) 4 BCLR 356 (T).

the grounds of reasonableness.[96] The government had failed, the Court found, to show any good reasons why the drug should be restricted to two sites per province as it had been shown to be safe and efficacious. The drug had also been made available to the government for free. The research around a program could not be allowed to inhibit the availability of a drug which would save thousands of lives. The Court found the government's program to be unreasonable and thus to violate its obligations in relation to the right to have access to health care services. It ordered the government to provide the drug in all health care facilities across the country, to provide counselling and to develop a comprehensive program to address mother-to-child transmission of HIV.

This decision is perhaps one of the most significant in the history of the Constitutional Court. Whilst the Minister of Health initially suggested that the department would disobey the order, it was implemented, albeit patchily across the country. The availability of nevirapine meant that many children did not develop HIV who otherwise would have. The Harvard School of Public Health published a study in which it estimated the number of people who could have been saved had the South African government implemented an ARV program earlier. It estimated that more than 330,000 people and approximately two million life years were lost because such a program was not implemented. The number of babies born with HIV amounted to 35,000 "resulting in 1.6 million person-years lost by not implementing a mother-to-child transmission prophylaxis program using nevirapine. The total lost benefits of ARVs are at least 3.8 million person-years for the period."[97]

The fact that the Constitutional Court forced the government to change its policy can thus be seen to have had concrete life-saving effects on thousands of children. Currently, the rate of transmission of HIV from mother-to-child has reduced to only 2.7 percent of children born.[98] The impetus created by the court case led to the questioning of the government's policy on antiretrovirals throughout the society and an inability on the part of the government to justify its refusal to provide such treatment in the case of all persons suffering from HIV/AIDS, including adults as well. The Department of Health began to make such drugs available and, today, South Africa has one of the largest antiretroviral programs in the world. Perhaps millions of people have been saved as a result of this change of policy which, to some extent, can be

96 Ibid. para. 36.

97 Chigwedere et al., "Estimating the lost benefits," 412.

98 K. Cullinan, "ARV programme saves 780 000 lives," *Health E-News* April 11, 2014 (available at www.health-e.org.za/2014/04/11/arv-programme-saves-780-000-lives/) (accessed date November 20, 2017).

connected to the Constitutional Court case. Recent estimates suggest that around 2.2 million lives have been saved by the change of policy by the government.[99] This case must for all time count as a strong reason in favor of constitutionalizing a right to have access to health care services which helped address a massive failure of government policy which was affecting the very survival of millions.

The Constitution has also helped guard against further irrational action by the government in the health care sector. In 1998, the government passed the South African Medicines and Medical Devices Regulatory Authority Act 1998, which controlled the flow of medicines on the market through placing medicines in particular categories.[100] To be effective, the Act required a complex regulatory structure to be in place which assigned medicines to particular schedules. Acting in good faith, the President signed the Act into law without the relevant schedules being in place. The result would have been that there would be no controls over medicines – no matter how dangerous – pending the passing of these schedules. The President himself asked for his action bringing the Act into force to be declared invalid by the courts.[101] The Constitutional Court held that all exercises of public power had to be rational and that the President's actions were objectively irrational in these circumstances. They were, as a result, invalid. Whilst the case was not decided in terms of the right to health, it demonstrates how a rule of law requirement may have important implications for protecting people's health.

The Constitutional Court has also had to address the problem of resource scarcity in the context of the right to health. It was faced with this problem in its very first case in this area relating to a Mr Soobramoney who suffered from chronic renal failure.[102] He needed kidney dialysis and argued that, in terms of the Constitution, he was entitled to be provided with it as he could not afford to pay for it himself. Given the limited number of dialysis machines, the state had adopted a rationing policy only to provide dialysis to those who had acute renal failure which could be treated and remedied or those eligible for a kidney transplant. The majority of the court dismissed the argument that Mr Soobramoney could claim a right to kidney dialysis in terms of the right of everyone to have access to health care services. Judge President Chaskalson found that the court needed to respect rational decisions taken in good faith

99 Ibid.

100 *Pharmaceutical Manufacturer's Association of South Africa: In re Ex parte President of the Republic of South Africa* [2000] 2 SA 674.

101 Ibid. para. 7. The President instituted this action after it came to light that the Government Notice purporting to publish the schedules to the Act was invalid.

102 *Soobramoney* (n.12).

by other branches of government in relation to the rationing of scarce health care resources. The following statement expressed the dominant approach of the Court to interpreting this right:

> What is apparent from these provisions is that the obligations imposed on the State by ss. 26 and 27 in regard to access to housing, health-care, food, water and social security are dependent upon the resources available for such purposes, and that the corresponding rights themselves are limited by reason of the lack of resources.[103]

The Court here signals that its understanding of the right in question can be limited by the resources that are available. It has been criticized severely for this ruling which has been said to be overly deferential.[104] The court only considered the existing provincial budgetary allocation to health. As Moellendorf argues, however, rights are meant to guide budgetary decisions and the focus of the Court on what resources were made available by the provincial tier of government was too narrow. The Court also only specified a rationality standard for evaluating rationing decisions which might offer people limited protection. *Soobramoney* was an earlier case than TAC and thus it is unclear whether or not the reasonableness standard might apply today when the courts are dealing with rights and scarce resources.

Nevertheless, given the poor state of public health, it is surprising there have been so few cases in this area and this may partly be explained by the conservative approach of the Court in *Soobramoney* and the difficulty of establishing that the government program has been irrational/unreasonable. In countries with a comparable right in their bill of rights such as Colombia, there have been many more claims in terms of the right to health as courts have been willing to entertain individual claims about continued failings in the health care system.[105] That approach has also been said to have many disadvantages, allowing those who can approach the court to be privileged over those who cannot.[106] In South Africa, the Court requires that the approach adopted be programmatic, which allows for better planning and less ad hoc effects. A programmatic approach, however, may be designed and yet still not place significant hurdles in the face of prospective litigants; the disadvantage

103 Ibid. para. 11.

104 D. Moellendorf, "Reasoning about resources: Soobramoney and the future of socio-economic rights claims" (1998) 14 *South African Journal on Human Rights* 327 at 331–33.

105 A. E. Yamin and O. Parra-Vera, "Judicial protection of the right to health in Columbia: From social demands to individual claims to public debates" (2010) 33 *Hastings International and Comparative Law Review* 431–59 at 443.

106 Ibid. 444.

of the existing approach of the court is thus that it sets a high barrier for any litigant to succeed in a claim given the complexity of the health care system. Moreover, litigation is discouraged as a successful challenge may not necessarily result in concrete benefits for litigants.

3.4.2.3. Performance of the Right to Have Access to Health Care Services

The inclusion of a right to have access to health care services was seen to be important both in addressing past inequities in the health care system and ensuring every South African has access to decent health care. Neither of these goals have been achieved fully in the past twenty years with vast inequities remaining in the health care system and poorer South Africans still often being able to access only sub-standard health care. There were, of course, significant challenges in expanding access, and the advent of an HIV/AIDS crisis just as South Africa was transitioning to democracy placed great strain on the health care system. Unfortunately, as we saw, the initial government response to the pandemic was not evidence based and led to a large number of unnecessary deaths. The constitutional right to health extended the battle lines within which advocacy and activism could take place and encouraged bolder steps on the part of social movements.[107] The constitutionalization of the right to health enabled courts to intervene in the face of a significant policy failure. The correction ordered catalyzed an overall shift in government policy which ensured drugs for millions of South Africans and saved their lives. If this were the only impact of the right to have access to health care services, its inclusion in the Constitution could be said to have been successful. The reasonableness approach of the Court and its decision in relation to scarce resources in the health care sector has though, arguably, inhibited much litigation. Whilst the right has made a difference, it could have made more of a difference if it were easier for litigants to approach the Court and highlight many of the unacceptable practices that occur within the health care sector. A re-consideration of the burden on litigants in accessing courts as well as a consideration of how there could be easier access would enable this right to reach its full potential for change. A dedicated, easy-to-access mechanism outside courts should also be considered to address situations where individuals in the public health sector are being denied adequate medical treatment or where they are treated with disrespect.

[107] M. Kavanagh, "The right to health: Institutional effects of constitutional provisions on health outcomes" (2016) 51 *Studies in Comparative International Development* 328–64 at 349–50.

3.4.3. *Right to Education*[108]

Schooling in South Africa became part of the implementation of the apartheid policy. There were separate schools for black and white learners. The education given to white learners was deliberately superior to that provided to black learners as part of the apartheid philosophy that whites would assume skilled and managerial positions in society with black people essentially becoming the unskilled labor work-force in the country.[109] Whilst there are some different accounts of apartheid history, the consistent message is that the schools and schooling were based on "inequalities, violations of human rights and were blatantly racist."[110] This philosophy left a concrete legacy. First, there was inadequate infrastructure to provide for the education of black people. Second, there was inadequate training of teachers who would provide education in black schools. Third, there were eighteen separate departments across the country which had to be merged into nine provincial departments. Fourth, the number of black students in higher education was relatively small and universities were often divided according to race.

In the face of these realities, the Constitution provided in subsection 29(1) that "[e]veryone has the right to (a) basic education including adult basic education; and (b) to further education, which the state, through reasonable measures, must make progressively available and accessible." A compromise clause was agreed upon concerning the right to receive an education in the official language of choice which was largely to protect Afrikaans-language education. A right was also enshrined to maintain, at one's own expense, independent educational institutions subject to a number of conditions. The focus of this section will largely be on subsection 29(1), although the other sections will be mentioned where relevant.

3.4.3.1. Thin Compliance

The South African government has passed much legislation since 1994 to realize the rights in section 29. It has passed the South African Schools Act 1996, which regulated the funding and governance of schools, and the National

[108] I am indebted to Linette Du Toit for her contribution to this section of the chapter.

[109] P. Christie and C. Collins, "Bantu education: Apartheid ideology or labour reproduction?" (1982) 18 *Comparative Education* 59–75 at 61.

[110] N. H. Carrim, "Human rights and the construction of identities in South African education," PhD thesis, University of the Witwatersrand, Johannesburg (2006), Chapter 6, 175 (available at www.wiredspace.wits.ac.za/bitstream/handle/10539/2032/CarrimN_Chapter%206.pdf?sequence=12) (accessed date November 20, 2017).

Education Policy Act 1996, which allows for the determination of a national policy for education. The government has also adopted a series of policies which attempt to make basic education free for all: see, for instance, the "Plan of Action for Improving Free and Quality Education for All."[111] This document seeks to outline plans through which the poorest 40 percent of learners can have the quality of their education improved and through which barriers to their access to education are removed.

In relation to higher education, the government passed the Higher Education Act 1997 to regulate universities, ensure proper governance and maintain standards; the Further Education and Training Colleges Act 2006 to regulate education and training that is higher than secondary schooling but lower than tertiary university education; and the National Qualifications Framework Act 2008, which is designed to ensure a national system of registration and accreditation of qualifications. It issued a National Plan on Higher Education[112] and set up a system known as the National Student Financial Aid Scheme, which is meant to provide loans to poorer students to enable them to gain access to higher education.

There are many other laws and policies and it is clear that, to the extent that the government has passed these, there is some thin compliance with the Constitution. Moreover, there has been an expansion of children in schooling and students in higher education since 1994 so, on a quantitative level, there is some compliance. Unfortunately, the implementation of the legislation and policies has been poor and the actual content of the education received by many learners, particularly the poor, is very limited. These points will be illustrated in relation to thick compliance.

3.4.3.2. Thick Compliance

BASIC EDUCATION. The right to basic education differs from the other constitutionally protected socio-economic rights in that it is not internally limited by qualifications such as "progressive realization," and "within available resources."[113] The Constitutional Court has confirmed in the case of *Governing Body of*

[111] Department of Education, South African Government, *Plan of action: improving access to free and basic education for all* (June 14, 2003) (available at www.education.gov.za/LinkClick.aspx?fileticket=IBMz%2fjGelkc%3d&tabid=390&mid=1124) (accessed date November 20, 2017).

[112] Ministry of Education, South African Government, *Draft national plan for higher education in South Africa* (February 2001) (available at www.dhet.gov.za/HED%20Policies/National%20Plan%20on%20Higher%20Education.pdf) (accessed date November 20, 2017).

[113] *Governing Body of the Juma Musjid Primary School* v. *Essay NO* [2011] 8 BCLR 761 (CC) para. 37.

Juma Musjid[114] that it is "immediately realisable" and can only be limited in terms of the general limitation clause.[115] This formulation of the right creates the expectation that more ought to be done to ensure the realization of its positive dimension than is the case with other "progressively realisable" rights. The government seems to take this "immediately realisable" right seriously in that it spends the largest proportion of the national budget on education. In 2015, it aimed to spend R265.7 billion, which is 18.5 percent of the total budget. Yet despite this large expenditure, the goals of the right to education do not seem to have been achieved in a thick sense.

One success of the right to basic education is that primary education has been made available to virtually everyone between the ages of seven and fifteen years.[116] Between 2002 and 2014, the percentage of learners who attend no fee schools increased from 0.4 percent of learners to 65.4 percent of learners.[117] Yet, the basic education offered in most schools in South Africa is not of a high quality and the inequality which apartheid created in the schooling system persists.

In 2009 the National Education Evaluation and Development Unit (NEEDU) was established as a unit within the National Department of Basic Education (DBE) to evaluate the quality of teaching and learning in South African schools.[118] NEEDU evaluated the numeracy and literacy skills of learners in foundational as well as intermediate grades and has found them to be falling short of the standards set by the curriculum.[119] NEEDU evaluated 215 Grade 2 classes and found that 72 percent of the three top learners in each of these classes were reading at a rate below the average benchmark for this group.[120] From a sample of 1790 Grade 5 learners from rural schools, 10 percent of students could not understand English (which was the medium of instruction in the schools they attended), 22 percent were illiterate and only

114 Ibid.

115 Section 36 of the Constitution provides that a right in the Bill of Rights can only be limited in terms of a law of general application that is "reasonable and justifiable in an open and democratic society based on human dignity, equality and freedom."

116 Statistics South Africa, *General household survey: 2014*, 18.

117 Ibid. 20.

118 National Education Evaluation and Developmental Unit (South Africa), *National Report 2013: teaching and learning in rural primary schools* (2013), 1 (available at www.cdn.mg.co.za/content/documents/2015/04/15/needureport2013.pdf) (accessed date November 20, 2017).

119 W. Louw and D. Isaacs, "Angie Motshekga sat on damning NEEDU Report – EE" (April 24, 2015) Politicsweb (available at www.politicsweb.co.za/politics/angie-motshekga-sat-on-damning-needu-report--ee) (accessed date November 20, 2017).

120 NEEDU, *National report: summary report* (2012), 10 (available at www.saqa.org.za/docs/papers/2013/needu.pdf) (accessed date November 20, 2017).

49 percent of learners had an acceptable reading capacity expected of a Grade 5 learner.[121]

Due to the legacy of apartheid, there is a large discrepancy between the performance of learners at 75 percent of South African schools, which still lack even basic resources, and the top 25 percent of schools, which achieve outcomes that are comparable to international standards.[122] Research conducted by Spaull suggests that the difference in performance between learners from the top 25 percent and the bottom 75 percent of schools is so stark that the top 25 percent's results have the effect of skewing the national results and create a misleading representation of the general performance of South African schools.[123] This difference in outcome can be attributed to the fact that many South African schools lack basic infrastructure and resources, such as a sufficient number of suitably qualified teachers, safe school buildings, desks and chairs, electricity and sanitation.[124] Despite the primacy of education and the large budgetary allocation to this area, the DBE has not made significant strides in reversing the effects of apartheid's deliberate education discrimination.

The constitutional right to basic education has given much room to civil society to make demands on the DBE for the improvement of conditions in former black-only schools. It has provided fertile ground for the involvement of courts in ensuring the adoption and implementation of policies guaranteeing the necessary conditions for the realization of the right. A few of the seminal cases in this regard will be elaborated upon below.

MUD SCHOOLS. As of 2010, there were hundreds of dilapidated and unsafe schools across the country and in the Eastern Cape in particular. Many of these schools were built by community members using mud and branches and left learners exposed to the elements. The schools furthermore had a shortage of desks and chairs and did not have access to potable water. The Centre for Child Law (CCL)[125] and the Legal Resources Centre (LRC)[126] instituted proceedings against the DBE on behalf of seven of these schools in the

[121] NEEDU, *National report 2013*, 41.

[122] N. Spaull, *South Africa's education crisis: the quality of education in South Africa 1994–2011* (2013), 36 (available at www.section27.org.za/wp-content/uploads/2013/10/Spaull-2013-CDE-report-South-Africas-Education-Crisis.pdf) (accessed date November 20, 2017).

[123] Ibid. 38.

[124] According to NEEDU, 2013, one of the main reasons for the below par performance of learner is a shortage of sufficiently qualified and capable teachers in rural areas in particular.

[125] A center of the University of Pretoria which advocates for children's rights.

[126] A public interest law nongovernmental organization.

Eastern Cape High Court. It was argued that the DBE's conduct and policies fell short of meeting the constitutional requirements in subsection 29(1)(a).[127] A settlement agreement was reached in 2011 in which the DBE undertook to spend more than R6.2 billion over three years to replace inappropriate structures at schools in the Eastern Cape. The program became known as the Accelerated Schools Infrastructure Delivery Initiative (ASIDI) and was aimed at upgrading 496 "mud schools" by the end of 2016.[128]

While the adoption of the program was a clear success for the constitutional right to basic education, there remain several hurdles in its way to full implementation. ASIDI aimed to have upgraded forty-nine schools by the end of the 2013 financial year, but only managed to complete the upgrading of ten.[129] The DBE spent a mere 10 percent of the School Infrastructure Backlog grant in the 2011/2012 financial year and 23 percent in the 2012/2013 financial year. The project deadline has been extended by a further three years. A monitoring exercise undertaken by the LRC and CCL at the end of 2014 also revealed that many schools which ought to have been included on the ASIDI list for upgrading have been left out. After repeated requests for the inclusion of these schools were ignored, the LRC once again instituted proceedings. Negotiations and court proceedings which might ensure the implementation of ASIDI are still ongoing.[130]

The "mud schools" cases serve as an example of how the right to basic education can provide the space for civil society to force the government to the negotiating table in order to provide a plan as to how it will fulfil its obligations. Social mobilisation, along with the involvement of the courts, has led to the adoption of a new government program and the drastic improvement of some rural schools in the Eastern Cape. It is also clear that ongoing civil society engagement is essential in ensuring that the goals of the right are achieved.

[127] S. Fredman and C. McConnachie, "Ready to Learn? A Legal Resource for Realising the Right to Education" (Johannesburg: Legal Resources Centre, 2013) 20 (available at www.lrc.org.za/lrcarchive/publications/books/item/ready-to-learn) (accessed date November 20, 2017).

[128] SA News "Infrastructure initiative to eradicate mud schools" SA news.gov.za (November 22, 2013) (available at www.sanews.gov.za/features/infrastructure-initiative-eradicate-mud-schools) (accessed date November 20, 2017).

[129] C. Abdoll and C. Barberton (eds.), *Mud to Bricks: A Review of School Infrastructure Spending and Delivery* (Pretoria: Pretoria University Press, 2014) iv.

[130] A second settlement agreement was reached and made an order of court. The DBE failed, however, fully to comply with the 2014 agreement. Contempt proceedings were instituted in early April 2015 to try and enforce compliance with the main aim of ensuring that the DBE updates the ASIDI list: see Legal Resources Centre "Further Litigation Launched After Department of Education Fails to Eradicate Mud Schools" (April 10, 2015) (available at www.lrc.org.za/lrcarchive/press-releases/3484-press-release-further-litigation-launched-after-department-of-education-fails-to-eradicate-mud-schools) (accessed date November 20, 2017).

MINIMUM NORMS AND STANDARDS FOR SCHOOL INFRASTRUCTURE. The right to basic education has also been instrumental in the adoption of Minimum Norms and Standards for School Infrastructure by the DBE in terms of section 5A of the South African Schools Act 1996. The purpose of these regulations is to provide a standard in terms of which school infrastructure can be measured and in terms of which the DBE can be held to account. Their absence, in turn, contributes to the failure to provide adequate infrastructure at public schools and undermines the right to basic education.

Proceedings were instituted against the Minister of Education in March 2012 by the LRC and Equal Education[131] on behalf of two Eastern Cape schools. An order was sought which would compel the Minister to set national binding norms and standards for schools in terms of classrooms, electricity, water, sanitation, libraries, laboratories, recreational facilities and security. A settlement agreement was reached in terms of which the Minister undertook to promulgate these regulations. The Minister kept her part of the agreement in publishing draft norms and standards. However, after comments were submitted on this draft by more than twenty organizations, the Minister failed to publish the final regulations within the agreed timeline. The Minimum Norms and Standards were only published in November 2013, after another court order was made compelling the Minister to fulfil her obligation.

The tireless social mobilization by Equal Education played an important role in the final adoption of these regulations and the organization remains active in ensuring their provincial implementation.[132] As a result of the combination of the adoption of the Minimum Norms and Standards for School Infrastructure and sustained activism, the provision of infrastructure at public schools has improved. The National Education Infrastructure Management System (NEIMS) Reports of 2011 and 2015 provides the figures contained in Table 3.1 on school infrastructure.[133] While the impact of the right to basic education is evident in the improvement in the provision of these facilities, the government's continued failure to provide the basic necessities for the fulfilment of the right means it still falls short of full thick compliance with its requirements.

131 Equal Education is an organization which advocates for quality and equality in education in South Africa.

132 Equal Education held numerous marches, vigils, public rallies and media statements in order to mobilise a "collective voice."

133 Figures obtained from NEIMS Reports of 2011 and 2015.

TABLE 3.1. *Number of schools lacking particular facility*

Fa Facility	2011	2015
Electricity	3544	913
Water	2401	452
Sanitation	913	128
Library	22,938	18,150
Laboratory	21,021	20,315
Computer lab	19,037	15,984

THE TEXTBOOK SAGA. The provision of textbooks has also been a stress point which has led to a recent pronouncement by the Supreme Court of Appeal on the content of the right to basic education. The DBE adopted a new education curriculum for the entire country in 2012. This new curriculum was to be phased in over a period of three years. During the phasing-in period, the DBE was simultaneously running two different curricula for different grades, which placed much pressure on its resources. Delays in the delivery of textbooks in the Limpopo province arose. In May 2012, an urgent application was brought to the North Gauteng High Court to compel the delivery of textbooks and the adoption of a catch-up plan. Kollapen J held that the DBE's failure to provide textbooks to schools in Limpopo is a violation of the right to basic education. The DBE was directed to deliver the outstanding textbooks for grades 1 to 3 and 10 by a certain date and to develop a catch-up plan. The DBE failed to ensure full delivery of the books in accordance with the court order. A settlement agreement was made an order of court on July 5, 2012. A fresh order was issued on October 5, 2012 extending the date of delivery to October 12, 2012. Considering that the school year had already started in January, it does not seem like much of a victory that textbooks were finally delivered to all of the learners by the middle of October in 2012. This litigation did, however, prepare the way for future challenges to the state's failure to deliver textbooks.

In 2014, the third and final stage of the roll-out of the new curriculum took place.[134] While most of the textbooks had been delivered, proceedings were nevertheless instituted against the DBE. The DBE's defense was that it had not violated the right to basic education because 97 percent of textbooks had

[134] The delivery of textbooks in the roll-out of the new curriculum in 2013 did not lead to any litigation.

been delivered by April 21, 2014. Tuchten J, in the North Gauteng High Court, confirmed rulings made by Kollapen J in 2012 that the right to basic education includes the right of *every* learner to be provided with a textbook for *every* learning area before the curriculum is due to commence. The DBE appealed directly to the Constitutional Court against this decision and the application for leave to appeal was dismissed. The DBE subsequently appealed to the Supreme Court of Appeal, where a full engagement with the obligations on the state in terms of subsection 29(1)(a) of the Constitution occurred.

The Supreme Court of Appeal held that the DBE's failure to deliver textbooks to 3 percent of students not only infringed upon their right to basic education, but also amounted to unfair discrimination. The Court held that the 3 percent of learners who were not provided with textbooks were adversely affected and that this differential treatment was not justifiable. The Supreme Court of Appeal confirmed that the subsection 29(1)(a) right entitles every learner to every textbook before the school year starts and that the DBE's failure to deliver *all* textbooks to *all* learners is a violation of this right.

Once again, the constitutional right to basic education provided a platform for litigation and allowed courts to order the enforcement of the right that enhanced access to the basic conditions for learning.

THE CRISIS IN FURTHER EDUCATION. Subsection 29(1)(b) provides that "[e]veryone has the right ... to further education, which the state, through reasonable measures, must make progressively available and accessible." Access to tertiary education has been made available to a very limited number of South Africans. In 2014, only 783,545 people out of a population of 53 million were enrolled at universities and universities of technology.[135] This is due to the failures in the primary and secondary school system as well as institutional capacity limitations. Tertiary education is also prohibitively expensive for the majority of South Africans.

The government has aimed to fulfil its subsection 29(1)(b) obligations by establishing the National Student Financial Aid Scheme (NSFAS) which provides loans and bursaries to students whose families earn below a defined income level. It has been suggested that this fund has been mismanaged and that it does not have effective mechanisms in place to disburse monies to students and to ensure the repayment of loans. It furthermore provides inadequate funding to cover all tuition fees (and living expenses) of qualifying students and some universities attempt to step in to address this shortfall.[136]

[135] Statistics South Africa, *General household survey: 2014*.

[136] The only criteria for funding are academic potential and financial need.

The state has also been taking steps in terms of its subsection 29(1)(b) obligations by funding public universities and technikons directly.[137] However, state funding per student has been decreasing by 1.1 percent every year from 2000 up to 2010.[138] In response to this decline in funding and increases in student numbers, universities have been increasing their tuition fees by 2.5 percent per student on an annual basis.[139]

In October 2015, the University of the Witwatersrand announced that its student fees for 2016 would increase by 10.3 percent.[140] Students reacted to this hike in fees by organizing protests and bringing activities on the campus to a standstill. Students from other universities, who were facing similar fee increases, joined the protests.[141] While most of the protests were conducted peacefully and orderly, there were instances of arson and destruction of university property on the part of the students, as well as claims of police brutality in response.[142] The protests eventually required the intervention of the President who responded by announcing that there would be no fee increase at any university in the country. The President also stated that provision would be made for the shortfall in funding for universities.[143] A task team was set up to review university funding but, unfortunately, no long-term solution to this problem had been developed at the time of writing.

3.4.3.3. Performance of the Right to Education

Despite the heightened urgency for compliance with the right to basic education (which is "immediately realisable"), the state has not fulfilled its

[137] In terms of s. 38G(1) of the Higher Education Act 1997. B. Fleisch and S. Woolman, "Education," in S. Woolman and M. Bishop (eds.), *Constitutional Law of South Africa*, 2nd edn (Cape Town: Juta, 2008), Chapter 57, 42.

[138] Department of Higher Education and Training, South Africa, *Report of the Ministerial Committee for the Review of the Funding of Universities* (Pretoria: October 2013) 152 (available at www.dhet.gov.za/SiteAssets/Latest%20News/Report%20of%20the%20Ministerial%20Committee%20for%20the%20Review%20of%20the%20Funding%20of%20Universities.pdf) (accessed date November 20, 2017).

[139] Ibid.

[140] A. Areff, "Student protests against fee hikes across South Africa" *TimesLive*, October 20, 2015 (available at www.timeslive.co.za/local/2015/10/20/Students-protest-against-fee-hikes-across-South-Africa) (accessed date November 20, 2017).

[141] Ibid.

[142] J. Duncan, "#FeesMustFall: A question of human rights violations" *Mail and Guardian*, November 9, 2015 (available at www.mg.co.za/article/2015-11-09-the-question-of-human-rights-violations-against-feesmustfall-protesters) (accessed date November 20, 2017).

[143] T. Gqirana, "There will be money for students next year, Zuma" *Sowetan*, November 19, 2015 (available at www.sowetanlive.co.za/news/2015/11/19/there-will-be-money-for-students-next-year--zuma) (accessed date November 20, 2017).

obligations adequately in this regard. The litigation which has led to the enforcement of certain aspects of this right can be counted as successes of the constitutional right. The right has provided a normative basis from which civil society and the courts could intervene to support the provision of basic education. At the same time, court interventions cannot fully succeed in improving the quality of education and crucial matters, such as the lack of well-trained teachers, are not easily susceptible to litigation.

The state has also failed to make further education progressively available but has adopted retrogressive measures instead by decreasing funding to tertiary institutions. The right to further education has "performed" in the sense that it has served as the basis for public protests against increased exclusion in tertiary education, but there have not been any cases on the exact requirements of the right.

3.5. CONCLUSION: OVERALL ASSESSMENT OF THE PERFORMANCE OF SOCIO-ECONOMIC RIGHTS IN SOUTH AFRICA

The South African government has put numerous policies and legislative schemes in place and has made a large proportion of its budget available for the fulfilment of its duties in respect of socio-economic rights. Yet, there remain major discrepancies between the socio-economic rights guaranteed in the Constitution and the reality faced by large numbers of the South African population who lack access to the goods promised. The socio-economic rights in the Constitution have had an impact, as has been shown, on the demands made by civil society and provided the basis for advances in policy to take place through litigation. Litigation has forced the adoption of policies where none existed, helped address a significant health crisis and forced the implementation of policies where the government has been dragging its feet. It has also strengthened the hand of civil society groups in negotiating with the government. Thus it is evident that these rights have had an impact on peoples' lives. These rights have effected significant changes even where they have not been interpreted by the courts to place an onerous and immediate burden on the state.

The South African experience with social rights thus provides strong support for the value of placing them in a bill of rights. The approach adopted by the courts toward their realization has also been of interest internationally and may offer some guidance as to a potential model for their adjudication in jurisdictions with a conservative approach to the separation of powers. At the same time, this experience highlights the disadvantages of such an approach, and engagement with comparative approaches in similar contexts of economic deprivation, such as India and Colombia, help to identify what alternatives may exist for enhancing thick compliance with the goals of including such rights in a bill of rights.

Indeed, arguably, a more expansive interpretation – such as that adopted in Colombia – would have encouraged even greater efforts to be expended in reducing absolute poverty and placed a greater focus on ensuring that those whose needs are most urgent would have been catered for. Rendering the courts more accessible and the path of litigation easier would have also facilitated more cases and perhaps greater legitimacy for the role of the courts in defending the poor. Indeed, the realization of socio-economic rights is a major challenge for the future stability of South African democracy. The overall picture that emerges in South Africa is one where there have been significant achievements through the inclusion of social rights in the bill of rights yet their full potential has not been realized. The reasons for this judgment are clearly not only to do with the weaker approach to enforcement adopted by the courts under the overhang of a conservative understanding of the separation of powers. The historical backlog, difficult global economic conditions, fiscal policies, the increase in corruption, the one-party dominance of the African National Congress and significant failures of the legislature and executive are but some of the factors that have contributed to the continued failure adequately to realize social rights for many. It is crucial to understand the deeper causes of the continued deprivation and for solutions to be proffered to these which could include a more robust approach to their enforcement in courts. The stakes are indeed high and the successful realization of social rights in South Africa will, in many ways, determine the success or otherwise of South Africa's constitutional democratic project.

4

Proceduralism's Promise: The Constitutional Court, Social and Economic Rights and Democracy

Steven Friedman

Does a constitutional court best serve democracy when it seeks to substitute for policy makers or when it strives to enable the agency of citizens?[1] The question is raised by an important debate in the pages of legal scholarly journals over the role of South Africa's Constitutional Court in extending social and economic rights. This is important in itself – but it also has wider application, for it raises broader questions about the role of courts in new democracies such as South Africa's as well as more general questions about the relationship between law and democracy in constitutional states.

The debate was initiated by scholars who question the view[2] that South Africa's Constitutional Court has come to the aid of the poor and the weak by effectively extending social and economic rights, a view which is widespread enough to prompt the observation that the court has been "remarkably successful, with a reputation among constitutional courts in new democracies second to none."[3] These critics[4] sharply criticize the Court for not doing enough to

[1] This chapter is born of a study of the courts and social policy undertaken for a project on Social Policy *in the BRICS Countries organize*d by the University of London. This generated a journal article, Steven Friedman "Enabling agency: the Constitutional Court and social policy" (2016) 91 *Transformation* 19–39 which this chapter uses as a point of departure.

[2] C. R. Sunstein, "Social and economic rights? Lessons from South Africa" (1999) 11 *Constitutional Forum* 123–32.

[3] T. Roux, "Principle and pragmatism on the Constitutional Court of South Africa" (2009) 7 *International Journal of Constitutional Law* 106–38 at 107.

[4] J. Dugard, "Courts and the poor in South Africa: a critique of systemic judicial failures to advance transformative justice" (2008) 24 *South African Journal on Human Rights* 214–39; J. Dugard, "Response to P. Danchin: 'A human right to water? The South African Constitutional Court's decision in the Mazibuko case'" (April 17, 2010) *EJIL: Talk! Blog of the European Journal of International Law* (available at www.ejiltalk.org/a-human-right-to-water-the-south-african-constitutional-court%E2%80%99s-decision-in-the-mazibuko-case/) (accessed date November 20, 2017); C. Albertyn, "Gendered transformation in South African jurisprudence: poor women and the Constitutional Court" (2011) 22 *Stellenbosch Law Review* 591–613.

extend the rights and entitlements of the poor – it has, they argue, backed away from handing down rulings which dictate strongly pro-poor outcomes. They are particularly critical of the Court for responding to the denial of social and economic rights with procedural remedies rather than by instructing offenders to remedy the violation by providing plaintiffs with specific goods or services. In this view, of course, it is the role of the court to come to the aid of the poor by instructing those who deny them rights on how they should remedy the violation. The more assertive it is in imposing standards which give content to social and economic rights, the more it does to advance the democratic and egalitarian values to which the Constitution is meant to give effect.

Their position is challenged on two grounds which are relevant here. First, by arguments which question whether it is appropriate to rely on courts to impose social and economic policy outcomes.[5] In this view, most of the decisions required of courts in adjudicating social and economic rights cases are not legal questions but distributional choices which are best made by democratically elected representatives. It warns that, while some judicial rulings on these issues may assist the poor and marginalized, courts are as likely to find against the poor[6] and that judicial authority could be a burden to people living in poverty rather than a boon. In many societies, courts have, at various times, delivered decidedly antipoor judgments (perhaps the most famous example in the global North is the clash between the Supreme Court and the Roosevelt administration in the United States of the 1930s in which the court sought to block the New Deal).[7] The obvious implication is that the poor may be better served by democratic politics than by judicial protection. The second, which shares some common assumptions with the first, sees the Court's preference for ordering parties to negotiate rather than imposing outcomes as a more likely route to promoting democracy and also to ensuring concrete gains for the poor.[8]

This chapter will discuss the debate and will argue in favor of the second proposition – that the Court's preference for negotiation over prescription has greater potential to enhance democratization and to realize the intention of the Constitution than one in which it would seek to dictate concrete outcomes. Since it is prepared for a gathering of legal scholars, it will assume

5 D. Davis, "The case against inclusion of socio-economic rights in a bill of rights except as directive principles" (1992) 18 *South African Journal on Human Rights* 475–90.

6 G. N. Rosenberg, *The Hollow Hope: Can Courts Bring About Social Change?* (Chicago, IL: University of Chicago Press, 1991).

7 W. E. Leuchtenberg, *Franklin Delano Roosevelt and the New Deal, 1932–1940* (New York, NY: Harper and Row, 1963).

8 B. Ray, "Proceduralisation's triumph and engagement's promise in socio-economic rights litigation" (2011) 27 *South African Journal on Human Rights* 107–26.

familiarity with the court's social and economic rights judgments and will not seek to explain the issues at stake or the court's rulings.

4.1. THE CRITIQUE AND ITS CONTEXT

The critique of the Court's stance on social and economic rights is grounded in a perceived shift in its approach from the halcyon days of the *Grootboom*[9] and *TAC*[10] judgments, in which it was seen to order government to take specific action to realize social and economic rights, to one in which it is seen to offer only procedural remedies, in particular the requirement that government action must be "reasonable." (Whether *Grootboom* can really be classed as a case in which the government was told to do something specific is open to debate. So too is the claim that the Court has done nothing since *TAC* to extend social and economic rights jurisprudence. For the purposes of this chapter, the relevant point is that this is what is perceived by the critics.)

The judgment which best illustrates the point of contention between the Court and its critics is *Mazibuko*,[11] in which it rejected the argument that it should force the state to provide the poor with a "minimum core" of services (in this case a significantly increased entitlement to free water). Instead, it ordered that the amount of free water to which the poor are entitled be negotiated. The Court's scholarly critics insist that this ignores the interests and needs of the poor[12] and have criticized the Court's failure to impose a judicially mandated minimum floor of entitlements for the poor.[13] In this view, the Court has, in its desire to avoid antagonizing government or private economic power-holders, failed to realize the promise of the earlier judgments.

A more general version of this argument is interested not in details such as "minimum core content" but in the Court's "transformative" role. It argues that the Constitution gives the Court latitude to re-engineer society by vigorously extending social and economic rights but that it has been unwilling to use it:

> [T]he South African Constitution, in sharp contrast to the classical liberal documents, is social, redistributive, caring, positive, at least partly horizontal, participatory, multicultural, and self-conscious about its historical setting and transformative role and mission.[14]

9 *Government of the Republic of South Africa* v. *Grootboom* (2001) 1 SA 46 (CC).
10 *Minister of Health* v. *Treatment Action Campaign (No. 2)* 2002 (5) SA 721 (CC).
11 *Mazibuko* v. *City of Johannesburg* (2010) 4 SA 1 (CC).
12 Dugard, "Response to Peter Danchin."
13 Ray, "Proceduralisation's triumph"; T. Roux, "Legitimating transformation: political resource allocation in the South African constitutional court" (2003) 1 *Democratization* 92–111.
14 K. E. Klare, "Legal culture and transformative constitutionalism" (1998) 14 *South African Journal on Human Rights* 146–88 at 153.

In this view, the Constitution enables the Court to engage in "transformative constitutionalism," which is required if the Constitution's values are to be realized. By implication, it is far from reaching the potential which the Constitution offers.[15] Catherine Albertyn is similarly concerned that the Court has not developed a jurisprudence appropriate to "the lived reality of poor women" and urges "a carefully crafted engagement" with its notion of reasonableness which "could be used to hold government to account for ensuring that its policies are appropriately 'engendered', and that the needs of women and men are built into the conceptualisation, resource allocation, budgeting … of … policies."[16]

Many (although not all) of the scholars who take this position are speaking from a left perspective which criticizes liberal jurisprudence and demands a far more assertive legal assault on poverty and inequality. Much of their position is a critique of what Brian Ray, following Danie Brand, describes as the "proceduralisation" of social and economic rights, a trend in the Court's rulings to insist on procedural fairness in social and economic rights cases rather than dictating specific outcomes.[17] This approach was spelled out by Justice O'Regan in the court's *Mazibuko* judgment:

> A reasonableness challenge requires government to explain the choices it has made. To do so, it must provide the information it has considered and the process it has followed to determine its policy … If the process followed by government is flawed or the information gathered is obviously inadequate or incomplete, appropriate relief may be sought.[18]

This is seen by the Court's critics as a retreat from substantive equality, for it leaves the final say in policy-setting to the government whose commitment to the poor they question. In all of these formulations, the Court is required to play an active role in dictating specific outcomes rather than processes and its failure to do so is seen as an abdication of responsibility.

In a similar vein to the critics, although not with the same pejorative intent, Theunis Roux has argued that the Court avoided endorsing "minimum core content" because it is aware of a strategic need not to place too great a burden on the government for fear of antagonizing it[19] – the Court's critics would no doubt see his argument as vindication of their view that it is motivated by prudence rather than principle. He has also located the Court's social and

[15] Klare, "Legal culture and transformative constitutionalism" at 146.
[16] Albertyn, "Gendered transformation," at 609.
[17] Ray, "Proceduralisation's triumph" at 107.
[18] *Mazibuko*, para. 71.
[19] Roux, "Principle and pragmatism."

economic rulings in a desire to assist the government to realize its change agenda which, he argues, the government and the Court broadly share.[20] Again, this could be seen to endorse the view that it seeks to co-operate with rather than confront the government.

Roux's work could, however, also be used to make an argument which the critics would reject – that the Court's perceived timidity in choosing procedure over prescription is born of an accurate estimate of the limits of what is possible. In this view, endorsing minimum core content would have painted a government with limited resources and many pressures on them into a corner, making it impossible for the Court's rulings to achieve anything for the poor. Prudence would then be not a failure to realize the Constitution's potential but a necessary means of ensuring at least limited progress in extending social and economic rights at all.

His stress on the values which the government and the Court held in common, at least during the time he discusses, could be understood to warn implicitly against the view that courts can alter the policy course of a government reluctant to address the social and economic needs of the poor. It suggests that a significant degree of stated government sympathy for addressing domination is needed before courts can nudge governments toward extending social and economic rights. There must, at the very least, be a consensus within the elite – judicial and political – that change is desirable. Constitutional courts are likely to be able to address poverty and equality only if there is consensus among the society's elites that this is necessary. If that view is accepted, a court which is careful to stay within the consensus is again doing all that it can to ensure that social and economic rights will be addressed, even if the result falls short of the change required. One way of doing this might be to concentrate on making it more likely that social policy will adhere to the new order's stated values and will be applied in a fair way which reduces the likelihood of resistance from the privileged. Albertyn points out that the "transformation consensus" in the courts "operates at a fairly high level of abstraction, and the differences that exist at the more detailed level of theory, concepts and strategies are not always apparent."[21] Given this, filling in the detail rather than challenging the principle of government actions might be an important role.

This also implies Roux's second point – that there are limits beyond which courts cannot go if they wish governments to listen to them rather than to close them down or pack them with compliant judges (presumably even if

[20] Roux, "Legitimating transformation."

[21] Albertyn, "Gendered transformation" at 595.

they share a consensus with them). Since it is surely true that the notion of following the instructions of judges is not self-evident to political power holders (and since, of course, the politicians have the power to close down constitutionalism and those who enforce it), a court serious about extending rights will also be cautious about pushing the political authorities too far for fear of undoing all its gains.

In practice, it is not possible to establish how far the Court could go before it is forced to retreat in the face of political reality – a core element of this line of argument is that the Court's influence and even perhaps its survival depend on never testing this. If a court is still functioning and handing down judgments which are accepted, it has presumably succeeded by definition in making sure that it does not find out how far it can push the government. This makes the argument about whether it could have gone further an interesting abstract exercise but not one which is likely to assist concrete judicial decision-making. More important for the purposes of this argument, the view that the Court was moved by prudence assumes that, if it was somehow assured that government would let it alone, it would be preferable for it to adopt minimum core content and to use it to order the government to adopt particular policies. This is, however, not a universally held view and it is also not the view expressed in this chapter. We need, therefore, to examine critiques of this view.

4.2. THE LIMITS OF PRESCRIPTION

There is an important irony about the debate among legal scholars on the court's role – the view which wants it to become far more assertive is less likely to extend social and economic rights in substance rather than form and to enable them to endure and is also much less likely to strengthen democracy.

Perhaps the key problem in this approach is that it almost entirely obliterates one of the key ingredients in any attempt to deepen democracy and ensure a fairer society – citizen agency. Democracy is not meant to be a system in which a small group of technically skilled people decide what is best for everyone else: on the contrary, this is precisely what it was meant to prevent. It is, rather, meant to be a system in which citizens play an active role in deciding not only who should govern but what government should do. An approach which wants jurists rather than citizens to decide how social goods are to be distributed is one which seeks to deny citizens the right to decide. In practice, democracy also depends on citizen agency: democracies are established by the actions of citizens and they become deeper and more enduring the more citizens are able to act to influence decisions.[22] So any workable program to realize the constitution's democratic values must place emphasis on encouraging citizen agency.

Since the call for the Court to give priority to substantive outcomes inevitably devalues citizen agency by relying on judicial decision-making rather than democratic politics, it is perhaps no surprise that scholars in this school pay scant attention to the agency of the poor who are, of course, the intended beneficiaries of minimum core content or "transformative constitutionalism." To cite one example (chosen because of its stress on the empowerment of the powerless, normally a process in which we would expect agency to play a key role), nowhere in Albertyn's analysis is there a mention of anything the courts might do to empower poor women to shape their own futures or even a suggestion that poor women are capable of doing this on their own (despite a rich history of women's agency in the fight against apartheid). She is concerned only to propose a jurisprudence which, as the citation above indicates, will instruct the government to take the needs of poor women seriously. The stress is purely on what enlightened jurists can do for poor women, not how jurisprudence could play a role in enabling them to do things for themselves.

This tendency to rely on the enlightenment of an elite rather than the agency of the poor to frame responses to poverty manifests in omission as well as commission. The critique entirely ignores a key reality: that, as Brian Ray points out, proceduralization has been accompanied by an equally important trend – "the Court's emphasis on participatory democracy and the ability of procedural remedies to democratise the rights-enforcement process."[23] A feature of emphasis on procedure has been a trend in judgments toward mandated engagement between hitherto powerless citizens and the public authorities: government is instructed to engage with those who its policies affect rather than imposing solutions unilaterally upon them.[24] Given the critique that the Court has been using proceduralization to escape its obligations, it is reasonable to assume that the stress on engagement, too, is seen by most radical (and some liberal) legal scholars as a retreat from the Court's core role – telling government what the minimum standards of social policy should be or ordering it to "transform" society. But, while it seems at first glance radical and "transformative" to argue that the Court should not leave the content

[22] S. Friedman, *Power in Action: Democracy, Collective Action and Social Justice* (Report for Institute for Democracy in South Africa and Ford Foundation, 2007).

[23] Ray, "Proceduralisation's triumph" at 107.

[24] Ibid.; S. Wilson, "Litigating housing rights in Johannesburg's inner city: 2004–2008" (2011) 27 *South African Journal on Human Rights* 127–51; R. Solange, "Transformative constitutionalism in a democratic developmental state" (2011) 22 *Stellenbosch Law Review* 452–565.

of social and economic rights to the vagaries of an uncertain negotiation process, the effect is to rely on the decisions of enlightened technical specialists rather than citizens.

Obvious objections of democratic principle could be leveled at this position. Judges are not elected and not accountable to those whose lives their rulings affect except in an extremely abstract way (judges are not punished by the electorate if their social policy rulings damage people's lives). Nor is it clear why legal training should, for example, enable anyone to say that 12 kl of free water is an appropriate level for indigent people, the lower court ruling which was overturned in *Mazibuko*. While Roux is dismissive of what he calls the "standard argument" that judges "are neither mandated nor institutionally equipped to undertake the complex economic and interest-balancing inquiries that inform the allocation of public resources" and that it is "therefore unwise to give them the power to review decisions taken by the political branch in this area, and foolish for judges to assume this power when they are not compelled to do so," he fails to demonstrate the flaws in this view.[25] Insisting that lawyers and judges have a greater right to decide than others is to claim that social policy should be made by those who presume to know better rather than by those who the policies affect.

Given this, it is certainly possible to insist, with Ray, that proceduralization of social and economic rights cases is not a flight from constitutional principle but a recognition of the democratic tenet that policy should be made by elected representatives, provided that they follow democratic procedures. It is in procedure that lawyers are trained and it seems far more consistent with democratic principles that they hold governments to account for procedural fairness in policy-making than that they make policy themselves.

A court which orders a public authority to engage with plaintiffs rather than deciding what the result of that engagement should be is doing far more to recognize the agency of the poor than one which sets an arbitrary "minimum core" for social services – hence Ray's observation that the trend towards mandated engagement can democratize the enforcement of social and economic rights. Rosa Solange, citing Amartya Sen, recommends engagement as a key element of "transformative constitutionalism" consistent with democratic values.[26] She notes a distinction between two understandings of this term among legal commentators: the first explains transformation as the "achievement of certain tangible results or outcomes" such as the reduction of poverty, through

[25] Roux, "Legitimating transformation" at 92.

[26] R. Solange, "Transformative constitutionalism in a democratic developmental state" 22 *Stellenbosch Law Review* (2011) 452–565.

adjudication; the second "refers to the radical change of the institutions and systems that produce results themselves."[27] The second approach, she argues, is more appropriate to Sen's stress on the need for policy to be formulated by democratic deliberation. And it is also, she suggests, more consistent with the norms which underpin a democratic constitution: "I argue here that at the heart of South Africa's transformative Constitution lies a participatory democratic culture that is integral to the achievement of social justice and development for all" and which is advanced by the engagement which the courts have mandated.[28] This understanding of transformative constitutionalism is almost entirely absent in the writing of the advocates of minimum core content.

As the preceding discussion has implied, democratic principle also requires placing a value on democratic governance which is also largely absent in the minimum core content approach. Elected governments require limiting by a constitution and those who interpret it. But this does not alter the point that, in democracies, policy is meant to be made ultimately by those elected to do so. This view does not contradict the stress here on citizen agency: elected governments may decide ultimately but in an effective democracy they do so only after citizens have acted and spoken. But it does mean that the popular mandates of elected governments are entitled to respect in constitutional democracies. This provides a further argument for negotiation rather than judicially imposed solutions since it gives elected government a role in determining the content of social and economic rights.

In a response to *Grootboom*, which would no doubt now seems quaint to radical legal scholars, Cass Sunstein hailed the ruling as "a powerful rejoinder to those who have contended that socio-economic rights do not belong in a constitution."[29] He argued that it had, uniquely (he insisted that he knew of no court elsewhere which had done the same), found an answer to the conundrum of how courts could intervene on the side of the poor without removing the prerogatives of elected governments. The ruling was "respectful of democratic prerogatives and of the limited nature of public resources, while also requiring special deliberative attention to those whose minimal needs are not met."[30]

It had thus answered the argument that social and economic rights litigation undermines democracy – the judgment "suggests that such rights can serve,

[27] Ibid. 456, citing D. Brand, "Courts, socio-economic rights and transformative politics" LLD thesis, Stellenbosch (2009).

[28] Solange, "Transformative constitutionalism" at 450.

[29] Sunstein, "Social and economic rights?" at 123.

[30] Ibid. 124.

not to preempt democratic deliberation, but to ensure democratic attention to important interests that might otherwise be neglected in ordinary debate."[31]

In hindsight, his assumption that South Africa's Court had broken new ground which was destined to lead international thinking proved excessively optimistic. Domestic legal scholars and housing rights activists would also question whether the judgment went as far as it could in giving attention to the interests of "those whose minimal needs are not met." But the principle which underlines his point is anything but quaint and outmoded – that social and economic rights jurisprudence is likely to sustain democratic social policy-making only if it seeks to enable rather than to override the agency of both elected governments and those who elect them.

4.3. RESPECTING CITIZEN AGENCY

The argument for giving primacy to negotiation processes is further strengthened by an examination of the concrete effects of the Court's rulings. This suggests that insisting on democratic process, which includes mandating negotiation, is most likely to realize social and economic rights because it is more likely to challenge the power relationships which prevent people enjoying these rights.

Analysis of the relative effectiveness of the two approaches is in some cases speculative. Evidence does not, for example, allow us to say with certainty what direct effect, if any, the only judgment in which the Court could be said to have adopted an approach similar to minimum core content, *TAC*, had on the government's decision, in 2003, to agree in principle to a comprehensive treatment regime for people living with HIV and AIDS. Research suggests that the campaign outside the courtroom was decisive and that the Court, important as its ruling may have been for other reasons, was not the key reason why the government shifted position.[32] But there is clearly no way this claim could be demonstrated conclusively. What the evidence does support is an important conclusion – that Court rulings on social policy have been most likely to contribute to change if they are a supplement to, rather than a substitute for, collective action by citizens seeking realization of their rights.

The point can be illustrated by a comparison between the outcomes of the two "stand-out" cases of the Court's "golden period," *Grootboom* and *TAC*. Besides the oft-made point that Irene Grootboom, the plaintiff who gave her

[31] Ibid. 123.

[32] S. Friedman and S. Mottiar, "A rewarding engagement? The Treatment Action Campaign and the politics of HIV/AIDS" (2005) 33 *Politics and Society* 511–65.

name to the judgment, died without receiving the accommodation to which the Court said she was in principle entitled, the fact that, almost a decade after the ruling, residents of the Johannesburg inner city were still fighting evictions,[33] that housing has remained a frequently contested issue since then and that, in 2012, the housing backlog was still estimated at more than two million,[34] surely indicates that, whatever its merits, the ruling has not fundamentally altered the problem it sought to address. By contrast, the achievements of the campaign to secure treatment for people living with HIV and AIDS have been striking. At the end of 2013, the Minister of Health reported that:

> 2.1 m people are on antiretroviral treatment (up from 923,000 in 2009), 3 540 HIV treatment sites have been established (up from 490 in 2009), and 23,000 nurses are able to initiate patients on treatment, compared to 250 four years ago.[35]

While, as noted above, it is possible that the *TAC* judgment had little or no influence on this outcome – that publicly-funded HIV and AIDS treatment is now no longer controversial is a product of a complex combination of political events and processes[36] – it clearly was seen by campaigners as an important supplement to collective action.[37] Just as the evidence suggests that the ruling did not usher in a serious government attempt to treat HIV and AIDS, it seems reasonable to assume that the Court ruling did play some role and that, in this case, using legal action as a means of reinforcing collective action has produced one of the great social policy advances of the democratic era.

There are obvious objections to this argument. One is that it is a great deal easier to induce governments to dispense medication for people living with a particular condition (even if they number several million) than to provide adequate shelter for all. Another is that the *TAC* ruling did order the government to take specific action while *Grootboom* did not. But neither of these factors are decisive enough to nullify the core point: the intent of *TAC* has become far

33 Wilson, "Litigating housing rights."

34 News 24 (2013) "Sexwale: Housing backlog at 2.1m" (March 13, 2014) (available at www.news24.com/SouthAfrica/News/Sexwale-Housing-backlog-at-21m-20130607) (accessed date November 20, 2017).

35 A. Thom, "Motsoaledi happy with HIV response" (December 11, 2013) *NSP Review* (available at www.spotlightnsp.co.za/2013/12/11/motsoaledi-happy-with-hiv-response/) (accessed date November 20, 2017).

36 S. Friedman, "Gaining comprehensive AIDS treatment in South Africa: the extraordinary 'ordinary'" in J. Gaventa and R. McGee (eds.), *Citizen Action and National Policy Reform* (London: Zed Books, 2010) 44–68.

37 Friedman and Mottiar, "A rewarding engagement?"

more a reality in the lives of citizens than that of *Grootboom* and, in the case which achieved much more concrete change, the ruling was a supplement to a campaign by citizens using the civil liberties established by the Constitution to seek their social and economic rights. If the realization of judicial intent in social and economic rights cases requires citizen agency, then "transformative constitutionalism" is surely bound to give priority to enabling this agency rather than relying on judicial prescription through the application of minimum core content.

The case for emphasizing negotiation is further supported if we examine the role of the law and citizen action in a successful campaign to prevent evictions in Johannesburg's inner cities.[38] This was a protracted attempt to prevent the city's council from depriving the occupants of "bad buildings" of their shelter and to compel it to recognize their housing needs. It is described and analyzed by Stuart Wilson, one of the lawyers who fought the legal battle on behalf of residents. The campaign ultimately halted the evictions and forced the council to engage with residents.

Wilson argues that recourse to the law was a product of the tenants' weakness – they had few other options. They "are not represented by, and do not constitute, a single agent" except in technical legal terms (and were impelled toward court action by the fact that the city needed to obtain court orders before evicting them).[39] "No matter how effective a grassroots campaign of direct action or political protest would have been, it seems unlikely that the occupiers of 'bad' buildings would have been able to resist their removal without engaging in litigation ..."[40] In any event, the "organisational resources" needed to sustain a successful campaign "were simply not present."[41]

But, despite the constraints to collective action, there were "grassroots organisations" operating in the inner city who attempted to link residents to legal assistance.[42] A period of legal trench warfare, in which evictions were contested in court apartment block by block, ensued. It culminated in the *Olivia Road*[43] case, which mandated engagement between the authorities and the plaintiffs. The Court handed down an interim order requiring the parties "to engage with each other meaningfully and as soon as it is possible for them to do so, in an effort to resolve the differences and difficulties aired in

38 Wilson, "Litigating housing rights."

39 Ibid. 137.

40 Ibid. 137–38.

41 Ibid.

42 Ibid. 140.

43 *Occupiers of 51 Olivia Road, Berea Township and 197 Main Street Johannesburg* v. *City of Johannesburg* 2008 (3) SA 208 (CC) (*Olivia Road*).

this application in light of the values of the Constitution, the constitutional and statutory obligations of the municipality and the rights and duties of the citizens concerned."[44]

Over the next weeks, the parties negotiated and reached a settlement which "represented an almost comprehensive surrender on the City's part." Its capitulation to almost all the occupiers' demands "was spectacular and was caused by a palpable ... fear of public censure from the Constitutional Court, which had made clear during argument that its sympathy lay with the occupiers." In early 2008, the Court ruled that the state was under a general obligation to "meaningfully engage" with persons it sought to evict "individually and collectively" and to "respond reasonably to the views and concerns raised during that engagement." Accordingly, the judgment "left little doubt that the only reasonable response to desperately poor persons who would be rendered homeless on eviction was to provide them with at least some alternative accommodation."[45] It might also be added, of course, that the judgment may also have left little doubt that the "only reasonable response" to people in the plaintiff's position was to negotiate with them.

This case has been quoted at some length for two reasons. First, while the inner-city residents' organization was weak – and Wilson is concerned to demonstrate, possibly in response to arguments that the poor should rely on organization rather than litigation, that they would have made little headway without court action – they were organized enough to sustain the campaign against evictions, with the help of lawyers, for a protracted period. Second, and perhaps more important, the Court's ruling mandating engagement is credited with ending the evictions and enabling residents to exert at least some influence on their future. This suggests that, even where citizens are weakly organized and therefore enjoy limited capacity to act to claim their rights, the court's stress on engagement can enable those over whom unaccountable power is wielded to acquire a voice. The Court followed by mandating engagement in two other cases: "In *Mamba* v. *Minister of Social Development*, [it] ordered the Gauteng government and others to engage with representatives of internally displaced refugees of the antiimmigrant violence that swept South Africa in early 2008 over the timing and procedures for closing the refugee camp"[46] and in the *Joe Slovo*[47] case, where again a "mass eviction" was

[44] *Olivia Road* cited in Wilson, "Litigating housing rights" at 148.

[45] Wilson, "Litigating housing rights" at 148.

[46] Ray, "Proceduralisation's triumph" at 111.

[47] *Residents of Joe Slovo Community, Western Cape* v. *Thubelisha Homes* 2010 (3) SA 454 (CC).

averted. A subsequent report by a nongovernmental organization on *Joe Slovo* observed:

> It was only after the Court ordered engagement over the details of the eviction process itself – including devising a detailed agenda of issues for that engagement and specifically requiring reservation of a set percentage of new homes for community residents – that the government finally took seriously the possibility of in situ upgrade that was a key demand of the residents.[48]

Far from falling short of minimum core content established by jurists, these judgments surely provide the model for extending social and economic rights built not on the beneficence of judges but on the only foundation on which it can be built – the collective action of citizens whose democratic rights enable them to contest attempts to relegate them to the margins. Court orders cannot substitute for citizen organization – but where organization exists (even in weak form), rulings have assisted attempts to use collective action to deepen and broaden social and economic rights. They can do so in the future if rulings empower citizens by mandating engagement.

4.4. MINIMUM CORE CONTENT OF ANOTHER TYPE

If the argument proposed here has rejected minimum core content as it is currently understood – a substantive set of entitlements formulated by a court and imposed on public decision-makers – it makes a case for a different form of minimum core: one which seeks to guarantee not a particular level of provision of public goods but the elements which ensure a negotiation process in which the power of the parties is equalized as much as possible, a real negotiation process rather than one in which one side alone decides.

The first reason for proposing this is the obvious possibility that the authorities who are not anxious to negotiate will simply go through the motions of talking and will not make any substantive compromises: the injunction to engage is not a guarantor of inclusive social policy-making. This is not a hypothetical: according to Sbu Zikode, the president of Abahlali baseMjondolo, a shack dweller organization:

> Engagement is usually a window-dressing exercise to show that government is listening to us but with no real results for the poor at the end of the day. Or it is a politicized process through ward councilors where if you are not an

[48] Cited in Ray, "Proceduralisation's triumph" at 113.

> ANC member, your opinion will not be heard and you do not have access to jobs or services.[49]

And even if the authorities are in earnest, the balance of power will inevitably favor them (just as it would businesses, if the Court ordered them to negotiate) since they have resources at their disposal which people seeking social and economic rights lack. Remedial action is therefore needed to ensure that the engagement is as close to one between equals as is possible – the balance of power is not simply redressed by an injunction to talk.

Ray who, as noted above, sees the Court's interest in engagement as an opportunity, argues, therefore, that it should take a more assertive stance – but to shape engagement rather than to determine outcomes:

> Government must commit to developing a robust infrastructure for engagement and to institutionalise engagement policies and procedures across the board. To ensure that institutionalisation, the Court itself must be willing to at times ... make substantive determinations of what these rights require as well as to prevent government from proceeding with policies where engagement was clearly inadequate. Civil society can assist ... through sustained pressure on government and by bringing cases ... to call attention to government's lack of sufficient institutionalisation.[50]

This suggests that effective social policy can best be protected by insisting on a "minimum core" – but one of engagement, not of substantive outcomes. This is unlikely to substitute for severe power imbalances – but it can act as a catalyst for effective collective action to achieve and maintain the extension of social and economic rights gains. An attempt to specify these requirements is beyond the scope of this chapter – although compelling power holders to supply accurate information (surely a core requirement for reasonableness criteria) would be an obvious starting point. But clearly it would require the Court to intervene more than it does now, to ensure a fair process rather than to decide on its outcome.

The Court's willingness – or reluctance – to take this route could be seen as a test of the turn in its social and economic rights jurisprudence which the minimum core content advocates criticize. If it simply mandates negotiation and does not intervene to ensure both that it happens in substance as well as

[49] N. Tolsi, "Grootboom Win a House of Cards" (March 9, 2012) *Mail and Guardian* (available at www.mg.co.za/article/2012-03-09-grootboom-win-a-house-of-cards) (accessed date November 20, 2017).

[50] Ray, "Proceduralisation's triumph" at 125–26.

form and that the balance of power between the parties is as even as it could be, then it is reasonable to conclude that it is indeed avoiding a confrontation with the government rather than charting a new democratic course which will turn the quest for social and economic rights into a stimulus for enhanced democratic participation. But, if it does rise to the challenge and begins to develop a jurisprudence which focuses on equalizing voice rather than distributing goods and services, it will be charting a new course more attuned, in the view of this chapter, to the requirements of democratic constitutionalism.

4.5. FERTILE SOIL? PARTICIPATION'S PEDIGREE

The South African Constitutional Court's stress on participation may not be unique – India's Supreme Court, for example, does not mandate negotiation between parties but it does negotiate with interested parties before framing its judgments on social and economic rights, which achieves a similar outcome.[51] But it is deeply rooted in the founding ethos of the democracy established in 1994.[52]

That formal channels were needed to enable citizens' organizations to communicate with the government was a canon of governance thinking at the establishment of the new democracy because it has strong roots in the fight against apartheid. As resistance grew in the 1980s, popular participation was a core rallying cry. In their fight against apartheid's exclusion of the majority from decision-making, activists frequently demanded "people's power," a slogan which could mean many things, but which clearly advocated popular participation in governance.[53] A balance of power between the resistance and the white authorities prompted negotiation between civic organizations representing disenfranchised black city-dwellers and the white authorities, and so the participatory forum as an element in local governance became a key instrument of the fight for majority rule.[54] During the negotiation period of the early 1990s, the insistence that the minority government not take unilateral

[51] S. Friedman and D. Maiarano (2017), "The limits of prescription: courts and social policy in India and South Africa," 55 *Commonwealth and Comparative Politics*, 353–76.

[52] S. Friedman, "Participatory governance and citizen action in post-apartheid South Africa" Geneva (International Institute of Labour Studies, Discussion Paper/164/2006, 2006).

[53] J. Rantete and M. Swilling, "Organization and strategies of the major resistance movements in the negotiation era" in R. Lee and L. Schlemmer (eds.), *Transition to Democracy: Policy Perspectives 1991* (Cape Town: Oxford University Press, 1991) 198–222.

[54] M. Swilling, "City politics comes of age: strategic responses to local government restructuring" in R. Schrire (ed.), *Critical Choices for South Africa: an agenda for the 1990s* (Cape Town, Oxford University Press: 1990) 411–27.

decisions which would bind the new democracy was a core concern of the African National Congress and its allies. A notable success of this campaign for shared decisions was agreement to the demand of the Congress of South African Trade Unions for a National Economic Forum which would allow for participatory decision-making in economic policy.[55] National sectoral negotiating forums dealing with social policy were a key feature of the process which negotiated an end to apartheid.[56]

The forums sought to balance the power of popular mobilization with the reality that the old order could not be defeated and therefore had to be negotiated out of power. Even after majority rule, the continued hold of the white minority over capital and skills made compromise with it an imperative. This reinforced enthusiasm for forums which would allow policy to be negotiated with a range of social interests because none could impose solutions unilaterally. Formal mechanisms of participation thus became an important feature of postapartheid governance. The National, Economic, Development and Labor Council (Nedlac) was established in 1995 as a statutory vehicle of negotiation between business, labor, government and "community" organizations.[57] Participatory forums were established to govern schools, oversee policing and to offer citizen groups a say in water distribution and health care. Local governments are compelled by law to consult citizens. The law also mandates public participation in the drafting of policy. While the ethos of participation withered as the postapartheid administration increasingly relied on management technique, as late as 2005 the local government minister responded to a wave of protest against municipal councils by urging the strengthening of participatory committees.[58] This is but one example of continued commitment to participation, at least on the level of rhetoric.

Participatory forums' contributions to democratic decision-making were very limited – they tended to privilege organized interest groups and they never became platforms for the negotiation envisaged by the Constitutional Court.[59] But the commitment in principle to negotiation and participation

55 O. Edigheji, "State-Society relations in post-apartheid South Africa: the challenges of globalisation on co-operative governance" in G. Mhone and O. Edigheji (eds.), *Governance in the New South Africa: The Challenges of Globalisation* (Cape Town: University of Cape Town Press, 2003) 77.

56 K. Shubane and M. Shaw, *Tomorrow's Foundations? Forums as a Second Level of a Negotiated Transition in South Africa* (Johannesburg: Centre for Policy Studies, 1993).

57 Edigheji, "State-Society relations" 78.

58 F. S. Mafumadi, "Address by Minister of Provincial and Local Government" (March 29, 2005) (available at www.dplg.gov.za/speeches/29Mar2005Min.doc) (accessed date November 20, 2017).

59 Friedman, "Participatory governance."

was central to the spirit of the founding years of South African democracy – many Constitutional Court Judges, who were human rights activists during the fight against apartheid, were steeped in this ethos, which is no doubt why it presented itself as a credible solution to the Court's desire to balance the protection of rights with respect for elected government.

4.6. ANOTHER CONSTITUTIONALISM?

It may be apparent by now that more is implied by this approach than a preference for negotiation as a means of settling social and economic rights disputes – or the view that people denied these rights are more likely to enjoy them fully if they claim them through their own agency. It also proposes a particular way of understanding constitutions and rights and their relationship to democracy.

A common approach to constitutionalism sees it as a necessary check on majority rule since it limits the power and freedom of action of democratic governments.[60] It is, of course, not controversial to point out that this is what constitutions do: the question is why they do it. Wittingly or unwittingly, the notion of minimum core content is consistent with the view that the decisions of majorities and those they elect cannot be trusted and that intervention is therefore needed to achieve the public good. While this view is advanced by scholars who consider themselves sympathetic to the poor and weak (whose social and economic rights are most likely to be denied), their view is ironically consistent with that of elitists who believe that some are more entitled to take decisions than others – in South Africa, of course, this is a popular view among members of racial minorities who feel threatened by majority rule. Whatever the motive, much legal writing on constitutionalism sees it as a check on, rather than an aid to, decision-making by the majority.

An alternative view is grounded in the rationale for minority rights, and thus for constitutionalism, offered by Hans Kelsen. He argued persuasively in the post-World War 1 period that, while majority rule was a core democratic concept, democracy also entailed the protection of minorities from the majority so that they can enjoy the freedoms which democratic participation requires.[61] For Kelsen, majoritarianism does not require constraint because there is an "objective" way of determining which policies are best. The core rationale for democracy is not that anyone's opinion is inherently "better" than anyone

[60] G. Sartori, *The Theory of Democracy Revisited* (Chatham, NJ: Chatham House, 1987).

[61] H. Kelsen, *The Essence and Value of Democracy*, H. Kelsen, N. Urbinati and C. Invernizzi Accetti (eds.) (Plymouth: Rowman and Littlefield, 2013).

else's but that, if the majority is enabled to do whatever it wishes it may well deprive the minority of its liberty. Since democracy is a system in which all citizens enjoy (in principle) an equal say, the effect would be to deprive some citizens of the say to which democracy entitles them.

There is an important difference between advocating constraints on majority decision-making because this is somehow not to be trusted and doing so because unrestrained majoritarianism would inhibit participation and hence reduce the circle of those enabled to decide. In this second view, the problem with allowing majority government to do as it pleases is not that it may act in ways which fail to meet the criteria of experts, but that it may use its majority to inhibit participation. It need not only do so by realizing Kelsen's fear – by muzzling the minority. It might also seek to use its legal mandate to govern as a rationale for silencing citizens between elections – this attitude is common among governments, particularly those beleaguered by citizen protest, who argue that the electorate chose them to govern and should, in effect, leave them to get on with it without interference. But democracy is meant to be an order in which everyone has an equal right to decide, not one in which everyone has an equal right to choose who decides; it therefore requires that citizen voice shapes policy between elections too.

In this view, human rights are also primarily seen as a means to realize full democratic citizenship – to which the right to decide is central – rather than to simply protect minorities from the harm that might be done to them by majorities. Democracy in this view requires everyone to enjoy rights not only because human beings are entitled to respect and consideration but because there cannot be full participation unless everyone's rights are respected. So rights become an essential ingredient of democratic citizenship, a point which is endorsed by thinkers in the global South who advocate action by the poor to redress inequalities of power and privilege. Arjun Appadurai observes in a discussion of popular politics in Indian cities: "there is no doubt that the global spread of the discourse of human rights has provided a huge boost to local democratic formations."[62] Issa Shivji, writing in Tanzania, urges that rights "... [not be] theorised simply as a legal right ..., but a ... standard-bearer around which people rally for the struggle from below."[63] It is important to note that for these writers, participation is the means by which those denied social and economic rights claim them.

62 A. Appadurai, "Deep democracy: urban governmentality and the horizon of politics" (2002) 14 *Public Culture* 21–47 at 25.

63 I. G. Shivji, *The Concept of Human Rights in Africa* (London: Council for the Development of Social Science Research in Africa (CODESRIA), 1989) 71.

Social and economic rights imposed from the bench cannot, in this view, trump the need for participation, for without the freedom to speak and associate, what will grassroots citizens use to both claim and defend their rights? Some advocates of minimum core content might argue that they cannot do the claiming because they cannot be fully effective citizens until they have achieved social and economic rights. The evidence presented here refutes that argument, since none of the social and economic rights cases on which the Court adjudicates would have been heard if citizens denied rights had not acted collectively to claim them.

In sum, relying on negotiation rather than prescription is not only more likely to ensure that those who are denied social and economic rights will be able to claim them. It also points the way to an understanding of constitutionalism's purpose which sees it as an enabler of, not a constraint to, free decision-making by all members of a political community. In principle, the Court's purported retreat is, therefore, potentially an enormous advance.

5

Corruption, the Rule of Law and the Role of Independent Institutions

Heinz Klug

5.1. INTRODUCTION

Faced with the prevalence of corruption in nearly all governments, this chapter explores whether the South African Constitution has in effect created a new separate branch of government that may be identified as an integrity branch distinct from the traditional three branches of constitutional government. While the 1996 Constitution has a separate chapter, which includes a set of six institutions whose role it is to strengthen democracy, I will argue that three of these chapter 9 institutions deserve to be understood as fitting the definition of "integrity institutions" that together constitute a fourth branch designed to expose and combat the corrosive spread of corruption in government at all levels. These three – the Auditor-General, the Independent Electoral Commission and the Public Protector – may be distinguished from the other "State Institutions Supporting Constitutional Democracy" in chapter 9 whose roles include the promotion and protection of human rights, gender equality, and the promotion and protection of the rights of cultural, linguistic and religious communities. Although these latter institutions also have mechanisms to accept and investigate complaints as well as to promote rights or community interests, it is the particular roles of the integrity institutions that both set them apart and provide the basis for identifying them as an integrity branch of government.

The existence of constitutionally independent institutions designed to ensure integrity with respect to key government functions, such as financial management, elections and procurement or "service delivery," raises important questions about the structural nature of the distribution and separation of powers created by the 1996 Constitution. Recent decisions in the courts, culminating in the Constitutional Court's 2016 decision in *EFF* v. *Speaker of the*

National Assembly,[1] which addressed President Jacob Zuma's constitutional failures in the Nkandla matter, highlight and clarify the nature of the checks and balances that will need to be understood and recognized if this fourth branch of constitutional government is to be an effective part of South Africa's scheme of constitutional governance. In the case of Nkandla, the name of President Zuma's home village in KwaZulu-Natal, there was clear evidence that public funds were used to refurbish his home, providing benefits beyond those justified by the security upgrade that the government was legitimately undertaking. Despite vigorous denials by both the President and various government ministers whose departments had been involved in the "upgrade" the Public Protector issued a report finding that the President had received unjustified benefits and that the President would have to repay the government the value of those benefits. This created the context in which it was necessary to clarify the constitutional status of a finding by the Public Protector.

Corruption is clearly a significant problem for governments around the globe, whether democratic or authoritarian. It is claimed that since 1994 South Africa has lost approximately US$50 billion to corruption.[2] While this is a staggering figure it is important to recognize that this figure includes the estimated cost of a range of corrupt activities from direct diversion of funds to overcharging on government procurement as well as the costs of nepotistic employment practices and the failure of financial management and reporting. Even as the ANC government questions whether particular decisions or expenditures should be considered corrupt, the government is charging a record number of lower level officials with corruption and trumpeting its determination to address malfeasance that all agree undermines effective governance and public confidence. In early 2016 President Zuma drew cheers from the crowd at the launch of the ANC's local government election manifesto when he stated that a "total of 234 government officials [had been] ... arrested, tried and convicted for corruption related offences since 2014," and that the government's antifraud and anticorruption campaign had recovered over R4-billion since 2009.[3]

1 *Economic Freedom Fighters* v. *Speaker of the National Assembly; Democratic Alliance* v. *Speaker of the National Assembly* (2016) 3 SA 580 (CC).

2 Al Jazeera, reporting on the anti-corruption marches on September 30, 2015: "How Corrupt is South Africa?," *Inside Story*, September 30, 2015 (available at www.aljazeera.com/programmes/insidestory/2015/09/south-africa-corruption-150930214450269.html) (accessed date November 20, 2017).

3 C. du Plessis, "'A vote for the ANC is a vote for the Constitution' – Zuma" (April 16, 2016) *Mail and Guardian* (available at www.mg.co.za/article/2016-04-16-a-vote-for-the-anc-is-a-vote-for-the-constitution-zuma?utm_source=Mail+%26+Guardian&utm_medium=email&utm_

The problem of corruption is entwined with a number of issues of significant constitutional importance including the public/private distinction – since it clearly takes two to tango – as well as democratic accountability and the separation of powers. In focusing on corruption, whether financial, political or administrative, this chapter begins by identifying the emergence of constitutional institutions that have been created or recently constitutionalized in the effort to address the scourge of corruption and maladministration. While the focus will be on the integrity institutions, the concern is to understand how these independent constitutional bodies may help to address the more general problem of holding the executive branch of government accountable and the implications these efforts have for the separation of powers which lie at the structural heart of a constitutional system. However, before focusing on these institutions, this chapter will provide a brief outline of the history of accountability in South Africa, focusing on Parliament as watchdog over the executive as well as the origins and emergence of the chapter 9 institutions and the Public Protector in particular. The chapter will then focus on the twenty-year history of the public protector as one of the three integrity institutions. It will describe the institutionalization of this institution and then explore the separation of power problems that have arisen and how these have been discussed in the jurisprudence of the courts. Finally, the chapter will discuss the most recent decision of the Constitutional Court in *EFF* v. *Speaker of the National Assembly*, identifying and evaluating how a system of checks and balances so central to the separation of powers is emerging. The chapter concludes that it is the emergence of this system of constitutionally recognized checks and balances that characterizes the constitutionalization of this fourth "integrity" branch of government.

5.2. ACCOUNTABILITY

While Parliament has always been the primary source of formal law-making in South Africa, it has historically never managed to serve as a very effective watchdog. This may, of course, be attributed to a number of both structural and conventional conditions. First, as a fused-system, in which the executive is part of a legislature dominated by the ruling party, it would be a surprise if it really was able to hold the government accountable in the face of party solidarity. Second, the parliamentary tradition has long seen major problems of accountability or disaster channeled into government-appointed Commissions

campaign=Daily+newsletter&utm_term=http%3A%2F%2Fmg.co.za%2Farticle%2F2016-04-16-a-vote-for-the-anc-is-a-vote-for-the-constitution-zuma) (accessed date November 20, 2017).

of Enquiry that are called upon to investigate and address questions of government failure and malfeasance. At Westminster, the parliamentary custom of ministerial responsibility – and quick, quiet resignation at the slightest hint of impropriety – has historically narrowed the institutional space for robust investigation or confrontation of a ruling party and its conduct in government. Instead, a government may fall or call an early election, but even in London there is an increasing tendency for the executive to brave its way through by actively attempting to "spin" public opinion while abandoning the custom of taking formal responsibility and accepting the resignation of those identified as culprits. Instead, governments are increasingly leaving the process of managing political and public service malfeasance to the courts through various processes of judicial review – either administrative law or, where appropriate, constitutional review.

Even if parliamentary systems have never served as effective watchdogs, given the dominance of the ruling party and members of government within the institution, this does not mean that parliamentarians do not at times take up this role with some forcefulness. South Africa's pre-1994 apartheid Parliament did not, however, have such a tradition. Instead, the colonial and apartheid regimes that governed until 1994 maintained an "entire social edifice ... structured to enrich a powerful few at the expense of the majority."[4] In the period between 1948 and 1994 Parliament served as a rubber stamp for the decisions of the National Party and executive. There were many pressure groups, "such as the wine farmers ... who used their close proximity to Parliament to "take people to parties" and provide them with a quota of wine annually – this continued in the immediate post-1994 period, when MPs had access to cost-price wines ... These were all subtle forms of influence buying that could be compared with contemporary private sector-subsidized golf days for politicians and public sector officials."[5] Furthermore, the increasing secrecy of the apartheid regime and the expansion of covert operations after 1976 – as well as the "history of routinised corruption"[6] in central government departments and the "homeland" administrations – provide ample evidence for the following claim by the Speaker of South Africa's first democratic Parliament, Frene Ginwala:

> [I]n South Africa we inherited an intrinsically corrupt system of governance ... To survive, it created a legal framework that was based on and

4 D. O'Meara, *Forty Lost Years: The Apartheid State and the Politics of the National Party, 1948–1994* (Athens, OH: Ohio University Press, 1996) 231.

5 H. van Vuuren, *Apartheid Grand Corruption: Assessing the Scale of Crime of Profit in South Africa from 1976–1994* (Cape Town: Institute for Security Studies, 2006).

6 T. Lodge, *South African Politics Since 1994* (Cape Town: David Philip, 1999) 60.

> facilitated corruption. It has taken years in Parliament to repeal old laws and introduce even the basic legal framework that would enable us to deal with corrupt bureaucrats, politicians and police. The private sector also operated in a closed society and profited by it. There were partnerships with international criminals and the corruption that was built into the system is very difficult to overcome.[7]

In contrast to this history, South Africa's first truly democratic legislature seemed in its early years to be committed to diligently exercising its duty to act as a public watchdog. The relative strength of the legislature during these early years may be attributed to two factors. First, the initial postapartheid Parliament, established under the interim Constitution, served simultaneously as the national legislature and as the Constitutional Assembly responsible for writing South Africa's final Constitution. Given this historic constitution-making responsibility, it is no surprise that many of the most prominent politicians and antiapartheid activists, from across three generations, were nominated and elected to serve in this first Parliament. Second, these individuals were held in high esteem and wielded enormous political authority within the ANC, which meant that there was a de facto as well as formal distribution of power between the legislature and the executive. This balance was also enabled by Nelson Mandela's explicit plea that even he, as President, be held accountable by the collective leadership of the ANC.

The confidence of these parliamentarians was evident in the early practice of the parliamentary committees, which would ask probing questions of high-ranking civil servants and Ministers and, at times, take them to task. At the same time, however, the committees lacked the resources to adequately research and investigate issues. This problem was exacerbated by the historic physical separation of government: the executive and administrative departments are located in Pretoria, while the legislature is situated more than one thousand miles away in Cape Town. In a short time, however, the tendency of the executive to recruit many of the most effective politicians into the Cabinet and the tendency of Committee Chairs to use their positions to promote their political careers meant that those members who were within the government increasingly dominated Parliament. The ruling party became correspondingly more centralized and concerned with protecting the image of the government rather than raising questions about the implementation of policy or the integrity of government programs and officials.

7 F. Ginwala, "Speaker of Parliament, Remarks to the Opening Session, Global Forum II, The Hague" (May 28, 2001), cited in Van Vuuren, *Apartheid Grand Corruption* 5–6.

Parliament's first major oversight challenge arose when it was revealed in the press that the Department of Health was spending R14.2 million on a musical that was to tour the country providing education on the growing HIV/AIDS pandemic. Commissioned from world-class South African playwright Mbongeni Ngema in 1995, the budget for the show represented a significant portion of the health department's HIV/AIDS prevention efforts. The musical itself, "Sarafina II" was criticized for failing to impart a clear public health message. But the scandal focused on the high costs of production – including the salaries, luxurious facilities and what was seen as the inappropriate grandeur of the production itself. When the Portfolio Committee first asked the Minister of Health, Dr Nkosazama Zuma, to justify this expenditure, she purportedly refused to attend the hearing. Dr Zuma's appearance before the committee, after government realized that her refusal to attend would be politically embarrassing, merely demonstrated how new the concept of oversight was for the legislature. First, the members of Parliament (MPs) relied mainly on press reports to challenge the Minister, instead of demanding access to the official documentation, which was their right. Second, the ANC members remained extraordinarily passive, caught between the exercise of their parliamentary duty and loyalty to the government. As one ANC member later admitted, "It was still early days. We did not know how to deal with something like this. Perhaps we should be condemned for it, perhaps we should be forgiven, but we were more concerned with damage control than we were with parliamentary accountability."[8] The Committee's failure was further highlighted when the Public Protector issued a report in June 1996 that documented the mismanagement of tender procedures and the "unauthorized expenditure of foreign aid" in this project.[9]

Parliament's ability to act as an effective watchdog was further undermined by its own dalliance in addressing a pattern of systematic abuse by MPs from across the political spectrum. The first inklings of what would come to be known as "travelgate" surfaced in the year 2000 when Speaker of the House Frene Ginwala publicly rebuked two MPs for abusing travel vouchers, granted annually in a check-book type format, so that MPs could travel between Parliament in Cape Town and their constituencies or homes around the country. When the issue was later raised in the ANC caucus, Essop Pahad, a close associate of President Mbeki, attacked the Speaker, objecting to the public reprimand on the grounds that the ANC MP involved had used the

[8] R. Calland, "The First 5 Years: A Review of South Africa's Democratic Parliament," *Political Information Monitoring Service* (Cape Town: IDASA 1999) 36.

[9] Ibid. 35.

travel vouchers for ANC Party business that the ANC leadership considered legitimate.[10] But this was only the tip of the iceberg, and by the time the scandal unraveled in 2007, it embroiled more than 100 MPs who were forced to resign, plead guilty and enter into plea-bargains to repay millions of Rands to Parliament for fraudulent claims; or were brought to trial and convicted as a result of their misuse or even the sale of their parliamentary travel allocations for private benefit. Even more damaging has been the fact that "senior ANC leaders and Cabinet members involved have, in most instances, quietly paid back the money that was defrauded from Parliament."[11] As a result, the integrity of the institution was severely compromised.

However, the most egregious and consequential failure of oversight occurred at the dawn of the new century when Parliament's attempt to assert its oversight of a major arms-procurement process led to repeated interventions by the executive, and the ANC's highest officials in the legislature, which effectively undermined the ability of the legislature to perform its constitutional role. The "arms deal," as it has been christened, involved a simple – if extremely expensive – government procurement process. But it was also a complex policy of military modernization and hoped-for economic investment for the country coupled with possible kickback funding for the ruling party and a plethora of secondary contracts providing multiple opportunities for simple old fashioned graft. Deputy-President Thabo Mbeki chaired the Cabinet sub-committee from 1996 to 1999, and headed the official procurement process that oversaw and "commissioned the purchase of R30 billion worth of armaments–specifically, submarines and frigates – from a French-German consortium and fighter-jets from a British-Swedish one."[12] The government justified such vast expenditures on armaments by arguing that they provided an opportunity for industrial investment and job creation, since the bidders promised that the deal would lead to investments in the South African economy worth approximately R104 billion and would create around 65 000 jobs. In the end, the arms deal cost twice the amount originally agreed upon, produced only 13 000 jobs by 1996, and became what Mark Gevisser has described as the "poisoned well of post-apartheid South African politics."[13] It led to the demise of some institutions, massive legal battles and the eventual ousting of Thabo Mbeki from the presidency.

[10] See, A. Feinstein, *After the Party: A Personal and Political Journey inside the ANC* (Cape Town, Jonathan Ball, 2007) 241–2.

[11] Ibid. 242.

[12] M. Gevisser, *A Legacy of Liberation* (New York, NY: Palgrave MacMillan, 2009) 256.

[13] Ibid.

The controversy that would become the arms-deal scandal had its roots in the early years of the democratic transition. Gevisser even suggests that the decision to modernize the military might have been based as much on concerns over a "disaffected military" and the threat of internal destabilization it posed, as it was on concern about external threats to national security. The scandal first hit the headlines when Member of Parliament Patricia de Lille (then of the opposition Pan Africanist Congress) stood up in the National Assembly and announced that she had in her possession a ten-page briefing authored by "concerned" ANC MPs accusing senior ANC politicians of corruption and questioning whether the promised "off-sets" would ever become a reality.[14] In fact, the Auditor-General had already raised questions about the arms deal in November 1998. And while Defense Minister Mosiuoa Lekota derided de Lille's claims in public, privately he gave approval for the Auditor-General to have access to all relevant documentation for audit purposes. However, within days, the Cabinet sub-committee countermanded the Defense Minister's decision, claiming that the Auditor-General first had to clear his terms of reference with the Committee. When the Auditor-General released the first official report on the arms deal on August 15, 2000, questioning the "off-sets" and arguing that the "practice of choosing the Hawk [aircraft] did not meet standard regulations on acquisitions,"[15] the issue was formally placed in the hands of the National Assembly's Standing Committee on Public Accounts (SCOPA).

While there is no constitutional duty to do so, the ANC's initial commitment to open government and accountability led to the practice of giving the chair of SCOPA to an opposition member of the National Assembly. When the Auditor-General's report came before SCOPA in late 2000, the chair, Gavin Woods of the Inkatha Freedom Party – together with the leading ANC member of the Committee, Andrew Feinstein and the remaining members – agreed that further investigation was necessary. When Feinstein reported this decision to senior ANC leaders in the legislature he was met with a mixed reaction. Jacob Zuma, then Deputy-President and the leader of Government's Business in Parliament was at first supportive and insisted to Feinstein that the Committee continue with its constitutional role, while the ANC's Chief Whip in Parliament Tony Yengeni argued that a public hearing was not a good idea and that the matter be considered an internal

[14] See, P. Holden, *The Arms Deal in Your Pocket* (Jeppestown, South Africa: Jonathan Ball, 2008) 38.

[15] Ibid. 40.

matter.[16] The government turned defensive when SCOPA insisted on continuing its investigation and recommended that Judge William Heath, who then headed the Special Investigating Unit (an independent statutory body reporting directly to Parliament and empowered to investigate maladministration and corruption in government at the President's request)[17] be brought in to investigate the arms deal. In a series of moves, the ruling party and government attacked the recommendation, contained in SCOPA's 14th Report to Parliament, and once President Mbeki rejected Judge Heath's application to investigate the arms deal, the ANC leadership in Parliament moved against SCOPA. First, Feinstein was removed from his role as head of the ANC Study Group in SCOPA; then the Committee was stacked with loyalists who would be sure to follow instructions. As ANC Chief Whip Tony Yengeni told a press conference, "there was no committee in respect of the ANC which is above party political discipline."[18]

5.3. ORIGINS OF THE CHAPTER 9 INSTITUTIONS

From early on in the negotiations toward a democratic transition the idea of creating an "ombudsman" to provide an avenue for complaints and for the investigation of malfeasance and maladministration in the state and its bureaucracy, and even to protect fundamental rights, was shared by the parties; however, the scope and nature of such an office remained a matter of debate.[19] Furthermore, the idea of creating independent governance institutions to address the high level of distrust between the parties and to enable specific aspects of the transition – such as the conducting of a free and fair election – was also being discussed.[20] The ANC Constitutional Committee's working document on "A bill of rights for a new South Africa," published in 1990 specifically included the establishment of an independent ombudsman as part of the section on the enforcement of rights and "[w]ith a view to ensuring that all functions and duties under the Constitution are carried out in a fair way with due respect for the rights and sentiments of those affected."[21] However, as circumstances proceeded the ANC also recognized the importance of creating transitional mechanisms, independent of de Klerk's

16 Feinstein, *After the Party* 160–1.

17 See Special Investigating Units and Special Tribunals Act 1996.

18 See Feinstein, *After the Party* 195, quoting *Business Day*, February 7, 2001.

19 See, South African Law Commission, *Report on Constitutional Models* (October 1991) ch. 23.

20 See, H. Klug, *Constituting Democracy: Law, Globalization and South Africa's Political Reconstruction* (Cambridge: Cambridge University Press, 2000) 119–21.

21 ANC Constitutional Committee, A *Bill of Rights for a New South Africa* (1990) 36–7.

government, as a means of ensuring the democratic transition. It is out of this legacy that the idea was born to incorporate independent institutions for accountability within the postapartheid constitutional order.

As South Africa prepared for its first democratic elections in the early 1990s questions arose about the management of the elections. Up until 1990, the government had organized and managed all elections. But many people raised serious concerns about the legitimacy of the first democratic election if the apartheid regime was to conduct it, especially if conflict were to arise over the results. The liberation movement sought to resolve this problem by calling for the installation of an interim government, as called for in the internationally sanctioned Harare Declaration. However, the incumbent regime argued that there could be no handover of power until a negotiated solution, insisting on legal continuity between the existing state and any future legal order. Faced with an irresolvable tension, the ANC embraced the option of creating a number of independent bodies to oversee the transition to democracy, including an independent electoral commission to manage the election itself. The democratic transition was further facilitated in the period leading up to the first democratic election by the establishment of three independent institutions: the Independent Electoral Commission, the Independent Media Commission and the Independent Broadcasting Authority.[22] The embracing of this idea and the legal institutions it spawned fit well in this period with the global emphasis on expanding democratic constitutionalism. And it set the stage for acceptance of the idea of "State Institutions Supporting Constitutional Democracy" that became an important innovation in South Africa's 1996 "final" Constitution. Thus, chapter 9 of the Constitution establishes six separate institutions: the Public Protector; South African Human Rights Commission; the Commission for the Promotion and Protection of the Rights of Cultural, Religious and Linguistic Communities; the Commission for Gender Equality; the Auditor General; and the Electoral Commission.

These institutions are set within a constitutional scheme that includes structural and institutional elements designed to fulfill the goals of democratic and accountable governance contained within an array of principles spread throughout the constitution. A key structural feature of the Constitution is the way in which power is both distributed and integrated in a system of governance that is designed to not only avoid the paralysis of a rigid separation

[22] See, H. Klug, "Constitution-making, democracy and the 'Civilizing' of irreconcilable conflict: what might we learn from the South African miracle?" (2007) 25 *Wisconsin International Law Journal* 269–99.

of powers, but also ensure that there are multiple avenues for democratic and legal contestation. This combination of distributed and integrated power extends from the system of cooperative government to the allocation of constitutional authority between distinct institutions whose task is to ensure that essential elements of good governance – clean elections, fiscal integrity, transparent procurement and just administration – are maintained at all levels of government as it grapples with the enormous task of addressing the crippling legacies of colonialism and apartheid. In fact, the Constitutional Assembly understood the role of these institutional features of the Constitution as key to the commitment to constitutional democracy, bringing them together in an innovative and unique fashion in chapter 9 as "State Institutions Supporting Constitutional Democracy." This is not to say that the Constitution is perfect or that these institutions have always played an effective role in this young democracy, but it is important to recognize that they do have a distinct role in ensuring that the promises of human rights and good governance reach down into the daily administration of the country and are not merely the subject of five yearly electoral contests or high profile legal disputes.

Just as the Constitution holds a twin promise, on the one hand, empowering government and protecting existing rights, while on the other hand providing a vision of a nonracial, nonsexist future in which all communities and members of South African society may flourish, chapter 9 establishes institutions that are designed to both secure existing rights and democratic achievements as well as provide an institutional mechanism for establishing the norms and capacities for moving toward the vision of a brighter future. At one end of the institutional spectrum the Electoral Commission, the Auditor General and the Public Protector are institutions that are primarily designed to ensure good governance today, while on the other end the Human Rights Commission, the Commission for Gender Equality and the Commission for the Promotion and Protection of the Rights of Cultural, Religious and Linguistic Communities look to the present, but are also designed to advance and extend these interests toward the achievement of the vision of a more equitable and sustainable society. In order to achieve these goals the Constitution establishes all these institutions as "independent, and subject only to the Constitution and the law," requiring them to be "impartial" and to "exercise their powers and perform their functions without fear, favour or prejudice[23]." The translation of this promise into the reality of functioning institutions has, however, not been without difficulty.

[23] Constitution of the Republic of South Africa 1996, s. 181(2).

From internal personnel conflicts to external challenges to their functioning, legitimacy and financial independence, these institutions have not avoided controversy. Apart from the Electoral Commission – which has now successfully managed four electoral cycles in addition to local government elections – and the Auditor-General – which, as a preexisting institution, had an institutional culture and staff in place – the remaining chapter 9 institutions have struggled to define and establish their institutional capacities and constitutional roles. At the same time, issues of adequate financing and accountability, as well as the political careerism and resulting caution of some of the office holders in these institutions led to debates over the degree of independence these institutions really enjoy or exercise. After the first decade, the government decided to initiate a review of these institutions; however, it soon realized that it would not be appropriate for the executive to conduct such a review. Instead, the executive called upon the National Assembly, to which the Constitution makes these institutions accountable, to conduct a review, and in September 2006 the National Assembly adopted a resolution appointing an ad hoc multiparty committee to review the chapter 9 institutions and the Public Service Commission. In its mandate the committee was asked "to assess in broad terms whether the current and intended legal mandates of the institutions are suitable for the South African environment, whether their consumption of resources is justified in relation to their outputs and contribution to democracy," and most significantly, "whether a rationalization of function, role or organization is desirable or will diminish the focus on important areas."[24]

The report of this committee, chaired by ANC stalwart and Member of Parliament, Kadar Asmal was issued in mid-2007 and called for significant reforms to some of these institutions.[25] Identifying an apparent "lack of consistency and coherence in approach" which the committee argued "is ultimately undermining of ... [these institutions] individual, and even common, efforts," the Report called on Parliament to conduct an urgent review "for the purposes of identifying a more systematic approach, particularly those regarding funding and budgets, the appointment of commissioners, collaboration between the institutions, internal governance arrangements and the relationship of the institutions with Parliament."[26] One recommendation of the Report was that a number of the chapter 9 and related institutions – such as the Pan-South African

[24] Republic of South Africa, *Minutes of Proceedings of National Assembly* (No. 46–2006, Third Session, Third Parliament, September 21, 2006) para. 4(2)(a).

[25] Parliament of the Republic of South Africa, Report of the ad hoc Committee on the Review of chapter 9 and Associated Institutions: A Report to the National Assembly of the Parliament of South Africa (Cape Town: July 31, 2007).

[26] Ibid. 19.

Languages Board and the National Youth Commission – be consolidated into the Human Rights Commission. Recognizing that the existing plethora of human rights institutions was the product of the particular circumstances of South Africa's democratic transition, the Report argued that "the present institutional framework has created fragmentation, confounding the intention that these institutions would support the seamless application of the Bill of Rights."[27]

However, the Report also notes that despite internal staff conflicts and a failure to amend the Human Rights Commission Act of 1994 – to make it consistent with the requirements of the 1996 Constitution – the Human Rights Commission has continued to expand and develop its activities. Complaints received from the public by the Human Rights Commission increased from 5762 in 1999/2000 to 11 710 in 2005/2006.[28] The Committee also noted the progressive improvement in the six Socio-Economic Rights reports issued by the Human Rights Commission, culminating in the 2006 report which showed a "vast improvement in the manner in which information is solicited from government departments and the accuracy with which that information is reported."[29] Despite the Report and concerns that the chapter 9 institutions continued to suffer internal tensions and overlapping mandates, there was no immediate effort to make reforms and two years later Kader Asmal, deeply distressed by the failure of the government, and National Assembly in particular, to take up the Report in a timely fashion, publicly "accused Parliament of having no interest in his review of chapter 9 institutions charged by the Constitution with protecting democracy, saying that the failure to debate the review was 'an appalling scandal'."[30] Despite Asmal's disappointment, a decade later the chapter 9 institutions have become an unquestioned part of the institutional landscape and despite the unique constitutional character of these institutions, including the integrity or "fourth" branch of government, they have proven to be a valuable part of what has become, from a global perspective, a vibrant and contentious young democracy.

5.4. INSTITUTIONAL DEVELOPMENT AND CONSTITUTIONAL IMPLEMENTATION

In contrast to this idealistic legal and constitutional framework it is clear that the work of ensuring accountability is much more complicated. In practice, the repeated framing of the law as a neutral arbiter of power must be

[27] Ibid. 37.
[28] Ibid. 179.
[29] Ibid. 179–80.
[30] M. Mateboge, "Asmal takes on Parliament" (July 20, 2009) *Mail and Guardian Online*.

understood in the context of the politics and institutions that are established and serve to breathe life into the law. In order to understand the place of specific institutions in this process we must recognize that institutions do not exist because they are named in the Constitution, but rather that institutions have histories, processes and individual participants that together shape their capacity to fulfill the roles assigned to them. If we take the Public Protector as a key example of one of the constitutional institutions for protecting democracy we will be able to reflect on the process of establishing the necessary institutional capacity as well as the resources, time and leadership that is necessary to achieve the goal of accountability.

While the Public Protector was first established by the "interim" 1993 Constitution and brought into existence through legislation – in the Public Protector Act 1994, the institution was given increased status by its inclusion as one of the independent "State Institutions Supporting Constitutional Democracy" that marked one of the unique features of the final 1996 Constitution. Once provided for by statute it fell to the first Public Protector, Advocate Selby Baqwa to begin the task of setting up the institution at its inception in 1995. If today the Public Protector has offices in all nine Provinces as well as a National Office in Pretoria, it took nearly ten years to create this institutional infrastructure. By 1999 there were only two regional offices, in the North West Province and in the Eastern Cape and it would only be in 2001 that additional offices were added in KwaZulu-Natal, Mpumulanga and the Western Cape. Two additional provincial offices, in the Northern Cape and Free State were added in 2002, while Limpopo and Gauteng were only established in 2003 and 2004, respectively. By 2016 there were twenty walk-in offices around the country as well as a toll-free line and other mechanisms aimed at making the institution accessible to the public.

This process of institution building is reflected too in the budget which grew steadily over a decade from R15.3 million in 1999 to just over R99 million in 2009. These expenditures included contributions from nongovernment sources in the form of grants to help the institution develop. As the Public Protector's office became institutionalized its budget and workload continued to expand. After the beginning of the new millennium expenditures doubled to just under R200 million in 2014 and the staff has grown from an initial 84 at its founding in 1999 to 314 in 2014. In addition to investigating and resolving complaints, the staff are actively involved in public outreach, education and communication activities, including clinics and information sessions in an "effort to bring its [the public protector's] services closer to communities."[31]

31 Public Protector South Africa, Public Protector Vision 2020 and Strategic Plan 2011–2014, 8.

Most of the complaints received by the Public Protector "involve service and conduct failure, including abuse of resources"[32] and the institution sees one of its key challenges as "positioning the office as a buffer between the state and ordinary people as opposed to an agency that primarily deals with high profile cases ... [so often focused on] by the media."[33]

Another way of viewing this developing institution is to consider its role through the number of cases that it has taken up and resolved since its creation. If we take the decade from 1999 until 2009 when the present Public Protector took office, we can see a pattern in which complaints rose from 9 085 in 1999 to a high of 22 323 in 2005 before falling back to 12 674 in 2008/2009. The steady increase in cases until 2005 probably reflects the growing infrastructure and capacity of the Public Protector as it opened offices around the country. By contrast the reason for the decline in cases from 2006 until 2009 is less obvious, although it might reflect the negative media attention that Public Protector Lawrence Mushwana received and the perception that while the resolution of cases rose dramatically after his appointment in 2002, there was a feeling that the Public Protector was not pursuing its mandate effectively. The throughput of cases of course increased in relation to the increase in complaints; however, there was a dramatic increase in resolutions in 2003, up from 13 234 to 21 704, raising concerns that cases were being disposed of without thorough investigation. The pace of resolution, however, settled into a fairly stable range of between 15 949 in 2004 and 13 949 in 2009. At the same time the jurisdiction of the Public Protector has continued to grow as additional legislation has been passed by Parliament to address issues of corruption and maladministration and which fall within the Public Protector's constitutional mandate.

In contrast to the Human Rights institutions, which have had internal problems but have remained largely outside of intense political controversy – except possibly for the Human Rights Commissions' investigation into racism in the media – the Auditor General and the Public Protector have both been directly involved in the intense conflicts over allegations of corruption in the "arms deal" and "oilgate," questions that implicate both the ANC as a party and senior members of government. While it was the Auditor-General who first raised concerns about the "arms deal" by declaring it a "high risk" and requesting permission to investigate it, the Auditor General has also avoided direct confrontation with the government agencies and institutions they are required to monitor by developing the practice of providing "qualified audits"

32 Ibid.
33 Ibid.

that are neither followed up upon nor seen to be as serious as those cases in which the Auditor-General declares that "severe problems have been detected."[34] The Public Protector, however, became a lightning rod for criticism by the media and nongovernment organizations during that period, both for the institution's unwillingness to confront government but most specifically for the 2005 Report that the Public Protector issued in response to complaints about the misappropriation of public funds by the Petroleum Gas and Oil Company of South Africa (PetroSA). PetroSA, a state oil company, was accused of advancing R15 million in public funds to a private company – Invume Investments – which in turn donated R11 million to the ANC.[35] Concerns about the unwillingness of the Public Protector to investigate some of these allegations and the report's perceived "whitewash" of other allegations were only heightened when the North Gauteng High Court set aside the Report in a ruling on July 30, 2009.[36] Concerns about the Public Protector were further heightened following strong public reaction to the news in early October 2009 that the outgoing Public Protector, Lawrence Mushwana, had received a golden handshake of R6.8 million in addition to the luxury car that he was entitled to purchase from the government at the end of his seven year nonrenewable term.

President Zuma's appointment, on October 19, 2009, of Thulisile Madonsela, a well-respected human rights advocate and constitutional lawyer led to public speculation that the Public Protector might yet fulfill the constitutional role it was envisioned to play. Indeed, during her seven-year term Public Protector Madonsela dramatically increased the capacity and profile of the institution. Madonsela adopted a number of strategies to both strengthen the institution as well as ensure a more effective response to growing public concerns over maladministration and corruption. Among a range of new initiatives, the Public Protector sought to both increase the capacity of staff through training (often through partnerships and links to ombudsman institutions around the globe) as well as through the reorganization of the office so as to improve the institution's functioning. One of the first innovations introduced was the creation of an Early Resolution Unit designed to employ the tools of Alternative Dispute Resolution – conciliation, mediation and negotiation – to

[34] See, Auditor-General of South Africa, "General Report on the Audit Outcomes for the Departments, Constitutional Institutions, Public Entities and Other Entities for the Financial Year 2007/2008."

[35] The Report of the Public Protector on an investigation into an allegation of misappropriation of public funds by the Petroleum, Oil and Gas Corporation of South Africa, trading as PetroSA (the PetroSA Report) submitted to Parliament as Report No. 30 on July 29, 2005.

[36] See, P. Zulu, *A Nation in Crisis: An Appeal for Morality* (Cape Town: Tafelberg, 2013) 96–104.

resolve complaints of "state maladministration and other forms of improper conduct."[37] At the same time investigations were separated into three categories: national investigations, provincial investigations and special investigations.[38] In addition the Public Protector faced an "ever expanding mandate" as Parliament passed additional legislation aimed at addressing the growing problem of corruption including: the Executive Members Ethics Act 1998; the Protected Disclosures Act 2000, the Promotion of Access to Information Act 2000, and the Prevention and Combating of Corrupt Activities Act 2004. In addition to these mandates the Public Protector also initiated her own investigations based on newspaper reports or concerns about systematic failures in specific government departments.

The success of the institution in this period is reflected most simply in the growing demand for its services. While the media and political process focused on the high profile "special investigations" being conducted by the Public Protector, it is the dramatic growth in everyday complaints – from 16,136 in 2009–10 to nearly 40,000 in 2014–15 – that demonstrates the impact of this institution. One explanation for this explosive growth is that in a political process based on proportional representation among political parties, members of the public do not feel that they have an elected representative to whom they can turn and that the political parties have been unable to provide this level of assistance to members of the public who feel mistreated by the bureaucracy or other official actors. Another explanation is that the high-profile cases against senior politicians and officials, including the Chief of Police, Cabinet Members and even the President, have produced a level of media and public exposure that has given the public confidence in this institution. As expressed in the Public Protectors Strategic Plan 2011–14, there is a "value of having this office as a buffer between citizens and government [in] that [it] seeks to strengthen constitutional democracy by promptly and impartially redressing administrative wrongs of the state."

From the perspective of the Public Protector the main focus of the office, as evident in the institution's publications and annual reports to Parliament, is on serving the public by "bringing much needed relief to the 'Gogo Dlaminis'" wronged by the state."[39] While this self-image of helping resolve the bureaucratic frustrations experienced by the prototype figure of "grandmother Dlamini" may in fact represent the vast bulk of service delivery, social grant and pension complaints resolved by the Public Protector around the

37 Public Protector South Africa Annual Report 2009–2010, 40.

38 Ibid. 42.

39 T. Madonsela, *Public Protector Annual Report 2012/2013*, Foreword, 4.

country, it is the Public Protector's direct engagement through self-initiated investigations that may have the broadest impact, especially in the context of increasingly violent service delivery protests. Speaking after initiating an investigation into conditions in Braamfisherville, Soweto, the Public Protector thanked the local community leadership for embracing the Constitution and working within its mechanisms to make local government accountable for service delivery, instead of demonstrating violently. Urging other communities to follow this example, Public Protector Tuli Madonesela added that "in giving the people a voice and serving as the conscience of the state, her office would seek answers from the City, with a view to holding those responsible for the situation to account."[40] The response was a surge in public confidence matched by increasing criticism by the legislature and a reluctance to meet the institutions budget and staffing demands.[41]

While the Public Protector may see its role as impartial, the political parties, and particularly the governing party and its senior officials often expressed concern that the institution is used by other parties and interests as part of continuing inter-party political conflict. While it is hardly a surprise that political opponents would attempt to discredit each other by pointing out their failures or initiating investigations, the Public Protector sought to retain a balance between high-profile, media-driven cases and the daily work of the institution. Despite these efforts, there has been increasing tension with the ruling party and government officials leading the Public Protector Madonsela to acknowledge that "[u]nfortunately, a number of organs of state are increasingly becoming adversarial in their dealings with the Public Protector."[42] Responding to this problem the Public Protector attempted to increase communication "with the government, highlighting the role of the Public Protector in reconciling the state and its people by giving the state a conscience ...[43]" Despite these efforts, tensions reached a climax in 2014 as the Public Protector conducted an investigation into allegations that excessive state resources had been used in an upgrade of President Zuma's private home at Nkandla.

The institutional consequences of this unavoidable tension between the Public Protector and the government officials the institution investigates have been threefold. First, it has brought increased media and even international

[40] Public Protector, *Public Protector Inspects Sewerage-Flooded Braamfisherville* (Media Release, March 27, 2012) (available at www.publicprotector.org/media_gallery/2012/27032012.asp) (accessed date November 20, 2017).

[41] T. Mokone, "Madonsela: No funds, no public protector" (October 23, 2014) *Times Live*.

[42] Public Protector South Africa, Public Protector Vision 2020 and Strategic Plan 2011–2014 (2011) 10.

[43] Ibid.

attention to the high-profile work of the Public Protector. Second, it has led to increased hostility from the ruling party, particularly from elements who refused to accept criticism of President Zuma. Finally, it led to an increasingly heated debate over the formal authority of the Public Protector, particularly in relation to the institutions' constitutional mandate to provide a remedy. It is this last issue which goes to the heart of the constitutional authority of the Public Protector and defines its status as a new integrity branch of government created by the Constitutional Assembly to promote constitutional democracy.

5.5. INTEGRITY INSTITUTIONS, GOOD GOVERNANCE AND THE RULE OF LAW

While these new institutions have proliferated since the late 20th century in new and amended constitutions, their development and role in the achievement of good governance and the rule of law raise important questions about their institutional authority and place in the constitutional system, and particularly within the realm of the separation of powers. Whether it is questions of appropriate investigative capacities, reporting and prosecutorial functions, or the appointment and institutional independence of officials within these institutions, the question of their constitutional status and relationship with the other branches or institutions of government quickly implicates the allocation and separation of powers within the constitutional system. Nowhere has this question been more salient than in South Africa where the implementation of the postapartheid constitutional order has been marked by the foibles of a dominant political party, a complex institutional structure and an active civil society that has sought to use the constitutional framework to hold the government accountable. Even if we try to maintain a very formal conception of the separation of powers, as a system of checks and balances between the three traditional branches of government – the legislature, executive and judiciary – or attempt to limit our conception of the separation of powers to a functionalist approach in which we distinguish between the making, implementing and interpreting of laws, our task will be impossibly complicated by the fact that in addition to the different coordinate branches of government, modern constitutions and even older constitutional orders, such as the United States, are laden with institutions of governance – such as the Federal Reserve in the United States and the chapter 9 institutions in South Africa – which do not fit neatly into either a purely formalistic or functionalist conception of the separation of powers. Instead these different institutions exercise public power relatively independent of the three traditional branches, or at least have a degree of constitutionally protected decisional autonomy and independence that is at odds with our traditional notions of the trilateral structure of government.

South Africa's first democratic government came into being at a moment when the technologies of governance and expectations about how government may more readily reflect the imagined efficiency of the market became dominant themes around the globe. Responding to the collapse of state socialism and the emergence of the United States as the sole super power, the new South African government embraced the latest technologies of governance, from the internet to negotiated rule-making as well as recognizing an extensive range of procedural obligations and rights in the administrative and procurement processes of the state. As a result, the South African legal framework establishing the rules and processes of good governance is among one of the most sophisticated in the world. From the unique structure of the Constitution to the adoption of a plethora of new statutes, including: The Public Finance and Management Act 1999; the Promotion of Administrative Justice Act 2000; the Promotion of Access to information Act 2000; the Preferential Procurement Policy Framework Act 2000; and at the local level, the Local Government: Municipal Systems Act 2000. The difficulty, however, is to ensure that this elaborate legal framework functions.

While the Constitution may attempt to distribute executive authority among a variety of institutions so as to mediate the effects of concentrated power – particularly within a polity in which the dominance of a single political party seemed relatively secure for the foreseeable future – the emergence of a unipolar democracy soon seemed to place limits on the relative independence of these institutions. Furthermore, the sophistication of the systems of governance created require a high degree of legal capacity, yet the legal field in South Africa, from the profession to academia has also been faced with the necessity of and obvious strains of transformation. In the case of legal doctrine, in the field of administrative law itself, there is still a degree of ambiguity and lack of clarity among legal academics and lawyers when it comes to understanding the relationship between the concepts and principles of administrative law that were part of the common law, and articulated by the courts prior to the new constitutional era and the adoption of the Promotion of Administrative Justice Act in 2000. Given South Africa's history, in which administrative law was creatively used by some progressive lawyers to oppose the arbitrary use of power by the old regime,[44] and the common lawyer's pride in the sources of administrative law principles, it is not a surprise that many

[44] See, A. Chaskalson, "Legal control of the administrative process" (1985) 102 *South African Law Journal* 419. See also, S. Ellmann, *In a Time of Trouble: Law and Liberty in South Africa's State*

continue to see these principles as in some way underlying or informing the new constitutional and statutory framework.[45] Despite the fact that the Constitutional Court has clearly indicated that the practice of governance is based solely on the new framework, our understanding of the new framework remains deeply influenced by both common law conceptions of administrative law as well as a conception of the separation of powers that is at odds with the more fluid distribution of power that characterizes the structure and institutional provisions of the Constitution.

These impediments and limitations on the transformation of law do not, however, fully explain the tensions within the governance system which has come under increasing stress since the latter years of President Thabo Mbeki's term in office. Issues of governance in this context became embroiled in the political struggles being waged between different political factions within the ANC at every level of government. Most dramatic were the accusations of corruption that led to the dismissal of the Deputy President Jacob Zuma and the counter-accusation that President Mbeki improperly influenced the National Prosecuting Authority in that case, an accusation that ultimately led to his resignation as President. The fact that a High Court judge endorsed these claims of political interference hastened Mbeki's departure and thus had powerful political consequences despite the fact that the High Court's decision was subsequently overruled and severely criticized by the Supreme Court of Appeals. Aside from this dramatic example of the way in which law and legal process was used to wage and resolve political struggles for power within the ruling party, there are also myriad examples of cases in which government officials, high and low, are accused of corruption or other wrong doing. In response to these accusations the assertion of legal and administrative process allows different factions to gain access to positions of power and authority while those accused are "suspended" on full-pay from their government positions. Among the most notorious cases during this period were: the suspension and later trial of then Deputy-President Jacob Zuma (for rape); the Commissioner of Police, Jackie Selebi (for corruption); the director-general of the National Intelligence Agency, Billy Masetlha (accused of withholding information from the inspector-general of intelligence and fraud); an official Commission of Enquiry into accusations against the former head of the

of Emergency (Oxford: Oxford University Press, 1992); R. Abel, *Politics by Other Means: Law in the Struggle Against Apartheid, 1980–1994* (New York, NY: Routledge, 1995).

45 See, H. Corder, "Administrative Justice" in D. van Wyk, J. Dugard, B. de Villiers and D. Davis (eds.), *Rights and Constitutionalism: The New South African Legal Order* (Cape Town: Juta, 1994) 387–400; Y. Burns and M. Beukes, *Administrative Law under the 1996 Constitution*, 3rd ed. (Durban: LexisNexis Butterworths, 2006) 3–25.

National Prosecuting Authority (NPA), Bulelani Ngcuka (accused of being an apartheid spy); and the Commission of Enquiry into whether Vusumzi "Vusi" Pikoli, Ngcuka's successor as head of the NPA, was fit to hold office despite his firing by President Mbeki. The net effect is that while some officials are excluded from processes of procurement and authority that have become the lifeblood of patronage and power, they continue to receive their government salaries and benefits, thus allowing them to continue to engage in the political struggles which led to their unmasking or possibly malicious denouement. Add to this the fact that the government has in many cases felt legally obliged to cover the legal costs of those accused of wrongdoing in their official capacities and the result is a new process of political struggle through law within the executive branches of the postapartheid state.

The formal legal framework within which these conflicts have played out is both clearly stated yet also ambiguously suspended between legal duties and ethical standards. While the President is duty bound to "uphold, defend and respect" the Constitution,[46] and Members of Cabinet are also formally responsible, "collectively and individually to Parliament,"[47] the task of achieving executive accountability remains a constant source of tension within the political and legal sphere. In addition to these general constitutional forms of accountability, Cabinet members are also required to abide by a code of ethics that the President published on July 28, 2000 as stipulated by s. 2 of the Executive Members Ethics Act adopted by Parliament in 1998. The Constitution specifies and the Executive Ethics Code reemphasizes that members of Cabinet must individually refrain from undertaking other paid work; use their positions to enrich themselves or others; or, act in ways that are inconsistent with their office or involve themselves in situations which might give rise to conflict of interests between their "official responsibilities and private interests."[48] The Ethics Code furthermore requires Cabinet members to declare any "personal or private financial interest" they might have in matters that are before the executive body, and in the case of a conflict of interests either withdraw from the decision-making process or ask the relevant Premier or President for permission to participate. In addition, there is a duty to report these interests to the Secretary of Cabinet. Nevertheless, accusations over violations of the Code of Ethics have led to a series of investigations by the Public Protector including a general investigation into reporting failures where the Public Protector concluded in 2006 that there had been no violation of the

[46] Ibid. Section 83(b).

[47] Ibid. Section 92(2).

[48] See, 1996 Constitution, s. 96(2) and para. 2.3 of the Executive Ethics Code.

Code because the data bases relied upon by the Auditor General were not always up to date and that there was a "misunderstanding in regard to the interests that Ministers and Deputy-Ministers are obliged to disclose."[49] Thus, despite an elaborate constitutional and legislative framework for ensuring executive accountability, the implementation of these processes is a continuing source of controversy which led President Zuma to create a new anticorruption Cabinet team in late November 2009.

While there has been widespread agreement that South Africa's Constitution is a progressive blueprint for addressing the legacies of apartheid, there seems at times to be less clarity about how this promise is to be achieved. On the one hand, it may be argued that the Constitution represents a vision of what might be – not unlike the 2030 National Development Plan – but on the other hand, the Constitution is the Supreme Law of the land, and by its own terms it declares that all "law or conduct inconsistent with it is invalid." The same section in the Founding Provisions of chapter 1 also states that "the obligations imposed by it must be fulfilled."[50] It is to this distinction, between the Constitution as a guarantee of minimum standards of governance and rights, and as the blueprint of a future that imposes obligations on our institutions of governance, that we must look, to understand both the frustrations of those who feel the Constitution stands in the way of transformation and those who believe that the country is failing to achieve the promise of the postapartheid rainbow. Law provides the basic mechanism through which government implements its policies, through which markets are created, and regulated, as well as a basis for claims against those who abuse power or fail to meet their legally defined obligations. In many cases this means that it is those with access to resources – the haves – who generally come out ahead, since they are able to most effectively mobilize legal resources, yet the legacy of mobilization, nongovernment organizations as well as progressive lawyering has meant that the Constitution has been repeatedly invoked to protect not only the well-to-do but also the more marginal sections of postapartheid society, and to this extent it has gained a reputation around the world as an example of how constitutions might serve as instruments of transformation.

When it comes to the statute book and regulatory framework, the post-1994 era has seen a raft of progressive policies and legislation from the very

[49] See, Report on an Investigation in Connection with Compliance by Ministers and Deputy Ministers with the Provisions of the Executive Ethics Code relating to the Disclosure of Financial Interests (Report of the Public Protector, No. 2/2006).

[50] Constitution of the Republic of South Africa 1996, s. 2.

first statute on the Restitution of Land to legal reform across a wide scope of law affecting both government and private interests. While there is legitimate debate over the policies and laws that have been adopted since the end of apartheid, the greatest area of concern has become the problem of effective governance – how are these progressive policies and the rhetoric of development and delivery being translated into reality. Governance from this perspective focuses on the institutions that are needed – from government agencies to the courts, from legal frameworks (including legislation and related regulations) to the elements of a functional market place – to implement these policies and achieve their goals. Within this context, the question of institutionalization becomes central to the question of good governance, since it lies at the heart of the matter. It is only through effective institutions that governance is possible. It is when institutions are undermined, lack capacity or are unable to function effectively that frustration leads to irregular methods, to shortcuts and ultimately to a level of maladministration and corruption that will undermine the sustainability of these institutions. At the same time, a persistent pattern of legal challenges, in which political conflict is conducted through legal claims, draws all institutions into what has been described by some as "lawfare": the pursuit of political goals through the abuse of legal processes, effectively paralyzing and frustrating regular processes of governance.

If what I have described reflects the conditions under which these institutions are laboring, what role is there for the Constitution and especially the unique institutional framework created by the 1996 Constitution? One popular conception of the Constitution seems to be that it belongs in the courts, particularly in the Constitutional Court, and that its purpose there is to be used as a tool to either claim rights or challenge government conduct. While this is of course an important dimension of the Constitution, and the Constitutional Court is indeed empowered to provide the defining interpretation of the Constitution's meaning, in fact the Constitution plays a much broader role in governance, a role that is essential to good governance. It is the Constitution that empowers all the institutions of government, providing an institutional framework through which power is to be exercised and controlled. While most constitutions today provide an institutional framework for the exercise of power within the nation state, it is a fairly unique feature of the South African Constitution that it provides for a range of interacting institutions, beyond the traditional three-way division of executive, legislature and courts, as a means to secure good governance and the rule of law.

5.6. SEPARATION OF POWERS AND THE NEW INTEGRITY BRANCH

As far as some in the ruling party were concerned the Public Protector is responsible to Parliament, which they feel has the right to both question the activities of the institution as well as decide whether the decisions of the Public Protector need to be implemented. In support of their claim they pointed to s. 181(5) of the Constitution, which states that the Public Protector, along with the other chapter 9 institutions, is "accountable to the National Assembly." In contrast to this broad claim of parliamentary authority the Public Protector has in each annual report since its founding pointed out that s. 182(1) empowers the institution to investigate, report and "take appropriate remedial action." Finally, the Public Protector has pointed to s. 181(2) of the Constitution which states that "[t]hese institutions [the chapter 9 institutions] are independent, and subject only to the Constitution and the law, and they must be impartial and must exercise their powers and perform their functions without fear, favor or prejudice." It is the confluence of these mandates and tensions over high profile cases, such as the security upgrades to President Zuma's home at Nkandla that brought the problem of the separation of powers to the fore.

The first opportunity for the courts to address this question with respect to the Public Protector came when the official political opposition, the Democratic Alliance, brought a suit demanding a court order that Mr Hlaudi Motsoeneng, the then Chief Operations Officer ("COO") of the South African Broadcasting Corporation ("SABC") – the government broadcaster – be immediately suspended. Their claim was based on the Report of the Public Protector into allegations of maladministration, systemic corporate governance deficiencies and abuse of power by the COO, as well as a claim that his appointment by the Board of the SABC was irregular. While the Western Cape High Court ordered that Mr Motsoeneng be suspended and that the SABC Board institute disciplinary proceedings against him, the Court's decision on the powers of the Public Protector led to some confusion. On the one hand, the Court ruled that the decisions of the SABC Board and the Minister of Communications to ignore the recommendations of the Public Protector were irrational and therefore unconstitutional. On the other hand, Judge Alvin Schippers also held that the Public Protector's findings are not directly binding and enforceable since they do not have the same legal status as court orders. Using the Supreme Court of Appeals and Constitutional Court's earlier decisions analogizing the Public Protector to the position of an ombudsman in other jurisdictions, Judge Schippers argued that while the recommendations of the Public Protector are not binding, the government officials to whom they are directed are not free to disregard them based on their own conclusion but rather need to either implement them or provide rational reasons for refusing to do so. This decision, an exercise of public power in its own right, would be subject to review by the courts as would any decision by the Public Protector that may be challenged by those affected by the Public Protectors findings or recommendations.

Both the ruling party and the Public Protector responded to the Court's decision claiming that their positions had been vindicated; however, Mr Motsoeneng took the judgment on appeal giving the Supreme Court of Appeal an opportunity to address the legal status of remedies agreed upon or imposed by the Public Protector. While the ruling party's claim that the Public Protector's recommendations were not binding seemed to be formally vindicated, this was a very narrow view of the Court's ruling and the role of the Public Protector in general. First, Judge Schippers made clear that the recommendations of the Public Protector may only be challenged before the courts if irrational, and may only be disregarded by the public authorities who are subject to the Public Protectors findings and recommendations if they have "cogent reasons for doing so, that is for reasons other than merely a preference for its own view." Second, the Court argued that the decision whether or not to accept the Public Protector's recommendation is an exercise of public power and thus must meet the minimum threshold requirement of rationality and that the principle of legality requires that any such decision "must be rationally related to the purpose for which the power was given, otherwise they are in effect arbitrary." Finally, the Court rejected the government's argument that the Public Protector needs to seek the assistance of Parliament – to which the Public Protector is accountable – to implement the findings and recommendations of her investigations. Noting that it is the government that in this case has refused without rational reasons to accept the findings or recommendations of the Public Protector, the Court went on to point out and that the intervention of the National Assembly is not an adequate remedy since "[t]he facts of this very case show that the constitutional and statutory provisions upon which they rely are inadequate to ensure that the Public Protector is not undermined."

The result produced distinctly different interpretations of the Court's decision. Apart from the government and the Public Protector reaching different conclusions, academics and other commentators also read different implications into the decision. On the one hand, Mtende Mhango of the University of the Witwatersrand Law School relied on Judge Schippers' analysis that the Public Protector is not an adjudicatory body and argued that the Court had "adopted English law, which distinguishes between the findings and recommendations of an ombudsman [so that] findings may be rejected only if there is a rational basis to do so. But recommendations are treated differently ... and are not binding at all." On the other hand, University of Cape Town law professor "Pierre de Vos interprets the judgment to say that because of the obligation on organs of state to 'assist and protect' the public protector, the threshold for rationality is set higher than usual," and an organ of state may only reject the view of the public protector for "'other, cogent reasons' – for example, if implementing the public protector's remedial action is impossible." At the same time neither of these academics agreed with the interpretation put forward by the named litigant, the Democratic Alliance, whose chairman James Selfe argued that the Court's decision meant that before an organ of state can reject the recommendations of the Public Protector it is required to get the approval of the courts.

It was this tension, between the constitutional mandate that "[o]ther organs of state ... must assist and protect these institutions to ensure the independence, impartiality, dignity, and effectiveness of these institutions,"[51] and the seeming inability of the Public Protector to ensure that the institutions findings and recommendations were addressed by the government that lay at the heart of the separation of powers question that the High Court's judgment in *Democratic Alliance* v. *SABC* did not effectively resolve. While the Court did note in defense of its own powers that "the rule of separation of powers cannot be used to avoid the obligation of a court to provide appropriate relief that is just and equitable to a litigant who successfully raises a constitutional complaint,"[52] its decision to equate the Public Protector with the British ombudsman failed to acknowledge that the legislative authority of the ombudsman in the United Kingdom is legally distinct from the constitutional status enjoyed by the chapter 9 institutions and the Public Protector in particular. Even if the Supreme Court of Appeal and the Constitutional Court analogized the Public Protector to similar ombudsmen institutions in other jurisdictions, these courts had not yet directly addressed the question of how the Constitution imagines the role of the chapter 9 bodies as "State Institutions Supporting Constitutional Democracy."

The difficulty of managing the relationship between the Public Protector and the government became acutely obvious when the Public Protector sort clarity over to whom she should submit her report on the expenditures on the President's home at Nkandla, since the Report was in part an investigation into benefits received by the President. The necessity of asking this question only served to highlight the more general question about the precise constitutional

[51] Constitution of the Republic of South Africa 1996, s. 181(3).

[52] *Democratic Alliance* v. *South African Broadcasting Corporation Soc Ltd* 2016 (3) SA 468 (WCC) para. 99.

status of the Public Protector and the other chapter 9 institutions. Even if we conceive chapter 9 as creating an additional branch of government, as I have argued, this does not resolve questions about the precise relationship of checks and balances that a separation of powers understanding requires. It is this challenge that first the SCA and then the Constitutional Court took up in both the *SABC* appeal and the *EFF* case.

When the case reached the Supreme Court of Appeals, the Court upheld the decision of the High Court requiring the SABC to subject its COO, Hlaudi Motsoeneng to a disciplinary hearing and noted that "[i]n modern democratic constitutional States, in order to ensure governmental accountability, it has become necessary for the guards to require a guard. And in terms of our constitutional scheme, it is the Public Protector who guards the guards."[53] The SCA then rejected the High Court's analogizing of the Public Protector to the British Parliamentary ombudsperson, noting that "the powers conferred on the Public Protector in terms of s. 182(1)(c) of the Constitution far exceeded those of similar institutions in comparable jurisdictions."[54] Responding to the government counsel's suggestion that the powers of the Public Protector are defined by legislation rather than the Constitution, the SCA argued that "[t]he problem with that suggestion is that the Constitution is the primary source and it stipulates and refers to 'additional' powers to be prescribed by national legislation"[55] and thus the suggestion that the Public Protector's powers are legislatively defined is "contrary to the constitutional and legislative scheme outlined above and would have the effect of the tail wagging the dog."[56]

Declaring the government's establishment of a parallel process to "investigate the veracity of the findings and recommendations of the Public Protector ... [to be] impermissible,"[57] the SCA argued that the "Public Protector cannot realise the constitutional purpose of her office if other organs of State may second-guess her findings and ignore her recommendations."[58] Summing up its judgment the SCA noted that:

> the office of the Public Protector, like all Chapter Nine institutions, is a venerable one. Our constitutional compact demands that remedial action taken by the Public Protector should not be ignored. State institutions are

53 *South African Broadcasting Corporation Soc Ltd* v. *Democratic Alliance* (2016) 2 SA 522 (SCA) (*SABC* v. *DA*), para. 3.

54 Ibid. para. 43.

55 Ibid.

56 Ibid.

57 Ibid. para. 47.

58 Ibid. para. 52.

> obliged to heed the principles of cooperative governance as prescribed by s 41 of the Constitution. Any affected person or institution aggrieved by a finding, decision or action taken by the Public Protector might, in appropriate circumstances, challenge that by way of a review application. Absent a review application, however, such person is not entitled to simply ignore the findings, decision or remedial action taken by the Public Protector.[59]

Referring back to the decision of the High Court the SCA drew a significant distinction between the status of the Public Protector under the 1993 interim Constitution and the final 1996 Constitution, arguing that the suggestion that the Public Protector had merely the power to recommend "appears to be more consistent with the language of the Interim Constitution and is neither fitting nor effective, denudes the office of the Public Protector of any meaningful content, and defeats its purpose." Noting that all parties to the litigation found the metaphor of a watchdog "a useful metaphor for the Public Protector" the SCA concluded that "this watchdog should not be muzzled."[60]

Unlike the *SABC* case, which wound its way up through the lower courts, the conflict over the failure of President Zuma to "pay back the money" and Parliament's decision that he owed nothing brought the question of the Public Protectors' powers directly to the Constitutional Court. In its dramatic decision – read out on national television by Chief Justice Mogoeng Mogoeng – the Constitutional Court linked the response to the Public Protector's report to the Constitution's foundational commitment to the rule of law, arguing that: "One of the crucial elements of our constitutional vision is to make a decisive break from the unchecked abuse of State power and resources that was virtually institutionalized during the apartheid era. To achieve this goal, we adopted accountability, the rule of law and the supremacy of the Constitution as values of our constitutional democracy. For this reason, public office-bearers ignore their constitutional obligations at their peril. This is so because constitutionalism, accountability and the rule of law constitute the sharp and mighty sword that stands ready to chop the ugly head of impunity off its stiffened neck."[61] Discussing the institution of the Public Protector, the Court noted that to achieve its objectives, "it is required to be independent and subject only to the Constitution and the law." This requirement the Court notes "would not ordinarily be required of an institution whose powers or decisions are by constitutional design always supposed to be ineffectual. Whether

[59] Ibid. para. 53.

[60] Ibid.

[61] *Economic Freedom Fighters* v. *Speaker of the National Assembly; Democratic Alliance* v. *Speaker of the National Assembly* (2016) 3 SA 580 (CC), para. 1.

it is impartial or not would be irrelevant if the implementation of the decisions it takes is at the mercy of those against whom they are made,"[62] and concluded that the "constitutional safeguards in s. 181 would also be meaningless if institutions purportedly established to strengthen our constitutional democracy lacked even the remotest possibility to do so."[63]

Detailing the constitutional place of the Public Protector the Constitutional Court argued that "[i]n the execution of her investigative, reporting or remedial powers, she is not to be inhibited, undermined or sabotaged"[64] and "[w]hen all other essential requirements for the proper exercise of her power are met, she is to take appropriate remedial action."[65] Justifying their conclusions in the name of strengthening constitutional democracy and "breathing life into the remedial powers of the Public Protector" the Court held that "she must have the resources and capacities necessary to effectively execute her mandate."[66] Rooting her powers within the Constitution, the Court made it clear that legislation is not able to "eviscerate" the powers provided by the Constitution as the "power to take remedial action is primarily sourced from the supreme law itself. And the powers and functions conferred on the Public Protector by the Act owe their very existence or significance to the Constitution."[67]

At the same time, the Constitutional Court recognized that the "Public Protector's power to take appropriate remedial action is wide but certainly not unfettered" and that the "remedial action is always open to judicial scrutiny."[68] Furthermore, "[w]hen remedial action is binding, compliance is not optional, whatever reservations the affected party might have about its fairness, appropriateness or lawfulness. For this reason, the remedial action taken against those under investigation cannot be ignored without any legal consequences."[69] The reason for this conclusion, the Court argued, is because "our constitutional order hinges also on the rule of law. No decision grounded on the Constitution or law may be disregarded without recourse to a court of law. To do otherwise would 'amount to a licence to self-help'."[70] According to the Court:

> The rule of law requires that no power be exercised unless it is sanctioned by law and no decision or step sanctioned by law may be ignored based purely

[62] Ibid. para. 49.
[63] Ibid.
[64] Ibid. para. 54.
[65] Ibid.
[66] Ibid.
[67] Ibid. para. 64.
[68] Ibid. para. 71.
[69] Ibid.
[70] Ibid. para. 74.

> on a contrary view we hold. It is not open to any of us to pick and choose which of the otherwise effectual consequences of the exercise of constitutional or statutory power will be disregarded and which given heed to. Our foundational value of the rule of law demands of us, as a law-abiding people, to obey decisions made by those clothed with the legal authority to make them or else approach courts of law to set them aside, so we may validly escape their binding force.[71]

In conclusion, the Court held that due to his manifest failure in disregarding the "remedial action taken against him by the Public Protector in terms of her constitutional powers" as well as his failure to "assist and protect the Public Protector so as to ensure her independence, impartiality, dignity and effectiveness by complying with her remedial action" the President has "failed to uphold, defend and respect the Constitution as the supreme law of the land."[72]

Addressing the actions of the national legislature the Court was careful to explain its own role within the checks and balances implicit in the constitutional structure. Noting that it "falls outside the parameters of judicial authority to prescribe to the National Assembly how to scrutinise executive action,"[73] the Court argued that the "mechanics of how to go about fulfilling these constitutional obligations is a discretionary matter best left to the National Assembly."[74] By comparison, the role of the Court, Chief Justice Mogoeng argued, "is a much broader and less intrusive role. And that is to determine whether what the National Assembly did does in substance and in reality amount to fulfilment of its constitutional obligations. That is the sum-total of the constitutionally permissible judicial enquiry to be embarked upon."[75] Describing these as "some of the 'vital limits on judicial authority and the Constitution's design to leave certain matters to other branches of government'" he concluded that "[c]ourts should not interfere in the processes of other branches of government unless otherwise authorised by the Constitution."[76] However, he went on to state that "[c]ourts ought not to blink at the thought of asserting their authority, whenever it is constitutionally permissible to do so, irrespective of the issues or who is involved. At the same time, and mindful of the vital strictures of their powers, they must be on high

71 Ibid.
72 Ibid. para. 83.
73 Ibid. para. 93.
74 Ibid.
75 Ibid.
76 Ibid.

alert against impermissible encroachment on the powers of the other arms of government."[77]

Despite these caveats, the Constitutional Court found that "there was everything wrong with the National Assembly stepping into the shoes of the Public Protector" and that by "passing a resolution that purported effectively to nullify the findings made and remedial action taken by the Public Protector and replacing them with its own findings and 'remedial action'," the National Assembly's action was "inconsistent with the Constitution and unlawful."[78] This, the Court stated, "the rule of law is dead against. It is another way of taking the law into one's hands and thus constitutes self-help."[79] While this decision clarifies the relationship between the Public Protector and the other branches of government, it does not guarantee the status of the integrity branch, which like all other constitutional institutions is both a product of law but also subject to its own institutional dynamics. The end of Thuli Madonsela's term as Public Protector in the midst of a political struggle over what is termed in the media "state capture" by business associates of the President left the institution particularly vulnerable. Even though it is only the very early stages of the new Public Protector's term, Advocate Busisiwe Mkhwebane has already indicated that she intends to refrain from the aggressive pursuit of high-profile cases that marked her predecessor's term. This has led to cries of fowl by some political parties, including the EFF who now regret having supported her appointment. However, the more serious consequence is that a number of the experienced personnel within the Public Protector's office have resigned. As a result, it seems that the integrity institutions are equally vulnerable to the institutional problems that have seen other governmental and constitutional institutions wax and wane during the first twenty years of South Africa's democracy.

5.7. CONCLUSION

The goal of establishing a constitutional design that includes the separation of powers is often described as a means to avoid the concentration of power and to "ensure accountability, responsiveness and openness"[80] in the practice of governance. While the separation of powers cannot be found explicitly enshrined in any single provision of the South African Constitution, or for that matter in most other constitutions, it is a core element in the structural

77 Ibid.

78 Ibid. para. 99.

79 Ibid. para. 98.

80 Constitution of the Republic of South Africa 1993, Constitutional Principle VI, sch. 4.

design of the Constitution and is expressed in the multiple provisions that create specific checks and balances between the different branches and institutions of government. As in most other constitutional systems that provide for constitutional review, the issue of the separation of powers soon emerges in constitutional jurisprudence as the different branches and institutions of government begin to exercise power and challenges are brought to test the extent of these powers in different contexts. Although traditional approaches to the political idea and legal doctrine of the separation of powers focus on the checks and balances between the legislature, executive and judiciary, the problem of political and legal accountability is no longer contained within these institutional parameters and, increasingly, constitutional designers have created additional mechanisms and institutions in their efforts in ensure the desired goals of accountability, responsiveness and openness in the exercise of governmental authority.

The revolutionary nature of the Constitution lies thus not only in the expansive framework of the rights it guarantees, or the unique system of cooperative government to manage the relationship between regional, local and national levels of government, but also in the constitutionalizing of a set of independent institutions whose role it is to uphold the progressive vision of the Constitution in the face of the ordinary pressures of political horse-trading and interest group politics. While it is these pressures that often tend to dominate the daily life of democracies, in which the voices heard are most often those who have the resources to command media, legal and other forms of attention, the design of the 1996 Constitution and its specific institutional framework is meant to provide a form of governance more responsive to the needs of those who have been historically excluded. The task of developing the checks and balances that are inherent in the creation of an "integrity" branch of government remains, this chapter suggests, an ongoing task that the Constitutional Court fully embraced in *EFF* and is essential to the building of a sustainable constitutional democracy in South Africa.

6

Violence against Women in South Africa: Constitutional Responses and Opportunities

Beth Goldblatt

6.1. INTRODUCTION

Violence against women, present in every society in the world, is deeply embedded in South Africa's past and is a central feature of the postdemocratic society. The South African Constitution is path-breaking in acknowledging this reality by providing a right to be free from violence in public and private realms. Over the past two decades since democracy, advocacy groups have been successful in lobbying and working with government to secure new legislation in the areas of domestic violence and rape. Implementation of these laws has, however, been mixed or poor and recourse to the law is limited for many, if not most, victims of this violence. A number of significant decisions have emerged from the Constitutional Court in relation to these laws and regarding aspects of the common law relevant to violence against women. This chapter surveys the jurisprudence on violence against women in assessing the Court's record in this area. While finding these decisions valuable in advancing the constitutional framework, the chapter suggests that fuller interpretation of the Constitution and more creative litigation and jurisprudence is necessary in contributing to the removal of the scourge of violence against South Africa's women.

Violence against women in South Africa is embedded in a history of brutality that has been central to the making of the country.[1] Many of the acts of

Associate Professor, Faculty of Law, University of Technology Sydney; Visiting Fellow, Faculty of Law, University of New South Wales; Visiting Associate Professor, School of Law, University of the Witwatersrand. I wish to thank the following people for their insightful observations in discussions on the topic of this chapter in February 2016: Cathi Albertyn, Elsje Bonthuys, Lisa Vetten, Rashida Manjoo and Bonita Meyersfeld.

[1] Patriarchy, race and class have been intimately connected in shaping the oppressive forms in which gender relations have played out in this country. For the classic article that developed this argument, see B. Bozzolli, "Marxism, feminism and South African studies" (1983) 9(2) *Journal of Southern African Studies* 139–71.

colonial dispossession, invasion, war, slavery and apartheid, as well as resistance to end this domination, have entailed violence to the bodies of women.[2] While most of the historical articulations of the wars against black South Africans are behind us, the war against women and girls lives on in the everyday occurrence of domestic violence, femicide, rape, sexual abuse, harassment and harmful cultural practices such as *ukuthwala* (abduction of girls for marriage)[3] and attacks on people labeled as witches.[4] Reported rape numbers in South Africa were the highest in the world in 2001.[5] Recent figures showed 43 195 cases of rape for the year 2014/15, although service providers estimate that as little as one in thirteen rapes are reported.[6] Rape takes a particularly brutal form in South Africa with a high rate of rape homicide and multiple perpetrator rape being very common.[7] In a recent Constitutional Court decision Khampepe J noted that:[8]

> Rape is perhaps the most horrific and dehumanising violation that a person can live through and is a crime that not only violates the mind and body of a complainant, but also one that vexes the soul. This crime is an inescapable and seemingly ever-present reality and scourge on the nation and the collective conscience of the people of South Africa.

The levels of female homicide as a whole are extremely high and domestic violence, though not adequately captured in official statistics, is epidemic.[9] South Africa has the dubious honor of being known as the "rape capital of the world"; as having a deputy president (now president) stand trial for rape of the daughter of his friend;[10] as having sporting hero Oscar Pistorius convicted of

2 For a discussion of the history of rape and its various forms in South Africa, see Pumla Dineo Gqola, *Rape – A South African Nightmare* (Johannesburg: MFBooks, 2015).

3 South African Law Reform Commission, "The practice of Ukuthwala" (Revised Discussion Paper 138, Project 138, 2015).

4 Both women and men are targeted: South African Law Reform Commission "The review of The Witchcraft Suppression Act 3 of 1957" (Discussion Paper 139, Project 135, 2014) (Review of Witchcraft legislation).

5 D. Smythe, *Rape Unresolved: Policing Sexual Offences in South Africa* (Cape Town: University of Cape Town Press, 2015).

6 AfricaCheck, *Factsheet: South Africa's 2014/15 assault and sexual crime statistics* (2016) (available at www.africacheck.org/factsheets/factsheet-south-africas-201415-assault-and-sexual-crime-statistics/#sthash.zuK16lgd.dpuf, www.africacheck.org/factsheets/factsheet-south-africas-201415-assault-and-sexual-crime-statistics/) (accessed date November 20, 2017).

7 Smythe, *Rape Unresolved* 17.

8 *Ndlovu* v. *The State* [2017] ZACC 19, at 53.

9 L. Vetten, "Deserving and undeserving women: a case study of South African policy and legislation addressing domestic violence" MA thesis, University of the Witwatersrand (2013) 5.

10 Although Jacob Zuma was acquitted of rape, his views and behavior, as they emerged from the trial, represented a troubling understanding of sex and power in a leader of the country. For a

murdering his partner; and as the place where so called "corrective rape" of lesbians occurs.[11] Many other high-profile cases are reported of horrific abuse of women and girls. While violence against women is a global problem it has a local character in South Africa that is shaped by the country's history and closely connected to the many social, economic and political challenges facing it today.[12]

Undoubtedly, legacies of structural violence live on for black and poor South Africans, regardless of gender, working on the mines, farms and factories and for those living in impoverished rural areas or urban settlements and slums, often separated from families and communities. Lack of health services, adequate nutrition and reliance on dangerous transport continue to determine the length of a person's life based on their race and class. Service delivery protests, workplace violence starkly displayed in the Marikana massacre, xenophobic bloodshed and everyday brutal crimes shape the South African reality. While this violent backdrop gives context to, and perhaps partly explains, the levels of violence against women,[13] it does not diminish the enormity of this issue – it is neither dramatic nor imprecise to characterize this violence as a war against women.[14]

It is clear that while violence against women is prevalent across social classes, the combination of poverty shaped by race has a fundamental impact on women's vulnerability to violence (and related to this, also to HIV infection). Lack of access to income and employment deepens women's dependency on men and limits their capacity to leave violent partners. Limited access to housing and social security also make escape impossible for many.

---

discussion of the politics of the Zuma trial see, S. Hassim, "Democracy's shadows: sexual rights and gender politics in the rape trial of Jacob Zuma" (2009) 68(1) *African Studies* 57–77.

11 L. Mwambene and M. Wheal, "Realisation or oversight of a constitutional mandate? Corrective rape of black African lesbians in South Africa" (2015) 15 *African Human Rights Law Journal* 58–88.

12 This violent context is the product of the way in which masculinity and femininity is culturally defined and gender inequality is produced. It should be noted at the outset that gender-based violence also affects men and boys, although women and girls are its major victims. This chapter chooses to use the term violence against women rather than more gender neutral terminology to keep the focus on the imbalance between men and women that reflects the underlying patriarchal roots of this violence.

13 For a discussion of the causes of violence against women in South Africa today see, L. du Toit, "Shifting meanings of postconflict sexual violence in South Africa" (2014) 40(1) *Signs* 101–23.

14 C. A. MacKinnon, *Are Women Human? And Other International Dialogues* (Cambridge, MA: Harvard University Press, 2006), has noted that: "Men violently dominating other men for control of states is called war; men violently dominating women within states is relegated to peace": 5. But note the concerns with this approach to sexual violence and the state: R. Kapur, "Gender, sovereignty and the rise of a sexual security regime in international law and postcolonial India" (2013) 14(2) *Melbourne Journal of International Law* 317–42.

Inadequate health care and social services mean that responses to violence often fall short of what is needed. Poor basic services such as transport, sanitation, water and electricity expose women to risks of attack in urban and rural environments. Similarly, girls face daily dangers in walking to school, at school where toilets may be some distance from classrooms or absent entirely, and where predatory teachers often behave with impunity. Certain groups facing additional challenges, such as women with disabilities, lesbians, elderly women, and women refugees and migrants, have greater exposure to abuse because of their intersectional disadvantage.[15]

This challenging context raises questions about how the country should respond with the necessary urgency in marshalling the resources to end this war. It also raises questions about the role of the Constitution in informing the boundaries and shape of the law as part of such a response. While some feminist scholars are skeptical about rights and laws in tackling violence against women, others suggest that law should be one, albeit limited, part of the approach to this challenging issue.[16] Law is seen by the latter as a contested arena that must be engaged with in the context of the broader project of ending sexual oppression and gendered power imbalances. Women's groups were central to efforts to include strong gender equality rights and protections against violence in the South African Constitution. This text has since been used to inform legislative development of rape and domestic violence laws and to defend and improve such laws through the courts. The Constitutional Court has been a focus of litigation on issues of violence against women and has produced sensitive and progressive jurisprudence in this area.

This chapter will briefly discuss the history and nature of the constitutional text as it pertains to violence against women (Section 6.2) before looking, also briefly, at the key legislative developments in the areas of domestic violence and rape (Section 6.3) over the past twenty years. Thereafter, it will survey the decisions of the Constitutional Court that dealt with this legislation as well as

[15] As noted at n.11, gender-based violence affects other vulnerable groups such as boys and gay men.

[16] In the latter category, in the South African context see, C. Albertyn et al., "Women's freedom and security of the person" in E. Bonthuys and C. Albertyn (eds.), *Gender, Law and Justice* (Cape Town: Juta, 2007) 295. In the US context see the foundational article by E. Schneider, "The dialectic of rights and politics: perspectives from the women's movement" (1986) 61 *New York University Law Review*, 589–652. For a discussion of human rights as a contested space in responding to violence against women, see S. E. Merry, *Human Rights and Gender Violence* (Chicago, IL: University of Chicago Press, 2006).

a series of decisions that dealt with the common law in cases where women were victims of male violence (Section 6.4). It will evaluate these decisions in terms of criteria set out in Section 6.4. The chapter will argue (Section 6.5) that a fuller interpretation of the Constitution and more creative litigation and jurisprudence is necessary in addressing violence against women, in particular through the use of social and economic rights.

This chapter is a domestic rather than comparative evaluation of the South African constitutional project that assesses the Court's performance within South Africa's specific historical and current context, and considers the unrealized opportunities that the constitutional text presents for those working to end violence against women. The chapter, nevertheless, provides insight for comparative scholars considering the value of different constitutional articulations of human rights and how these support (or fail to support) efforts to address violence against women. It also provides a view of the jurisprudential opportunities and pitfalls in this area that may be applicable elsewhere. Gender equality, and central to this, the right of women to live lives free of violence, is a precondition for full democratic participation[17] and is a universal goal.[18] The South African experience contributes to a wider understanding of the possibilities and limits of constitutions in challenging the ubiquity of violence against women.

6.2. THE CONSTITUTIONAL TEXT

The involvement of women as a lobby group in shaping the content of South Africa's new Constitution focused on ensuring that gender equality was strongly protected.[19] There was no specific acknowledgement of rights for women facing violence in and outside of the home in the Interim Constitution 1993. However, with input from the women's lobby,[20] feminist parliamentarians and technical experts involved in the drafting of the Final Constitution 1996 succeeded in including the words "to be free from all forms

[17] See, e.g., N. Fraser, *Justice Interruptus: Critical Reflections on the "Postsocialist" Condition* (New York, NY: Routledge, 1997); M. Nussbaum, *Women and Human Development: The Capabilities Approach* (Cambridge: Cambridge University Press, 2000).

[18] United Nations, *Sustainable Development Goals*, Goal Five.

[19] C. Albertyn, "Women and the transition to democracy in South Africa" (1994) *Acta Juridica* 39–63.

[20] C. Albertyn (ed.), *Engendering the Political Agenda: A South African Case Study* (Johannesburg: University of Witwatersrand, Centre for Applied Legal Studies, 1999), 120–21, 66–68.

of violence from either public or private sources"[21] in s. 12 of the Bill of Rights which deals with freedom and security of the person as well as significant reproductive and sexual rights within the same section. These notable additions aligned with and were informed by international developments of the same period. In 1994, the United Nations General Assembly adopted the Declaration on the Elimination of Violence Against Women[22] and in the same year the Cairo Programme of Action articulated women's reproductive rights at the International Conference on Population and Development.[23] Both of these statements on women's rights reflected a shift toward recognizing women's agency over their bodies and required the breaking down of some of the harmful public/private divisions in law that had rendered violence against women invisible.[24] The international law has been specifically referenced by the Constitutional Court in some of the key decisions on violence against women.[25]

[21] Constitution of the Republic of South Africa 1996, s. 12(1)(c). The whole section reads as follows:

Section 12 Freedom and security of the person

1. Everyone has the right to freedom and security of the person, which includes the right –
   a. not to be deprived of freedom arbitrarily or without just cause;
   b. not to be detained without trial;
   c. to be free from all forms of violence from either public or private sources;
   d. not to be tortured in any way; and
   e. not to be treated or punished in a cruel, inhuman or degrading way.
2. Everyone has the right to bodily and psychological integrity, which includes the right –
   a. to make decisions concerning reproduction;
   b. to security in and control over their body; and
   c. not to be subjected to medical or scientific experiments without their informed consent.

[22] UN GAOR 48th sess., U.N. Doc. A/Res/48/104 (1994).

[23] A/CONF.171/13, *Report of the International Conference on Population and Development: Cairo 5–13 September 1994* (94/10/18) (October 18, 1994).

[24] E. Bonthuys and W. Domingo, "Constitutional and international law context" in E. Bonthuys and C. Albertyn (eds.), *Gender, Law and Justice* (Cape Town: Juta, 2007) 51, 64–8. For a discussion of South Africa's international human rights compliance see: M. Govender, "Domestic violence: is South Africa meeting its obligations in terms of the Women's Convention?" (2003) 19 *South African Journal on Human Rights* 663–78. For a broader discussion of human rights as a response to violence against women see: R. Manjoo, "Violence against women as a barrier to the realisation of human rights and the effective exercise of citizenship" (2016) 112 *Feminist Review* 11–26.

[25] *Bothma* v. *Els and Others* (2010) 1 BCLR 1 (Constitutional Court), at para. 55–6; S v. *Baloyi* [2000] 1 BCLR 86 (Constitutional Court), at para. 13; *Masiya* v. *Director of Public Prosecutions Pretoria (The State) and Another* [2007] 8 BCLR 827, at para. 37; *Carmichele* v. *Minister of Safety and Security* [2001] 10 BCLR 995 (Constitutional Court), at para. 62.

The inclusion of freedom and security and bodily integrity rights was part of a broader constitutional commitment to nonsexism[26] as evidenced by the strong equality right which includes sex, gender, pregnancy and marital status as grounds of unfair discrimination.[27] The antidiscrimination legislation, mandated by the Constitutional equality right, prohibits unfair discrimination based on gender, which includes gender-based violence and female genital mutilation.[28] The Act also prohibits harassment based on sex and gender[29] and gender-related hate speech.[30] Its preamble makes reference to patriarchy, alongside colonialism and apartheid, as systems that generated inequality and caused pain and suffering to the majority of South Africans.[31] The Constitution also established a Commission for Gender Equality as an independent body to promote and protect gender equality.[32] The Constitution contains a provision regarding the role of the police service in protecting the public.[33]

6.3. LEGISLATIVE DEVELOPMENTS

It was this broad and hard-won constitutional framework that informed the development of new postapartheid laws on violence against women. In the first decade of democracy, huge effort was expended in creating strong legislative measures to address and respond to violence against women. This resulted in the enactment of the Domestic Violence Act[34] to allow courts to provide protection orders and the Sexual Offences Act, which expands the definitions of rape and other sexual offences.[35] Both pieces of legislation were informed by the urgent need to address violence against women and by the constitutional promise of freedom and security.

The Domestic Violence Act replaced the Prevention of Family Violence Act,[36] which was hurried through in the last days of the Apartheid Government. The new Act was framed in terms of South Africa's constitutional commitments to freedom and security of the person and equality and its international

[26] Constitution of the Republic of South Africa 1996, preamble, s. 1(b).

[27] Ibid. s. 9.

[28] Promotion of Equality and Prevention of Unfair Discrimination Act 2000, ss. 8(a)–(b).

[29] Ibid. s. 1.

[30] Ibid. s. 2(c).

[31] Ibid. preamble.

[32] Constitution of the Republic of South Africa 1996, s. 187.

[33] Ibid. s. 205(3). This role is elaborated by O'Regan J in *K* v. *Minister of Safety and Security* [2005] 9 BCLR 835 (Constitutional Court), at para. 52.

[34] Domestic Violence Act 1998.

[35] Criminal Law (Sexual Offences and Related Matters) Amendment Act 2007.

[36] Prevention of Family Violence Act 1993.

obligations to end violence against women and children. The Act contains a broad and progressive definition of domestic violence that includes economic abuse, damage to property and controlling or abusive behavior alongside more traditionally recognized forms such as physical abuse and sexual harassment.[37] Complainants can obtain interim and final protection orders from courts that can include a wide range of conditions limiting the respondent's access to the home or workplace of the complainant and requiring the payment of rent and emergency relief.[38] The protection order is accompanied by a warrant of arrest that can be used if the order is breached and criminal sanctions can be imposed on contravention of an order.[39] Despite its positive features, the *Domestic Violence Act* has been criticized for its piecemeal approach (it neglects issues of child custody and matrimonial property), as well as for focusing on policing and the courts without also legislating in areas such as health care, housing and income support.[40]

The Sexual Offences Act was introduced after a lengthy consideration by the South African Law Reform Commission and an extended consultation process that took a decade to produce changes to the law. The Act aimed to bring the out-dated definition of rape and related offences in line with the rights in the Constitution. This led to changes in the definition that recognized rape could involve penetration into the vagina, anus or mouth of the victim with any body part or object.[41] It also introduced gender neutrality into the definition of rape by recognizing that anyone, men included, could be a victim of the crime. The Act expanded on sexual crimes against children and people with mental disabilities and introduced laws related to trafficking. The Act also provided some rights to victims for postexposure prophylaxis to avoid HIV infection and introduced a sexual offences register. While many feminists were actively involved in lobbying for the new legislation, some felt despondent about the eventual content of the law. Artz and Smythe, commenting shortly before the Sexual Offences Bill was enacted, argued that the focus on the constitutional right to equality rather than the right to be free from all forms of violence led to law with a "peculiarly liberal feminist flavour."[42] This is particularly evident in the gender neutral definition of rape,

37 Domestic Violence Act 1998, s. 1.

38 Ibid. s. 7.

39 Ibid. ss. 8, 17.

40 Vetten, "Deserving and undeserving women," 43.

41 Criminal Law (Sexual Offences and Related Matters) Amendment Act 2007, s. 1 (definition of sexual penetration).

42 L. Artz and D. Smythe, "Feminism vs. the State? A decade of sexual offences law reform in South Africa" (2007) 74 *Agenda* 6–13 at 10.

taken together with the lack of measures to protect victims, that has "muted the distinctly gendered experience of sexual assault."[43] They suggested that the removal of gendered language has "edited out the structural reality of gender-based violence" and the uneven gender power relations between men and women.[44] Artz and Smythe were also critical of the failure to remove "consent" from the definition of rape. They were particularly concerned with the relegation of measures to protect victims in the criminal justice system to the policy framework of government rather than being located within the Act, as originally intended. Their conclusion was that the reform of rape law has been somewhat symbolic but has had some value in terms of public education. However, huge challenges remain to shift practices within the justice system and the jurisprudence and to improve the experiences of victims.

Both Acts have been accompanied by various policy plans by government to give effect to these laws and develop wider responses. Dishearteningly, many commentators have bemoaned the poor implementation of these laws and plans in the period since their enactment. Dee Smythe has noted in relation to rape laws and policies that:[45]

> South Africa is paper rich when it comes to dealing with sexual violence. It has ratified the leading international and regional human rights treaties and instruments seeking to address these problems, and enshrined a constitutional protection against privately perpetrated violence, applied and enforced through decisions of our highest courts. At a policy level, the South African government and the police service have identified violence against women as a critical policing priority and enacted institutional safeguards against inappropriate responses to rape complainants through National Instructions and Standing Orders. The problem is not with the law in the books but with criminal justice practice. It is in the practical realities of everyday policing and in the attendant discretionary choices, that police responses to rape crumble, reinforcing the pretext that rape is, essentially, a crime that is impervious to policing.

There is less despondency about the implementation of the Domestic Violence Act, but concerns remain about the training of government officials, access to justice for poor women, as well as the lack of options for women fleeing violence.[46] These two laws have been the subject of litigation in the

43 Ibid. 11.

44 Ibid.

45 Smythe, *Rape Unresolved*, at pp. 46–7.

46 H. Combrinck, "The dark side of the rainbow: violence against women in South Africa after ten years of democracy" (2005) *Acta Juridica* 171–99; L. Artz and D. Smythe, "Bridges and

Constitutional Court, in some cases leading to their improvement and in others defending their provisions. The next part examines this jurisprudence as well as three decisions relating to the interpretation of the common law where the state failed to protect women from violent assault and rape.

6.4. CONSTITUTIONAL COURT JURISPRUDENCE

This part evaluates the jurisprudence of the Constitutional Court over the past twenty years on the subject of violence against women.[47] While the Supreme Court of Appeal and the provincial High Courts have handed down some very important constitutional judgments on this subject, mostly dealing with criminal law and procedure, this broader jurisprudence will not be canvassed here.[48] The Constitutional Court decisions are evaluated in terms of a number of criteria: first, whether the jurisprudence pursues the transformatory mandate inherent in the Constitution in ensuring laws aimed at achieving

barriers: a five year retrospective on the Domestic Violence Act" (2005) *Acta Juridica* 200–26; Vetten, "Deserving and undeserving women."

47 The following decisions, in chronological order, are considered here: *S* v. *Baloyi* [2000] 1 BCLR 86 (Constitutional Court); *Carmichele* v. *Minister of Safety and Security* [2001] 10 BCLR 995 (Constitutional Court); *Ex Parte Omar* [2003] 10 BCLR 1087 (Constitutional Court); *K* v. *Minister of Safety and Security* [2005] 9 BCLR 835 (Constitutional Court); *Masiya* v. *Director of Public Prosecutions Pretoria (The State) and Another* [2007] 8 BCLR 827; *Director of Public Prosecutions, Transvaal* v. *Minister for Justice and Constitutional Development and Others* [2009] 7 BCLR 637 (Constitutional Court); *Bothma* v. *Els and Others* [2010] 1 BCLR 1 (Constitutional Court); *F* v. *Minister of Safety and Security and Another* [2012] 3 BCLR 244 (Constitutional Court); *Teddy Bear Clinic for Abused Children and Another* v. *Minister of Justice and Constitutional Development and Another* [2013] 12 BCLR 1429 (Constitutional Court) (*Teddy Bear Clinic*); *J* v. *National Director of Public Prosecutions and Another* [2014] 7 BCLR 764 (Constitutional Court). The case of *S* v. *Marais* [2010] 12 BCLR 1223 (Constitutional Court), dealing with an appeal by a woman who arranged for her husband to be killed will not be included in the discussion. Her unsuccessful appeal concerned her wish to bring further evidence of her status as a battered women as a defense against her conviction and sentence. The Constitutional Court's decision is primarily procedural and the substantive issue of the battered woman defense had already been decided by the Supreme Court of Appeal in the case of *S* v. *Ferreira and Others* [2004] 2 SACR 454 (SCA). The decisions in *National Coalition for Gay and Lesbian Equality and Another* v. *Minister of Justice and Others* [1998] 12 BCLR 1517 and *Geldenhuys* v. *National Director of Public Prosecutions and Others* [2009] 5 BCLR 435 (Constitutional Court), although concerning definitions of sexual offences, are not included here since they do not concern violence against women. Both cases, formal equality decisions, related to the unfairly discriminatory criminalization of male to male sexual conduct.

48 For a discussion of some of these decisions see, Albertyn et al., 'Women's freedom'; M. J. Maluleke and T. Madonsela, *Gender Equality Jurisprudence in Landmark Court Decisions* (Department of Justice and Constitutional Development, 2009).

far-reaching social change including substantive gender equality.[49] Second, and related to this, whether the Court's decisions infuse the interpretation of the law and the rights in the Bill of Rights of the Constitution with the democratic values underlying the Constitution of dignity, equality and freedom.[50] Third, whether they effectively engage with and provide guidance on the legal responses to violence against women and advance the law in this area. Fourth, whether they provide a consistent, coherent and convincing jurisprudence on violence against women that fairly balances sometimes competing constitutional rights. These are narrow criteria, judged qualitatively, that do not attempt to evaluate the possible impact that the Constitution or the Court has had on governmental or public responses toward violence against women, let alone on the reduction of this violence.[51]

Before examining the Court's decisions it is worth noting the factual issues in nine of the leading judgments lest the real people involved become lost in the legal discussion.[52] The following is a brief description, in chronological order, of the types of violence that led to the judgments under discussion.

The complainant in *Baloyi's* case alleged that her husband, an army officer, assaulted her and threatened to kill her following the granting of an interdict where he had been ordered not to assault her and their child or prevent them from leaving or entering their joint home.[53] Alix *Carmichele* was brutally assaulted by Francois Coetzee who had previously been convicted of the indecent assault of one woman, and attempted rape of a seventeen-year-old girl. He attacked Carmichele with a pick handle and stabbed her with a knife after breaking into the house where she was staying. In *Omar's* case, the applicant was arrested for breaching a domestic violence order in which he had been prohibited from "threatening, assaulting, harassing, intimidating, stalking or abusing" his estranged wife and their children. In *K's* case a twenty-year-old woman was stranded without transport and was offered a lift by three policemen who then assaulted and took turns raping her. *Masiya* was accused of

49 See, K. Klare, "Legal culture and transformative constitutionalism" (1998) 14 *South African Journal on Human Rights* 146–88; C. Albertyn and G. Beth, "Facing the challenge of transformation: difficulties in the development of an Indigenous jurisprudence of equality" (1998) 14 *South African Journal on Human Rights* 248–76.

50 As set out in s. 39(1)(a) of the Constitution of the Republic of South Africa 1996 and informed by ss. 7(1) and 36(1).

51 See the discussion of the evaluation of causation in the introductory chapter by Dixon and Roux.

52 In the *Teddy Bear Clinic* case there were no individual applicants or respondents as the case was brought directly by organizations challenging the constitutionality of laws.

53 He alleged, although this version was not accepted, that his wife and her brother had assaulted him.

anal penetration of a nine-year-old girl. In *DPP* v. *Minister for Justice and Constitutional Development and others*, Phaswane was convicted of the rape of a thirteen-year-old girl who was the sister of his cohabiting partner. In the same case, Mokoena was convicted of the rape of an eleven-year-old girl. *Bothma's* case concerned a woman who claimed she was repeatedly raped over two years from the age of thirteen by a much older family friend. In *F's* case, a thirteen-year-old girl was given a lift home by a policeman who assaulted and raped her. In the case of *J*, a fourteen-year-old boy was convicted of the rape of a seven-year-old boy and two six-year-old boys. He was also convicted of assault for stabbing a twelve-year-old girl.

The facts in the cases that have reached the Constitutional Court reflect the reality of vicious crimes against women, girls and boys. Most of the victims were female and many were children. Aside from age, other indicators of vulnerability include the lack of access to transport, women's fear for their safety on the streets, and poverty that forced a young girl and woman to seek lifts from policemen. A number of the victims were women and children who were unable to find safety from violence in their own homes. All of the perpetrators were male.

The Constitutional Court's ten decisions on violence against women broadly concern three areas: sexual offences and how the criminal law and procedure treat victims and perpetrators of sexual crimes; the constitutionality of domestic violence legislation; and the boundaries of civil liability of the state where it fails to protect victims from physical and sexual harm by employees and other offenders.

6.4.1. *Sexual Offences*

The sexual offences judgments deal with one decision that arose before the coming into force of the Sexual Offences Act concerning the common law definition of rape; a decision concerning the time delay in the prosecution of child abuse; and three decisions arising from the reforms to the law after 2007.

Masiya's case concerned the common law definition of rape which excluded anal penetration and was gender specific. The case reached the Court shortly before the long awaited Sexual Offences Act created a statutory crime of rape "applicable to all forms of sexual penetration without consent, irrespective of gender."[54] It is an important judgment in setting out the patriarchal history of rape (in both its colonial and customary origins) that saw the crime in terms

[54] Criminal Law (Sexual Offences and Related Matters) Amendment Act 2007, preamble. See ch. 2, pt. 1, s. 3 for the definition.

of the interests of male protectors of women rather than in terms of the rights of the women themselves; and understanding this history in terms of male dominance and power, objectification of women and gender stereotyping.[55] The judgment noted that the new Constitution provides a different foundation for the law of rape based on the democratic values of the Constitution of human dignity, equality and freedom.[56] In particular, the rights to freedom from violence, equality and dignity are implicated in relation to this crime.[57] The Court acknowledged the role of women's activism in challenging patriarchal notions of rape and in ensuring the wide acceptance that "sexual violence and rape not only offends the privacy and dignity of women but also reflects the unequal power relations between men and women in society."[58] This led the Court to extend the definition so as to "promote the spirit, purport and objects of the Bill of Rights"[59] and the "principles, ideals and values underlying the Constitution."[60]

The majority decision of Nkabinde J (followed by eight judges) did, however, refuse to extend the definition of rape to nonconsensual intercourse between men because in terms of the facts of the case this matter was not before the Court. It hinted, however, that law reform was needed in this regard.[61] This was disputed by Langa CJ in a minority decision (Sachs J concurring) where he found that the absence of men in the definition of the crime failed to give "effect to the constitutional values of dignity, equality and freedom: dignity through recognition of a violation; equality through equal recognition of that violation; and freedom as rape negates not only dignity, but bodily autonomy."[62] While Nkabinde J highlighted the particular vulnerability of women and girls to rape,[63] Langa CJ focused on the protection of all people, regardless of gender.[64] He stressed that this recognition would not detract from the understanding that women are the "primary target of rape" and that "male domination of women is an underlying cause of rape."[65] He went further to argue that limiting rape as a crime against women might entrench stereotypes

55 *Masiya* v. *Director of Public Prosecutions Pretoria (The State) and Another* [2007] 8 BCLR 827, at para. 24.
56 Ibid. para. 25.
57 Ibid. para. 27.
58 Ibid. para. 28.
59 Ibid.
60 Ibid. para. 45.
61 Ibid. para. 31.
62 Ibid. para. 80.
63 Ibid. para. 37.
64 Ibid. para. 84.
65 Ibid.

of women as vulnerable, hence reinforcing their subordinate position.[66] He argued that male rape is as much about "gender-supremacy" as female rape and, hence, from an equality perspective, requires equal protection.[67] Langa CJ justified the development of the common law beyond the facts presented in the case on the basis that curing the gender defect in the law was a necessary part of the development of the crime of rape based on the underlying constitutional principles, as necessitated by the case before the Court.[68]

Langa CJ's decision is more deeply aligned with a substantive understanding of gender inequality since it recognizes the concurrence of male and female gender-based harm while acknowledging the patriarchal underpinnings of and manifestation of the crime. Ultimately, it offers more transformatory possibilities than the minority decision in requiring gender equality to include more far-reaching and systemic cultural, social and psychological change if sexual violence is to be addressed.[69] Commenting on this decision, Bonthuys argued that the majority incorrectly focused on "the sex of the victims and perpetrators, rather than on a proper understanding of gender."[70] She suggested that the majority's approach in *Masiya* reflected a similarly conservative approach followed by the Court in the *Jordan*[71] case where it failed to acknowledge that the criminalization of the sale of sex but not its purchase was unfair gender discrimination.[72] The Court appeared to be favoring a safe and narrow approach to issues of sexuality where "bad" women and male rape victims do not fit the image of the victim requiring protection.[73] The Langa CJ judgment, in succinctly capturing the implications of rape as a violation of the core values of the Constitution, led to a more nuanced and progressive re-interpretation of the common law.

In *Bothma's* case the Constitutional Court balanced the accused's right to a fair trial against the interests of a complainant alleging child sexual abuse and society's need for justice. The High Court had permanently stayed a private prosecution by Mrs Bothma who alleged she had been raped as a child. It found that she had waited an unreasonable length of time (39 years), which

[66] Ibid. para. 85.

[67] Ibid. para. 86.

[68] Ibid. para. 90.

[69] See also, C. Albertyn, "Substantive equality and transformation in South Africa" (2007) 23 *South African Journal on Human Rights* 253–76.

[70] E. Bonthuys, "Putting gender into the definition of rape or taking it out? *Masiya* v. *Director of Public Prosecutions (Pretoria) and Others*, 2007 (8) BCLR 827 (CC)" (2008) 16 *Feminist Legal Studies* 249–60 at 254.

[71] *Jordan* v. S [2002] 11 BCLR 1117 (Constitutional Court).

[72] Bonthuys, "Putting gender into the definition of rape," at 258.

[73] Ibid.

prejudiced the right to a fair trial of the man she accused. The Constitutional Court granted Mrs Bothma's appeal against the High Court decision on the basis that victims of child sexual abuse can take many years to acknowledge, report and pursue complaints. The Court referred to Nkabinde's strong statements on the crime of rape in the *Masiya* decision and added the context of unequal power arising from age differences that impact on the silencing of children who have been sexually abused.[74] Sachs J found that:[75]

> Without pronouncing on the veracity of her charges, it should be noted that there also exist strong public policy reasons for allowing the nature of the crime to weigh heavily in favour of allowing these charges to be aired in court. Adults who take advantage of their positions of authority over children to commit sexual depredations against them, should not be permitted to reinforce their sense of entitlement by overlaying it with a sense of impunity. On the contrary, the knowledge that one day the secret will out, acts as a major deterrent against sexual abuse of other similarly vulnerable children.

The decision is a further demonstration of the Court's contextual understanding and firm stance on sexual violence.

The following cases came to the Court after the enactment of the Sexual Offences Act in 2007. The *Teddy Bear Clinic* case was an attempt to correct a defect in the new Act that was overly broad in restricting consensual sexual activity between adolescents leading to inappropriate and harmful criminalization of children. It was brought by not-for-profit organizations working with victims of child abuse. The applicants argued that the Act violated the rights of children to dignity, privacy and bodily integrity, and was not in their best interests.[76] They argued that the provisions of the Act would unnecessarily expose children to the criminal justice system and would constrain "healthy attitudes to sexual behaviour."[77] The position taken by the applicants was supported by two amici curiae representing women's interests who argued that girls would be disproportionately affected by the provisions and that the provisions resulted in indirect discrimination based on sex.[78] Khampepe J, in a unanimous decision, found that the provisions impaired the dignity of adolescents by leading to stigma and shame with potentially traumatic and harmful

[74] *Bothma* v. *Els and Others* (2010) 1 BCLR 1 (Constitutional Court), para. 47.
[75] Ibid. para. 66.
[76] *Teddy Bear Clinic for Abused Children and Another* v. *Minister of Justice and Constitutional Development and Another* [2013] 12 BCLR 1429 (Constitutional Court) para. 29 (*Teddy Bear Clinic*).
[77] Ibid. para. 28.
[78] Ibid. para. 36.

consequences.[79] Dignity was closely linked to privacy and was also negatively impacted by the provisions.[80] The provisions were not in the best interests of children who should not be held criminally responsible for consensual sexual behavior. Criminalization would drive behaviors underground and prevent children from having open discussions with parents.[81] The Court thus found the provisions to be invalid to the extent of their inconsistency but suspended this declaration for eighteen months to allow Parliament to rework the statute. During this period of suspension, the Court ordered a moratorium on investigations, arrests and prosecutions of adolescents and to expunge any convictions or sentences under the Act and remove these from the sexual offences register. The Court refused to consider the additional contention of the applicants regarding the undesirable absence of a "close in age" defense for sixteen and seventeen year olds who engage in sexual conduct with adolescents.

The decision, while not directly following an instance of violence against women, was important in addressing a problem with the newly enacted Sexual Offences Act. The Act had intruded too far into the realm of consensual sex in attempting to protect children from violence by criminalizing normal sexual activity between adolescents. The judgment, in going against this somewhat conservative sentiment, was more realistic and enlightened with regard to sexual behaviour of adolescents. While it hinted that sex education was more appropriate than criminalization,[82] it was careful not to prescribe any particular policy response to the State.[83] The judgment is disappointing in failing to engage with the value of freedom or the right to freedom and security of the person. While it examined issues of privacy and dignity in relation to children with some sensitivity, it would have been beneficial if it had given greater consideration to the positive dimensions of the rights to bodily integrity and freedom and security of the person in line with the Constitutional values.

As with the *Teddy Bear Clinic* case, *J*'s case related to the rights of children, in this case those of child offenders. Here, there was mandatory inclusion of children convicted of sex offences against children or persons with a mental disability on the National Register for Sex Offenders.[84] The inclusion on the Register meant that listed people were precluded from working with, supervising or assuming caring responsibilities for children. The Constitutional Court

79 Ibid. paras. 52–8.
80 Ibid. paras. 59–64.
81 Ibid. para. 89.
82 Ibid. para. 99.
83 Ibid. para. 100.
84 In terms of s. 50(2) of the Criminal Law (Sexual Offences and Related Matters) Amendment Act 2007 (Sexual Offences Act).

found that the legislation resulted in serious violations of the best interests of children. In weighing up whether limitations of the rights of these children were justified, the Court acknowledged the competing rights of child offenders and other vulnerable groups to be safe from abuse. The Court stressed that:[85]

> Sexual violence threatens a victim's rights to freedom and security of the person, privacy and dignity in a profound way. Sexual offences have effects that ripple far beyond the horrific immediacy and physicality of the crime. Our success or failure as a community to prevent and protect against sexual violence has bearing on us all, collectively and individually. (footnotes omitted)

Nevertheless, the Court decided that the limitation of the rights of child offenders was not justified as there were less restrictive means to achieve the purpose of the legislation. However, the Court was unable to craft an order that would remedy the situation without a broader re-examination of the Act as a whole. It therefore declared the section invalid but suspended the declaration of invalidity for fifteen months to enable the legislature to remedy the defect. The Court was mindful of the fact that the Act was already being reconsidered following the *Teddy Bear Clinic* case. It also ordered, as an interim measure, that the government provide details of children listed in the Register to the Court to make available to organizations assisting offenders. The Court demonstrated flexibility and the capacity to provide creative responses in its order in this case, whilst avoiding stepping on the toes of the legislature.

In 2015 Parliament made the necessary amendments to the Sexual Offences Act in response to both the *Teddy Bear Clinic* case and *J*'s case.[86]

The case of *DPP* v. *Minister of Justice* involved a somewhat more hands-on response by the Constitutional Court. The case involved statutory provisions dealing with the protection of child complainants in sexual offences cases. The Court refused to set aside the impugned provisions but acknowledged concerns with the administration of justice in regard to child complainants in sexual offences cases (as supported by evidence from the amici in the matter). One of the concerns was the lack of appointment of intermediaries for child complainants. Another was the lack of specialist sexual offences courts and officers to prepare child witnesses. Only a small number of regional courts had facilities to permit the use of intermediaries and even in those courts equipment was often not working. Intermediaries were poorly trained and unable to perform their functions adequately. Similarly, interpreters or prosecutors, used

[85] *J* v. *National Director of Public Prosecutions and Another* [2014] 7 BCLR 764, para. 48.

[86] *Criminal Law (Sexual Offences and Related Matters) Amendment Act Amendment Act* 2015.

because they were easier to obtain than intermediaries, were not equipped to deal with child witnesses. Very few prosecutors had received appropriate training for these types of cases and magistrates were also lacking in specific training. The Court found this state of affairs to be inconsistent with the statutory promise of intermediaries or the constitutional promise of the centrality of the child's best interest.[87] The Court pointed to the vulnerability of child sexual offences complainants who are not parties to criminal proceedings but who do have constitutional rights that must be protected. The Court stressed, in relation to poor implementation of the new laws, that:[88]

> Compliance with the Constitution requires not only that laws be enacted to give effect to the rights in the Constitution, but also requires that these laws be implemented. Failure to implement laws that protect constitutional rights is a violation of the Constitution.

The Court also noted that the relevant subsections of the Criminal Procedure Act envisaged that the state would "commit the necessary resources" to achieve the objectives of the Act and the Constitution. In a supervisory order, the Court called for information as a first step in the supervisory process, requiring the Department of Justice to list, within ninety days, the number of intermediaries and facilities (CCTV, separate rooms for testimony, one-way mirrors) available and needed; and the steps being taken to meet these needs. The Court gave the DPP and the amici the opportunity to comment on the information provided by the Minister. It left open the possibility that further directions might be needed to ensure supervision of its orders.

In following this decision, the Department of Justice provided the information as ordered. The Court then directed the Department to provide a further report in response to the comments on their first report by the DPP and some of the amici. The second report was required to provide information on the huge shortage of intermediaries and the many postponements in child rape cases resulting from this; whether the Department was considering increasing the rate of pay for intermediaries to "an appropriate professional" level; the extent of the problem of malfunctioning equipment and what steps were being taken to address this quickly. The Department provided this report and made further information available in 2012.[89]

87 *Director of Public Prosecutions, Transvaal* v. *Minister for Justice and Constitutional Development and Others* [2009] 7 BCLR 637, para. 198.

88 Ibid. para. 201.

89 Centre for Child Law, *Making Room: Facilitating the Testimony of Child Witnesses and Victims* (Pretoria: Pretoria University Law Press, 2015), 5–6.

A 2015 report by the Centre for Child Law, one of the amici in the *DPP* case, examined the extent to which the supervisory order was followed by the Department of Justice five years later and whether the situation had improved.[90] The report found that while there had been a quantitative improvement in the provision of services this was not adequately or consistently documented so it was hard to evaluate this provision based on available evidence. It called for better and clearer data collection. From a qualitative perspective the report found some positive examples of good practice but a lack of consistency and variations in the available resources. It called for a "set of norms and standards applicable to the provision of acceptable court services for child victims and witnesses."[91] In relation specifically to the provision of intermediaries, the report found greater use and availability of these service providers, but it recommended the need to revise salaries and move away from contract appointments to address the shortage of intermediaries.[92]

The decision is commendable in taking a firm stand on lack of implementation of statutory provisions protecting sexual offence complainants. The Court's use of its supervisory jurisdiction was necessary and important in a context where good legal frameworks were failing through poor administration. However, it appears that despite the Court's role, implementation remains inadequate. This raises two possibilities: first, that the Court may have needed to pursue its remedies more expansively; and second, that lack of resources and state capacity may remain challenges that cannot be immediately or easily addressed. The latter point suggests the unwelcome possibility that despite a responsive Constitutional Court, certain problems may be immune to judicial intervention.

Overall, the five sexual offences cases decided by the Court led to improved substantive and procedural law and, to some extent, to better administration of justice.

6.4.2. *Domestic Violence*

In two cases concerning domestic violence, one brought under the old legislation and the other under the newer Domestic Violence Act, the Court was strong in its defense of laws under attack from men named in court orders.

The case of *S* v. *Baloyi* concerned the predecessor to the Domestic Violence Act 1998, the Prevention of Family Violence Act 1993. It related

[90] Ibid.
[91] Ibid. 70.
[92] Ibid. pp. 64–5.

to whether a provision requiring a person charged with breaching a family violence interdict to prove that they were not guilty violated their right to be presumed innocent. Sachs J, in a unanimous judgment, found that the provision did not introduce a reverse onus and did not violate the rights of the person charged with breaching an interdict. The decision is significant in presenting a sophisticated argument, informed by feminist theory, for viewing domestic violence laws as different from other criminal law in the balancing of the rights of women to be safe from domestic violence against the rights of men accused of such crimes. In interpreting the s. 12 right to be "free from all forms of violence from either public or private sources," Sachs J noted that:[93]

> The specific inclusion of private sources emphasises that serious threats to security of the person arise from private sources. Read with section 7(2), section 12(1) has to be understood as obliging the state directly to protect the right of everyone to be free from private or domestic violence. Indeed, the state is under a series of constitutional mandates which include the obligation to deal with domestic violence: to protect both the rights of everyone to enjoy freedom and security of the person and to bodily and psychological integrity, and the right to have their dignity respected and protected, as well as the defensive rights of everyone not to be subjected to torture in any way and not to be treated or punished in a cruel, inhuman or degrading way. (footnotes omitted)

The right to be free from violence has thus been interpreted by the Court as placing a positive obligation on the state to protect women from domestic violence.[94] The right is read together with s. 7(2) of the Constitution which requires the state to "respect, protect, promote and fulfil the rights in the Bill of Rights." Sachs J alluded to the distinction in the wording of s. 12 where the overall rights to freedom and security of the person (s. 12(1)) and to bodily and psychological integrity (s. 12(2)) are seen as essential features of personhood to which everyone is entitled to receive protection. Most of the sub-sections of ss. 12(1) and (2) contain the types of harms that people should not be subjected to – what Sachs J calls "defensive rights." Thus, people must expect the state to defend them against such harms while protecting their freedom, security and integrity.

Interestingly, Sachs J added the issue of dignity here to his discussion of the right. It is unclear whether he was referring to dignity as one of the three central values of the Bill of Rights set out in s. 7(1) of the Constitution or dignity as a right articulated in s. 10, or both. It seems curious to single out the value of

93 S v. *Baloyi* [2000] 1 BCLR 86 (Constitutional Court), at para. 11.
94 As discussed in Albertyn et al., "Women's freedom" 322.

dignity from the list of dignity, equality and freedom when freedom is so obviously central to the right in s. 12. Sachs J did, however, go on to consider equality when he argued that domestic violence "compels constitutional concern" because it is "gender-specific" and a product of a patriarchal society.[95] This, he noted, meant that "the non-sexist society promised in the foundational clauses of the Constitution, and the right to equality and nondiscrimination guaranteed by section 9, are undermined when spouse-batterers enjoy impunity."[96]

Sachs J came to the issue of freedom when considering what autonomy means for women facing domestic violence. Drawing on feminist legal theory he noted that both autonomy and privacy have been used to shield men and prevent intervention to protect women in the home. He thus praised the idea behind domestic violence protection laws which are aimed at addressing the complexities of intimate partner abuse without immediate recourse to the criminal law. Sachs J pointed to the laudable purpose of protection legislation which "at its most optimistic ... seeks preventive rather than retributive justice, undertaken with a view ultimately to promoting restorative justice."[97] The judgment has been rightfully lauded for its sensitive but firm elaboration of women's rights to be protected from domestic violence by the state.

Unlike *Baloyi* the *Omar* case was brought in terms of the newer Domestic Violence Act of 1998. It concerned a similar issue of the constitutionality of the provision of the Act that allowed a Court, when issuing a protection order, to authorize a warrant of arrest that would be suspended unless there was a breach of the protection order.[98] The Court stated that:[99]

> The high incidence of domestic violence in our society is utterly unacceptable. It causes severe psychological and social damage. There is clearly a need for an adequate legal response to it. Whereas women, men and children can be victims of domestic violence, the gendered nature and effects of violence and abuse as it mostly occurs in the family, and the unequal power relations implicit therein, are obvious. As disempowered and vulnerable members of our society, women and children are most often the victims of domestic violence.

The Court stressed that domestic violence "brutally offends the values and rights" of the Constitution.[100] Because of the "complex public ... (and private)

95 S v. *Baloyi* [2000] 1 BCLR 86, at paras. 11–12.
96 Ibid. para. 12.
97 Ibid. para. 17.
98 Domestic Violence Act 1998, s. 8.
99 *Ex Parte Omar* [2003] 10 BCLR 1087 (Constitutional Court), at para. 13.
100 Ibid. para. 17.

character" of domestic violence, measures were needed that differed from the general criminal laws.[101] The Court examined the workings of the legislation and Omar's arguments that his rights of access to court and to a fair trial and against arbitrary arrest were affected negatively. It found that none of these rights were compromised by the scheme of the Act and, as with *Baloyi's* case, there was no issue of a reverse onus.[102] Since the Court found that none of the rights of a respondent in a domestic violence matter were infringed by the Act, it did not need to undertake any kind of balancing exercise. The *Omar* case did not significantly deepen the interpretation of the Constitutional framework on domestic violence as developed in *Baloyi*. It did, however, confirm the value and integrity of the Domestic Violence Act as a necessary and appropriate means of protecting women and children (primarily) from harm in the home.

Both decisions use the Constitution to defend women's rights to freedom and security and affirm the state's obligations to protect them. They do not, of course, consider how the Constitution might oblige the state to take measures to prevent violence against women from arising in the first place or to protect women by ensuring that they have access to the resources needed to avoid the violence that emerges in situations where poverty and disadvantage leave them defenseless.

6.4.3. *State Liability Under the Common Law*

While the above cases deal with the state's obligations to protect women from violence in the home, the Court has given a series of decisions regarding the state's obligations to protect women from violent men outside of the home under the common law. The three cases of *Carmichele* (2001), *K* (2005) and *F* (2012) concern the way in which the Constitution informs the interpretation and development of the common law in situations where the state fails to protect people from criminal acts. In all three cases, the criminal acts concerned violent attacks on women and girls. These cases have proved highly significant, not just to the law of delict (torts), but more generally to the understanding of the role of the Constitution in reshaping the common law. The *Carmichele* case dealt with the question of whether the state was liable for the conduct of police and prosecutors that led to a member of the public being harmed by a criminal who should not have been released on bail. It raised the

101 Ibid. para. 18.

102 The Court declined to consider whether the definition of economic abuse in the Act was constitutionally valid.

question, of importance to this discussion, of the nature of the state's obligations to protect women from harm. The *K* and *F* cases were more narrowly focused on the vicarious liability of the state for victims of violent acts against women by policemen.

In a unanimous decision in *Carmichele*, the Constitutional Court stressed that the courts have an obligation to develop the common law having regard to the "spirit, purport and objects of the Bill of Rights."[103] In determining whether police officers were under a legal duty to act, the Court said that the weighing up of the interests of the parties and the community involved a proportionality exercise that would need to be considered in the context of a "constitutional state founded on dignity, equality and freedom and in which the government has positive duties to promote and uphold such values."[104] This could entail both a duty not to perform an act that violates rights and a positive duty to provide protection.[105] This echoes the comments of Sachs J in *Baloyi* regarding the state's obligations to protect people from domestic violence and promote their rights to freedom and security.[106] The Constitutional Court found that the values underlying the Constitution pointed to the possible extension of liability to the state since the state, under the Constitution, has obligations to "respect, protect, promote and fulfil the rights," "and in particular, the right of women to have their safety and security protected."[107] It further noted that for police approaching their positive obligations arising from legislation and the Constitution, in relation to the rights to dignity and freedom and security of the person, "few things can be more important to women than freedom from the threat of sexual violence."[108]

The Court upheld Carmichele's appeal and referred the matter back to the trial court to conclude the trial and determine the factual and legal issues. The trial court found the Minister of Safety and Security was liable and this was confirmed by the Supreme Court of Appeal,[109] effectively reversing the finding of the same court in an earlier hearing of the case. In the intervening period the test for wrongfulness in delict had been developed in light of the Constitution in the cases of *Van Eeden*,[110] which concerned an escaped repeat

[103] As stated in the Constitution of the Republic of South Africa 1996, s. 39(2); *Carmichele* v. *Minister of Safety and Security* [2001] 10 BCLR 995 (Constitutional Court) at paras. 38–9.
[104] *Carmichele* at para. 43.
[105] Ibid. para. 26.
[106] *Baloyi* at para. 11.
[107] Ibid. para. 57.
[108] Ibid. para. 62.
[109] *Minister of Safety and Security* v. *Carmichele* [2004] 2 BCLR 133 (Supreme Court of Appeal).
[110] *Van Eeden* v. *Minister of Safety and Security* [2002] 4 All SA 346 (Supreme Court of Appeal).

rapist and *Van Duivenboden*,[111] which concerned a man who killed his wife and child and shot a neighbor where he should not have been allowed to possess firearms.

The *Carmichele* decision of the Constitutional Court has been broadly applauded for its focus on the centrality of the values and rights within the Constitution in shaping the development of the common law. In comparing the case with a similar case in the US courts, Roederer noted:[112]

> The contrast is between a court that views its constitution as a progressive covenant between the people and its government, which fosters a culture of justification and accountability, and a court that views its constitution as a charter of negative liberties, which will go to great lengths to conserve the status quo distribution of rights and entitlements. One is intent on protecting the vulnerable members of its society, and the other is skeptical of attempts by the legislature to do so through the creation of new rights. (footnotes omitted)

Commenting on the latter case of *K*, Roederer argued that it showed, like *Carmichele*, a similar value-based response to state accountability and the obligation to protect vulnerable members of society. *K*'s case concerned the nature and scope of vicarious liability in the situation where three policemen, while on duty, raped a young woman to whom they had offered a lift home. O'Regan J, in a unanimous decision overturning the decision of the Supreme Court of Appeal, found the Minister of Safety and Security liable. The judgment developed the vicarious liability rule in line with the "spirit, purport and objects of the Bill of Rights," following the *Carmichele* requirement that the normative values of the Constitution must inform the development of the common law.[113] The court recognized that the principle of vicarious liability poses difficulties where the delictual act deviates from an employee's normal duties, and is even more difficult where it is an intentional wrong.[114] The Court explained that the test for vicarious liability[115] involves a subjective question of whether the wrongful acts were done purely for the benefit of the employee. Even where they were, there is still a further objective test of the sufficient

[111] *Minister of Safety and Security* v. *Van Duivenboden* [2002] 6 SA 431 (Supreme Court of Appeal).

[112] C. J. Roederer, "The constitutionally inspired approaches to police accountability for violence against women in the U.S. and South Africa: conservation versus transformation" (2005) 13 *Tulsa Journal of Comparative and International Law* 91–140 at 93.

[113] *K* at para. 15.

[114] Ibid. para. 25.

[115] As set out in *Minister of Police* v. *Rabie* [1986] 1 SA 117 (A).

closeness of the link between the employee's acts to further his or her own interests and the "purpose and business of the employer."[116] This part of the test is both factual and legal – the legal component of sufficient closeness requires examination in terms of the "spirit, purport and objects of the Bill of Rights."[117] In applying the redeveloped test to the facts of *K*'s case the Court found that the policemen, in *committing* the rape against K, "were simultaneously *omitting* to perform their duties as policemen."[118] O'Regan J noted that by offering K a lift, the policemen had induced her to trust them, something she was entitled to expect from the police in terms of the Constitution. They failed to meet their general duty to protect K from harm and their special duty in the particular situation of the case. "The close connection between the wrongful conduct of the policemen and the nature of their employment" led to the Minister of Police being liable for K's damages.[119] The policemen infringed K's constitutional rights to dignity and security of the person.

The decision sent a strong message to the governing bodies of the police that police personnel who abuse their positions of power remain the responsibility of the force. In a country where women live in fear of sexual violence, it is critical that they must be able to both expect protection from the police and feel confident that the police themselves will not abuse their authority and take criminal advantage of women.

The final and most recent case in the sequence of cases dealing with the common law in relation to liability following violent crimes against women is the case of *F*. Here, a thirteen-year-old girl was raped and assaulted by a policeman on standby duty who had given her a lift home. The case reached the Constitutional Court on appeal from the Supreme Court of Appeal (SCA) which had decided not to hold the Minister of Safety and Security liable. The majority decision of the SCA distinguished this case from *K*'s case on the basis that a policeman on standby duty was not on duty and hence had not committed a delictual omission. It (mis)understood *K*'s case to mean that an intentional commission such as rape could not result in vicarious liability for the state.

The Constitutional Court (Mogoeng J) considered the boundaries of the test for vicarious liability as set out in *K* in the situation where a policeman on standby duty "deviates from his employer's constitutional obligation to protect the public and engages in conduct that constitutes 'the single greatest threat to

[116] *K* at para. 32.
[117] Ibid. paras. 32, 44.
[118] Ibid. para. 48 (emphasis added).
[119] Ibid. para. 57.

the self-determination of South African women', namely rape."[120] The Court followed the *K* approach to determining vicarious liability in examining the facts of *F*'s case. It looked at the following factors:[121]

> the state's constitutional obligations to protect the public; the trust that the public is entitled to place in the police; the significance, if any, of the policeman having been off duty and on standby duty; the role of the simultaneous act of the policeman's commission of rape and omission to protect the victim; and the existence or otherwise of an intimate link between the policeman's conduct and his employment.

Mogoeng J noted that rape by men of women and girls, which is common and ongoing, and often goes unpunished, is a violation of a range of women and children's rights.[122] He went on to say that:[123]

> The threat of sexual violence to women is indeed as pernicious as sexual violence itself. It is said to go to the very core of the subordination of women in society. It entrenches patriarchy as it imperils the freedom and self-determination of women. It is deeply sad and unacceptable that few of our women or girls dare to venture into public spaces alone, especially when it is dark and deserted. If official crime statistics are anything to go by, incidents of sexual violence against women occur with alarming regularity. This is so despite the fact that our Constitution, national legislation, formations of civil society and communities across our country have all set their faces firmly against this horrendous invasion and indignity imposed on our women and girl-children.

Mogoeng J stressed that courts must accept that common law rules are now subject to constitutional values and "it is their duty to ensure that the fundamental rights of women and girl-children in particular are not made hollow by actual or threatened sexual violence."[124]

The Court found that the standby duty status of the policeman did not preclude the state from liability, as the focus of vicarious liability, following *K*'s case, was the trust placed by the member of the public in the police. It also found that the SCA has misinterpreted the decision in *K* that vicarious liability related not just to omissions of employees but commissions as well.

[120] *K* v. *Minister of Safety and Security* [2005] 9 BCLR 835 (Constitutional Court) para. 37. The Court was quoting counsel for the Centre for Applied Legal Studies, as cited in *Carmichele* at para. 62.

[121] Ibid. para. 52.

[122] Ibid. para. 55.

[123] Ibid. para. 56.

[124] Ibid. para. 57.

It explained that rape by a policeman and his failure to protect the woman are "two sides of the same coin" and are "inseparable."[125] The Court accepted that the "closeness of the connection" between the wrongful conduct of the policeman and his employment was more tenuous on the facts of this case than in *K*'s but that the link was still sufficient to find the state vicariously liable.

The three cases clarify and extend the obligations of the state under the common law of delict to compensate women who have been harmed by violent men due to the inaction and action of state officials, particularly police and prosecutors. It remains to be seen whether the common law will be developed further, in light of the Constitution, in requiring state responsibility for the protection of women from public and private sources of violence. Dee Smythe notes that the "full ambit of state obligations to protect, investigate, punish and compensate victims of sexual violence has not been fully explored in South African courts"[126] and that "the cases have dealt with harm suffered consequent to a failure by the police to comply with their obligations, rather than the harm intrinsic in such a failure."[127] This points to the need for a consideration of the way in which the Constitution might be used to greater effect in tackling violence against women and to create the conditions for violence to be reduced and prevented.

6.5. EXPANDING CONSTITUTIONAL OPPORTUNITIES TO ADDRESS VIOLENCE AGAINST WOMEN

An evaluation of the jurisprudence indicates that the Constitutional Court sees violence against women as an extremely serious infringement of human rights that is at odds with the values that underlie the Constitution. The Court has shown a willingness to develop the common law and require the improvement of statutes where these are failing to appropriately tackle this urgent social crisis. The Court has made it clear that the state has obligations in terms of the Constitution and international law to protect women from violence. The cases also point to the Court's preparedness to use its remedial jurisdiction to order remedies that require the state to expend resources and take actions to meet its obligations under the law. Most of the decisions are contextual in approach and situate legal development within an understanding of the extent, nature and impact of violence against women. This ensures

[125] Ibid. para. 72.
[126] Smythe, *Rape Unresolved* (n. 5) 30.
[127] Ibid. 224, n. 117.

that the decisions avoid conservative, inappropriate or formalistic approaches to law. The combination of a progressive Court and a strong constitutional text has resulted in jurisprudence and a constitutional model worth emulating elsewhere.[128]

The judgments discussed demonstrate an engagement with the rights to freedom and security of the person alongside dignity and equality as key rights contravened by acts of violence against women and children. The values of human dignity, equality and freedom have been given prominence in some of the leading decisions set out above. Compared to some of the gender equality jurisprudence that has attracted criticism by feminist scholars,[129] the violence against women jurisprudence is broadly progressive. However, the ten decisions in the twenty years of the Constitution have dealt only with the protection of women from harm and their treatment within the legal system or in claiming damages once such harm has occurred. No case dealing with the obligations of the state to take active measures to prevent violence against women has reached the Court, and this leads to a jurisprudential gap that should be remedied. It is a concern that a limited range of cases has reached the Court and that there has been a lack of opportunity for the Court to deepen its jurisprudence and provide far-reaching responses. Advocacy and service organizations representing violence victims have thus far played a mostly responsive role in assisting the Court (with the exception of the parties who brought the challenge to the provisions criminalizing under-age sexual conduct).[130] There appear to be opportunities for such groups to creatively formulate new public interest litigation that engages the Constitution and the courts more effectively. The lack of litigation may reflect a number of things, including despondency within the sector about the value of good judgments when implementation remains so poor. Aside from looking to the Constitution for opportunities to litigate further in this area, the Constitution should be used as a framing document for new policy and law reform initiatives by the sector.

The South African constitutional experience on violence against women reflects some important successes but these must be taken further to expand

[128] Note, however, that although s. 12 was path-breaking in referring to public and private violence, constitutional provisions on violence against women could be even more explicit and expansive, for example, The Constitution of the Tunisian Republic 2014, Art. 46, which says: "The state shall take all necessary measures in order to eradicate violence against women."

[129] E. Bonthuys, "Institutional openness and resistance to feminist arguments: the example of the South African Constitutional Court" (2008) 20 *Canadian Journal of Women and the Law* 1–36; C. Albertyn, "Law, gender and inequality in South Africa" (2011) 39 *Oxford Development Studies* 139–62.

[130] The Teddy Bear Clinic for Abused Children and RAPCAN in the *Teddy Bear Clinic* case.

the legal frameworks and the state's obligations in this area. There are real questions about the ability of the Court to address lack of state capacity in implementing its laws in the face of massive social and economic problems, including the epidemic of violence against women. Clearly, the Constitution alone is not sufficient to solve this issue. Nevertheless, it is a text with the capacity to contribute further, in tandem with a range of other mechanisms and actors to tackle this major challenge.

This last part of the chapter considers some of the constitutional possibilities that could be explored to expand the Constitution's reach in both protecting women from violence and responding to it. These include: developing the meaning and content of the right to freedom and security of the person in s. 12; deepening the interpretation of the constitutional values and considering their substantive content; drawing on the social and economic rights, in combination with s. 12 and the right to equality to obtain the necessary resources and action by the state in addressing violence that is closely tied to gendered poverty. Other rights such as rights to culture and religion may also prove important in challenging practices that lead to violence and abuse of women.

6.5.1. *Developing the Interpretation of* s. 12

The right to freedom and security of the person in s. 12 of the Constitution is capable of further interpretation and elaboration by the courts. The positive and negative dimensions of the right could be more fully spelt out as a basis for expanding the boundaries of state obligations to address violence against women. The various dimensions of the right have implications for women facing violence. Thus, deprivation of freedom referred to in s. 12(1)(a) may result from controling partners or parents who prevent women and girls from working, socializing or participating in their communities, using physical, psychological, economic and other forms of control. The idea of freedom from violence from public or private sources referred to in s. 12(1)(c) may involve some definition with regard to acts of abuse by teachers, religious leaders or employers. In the employment context, sexual harassment is prohibited but this does not necessarily mean that employers are taking active steps to prevent its occurrence. In situations where people face job insecurity, which is common in the high-unemployment context of South Africa, the right might need to be used to require measures to prevent harassment and abuse of female workers. Similarly, in the schooling context where power inequalities, together with poverty, shape girls' capacities to challenge teachers who abuse them, the right should be used to expand the available preventative and responsive measures. Sadly, the references in s. 12 to torture and cruel, inhuman and degrading treatment are relevant to women in South Africa where rape, domestic violence and other forms of abuse can be categorized in these terms. Strong statements by the Court on these definitional overlaps would be important in clarifying the conceptual boundaries of violence against women as a violation of human rights.[131] Similarly, bodily and psychological integrity, the second part of s. 12, has important meaning in the context of violence against women, particularly the sub-right of "security in and control over their body." In a country where many young people of both sexes believe that nonconsensual sex is normal,[132] fulfilling the s. 12 right might entail educational program to address these alarming perceptions.[133] Pieterse discusses the possibilities of using s. 12 to obtain material outcomes in the health sphere and points to judicial decisions in South Africa and Canada that might support this interpretation. Similar arguments could be applied in the area of violence against women.[134]

6.5.2. *Deepening the Substantive Interpretation and Application of the Constitutional Values*

The values of dignity, equality and freedom underlying the rights in the Bill of Rights require ongoing interpretation and development in the context of the particular rights they inform and the circumstances of the cases reaching the courts. In considering the development of the right to equality in its engagement with culture, Albertyn has proposed an interpretation of the fundamental constitutional values as follows:[135]

> dignity as affirming the humanity of each person and their entitlement to equal concern and respect; equality as remedying of disadvantage and enabling redistribution (difference should not be a basis for disadvantage); an

[131] On the relationship between violence against women and human rights, see Manjoo, "Violence against women."

[132] R. Jewkes and N. Abrahams, "The epidemiology of rape and sexual coercion in South Africa: an overview" (2002) 55 *Social Science and Medicine* 1231–44.

[133] For recommendations of the types of programs to address these attitudes see E. Fulu et al., *Why Do Some Men Use Violence Against Women and How Can We Prevent It? Quantitative Findings from the United Nations Multi-Country Study on Men and Violence in Asia and the Pacific* (Bangkok: UNDP, UNFPA, UN Women and UNV, 2013).

[134] M. Pieterse, "The interdependence of rights to health and autonomy in South Africa" (2008) 125 *South African Law Journal* 553–72. See also, D. Bhana, "The substance of contractual autonomy in the twenty-first century: the South African experience" (2015) 48(4) *VRÜ Verfassung in Recht und Übersee*, 491–515.

[135] C. Albertyn, "The stubborn persistence of patriarchy'? Gender equality and cultural diversity in South Africa" (2009) 2 *Constitutional Court Review* 165–208 at 187.

affirmation of difference and diversity (positive differences should be recognised and developed); and freedom as autonomy, participation and the establishment and nurturing of conditions for substantive choice.

She notes that freedom is the least developed constitutional value and, like Pieterse, argues for a substantive conception of freedom that enables choice, agency and participation. Violence is multi-dimensional in its impact on women, limiting their opportunities, life choices, access to resources and to full participation in society. Understanding dignity, freedom and equality substantively involves addressing these various dimensions of the impact of violence on women. The development of substantive freedom as a fundamental value underlying all rights in the context of violence against women is a critical conceptual constitutional project that may lead to practical outcomes for victims. For example, if sex workers who face regular sexual violence are not provided with the mechanisms to resist attack because the employment "choices" they make are frowned upon, then freedom is given a meaning that is narrow and unresponsive.[136]

6.5.3. *Drawing on the Social and Economic Rights (Together with Other Rights)*

Scholars examining the Constitutional Court's jurisprudence on violence against women have pointed to the need to look to the social and economic rights in the Constitution to address the conditions of poverty that expose women to violence and limit their access to appropriate services.[137] A study by Elsje Bonthuys has considered the issue of domestic violence in particular and the ways in which social and economic rights might be used to overcome the implementation deficiencies of the *Domestic Violence Act*.[138] This is innovative research both within South Africa and beyond where the links between violence against women and social and economic rights have not been fully theorized in constitutional or international human rights law. Conceptually, Bonthuys brings together the right to gender equality and socio-economic

[136] See research on the relationship between freedom, access to property and resources, and domestic violence in the Indian context: B. Aggarwal and P. Panda, "Toward freedom from domestic violence: the neglected obvious" (2007) 8 *Journal of Human Development* 359–88.

[137] P. Andrews, "Learning to love after learning to harm: post-conflict reconstruction, gender equality and cultural values" (2007) 15 *Michigan State Journal of International Law* 41–62 at 62; Combrinck, "The dark side of the rainbow" at 196–8.

[138] E. Bonthuys, "Domestic violence and gendered socio-economic rights: an agenda for research and activism" (2014) 30 *South African Journal on Human Rights* 111–33.

rights to focus on the issue of domestic violence against women specifically. She draws on work that has combined substantive gender equality with socio-economic rights to address the conditions of material disadvantage and status-based discrimination that adversely affect women.[139]

While Bonthuys' argument provides a fruitful framing of the issues and the basis for further research, litigation and advocacy on domestic violence it leaves certain conceptual and substantive questions open for further development. At a conceptual level, the reliance on gender equality, together with socio-economic rights, to provide the substantive responses to domestic violence against women overlooks the need to theorize the relationship between the right to freedom and security of the person and socio-economic rights. The rights in s. 12 need to be given substantive content based on a rich conception of the value of freedom that requires state and private provision of the means to exist as free and autonomous members of society. At a substantive level, Bonthuys' paper only addressed domestic violence and there would be value in a similar study that considers the role of social and economic rights in addressing other forms of sexual or gender-based violence. Such a study might lead to ideas for creative litigation including the installation of lighting in informal settlements to make streets safer for women, education programs in school to address male and female attitudes to sex, transport for girls to reach school safely or, as required by the Bombay High Court, the provision of women's toilets in public places that has a positive impact on their safety.[140] Private provision of services and supports might also be required in terms of social and economic rights, for instance, to address violence against women and sexual harassment in the workplace.

We know there are problems with state capacity and implementation and that solving these problems takes time. Constitutional rights can create the enabling framework for community-based responses that are less resource-dependent than orders requiring state provision of services. An example of

[139] S. Fredman, "Engendering social and economic rights" in B. Goldblatt and K. McLean (eds.), *Women's Social and Economic Rights – Developments in South Africa* (Cape Town: Juta, 2011) 4. This involves an application of Fredman's focus on both distributive and status-based features of equality, to violence against women. Fredman's conception of four-dimensional substantive equality includes these recognition and redistribution dimensions but also requires a focus on participation and transformative approaches. It would be valuable to map all of Fredman's equality dimensions of socio-economic rights as a response to violence against women. It would also be important to think about intersectional discrimination and how violence against women has different implications for a variety of different groups such as women with disabilities, lesbians, and women in religious communities.

[140] *Milun Saryajani* v. *Pune Municipal Corporation and Others*, P. I. L. No. 98 of 2011, H. C. Bom (December 23, 2015).

this might be a program undertaken by school students, parents and teachers to ensure girl students are accompanied to school by protective groups based on a roster system. Creative local responses can be defended by courts where they face regulatory challenges or can be rolled out to other areas by courts. Such strategies should not, however, be seen as transferring state obligations to women and communities, themselves time and resource poor.[141]

6.6. CONCLUSION

This chapter, in examining the jurisprudence of the Constitutional Court on violence against women over the past twenty years, has noted the valuable framework created by the Court in defining the state's obligations in this area. It has argued that this framework requires expansion if it is to offer additional space for attempts to use the law to challenge systemic and ongoing violence. The chapter has made some suggestions for ways in which this jurisprudential framework might be developed and where creative litigation might bring new issues into focus for the Court. These areas of development would be aided by considering comparative and international jurisprudence and might also impact on debates in these terrains. It is clear that it is a difficult economic and political context in which to demand more from a state whose capacity to implement existing laws and policies is limited. But it is always a difficult time for women facing violence or its threat on a daily basis. It is necessary to use all available measures to end the war against South Africa's women and the Constitution remains one of the important tools for this task.

[141] For a discussion of some of the dangers of placing obligations on poor women to address social problems that should be fixed by the society as a whole, see S. Chant, "The 'feminisation of poverty' and the 'feminisation' of anti-poverty programmes: room for revision?" (2008) 44 *Journal of Development Studies* 165–97; M. Molyneux, "Mothers at the service of the new poverty agenda: progresa/oportunidades, Mexico's conditional transfer programme" (2006) 40 *Social Policy & Administration* 425–49.

7

Toward Reparative Transformation: Revisiting the Impact of Violence Against Women in a Post-TRC South Africa

Andrea Durbach

> Sexual and gender-based violence does not begin with conflict or political instability and end with a transition to peace or democracy.[1]

7.1. INTRODUCTION

> South Africa has not even begun to understand the deepest social crisis ... systematically implemented along decades and decades by the apartheid system ... I don't believe that in 18 years of freedom, this nation took the time to seriously revisit what kind of psychological and emotional damage has been inflicted on men and women in this society ... We are harming one another because we cannot control our pain.[2]

As South Africa marked twenty years of democracy, the disparities that existed under apartheid had shifted with some positive, although fragmented, results. Their long-term impact had taken its toll on black South African women,

This chapter is based on research supported by the Australian Research Council Discovery Projects funding scheme (DP140102274), "Combating Sexual Violence against Women Post-Conflict through 'Transformative' Reparations: Problems and Prospects." My appreciation to all the extraordinary people I interviewed in South Africa and in Australia who gave their time and shared their experiences, expertise and insights and agreed to be part of the project. My thanks also to Lucy Geddes – particularly for her invaluable support in South Africa – and Natalie Hodgson for their superb research and editing assistance.

This chapter was previously published under the same title in (2016) 10 *International Journal of Transitional Justice* 366–87. It is republished here with the kind permission of Oxford University Press.

1 R. Sigsworth and N. Valji, "Continuities of violence against women and the limitations of transitional justice: the case of South Africa" in S. Buckley-Zistel and R. Stanley (eds.), *Gender in Transitional Justice* (Basingstoke: Palgrave Macmillan, 2011) 115.

2 G. Machel, "2nd Annual Desmond Tutu International Peace Lecture" (presented at the University of the Western Cape, Cape Town, October 2, 2012).

who suffered discrimination, oppression, economic marginalization and violence. In postapartheid South Africa, the majority of black women "remain mired down in poverty, without resources, without economic security, with no way out."[3] The brutality of apartheid and the violence invoked to reinforce its reach was manifest not only in the conduct of apartheid's executioners (police, army, security forces) but in its systemic and structural foundations which exacted cheap supplies of labor and controlled the movement and day-to-day lives of the majority of citizens. The migrant labor system, the "pass" laws that excluded black people from white-designated urban areas, the forced removals of whole communities under the Group Areas Act and the creation of bantustans (homelands) which stripped black South Africans of their citizenship, combined to dismantle relationships, break families apart, uproot communities and force millions of women to the margins of existence.[4] Attempts to resist or circumvent these tiers of structural violence were met with arrest, detention, torture, rape and death.

Despite this long history of gendered violence and violations by security forces and opposition political forces, the Truth and Reconciliation Commission (TRC) was limited to investigating and establishing the nature, causes and extent of specified gross violations of human rights committed between 1960 and 1994. It focused on events "which emanated from the conflicts of the past, rather than from the policies of apartheid" and excluded egregious abuses caused, inter alia, by "the denial of freedom of movement ... [and] the franchise to citizens, ... and by discrimination."[5] The TRC categories of human rights violations were "the killing, abduction, torture or severe ill-treatment of any person," committed primarily to secure a political objective.[6] This focus on "political" offences[7] and the absence of sexual violence as a distinct category within the definition of "political" crime, resulted in the TRC "neglecting the link between what was considered 'extraordinary' [political] and "ordinary" [criminal] violence," missing "the opportunity to

3 Khulumani Support Group, How the TRC failed women in South Africa: a failure that has proved fertile ground for the gender violence women in South Africa face today (October 3, 2011) (available at www.khulumani.net/truth-memory/item/527-how-the-trc-failed-women-in-south-africa-a-failure-that-has-proved-fertile-ground-for-the-gender-violence-women-in-south-africa-face-today.html) (accessed date November 20, 2017).

4 T. Sideris, "Women and apartheid: collective trauma and social reconstruction" (1998) 93 *The Way Supplement* 80–91.

5 Truth and Reconciliation Commission (TRC), *Truth and Reconciliation Commission of South Africa Report* (1998), vol. 5, ch. 1, para. 48.

6 Promotion of National Unity and Reconciliation Act 1995 (TRC Act), ch. 1, s. 1.

7 Ibid. preamble.

examine the structural, ideological and systemic ... abuses against women"[8] and to analyze their long-term impact.

In January 2015, almost twenty years after the TRC hearings commenced, I visited South Africa to conduct research as part of a project on the capacity and potential of court- and tribunal-awarded reparations to prevent the postconflict recurrence of sexual violence against women. I interviewed twenty-five women and men over three weeks, many of whom had been associated with the work of the TRC and were working on issues related to gender discrimination, inequality and sexual violence.[9] They included former TRC commissioners, lawyers, psychologists, academics, health practitioners and representatives from government, nongovernmental organizations (NGOs), the South African Human Rights Commission and the Commission for Gender Equality (CGE). The focus of the interviews was, first, to examine the consequences of the TRC's failure to investigate the impact of sexual violence against women in a post-TRC South Africa and, second, to offer a retrospective analysis of the capacity of transformative institutions, such as the TRC and the Constitutional Court, to address the conditions that enabled the violence with a view to preventing its repetition. The reflections of people with recognized links to South Africa's political, economic and social history and the specific issue of gender violence, afforded observations and analysis that highlighted the urgent quest to attempt the repair of this "deepest social crisis."

The chapter begins by examining the historical and political factors which might explain the extent of sexual violence against women in South Africa, currently regarded as higher "than anywhere else in the globe not at war or embroiled in civil conflict."[10] It then examines the evolution of the legislation establishing the TRC and its ultimate design. The interviews bring a contemporary perspective to the analysis of reasons proffered for the TRC's omission to assign sexual violence against women a distinct category of investigation within the definition of gross violation of human rights and explore whether this "absence of a truly inclusive gender perspective" has undermined the prospect of "establish[ing] firm grounds for a society free of gender-based

[8] A. Kusafuka, "Truth commissions and gender: a South African case study" (2009) 9(2) *African Journal on Conflict Resolution* 45–67 at 51.

[9] All interviews were conducted on a confidential basis. Permission was granted by all interviewees to publish extracts from their interviews contained in this article without disclosing their identity. Unless indicated otherwise, all interviews took place in South Africa.

[10] H. Moffett, "The Political Economy of Sexual Violence in Post-Apartheid South Africa" (paper presented at the Harold Wolpe Memorial Trust's Tenth Anniversary Colloquium: *Engaging Silences and Unresolved Issues in the Political Economy of South Africa*, Cape Town, South Africa, September 21–23, 2006).

violence."[11] Finally, the chapter considers the TRC's transformative role and its legislative requirement to recommend reparations to a government mandated to restructure social and economic conditions. It does so in the context of increasing calls by gender justice scholars for international justice tribunals to adopt a "transformative" approach to the design of reparations when seeking to address the harm of women victims of sexual violence. The chapter includes a brief commentary on the role of the Constitutional Court as a potential vehicle for developing measures of redress. It ends with endorsement for a process of national engagement on the extent and impact of sexual violence against women as the essential precursor to any broad-based transformative enterprise, in the hope of giving "the problem of violence against women ... the consideration it deserves in the construction of a new democratic society"[12] in alignment with the nation's transformative promise.

7.2. "THE DEEPEST SOCIAL CRISIS": TRACING A HISTORY OF SEXUAL VIOLENCE

7.2.1. *Violence is a Form of Communication in South Africa*[13]

The execution of violence endemic to the apartheid system, and the impunity that accompanied its manifestation, are two recurrent explanations for the high levels of sexual violence against women postapartheid. South Africa's preapartheid history suggests that these factors had their origins in a past that shaped apartheid's foundations, establishing clear lines of domination and exclusion based on race and gender that would harden and survive the country's transition to democracy. The lives of indigenous inhabitants of South Africa's founding Cape Colony, who suffered displacement and exploitation at the hands of Dutch colonists in the mid-1600s, and the slaves imported from east Africa and South East Asia to supplement local labor supplies, were similarly "marked by brutality," and "extreme violence, including systemic sexual violence, became the norm under slavery."[14] Although there are accounts of

[11] Global Gender Justice, *The ugly truth about the TRC: Are black women of the LGBTI community in South Africa paying the price?* (December 11, 2013) (available at www.globalgenderjustice.wordpress.com/2013/12/11/the-ugly-truth-about-the-trc-are-black-women-of-the-lgbti-community-in-south-africa-paying-the-price/) (accessed date November 20, 2017).

[12] L. Vogelman and G. Eagle, "Overcoming endemic violence against women in South Africa," (1991) 18 *Social Justice* 209–29 at 209.

[13] Personal interview, 01SAET (Johannesburg, January 12, 2015).

[14] G. Baderoon, "Remembering slavery in South Africa,"' (December 7, 2014) *Africa Is a Country* (available at www.africasacountry.com/?p=85664) (accessed date November 20, 2017).

women slaves instigating charges of rape, many were not pursued and few, if any, convictions were secured.[15] While the abolition of slavery by the British somewhat ameliorated the lives of black communities in the Cape and further north (with British expansion), British colonial rule reinforced the bond between racial and sexual power and control, a "racially constructed sexual right [of primarily white men] to the bodies of black women."[16]

> We've been a country of sexual violence with very deep, historical roots ... [This country] started off as a sort of a trading post with the VOC [Dutch East India Company]. Men would use slave women and Khoi women, and exploit them ... [At] night they would unlock the slave quarters – the women's quarters – for the men to go in. So rape as something socially accepted has a very long history in this country and we should ... look back a bit further, and not start our story always with the transition as if rape was invented there and the apartheid regime was better somehow.[17]

Under apartheid, black South African women suffered compound harm by virtue of their gender, race and class. Their legal capacity, access to education, employment, property and basic social services, freedom of movement and right to relationships and family were all regulated and curtailed by customary and discriminatory laws, policies and practices that entrenched exclusion and deprivation, confining most black women to lives of domestic labor or hawking. This gendered harm was exacerbated by the impact of the structural hallmarks of apartheid – the "pass" laws, the migrant labor system, forced removals, job reservation, bantu education and social segregation – which eroded the integrity of the family and marginalized women socially and economically, many of whom lived in rural impoverishment. Additionally, black women were the predominant victims of sexual violence, a tactic employed by police, prison personnel and soldiers to instil fear, humiliate, control and silence or punish women, particularly those who resisted the system or supported its opponents.[18] There are also reports of sexual abuse of women in the African National Congress (ANC) exile communities and liberation camps.

15 R. L. Watson, *Slave Emancipation and Racial Attitudes in Nineteenth-Century South Africa* (New York, NY: Cambridge University Press, 2012).

16 P. Scully, "Rape, race, and colonial culture: the sexual politics of identity in the nineteenth-century cape colony, South Africa" (1995) 100 *American Historical Review* 335–59 at 356.

17 Personal interview, 22SAMU (Stellenbosch, February 4, 2015).

18 B. Goldblatt and S. Meintjes, "Gender and the Truth and Reconciliation Commission," submission to the Truth and Reconciliation Commission (May 1996): "Men and women experienced sexual torture: electric shocks to genitals, and to women's breasts were commonplace ... But the nature of these experiences ... were *felt differently*. Assaults on pregnant women, which led to miscarriage, body searches, vaginal examinations, were all assaults on the sexuality and sexual identity of women" (original emphasis).

In a 2014 study on the lives of children who grew up in these communities and camps, respondents spoke of acts of rape and how the "movement" was prioritized "above the needs of girls and women."[19]

The first chairperson of the CGE and former senior member of the ANC in exile, Thenjiwe Mtintso, argues that the "aggression and attitudes towards women" by men in the ANC camps was shaped by their treatment at the hands of the South African Police, many of whom were psychologically "dented." She also speaks of the "double-barrelled" oppression of women at the hands of

> the boers [Afrikaners] because they don't want you to [resist] and ... from your own comrades because they don't expect you to perform better [beyond the female stereotype]. It's a can't-win situation.[20]

This "double-barrelled" oppression along gender lines, reflecting a patriarchal culture that permeated the ideology of Afrikaner nationalism and African customary laws or traditional practice,[21] coalesced with the country's stratification along race lines.

South Africa's "masculinized national narrative"[22] was reinforced by decades of state sponsorship and legitimization of violence to entrench political power and the popularization of violence by resistance movements to provoke political change.[23] The systemic violence extended across race lines as white South African men were conscripted into an army which executed "large-scale massacres" in neighboring states[24] and was deployed in the bantustans (homelands),[25] black townships[26] and rural areas "to maintain a low-level war

19 Z. O. De Sas Kropiwnicki, "Childhood in exile: the agency of second-generation exiles seeking refuge from apartheid," (2014) 30 *Refuge: Canada's Journal on Refugees* 35–46 at 42.

20 Goldblatt and Meintjes, "Gender and the Truth and Reconciliation Commission."

21 In "Marxism, feminism and South African studies" (1983) 9 *Journal of Southern African Studies* 139–71 at 149, Belinda Bozzoli refers to the "'patchwork quilt' of patriarchies" that existed in nineteenth-century South Africa, "each connected with a particular society" (e.g., pre-industrialist African societies) and shaped by "the penetration of merchant capital and colonial conquest."

22 Personal interview, 22SAMU (Stellenbosch, February 4, 2015).

23 G. Simpson, "Women and children in violent South African townships," in M. Motshekga and E. Delport (eds.), *Women and Children's Rights in a Violent South Africa* (Pretoria: Institute for Public Interest, Law and Research, 1993).

24 See generally TRC, *Report* (n. 5) vol. 2, ch. 2. "[P]hysical beatings, the destruction of property, sexual assault and various forms of torture ... [were used] as a means of coercion, intimidation and the extraction of information. Rape was common, and women and girls of all ages were victims" (at para. 122).

25 Personal interview, 03SANK (Johannesburg, January 12, 2015).

26 Ibid.: "In [19]92 ... [the SADF] stationed the 32 Battalion in Phola Park [a township] and actually took them out because there was so much violence and rape."

between the state and comrades."[27] This sanctioning of and reliance on political violence, coupled with the dehumanizing features of apartheid – disenfranchisement, racism and "the powerlessness of poverty"[28] – resulted in violence becoming "a form of communication" which "seeped into your relationships as well as your social and community relationships."[29] This culture of violence so endemic to apartheid South Africa is a key factor in the overall explanation of the "epidemic" of violence against women that was evident even at a time when "the country's prospects for peace and of negotiated solutions [were] more attainable than ever before in the history of apartheid."[30]

South Africa's transition to democracy heralded considerable gains for women, including the constitutional protection of gender rights, significant parliamentary representation,[31] employment equity, domestic violence and sexual offences legislation[32] and the establishment of the CGE. Despite these advances, the country "entered a transition in a culture of very serious ... interpersonal violence, political violence."[33] The levels of sexual violence that have sustained, and arguably increased,[34] in postapartheid South Africa suggest that entrenched gender disparities have outlived political developments and institutional restructuring. As women "became more empowered professionally and socially,"[35] they encountered a "backlash" against their increasing economic emancipation:

> After the revolution, win or lose, there was a reaction against [economic empowerment] and women were basically forced back into a more domesticated role, often using violence. So there's a spike in violence with pushing women back into [traditional roles].[36]

[27] P. D. Gqola, "How the 'cult of femininity' and violent masculinities support endemic gender based violence in contemporary South Africa," (2007) 5 *African Identities* 111–24 at 113.

[28] Personal interview, 21SABH (Stellenbosch, February 4, 2015).

[29] Personal interview, 01SAET (Johannesburg, January 12, 2015).

[30] Simpson, "Women and children" 3.

[31] The ANC stipulates that at least 30 percent of its candidates must be women. In the 1994 election, ANC women won 27.7 percent of the seats in parliament. Ten years later, women held 33 percent of parliamentary seats in both houses.

[32] Domestic Violence Act 1998; Criminal Law (Sexual Offences and Related Matters) Amendment Act 2007.

[33] Personal interview, 21SABH (Stellenbosch, February 4, 2015).

[34] A. Gouws, "Recognition and redistribution: state of the women's movement in South Africa 20 years after democratic transition" (2014) 28 *Agenda* 19–32 at 22–3: "South Africa [has] one of the highest rape rates in the world, if not the highest ... [and] according to the 'One in Nine Campaign' only 1 in 9 rapes are reported."

[35] Personal interview, 05SAOX (Johannesburg, January 13, 2015).

[36] Personal interview, 03SANK (Johannesburg, January 12, 2015).

The perceived shift in the control of and access to economic resources, perhaps exacerbated by the "shock of transition"[37] and the uncertainty that accompanies accelerated political change, appeared to generate "economic violence ... between men and women."[38] This attempt to curb or contest the disruption of gender patterns that happened during the conflict "[was] a foundational violence – laying the foundations for the new state as patriarchal, as male-centred ... to create the political space as a masculine space again."[39]

Despite the creation of laws and institutions designed to transform gender iniquities, the reality for many women victims of sexual violence was that South Africa's democratic transition failed to take account of the extent to which they "experienced so much chronic and institutionalized violence" that was left "unmet, unscrutinized and untreated"[40] and was increasingly internalized and normalized:

> I feel the violence in this country and the way people have taken it on, is almost in camouflage. It's always there. It's lurking but we've stopped seeing it. And if you don't see something you're never going to be able to address it.[41]

The pervasiveness of sexual violence against women during apartheid and the political context in which it was employed, has led to a criticism of the TRC that its "privileging of particular violations" (torture, abductions, killings) and failure to examine sexual violence as a distinct category, "not ... just [through] the lens of torture but ... as a violation on its own,"[42] essentially failed women, "prov[ing] fertile ground for the gender violence that women face [in South Africa] today."[43] The next section considers this claim against the history of the TRC's design and creation, its multiple mandates, and the capacity of a transitional justice mechanism to stem the recurrence of sexual violence against women postconflict.

37 Rape Crisis Cape Town Trust, *Causes of Rape* (available at www.rapecrisis.org.za/rape-in-south-africa/) (accessed date November 20, 2017): "As South Africa began its transition to democracy in the early 1990s, it again saw a rapid increase in reported rapes and other violent crimes. Cases of reported rape increased from 27 056 in 1993 to a peak of 55 114 between April 2004 and March 2005."

38 Personal interview, 14SAIR (Cape Town, January 20, 2015).

39 Personal interview, 22SAMU (Stellenbosch, February 4, 2015).

40 Personal interview, 05SAOX (Johannesburg, January 13, 2015).

41 Ibid.

42 Personal interview, 23SAZT (Cape Town, February 5, 2015).

43 J. Seidman and N. Bonase, *Tsogang Basadi: finding women's voice from South Africa's political conflict* (July 6, 2016) (available at www.judyseidman.com/tsogang%20basadi%20paper.html) (accessed date November 20, 2017).

7.2.2. *The TRC: Blind to Gender Violence*

> Although there is no single definition of transitional justice ... predominant views construct human rights violations fairly narrowly to the exclusion of structural and gender-based violence.[44]

The complex negotiations that ultimately enabled South Africa's transition produced a number of "experimental institutions [which were the product] of political compromises."[45] The TRC's objectives, established by the Promotion of National Unity and Reconciliation Act 1995 (the TRC Act), were to encourage victims to make statements about the human rights violations they suffered under apartheid, to award amnesty to perpetrators in exchange for full disclosure of conduct associated with a political objective, and to make recommendations to the government on measures of reparation aimed at rehabilitating and restoring the "human and civil dignity" of victims.

The TRC's mandate to investigate and establish the nature, causes and extent of gross violations of human rights committed between 1960 and 1994 was the subject of extensive debate given the definitions and scope of the TRC Act. "Gross violations of human rights" were defined as "the violation of human rights through the killing, abduction, torture or severe ill-treatment of any person."[46] The TRC Act defined victims as individuals who

> suffered harm in the form of physical or mental injury, emotional suffering, pecuniary loss or a substantial impairment of human rights (i) as a result of a gross violation of human rights; (ii) or as a result of an act associated with a political objective for which amnesty has been granted.[47]

Despite evidence that sexual violence was used to "undermine resistance and enforce political acquiescence,"[48] during the period of focus for the TRC, it was not accorded a distinct category of human rights violation within the TRC legislation.

One justification for this omission was that "rape was such a horrible personal crime that it couldn't possibly be considered a political crime for which

[44] R. Nagy, "Transitional justice as global project: critical reflections" (2008) 29 *Third World Quarterly* 275–89 at 276.

[45] Personal interview, 23SAZT (Cape Town, February 5, 2015).

[46] TRC Act. The definition of "severe ill-treatment" evolved to include violations such as rape, sexual assault and abuse, and sexual harassment. See, TRC, *Report* vol. 1, and "Coding frame for gross violations of human rights" at vol. 5.

[47] The TRC received statements from 21,290 people and held that more than 19,050 were victims of a gross violation of human rights with a further 2975 emerging from the amnesty process. See, TRC, *Final Report* vol. 7, pt. 1, para. 1.

[48] C. Nordstrom, *A Different Kind of War Story* (Philadelphia, PA: University of Pennsylvania Press, 1997) 148.

amnesty [could be granted]."[49] This decontextualizing of "the act [of rape] from a situation of systemic violence and terror"[50] allowed the delinking of what was considered "ordinary" or common crime from "extraordinary" or political violence.[51] This severing further permitted an assessment that either accepted sexual violence as the norm or denied its extent:

> It comes from two perspectives: one is so, it happened – it's just par for the course; but, on the other side, it's also the refusal to admit that it could have happened.[52]

The TRC's focus on forgiveness and the influence of Archbishop Desmond Tutu's "orientation towards reconciliation," and the "creation of a collective narrative ... even at the expense of a forensic truth,"[53] might have played a role in understating the extent of sexual violence in the Commission's account of apartheid.

Additionally, to demonstrate that an act of sexual violence had a political

> objective required proof and consequently, the responsibility got put back on the women to prove it was a political act ... The fact that six soldiers in uniform came into your house in the middle of the night and raped you, and raped your sister, and your daughter, does it make it a political act?[54]

While a perpetrator's admission of sexual violence might have thwarted a grant of amnesty, a victim's ordeal of proving such violence was often their rationale for silence. These two factors "colluded"[55] to maintain minimal exposure of systemic sexual violence before the TRC. For some women who might have testified, particularly those who held public positions, "giving evidence before the Commission [was seen] as giving public evidence"; for others, guarantees of private hearings were insufficient as "they wanted to be seen as strong, competent, healed women, even if they weren't."[56] The reluctance to talk about

49 Personal interview, 03SANK (Johannesburg, January 12, 2015).

50 J. Boesten, "The state and violence against women in Peru: intersecting inequalities and patriarchal rule" (2012) 19 *Social Politics* 361–82 at 368.

51 Kusafuka, "Truth commissions and gender"; Personal interview, 15SAIN (Cape Town, January 20, 2015): "[In] South Africa ... political violence didn't take on quite the overt gender dimension that it did in many ... other countries, [where] for example, mass rape is part of that dynamic. There was a sense of gender violence being much more just the norm."

52 Personal interview, 23SAZT (Cape Town, February 5, 2015); Personal interview, 14SAIR (Cape Town, January 20, 2015): "If you talked to any of the TRC commissioners, they still don't really believe that rape was used as a political tool. They don't believe the apartheid police were using it ... that intimidation of a sexual nature was the norm."

53 R. E. Howard-Hassmann and A. P. Lombardo, *Reparations to Africa* (Philadelphia, PA: University of Pennsylvania Press, 2008) 163.

54 Personal interview, 03SANK (Johannesburg, January 12, 2015).

55 A. Krog, *Country of My Skull* (London: Vintage, 1999) 277.

56 Personal interview, 18SANA (Cape Town, January 22, 2015).

sexual violence was often a consequence of the shame and stigma that might attach to women socially and culturally (within their families and community) or politically:

> You didn't want to be judged as that woman who was raped and not be taken seriously. [And if] you were going to be a government minister why would you want to be the government minister that was raped?[57]

The stigma was even more pronounced in cases where women were raped in the liberation camps: "to speak out against your experience at the hands of comrades was a betrayal."[58] And when women did testify before the TRC, "it's often been said that they [spoke] about their husbands and their sons, and their lovers, and their brothers, rather than about themselves."[59]

The political environment at the time of drafting the TRC Act might have further explained the omission of sexual violence from the categories of human rights violations. Although "during [constitutional] negotiations between the ANC and the apartheid government, the easiest area of commonality they found was patriarchy,"[60] the mobilization around issues of gender significantly influenced a constitution and bill of rights that incorporated a clear gender rights and equality dimension. This contribution was in large part due to

> the power of feminists within the ANC ... and the Women's National Coalition between 1992 and 1994 ... You had greater mobilization around the constitutional period than around the TRC period.[61]

The commitment to gender rights, however, did not permeate negotiations around the development of the TRC, perhaps due to the perception that the TRC was "a somewhat back-ward looking project":[62]

> If you look back at the way in which the constitution itself was written and who was intervening and who was engaged ... some of those intersectional

57 Personal interview, 14SAIR (Cape Town, January 20, 2015).

58 Personal interview, 18SANA (Cape Town, January 22, 2015).

59 Ibid. See also, F. C. Ross, "Using rights to measure wrongs: a case study of method and moral in the work of the South African Truth and Reconciliation Commission," in R. A. Wilson and J. P. Mitchell (eds.), *Human Rights in Global Perspective: Anthropological Studies of Rights, Claims and Entitlements* (New York, NY: Routledge, 2003).

60 Personal interview, 15SAIN (Cape Town, January 20, 2015). See also, A. Sachs, *Protecting Human Rights in a New South Africa* (Cape Town: Oxford University Press, 1990).

61 Personal interview, 09SAQH (Johannesburg, January 15, 2015).

62 B. Goldblatt, "Evaluating the gender content of reparations: lessons from South Africa" in R. Rubio-Marin (ed.), *What Happened to the Women? Gender and Reparations for Human Rights Violations* (New York, NY: Social Science Research Council, 2006) 53.

> thinkers were there ... The research ... was analyzed by the feminists and some of that went into the constitution itself through the Bill of Rights. But somehow [in] the setting up of the TRC Act, [it] was missed. I don't know how ... There was a critique but it came after the Act was already implemented.[63]

Priscilla Hayner notes that, although not a substitute for prosecution, truth commissions should ignite a "push for accountability, ... reinforce the rule of law and combat continued impunity."[64] Hayner also cautions that if truth commissions fail to address women's experiences of violence, these will "remain largely shrouded in silence and hidden from the history books."[65] The TRC amnesty provisions were perceived as a "very weak form of accountability,"[66] and the lack of prosecutions[67] "contributed to impunity as there's a sense of we're giving victims the voice and then we don't do anything about following up on prosecutions."[68] It appeared that much of the energy channeled into developing the TRC Act was employed to mediate issues of accountability in a framework that positioned amnesty as a core principle. An interviewee conceded:

> I was so focused on the question of how to avoid the amnesties and the accountability issue that, even though I was part of a women's movement, it didn't strike me to look for the gender dimensions in the truth commission law. [It] was quite a shock when I ... realized there was a real absence of reference to anything about gender-based violence and ... the women [civil society] very quickly pointed that out ... And it really became a big question: how were we going to address it?[69]

The failure to engage victims directly at the design stage of the TRC might have also undermined a focus on gender violence. When the draft legislation

[63] Personal interview, 12SATN (Johannesburg, January 16, 2015).

[64] P. B. Hayner, *Unspeakable Truths: Facing the Challenge of Truth Commissions* (New York, NY: Routledge, 2002) 202.

[65] Ibid. 79.

[66] Personal interview, 15SAIN (Cape Town, January 20, 2015).

[67] Of the 7,116 amnesty applications, over two-thirds (5,143) of the cases were rejected. Although 800 cases were forwarded to the National Prosecuting Authority, few have been prosecuted: South African History Archive and Historical Papers, "TRC Category – 3. Amnesty: Category Description," *Traces of Truth* (available at www.truth.wwl.wits.ac.za/cat_descr.php?cat=3) (accessed date November 20, 2017).

[68] Personal interview, 15SAIN (Cape Town, January 20, 2015).

[69] Personal interview, 23SAZT (Cape Town, February 5, 2015).

was debated in parliament, women's voices "were not the strongest ones being heard,"[70] and while consultation took place

> at the highest levels of the NGO leadership, religious leadership, nobody [was] talking to the victims direct ... who were actually at the forefront of the mass struggle and severely harmed in the process.[71]

In addition, despite the fairly "generous"[72] representation of women and "broad-minded and progressive" men on the TRC,

> the men slip[ped] back into old patterns. And [gender] just never made it to the top of the agenda. Part of that was a question of time and pressure to deliver work quickly, but I think we should have worked harder at doing that.[73]

The harm experienced by women was highlighted through work undertaken by a group of academics, lawyers and representatives from women's and victims' support NGOs, TRC staff and psychologists. Their submission to the TRC explored how the political violence of apartheid had distinct impacts on and consequences for women.[74] It recommended that the Commission adopt an "overall gender sensitive approach" to all aspects of its functions – amnesty, truth telling and reparations – and address the physical and psychological torture used against women, which "target[ed] [their] femininity and sexuality."[75] The recommendations in the submission and discussions with the TRC's Human Rights Violations Committee resulted in the Commission convening three special women's hearings[76] – in Cape Town (August 1996), Johannesburg (July 1997) and Durban (October 1996) – to elicit women's accounts of violations, particularly sexual violence.[77] Not all members of the TRC embraced this development and attempts to secure a budget for the hearings were met with "a kind of ... amused tolerance. Like, you know, 'Let ... these girls get on with it'."[78] Despite the provision of a safe forum and

70 Personal interview, 18SANA (Cape Town, January 22, 2015).
71 Personal interview, 03SANK (Johannesburg, January 12, 2015).
72 Personal interview, 18SANA (Cape Town, January 22, 2015).
73 Personal interview, 03SANK (Johannesburg, January 12, 2015).
74 Goldblatt and Meintjies, "Gender and the Truth and Reconciliation Commission."
75 Kusafuka, "Truth commissions and gender" 50.
76 A TRC statement released in August 1996 endorsed the special hearings and encouraged women "to break the silence" about their "abuse in a political context": African Studies Center, University of Pennsylvania, *South Africa: TRC and gender* (August 15, 1996) (available at www.africa.upenn.edu/Urgent_Action/apic_823.html) (accessed date November 20, 2017).
77 This testimony appears in volume 4 of the final report.
78 Personal interview, 23SAZT (Cape Town, February 5, 2015).

the design of gender-sensitive statement-taking protocols for women who preferred not to speak,[79] perhaps unsurprisingly, only a limited number of women testified before the all-women panel of commissioners.[80] Fear of incrimination, retaliation and humiliation, compounded by external factors of "impunity, lack of accountability,[81] the distortion of statistics, [and] the deeply entrenched patriarchy which continues," combined to inhibit women's participation in the hearings.[82] Even in a "safe" environment, there was no guarantee that women who testified would be spared the trauma that often accompanies such recounting.[83] Rather than restoring their "human and civil dignity," the experience often left women feeling "a loss of dignity."[84] Although "creating one sort of safe forum right after the end of apartheid isn't going to uncover what actually went on, … for the most part," the TRC did, however, perform a "critical role … in claiming a story about our past that would be undisputable … [and] it had a healing function."[85]

While the women's hearings offered the TRC a "non-gendered way of dealing with the testimonies of women"[86] and ensured that its final report did not hide or excise women's experience of sexual violence "from the history books," some commentators viewed the hearings as "tacked on as an afterthought:"[87]

> [They were] intended to allow women to speak freely and deal with the private nature [of sexual violence] and the prurient watchers. But I think perhaps it would have been better to have a careful analysis of why and how, and what the outcomes were … what their importance was going to be.[88]

79 From April 1997, the TRC statement-taking form contained the following: "IMPORTANT: … Don't forget to tell us what happened to you yourself if you were the victim of a gross human rights abuse": Statement Concerning Gross Violations of Human Rights, Version 5 (1997), 3. TRC, *Report*, vol. 4, ch. 10, para. 5.

80 "Some women made statements but could ultimately not bring themselves to appear before the hearings." See, B. Goldblatt and S. Meintjes, "Dealing with the aftermath: Sexual violence and the Truth and Reconciliation Commission" (1997) 13(36) *Agenda* 7–18 at 9.

81 See J. Duarte, quoted in B. Goldblatt and S. Meintjes, "Dealing with the aftermath": "The woman knows that in coming forward to say so-and-so raped me that she may not necessarily see justice being done" (at 11).

82 Personal interview, 17SASN (Cape Town, January 21, 2015).

83 Ibid.

84 TRC, *Report*, vol. 4, ch. 10, para. 44. At the special hearings, women could choose to testify on-camera before a women-only panel of commissioners.

85 Personal interview, 25AusCH (Sydney, Australia, February 19, 2015).

86 Personal interview, 17SASN (Cape Town, January 21, 2015).

87 Personal interview, 06SAFC (Johannesburg, January 14, 2015).

88 Personal interview, 18SANA (Cape Town, January 22, 2015).

The criticism that the women's hearings, however important, were an "add-on" and failed to inculcate a gendered analysis by the TRC commissioners overall, was also made in relation to the TRC's inclusion of the women's testimonies in its final report, "relegated to a [short] chapter at the end."[89] Perhaps more significantly, the report failed

> to integrate the issues that [NGOs and academics] had raised around gender into an analysis of why society was so violent and so masculinist ... [And] what generates violence ... sexual violence in particular.[90]

However, in the absence of this critical initiative by academics and NGOs, the TRC report might have been completely silent about "women's experiences in the political conflicts of the past."[91] Indeed, the final report on the Findings and Conclusions of the Committee on Human Rights Violations acknowledged that women "suffered direct gross violations of human rights, many of which were gender specific in their exploitative and humiliating nature."[92] Additionally, the TRC held the state responsible for the "severe ill treatment of women in custody" and for their abuse by

> security forces in ways which specifically exploited their vulnerabilities as women, for example [by] rape or threats of rape and other forms of sexual abuse, ... and humiliation and abuse around biological functions such as menstruation and childbirth.[93]

It acknowledged that "women in exile, particularly those in camps, were subjected to various forms of sexual abuse and harassment, including rape,"[94] and noted that although

> rape formed part of the fabric of political conflict in the East Rand townships and in the bloody battles in KwaZulu-Natal during the early nineties, it was infrequently reported in HRV [human rights statements] to the Commission.[95]

89 B. Goldblatt and S. Meintjes, "Women: One chapter in the history of South Africa? A critique of the Truth and Reconciliation Commission Report" (paper presented at the CSVR/History Workshop Conference: *The TRC: Commissioning the Past*, University of the Witwatersrand, South Africa, June 11–14, 1999).

90 Personal interview, 12SATN (Johannesburg, January 16, 2015).

91 TRC, *Report*, vol. 7, pt 1, at 9. Although TRC researcher Vanessa Barolsky was commissioned to draft an extensive report on "gender and gross human rights violations," her draft was "sparingly and fragmentally incorporated in the TRC's final report." See, Kusafuka, "Truth commissions and gender" 59, 60.

92 TRC, *Report* (n. 5) vol. 5, ch. 6, para. 161.

93 Ibid.

94 Ibid.

95 TRC, *Report*, vol. 7, pt 1, 8.

These observations clearly underscore the TRC's admission that it failed to "adequately capture the story of thousands of women ... who experienced the brutality of the apartheid system," including sexual torture.[96] Despite these acknowledgments and urgings from women's groups and academics to the Reparation and Rehabilitation Committee that they draw on the testimony of women when determining reparations recommendations for reparations,[97] the TRC's report gave "limited consideration" to "women's special needs and interests"[98] and failed to specifically address the harm suffered by victims of sexual violence. The only apparent, and disappointing, reference to any form of targeted assistance appears in the TRC's Administrative Report on the implementation of categories of reparation. Under a provision on referrals to government departments, the report minimally recommends that "provincial networks on violence against women coordinate related services to abused women."[99]

Although the special hearings and the findings of the Committee on Human Rights Violations gave some consolation, thousands of women – victims of violence in townships, prisons, police stations and liberation camps – were unable to "give voice to their past" due to social, cultural and political constraints; physical distance from the hearings, particularly for rural women; illiteracy or lack of information; and the multiple and enduring manifestations of the violence which rendered articulation of their harm "unspeakable."[100] This explicable absence of testimony from women, "to talk about what had happened to [them] as ... women,"[101] speaks more critically to the magnitude of its impact rather than the scale of its prevalence. It also suggests important indicators of focus for the design, content and implementation of measures of redress and reparation and questions a reliance on victims' testimony to shape reparations directed at transforming the conditions that enable the perpetuation of the violence.

Given that the long-term impact of sexual violence can erode the capacity to speak and preclude effective participation in postconflict life, it became apparent from the interviews that the TRC would have needed to "bring [women's] extreme experiences of negation into the realm of

96 Ibid.

97 The TRC reparations policy provided for urgent interim, individual, symbolic, community and institutional measures of reparation.

98 Kusafuka, "Truth commissions and gender" 63.

99 TRC, *Report*, vol. 6, sec 2, ch. 8, para. 29 (2), 171.

100 T. L. Tompkins, "Prosecuting rape as a war crime: speaking the unspeakable" (1995) 70 *Notre Dame Law Review* 845–90 at 852.

101 Personal interview, 24SAGN (Cape Town, February 6, 2015).

representation"[102] for any effective exploration of violence against women. The inability to do so was perhaps because

> we didn't develop the language for it [sexual violence]. That was a moment to do it. It would have been a radical act and ... a historical act, and it would have contributed to enabling some process post the TRC.[103]

The omission of sexual violence as a primary category of gross violations of human rights in the founding legislation of the TRC was not due to "the drafters intentionally leav[ing] out those clauses. It's how we've normalized patriarchy ... as though it's natural."[104] And its exclusion as an "act associated with a political objective" and as a violation warranting distinct measures of reparation "was a lost opportunity reflect[ing] the inability of progressive forces to grasp the seriousness of the issue."[105]

7.3. REPARATIVE TRANSFORMATION: PREVENTING THE PAST BY TRANSFORMING THE FUTURE

> Rape, like genocide, will not be deterred unless and until the stories are heard. People must hear the horrifying, think the unthinkable and speak the unspeakable.[106]

> A lot of people got money ... and the money is finished. But they're still in the same spot.[107]

In postapartheid, democratic South Africa, "even after [the] forms of social stratification" have been evidently "dismantled or transformed in line with rights-based principles," the "racially ranked hierarchies" central to a system of enforced segregation have persisted with "profound implications for women and their experience of gender-based and sexual violence."[108] The final section of this chapter considers the capacity of transitional justice mechanisms, such as the TRC and the Constitutional Court, to transform entrenched manifestations of structural violence that continue to have damaging consequences for women postapartheid. It argues that the absence of recommendations by the TRC for

[102] N. Motsemme, "The mute always speak: on women's silences at the truth and reconciliation commission" (2004) 52 *Current Sociology* 909–32 at 916.
[103] Personal interview, 10SATI (Johannesburg, January 15, 2015).
[104] Personal interview, 24SAGN (Cape Town, February 6, 2015).
[105] Ibid.; personal interview, 10SATI (Johannesburg, January 15, 2015).
[106] Tompkins, "Prosecuting rape as a war crime."
[107] Personal interview, 01SAET (Johannesburg, January 12, 2015).
[108] H. Moffett, "'These women, they force us to rape them': rape as narrative of social control in post-apartheid South Africa" (2006) 32 *Journal of Southern African Studies* 129–44 at 131.

reparations aimed specifically at female victims of sexual violence – impeded to some degree by its failure to explicitly investigate the extent and impact of sexual violence against women during apartheid – has enabled a perpetuation of key "structural conditions" that continue to make women vulnerable to sexual violence.[109]

The Committee on Reparation and Rehabilitation was mandated to determine measures of reparation[110] and rehabilitate, to restore the "dignity of victims" and to make recommendations to the government "aimed at the prevention of the commission of gross violations of human rights."[111] The legislation defined reparations as including "any form of compensation, ex gratia payment, restitution, rehabilitation or recognition"[112] and distinguished between urgent and immediate measures of reparations and a broad, longer-term reparations policy. Only those who appeared before the TRC in public hearings or submitted a victim's statement before December 15, 1997 were eligible for reparations (known as a "closed-list" policy).[113] Unlike the Amnesty Committee, the Reparation and Rehabilitation Committee had no powers of enforcement and implementation of its recommendations was not guaranteed. Two key considerations influenced its final reparations and rehabilitation policy:[114] that reparations (and rehabilitation) were prerequisites for healing and reconciliation, and that these were necessary to counteract or offset the provision of amnesty.

The implementation of the reparations policy has been slow, sporadic and in some cases nonexistent.[115] One-off financial payments of compensation failed to differentiate between harm:

> [It] doesn't matter whether you suffered violence of a sexual nature ... whether your father disappeared or your cattle was stolen by the apartheid

109 Personal interview, 20SAER (Cape Town, January 23, 2015).

110 TRC Act ch. 5. The TRC's recommended reparations and rehabilitation policy contained five key components: redress, restitution, rehabilitation, restoration of dignity, and reassurance of nonrepetition. See, TRC, *Report*, vol. 6, sec. 2, ch. 1 at 93–4.

111 TRC Act, preamble.

112 Ibid. sec. 1.

113 See, TRC, *Report*, vol. 6, sec. 5, ch. 7 at 732.

114 TRC, *Report*, vol. 6, sec. 2, ch. 2 at 100–111.

115 The President's Fund, established in 2003 to fund reparations, had an initial allocation of R800 million from the South African government and additional contributions from foreign governments. Many victims identified by the TRC as eligible for reparations "have still received nothing. Some have died waiting." M. Gontsana, "Over R1 Billion in Fund – Yet Apartheid Victims Still Await Compensation," *GroundUp* (November 5, 2013) (available at www.groundup.org.za/article/over-r1-billion-fund-yet-apartheid-victims-still-await-compensation/) (accessed date November 20, 2017).

> government ... you [got] 30,000 [South African rand].[116] How does that deal with gender violence, which is both psychological and material?[117]

Although the TRC did uncover acts of sexual violence against women, the lack of this specific category of violation in the TRC legislation, combined with comparatively low numbers of women testifying to this violence,[118] appears to have influenced the absence of TRC reparations recommendations to redress and prevent sexual violence. Moreover, calls on the government to fund reparations for victims of apartheid and to "have regard to the 'untold suffering' of individuals and families whose fundamental rights had been invaded during the conflict of the past"[119] have had to compete with the government's broader notion of reparations, defined by the social and economic imperatives of the reconstruction and development of a deeply unequal society. The government's reliance on arguments favoring a development agenda as a way of subsuming reparations[120] or discounting their validity undermined the specific "challenges that victims face"[121] and failed to provide a measure of justice that "targets the form of violence"[122] and which "the victim can recognize as restorative."[123]

The Nairobi Declaration is clear in its aspiration that the goals of reparative justice for women and girl survivors of violence postconflict move beyond compensatory, restorative and rehabilitative measures and "drive postconflict transformation of [the] socio-cultural injustices, and political and structural inequalities that shape the lives of women and girls."[124] The Declaration further asserts that "reintegration and restitution by themselves are not sufficient goals of reparation, since the origins of violations of women's and girls' human rights predate the conflict situation."[125] This idea was subsequently echoed in the *Cotton Fields* judgment by the Inter-American Court of Human Rights,

[116] On April 15, 2003, then South African president Thabo Mbeki announced payment of a once-off government grant of R30 000 (US$3900) to 22 000 victims designated by the TRC.

[117] Personal interview, 07SAUN (Pretoria, January 14, 2015).

[118] The TRC heard testimonies about rape from 140 women. T. A. Borer, "Gendered war and gendered peace: Truth Commissions and Post-Conflict Gender Violence: Lessons from South Africa" (2009) 15 *Violence against Women* 1169–93.

[119] *Azanian People's Organization (AZAPO)* v. *President of the Republic of South Africa* (1996) 4 SA 671 (July 25, 1996) at para. 45.

[120] Personal interview, 14SAIR (Cape Town, January 20, 2015).

[121] Personal interview, 03SANK (Johannesburg, January 12, 2015).

[122] Personal interview, 11SAUL (Johannesburg, January 15, 2015).

[123] Personal interviews 13SAGU (Cape Town, January 19, 2015).

[124] "Nairobi Declaration on Women's and Girls' Right to a Remedy and Reparation" (drafted at the *International Meeting on Women's and Girls Right to a Remedy and Reparation*, March 19–21, 2007) at para. 3.

[125] Ibid.

which articulated the necessary effect of reparations for women victims of sexual violence to be "not only of restitution, but also of rectification," rejecting any "re-establishment of the same structural context of violence and discrimination" that facilitated the harm.[126] Former UN Special Rapporteur Rashida Manjoo argues that in addition to states' obligations to eliminate (or prevent) violence against women and girls and hold perpetrators to account, they must "ensure comprehensive reparations for women victims of violence and their relatives"[127] that "subvert instead of reinforce preexisting patterns of … structural subordination, gender hierarchies, systemic marginalization and structural inequalities"[128] that perpetuate violence against women.

Relying on the "cluster of interlinked fundamental rights treasured by our Constitution,"[129] the South African Constitutional Court has established and confirmed the state's obligation to prevent discrimination against women to protect their life, dignity, freedom and security.[130] Although most cases have concerned individual perpetrators with histories of committing sexually violent acts and the accountability of the state where, for example, they reoffend, the Court has established the clear principle that the state has a duty under the country's Constitution and international law to take steps to prevent sexual violence against women.[131] However, the reparative dimension of many of these cases is often, perhaps legitimately, confined to rehabilitative or remedial aspects of redressing individual harm. In considering a transformative approach toward addressing violence against women, the preventive dimension is critical. The challenge for courts is to focus at the

> institutional and structural levels … At the structural level, transformative remedies should help in some way to change the realities of people that are impacted. Do courts and judges understand the importance of transformative remedies? I think largely not.[132]

[126] *Case of Gonzáles et al. ("Cotton Field")* v. *Mexico* (preliminary objection, merits, reparations, and costs) I/ACourt H.R, ser. C no. 205 (November 16, 2009) para. 450.

[127] R. Manjoo, "Statement by Ms. Rashida Manjoo, special rapporteur on violence against women, its causes and consequences," (delivered at the Commission on the Status of Women: fifty-seventh session, New York, March 4, 2013) (available at www.un.org/womenwatch/daw/csw/csw57/statements/statement-rashida-manjoo.pdf) (accessed date November 20, 2017) 3.

[128] Ibid. para. 75.

[129] *F* v. *Minister of Safety and Security* (2012) 1 SA 536 (CC).

[130] *Constitution of the Republic of South Africa 1996*, s. 12(1)(c): "everyone has the right to freedom and security of the person, which includes the right to be free from all forms of violence from either public or private sources."

[131] *Carmichele* v. *Minister of Safety and Security* (2001) 4 SA 938 (CC); *S* v. *Baloyi (Minister of Justice Intervening)* (2000) 2 SA 425 (CC).

[132] Personal interview, 17SASN (Cape Town, January 21, 2015).

Manjoo has noted that reparations aimed at "non-recurrence ... trigger a discussion ... about the broader institutional or legal reforms that might be called for to ensure non-repetition."[133] In the current South African context, rather than "trying to overload reparations to play the transformative role,"[134] our empirical research demonstrated support for an approach that seeks to "trigger the discussion" to which Manjoo refers. Interviewees were overwhelmingly of the view that a critical precursor to and component of reparations directed at transforming the structural conditions that enable sexual violence against women, is an acknowledgment of the violence and its impact on women's lives "that does something for the self-esteem or the self-healing of the individual [and] can then lead to talking about systemic, structural aspects."[135] Following acknowledgment and analysis, the resetting of norms that facilitate the violence, such as normalization and resignation, becomes possible, as does the design of reparations directed at the nonrepetition of harm.

In 2013, following the rape and murder of seventeen-year-old Anene Booysen in the Western Cape, a group of NGOs led by Sonke Gender Justice wrote to President Jacob Zuma requesting a government inquiry into sexual violence:

> We issued a call for a national commission of inquiry on gender-based violence ... We know enough about the causes of violence ... So we really wanted to convene a commission that helped us understand people's experience with the failure of the state to act on its obligations.[136]

Despite some "pushback" at the time from civil society groups[137] fatigued and disappointed by the government's consistent failure to act on recommendations of commissions of inquiry and of the TRC, most interviewees endorsed the idea of a special commission or tribunal, designed, implemented and conducted by women to expose the extent, nature and impact of sexual violence and the failure of government to address a national crime. While impetus for the mechanism was evident and viewed as essential for "the flourishing of all people, particularly women, to contribute economically and socially, and

[133] R. Manjoo, Report of the special rapporteur on violence against women, its causes and consequences, Rashida Manjoo, UN Doc. A/HRC/14/22 (April 23, 2010), 26.

[134] Personal interview, 15SAIN (Cape Town, January 20, 2015).

[135] Personal interview, 17SASN (Cape Town, January 21, 2015).

[136] Personal interview, 16SAEQ (Cape Town, January 21, 2015). See also, Women under Siege, "Gender justice group urges South Africa's Zuma to create commission to stop sexualized violence" (February 13, 2013) *Women Under Seige Blog* (available at www.womenundersiegeproject.org/blog/entry/Gender-justice-group-urges-South-Africa-Zuma-to-create-commission) (accessed date November 20, 2017).

[137] Ibid.

politically to the country's development,"[138] many interviewees spoke of the need for women across South Africa to mobilize and rebuild a political base to ensure its long-term impact.

> We need to stand in solidarity across the board. So women who are employed standing with women who are unemployed. Women who are wealthy and middle-class standing with women who are poor. Women in urban areas standing with women in rural areas.[139]

7.4. CONCLUSION

Twenty years after the TRC was established as the key mechanism for "dealing with the past … for a lot of women, there's [been] no change from 1994 up to now. … They still live in fear."[140] The new democracy continues to wrestle with intergenerational violence spawned by apartheid and intergenerational trauma, often the consequence of unacknowledged harm. When a primary process seeking to chart the map for South Africa's transition omits to include a critical site for recognition and redress, such as sexual violence against women, development, transformation and reparation have little prospect of impacting on the restoration of the dignity of individuals who suffered harm or of contributing to a reduction and prevention of the violence.

Despite claims of "women's empowerment" that accompanied South Africa's political transition, this apparent enfranchisement of women has failed to translate into the transformation of women's lives, evidenced by "rape and other gender based violence statistics, rampant sexual harassment at work and public spaces, the siege on black lesbians and raging homophobia."[141] Luke Moffett argues that the "transformative potential of reparations rests in their ability to prioritise and publicise victimisation and underlying structural inequalities that precipitated or compounded violence."[142] As South Africa faces levels of sexual violence that rank among the highest in the world, the imperative to publicly acknowledge, examine and prioritize the "underlying structural inequalities that precipitated or compounded" sexual violence against women, has surfaced as a critical first step in developing reparations

[138] Personal interview, 08SACN (Johannesburg, January 15, 2015).

[139] Personal interview, 09SAQH (Johannesburg, January 15, 2015).

[140] Personal interview, 07SAUN (Pretoria, January 14, 2015).

[141] Gqola, "Cult of femininity" at 115.

[142] L. Moffett, "Transitional Justice and Reparations: Remedying the Past?," School of Law Research Paper No. 201506, Queen's University Belfast, School of Law Research Paper No. 2015-06, 10.

that are appropriate in design and transformative in substance. A precursor to and component of such reparations is national acknowledgment of the impact of violence on women's lives. Failure to name the violence and recognize its debilitating impact on society, particularly on women victims, risks entrenching a destructive silence and facilitating a perception of violence as routine.

The "hierarchies" of harm investigated by the TRC inhibited a comprehensive examination of sexual violence: "community violence or the political violence [was] justified violence and other violence had less of a say."[143] The inclusion of gender equity principles in South Africa's Bill of Rights, the establishment of the CGE and the implementation of legislation to promote equality and address sexual offences and domestic violence have "perhaps [meant] that it's now more part of the national conversation."

> There's a constitution that guides people and [an] understanding [of] what their rights are more and more, especially within gender violence issues [and] we're able to start articulating what they are ... We talk about it more. But we're just failing to respond to it.[144]

Establishing a public process that would invite the nation to revisit the enduring impact and persistence of violence against women in a post-TRC South Africa has the potential to begin "transforming gender norms, not just ... transforming services for survivors."[145] In addition, it would reach beyond the women who testified before the TRC and recognize those "who had been excluded, marginalized, or silenced under the previous regime"[146] and were now able to "give voice to their past"[147] and "talk about what had happened to [them] as wom[en]."[148]

Although the TRC opened up the possibility of documenting the prevalence and impact of sexual violence, most victims were absent from the process. While those identified as victims under the TRC process could point to the harm, they were not fully representative of its multiple forms and effects.[149] It is envisaged that the public process described above – designed and implemented by civil society organizations and specialists in the fields of women's rights; gender violence; transitional justice; social, economic

143 Personal interview, 05SAOX (Johannesburg, January 13, 2015).

144 Personal interview, 01SAET (Johannesburg, January 12, 2015).

145 Personal interview, 16SAEQ (Cape Town, January 21, 2015).

146 Rosemary Nagy, "Post-apartheid justice: Can cosmopolitanism and nation-building be reconciled?" (2006) 40 *Law & Society Review* 623–52.

147 Motsemme, "The mute always speak" at 915.

148 Personal interview, 24SAGN (Cape Town, February 6, 2015).

149 Kusafuka, "Truth commissions and gender."

and cultural rights and psychosocial trauma – would provide the space for discussion and analysis of the structural causes of the violence, its gendered manifestations and the obligations of the state. It would also revisit some of the critical writings and ideas that emerged from the work of the TRC[150] and initiate the deliberation and planning essential to the design of transformative measures that might serve the objective of a nonrepetition of harm.

That victims are central to the design and content of reparations directed at compensation, restitution, rehabilitation and satisfaction is unquestioned. However, the progressive and transient manifestation of sexual violence over time, the intergenerational trauma associated with this form of violence and its crippling effects on productive lives suggest that transformative reparations aimed at preventing the recurrence of such violence require the parallel participation and investment of multiple players from different disciplines and perspectives if reparations are to erode systematic forms of inequality. This assessment accords with the International Criminal Court's decision in the case of *Lubanga*, with the Trial Chamber noting that the complex consequences of crimes of sexual violence, which "operate on a number of levels" with enduring impact, "require a specialist, integrated and multidisciplinary approach."[151]

This transformative approach to formulating reparations is directed at a postconflict society where "the scars of its past are still very much alive in its [contemporary] social fabric"[152] and where the country's capacity and commitment to implement compensatory and restorative reparations, have been negligible and insubstantial.[153] The proposed process sees the development of reparations move away from "an individualized context"[154] and "beyond

[150] Many of which I draw on in this article, as reflected in the work of Barolsky, Goldblatt and Meintjes and in the confidential interviews conducted for this study.

[151] *Situation in the Democratic Republic of the Congo in the Case of the Prosecutor* v. *Thomas Lubanga Dyilo* (International Criminal Court, Trial Chamber I, Case No. ICC-01/04-01/06, August 7, 2012) 72 para. 207.

[152] Office of the United Nations High Commissioner for Human Rights, *Special Rapporteur on violence against women, its causes and consequences finalizes country visit to South Africa* (December 11, 2015) (available at www.ohchr.org/EN/NewsEvents/Pages/DisplayNews.aspx?NewsID=16877&LangID=E) (accessed date November 20, 2017).

[153] As partially argued in M. U. Walker, "Transformative reparations? A critical look at a current trend in thinking about gender-just reparations" (2016) 10 *International Journal of Transitional Justice* 108–25.

[154] M. Turshen, "The political economy of war: what women need to know" in D. Buss et al. (eds.), *Sexual Violence in Conflict and Post-Conflict Societies: International Agendas and African Contexts* (Abingdon: Routledge, 2014) 28.

[women's] victim status"[155] into the realm of broad-based social, economic and political planning to allow women

> to have a full, dignified life, regardless of what characteristics [they] may carry. You do not need to have been raped in order to have a society in which you are protected from rape.[156]

The contribution by victims' support groups and women's organizations, economists, health practitioners and psychologists, educators, artists, human rights and gender advocates, lawyers and sociologists to this initiative can usefully assist to craft "reparations that drive postconflict transformation of sociocultural injustices, and political and structural inequalities that shape the future lives of women and girls."[157] The process envisaged – a national commission on violence against women – is directed at a "locally grounded process of social change ... to foster dialogue about, and help contribute to, a long-term, endogenous gender justice agenda" and build on appropriate "pre-existing priorities, programmes and advocacy efforts"[158] of government and NGOs.

> The pain and the grief and the damage goes on ... for a lifetime. That you can get over it and live with it but it doesn't ever leave you alone completely. So how can reparations, financial or other practical reparations, make a difference? I think "transformative" is really the perfect word because it has to change the society. It has to change the world you live in. Then maybe you can believe that what you went through ... is not going to happen again. It's not going to happen to your daughter and your sister, and your granddaughter, and so on. That's got to be the transformative aspect of it.[159]

[155] Personal interview, 10SATI (Johannesburg, January 15, 2015).

[156] Ibid.

[157] Nairobi Declaration.

[158] L. Kent, "Narratives of suffering and endurance: coercive sexual relationships, truth commissions and possibilities for gender justice in Timor-Leste," (2014) 8 *International Journal of Transitional Justice* 289–313 at 312.

[159] Personal interview, 18SANA (Cape Town, January 22, 2015).

8

The Constitutional Goal of Transforming Education: The South African Constitutional Court in Comparative Perspective

Julie C. Suk

South Africa's 1996 Constitution was intended to consolidate the transition from apartheid to democracy, based on principles of equality and nondiscrimination. Apartheid was significantly manifested in enormous inequalities in education. So, the constitutional right to education in section 29 of the 1996 Constitution, as well as the guarantees of equality and nondiscrimination in section 9, were central to the Constitution's project of transformation and the transition to democracy.[1] In evaluating the performance of South Africa's constitution, the reduction of inequality in educational opportunity and achievement is thus a self-declared internal goal[2] by which its success can be measured. Taken together, the constitutional guarantee of equality and the constitutional right to education were written to dismantle the regime of unequal education by reducing inequality. This chapter assesses the success of the constitutional right to education with regard to the South African Constitution's internal goal of transformation. Success must be understood and measured in relation to the apartheid past and not abstractly based on educational adequacy or performance alone. Thus, the success of the constitutional right to education in South Africa would be defined, in light of the project of transformation, as the eradication of educational inequalities stemming from apartheid. Partial

[1] In its education rights cases, the South African Constitutional Court has acknowledged the importance of these rights to the nation's post-apartheid transition to democracy. See, e.g., *Hoërskool Ermelo, Head of Department, Mpumalanga Department of Education* v. *Hoërskool Ermelo* [2010] 2 SA 415 (CC).

[2] In the project, *Assessing the Performance of the South African Constitution*, David Bilchitz et al. identify the fundamental transformation of South African society as a broad internal goal of the 1996 constitution, which includes an ambitious vision of social justice. See D. Bilchitz et al., *Assessing the Performance of the South African Constitution* (International Institute for Democracy and Electoral Assistance, 2016) 8. See also Bilchitz's chapter in this volume.

success could be identified when these inequalities are disrupted and reduced through constitutional enforcement.

During apartheid, white South Africans had a monopoly over high-quality schools, and the best educational resources were seldom within the reach of nonwhites.[3] Poor black children were formally excluded from good schools, and many were and continue to be educated in low-quality schools that lack basic infrastructure and necessities such as running water and textbooks. Recent litigation, enforcing both the constitutional right to education as well as statutory rights under the South Africa Schools Act, has challenged many different manifestations of education inequality. Some cases enforcing the right to basic education in courts have focused on whether the most disadvantaged students are receiving an adequate basic education; these cases have focused on the lack of infrastructure, and, when successful, have required government actors to provide running water, electricity and textbooks so that the poorest students can receive an education that more closely approximates an adequate basic education.[4] Other cases have focused on opening up access to the high-quality schools that were exclusively white during apartheid.[5] This litigation attempts to broaden access to the best schools, rather than improve the baseline of the worst schools. These cases focus more on equality than on adequacy of education. This chapter analyzes the cases concerned with education equality in comparative context.

Reducing inequality by diminishing unjustified privilege is one important way in which authoritarian societies attempt to transition to democracy. A new democratic constitutional order, founded on principles of equality, with guarantees of social rights including education, becomes an instrument of this transformation. Yet, attempts to do away with incumbent privilege come with heightened risks of resistance and backlash. When transformative constitutionalism is met with backlash, the legitimacy of the constitutional project and of the courts facilitating the transformation may be called into question. At the same time, the persistence of inequalities that can be traced to apartheid may

[3] See E. B. Fiske and H. E. Ladd, *Racial Equality in Education: How Far Has South Africa Come?* (Terry Stanford Institute of Public Policy, September 2004).

[4] See, e.g., *Minister of Basic Education* v. *Basic Education for All* [2015] ZASCA 198 (December 2, 2015) (holding that the right to basic education under s. 29(1)(a) requires the Department of Basic Education to provide a textbook in each subject to each learner at the beginning of each academic year.

[5] See *Hoërskool Ermelo, Head of Department, Mpumalanga Department of Education* v. *Hoërskool Ermelo* [2010] 2 SA 415 (CC) (*Hoërskool Ermelo*); *MEC for Education in Gauteng Province* v. *Governing Body of the Rivonia Primary School* [2013] 5 SA 582. See discussion at infra, text accompanying nn. 19–34.

also threaten the legitimacy of a constitution that consciously aimed to end apartheid.

In evaluating the success of South Africa's constitutional education rights from the internal criterion of postapartheid transformation, a comparative perspective can illuminate the dynamics of resistance. The experience of United States ("US") courts' attempts to enforce equality in public education illustrates how the dynamics of resistance can influence and distort the constitutional order's articulation of its own internal goals and criteria of success. *Brown* v. *Board of Education* introduced a transformative conception of the Equal Protection Clause as requiring the racial integration of public schools, but sixty years afterwards, very few American public schools are actually integrated. Yet, the persistence of racial separation and academic achievement gaps does not necessarily signal the failure of the American Equal Protection Clause, largely because, from 1954 to the present, the Supreme Court abandoned the transformative ideal of equal education as real integration. Responding in part to the backlash against courts' integration remedies, the Court substantively redefined the goal of Equal Protection in education more modestly, to require only desegregation and nondiscrimination as distinct from the more ambitious goals of integration and the eradication of de facto segregation.

A growing literature documents the persistence of racial disparities in American public education six decades after *Brown*. Recent studies document both the persistence of academic achievement gaps between black and white students at all levels, as well as patterns of de facto segregation. As for the black–white achievement gap, the gap in reading and math scores has not decreased significantly since 1965.[6] A new study indicates that in both math and reading, the national test-score gap in 1965 was 1.1 standard deviations. The average black student, in the final year of high school, placed at the 13th percentile of the score distribution for white students in math. Fifty years later, the average black student is only at the 19th percentile of the white distribution. A similar gap exists in reading test scores. If progress occurs at roughly the same pace, it will take two and a half centuries to close the black-white math score gap.[7]

In addition, white and black students are generally not educated in racially integrated settings. Recent reports suggest that black children in the American South are twice as likely today than they were forty years ago to attend a school

6 See E. A. Hanushek, "What matters for student achievement: updating Coleman on the influence of families and schools" (Spring 2016) 16(2) *Education Next* 18–26 at 19, 21.

7 Ibid.

in which at least nine out of ten students are racial minorities.[8] A 2014 study of New York City schools by the UCLA Civil Rights Project declared it "home to the largest and one of the most segregated public school systems in the nation."[9] In New York City, a third of public schools serve more than 80 percent white students, and another third serves less than 40 percent white students. Ninety percent of black students in New York attended majority-minority schools in 2010, that is, schools with 50 percent or greater minority students. A majority of these students (75 percent) attended schools with 90 percent or greater minority students. The transformative goal of integration has not been achieved.

Read alongside the U.S. Supreme Court's desegregation cases, the South African Constitutional Court's education equality cases illustrate a different path of doctrinal response to the practical realities of white resistance to the actual prospect of integrating their own children. In both South Africa and the United States, constitutional education litigation has sought, inter alia, to open up access to good schools. If successful, this litigation proposes to alter and perhaps constrain the educational landscape of the currently privileged. Hence, the highly salient risk of resistance and backlash. Courts may be ill-equipped to deal with the wrath and flight of incumbently privileged parents who make reasonable efforts to optimize the educational opportunities of their offspring. While the U.S. Supreme Court retreated from the transformative approach attempted by *Brown* v. *Board of Education* in the face of resistance to strong judicial remedies, the South African Constitutional Court has sustained a transformative vision of postapartheid constitutional education rights by employing weak remedies accompanied by strong norm articulation.

8.1. THE CONSTITUTIONAL RIGHT TO EDUCATION AFTER APARTHEID

For the framers of the 1996 Constitution, education was a central domain in which apartheid was to be dismantled. In addition to principles of nonracialism,[10] equal citizenship,[11] equal protection and nondiscrimination,[12] human

[8] N. Hannah-Jones, "Segregation Now" (May 2014) *The Atlantic Monthly* (available at www.theatlantic.com/magazine/archive/2014/05/segregation-now/359813/) (accessed date November 20, 2017).

[9] J. Kucsera, *New York State's Extreme School Segregation: Inequality, Inaction and a Damaged Future* (UCLA Civil Rights Project, March 26, 2014).

[10] Constitution of the Republic of South Africa 1996, s. 1(b).

[11] Ibid. s. 3(2).

[12] Ibid. s. 9.

dignity,[13] and the best interests of children, education rights are specifically enumerated[14] in the constitutional text. In addition to the constitutional guarantee of the right to a basic education, the South African Schools Act, also adopted in 1996, established a "new national system for schools which will redress past injustices in educational provision."[15] The statute prohibits unfair discrimination in admission to public schools,[16] and provides that learners may not be refused admission to a public school on the grounds that their parents are unable to pay school fees.[17] Twenty years onward, while official policies of racial apartheid are no longer in force, racial disparities persist: black South African students significantly underperform white students academically, and are more likely to attend schools that are under-resourced and academically deficient than white South Africans. Numerous studies document the black–white academic achievement gap in South Africa by various measures.[18] In addition, despite being somewhat integrated, high-quality schools have an over-representation of whites as compared to whites' proportion of the learner population.

Although the United States is sixty years past the moment at which the Supreme Court declared racial segregation in education unconstitutional, and South Africa is only twenty years past constitutional and statutory repudiation of racial apartheid in education, commentators are observing the same phenomenon in both countries: decades after the official policies of segregation or apartheid were abandoned, racial inequalities in education persist, as measured by academic achievement or by the degree of integration. Should this state of affairs be understood as a constitutional failure in either or both countries?

In just the last few years, several decisions of the South African Constitutional Court have invoked the right to basic education to challenge some educational

[13] Ibid. s. 10.

[14] Section 29 provides, inter alia, that everyone has a right to a basic education, and the right to receive education in the official language or languages of their choice: see ibid. s. 29.

[15] South African Schools Act 1996, preamble ("SASA" or "Schools Act").

[16] SASA ch. 2(5)(1).

[17] SASA ch. 2(5)(3)(1).

[18] See, e.g., E. Fiske and H. Ladd, *Racial Equality in Education: How Far Has South Africa Come?* (Working Paper, Terry Sanford Institute of Public Policy, Duke University, 2004); T. B. Heaton, A. Y. Aomateng, and M. Dufur, "Race Differences in Educational Attainment in Post-Apartheid South Africa" (*Working paper*, Brigham Young University, 2012); S. van der Berg, "How effective are poor schools? Poverty and educational outcomes in South Africa," (2008) 34 *Studies in Educational Evaluation* 145–54; N. Spaull, "Poverty & privilege: primary school inequality in South Africa" (2013) 33 *International Journal of Educational Development* 436–47; Equal Education *Upcoming 2015 Matric Results Require Careful Scrutiny!* (Press Statement, January 2, 2016) (available at www.equaleducation.org.za/article/2016-01-03-upcoming-2015-matric-results-require-careful-scrutiny) (accessed date November 20, 2017).

practices that help maintain the over-representation of whites in excellent public suburban schools. These schools, formerly all-white schools during apartheid, engage in practices and policies that tend to limit the numbers of blacks admitted. The policies and practices are adopted by the schools' governing bodies, which are explicitly authorized to regulate the schools under the South Africa Schools Act. Since 2009, the South African Constitutional Court has elaborated the constitutional right to basic education and to education in the official language of one's choice to alter the power of school governing bodies over decisions that affect equal access to high-quality education. The South African Constitutional Court's strong articulation of the constitutional rights norms, accompanied by its cautious and light use of remedies, is paving an incremental path toward the transformative constitutional goal of education equality. When compared to the current American situation of education inequality and the lack of currently viable constitutional arguments to challenge its manifestations, the South African jurisprudence could be understood as a partial success.

The *Hoërskool Ermelo* case from 2009 is a good example. The *Ermelo* litigation challenged a high-quality public school's policy, adopted and maintained by the school's Governing Body, of designating Afrikaans as the only language of instruction.[19] Hoërskool Ermelo, despite its enviable academic record by many measures, had a declining enrollment, even as the town of Ermelo was growing. Surrounding public schools with English as the language of instruction were full beyond classroom capacity. In one English language school, students had to be accommodated in a converted laundry. Under these circumstances, the Mpumalanga Department of Education attempted to persuade the Governing Body of Hoërskool Ermelo to admit English-language learners and provide education in English. But the schools' Governing Body insisted on providing instruction only in Afrikaans. Eventually, the Head of the Mpumalanga Department of Education revoked the power of the school's Governing Body to set the language of instruction, and conferred the power on an interim body. The interim body altered the language policy to offer instruction in English and Afrikaans, and then admitted 113 learners to the school.

The litigation focused on the authority of the Head of Department (HoD) to constitute an interim committee to displace the school Governing Body's role in setting the language policy of the school. The HoD justified its actions

[19] Prior to the Constitutional Court's decision, Brahm Fleisch and Stuart Woolman argued that single-medium public schools raised constitutional problems from the standpoint of adequacy and equality of education: B. Fleisch and S. Woolman, "On the constitutionality of single-medium public schools" (2007) 23 *South African Journal on Human Rights* 34–67.

by invoking constitutional education rights. The Constitutional Court recognized that constitutional issues were at stake, responding to the HoD's concern that Hoërskool Ermelo's Afrikaans language policy had a disparate impact on learners who chose to be taught in English, who, in this case, were exclusively black learners.[20] While the school's Governing Body framed the case as a simple administrative-law matter as to who had authority to set language policy, the Constitutional Court explained the dispute's constitutional matrix in the following way:

> Apartheid has left us with many scars. The worst of these must be the vast discrepancy in access to public and private resources. The cardinal fault line of our past oppression ran along race, class and gender. It authorized a hierarchy of privilege and disadvantage. Unequal access to opportunity prevailed in every domain. Access to private and public education was no exception. While much remedial work has been done since the advent of constitutional democracy, sadly deep social disparities and resultant social inequity are still with us.[21]

Thus, while the issue is who has authority to set language policy in one school, the Constitutional Court suggests that this decision implicates the black–white academic achievement gap which remains twenty years after the end of apartheid:

> It is so that white public schools were hugely better resourced than black schools. They were lavishly treated by the apartheid government. It is also true that they were served and were shored up by relatively affluent white communities. On the other hand, formerly black public schools have been and by and large remain scantily resourced. They were deliberately funded stingily by the apartheid government. Also, they served in the main and were supported by relatively deprived black communities. That is why perhaps the most abiding and debilitating legacy of our past is an unequal distribution of skills and competencies acquired through education.[22]

Although the South Africa Schools Act section 6(2) clearly delegated to school governing bodies the power to determine a school's language of instruction, the Constitutional Court held that this power had to be exercised reasonably, taking into account other duties imposed by the Schools Act.[23] For instance,

[20] *Hoërskool Ermelo* para. 38.

[21] Ibid. para. 45.

[22] Ibid.

[23] Stuart Woolman suggests that *Ermelo* establishes the lack of a right to a single-medium public school under s. 29(2) of the Constitution. See S. Woolman, "Between norms and facts: The Constitutional Court's commitment to pluralism in South Africa's radically

section 3(3) of the statute imposes on the state the duty to ensure that there are enough school places for every child, and section 29(2) of the Constitution entitles every learner to receive education in the official language of one's choice. Also, very importantly, the Schools Act requires schools to admit learners without unfairly discriminating, and here, it is suggested that the school's refusal to offer English-language instruction under the circumstances disproportionately disadvantages blacks.

Yet, instead of framing the problem as one of unfair discrimination, the Court used the Constitution's section 29 education rights to articulate a duty of school governing bodies to act in the public interest, and not merely in the interests of its current stakeholders:

> A school cannot be seen as a static and insular entity. Good leaders recognize that institutions must adapt and develop. Their fiduciary duty, then, is to the institution as a dynamic part of an evolving society. The governing body of a public school must in addition recognize that it is entrusted with a public resource which must be managed not only in the interests of those who happen to be learners and parents at the time but also in the interests of the broader community in which the school is located and in the light of the values of our Constitution.[24]

The Court determined, based on its construction of the postapartheid normative grounding of education rights, that the newly admitted students to Hoërskool Ermelo were entitled to continue being taught in English through Grade 12.

Although the Constitutional Court did not explicitly develop a disparate impact construction of constitutional equality to arrive at its conclusions, the rhetoric about understanding basic education rights in light of apartheid only makes sense in this case in light of the Court's observation that the language policy had the "disparate impact" of excluding English-language learners who happened, in this case to be exclusively black.[25] These black learners were excluded from a ninety-three-year-old school that had an "excellent and enviable academic record"[26] and generous teacher–student ratios.[27] Prior to the HoD's interventions to enroll the English-language learners, the school had included only thirty-four black learners out of 685 enrolled.[28]

heterogeneous public schools" (2015) 18 *Potchefstroomse Elektroniese Regsblad* 2080–107 at 2089.

[24] *Hoërskool Ermelo* para. 80.

[25] Ibid. para. 38.

[26] Ibid. para. 1.

[27] Ibid. paras. 7–8.

[28] Ibid. para. 9.

While suggesting here that the Governing Body acted at odds with constitutional rights to receive basic education and to be taught in the language of choice, the Constitutional Court nonetheless declined to bless the particular procedure by which the HoD attempted to give effect to constitutional education rights, namely, by withdrawing the school's Governing Body's decision making power and constituting an interim committee that adopted a dual-language policy. HoD did not have the statutory power to withdraw a function from the school's Governing Body under a statutory provision that granted that power for enumerated reasons that did not include language policy. Another provision of the South Africa Schools Act (s. 25) authorizes the HoD to appoint a committee when a school's governing body fails to fulfill its functions. Here, the Constitutional Court noted that the Ermelo Hoërskool School Governing Body had not ceased to perform a function, nor had it failed to adopt a language policy. HoD did not like the language policy, and the language policy may have been unconstitutional, but this situation did not fall within the statute's authorization to HoD to constitute a new committee to make a new policy. In short, the Constitutional Court found fault with both the Hoërskool Ermelo's School Governing Body's language policy, and also with the unlawful manner by which the HoD attempted to impose a constitutionally acceptable one. Accordingly, the Constitutional Court invalidated the new language policy adopted by the HoD's illegitimately constituted interim committee – that of offering instruction in Afrikaans and English.

The Constitutional Court therefore gave effect to the learners' section 29 right to basic education in the language of choice without upholding the legitimacy of the interim committee's new dual language policy. In so doing, it imposed a constitutional duty on the school's Governing Body while also giving the HoD a slap on the wrist for attempting to enforce the constitutional duty. In addition, the Court's order enforcing the school's Governing Body's constitutional obligations did not dictate the same policy outcome as that adopted by the interim committee. The court simply issued an order directing the school's Governing Body to "reconsider the school language policy in the light of considerations set out in this judgment," and in a manner consistent with the Constitution and the Schools Act.[29] The school's Governing Body was required to report to the Court the steps it had taken to review its language policy and the outcome of the review process.[30] In addition, the Court ordered the HoD to file a report setting out the demand for grade eight English places, and the steps taken by the Education Department to satisfy this demand. The report was to include information and statistics on levels

[29] Ibid. para. 98.
[30] Ibid. para. 101.

of enrollment in other high schools in the area. In less than a month following the Constitutional Court's decision, the Chairman of Hoërskool Ermelo's Governing Body reported to the Constitutional Court that it would change its language policy to accommodate English-speaking pupils.[31]

The *Ermelo* case interpreted the statutory powers given to various institutions in the South Africa Schools Act as being constrained by the constitutional commitment to equal education. Since *Ermelo*, the Constitutional Court has read a school's governing body's powers under the South African Schools Act as being constrained by the duties arising from the constitutional rights of learners. These interpretations ultimately broaden access for more black learners to high-performing formerly white schools. In 2013, in *Member of the Executive Council for Education in Gauteng Province* v. *Governing Body of the Rivonia Primary School*, the Constitutional Court, using the right to basic education as its starting point, reached a ruling that upheld the Department of Education's power to instruct a primary school to admit a learner even when doing so exceeded the limit on the number of students articulated by the school's Governing Body. The *Rivonia* case continues the Constitutional Court's trajectory of imposing constitutional duties on a school's governing body, while also constraining the extent to which education authorities can interfere with a school's governing body to enforce constitutional rights on their own.

The *Rivonia* decision begins:

> Section 29 of the Constitution guarantees everyone the right to a basic education. That is a promise. In reality, a radically unequal distribution of resources – related to a history of systematic discrimination – still makes this constitutional guarantee inaccessible for large numbers of South Africans.[32]

The dispute centered on the admission policy of Rivonia Primary School, a school located in an affluent, historically white suburb.[33] As Jaftha J put it in his concurring opinion, "[t]his case concerns a little black girl whose dream was to obtain education at the school closest to her home."[34] The girl was placed on a waiting list for admission to the school because the school Governing Body had set the limit on the number of students for grade one at 120 learners. The mother of the child complained to the Gauteng Department

31 "School Welcomes English Pupils," *IOL News South Africa*, November 19, 2009.

32 *MEC for Education in Gauteng Province* v. *Governing Body of the Rivonia Primary School* [2013] 6 SA 582 (CC) para. 1 (*Rivonia*).

33 Ibid.

34 See *Rivonia* para. 82 (Jaftha J., concurring).

of Education, and the Department of Education determined that the school had room for an additional student and instructed the school to admit the child immediately. When the school Governing Body refused, a Department representative physically placed the student in a first-grade classroom at a desk which was unoccupied but intended for a child with learning disabilities. The HoD carried out the enrollment of this girl a few weeks after the school year had already begun.

In the decision below, the Supreme Court of Appeal had invalidated the actions of the Gauteng Education Department in enrolling the girl contrary to the school Governing Body's policy. The Supreme Court of Appeal did not recognize the salience of racial disparity to the issues in this case. It stated that the dispute "happens" to occur "at a school located in an affluent, historically white suburb, where a little more than half the learners were white … but none of it is relevant to this appeal."[35] The Supreme Court of Appeal noted, "There was not one bit of evidence to suggest that the school has ever refused admission to a child – including this child who happens to be black – on the grounds of race or has unfairly discriminated against any child on this basis … The school's refusal to admit the learner in this case had nothing to do with her race or her background."[36] The applicants, however, had advanced a disparate impact argument, pointing out that the school was in a "peculiarly privileged position that can primarily be linked to the historical disparities in the resourcing of public education under Apartheid," and that the school's enrollment was "disproportionately 'white' when compared to the overall demographic profile of the province."[37] They argued that the Constitution prohibited "privileged governing bodies in historically white areas to entrench racially discriminatory privileges bequeathed by Apartheid,"[38] but the Supreme Court of Appeal had rejected the suggestion that the Rivonia School Governing Body's enrollment limits were discriminatory.

The Constitutional Court reversed this part of the Supreme Court of Appeal's holding. The Constitutional Court focused on the limits to the school Governing Body's powers under the South African Schools Act. It held that, while the Governing Body clearly had power to determine its admissions policy under the statute, that power was limited by other provisions of the statute and, by the statute's own formulation, provincial law. Furthermore,

35 *Governing Body of the Rivonia Primary School* v. *MEC for Education: Gauteng Province* [2013] 1 SA 632 (CC) para. 1.

36 Ibid. para. 52.

37 Ibid. para. 53.

38 Ibid.

the Court, citing *Ermelo*, noted that any powers exercised by a school governing body had to be understood, "within the broader constitutional scheme to make education progressively available and accessible to everyone."[39] The Constitutional Court concluded that the Department of Education could legitimately instruct the school to admit this additional learner, exceeding the school Governing Body's limit, based on the learner's section 29(1) right to basic education.[40] In their amicus brief to the Constitutional Court, Equal Education and the Centre for Child Law argued, "[i]t is not necessary to establish that Rivonia Primary has unfairly discriminated against learners in order to contend that laws applicable to the school should be interpreted so as to best address the systemic inequality in education. To the extent that schools that are in a relatively better position may perceive this approach to impose an unfair burden, it is a burden that the Constitution requires."[41] Essentially, they urged that members of the advantaged group had equality duties that went beyond the duty not to discriminate intentionally or unfairly. White flight is a constitutional problem.

At the same time, the Constitutional Court agreed with the Supreme Court of Appeal that the Department had employed unreasonably and procedurally unfair means to enroll this learner at the school. Because the Schools Act and the Constitution both set out a "co-operative governance scheme … the relevant functionary and the school governing body are under a duty to engage with each other in good faith on any disputes, including disputes over policies adopted by the governing body."[42] The Constitutional Court was particularly critical of the HoD's administrative failures which led to enrolling the learner disruptively after the school year had begun, without sufficient attention to the "partnership and cooperation framework envisaged in the Schools Act."[43] While the HoD had the statutory authority to require a school to admit more learners than the school Governing Body's policy allowed, "there must be proper engagement between all parties affected."[44] On this score, the Court was equally critical of the Rivonia School Governing Body, which "failed to place the interests of the learner first," by resorting to

[39] Ibid. para. 41.

[40] *MEC for Education in Gauteng Province* v. *Governing Body of the Rivonia Primary School* [2013] 6 SA 582 (CC) para. 56.

[41] Equal Education and the Centre for Child Law (Amici Curiae), Written Submission in *MEC for Education: Gauteng Province* v. *Governing Body of the Rivonia Primary School*, Case No. CCT 135/2012, para. 16.

[42] *Rivonia* para. 49.

[43] Ibid. para. 68.

[44] Ibid. para. 72.

litigation.[45] The Constitutional Court concluded that "the Gauteng HoD should have afforded the school an opportunity to make representations and respond to the tenth-day statistics report, before the learner was forcibly placed in the school."[46] With regard to both parties, the Constitutional Court held, "[t]he duty on the parties to cooperate and attempt to reach an amicable solution is intimately connected to the best interests of the child ... I would imagine that starting Grade 1 is a stressful and scary time for any child. Due to the failure of the parties to engage and reach agreement, the learner was physically placed at a desk and was caught in the middle of a disagreement which may well have been very traumatizing for her."[47] Thus, the Court concluded that "disagreement is not necessarily a bad thing ... But one organ of state cannot use its entrusted powers to strong-arm others. All sides are required to work together in partnership to find workable solutions to persistent and complex difficulties – and resorting to court in every skirmish is not going to help in that process."[48]

While making it clear that the school Governing Body had a constitutional duty to make education progressively available and accessible to everyone, the Court refuses to bless the regional education authority's forcible enrollment of a learner as a means of enforcing education rights. Like the *Hoërskool Ermelo* decision, the *Rivonia* decision becomes an opportunity to articulate constitutional norms of education rights and duties without ruling decisively in favor of any party to the litigation. The norm is thus articulated without providing the party who would be most likely to resist the norm with a concrete judgment to defy.

Decisions like *Hoërskool Ermelo* and *Rivonia*, articulating rights without displacing the authority of school governing bodies, illustrate a judicial strategy of preserving legitimacy against the dynamics of resistance and resentment. Such decisions paved the way for the Constitutional Court's most recent decision affecting the admissions policies of privileged schools. The Court upheld regulations that limit school governing bodies' power to control admissions. In *Federation of Governing Bodies for South African Schools* v. *Member of the Executive Council for Education, Gauteng and Another*, a unanimous court has also recently upheld regulations that limit school governing bodies' powers to control admissions. The unanimous judgment in this case begins by extolling the importance of education in postapartheid transformation.

[45] Ibid. para. 76.
[46] Ibid. para. 68.
[47] Ibid. para. 77.
[48] Ibid. para. 78.

Quoting a range of thinkers from Aristotle, Kant, Gandhi, Mandela to Malala Yousafzai, the Court noted:

> The uneven power relations that marked slavery, colonialism, the industrial age and the information economy are girded, in great part, by inadequate access to quality teaching and learning. At the end of a long and glorious struggle against all forms of oppression and the beginning of a democratic and inclusive society, we, filled with rightful optimism, guaranteed universal access to basic education. We collectively said: "[e]veryone has the right to basic education, including adult basic education."[49]

In the decisions being appealed, the High Court had initially struck down several of the regulations, which were challenged by school governing bodies on the grounds that they departed from the South African Schools Act or the constitutional power of provincial governments. Regulation 3(7) prohibited the school from requesting a learner's current school to furnish confidential reports about that learner in the context of an application for admission to a new school. Regulation 4 permitted but did not require the provincial government to determine the "feeder zone" for schools, after consultation with relevant stakeholders (including presumably the school governing bodies). Regulation 5 authorized the provincial government to place unplaced learners at any school, even if contrary to school admissions policies. Regulation 8 authorized the provincial government to determine independently of school governing bodies whether the school had reached its enrollment capacity.

The Constitutional Court upheld all but regulation 4, holding that the provincial government was required, not merely permitted, to determine feeder zones in consultation with relevant stakeholders. With regard to regulation 4, the Constitutional Court agreed with the school governing bodies' positions. But with regard to all the other regulations, which the school governing bodies had challenged, the Constitutional Court determined that they were reasonable, especially considering the goals of nondiscrimination and postapartheid transformation through education. The federation of school governing bodies that initiated this litigation did not invoke constitutional education rights or these transformative goals. Nonetheless, the Constitutional Court acknowledged:

> The application engages important constitutional questions of equitable access to education – a promise made by section 29 of the Constitution. We

49 *Federation of Governing Bodies for South African Schools* v. *Minister of Executive Council for Education, Gauteng* [2016] ZACC 14 (CC) para. 3.

> are also required to interpret national and provincial legislation in light of our supreme law. The contrast between the applicant, representing certain school governing bodies, and provincial government is neither new nor of passing public interest. The concern of equitable access to quality basic education is of vast public importance.[50]

In light of this background norm, the court upheld regulation 3(7) disallowing a learner's prospective school from requesting confidential information from her current school, noting that the rule's purpose was to prevent unfair discrimination against a learner.[51] Regulations 5 and 8, which represent the most significant limitation on the typical functions of school governing bodies, were upheld against the school governing bodies' contentions that these regulations were inconsistent with national statutes that gave school governing bodies control over their schools' admissions policies. Here, the Constitutional Court held that "[t]he Constitution anticipates the possibility of overlapping and conflicting national and provincial legislation on concurrent provincial and national competences."[52] More importantly, the Court invoked "the vision of universal access to education embraced by the Constitution" to justify as reasonable the regulations authorizing the provincial government to place unplaced learners at any school, and also to revisit the schools' own determination as to whether enrollment is at capacity:

> It is also quite in order that a school seeks to be a center of excellence and to produce glittering examinations and other good outcomes. But public schools are not rarefied spaces only for the bright, well-mannered and financially well-heeled learners. They are public assets which must advance not only the parochial interest of its immediate learners but may, by law, also be required to help achieve universal and non-discriminatory access to education.[53]

While ruling against school governing bodies, the Court acknowledged their important role and responsibility with regard to the realization of constitutional education rights. School governing bodies were "democratic and participatory" and "ordinarily would advance the legitimate interests of learners at a school."[54] Thus, in previous decisions like *Ermelo* and *Rivonia*, the Court had "correctly cautioned against undue dominance of the school

50 Ibid. para. 23.
51 Ibid. para. 33.
52 Ibid. para. 35.
53 Ibid. para. 44.
54 Ibid. para. 47.

governing bodies by the provincial Executive." The Court sums up its approach to education equality in the following sentence: "[w]e have called for the cooperative governance between statutory creatures – school governing bodies and the MEC and HoD – entrusted with effective and universal access to basic education."[55] By avoiding strong, coercive remedies, the Court is trying to get stakeholders to choose to act in accordance with the constitutional commitment to equal education. This project of persuasion is aided by the Court's strong pronouncements of the constitutional commitment. The weak remedies seem to enable strong norm articulation, by tempering the potential resistance to coercive judicial remedies. The Court's articulation of the constitutional norm catalyzes a dialogical process of transformation, instead of ordering immediate transformative action. To fully appreciate this approach as a successful one, or at least a step toward the internal goal of education transformation, a comparison with the U.S. Supreme Court's management of white flight since *Brown* v. *Board of Education* is illuminating.

8.2. *BROWN*: TRANSFORMATIVE CONSTITUTIONALISM AND RETRENCHMENT

In U.S. constitutional law, *Brown* v. *Board of Education* has iconic status because the Supreme Court boldly invalidated racial segregation in public schools. *Brown*, like the 1996 Constitution of South Africa, articulated a transformative vision for equal protection. In declaring that "separate educational facilities are inherently unequal,"[56] the Court declared unconstitutional the public education institutions of Southern states. Complete transformation of these institutions appeared to be constitutionally required.

Yet, measured by the black–white achievement gap, or by the lack of racial integration in public schools, the goal of transformation embraced by *Brown* has not been reached. These outcomes would suggest that the U.S. constitutional guarantee of Equal Protection, as interpreted by *Brown*, is a failure. Legal scholar James Ryan, until recently the Dean of Harvard School of Education, has shown how the current situation of racial segregation in public education is largely the result of the boundary between urban and suburban school districts, across which the Supreme Court has declined to require integration.[57] Ryan writes: "[t]his boundary has been the fault line of public education for half a century, doing more than anything else to define and shape

[55] Ibid.

[56] *Brown* v. *Bd. of Educ. of Topeka* 347 U.S. 483, 495 (1954).

[57] *See Milliken* v. *Bradley* 418 U.S. 717 (1974).

the educational opportunities of public school students. On one side stand predominantly white, middle-income, and relatively successful schools. On the other side stand predominantly minority, poor, and relatively unsuccessful schools."[58] Following *Brown*, as documented by the Kerner Commission Report in 1967, the white population in cities declined as many whites moved to the suburbs. Seventy-eight percent of white population growth from 1960 to 1966 occurred in suburbs, while 98 percent of African American population growth in the same period occurred in central cities. In a series of cases decided in the early to mid-1970s, the U.S. Supreme Court refused to view the de facto segregation of black and white pupils resulting from these patterns as constitutional violations.

The persistence of the racial achievement gap and de facto racial segregation in U.S. public schools despite *Brown* v. *Board of Education* is largely attributable to "white flight." As Dean Ryan points out, the failure to integrate suburban and urban school districts is a significant source of unequal educational opportunity. Parents who have the resources to choose the best educational options for their children, mostly white and Asian, move to suburban school districts and make efforts to have their children tested and placed in gifted and talented programs. They avoid placing their children in schools that are under-resourced or academically failing. They raise money to make enrichment programs like art, sports and music available in the schools their children attend.[59] Many opt out of the public school system altogether, choosing private schools where tuition can cost over $40,000 a year per child. All of these behaviors seem reasonable, if not obligatory, from the standpoint of parents seeking to optimize their children's chances of living a good life.[60] Therefore, legislatures are unlikely to disrupt white flight, and courts risk resistance and challenges to their legitimacy when they attempt to do so.

The U.S. Supreme Court responded to this risk by driving a conceptual wedge between desegregation, on the one hand, and integration, on the other, in its education Equal Protection cases less than two decades after *Brown*. It eventually held that only desegregation – and not integration – was constitutionally required. In recent years, the Supreme Court has scrutinized and struck down voluntary state efforts to integrate schools, holding the salient

58 J. Ryan, *Five Miles Away, A World Apart: One City, Two Schools, and the Story of Educational Opportunity in Modern America* (New York, NY: Oxford University Press, 2010) 3.

59 L. McKenna, "How Rich Parents Can Exacerbate School Inequality" (January 28, 2016) *The Atlantic* (available at www.theatlantic.com/education/archive/2016/01/rich-parents-school-inequality/431640/) (accessed date November 20, 2017).

60 See A. Swift, *How Not to Be a Hypocrite: School Choice for the Morally Perplexed Parent* (London: Routledge, 2003).

consideration of race in these efforts to be contrary to Equal Protection. The U.S. Supreme Court's understanding of Equal Protection's relationship to racial integration changed. While *Brown* v. *Board of Education* viewed the Constitution as requiring a transformation from racial segregation to racial integration in public education, subsequent cases revised and rejected this internal criterion of constitutional success.

The understanding that equal protection imposed an imperative to integrate public schools permeated *Brown* v. *Board of Education* and the U.S. Supreme Court's initial school desegregation cases, but it eroded in the early 1970s. While *Brown* v. *Board of Education* famously declared that separate education for black and white children was "inherently unequal," it postponed the determination of appropriate remedies,[61] such as integration. In *Brown II*, the Supreme Court equated desegregation with integration initially. In that decision, lower courts were instructed to adopt measures that were "necessary and proper to admit to public schools on a racially nondiscriminatory basis with all deliberate speed the parties to these cases."[62]

The Supreme Court authorized strong remedies in the decade following *Brown*. In *Cooper* v. *Aaron*, responding to violent resistance to integration, the Court upheld a school board's desegregation efforts citing "the right of a student not to be segregated on racial grounds."[63] The duty to end unconstitutional segregation could not, in *Griffin* v. *County School Board of Prince Edward County*, be met by a state by simply closing down its public schools. Nor could a state fulfill its duty to desegregate by allowing white and black pupils to choose which school to attend postsegregation.[64] In observing that no white child had chosen to attend a former black school in the "freedom of choice" plan, the Court noted that its inquiry was "whether the Board has taken steps adequate to abolish its dual, segregated system."[65] In that case, the Court declared that school authorities are "clearly charged with the affirmative duty to take whatever steps might be necessary to convert to a unitary system in which racial discrimination would be eliminated root and branch."[66] In the context of past segregation by the state, there was a positive duty to remedy the situation through integration. In *Alexander* v. *Holmes County Board*

61 *Brown* v. *Bd of Educ. of Topeka* 347 U.S. 483, 495 (1954).

62 *Brown* v. *Bd. of Educ. of Topeka* 349 U.S. 294 (1955) ("Brown II").

63 *Cooper* v. *Aaron* 358 U.S. 1, 19 (1958). In *Weak Courts, Strong Rights*, Mark Tushnet notes that *Cooper* v. *Aaron* provides "[t]he modern articulation of strong-form judicial review" (M. Tushnet, *Weak Courts, Strong Rights* (Princeton, NJ: Princeton University Press, 2008) 21).

64 *Green* v. *County School Bd. of New Kent County* 391 U.S. 430, 437 (1968).

65 Ibid.

66 Ibid. 437–8.

of Education, the Court reiterated that "the obligation of every school district is to terminate dual school systems at once and to operate now and hereafter only unitary schools."[67] The Court ordered the Court of Appeals to issue an order directing the school districts to begin operating immediately as unitary school systems.[68] In these formulations of the late 1960s, the duty to desegregate seems equivalent to the duty to operate an integrated school system, and it is backed up by court orders requiring school districts to operate immediately on an integrated basis.

Yet, in 1971, the Court began to distinguish between the duty to desegregate and the duty to integrate. In *Swann* v. *Charlotte-Mecklenburg Board of Education*, the Court held that states that had maintained separate schools based on race as a governmental policy must desegregate, and upheld courts' broad equitable remedial powers to correct constitutional violations. While the *Swann* Court upheld judges' power to order busing to desegregate, it also began to narrow the meaning of desegregation. Title IV had defined "desegregation" as "the assignment of students to public schools and within such schools without regard to their race, color, religion, or national origin, but 'desegregation' shall not mean the assignment of students to public schools in order to overcome racial imbalance."[69] The Court also declared, "We are concerned in these cases with the elimination of the discrimination inherent in the dual school systems, not with myriad factors of human existence which can cause discrimination in a multitude of ways on racial, religious, or ethnic grounds … The elimination of racial discrimination in public schools is a large task and one that should not be retarded by efforts to achieve broader purposes lying beyond the jurisdiction of school authorities."[70] Thus, the Court "does not and cannot embrace all the problems of racial prejudice, even when those problems contribute to disproportionate racial concentrations in some schools."[71] The Court explicitly noted that "the existence of some small number of one-race, or virtually one-race, schools within a school district is not in and of itself the mark of a system that still practices segregation by law."[72]

Swann, a unanimous decision authored by a newly inaugurated Chief Justice Burger, signaled the beginning of an ideological drift away from the Warren Court's steadfast commitment to the implementation of Brown's vision of racial integration. By articulating the possibility of desegregating

67 *Alexander* v. *Holmes County Bd. of Ed.* 396 U.S. 19 (1969).

68 Ibid. 30.

69 *Swann* v. *Charlotte-Mecklenburg Bd. of Ed.* 402 U.S. 15, 17 (1971) (citing Title IV) (*Swann*).

70 Ibid. 22–3.

71 Ibid. 23.

72 Ibid. 26.

public schools without fully integrating them, a court with a changing composition imagined a different normative vision of constitutional equality in education, one which was compatible with some forms of racial stratification, such as the separation resulting from white families' flight to the suburbs. But as it took its first steps in this shift, the Court's opinions spoke a prudential language, not an ideological one. Of primary concern was the Court's inability to transform institutions, and the threat to judicial legitimacy arising from judicial orders that were not obeyed. In *Swann*, the distinction between the duty to desegregate and the duty to integrate was articulated in the same breath as the Court's acknowledgment of the practical difficulties encountered in the implementation of *Brown*:

> Over the 16 years since *Brown II*, many difficulties were encountered in implementation of the basic constitutional requirement that the State not discriminate between public school children on the basis of their race. Nothing in our national experience prior to 1955 prepared anyone for dealing with changes and adjustments of the magnitude and complexity encountered since then. Deliberate resistance of some of the Court's mandates has impeded good-faith efforts of others to bring school systems into compliance. The detail and nature of these dilatory tactics have been noted frequently by this Court and other courts.[73]

The Court acknowledged "[t]he problems encountered by the district courts and courts of appeals" and "the massive problem of converting from the state-enforced discrimination of racially separate school systems." This process was "rendered more difficult by changes since 1954 in the structure and patterns of communities, the growth of student population, movement of families, and other changes, some of which had marked impact on school planning, sometimes neutralizing or negating remedial action before it was fully implemented."[74] The Court attempted to define the proper limits of judicial power: "Remedial judicial authority does not put judges automatically in the shoes of school authorities whose powers are plenary."[75]

Swann's concerns about both the practical inability of courts to bring about full integration, and the illegitimacy of courts' displacement of the school board's role, laid the groundwork for the Court's later normative justification of nonintegration. In 1973, the Supreme Court decided two cases that effectively protected the structures enabling well-resourced white parents and

[73] *Swann* 13.
[74] Ibid.
[75] Ibid. 16.

communities to educate their children in isolation from poor black and brown children. Litigants in *Keyes* v. *School District No. 1* challenged the maintenance of "neighborhood" schools that had the effect of separating black and white students. Litigants in *San Antonio* v. *Rodriguez*, argued on the same day as Keyes, challenged the use of local property taxes to fund a public school. The *Rodriguez* litigants pointed out that this practice led to high concentrations of minority students in some schools. While *Keyes* authorized judges to scrutinize schools that were disproportionately one race when they were part of a school district that had intentionally segregated some of its schools in the past, it ultimately affirmed the distinction between desegregation and integration.[76] Only desegregation was legally required, and could only be obligatory if the racial separation was the consequence of official segregation. As for *Rodriguez*, it famously held that education was not a fundamental right guaranteed by the federal constitution.[77] Therefore, the state could constitutionally distribute education on any rational basis, and because property tax was a wealth classification rather than a race classification, the Court declined to strictly scrutinize it as a basis for funding education.

In *Swann*, *Rodriguez* and *Keyes*, the Supreme Court moved away from transformative constitutionalism in the area of education equality. These cases were decided after almost twenty years of attempts by courts to enforce a constitutional right to education equality. Courts' strong efforts to integrate schools were met with resistance, which threatened to undermine the legitimacy of the judiciary. Less than twenty years after *Cooper* v. *Aaron*, the Court abandoned its earlier effort to assert the legitimacy of its authority to impose its constitutional vision on resistant state officials. The South African Constitutional Court's decisions in *Ermelo*, *Rivonia* and FEDSAS similarly encompass the period of roughly twenty years past the moment of constitutional commitment to transformation, from apartheid to open access to excellent schools. By contrast to the U.S. Supreme Court at an analogous moment, the South African Constitutional Court has strongly reaffirmed the transformative vision of education equality after apartheid, while promoting a dialogical process between stakeholders and government by which the vision is progressively realized.

In the United States, not only did the transformative vision fade away, but in the next twenty years, the transformative vision came to be prohibited. The Supreme Court invalidated several attempts to desegregate, holding that they engaged in integration beyond what was required to remedy the wrong of segregation. In *Freeman* v. *Pitts*, for instance, the Court noted, "Where

[76] *Keyes* v. *Sch. Dist. No.* 1 413 U.S. 189 (1973).

[77] *San Antonio Indep. Sch. Dist.* v. *Rodriguez* 411 U.S. 1, 54 (1973).

resegregation is a product not of state action but of private choices, it does not have constitutional implications."[78] Again, the Court observed that it was "beyond the practical ability of the federal courts to try to counteract these kinds of continuous and massive demographic shifts."[79] In *Missouri* v. *Jenkins*, the Court struck down various measures undertaken by the state to achieve racial integration across geographic school districts pursuant to court desegregation orders. The Supreme Court held that the District Court's attempts to integrate exceeded its authority to desegregate. Finally, in 2007, the U.S. Supreme Court struck down integration plans in Seattle and Louisville that took the race of children into account when placing them in schools within a school district. The school district's goal was to maintain a diverse racial composition in primary and secondary schools, but the Supreme Court held this practice to be constitutionally problematic.

How did federal constitutional education equality law in the United States evolve from requiring to prohibiting integration? Judges responded, in part, to the dynamics of resistance and white flight, seeing how they threatened courts' legitimacy. In the beginning, American judges exerted extensive powers to order busing and other specific plans to integrate schools. Judges' frustrations with the resistance to integration orders have influenced their articulation of the constitutional demands of equality in education. The conceptual wedge between desegregation and integration was an ideology that converged with practical considerations. Resistance to integration orders challenged the legitimacy of courts, and judges opted to preserve their own legitimacy and authority as desegregation began to mean something less than integration. The absence of integration – for instance, an urban American school where a large majority of the students are of the same race – is only pronounced wrong by courts if it can be directly traced to a state policy of racial separation.

The Supreme Court's implicit rejection of the imperative to integrate Texas public schools in *San Antonio* v. *Rodriguez* was partially driven by the acknowledgment, as in *Swann*, of likely resistance to implementation: "It cannot be questioned that the constitutional judgment reached by the District Court [striking down Texas's policy of tying school funding to local property tax] and approved by our dissenting Brothers today would occasion in Texas and elsewhere an unprecedented upheaval in public education."[80] Finding a constitutional violation in this education scheme due to its segregative effects would lead to "massive change in the financing and control of

[78] *Freeman* v. *Pitts* 503 U.S. 467 (1992).

[79] Ibid.

[80] *San Antonio Indep. Sch. Dist.* v. *Rodriguez* 411 U.S. 1, 54 (1973).

public education."[81] At the same time, the Court insisted that "[t]hese practical considerations, of course, play no role in the adjudication of the constitutional issues presented here."[82]

The South African Constitutional Court, by contrast, has been conscious of the practical considerations regarding the dynamics of control of public education. While acknowledging the rights of learners to "universal access to basic education," the Court is constantly acknowledging the "continuing contests on the governance of public schools and policies on admission of learners."[83] Sandra Fredman has criticized the South African Constitutional Court's recent education equality cases, on the grounds that, despite recognizing the constitutional rights at stake, the Court's decisions imposed procedure but not substance on school governing bodies.[84] Without giving specific guidance as to how the constitutional right should be effectuated by the school governing body, it remains possible for these entities to carry on in a complacent manner in maintaining admissions regimes that exclude too many of the most vulnerable learners. This proceduralization is an implicit recognition of the challenges facing courts that attempt to enforce the transformative agenda of postapartheid education rights.

8.3. CONCLUSION

When viewed in comparative context, the South African Constitutional Court's education equality jurisprudence of the past decade should be regarded as a partial success. On the one hand, the persistence of racial disparities in educational attainment and the inadequacy of the education infrastructure for vast numbers of black learners indicate that South Africa has not moved far enough away from its apartheid past in the last twenty years. At the same time, by comparison with the U.S. Supreme Court's education equality jurisprudence twenty years after *Brown* and its aftermath, it is remarkable that the South African Constitutional Court maintains a robust rhetoric of equality and universal access to schools that were inaccessible under apartheid. It appears that the Court maintains its legitimate authority to articulate these normative positions precisely because it refrains from rulings that coerce integration by way of new admissions policies formulated by the judiciary or

81 Ibid. 58.

82 Ibid.

83 *FEDSAS*, SACC 209/15. 20 May 2016, para. 4.

84 S. Fredman, "Procedure or principle: The role of adjudication in achieving the right to education" (2015) 6 *Constitutional Court Review* 165–98.

by regional education departments. The U.S. Supreme Court, by contrast, rewrote its trajectory of failure by changing the internal criteria by which courts would evaluate the facts of continuing racial separation and white resistance to integration. For the next twenty years of interpreting the right to basic education, South African courts will have a strong judicial articulation of the constitutional transformation required by this right upon which to draw in shaping appropriate remedies. In assessing constitutional performance and potential, the creation of this possibility should not be underestimated.

9

Race, Inclusiveness and Transformation of Legal Education in South Africa

Penelope Andrews

9.1. INTRODUCTION

In many ways 2015 was a watershed year in South Africa's postapartheid constitutional democracy. This was the year in which South Africa's university students – after a fairly long period – resurfaced as a potent political force, especially on the campuses of what were historically white universities.[1] Although there had been protests on many campuses since 1994, the last time university students protested loudly and consistently was throughout the apartheid era, especially during the dying days of apartheid.[2]

The protests came in the wake of widespread civil unrest in postapartheid South Africa that had been part of the political landscape since the late 1990s and the advent of democracy.[3] Barely had South Africa entered a democratic era, with a government (formerly a national liberation movement) committed to a range of political and socio-economic goals, when protests once again became a staple feature of the South African political landscape. Relating mostly to service delivery by governmental and parastatal entities, these protests highlighted the gap between the socio-economic rights embodied in the

Thank you to Professors Rosalind Dixon and Theunis Roux for the invitation to participate in the University of New South Wales conference on Comparative Constitutionalism in April 2016. Thank you also to Joshua Davis, UCT LL.B. Intermediate Year student, for research assistance with this chapter.

1 D. Cooper, "Social justice and South African university student enrolment data by 'race', 1998–2012: from 'skewed' revolution to 'stalled' revolution" (2015) 69 *Higher Education Quarterly* 237.

2 B. Hirson, *Year of Fire Year of Ash: The Soweto Schoolchildren's Revolt That Shook Apartheid* (London: Zed Press, 1979).

3 A. Desai, *We Are the Poors: Community Struggles in Post-Apartheid South Africa* (New York, NY: Monthly Review Press, 2002).

Constitution and the continued reality of the lives of a significant number of South Africans, who are overwhelmingly black.[4]

The past two years have seen waves of disruptions by student protestors at South African universities. The first wave in 2015 focused on the removal of colonial symbols, including the removal of the statue of Cecil John Rhodes at the University of Cape Town, and a call for no university fee increases.[5] The second wave of protests in 2016 embraced a call for transformation of universities and free and decolonized tertiary education.[6] Student protesters also made a range of localized demands at various universities, mostly related to university actions against protesting students who had engaged in violent activities and the destruction of property.[7]

Giving rise to what has been termed "fallism," these protests occurred under various labels, including #RhodesMustFall, #FeesMustFall, #Decolonise UCT and others. At times the protestors turned their rage against the political and legal arrangements negotiated by President Nelson Mandela and others during South Africa's transition to democracy, interpreting such arrangements as "selling out" the interests of the black majority population.[8] They also leveled particular criticism at the Constitution itself, seeing the document as irrelevant to the struggle for social and economic justice.[9] A recent posting noted that the following:

> The rise of Fallism on the nation's campuses is, at heart, a local manifestation of a global phenomenon. It is a rage against the machine of liberal democracy and its corollary, a market economy. Already, there are disturbing signs that this fury is being turned towards the Constitution.[10]

4 R. Ballard, A. Habib and I. Valodia (eds.), *Voices of Protest: Social Movements in Post-Apartheid South Africa* (Pietermaritzburg: University of KwaZulu-Natal Press, 2006); N. Davids and Y. Waghid, "History of South African student protests reflects inequality's grip" (October 9, 2016) *The Conversation* (available at www.theconversation.com/history-of-south-african-student-protests-reflects-inequalitys-grip-66279) (accessed date November 20, 2017).

5 Some brief facts about South African universities: Like their counterparts elsewhere, they are underfunded. Like public universities elsewhere as well, the impact of underfunding has been transferred to consecutive fee increases. In South Africa, this has resulted in a disproportionate burden on black (primarily African and colored) students. See Council of Higher Education, *South African Higher Education Reviewed: Two Decades of Democracy* (Pretoria: Council of Higher Education, 2016) 321.

6 See N. Badsha, *No-Fee Universities Will Not Serve Us Well*, Business Day, October 5, 2016.

7 See T. Petersen, UCT Shutdown Will Last Until University Agrees to #Shackville TRC Student Leader, News 24, September 16, 2016/.

8 See E. Fairbanks, "Why South African students have turned on their parents' generation" *The Guardian*, November 18, 2015.

9 See UCT Rhodes Must Fall Mission Statement, The Salon, Volume 9, 2015 (available at www.jwtc.org.za/resources/docs/salon-volume-9/RMF_Combined.pdf) (accessed date November 20, 2017).

10 M. Cardo, 'Fallism: at the totalitarian tipping point?' (November 14, 2016) *Politicsweb* (available at www.politicsweb.co.za/news-and-analysis/fallism-at-the-totalitarian-tipping-point) (accessed date November 20, 2017).

At the conclusion of this paper in December 2016, the protests have abated for a month as universities close for the summer holidays.[11] Responding in divergent ways to the demands of the students, universities have embarked on transformation agendas and strategic initiatives, as well as pursuing the project of affordable and decolonized education.[12] Under the auspices of the Nelson Mandela Foundation, a National Education Crisis Forum has been set up to deal with the crisis in education and to pursue a path forward. At the University of Cape Town (UCT) a strategic planning focus has just been completed which embodies the commitment of UCT to continue its role and status as Africa's leading university, as well as embracing many of the concerns raised by the student protestors.[13] UCT has also set up an institutional reconciliation mechanism to embark on a reconciliation and healing process between students, staff and the university administration.[14]

In addition to the protests on university campuses, in law faculties across South Africa a national review of the undergraduate LL.B. program commenced in 2012 and will be completed in 2017. The purpose of the review is to assess, among others, the inclusion of constitutional principles and ethics in the curriculum, experiential learning and the pursuit of technological

[11] There was a protest at the UCT Convocation on December 15, 2016, when a group of about eight protesters attended the Convocation meeting carrying placards related to a range of issues including insourcing, the agreement reached by students with Vice-Chancellor Max Price, decolonized education and others. See Royston Pillay, Secretary of Convocation, *Campus Announcement* (December 28, 2016) (available at www.uct.ac.za/dailynews/?id=10139) (accessed date November 20, 2017).

[12] Regarding the demographic transformation of South Africa's universities, data provided by the Department of Higher Education and Training in 2012 provided the number of enrolments at universities by racial category: 69 percent of students enrolled in public universities were black Africans; 6 percent colored; 6 percent Indian and 18 percent white: South African Human Rights Commission, *SAHRC Report: Transformation at Public Universities in South Africa* (December 9, 2016) 25. But this number is uneven across the various universities, a legacy of the apartheid higher education landscape. Under apartheid, universities were racially demarcated, with the historically black universities underfunded and consisting of an almost 100 percent black student population. For those universities, the racial demographics have hardly changed. At the historically white universities, the racial demographics have shifted from a majority white student population to an increasingly majority black student population. The racial demographics of the academic staff have been slower in terms of transformation. For example, according to the SAHRC Report, in 2014 only 29 percent of Instruction and Research Staff were black, while 45 percent were female: at 34.

[13] See *the University of Cape Town's strategic planning framework 2016–2019* (December 10, 2016) (available at www.uct.ac.za/usr/about/governance/council/2016-12-10_UCTCouncil_StrategicPlanningFramework.pdf) (accessed date November 20, 2017).

[14] See Y. Omar, 'Reconciliation and transformation commission kicks off' (February 3, 2017) *Daily News* (available at www.uct.ac.za/dailynews/?id=10163) (accessed date November 20, 2017).

competence and literacy within the various programs of legal education across the country. It is apparent therefore that the project of legal education is confronting widespread changes and challenges.

Since 1994, the most fundamental driver of change on legal education has been the Constitution. An examination of the demands of the student protesters in 2015 and 2016 and the LL.B. Review suggest that in combination they have highlighted the possibilities and limitations of the Constitution, especially as they relate to the implementation and enforcement of social and economic rights. In their own distinct interface with legal education, these latest drivers of change embody the imperatives of the South African Constitution and its transformative vision. Karl Klare describes this transformative vision as:

> ... a long-term project of constitutional enactment, interpretation, and enforcement committed (not in isolation, of course, but in a historical context of conducive political developments) to transforming a country's political and social institutions and power relationships in a democratic, participatory, *and egalitarian* direction.[15]

The student protests and the LL.B. review have once again focused the attention of legal educators on the urgent need to address transformation as envisioned in the constitution.[16]

This chapter addresses the following issues: the adoption of the South African Constitution was about upending and disrupting a colonial and racist legal system, thereby mandating a fundamental paradigm shift. The express goal was to transform the content, patterns, processes, symbols and meaning of law and the Constitution for all South Africans, but especially for the majority black population for whom the impact of the Constitution was expected to be most profound. Consequent to that mandate, my chapter examines whether a paradigm shift implicit in the postapartheid Constitution impelled legal education sufficiently to transform its major tenets and operations? In investigating this paradigm shift I apply an analysis centered on critical race theory.

This chapter is written against the backdrop of extraordinary changes and shifts within the legal profession globally, resulting from the aftermath of the

[15] K. E. Klare, "Legal culture and transformative constitutionalism" (1998) 14 *South African Journal on Human Rights* 146–88.

[16] At the UCT Law Faculty issues of transformation have been discussed and pursued since 1994, with limited success. Indeed, the last strategic plan of the Law Faculty explicitly addresses the need for change and transformation. See *Strategic Plan for the Law Faculty 2010–2014* (available at www.uct.ac.za/googlesearch/?q=law+faculty+strategic+plan) (accessed date November 20, 2017).

2008 global financial crisis, the globalization of legal services, including the outsourcing of legal services and technology. These changes have significantly weighed upon legal education, indeed have transformed legal education, and have been documented in some detail.[17] These changes too, however, as elsewhere, will in time have a broader impact on South African legal education. Because I concern myself solely with the contemporary South African context, the issues of the 2008 global financial crisis, globalization and technology, and their impact on legal education are not considered for this chapter.

9.2. THE CONSTITUTION, EQUALITY AND THE RIGHT OF ACCESS TO EDUCATION

The Preamble to South Africa's Constitution states:

> We adopt this Constitution ... so as to:
>
> - Heal the divisions of the past and establish a society based on democratic values, social justice and fundamental human rights;
> - Lay the foundations for a democratic and open society in which government is based on the will of the people and every citizen is equally protected by law;
> - Improve the quality of life of all citizens and free the potential of each person ...[18]

From its Preamble to the text and structure of the South African Constitution, including the comprehensive Bill of Rights, it is clear that those who drafted the text were committed to the goal of a society based on equality and dignity. This goal was about overcoming the legacy and destruction of colonialism and apartheid in all its social, political, economic and cultural manifestations.[19]

Indeed, Justice Arthur Chaskalson, former Chief Justice, noted in one of the first socio-economic rights cases before the Constitutional Court:

> We live in a society in which there are great disparities in wealth. Millions of people are living in deplorable conditions and in great poverty. There is a high level of unemployment, inadequate social security, and many do not

[17] For a thoughtful account of these changes see, e.g., R. Susskind, *Tomorrow's Lawyers: An Introduction to Your Future* (Oxford: Oxford University Press, 2013); R. Susskind, *The End of Lawyers? Rethinking the Nature of Legal Services* (New York, NY: Oxford University Press, 2010).

[18] Constitution of the Republic of South Africa 1996 ("Constitution").

[19] H. Klug, *The Constitution of South Africa: A Contextual Analysis* (Oxford: Hart Publishing, 2010).

> have access to clean water or to adequate health services. These conditions already existed when the Constitution was adopted, and a commitment to address them, and to transform our society into one in which there will be human dignity, freedom and equality, lies at the heart of our new constitutional order.[20]

In short, both text and its interpretation are incontrovertible mandates to transform social and economic relations.

Heralded as one of the most impressive and expansive human rights documents of the twentieth century,[21] the Constitution outlines a clear commitment to equality.[22] Chapter 2 states that:

> The state may not unfairly discriminate directly or indirectly against anyone on one or more grounds, including race, gender, sex, pregnancy, marital status, ethnic or social origin, colour, sexual orientation, age, disability, religion, conscience, belief, culture, language and birth.[23]

Strengthening the commitment to equality, the Constitution also incorporates a provision mandating affirmative action or measures of historical redress.[24] Direct and indirect discrimination are prohibited and the intersectionality of various forms of discrimination is explicitly recognized.[25] By creating a presumption of unfair discrimination linked to the listed grounds, the equality section removes a huge obstacle to complainants who allege discrimination.[26]

But arguably the impact of the Constitution is most pronounced in the sections that address social and economic rights. It is through a combination of equality and access to socio-economic rights that South Africa's fault line of race may be comprehensively and aggressively addressed. The Constitution provides that the state must, through reasonable measures and within its

20 *Soobramoney* v. *Minister of Health, KwaZulu-Natal* (1998) 1 SA 765 (CC) para. 8.

21 H. Klug, "Constitution-making, democracy and the 'civilizing' of irreconcilable conflict: what might we learn from the South African miracle?" (2007) 25 *Wisconsin International Law Journal* 269–99; A. K. Wing, "The South African Constitution as a role model for the United States" (2008) 24 *Harvard Blackletter Law Journal* 73–80.

22 For the purposes of this chapter only, the equality and certain of the socio-economic rights clauses are highlighted. The Bill of Rights, however, incorporates a range of civil and political rights that have a direct and indirect impact on the enjoyment of the equality and socio-economic rights provisions.

23 *Constitution* ch. 2 s. 9(3).

24 Ibid. s. 9(2) provides that: To promote the achievement of equality, legislative and other measures, designed to protect or advance persons, or categories of persons, disadvantaged by unfair discrimination may be taken.

25 Ibid. s. 9(4). Discrimination on one or more of the grounds listed in subsection (3) is unfair unless it is established that the discrimination is fair. Ibid.

26 Ibid. s. 9(5).

available resources, progressively ensure a range of socio-economic rights, including access to housing,[27] health care, food, water and social security.[28] The right to education is specifically provided for in the Constitution, the relevant section stating that:

> Everyone has the right
>
> a. to a basic education, including adult basic education, and
> b. to further education, which the state, through reasonable measures must make progressively available and accessible.[29]

Whereas the other socio-economic rights provide for *access* to the relevant right, the right to education is stated more directly.

Moreover, included in the Constitution is recognition of the multiplicity of languages spoken in the country. To cater to such diversity of languages, the Bill of Rights provides the right for South Africans to "receive education in the official language or languages of their choices" at state schools "where such education is reasonably practicable."[30]

The Bill of Rights further provides that in implementing this right, and making it accessible, the government "must consider all reasonable educational alternatives" within considerations of "equity and practicability" and "the need to redress the results of past racially discriminatory laws and practices."[31] The Bill of Rights also provides for those who wish to pursue the establishment and maintenance of private schools, on the condition that such educational institutions register with the government and "do not discriminate on the basis of race."[32] In addition, these private educational institutions are required to "maintain standards that are not inferior to standards at comparable public educational institutions."[33]

The Constitution mandates that in its interpretation regard must be had to international law and foreign law.[34] The South African government is therefore obligated to recognize the range of rights under various international human rights instruments.[35]

[27] Ibid. s. 26.
[28] Ibid. s. 27.
[29] Ibid. s. 29.
[30] Ibid. s. 29(2).
[31] Ibid.
[32] Ibid. s. 29(3).
[33] Ibid.
[34] Ibid. s. 39(1).
[35] J. Foster, "The use of foreign law in constitutional interpretation: lessons from South Africa" (2010) 45 *University of San Francisco Law Review* 79–139.

In addition to the Constitutional text providing the right to education, South Africa is also party to a number of key international human rights instruments that reference the right to education, including the International Covenant on Economic, Social and Cultural Rights (ICESCR), which explicitly highlights the right to education.[36] The ICESCR states that:

> ... education shall be directed to the full development of the human personality and the sense of its dignity, and shall strengthen the respect for human rights and fundamental freedoms ... education shall enable all persons to participate effectively in a free society, promote understanding, tolerance and friendship among all nations and all racial, ethnic or religious groups, and further the activities of the United Nations for the maintenance of peace.[37]

Regarding higher education, the ICESCR states that higher education shall be made, "equally accessible to all, on the basis of capacity, by every appropriate means, and in particular by the progressive introduction of free education."[38]

Other relevant international documents that highlight the right to education include the Convention on the Elimination of All Forms of Discrimination Against Women[39] and the International Convention on the Elimination of Racial Discrimination.[40] Notably, the African Charter of Human and Peoples Rights only states the principle that everyone shall have the right to education, without elaborating on the meaning and the content of the right.[41]

The provision of the right to education in the South African Constitution is premised on the truism that education is fundamentally a precondition for the exercise of other rights. Moreover, the overarching principle of the

36 *International Covenant on Economic, Social and Cultural Rights*, opened for signature December 16, 1966, 993 UNTS 3 (entered into force January 3, 1976) art. 27.

37 Ibid. art. 13(1).

38 Ibid. art. 13(2).

39 *Convention on The Elimination of All Forms of Discrimination Against Women*, opened for signature December 18, 1979, 1249 UNTS 13 (entered into force September 3, 1981) art. 27(1), art. 10 (calling for the elimination of discrimination against women in education).

40 *International Convention on The Elimination of Racial Discrimination*, opened for signature December 21, 1965, 660 UNTS 195 (entered into force January 4, 1969) art. 19, art. 5 (calling for the elimination of racial discrimination in education).

41 *African Charter on Human and People's Rights*, adopted June 27, 1981, CAB/LEG/67/3 rev. 5, 21 I.L.M. 58 (1982) (entered into force October 21, 1986) art. 17.

Constitution, the right to equality, has to be contextualized in the social and historical context of South Africa and its legacy of dispossession, discrimination and subordination.[42] To reduce the devastating impact of the legacy of apartheid on education remains a Sisyphean challenge.

Regarding implementation and enforcement, in addition to the key role of the Constitutional Court, under chapter 9 there are a range of institutions authorized to pursue, implement and enforce the rights in the Constitution.[43] For example, the South African Human Rights Commission is directed to pursue the enforcement of rights through education, lobbying and monitoring of human rights progress. Specifically, s. 184 mandates that the South African Human Rights Commission promote respect for human rights and a culture of human rights; promote the protection, development and attainment of human rights; and monitor and assess the observance of human rights. This section also empowers the Commission to investigate and to report on the assessment of human rights; to educate, carry out research and to redress human rights violations.

That twenty-one years later the goal and vision of the constitutional drafters have not materialized, or that the limitations of constitutional and legal processes to address and enforce social and economic justice have surfaced and are now more apparent, does not detract from the intention or the commitment of the drafters of the document under the leadership of President Nelson Mandela. Consequently, the Constitution continues to be ripe for critique and review. I address these concerns later in this chapter.

In the next section I briefly cover some of the notable decisions of the Constitutional Court as they relate to equality, social and economic rights, and especially the right to education.

[42] It is no accident that the major protests against apartheid emerged from an unequivocal rejection by students of the grotesquely unequal system of education which typified the policies of the apartheid government. In June 1976, students in the black township of Soweto just outside of Johannesburg commenced a strike to protest the teaching of Afrikaans in schools – a compulsory requirement for matriculation. The rioting soon spread from Soweto to other towns on the Witwatersrand, Pretoria, to Durban and Cape Town, and developed into the largest outbreak of violence South Africa had experienced. The police used brutal force to quell the riots and several students died in the protests. See E. Brink, *Soweto 16 June 1976* (Cape Town: Kwela Books, 2001).

[43] The chapter 9 institutions include: The Public Protector, the South African Human Rights Commission, the Commission for the Promotion and Protection of the Rights of Cultural, Religious and Linguistic Communities, the Commission for Gender Equality, the Auditor-General and the Electoral Commission.

9.3. CONSTITUTIONAL COURT JURISPRUDENCE

In a series of cases the Constitutional Court has adopted and outlined a version of equality that eschews a merely formalistic approach to embrace substantive equality, in effect rejecting the approach of equal treatment that reinforces inequalities.[44] As Justice Mokgoro noted in a 2004 decision challenging an aspect of the Pensions Fund:

> It is no mistake that our Constitution uses the phrase "achievement of equality." The tremendous indignity and political oppression that characterized the years of apartheid was coupled with the systemic entrenchment of economic disadvantage for millions of South Africans. The vast majority of this country's wealth remained then and remains still, as a consequence of the entrenched disadvantage, in the hands of a minority ... The use of the phrase 'achievement of equality' therefore recognizes that the creation of democracy and equal treatment before the law are not enough to foster substantive equality.[45]

Similarly, Justice O'Regan has noted that:

> ... although the long-term goal of our constitutional order is equal treatment, insisting upon equal treatment in circumstances of established inequality may well result in the entrenchment of that inequality.[46]

It is clear therefore that the Constitutional Court's interpretation of equality recognizes the structural underpinnings of inequality and disadvantage in

[44] For example, in *Fraser* v. *Naude* (1998) 11 BCLR 1357 (CC), the Court struck down a statute that disposed of a father's consent for adoption of a child born out of wedlock, while conversely requiring the consent of a father when the parents are married. Similarly, in *President of the Republic of South Africa* v. *Hugo* (1997) 6 BCLR 708 (CC), the Court allowed a facially gender discriminatory presidential pardon to stand where mothers of minor children would benefit. In a controversial decision, the Court contextualized the role of mothers in child-bearing and child-rearing, and concluded that a presidential pardon which benefited mothers in prison did not violate the rights of fathers in similar situations. In a 2004 decision which validated the affirmative action provision in the Bill of Rights, *Minister of Finance* v. *Van Heerden* (2004) 11 BCLR 1125 (CC) (*Van Heerden*), the Court stated:

> As we have seen a major constitutional object is the creation of a non-racial and non-sexist egalitarian society underpinned by human dignity, the rule of law, a democratic ethos and human rights. From there emerges a conception of equality that goes beyond mere formal equality and mere non-discrimination which requires identical treatment, whatever the starting point or impact: Ibid.

[45] *Minister of Finance & Anor* v. *Van Heerden* (2004) 11 BCLR 1125 (CC) para. 73 (opinion of Mokgoro J.).

[46] *President of the Republic of South Africa* v. *Hugo* (1997) 6 BCLR 708 (CC) para. 49.

South Africa and that purposive steps need to be taken to address such inequality and disadvantage.[47]

The Court has continued to confirm that affirmative action measures are required to achieve equality and that such measures are not a departure from the right to equality, but a necessary requirement for its achievement.[48]

In the Court's decisions on affirmative action, one observes the judges grappling to give effect to the meaning and limits of affirmative action, while confirming its constitutionality and necessity to redress the structural disadvantages wrought by apartheid.[49] Notably, in a significant 2014 judgment,[50] then Deputy Chief Justice Moseneke remarked that affirmative action measures are important mechanisms to effect equity.[51] But he also cautioned that government programs need to do more than merely overseeing the implementation of affirmative action.[52]

Arguably, the adjudication of socio-economic rights in pursuit of social justice has increasingly become fraught, as the promise of economic justice meets the reality of government resources and spending priorities.[53] Initially, the implementation of socio-economic rights in the Constitution held much promise, suggesting that such inclusion may bring meaningful relief to the poorest in the country. But the Court's jurisprudence regarding the promise has been mixed. One observes a somewhat more cautious approach in

47 *South African Police Service* v. *Solidarity obo Barnard* (2014) 10 BCLR 1195 (CC).

48 Ibid.

49 See, e.g., *Van Heerden* and *Harksen* v. *Lane NO* (1998) 1 SA 300 (CC).

50 *South African Police Service* v. *Solidarity obo Barnard* (2014) 10 BCLR 1195.

51 Justice Moseneke noted:

> We must remind ourselves that restitution measures, important as they are, cannot do all the work to advance social equity. A socially inclusive society idealised by the Constitution is a function of a good democratic state, for the one part, and the individual and collective agency of its citizenry, for the other. Our state must direct reasonable public resources to achieve substantive equality "for full and equal enjoyment of all rights and freedoms." It must take reasonable, prompt and effective measures to realise the socio-economic needs of all, especially the vulnerable. In the words of our Preamble the state must help "improve the quality of life of all citizens and free the potential of each person." That ideal would be within a grasp only through governance that is effective, transparent, accountable and responsive. Our public representatives will also do well to place a premium on an honest, efficient and economic use of public resources: ibid. para. 33.

52 Ibid.

53 See E. Christiansen, "Adjudicating non-justiciable rights: socio-economic rights and the South African Constitutional Court" (2007) 38 *Columbia Human Rights Law Review* 321–86 and R. Dixon and T. Ginsburg, "The South African Constitutional Court and socio-economic rights as 'insurance swaps'" (2013) University of Chicago Law School, Coase-Sandor Working Paper Series in Law and Economics.

the Court's jurisprudence as it considers its own institutional competence as well as not infringing government prerogatives regarding resource allocation.[54] The Court's analysis in cases involving socio-economic rights has seen the Court interpret socio-economic claims, including the right to education, against the government on the basis of "reasonableness."[55]

One of the Constitutional Court's earliest decisions regarding the right to health demonstrates the limitations to litigants based on the available resources of the state.[56] Similarly, in 2000 when the Court had to consider the right to housing,[57] the judgment and its implementation once again highlighted significant limits to the Court's ability to meaningfully impact the socio-economic conditions of many of South Africa's poorest communities.[58]

In its decision the Court affirmed that the government had a duty in terms of s. 26 of the Constitution (the right to adequate housing) to adopt reasonable policy, legislative and budgetary measures to provide relief for people who have no access to land, no roof over their heads, and who are living in intolerable conditions.[59] However, due to a combination of factors, including bureaucratic inefficiency and indifference, the applicant in this case died a few years later, without ever receiving reasonable accommodation from the state.[60] Despite this, the decision had an impact on government policy regarding the provision of housing to those left without any means of accommodation.

Six months after the *Grootboom* decision, the right to housing was again considered by the Court.[61] The case involved a group of poor residents in aninformal settlement located on the banks of a stream. When the stream flooded and washed away their residences, the government established a cabinet

[54] See, e.g., *Mazibuko* v. *City of Johannesburg* (2010) 4 SA 1 (CC).

[55] See, e.g., *Government of the Republic of South Africa* v. *Grootboom* (2001) 1 SA 46 (CC) (*Grootboom*).

[56] *Soobramoney* v. *Minister of Health, KwaZulu-Natal* (1998) 1 SA 765 (CC).

[57] *Grootboom*.

[58] T. Madlingozi, "Post-Apartheid social movements and the quest for the elusive 'new' South Africa" (2007) 34 *Journal of Law and Society* 77–98.

[59] The case concerned an application for temporary shelter brought by a group of people, including a number of children, who were without shelter following their brutal eviction from private land on which they were squatting. The conditions under which the community lived were deplorable; they had access to one tap and no sanitation facilities: ibid.

[60] Although this decision has been widely hailed as setting an important precedent for the enforcement of socio-economic rights at both the local and global level, many commentators have expressed disappointment in the Court's focus on "reasonableness." They instead argue that the Court should have applied the "minimum core approach" as adopted in the interpretation of the *International Covenant on Economic, Social and Cultural Rights*. See M. Pieterse, "Resuscitating socio-economic rights: constitutional entitlement to health care service" (2006) 22 *South African Journal on Human Rights* 473.

[61] *Minister of Public Works* v. *Kyalami Ridge* (2001) 7 BCLR 652 (CC).

committee and allocated a considerable amount of money to assist the informal settlement dwellers (in furtherance of the policy enunciated in *Grootboom*).[62] The committee decided to give the settlement dwellers temporary prefabricated homes with bathroom facilities on the grounds of a large farm prison, near an upper-middle class white residential suburb. Property owners of the suburb brought a claim before the Constitutional Court, arguing that placing these settlement dwellers half a mile from the suburb would depress their property values, and that the government had no right to take this action but had to pass special legislation to this effect. The Constitutional Court found that the government had acted properly in providing housing to the squatter-dwellers. It concluded that where there is a constitutional demand, no special legislation is necessary because the demand itself is sufficient legislative authority to authorize government action.[63]

The limitations in the enforcement of the Court's decision in the *Grootboom* decision suggest that litigants supported by social action movements are far more likely to not only receive a favorable decision, but also successful implementation of that decision.[64] In the *Treatment Action* case,[65] the appeal to the Constitutional Court was directed at reversing orders made in a high court against the government because of perceived shortcomings in its response to an aspect of the HIV/AIDS challenge. In its lengthy decision, the Constitutional Court found that the government had not reasonably addressed the need to reduce the risk of HIV-positive mothers' transmitting the disease to their babies at birth. More specifically, the finding was that the government had acted unreasonably in refusing to make an antiretroviral drug called nevirapine available in the public health sector where the attending doctor considered it medically necessary, and in not setting out a time frame for a national program to prevent mother-to-child transmission of HIV.[66]

The implementation of the Court's decision, despite initial hitches, was relatively successful because of the involvement of the Treatment Action

62 Ibid.

63 Ibid. para. 52.

64 See J. M. Berger and A. Kapczynski, "The story of the TAC Case: the potential and limits of socio-economic rights litigation in South Africa" in D. R. Hurwitz and M. L. Satterthwaite (eds.), *Human Rights Advocacy Stories* (New Delhi: Foundation Press, 2009) (available at www.www.ssrn.com/abstract=1323522 *or* www.dx.doi.org/10.2139/ssrn.1323522) (accessed date November 20, 2017); see also M. Pieterse, "Health, social movements and rights-based litigation in South Africa" (2008) 35 *Journal of Law and Society* 364–88.

65 *Minister of Health* v. *Treatment Action Campaign (1)* (2002) 10 BLCR 1033 (CC).

66 Ibid. para. 95.

Campaign, South Africa's most visible post-1994 advocacy movement.[67] Their efforts ensured the roll-out of nevirapine to HIV-positive pregnant women in public hospitals throughout South Africa.

In addition to focusing on the positive aspects of socio-economic rights, that is, the obligation of the state to provide certain rights, the Court has also focused on what has been seen as the negative component of socio-economic rights. For example, in a case involving the protection of a tenant against eviction in the process of executing a judgment on debts, the Court held that such a process violated the constitutional right to housing.[68]

The Court has not had occasion to consider the substance of the right to education. Most of the cases, except for one or two, raised questions not central to the content of the right to education. For example, the Court has considered the constitutionality of disallowing non-South African citizens permanent employment in public schools.[69] The Court has also considered the implications and validity of government spending in education,[70] as well as the regulation of admission of learners to public schools.[71] It has also considered the rights of learners to practice their religious and cultural traditions.[72]

A cursory scan of the Court's twenty-year socio-economic rights jurisprudence suggests that, even though litigants seeking economic justice in the courts may ultimately receive some relief, court action has a greater chance of success if accompanied by nonlegal strategies, including civil society engagement, lobbying to government, and educational and other initiatives. In other words, economic justice is possible and sustainable only when litigation is one part of a more comprehensive struggle.[73]

67 See M. Heywood, "TAC Builds Civil Society Support for a Successful ARV Rollout," *Aids Analysis Africa*, January 2004; M. Mabali, "TAC in the History of Rights-Based, Patient Driven HIV/AIDS Activism in South Africa," (Ann Arbor, MI: University of Michigan, June 2005) (available at www.quod.lib.umich.edu/p/passages/4761530.0010.011/–tac-in-the-history-of-rights-based-patient-driven-hivaids?rgn=main;view=fulltext) (accessed date November 20, 2017).

68 *Jaftha* v. *Schoeman* (2005) 1 BCLR 78 (CC).

69 *Larbi-Odam* v. *Members of the Executive Council for Education (North-West Province)* (1997) 12 BCLR 1655 (CC).

70 *Bel Porto School Governing Body* v. *Premier of the Western Cape Province* (2002) 3 SA 265 (CC).

71 *Federation of Governing Bodies for South African Schools* v. *Member of the Executive Council for Education, Gauteng* (2016) 8 BCLR 1050 (CC).

72 *Christian Education South Africa* v. *Minister of Education* (2000) 4 SA 757 (CC); *MEC for Education: KwaZulu-Natal* v. *Pillay* (2008) 2 BCLR 99 (CC).

73 See Pieterse, "Health, social movements and rights-based litigation in South Africa." See also Ballard, Habib and Valodia, *Voices of Protest*.

9.4. SKEPTICISM ABOUT THE TRANSFORMATIVE POSSIBILITIES OF THE CONSTITUTION

The seeds of disillusionment with the Constitution among many sectors of the population, particularly the black population, can be found in the growing and seemingly persistent levels of economic inequalities that continue to reinforce apartheid's racial narrative. In other words, as the markers of affluence in South Africa become more multi-racial, the face of poverty continues to be black.[74] In addition, the party of liberation, the African National Congress, which established the first democratic government under the leadership of Nelson Mandela, has increasingly lost its moral status as corruption scandals and reports of unbridled venality in its ranks continue to besmirch its name and reputation.[75] Moreover, the bargain struck by the Truth and Reconciliation Commission, namely truth and forgiveness in exchange for justice, now rankle young South Africans who believe that the negotiated settlement resulted in too much compromise for black South Africans with no concomitant sacrifice on the part of whites.[76]

Before and during the constitutional drafting process, the potential of the Constitution to transform the lives of all South Africans had almost been an item of faith. Not just admired globally, the Constitution also infused judges, lawyers and scholars within South Africa with a kind of zealous faith and passionate devotion to its transformational prospects. As one of South Africa's most celebrated jurists has noted:

> It is argued here that a creative jurisprudence of equality coupled with substantive interpretation of the content of "socio-economic" rights should restore social justice as a premier foundational value of our constitutional

[74] Madlingozi, "Post-apartheid social movements." S. Sibanda, "Not purpose-made! Transformative constitutionalism, post-independence constitutionalism and the struggle to eradicate poverty" (2011) 22 *Stellenbosch Law Review* 482–500.

[75] See C. Bundy, *Short-Changed? South Africa Since Apartheid* (Athens, OH: Ohio University Press, 2015); see also IPSOS, *Election Outlook: IPSOS Poll of Polls* (Press Release, August 2, 2016) (available at www.pressoffice.mg.co.za/ipsos/PressRelease.php?StoryID=269032) (accessed date November 20, 2017).

[76] As an op-ed piece in the New York Times in December 2016, noted: South Africans are beginning to reclaim their power over a sentimental mythology about forgiveness and racial harmony that has been, for at least a decade, inauthentic and out of step with the realities of most people's lives. They have accepted that the exceptionalism of South Africa's rosy story of transformation to a rainbow nation has threatened to undermine their capacity to challenge authority and ask deeper questions. S. Msimang, "Making South Africa great again" (December 8, 2016) *New York Times*.

democracy side by side, if not interactively with, human dignity, equality, freedom, accountability, responsiveness and openness.[77]

But at the same time the possibilities of the Constitution to redress the structural economic inequalities in South Africa have been met with some skepticism and have been the source of much debate since its adoption.[78]

The replacement of the language of rights with the language of redistribution, particularly after 1989, was the context in which the South Africa Constitution was adopted. The dominant legal paradigm culminated in what De Sousa Santos has termed the judicialization of politics and the prioritization of legal institutions as the primary venues for securing rights.[79] As I have argued elsewhere:

> Despite its importance in strengthening state institutions, legal formalism plays a powerful ideological role in channeling political aspirations and immobilizing grassroots political struggle.[80]

The seductive possibilities generated by litigation for social and economic rights may disproportionately influence communities to redirect their attention from nonlegal transformative strategies that may produce a deeper and more enduring economic, political and social justice. Translating formal legal rights into substantive socio-economic rights remains the biggest challenge in South Africa. There is a causal link between this challenge and contemporary struggles, particularly in relation to higher education.

Skepticism about the transformative possibilities of the South African Constitution has been reinforced with respect to some of the jurisprudence of the Constitutional Court, especially the jurisprudence around social and economic rights.[81] Some critics have argued that the Court has been too

77 D. Moseneke, "Transformative adjudication" (2002) 18 *South African Journal on Human Rights* 309–19, 314.

78 See K. van Marle, "Transformative constitutionalism as/and critique" (2009) 20 *Stellenbosch Law Review* 286–301; K. G. Young, "The minimum core of socio-economic rights: A concept in search of content" (2008) 33 *Yale Journal of International Law* 113–75.

79 B. De Sousa Santos, *Toward A New Common Sense: Law Science and Politics in The Paradigmatic Transition* (New York, NY: Routledge, 1995) 266–7. See also U. Baxi, "Voices of suffering and the future of human rights" (1998) 8 *Transnational Law & Contemporary Problems* 125–69.

80 P. Andrews, "Making room for critical race theory in international law: some practical pointers" (2000) 45 *Villanova Law Review* 855–85 at 865.

81 P. Bond, "Constitutionalism as a barrier to the resolution of widespread community rebellions in South Africa" (2014) 41 *Politikon* 461–82; M. Pieterse, "Eating socio-economic rights: the usefulness of rights talk in alleviating social hardship revisited" (2007) 29 *Human Rights Quarterly* 796–822.

reticent in its approach and should have shown less deference to the legislative and executive branch with regard to the enforcement of social and economic rights.[82]

Among a new generation of legal academics, there is also some criticism of what is termed "constitutional worship."[83] Referring to the scholarship of Jean and John Comaroff, they bemoan "the fetishism of law and constitutionality" and the "fetishism of the legal ... in constitution-obsessed South Africa."[84] As Joel Modiri observes:

> To replace one legal "master-narrative" (the common law) with another (the Constitution) seems to me to only reproduce the problem. And it is always worth remembering that the roots of totalitarianism – of the mind and of the body politic – lie precisely in this pathological attachment to the reigning legal and political order.[85]

In this he has found common cause with other critical scholars of the global South. For example, Makau Mutua has for some time cast a rather dubious eye on the possibilities of societal transformation in a constitutional democracy like South Africa in which structural economic and social disadvantage is deeply entrenched. Noting that the constitutional arrangement signified the triumph of liberal legalism culminating in over half a century's human rights activism, Makau Mutua observes that:

> The construction of the post-apartheid state represents the first deliberate and calculated effort in history to craft a human rights state—a polity that is primarily animated by human rights norms. South Africa was the first state to be reborn after the universal acceptance, at least rhetorically, of human rights ideals by states of all the major cultural and political traditions.[86]

82 See L. A. Williams, "The justiciability of water rights: Mazibuko v. City of Johannesburg" (2010) 18 *Willamette Journal of International Law and Dispute Resolution* 211; S. Liebenberg and K. Young, "Adjudicating social and economic rights: can democratic experimentalism help?" in H. Garcia et al. (eds.), *Social and Economic Rights in Theory and Practice: Critical Inquiries* (London: Routledge, 2015) (available at www.ssrn.com/abstract=2799906) (accessed date November 20, 2017).

83 J. Modiri, "The time and space of critical legal pedagogy" (2016) 27 *Stellenbosch Law Review* 507–34, 513.

84 Ibid. citing J. Comaroff and J. Comaroff, "Law and disorder in the postcolony: an introduction" in J. Comaroff and J. Comaroff (eds.), *Law and Disorder in the Postcolony* (Chicago, IL: University of Chicago Press, 2006).

85 Modiri, "Time and space" 514.

86 M. wa Mutua, "Hope and despair for a new South Africa: the limits of rights discourse" (1997) 10 *Harvard Human Rights Law Journal* 63–114, 65.

That the South African Constitution is a compromise document located within the context of the triumphalist ascendancy of a global liberal legal ideology at the end of the twentieth century does not detract from its transformative potential. To discount this possibility and what it has meant for South Africans, especially black South Africans, is almost to ignore the potency of rights and dignity. The fundamental legacy of apartheid was a complete erasure of humanity, of dignity, of all rights. The Constitution with its extensive listing of rights and its anchor in dignity is the foundation and the architecture to restore and give back to South Africans humanity, dignity and rights that were erased under apartheid.

As Patricia Williams noted so poignantly regarding a similar critique from critical legal scholars about civil rights law in the United States:

> "Rights" feels new in the mouths of most black people. It is still deliciously empowering to say. It is the magic wand of visibility and invisibility, of inclusion and exclusion, of power and no power. The concept of rights, both positive and negative, is the marker of our citizenship, our relation to others.[87]

For black South Africans, her words are entirely appropriate. Denied the most basic and fundamental rights, ought the starting point not to be the "deliciously empowering" Preamble to the Constitution and all the rights contained therein?

Critics of the constitutional framework point to its paradigmatic limits, particularly its genesis in liberal legalism. But those limits should be contextualized in the historic moment of the political transition and do not detract from the Constitution's ability to make a difference to the lives of people, whether HIV/AIDS sufferers, gay married couples, women who suffer from violence, the poor and others.[88] There is no doubt that many limitations, including the doctrine of separation of powers, render the judicial enforcement of socio-economic rights especially vexing. But by including justiciable social and economic rights in the Constitution, the needs of the poor are converted into the realm of legal entitlement.[89]

87 P. J. Williams, *The Alchemy of Race and Rights* 164 (Cambridge, MA: Harvard University Press, 1991).

88 T. Roux, *The Politics of Principle: The First South African Constitutional Court, 1995–2005* (Cambridge: Cambridge University Press, 2013); H. Klug, *The Constitution of South Africa.*

89 Danie Brand noted that:

> First, courts' adjudication of socio-economic rights claims becomes part of the political discourse, even a medium through which this discourse partly plays out ... Second, courts also occupy a symbolic, or perhaps more accurately, an exemplary, role with

In the final analysis, the limits of translating formal legal rights into socio-economic realities stem from a range of factors, including the lack of implementation and enforcement because of an absence of will, commitment, inertia and incompetence on the part of government, the private sector and the wider society. This limitation also includes lack of access to legal resources on the part of those whose rights ought to be pursued. Another limiting factor comprises deeply ingrained illiberal philosophical ideas and attitudes, including racism, sexism, patriarchy, homophobia and xenophobia leading to the lack of a shared human rights culture across the entire society. Widespread poverty and economic inequality severely test the sustainability of the constitutional framework, and if not adequately addressed, the skeptics of "constitutional worship" may prevail and render the Constitution a casualty.

9.5. THE NATIONAL REVIEW OF THE LL.B. DEGREE

A national review of the LL.B. degree at law campuses across South Africa commenced in 2012. Mandated by the Council of Higher Education, a statutory body, the review will complete its work later in 2017 and a national report card of law faculties will be issued. Although generated by concerns raised by the legal profession regarding the role of law faculties in adequately preparing candidate attorneys, the review provided a timely and welcome exercise of self-reflection on the part of law faculties. The review process required each law faculty to write a self-assessment report responding to a series of questions that focus on the impact of the Constitution on the entire program of legal education.

Setting its sights on a range of weighty issues, including transformative constitutionalism and responsiveness to social justice, the LL.B. review is particularly concerned about the manner in which the values and ethos embodied in the Preamble to South Africa's Constitution occupies a central place in the law school curriculum as well as in teaching methodologies and student engagement. The review is also paying close attention to the teaching of ethics across the entire program of legal education and especially how ethics is inculcated into law student learning and professional development.

---

respect to poverty and need discourses – their vocabulary, the conceptual structures they rely on, the rhetorical strategies they employ infiltrate and so influence and shape the political discourses around poverty and need.

D. Brand, "The politics of need interpretation and the adjudication of socio-economic rights claims in South Africa" in A. J. Van der Walt (ed.), *Theories of Social and Economic Justice* (Stellenbosch: Sun Press, 2005) 17, 24.

Mindful of the changing nature of law practice and the diverse array of career choices unfolding fairly rapidly, the review raises a series of questions about the nature and manner of preparation in law school for the various graduate career pathways. Included in these pathways is the availability of post-graduate studies in law, including academic career pathways. Although much attention is paid in the review to teaching students the history, underlying values and knowledge of the South African legal system, a series of questions include the responsiveness of law faculties to the imperatives of globalization. Included as well is the inquiry about the responsiveness of law faculties to the evolving information technology.

Of vital concern in the review is the question of the profile of the staff and students, especially the academic staff, as noted in the following question:

> How is the academic staff profile, in terms of qualification, experience and levels of appointment, aligned with the program structure and content to ensure that students are exposed to a diversity of expertise, ideas, styles and approaches, as well as the achievement of all the graduate attributes?[90]

The review process entailed site teams visiting all of South Africa's law faculties to gather facts on the ground and to confirm the information provided for in the self-evaluation reports submitted by each faculty. The report card for each law faculty is likely to be issued in mid-2017 and will determine the accreditation status of each law faculty.

9.5.1. *Exploring the Meaning of Transformation for Universities*

> ... Transformation is a complex, multi-layered and dynamic process which not only encompasses the need to change demographics, but encompasses the need to promote substantive change in the culture of institutions of higher learning, as well as the attitudes and perceptions within institutions of higher learning[91]

As the above quotation signifies, the project of transformation embraces a range of concerns and is a multifaceted one. At its core is the attempt to take decisive steps to overcoming the legacy of centuries of colonialism and

[90] Council of Higher Education, *National Review of Bachelor of Laws (LLB) Programmes: The Institutional Self-Evaluation Report* (available at www.che.ac.za/sites/default/files/LLB%20Self%20Evaluation%20Report%20Template_%20(%20Updated%20Version)_2.pdf) (accessed date November 20, 2017).

[91] South African Human Rights Commission, *SAHRC Report* 29.

decades of apartheid and their effect on all institutions in South Africa, including institutions of higher education.[92]

For universities, there are several issues to be considered in transformation, among them institutional identity, culture, structure and organization. In addition, issues such as the curriculum, faculty research and scholarship, teaching and learning methods, and physical spaces are also ripe for examination.[93]

One aspect of the transformation agenda includes the imperative to decolonize institutions and education. The issue of decolonization is not of recent vintage and can be found in the literature analyzing events leading to the end of colonialism, as seen in the writings of Franz Fanon[94] and Paul Robeson,[95] as well as in literature examining the postcolonial period.[96] Still a contested concept and embodying several definitions, decolonization has been described as a project of "re-centering,"[97] raising the question "had our law developed with the national public interest at its core, rather than colonial and neo-colonial interests, what would it look like?"[98] Mahmood Mamdani argues that decolonization "has moved from one limited to political independence" and external domination "to a broader transformation of institutions."[99] This is especially so for those institutions that were "critical to the reproduction of racial and ethnic subjectivities legally enforced under colonialism," as universities arguably were.[100]

92 C. Suransky and J. C. van der Merwe, "Transcending apartheid in higher education: transforming an institutional culture" (2016) 19 *Journal of Ethnicity Race and Education* 577–97.

93 For a thoughtful reflection on transformation in legal education, see P. Maisel and S. R. Jones, "Implementing the social and economic promise of the Constitution: the role of South African legal education" in P. E. Andrews and S. Bazilli (eds.), *Law And Rights: Global Perspectives On Constitutionalism And Governance* (Lake Mary, FL: Vandeplas Publishing, 2008) (available at www.ssrn.com/abstract=1507947) (accessed date November 20, 2017).

94 F. Fanon, *Wretched of The Earth* (1961) trans. C. Farrington (Harmondsworth: Penguin, 1967).

95 P. Andrews, "A champion for African freedom: Paul Robeson and the struggle against apartheid" (2014) 77 *Albany Law Review* 473–98.

96 See A. Loomba, *Colonialism/Postcolonialism* (London: Routledge, 1998); I. G. Shivji, *Where Is Uhuru? Reflections on the Struggle for Democracy in Africa* (Cape Town: Fahamu Books, 2009).

97 A. Mbembe, *Decolonizing Knowledge and The Question of the Archive* (available at www.wiser.wits.ac.za/system/files/Achille%20Mbembe%20-%20Decolonizing%20Knowledge%20and%20the%20Question%20of%20the%20Archive.pdf) (accessed date November 20, 2017).

98 C. B. Ncube, "Decolonizing Intellectual Property Law in Pursuit of Africa's Development" (2016) 8 *WIPO Journal* 34–40, 36 (available at www.wipo.int/edocs/pubdocs/en/wipo_journal_wpj8n1.pdf) (accessed date November 20, 2017).

99 M. Mamdani, "Between the public intellectual and the scholar: decolonization and some post-independence initiatives in African higher education" (2016) 17 *Inter-Asia Cultural Studies* 68–83.

100 Ibid.

But why the demands for transformation now, and why with such urgency and vehemence? To address this question requires a look back to 1994 and the compact to destroy the old apartheid order and the birth of the new democratic order as embodied in the expansive Constitution and Bill of Rights. Explicit in the spirit and text was the promise of a decent life for all, especially as encapsulated in the sections on equality and dignity as well as those sections listing a range of political, social and economic rights.

In 1994, at the end of legal apartheid, the higher education system comprised twenty-six universities in South Africa arranged strictly and systemically along racial and ethnic lines. Nine universities were designated for white South Africans, one each was set aside for "colored" and Indian South Africans, and the rest were reserved for ethnically designated black South Africans. Most of those universities, sometimes referred to as "tribal colleges," were located within the former bantustans.[101]

After 1994, it was apparent that to dismantle this highly stratified and unequal infrastructure of higher education required a fundamental rethink and a radical disruption. Flowing from the constitutional imperatives was a call to all universities to change the demographic profile of the staff and student bodies, in particular at those universities that were classified as white in the apartheid era. Not only were they the best resourced and most elite of South African universities, they were also largely located in the major urban areas linked to career possibilities and other societal structures of upward mobility. They *were* the key to a sustained trajectory of economic advancement and social mobility.

Conversely, this call for demographic transformation generated a different set of concerns for the previously disadvantaged black universities. At those institutions the racial demographics in 1994 were for the most part representative, but the historical lack of resources, authoritarian institutional cultures and a range of other factors served to impede transformation in line with constitutional imperatives of equality and dignity.[102] In short, they were not equipped to give effect to the exhortation in the Preamble to the Constitution to *improve the quality of life of all citizens and free the potential of each person.*[103]

Transformation initiatives at South African universities have included changing the demographics of staff and students, thereby paying particular attention

[101] I. Bunting, "The higher education landscape under apartheid" in N. Cloete et al. (eds.), *Transformation in Higher Education: Global Pressures and Local Realities in South Africa* (Dordrecht: Springer, 2002) 35–52.

[102] Ibid.; C. Napier, "The Transkei Bantustan and its university: A crisis of legitimacy" (1985) 18(2) *Reality* 15–8 (available at www.sahistory.org.za/sites/default/files/DC/remar85.5/remar85.5.pdf) (accessed date November 20, 2017).

[103] Constitution, Preamble.

to the recruitment and retention of a more diverse cohort of academic staff to reflect South Africa's racial and gender demographics. Universities have examined teaching and learning methodologies to ensure that they are able to educate graduates who are competent and skilled. They have also turned their attention to the learning environment, to student engagement, to institutional culture and to staff professional development.[104]

Transformation initiatives have also included a determined response to manifestations of racism, sexism, homophobia and other forms of conduct that impede the dignity of individuals.[105] In the words of Judge Dennis Davis:

> A transformed system of higher education is one that is free from all forms of unfair discrimination ... and artificial barriers to access and success, as well as one that is built on the principles of social inclusivity, mutual respect and acceptance.[106]

Slowly gathering steam since 1994, but especially since 2010, a series of steps have been taken to accelerate the process of transformation in South Africa.[107] Arguably, the 2015 and 2016 student protests have fast-tracked the need for transformation.

9.5.2. *Transformation and Law Faculties*

For law faculties, the transformative vision embodied in South Africa's Constitution provides a potent driver for change.[108] Law faculties are authorized to educate and train future generations of legal professionals with the

[104] Groundup Staff, "The debate over what is taught" (May 14, 2015) *Mail and Guardian* (available at www.mg.co.za/article/2015-05-14-uct-and-transformation-the-debate-over-what-is-taught) (accessed date November 20, 2017).

[105] See B. Gumede, "Feminist groups take over sexism fight on campuses" (11 January 2016) *Sowetan* (available at www.pressreader.com/south-africa/sowetan/20160111/281728383508598) (accessed date November 20, 2017); S. Msimang, "South Africa's topless protesters are fighting shame on their own terms" (May 5, 2016) *The Guardian* (available at www.theguardian.com/world/2016/may/05/south-africas-topless-protesters-are-fighting-shame-on-their-own-terms) (accessed date November 20, 2017).

[106] South African Human Rights Commission, *SAHRC Report* 8.

[107] See C. Soudien, Development Bank of South Africa, *Transformation in Higher Education In South Africa: A Briefing Paper* (2010) (available at www.dhet.gov.za/summit/Docs/2010Docs/Transformation%20in%20higher%20education-%20A%20briefing%20paper%20by%20Crain%20Soudien.pdf) (accessed date November 20, 2017); see also L. V. Mazwi-Tanga, "Gender and transformation in higher education" in Council on Higher Education, *Reflections Of South African University Leaders 1981 To 2014* (Cape Town: African Minds, 2016) 159–81.

[108] See L. Greenbaum, "Legal education in South Africa: harmonizing the aspirations of transformative constitutionalism with our educational legacy" (2015) 60 *New York Law School Law*

knowledge, expertise, empathy and skill needed to give effect to the range of political, socioeconomic and cultural rights embedded in the Constitution. The former Chief Justice Pius Langa noted that "the change to legal education is a change in mind-set, not simply a change in laws."[109]

It is not possible to eradicate colonial and apartheid laws, legal processes and legal culture without transforming all legal institutions, including law faculties. They are preeminent sites of constitutional transformation by their capacity and resources to embark on imaginative and sustainable approaches to training future generations of legal professionals who will give meaning to the text and spirit of the Constitution. It is arguable that in the past two decades of democracy, despite progress in some areas, transformation at law faculties has been somewhat limited. As so stridently noted by the legal scholar, Joel Modiri:

> If the shortcomings, inadequacies and failings ... in legal education could be traced to one central problem, it would be the failure of law teachers and law faculties or schools to adapt to the present-day context – to recognize and respond to the complexity and character of living, knowing and doing in post-1994 South Africa.[110]

In the words of the late former Chief Justice Pius Langa, constitutional transformation is:

> A permanent ideal, a way of looking at the world that creates a space in which dialogue and contestation are truly possible, in which new ways of being are constantly explored and created, accepted and rejected and in which change is unpredictable but the idea of change is constant. This is perhaps the ultimate vision of a transformative, rather than a transitional Constitution.[111]

According to the former Chief Justice therefore, the transformative nature of the Constitution "envisions a society that would always be open to change and contestation," and one "that will always be defined by transformation."[112]

This is no doubt the directive for law faculties to embrace change and contestation across the entire program of legal education and to do so constantly.

Review 463–91; G. Quinot, "Transformative legal education" (2012) 129 *South African Law Journal* 411–33.

[109] Chief Justice P. Langa, "Transformative constitutionalism" (2006) 17 *Stellenbosch Law Review* 351–60, 356.

[110] Modiri, "Time and space" 507.

[111] Chief Justice Pius Langa, "Transformative constitutionalism" 354.

[112] Ibid.

Indeed, nothing short of "a new imagination: new definitions, new categories, new lines of enquiry, new practices and new mind sets" will suffice.[113]

Of significance is a rethinking of the content of legal education and the various ways that the program of legal education may reinforce colonial and apartheid mentalities. Central to this rethinking is the undertaking that the entire corpus of South African law, namely, private, commercial, public, religious and indigenous law, is to be subjected to the imperatives of the Constitution. This rethinking also requires an examination of the infrastructure of law faculties, including a look at departmental segmentation that may immunize various parts of the curricula from the transformative possibilities of the Constitution.

In light of the constitutional directive that the common law be developed in line with the values of the Constitution, this is particularly pertinent regarding the menu of private law offerings.[114] The various areas of private law, including contract, tort and property, are constitutionally obligated to marginalize or eradicate the vestiges of South Africa's colonial past in their curricula offerings. The constitutional mandate to develop the common law in line with constitutional values is a recognition that it is in the private realm that disadvantage and discrimination abounds, and where eradication of such disadvantage and discrimination is hardest to dislodge.

Transformation in legal education therefore requires that there be no analytical curtain between any area of law and the Constitution. As Judge Dennis Davis has noted, "The entire body of law must be analyzed from the perspective of congruence or lack thereof with the core normative framework of the constitution."[115]

Although eloquently challenged by Professor Anton Fagan in his inaugural lecture,[116] the Constitutional Court has reaffirmed the view articulated by Judge Davis. Noting that in South Africa there is only one system of law, the supreme law which is the Constitution, and "all law, including the common law, derives its force from the Constitution and is subject to constitutional control."[117] In his writing Professor Barnard-Naude has also made these points

[113] Modiri, "Time and space" 507.

[114] Constitution, s. 39(2).

[115] D. Davis, "Legal transformation and legal education: Congruence or conflict?" in A. Price and M. Bishop (eds.), *A Transformative Justice? Essays in Honour of Pius Langa* (Cape Town: Juta, 2015) 172.

[116] A. Fagan, "The secondary role of the spirit, purport and objects of the Bill of Rights in the common law's development" (2010) 127 *South African Law Journal* 611–24.

[117] *Pharmaceutical Manufacturers Association of SA: In Re Ex-Parte President of the RSA* (2000) 2 SA 674 (CC). See also *Carmichele* v. *Minister of Safety and Security* (2001) 4 SA 938 (CC).

persuasively, citing Kelsen to argue that the transition from apartheid to constitutional democracy was a legal revolution, with all the consequences of disruption of and disconnection with the old order that accompanies such revolution.[118]

It can and has, nevertheless, been forcefully argued that it cannot be denied that the substantive break with the apartheid legal order that the interim Constitution represented, amounted to a "constitutional revolution."[119]

In summary, therefore, the process of transformation for law faculties entails attention to changing the racial and gender demographics of academic staff and students, rethinking curricular offerings, research agendas and priorities, institutional processes and culture,[120] and paying closer attention to teaching and learning and to student engagement.[121]

9.6. VIEWING TRANSFORMATION THROUGH A CRITICAL RACE LENS

The struggle for transformation and decolonization at South African universities has found contemporary and historical reverberations elsewhere, especially in the United States.[122] Today's protests in the United States around the banner *Blacks Lives Matter* and the earlier *Occupy Wall Street* (and its several spinoffs) have resonated strongly with this generation of South African

[118] J. Barnard-Naude, "The pedigree of the common law and the unnecessary Constitution: a discussion of the Supreme Court's decision in *RH* v. *DE*" (2016) 133 *South African Law Journal* 16–28.

[119] Ibid. 18. The contention of a legal revolution has also been made by former Justice of the Constitutional Court, Justice Laurie Ackermann. See L. Ackermann, "The legal nature of the South African constitutional revolution" (2004) *New Zealand Law Review* 633–79.

[120] J. Teboho Lebakeng et al., "Epistimicide, institutional cultures and the imperatives for the Africanisation of universities in South Africa" (2006) 13 *Alternation* 70.

[121] This is not new in the current South African context, but it has become far more relevant because of the demands of transformation. Indeed, many universities have expended significant resources on innovative and collaborative methods of teaching to enhance student engagement and participation. These endeavors are particularly pertinent to accommodate the different learning styles of students and to acknowledge the learning of students for whom English is not a first language. At the UCT the Centre for Higher Education and Development has been instrumental in generating a culture of teaching and learning to accommodate some of the concerns. See University of Cape Town, *CHED* (available at www.ched.uct.ac.za/) (accessed date November 20, 2017).

[122] See R. Maart, "When black consciousness walks arm-in-arm with critical race theory to meet racism and white consciousness in the humanities" (2014) 21 *Alternation* 54–82. One could probably see reverberations in the Arab Spring or other pro-democracy movements of the past decade, but the racial comparisons and the issues that they generate make a comparison with the USA more compelling. See J. Modiri, "Towards a post-apartheid critical race jurisprudence: 'divining our racial themes'" (2012) 27 *South African Public Law* 229 (2012).

students both with respect to the racial realities as well as the economic inequalities that continue to haunt both societies. In addition, the symbols as displayed in social media and other forms of popular communication suggest a strong affinity with *Black Lives Matter* and *Occupy Wall Street*.[123]

Because the South African university protests reverberated so strongly with their American counterparts, and because race and racial transformation are so central to the demands of the protesters, the following questions surface: What relevance might a critical race perspective bring to our understanding of transformation and decolonization at South African universities and what is the transformative potential of such a perspective? Although several theoretical perspectives may have application regarding the contemporary struggle for access to decolonized higher education, the perspectives of critical race theory ("CRT") seem most pertinent. CRT seeks to speak directly to this historical moment in South Africa and the need to realign and readjust the racial (and economic) order. CRT invites a radical approach to South African social and economic relations that advances the centrality of race as key to that approach, in the same way that Franz Fanon and Steve Biko postulated.[124]

Embraced by a growing number of legal scholars of color in the United States beginning in the late 1980s,[125] CRT incorporates "an experientially grounded, oppositionally expressed, and transformatively aspirational concern with race and other socially constructed hierarchies."[126] Displaying skepticism of liberalism, much of critical race theory is characterized as well by "deep discontent" with "civil rights litigation and activism, faith in the legal system, and hope for progress."[127]

The genesis of much of CRT suggests a hybrid of critical theories and perspectives with race at the core.[128] CRT thus builds upon and is the theoretical progeny of a range of global critical legal theorists represented in the works

[123] A. Akbar, *Law's Exposure: The Movement and the Legal Academy, Public Law and Legal Theory* (Working Paper Series No. 320, November 13, 2015) (available at www.jle.aals.org/cgi/viewcontent.cgi?article=1325&context=home) (accessed date November 20, 2017).

[124] F. Fanon, *Wretched of The Earth*; S. Biko, *I Write What I Like* ed. A. Stubbs (Chicago, IL: University of Chicago Press, 2002).

[125] R. Delgado, "Legal scholarship: insiders, outsiders, editors" (1992) 63 *University of Colorado Law Review* 717–23, 721.

[126] D. A. Bell, "Who's afraid of critical race theory?" (1995) *University of Illinois Law Review* 893–910, 906.

[127] See R. Delgado, "Critique of liberalism" in R. Delgado and J. Stefancic (eds.), *Critical Race Theory: The Cutting Edge*, 1st ed. (Philadelphia, PA: Temple University Press, 2000) 1.

[128] See K. Crenshaw et al. (eds.), *Critical Race Theory: The Key Writings That Formed the Movement* (New York, NY: The New Press, 1995).

of Boa De Sousa Santos,[129] Upendra Baxi,[130] Duncan Kennedy[131] and Ratna Kapur.[132] As the late CRT scholar Jerome McCrystal Culp noted:

> Critical race theory is not uni-perpectival; there is no single consensus of a characterization of the theory. Certainly, the name "critical race theory" suggests some connection to critical legal theory, yet its name derives more directly from the name "critical theory" by which some refer to the tenets of Habermas and Marcuse. The contributors to critical race theory have resisted defining themselves.[133]

Critical race scholars are also bedfellows of a cohort of critical scholars of international law who have enriched the field by embedding the identity and experiences of the global south. Scholars of this genre include Anthony Anghie,[134] Makau Mutua,[135] James Gathii,[136] Caroline Ncube[137] and several more who are located both in the global south and elsewhere.[138]

Despite diverse methodologies and perspectives of those whose work falls under the umbrella of CRT, the unifying theme of this body of work is a

[129] B. De Sousa Santos, *Epistemologies of The South: Justice Against Epistemicide* (Boulder, CO: Paradigm Publishers, 2014); B. De Sousa Santos, *Toward A New Legal Common Sense: Law, Globalization, and Emancipation*, 2nd ed. (Cambridge: Cambridge University Press, 2002).

[130] U. Baxi, "Voices of suffering and the future of human rights" (1998) 8 *Transnational Law and Contemporary Problems*, 125–69; U. Baxi, "Enculturing law? Some unphilosophic remarks" in M. John and S. Kakarala (eds.), *Enculturing Law: New Agendas in Legal Pedagogy/Ethics* (New Delhi: Tulika Books, 2007) 221.

[131] D. Kennedy, "Legal education and the reproduction of hierarchy" (1982) 31 *Journal of Legal Education* 591–615.

[132] R. Kapur and B. Cossman, *Subversive Sites: Feminist Engagements with Law in India* (London: Sage Publications, 1996).

[133] J. M. Culp, "Posner on Duncan Kennedy and racial difference: white authority in the legal academy" (1990) 41 *Duke Law Journal* 1095–114.

[134] A. Anghie, *Imperialism, Sovereignty and The Making of International Law* (New York, NY: Cambridge University Press, 2005); A. Anghie, *The Third World and International Order: Law, Politics and Globalization* (Boston, MA: Martinus Nijhoff Publishers, 2003).

[135] M. Mutua, *Human Rights: A Political and Cultural Critique* (Philadelphia, PA: University of Pennsylvania Press, 2007).

[136] J. T. Gathii, *African Regional Trade Agreements as Legal Regimes* (New York, NY: Cambridge University Press, 2013).

[137] C. B. Ncube, "Decolonising intellectual property law in pursuit of Africa's development" (2016) 8 *The Wipo Journal: Analysis of Intellectual Property Issues* 34–40 (available at www.wipo.int/edocs/pubdocs/en/wipo_journal_wpj8n1.pdf) (accessed date November 20, 2017). See also W. J. Du Plessis and C. Ncube (eds.), *Indigenous Knowledge and Intellectual Property* (Cape Town: Juta, 2016).

[138] I. Gassama, "Transnational critical race scholarship: transcending ethnic and national chauvinism in the era of globalization" (1999) 5 *Michigan Journal of Race and Law* 133–60; H. Lewis, "Reflections on 'blackcrit theory': human rights" (2000) 45 *Villanova Law Review* 1075–90.

concern with the legacy of racial subordination in the United States and its reflection in law's edifice.[139] Under the label, Critical Race Feminism, CRT also includes a critique of the underbelly of patriarchy, sexism and homophobia in the United States and globally.[140] CRT has also seen offshoots in Canada, Australia and the United Kingdom.[141]

Although redressing poverty and economic inequality will remain the core of the goals of social justice advocates, it is the continuous tethering of blackness to poverty and economic inequality that mandates a racialized analysis. This is why the tenets of CRT are so apposite in South Africa today.

9.7. CONCLUSION

The lingering effects of colonialism and apartheid bedevil the constitutional project in South Africa. They are not aberrations nor are they temporary, but are built into the political, social and economic fabric thereby marginalizing large sectors of the population. This is the reality for many black South Africans. Escape from this reality has proven to be illusive since 1994, despite many steps taken by successive postapartheid governments.[142]

Access to education provides the possibility of an escape from such marginalization. It is therefore an urgent constitutional imperative. The student protests have highlighted the urgency.

139 See R. A. Williams Jr. "Documents of barbarism: the contemporary legacy of European racism and colonialism in the narrative traditions of Federal Indian Law" (1989) 31 *Arizona Law Review* 237–78; see also E. M. Iglesias, "Out of the shadow: marking intersections in and between Asian Pacific American critical legal scholarship and Latina/o critical Legal Theory" (1998) 19 *Boston College Third World Law Journal* 349–83; P. Williams, *The Alchemy Of Race and Rights* (Cambridge, MA: Harvard University Press, 1991).

140 See Critical Race Feminism: A Reader, Adrien Katherine Wing Ed. (New York, NY: New York University Press, 2003); see also Global Critical Race Feminism: An International Reader, Adrien Katherine Wing Ed. (New York, NY: New York University Press, 2000) and States of Race: Critical Race Feminism for the 21st Century, Sherene Rezack, Malinda Smith and Sunera Thobani, eds. (Toronto: Between the Lines Press, 2010).

141 See C. A. Aylward, *Canadian Critical Race Theory: Racism and the Law* (Halifax: Fernwoord Publishing, 1999); D. Gillborn, "Education policy as an act of white supremacy: whiteness, critical race theory and education reform" (2005) 20 *Journal of Education Policy* 485–505; N. K. Denzin, Y. S. Lincoln and L. T. Smith (eds.), *Handbook of Critical and Indigenous Methodologies* (New York, NY: Sage Publications, 2008).

142 See E. Maloka, *The Fruits of Freedom in Turning Points in History: Negotiation, Transition and Freedom, Book 6* (Cape Town: STE Publishers, 2004) (available at www.sahistory.org.za/archive/book-6-negotiation-transition-and-freedom-chapter-4-fruits-freedom-eddy-maloka) (accessed date November 20, 2017).

10

The Contribution of the South African Constitution to Kenya's Constitution

Jill Cottrell Ghai and Yash Ghai

There is no such thing as an original constitution. And there is no sin in plagiarizing another country's constitutional ideas (or more importantly, learning from their experience). South Africa's own debt to other countries' constitutions – particularly those of India, Canada and Germany – is evident. In the last seventy or eighty years, probably more constitutions have been enacted than in all the centuries before. These constitutions are widely available and their performance widely analyzed. There are numerous books on these (and past constitutions) and some handbooks on the best strategies and procedures for making a constitution, and how to design them for effectiveness.[1] A number of significant regional and international treaties have been adopted in the last fifty or more years imposing obligations on states that influence the orientation of constitutions. International consultants (mostly from the West) on how to write constitutions and even who will "do it for you" have proliferated at an alarming rate. All these developments lead to borrowing of ideas and structures for constitutions. South Africa has both borrowed from some other countries and has had its own constitution copied.

Constitutional borrowing (an odd word, since the debt is never repaid) is by no means restricted to situations where foreigners were intimately involved in a country's constitution-making process. Propinquity (in space and time), similarity of history, tradition and experience, of political orientation and vision, and of legal tradition, all play their parts. And so do personal factors: local constitution makers do not come to their tasks as personal blank slates. They have expectations of how things ought to be done, perhaps rooted in their own

[1] See, e.g., M. Brandt et al., *Constitution-Making and Reform: Options for the Process* (Geneva, Switzerland: Interpeace, 2011) (available at www.constitutionmakingforpeace.org/) (accessed date November 20, 2017). This has been translated into Arabic, English, French, Vietnamese and is being translated into Ukrainian and Russian.

country's history, or they may reject how things were done in the past and look to other countries for inspiration on how to do them differently. They have studied, perhaps in another country, have perhaps worked in another country, have academic knowledge of other countries, even friends in other countries.

South Africa's constitution-making process came early, though not the earliest, in the post-Cold War spate of processes. Its emergence from apartheid was an inspiration to other countries, especially in Africa. The country became a place of pilgrimage, literally and virtually, for other countries emerging from autocracy.

Kenya's process did not really begin in 2000 when the first official constitution-making body (the Constitution of Kenya Review Commission or CKRC) was appointed. It began just over a decade earlier, and thus ran somewhat in parallel with South Africa's. One of the leading early activists, and chronicler of the Kenyan process, records that, in 1994, three organizations that had been working toward a new constitution held a workshop (funded by two German bodies); they reflected on the Constitutions of Uganda, Ghana, Namibia and South Africa. But they also discussed ideas from the USA and Germany.[2]

South Africa's final Constitution was adopted only four years before the official Kenyan process began. But there were other, more direct and more personal, influences. The Chair of the CKRC[3] had been somewhat involved in the South African process, and had been very much inspired by the experience, and also had a number of South African contacts. A member of the CKRC had spent time as an intern at the Kenyan High Commission in South Africa and drew on what he learned especially in contributing to the debates on devolution. In phase two of the Kenyan process, when three foreigners joined the Committee of Experts (2009–10) (CoE), one of those foreigners was South African (Christina Murray). Another was Ugandan and the third Zambian, resident in the United Kingdom.

South Africans came to Kenya at the invitation of Kenyans. Yvonne Mokgoro, Judge of the Constitutional Court, was a member of a panel of Commonwealth experts that advised on how to deal with the issue of a compromised judiciary – including a proposal for a vetting process to weed out the corrupt, incompetent and executive-dependent members of the judiciary. This was not a process inspired by South Africa.

2 W. Mutunga, *Constitution-Making from the Middle: Civil Society and Transition Politics in Kenya, 1992–1997* (Nairobi/Harare: Sareat/MWENGO, 1999) 54.

3 Yash Pal Ghai. He was invited to facilitate the first ever meeting between the lawyers of the ANC and the National Party, and was later among the advisers to the advisers to the Constitutional Assembly.

The CKRC held various workshops to educate itself about dimensions of the issue, including speakers on economic social and cultural rights in South Africa,[4] and other aspects of human rights,[5] on devolution in South Africa, and on electoral systems with considerable discussion of PR in South Africa.

Another influence is almost certainly that of a drafter: Philip Knight is a Canadian legal drafter who played a significant role in the final stages of drafting the South African Constitution with the specific brief of making that document as "plain English" as possible.[6] Yash Ghai admired the style, and thus proposed him for the Kenya process, phase 1. And he was also a major drafter in the CoE phase. Clearly the decision to draw on the South African experience had already been made; it was not Knight's initiative. But he almost certainly introduced some phraseology from that country.

There were significant differences between the South African and Kenyan constitutional and political situation. The former was more like Kenya at independence: a past, in many ways alien, regime was being shaken off, and there was faith in the new leaders of the majority. But Kenya in 2000 was not a newly independent country: though it was capable of short periods of wild optimism, it was basically a country disillusioned by politicians, and determined that a new constitution would contain as many constraints on abuse of power, corruption and land grabbing as possible. And women, persons with disability and other groups that had felt marginalized over the preceding forty-seven years were equally enthusiastic to ensure that everyone was

4 For the reported versions of the papers presented, see S. Liebenberg, "South Africa's evolving jurisprudence on socio-economic rights" (2002) 6 *Law, Democracy and Development* 159–91; G. Budlender, "Justiciability of the right to housing: the South African experience" in S. Leckie (ed.), *National Perspectives on Housing Rights* (The Hague: Martinus Nijhoff Publishers, 2003) 207; *Report of The Constitution of Kenya Review Commission: Volume Five: Technical Appendices* (Nairobi: Constitution of Kenya Review Commission, 2003).

5 H. Corder, "From administrative law to administrative justice" and J. Kollapen, "The role of law enforcement agents – the police force," in *Report of the Constitution of Kenya Review Commission: Volume Five: Technical Appendices: Part Three* (Nairobi: Constitution of Kenya Review Commission, 2003) (available at www.katibainstitute.org/Archives/images/CKRC%20Final%20Report.pdf) (accessed date November 20, 2017).

6 On Knight's drafting philosophy see P. Knight, *The Role of the Constitutional Drafter: Thoughts on the Art of Expressing Constitutional Visions Philip Knight* (Geneva: Interpeace, 2010) (available at www.constitutionmakingforpeace.org/wp-content/uploads/2015/04/InFocus_Knight_FINAL.pdf) (accessed date November 20, 2017). One author comments, in relation to the CSA, "Besides the crucial presence of Phil Knight, the Canadian lawyer and proponent of the Plain Language Movement on the Constituent [sc. Constitutional] Assembly while the text was actually being drafted (which presumably explains the total absence of *shall*)": C. Williams, *Tradition and Change in Legal English: Verbal Constructions in Prescriptive Texts*, 2nd rev. ed. (Bern: Peter Lang, 2007) 191. Note that Knight served the Assembly, but was not a member of it.

included in the new Kenya that they believed a new constitution (and the end of President Moi after twenty-four years) would – or should – bring. This disillusionment accounts for many of the differences between the South African and Kenyan constitutions. Another difference between the two countries was in the position of the political leaders. While the ANC wanted a liberal-democratic constitution, the Kenyan leaders wanted maximum powers and perks for themselves; their primary interest was to get rid of President Moi so they could assume government with the extensive powers that Moi had assumed for himself. The same differences were reflected in the implementation of the constitutions: South Africa's enthusiastically by political leaders, Kenya's the object of sabotage efforts.

Between 2000 and 2010 when a new constitution was finally adopted there were seven official drafts of a constitution (a process of development but sometimes regression from the first draft in September 2002 to the one of May 2010 that was adopted in a referendum in August that year).[7] There was no "big bang" acceptance of South African ideas.

Some things came in early and stayed, like provisions of the Bill of Rights, notably s. 27 of the South African and Article 24 of the Kenyan on limitation of rights, and s. 38/Article 22 on right to standing to sue for breach of human rights – the constitutional basis for public interest litigation. The occasional thing came and went, like the terminology of "State President," used only in the fifth version of a new constitution, and a constitutional court – in the fourth and fifths drafts; both were removed by the Parliamentary Select Committee (PSC). Some topics became gradually more South African, like devolution, which we discuss in some detail.

It is important to distinguish between language and substance, while recognizing their profound interlinkages. That language is similar between two constitutions does not mean that the latter took the idea of substance from the earlier, even if they share formulations not used elsewhere. An example is s. 38/Art. 22. The inspiration for the South African provision on expanded standing is obviously public interest/social action litigation in India. But lawyers in Kenya were also aware of the Indian developments,[8] and it was a great

7 (i) The CKRC Draft of 2002; (ii) the National Constitutional Conference (Bomas) draft of 2004; (iii) the Government mutilation (or Wako Draft) of 2005 (rejected in a referendum); (iv) the CoE Harmonised Draft of 2009; (v) its Revised Harmonised Draft of 2010; (vi) the Parliamentary Select Committee revision of the RHD; and (vii) the CoE's Proposed Draft of May 2010, accepting some of the PSC changes but not others.

8 Jill Cottrell wrote various articles about it as long ago as the 1990s. See, e.g., J. Cottrell, "Courts and accountability: public interest litigation in the Indian High Courts" (1992) 11 *Third World Legal Studies* 199–213.

convenience to find a country that had worked out a neat encapsulation of enhanced standing.

10.1. PROCESS

The two processes were very different. Kenya did not have an interim Constitution, but arrived at its document through an independent commission followed by a sort of constituent assembly – the National Constitutional Conference or NCC. That draft having not been adopted, there was later an expert committee followed by a referendum. In each phase, Parliament played a part (and MPs were members of the NCC). Put crudely, Parliament's role was to remove some of the better provisions of each draft. In South Africa, the interim Constitution was a negotiated document between two powerful political forces and the final Constitution was developed by the constitutional assembly, which was also parliament.

The only aspect that might seem similar was the degree of public participation. But this owed little to South Africa. Yash Ghai had been involved in a process of constitution making for Papua New Guineas as long ago as the 1970s and was determined that any process he was responsible for or was in a position to influence would be very participatory. No inspiration from the south of the continent was required.

10.2. OVERALL PHILOSOPHY AND APPROACH

Both documents are readily identifiable as "transformative constitutions" – a phrase used freely in both countries. Both are heavily value laden, and explicit about values. The Constitution of South Africa (CSA) includes in its very first section: human dignity, the achievement of equality and the advancement of human rights and freedoms; nonracialism and nonsexism; supremacy of the Constitution and the rule of law; universal adult suffrage, a national common voters roll, regular elections and a multi-party system of democratic government, to ensure accountability, responsiveness and openness.

Kenya had had universal suffrage since independence, so did not feel the need to stress elections so prominently, though it was concerned about rigging and though tribalism (usually these days called ethnicity) was recognized as a problem, racialism was not. So, the Kenyan values and principles include patriotism, national unity, sharing and devolution of power, the rule of law, democracy and participation of the people; human dignity, equity, social justice, inclusiveness, equality, human rights, nondiscrimination and protection of the marginalized; good governance, integrity, transparency and accountability; and sustainable development.[9]

The drafting of the Constitution of Kenya (CoK) lacks some of the straightforwardness of its South Africa counterpart. This is a result, not of lack of effort on the part of the technical drafters, but of various factors including some element of rush at some stages, and of the nature of the Kenyan process. The involvement of many actors through the NCC, a body that was not also the national parliament and in which party discipline was ineffective, and which was not dominated by political parties, was one factor.[10] A second factor was a certain conservatism in Kenya (politically more right-wing, to the extent that there is any ideology in Kenya, legally conservative, and powerful influences from the church and the mosque). Legal conservatism had its way on some; for example, Phil Knight failed to persuade Kenyans to adopt the "revolutionary"[11] approach of using "must" rather than "shall" where appropriate.[12] And while the Kenyan draft is gender neutral (never using "he" or "him" but "their," even occasionally ungrammatically as in "(2) In addition to a person acting in their own interest ..."[13]) it did not adopt the women visible approach of the CSA ("a woman or a man"). In fact, some women have complained about the invisibility of women in the CoK.

Popular determination to see (as people hoped) every loophole stopped and every voice visible won over legal conservatism (or even legal rigor) and accounts for much of the prolixity. Conservatism of various types accounts for the attempts to preserve the death penalty and ban gay marriage and abortion. The presence of the existing ruling class (despite an election that seemed to introduce a new era and for a while produced a reforming government) probably accounts for the deletion of proposals limiting evictions and possibly of any element of proportional representation. The last is also perhaps attributable to the difficulty of persuading people to accept new electoral systems. Whereas in South Africa most of the majority community had not voted before, in

9 Constitution of Kenya 2010, art. 10 (CoK).

10 One third of the members were MPs, but parties were weak in terms of clear vision of a new constitution and ethnic concerns dominated: see J. Cottrell and Y. Ghai, "Constitution making and democratisation in Kenya (2000–2005)" (2007) 14 *Democratisation* 1–25. One third of the members were elected by districts locally, but under the previous regime, and one-third was from civil society.

11 The word is that of Christopher Williams, "Legal English and the 'modal revolution'" in R. Salkie, P. Busuttil, and J. van der Auwera (eds.), *Modality in English: Theory and Description* (Berlin: Walter de Gruyter, 2009) 200.

12 Personal information from Philip Knight.

13 CoK art. 258.

Kenya people thought they knew how elections worked, and their expectations were of a first past the post system.

To determine the impact of the SAC on the CoK, we restrict ourselves to examining the Bills of Rights and the structuring and functions of institutions, with particular reference to devolution. We also examine the impact of the jurisprudence of South Africa on the approach and decisions of Kenyan judges, and briefly refer to intellectual intercourse between the two countries.

10.3. THE BILL OF RIGHTS

At a Workshop on Human Rights attended by distinguished South Africans[14] (as well as Ugandan, Tanzanian and Indian speakers), Yash Ghai said,[15]

> My own approach to some extent in organizing this workshop has been to look very closely at the bill of rights of the South African Constitution and the experiences in South Africa of implementing that bill. I believe myself that the bill of rights in the South African Constitution is one of the best in the world, it is innovative, it tries to integrate economic-social with civil-political, it provides clear guidance or provides guidance to state organs, about their responsibilities in respect of the bill of rights and it speaks to many of the concerns that we have in this country, many of the goals which are set out in the review act. And we will be very interested to learn as much as we can about the South African bill of rights and to hear from you, those of you from South Africa whether you would draft the bill differently today and with hindsight, so that we can fully benefit from your experience.

The debt to South Africa is very clear. Both in terms of coverage (extent of rights recognized) and in terms of the philosophical and practical framework of rights the ancestry is evident.

It was not that Kenya had not had a Bill of Rights. Its independence Constitution had what Stanley de Smith called a "neo-Nigerian Bill of Rights."[16] The Nigerian one was based on the European Convention on Human Rights; the neo-Nigerian ones had some modifications. But what strikes the modern reader about these Bills of Rights is, first, that there is no

[14] Geoff Budlender and Justice Pius Langa.

[15] "Verbatim Report of Workshop on Human Rights at The Safari Park Hotel, Nairobi on Thursday August 1st, 2002" (Nairobi: Constitution of Kenya Review Commission) (available at www.katibainstitute.org/Archives/) (accessed date November 20, 2017).

[16] S. de Smith, *The New Commonwealth and its Constitutions* (London: Stevens and Sons, 1964) 193.

clear statement that the people have the rights, but a preambular statement that assumes they have certain rights:

> Whereas every person in Kenya is entitled to the fundamental rights and freedoms of the individual, that is to say, the right, whatever his race, tribe, place of origin or residence or other local connexion, political opinions, colour, creed or sex, but subject to respect for the rights and freedoms of others and for the public interest, to each and all of the following, namely:
>
> a. life, liberty, security of the person and the protection of the law;
> b. freedom of conscience, of expression and of assembly and association; and
> c. protection for the privacy of his home and other property end from deprivation of property without compensation … (s. 14)

Technically – in terms of the theory that rights are inherent and not granted – this may be accurate. But it lacks the ringing simplicity of the South African: "Everyone has the right …"

Second, and most strikingly, most of the rest of the Bill of Rights was devoted to limitations on rights. For example, "No person shall be deprived of his personal liberty save as may be authorized by law in any of the following cases …" and there follow ten exceptions (or 380 words worth) (s. 16(1)), although they must also be justified in a democratic society.

Third, in the Kenyan Bill of Rights the scope of prohibited discrimination was rather narrow – notably, from more modern perspectives, neither age nor disability was mentioned. And, though the right not to be discriminated against was assumed, as we have seen, when it came to forbidding law that discriminates, or to forbidding discrimination by anyone acting under the authority of law or as a public servant or authority, sex discrimination was not outlawed (s. 26(1)–(3)). This was rectified by the time a new constitution came to be written in 2000. But by 2000 it was still the case that the benefit of non-discrimination provisions did not apply to noncitizens, or in connection with personal law (mainly marriage, divorce, or succession).

10.4. THE KENYAN BILL OF RIGHTS

Three fundamental design issues characterize the South African and the Kenyan Bills of Rights. The first is that human rights are not binding only on the state, but also, to a considerable extent, on other people and bodies. The second is that, although most rights can be limited, limitations are not spelled out for each right, but are based on a general principle. The third is the inclusion of justiciable economic, social and cultural rights.

10.4.1. *Horizontal Application*

Previously only antidiscrimination provisions applied horizontally in Kenya – and only to access to facilities for the public such as shops, restaurants or places of entertainment, or to those acting under law. Now all rights apply horizontally. Underlying this was a sense that society is a major source of rights violation in many countries in terms of discrimination. The formulation about nonhuman persons is a bit different in Kenya. Whereas the SA Constitution clearly has in mind that especially the rights of a nonhuman person might be different from those of a human person, this does not seem to have been fully understood in Kenya. So, while the former says that "[a] juristic person is entitled to the rights in the Bill of Rights to the extent required by the nature of the rights and the nature of that juristic person (s. 8(4))," which compels the user to consider the issue of how the artificial person might be different in terms of rights from the human, the Kenyan equivalent is: "Every person shall enjoy the rights and fundamental freedoms in the Bill of Rights to the greatest extent consistent with the nature of the right or fundamental freedom" (Art. 20(2)). This does not highlight the issue of juristic persons, and is actually hard to understand, and has not really been considered by the courts, unlike the situation in South Africa.[17] Arguably a provision more akin to the South African one might focus minds a bit more on issues such as whether a nonhuman person has a right to property.

And in terms of the liability side of horizontal application, the CoK is blunter than the CSA, saying that it binds everyone, without any hint that this may be problematic. The motive may have been to avoid the somewhat obscure provision in the CSA: "A provision of the Bill of Rights binds a natural or a juristic person if, and to the extent that, it is applicable, taking into account the nature of the right and the nature of any duty imposed by the right" (s. 8(2)). There have been a number of Kenyan case that have held rights to be binding horizontally, but so far these have not tended to be socio-economic rights. It may well be that courts will hold that the positive obligations (protect, promote and fulfil) are not appropriately applied to nonstate actors. In this the provision (virtually identical to the CSA) that the state must respect, protect, promote and fulfil all the rights, will help. But to assume that no socio-economic rights should be horizontally applicable[18] overlooks

[17] In cases such as *Investigating Directorate: Serious Economic Offences* v. *Hyundai Motor Distributors (Pty) Ltd* (2001) 1 (SA) 545 (CC) juristic persons have right to privacy (though not as intense as for private person) but no right to dignity.

[18] Which seems to be the position of Christina Murray commenting on the difference between the CSA and the CoK: "Kenya's 2010 Constitution" (2013) 61 *Jahrbuch des öffentlichen Rechts*

the element of the duty to respect – which everyone should arguably be capable of.

10.4.2. *Limitation of Rights*

Article 24 of the CoK is very similar indeed to s. 36 of the SA document. In other words, rights may be limited but only by law, and that the "limitation is reasonable and justifiable in an open and democratic society based on human dignity, equality and freedom." And to make the decision various factors are to be considered, including "the nature of the right or fundamental freedom"; "the importance of the purpose of the limitation," "the nature and extent of the limitation," and "the relation between the limitation and its purpose and whether there are less restrictive means to achieve the purpose."

But it proved impossible to wean Kenyan lawyers away from some of the phrases they were used to including "the need to ensure that the enjoyment of rights and fundamental freedoms by any individual does not prejudice the rights and fundamental freedoms of others." The inclusion of this is unfortunate. As a phrase, it overlooks the possibility that a case may involve competing rights each limiting the rights of the other right holder. And it offers an easy and unthinking way out to lawyers and judges who care to avoid the more rigorous analysis that the other factors demand.

Another interesting distinction between the two constitutions is the existence in Kenya of an article prohibiting any limitation of certain rights. These (art. 25) are "freedom from torture and cruel, inhuman or degrading treatment or punishment; freedom from slavery or servitude; the right to a fair trial; and the right to an order of habeas corpus." This provision first appeared in the first draft of the CoE (exceptionally, not based on the Bomas draft). While the origins of the complete ban on torture are clear,[19] the rest of the prohibitions are less usual. There may have been some confusion between limitation and derogations from rights in the case of declaration of a state of emergency. The CSA Constitution has an elaborate provision on the latter; CoK has none.[20] This means that if a state of emergency is declared in Kenya, any limitation on rights must satisfy Article 24's requirements.

The second half of Article 24 is not found in the CSA: it requires that post-Constitution legislation that limits rights specifies that it does so. This

der Gegenwart. Neue Folge 747–88. We are grateful to Victoria Miyandazi for drawing this chapter to our attention, as well as for other helpful observations. Christina Murray was the South African member of the Kenyan CoE.

19 In the ICCPR, the Convention Against Torture (to which Kenya is a party) and the ECHR.

20 The CoE discussed this and decided (in 2009) to leave the issue to the constitutional court.

provision is inspired by one in the Papua New Guinea Constitution.[21] The idea is that legislators give focused consideration to the fact that they are limiting rights and make it clear that they intend to do so.

Article 24 includes a provision with antecedents in the European Convention, the Namibian Constitution and the Interim CSA. The Kenyan version reads: "a provision in legislation limiting a right or fundamental freedom ... (c) shall not limit the right or fundamental freedom so far as to derogate from its core or essential content" (art. 24(2)). It is interesting that this was adopted, although SA had abandoned it.

10.4.3. *Economic Social and Cultural Rights*

The CKRC was clear that it wanted justiciable socio-economic rights, aware of the institution of directive principles, used in the constitutions of Ireland, India and PNG, for example, and of the way in which the Indian courts had been turning those nonbinding principles into rights in the years since 1975. The language of the CSA, drawing on the International Covenant on Economic, Social and Cultural Rights, proved a useful starting point.

The actual formulation of the individual rights changed over time. The first four drafts contained separate articles for social security, health, education, housing, food, water, sanitation and environment,[22] while the CSA puts health care, food, water and social security together,[23] and does not mention sanitation. The PSC took a minimalist approach:

> The State shall take legislative, policy and other measures, including the setting of standards to achieve the progressive realization of the rights of every person to-
>
> a. social security;
> b. health;
> c. education;

[21] Section 38(2) of which says:

> For the purposes of Subsection (1), a law must:
>
> a. be expressed to be a law that is made for that purpose; and
> b. specify the right or freedom that it regulates or restricts; and
> c. be made, and certified by the Speaker in his certificate under Section 110 (certification as to making of laws) to have been made, by an absolute majority.

[22] Draft arts. 55–62.

[23] CSA s. 27.

d. housing;
e. food; and
f. water.

The CoE, faced with what it felt was the dilemma of wanting to assert what it considered appropriate while not seeming to reject the PSC's suggestions, left these provisions in one article but spelled out what was intended in more detail. So, for example, they reinserted "the highest attainable standard of health" and "reproductive health," "accessible and adequate housing." And an article on the rights of the child (deleted by the PSC) was reinstated with its provision on "free and compulsory basic education," as well as "to basic nutrition, shelter and health care."

There are a number of differences from the SA provisions. An initial proposal – based on the CSA – that:

2. No person may be evicted from their home, or have their home demolished, without an order of court made after considering all the relevant circumstances.
3. Parliament may not enact legislation that permits or authorizes arbitrary eviction (Art. 38)

was removed at the NCC, at the instance of the landowning (and grabbing) class. The proposal resurfaced before the CoE but was rejected again.[24]

The CSA provision on health is for "access to health care services, including reproductive health care." The Kenyan process, from the beginning, preferred the International Covenant's more expansive right to the "highest attainable standard of health." This version of the right makes the achievement of health more than the responsibility of the health care system, making the right something to be respected and fulfilled by the whole range of government, and the private sector and citizens. And while the CSA recognizes the right to access to housing, the Kenyan recognizes the right to housing as such, Kenyans not being convinced by the arguments in South Africa and fearful that the right to access diminishes the right. A member of the NCC said, "the current formulation of, 'Every person has a right to have access to adequate housing', limits the right in a ridiculous way."[25]

[24] "Minutes of the Meeting of The Committee of Experts Held at The Great Rift Valley Lodge, Naivasha on the September 18th–20th, 2009" (manuscript on file with the authors).

[25] Lawrence Mute (later Commissioner with the Kenyan National Commission on Human Rights) at the NCC "Verbatim Report of Plenary Proceedings on Decisions on Draft Bill by The Committee of the Whole Conference Held at the Plenary Hall, Bomas of Kenya on March 09, 2004" (manuscript on file with the authors and www.katibainstitute.org/Archives) (accessed date November 20, 2017).

Another difference based on fear of diminishing ESC rights is the refusal (at the CKRC stage) to include certain language about "available resources." The CSA constitution makers found themselves unable to commit to the Covenant's language of "[e]ach State Party to the present Covenant undertakes to take steps ... to the maximum of its available resources, with a view to achieving progressively the full realization of the rights recognized in the present Covenant by all appropriate means" (art. 2.1). They adopted the phrase "within its available resources." The NCC rejected any such provision as being too much of a "get-out" for the government. However, effectively the concept was re-introduced by providing that:

> 22 (5) In applying any right under Article 43, if the State claims that it does not have the resources to implement the right, a court, tribunal or other authority shall be guided by the following principles—
>
> (a) it is the responsibility of the State to show that the resources are not available;
> (b) in allocating resources, the State shall give priority to ensuring the widest possible enjoyment of the right or fundamental freedom having regard to prevailing circumstances, including the vulnerability of particular groups or individuals; and
> (c) the court, tribunal or other authority may not interfere with a decision by a State organ concerning the allocation of available resources, solely on the basis that it would have reached a different conclusion.

Sub-clause (a) is really a burden of proof provision on whether resources were available. Sub-clause (b) is inspired by the *Grootboom* case: the idea that a scheme that does not cater for the most desperate is defective. This was emphatically described by Geoff Budlender in a presentation in Nairobi:

> The constitutional court said it is not reasonable to have a program which pretends that everyone is in the same position, and which doesn't have regard to the special needs of the most vulnerable or most desperate or the people living in intolerable circumstances.[26]

And (c) was perhaps a reaction to comments such as those of Budlender, who said, on the same occasion, "[w]e don't expect the courts to re-write the national budget."[27]

[26] "Verbatim Report of Workshop on Human Rights at The Safari Park Hotel, Nairobi."
[27] Ibid.

Before leaving ESCR, there is another difference of drafting: whereas the CSA makes it clear that the prohibition on refusing emergency medical care is not subject to progressive realization (s. 27(3)), the Kenyan provision is more equivocal: it appears in an Article the whole of which is made subject to progressive realization: "21 (2) The State shall take legislative, policy and other measures, including the setting of standards, to achieve the progressive realisation of the rights guaranteed under Article 43."

10.4.4. *Two New Rights*

Two less commonly seen rights are recognized in the CoK in language very similar to the CSA. The first is the right to information (or of access to information). A significant difference – and a regrettable one – is that the Kenyan version recognizes the right of citizens only. This goes back to the very first draft, but it is not clear precisely why this was done (personal recollection suggests that it was the result of fears of foreigners getting at Kenyan secrets). Another distinction is that the CSA requires law to be passed to operationalize the right. A similar provision (with a six-month deadline) was in the CKRC draft, but disappeared in the CoE's first draft (not without some misgivings).[28] The motive was the fear that the right would be meaningless if law was required and law was not passed.[29] That legislators are indeed not enthusiastic about such a right is shown by the fact that the PSC deleted the Article and just provided that Parliament must "provide for the right of access to information."

The other less usual right is that to fair administrative practice: the constitutionalization of an expanded concept of administrative law. The CoK provision is basically the same but while the original provides "[e]very person has the right to administrative action that is lawful, reasonable and procedurally fair (s .33)," the CoK adds "expeditious, efficient" before lawful.

10.4.5. *Supporting Structures*

There are many other situations in which a South African reader of the Kenyan Bill of Rights would say "I recognize that." Notable is the place of dignity: the Kenyan "[e]very person has inherent dignity and the right to have that dignity respected and protected" (art. 28) is almost identical to the CSA (s. 10).

28 Personal information.

29 The authors (who were not of course involved in the CoE exercise) note than in Nepal it took seventeen years for a constitutional requirement of access to information legislation to be satisfied, from the 1990 Constitution to an Act of 2007.

The Kenyan freedom of expression article (art. 33) adopts the exclusion from the protection of the constitution of propaganda for war, incitement of violence and advocacy of hatred in the CSA (s. 16).

The substantive rights are supported by a scaffolding of other provisions about processes and approaches, many of which are easily traced to the CSA. The notion of the Bill of Rights (BoR) as a "cornerstone of democracy" (CSA 7(1)) is echoed in the CoK's "integral part of Kenya's democratic state and is the framework for social, economic and cultural policies" (art. 19(1)). The conception of state responsibilities, derived from the work of special rapporteurs on ESC rights, but extended to all rights in the CSA is also used in the CoK: the duty of the state to "respect, protect, promote and fulfil the rights" (art. 21(1)). Again, Geoff Budlender explained this well in the Nairobi workshop, and commented that:

> It helps to guide Government and it helps to guide the court in understanding what the rights mean, when you don't simply say this a right to access to adequate housing, but you say that Government duties are duties to respect, protect, promote and fulfill, that is the way we have articulated it ... Very helpful to give some texture to the rights.[30]

But the CoK adds, inexplicably, "observe" at the beginning of the list, an innovation that survives.

Both have principles of interpretation, designed to ensure the maximal application of the BoR to the law, spelled out in similar though not identical terms. The CSA says that the courts must – when interpreting the BoR – "promote the values that underlie an open and democratic society based on human dignity, equality and freedom" while the CoK adds "equity" to the values. The CSA says that in that process the courts must consider international law and may consider foreign law, but identical provisions were removed from the Kenyan draft at the NCC. Both want the courts to promote the spirit, purport and objects of the BoR (s. 39(2)/art. 20(4)(b)) though the CSA is referring to interpreting any legislation or developing the common law or customary law, while the CoK is just referring to interpreting the BoR itself.

The provisions about developing the law to achieve the BoR are not quite the same. The CSA requires the courts to apply the common law if legislation does not give effect to the BoR; if necessary the courts must develop the common law for this purpose. The South African courts may use the common law to create limitations on rights – provided they satisfy s. 36. However, the CoK

30 "Verbatim Report of Workshop on Human Rights at The Safari Park Hotel Nairobi."

says the courts must "develop the law to the extent that it does not give effect to a right or fundamental freedom" – no mention of the common law. Yet the courts do not "develop" statute law, though they interpret it, and under the CSA BoR must, as we have seen, do so if possible to promote the BoR.

Neither constitution, it is suggested, gets to grips with issues like how far and how fast can the common law be developed, and the legitimacy of techniques for interpreting statutes like reading down and reading in.

A novel provision of the CoK is "[a]ll State organs and all public officers have the duty to address the needs of vulnerable groups within society, including women, older members of society, persons with disabilities, children, youth, members of minority or marginalized communities, and members of particular ethnic, religious or cultural communities."[31] This began with "understand" where the word "address" now appears and was intended to deal with the sort of incomprehension, even hostility, that minority groups, women, etc., often find when they approach the police and other public servants.

Both chapters have provisions encouraging public interest litigation, though, as explained earlier, this was no novel idea to the Kenyan drafters. And they introduced a provision direct from the Indian jurisprudence: "the court shall, if necessary, entertain proceedings on the basis of informal documentation" (art. 22(3)(b)).[32]

Both constitutions recognize the importance of a national human rights institution in the implementation of human rights. As Budlender said, "[w]e also have concluded that we shouldn't put all our eggs in the judicial basket. The courts are fundamentally important in this process, they have to lead and sometimes they have to act as a backdrop and a safety net at other times."

There was already (as a result of recent legislation) a human rights commission in Kenya. There was no hesitation in incorporating that in the Constitution. But the CoK (and the various drafts) did not go so far as to emulate the CSA provision about the specific role of the South African Human Rights Commission (SAHRC) in monitoring ESCR. This is perhaps

[31] CoK art. 21(3).

[32] The inspiration is what Indians sometimes call "epistolary jurisdiction": see B. Neuborne, "The Supreme Court of India" (2003) 1 *International Journal of Constitutional Law* 476–510 at 502. "[T]he Court treated letters, even newspaper clippings, as article 32 petitions for the protection of fundamental rights. Although the initial burst of informal epistolary pleading diminished somewhat over time, in part because the Court has evolved somewhat more formal procedures to process PIL cases, the pleading rules remain extremely flexible" quoted by Mutunga CJ in *Nicholas Kiptoo Arap Korir Salat* v. *Independent Electoral and Boundaries Commission* Petition No. 23 of 2014, [2015] eKLR, para. 106 (available at www.kenyalaw.org/caselaw/cases/view/114738/) (accessed date November 20, 2017).

regrettable, because there has been no equivalent in Kenya of the SAHRC reports.[33]

The CSA chapter 9 institutions include the SAHRC, the Gender Commission and the Public Protector. There was a good deal of controversy in Kenya about the desirability of a multiplicity of human rights commissions, informed to a considerable extent by reports of difficulties experienced by the South African Commission on Gender Equality, as well as discussion in other countries. The CKRC draft proposed a single commission with commissioners designated as Gender Commissioner and People's Protector (Ombudsman) among others, with a requirement that others include those with expertise in disability, children and basic needs. A separate People's Protector appeared in the Revised Harmonized Draft, alongside a Human Rights and Gender Commission. The PSC would have merged the former into the latter and renamed the latter only the Equality Commission. The final version has one Human Rights and Equality Commission but allowed for a de-merging. In no time at all the Commission was split into three. And the relations between the three have not always been cordial.

10.4.6. *Equality and Affirmative Action*

The CoK equality provisions contains the same basic ideas as the CSA: equality before the law, true equality to be achieved through affirmative action, a nonexhaustive list of prohibited grounds of discrimination, prohibition of both direct and indirect discrimination (though this was in the 1963 Kenya Constitution too) and some similar language.

The first difference is the absence of the word "unfair" in relation to discrimination. It was there in the CKRC but Philip Knight could not persuade the NCC to keep it: Kenyans were not persuaded that the concept added value; they believed that discrimination is of necessity unfair. The practical result is that even gender-separate toilets (Knight's favorite example) would have to be justified in terms of art. 24. However, the absence of this word in the CoK has spared the country's courts the difficult task of deciding just what "unfair discrimination" means.[34]

Among the listed prohibited grounds of discrimination, "sexual orientation" is notably missing in the CoK. Kenya is a less risky place to be gay than Uganda, but is not really a tolerant society. This is shown by the inclusion,

[33] South African Human Rights Commission, *Section 184(3) Reports* (available at www.sahrc.org.za/index.php/sahrc-publications/section-184-3-reports) (accessed date November 20, 2017).

[34] For a recent article, see C. McConnachie, "Human dignity, 'unfair discrimination' and guidance" (2014) 34 *Oxford Journal of Legal Studies* 609–29.

during the NCC proceedings, of provisions that partly remain: "everyone ... has the right to marry a person of the opposite sex, based upon the free consent of the parties. A person shall not marry another person of the same sex."[35] The second part of this disappeared in subsequent drafts. A foretaste of likely reaction to any attempt specifically to list sexual orientation was experienced very early on. Invited to work with the CKRC on the drafting, Philip Knight proposed that he make himself useful while waiting for the drafting retreat to begin, by doing a sort of dummy draft of a possible document drawing on the issues that he understood would be addressed by a new constitution.[36] His dummy document naturally included a BoR, in which he inserted "sexual orientation." This document, clearly marked on the cover page as a nondraft, was stolen from the chair's office by a CKRC commissioner, and given to the media and President Moi, a man with no enthusiasm for a new constitution or even democracy. One commissioner attributed to this the President's refusal to give his own views to the Commission.[37]

Another provision that has attracted comment is that: the right to equality "shall be qualified to the extent strictly necessary for the application of Muslim law before the Kadhis' courts, to persons who profess the Muslim religion, in matters relating to personal status, marriage, divorce and inheritance." This was in response to clear requests of Muslim women made to CKRC commissioners in meetings for women only and chaired by women commissioners. Christina Murray comments "[i]ts insistence that qualifications be 'strictly necessary' might be read to permit no greater invasion of the right to equality than is in any event permitted by clause (1) which allows reasonable limitations that are proportionate to their goals and its specific reference to the Kadhis' Courts raises the question what happens when cases are appealed from those courts." On the second point: one wonders what the CoE, of which Murray was a member, had in mind when they "raised this question by inserting 'before the Kadhis' courts'" in their second draft.

Another difference is the *requirement* of affirmative action rather than it being permitted as a technique for achieving substantive equality. Such a provision is very hard to conceptualize in terms of practical implementation.[38]

35 Draft arts. 41(2)–(3).

36 The Act under which the CKRC operated, the Constitution of Kenya Review Act 2000, listed many issues that were to be addressed in a new constitution, and the CKRC had already collected public views across the country.

37 See B. Kikechi, "Politicians stand in the way to new set of laws" (1 June 2010) *The Standard* (available at www.standardmedia.co.ke/article/2000010592/politicians-stand-in-the-way-to-new-set-of-laws?categoryID=0) (accessed date November 20, 2017).

38 As we have said in "Constitutionalising affirmative action in the Fiji Islands" (2007) 11 *The International Journal on Human Rights* 227–57.

Though affirmative action is a key tool in the de-apartheidization of South Africa, the CSA contains far fewer explicit provisions than the CoK. The latter has a plethora of provisions about women, persons with disability and minorities and marginalized groups and communities. The "no more than two thirds of either gender"[39] rule applies to all elected and appointed public bodies.[40] There is a separate Article on the rights of persons with disability including "The State shall ensure the progressive implementation of the principle that at least 5 percent of the members of the public in elective and appointive bodies are persons with disabilities."[41] There are special legislative seats for underrepresented groups including persons with disability,[42] and "[t]he values and principles of public service include – ... affording adequate and equal opportunities for appointment, training and advancement, at all levels of the public service, of – ... persons with disabilities."[43] All this contrasts markedly with the CSA's single mention of disability.

There are also a number of provisions in the CoK about marginalization – a word that does not appear in the CSA. "Protection of the marginalised" is a national value; there is a specific Article requiring affirmative action for minorities and marginalized groups, mentioning participation, special opportunities in educational and economic fields and employment, development of their cultural values, languages and practices and access to water, health services and infrastructure.[44] This has some oddities, such as the idea of affirmative action to develop their practices. And it could be considered redundant in the light of the general equality and affirmative action provisions. But it reflects the desire of all groups to see themselves in the new document and the new Kenya. South Africans might be surprised to see the lack of specific references to language other than English (official) and Kiswahili (national and official). There is a provision requiring the state to promote and protect the diversity of language of Kenya and promote the development of indigenous languages, but no equivalent of the SA recognition of eleven official languages and the listing of three indigenous languages and eleven nonindigenous ones.[45] This is partly

[39] The very clumsiness of this formulation is testimony to the dynamics of the NCC, and its content to some degree of push-back from men. But, in fact, women have found it useful in argument: that it does not permit rounding up of women to one-third; there must be absolutely no more than two-thirds men.

[40] In the CoK this formulation appears in four articles: 27(8), 81(b), 175(c), 197(1).

[41] CoK art. 54(2).

[42] Ibid. arts. 97–8, 177.

[43] Ibid. art. 232(1)(i).

[44] Ibid. art. 56.

[45] CSA s. 6(5).

because of a reluctance to undermine the uniting role of Kiswahili – an indigenous language albeit of a group often marginalized – but also, perhaps, because Kenya has many languages. Ethnologue's, *Languages of Kenya* summarizes the situation as: sixty-seven living languages of which sixty are indigenous, while "34 are developing, 15 are vigorous, 2 are in trouble, and 4 are dying."[46]

10.4.7. *Right to Life*

South Africa chose to leave the right to life unqualified and unelaborated, though both abortion and the death penalty were issues raised during the constitution-making process. As far as the death penalty was concerned, the decision was deliberate precisely because agreement could not be reached. On abortion, the background in Kenya was legally, and indeed politically, very different. Kenya's law simply referred to "unlawfully" inducing abortion. South Africa had had law permitting termination of pregnancy in certain circumstances since 1975.[47] The ANC campaigned in the 1994 elections supporting abortion, and ensured the enactment of new, even more liberal, legislation in 1995 despite majority opposition in society.[48] Kenya seems to have lacked the "combination of advocacy by civil society organizations and pressure by [dominant party] feminists" observed by Albertyn in South Africa. And while that country "included a guarantee of the '"right to bodily and psychological integrity', including 'the right to make decisions concerning reproduction' and to 'security in and control over their body' in section 12(2)," Kenyan women had to be satisfied with a general inclusion of reproductive health.

The CoE proposed:

1. Every person has the right to life.
2. A person shall not be arbitrarily deprived of life.

But the PSC added that the right to life begins at conception and "[a]bortion is not permitted unless in the opinion of a registered medical practitioner, the life of the mother is in danger." The CoE was reluctantly persuaded by the parliamentary committee that the life begins at conception provision was a

46 It is described as based on information from M. P. Lewis, G. F. Simons, and C. D. Fennig (eds.), *Ethnologue: Languages of the World*, 19th ed. (Dallas, TX: SIL International, 2016).

47 The Abortion and Sterilization Act 1975, amended in 1982 permitted abortions, for example: if necessary to protect the life or health of the mother; if the child would be seriously handicapped; or if the pregnancy was the result of rape or incest: see C. Albertyn, "Claiming and Defending Abortion Rights in South Africa" (2015) 11 *Revista Direito GV* 429–54.

48 Ibid.

deal breaker as far as the Catholic Church was concerned.[49] But they modified the other provision to read, "[a]bortion is not permitted unless, in the opinion of a trained health professional, there is need for emergency treatment, or the life or health of the mother is in danger, or if permitted by any other written law." The Chair described this as struggling "to rephrase the clause so as to accommodate all competing interests."[50] The influence of conservative forces, including the Catholic Church is still felt, to the extent that the Ministry of Health, having prepared useful guidelines for safe abortion within the constitution, withdrew them and has so far failed to reintroduce revised guidelines.

On the death penalty, however, the CoE carried out no such sleight of hand. The words added by the PSC – so that the provision read "[a] person shall not be deprived of life intentionally except as may be authorized by this Constitution or any other written law" – remain. While the Supreme Court has recently decided that the mandatory death penalty is unconstitutional, a challenge to the death penalty as such is thought to be less likely to succeed and is made harder by the wording. Kenya does not anticipate having its *Makwanyane* case for a while yet.[51]

10.4.8. *Comments on the Bill of Rights*

To the extent that there are differences between the two constitutions in their Bills of Rights, the CoK though later, is often not an improvement. Sometimes this is because of what the present authors at least consider a retrograde decision – like removing the provision about arbitrary evictions. Sometimes the motive is less clear: CSA s. 16 removes from the umbrella of constitutional protection "advocacy of hatred that is based on race, ethnicity, gender or religion, and that constitutes incitement to cause harm." The CoK rewords this as "*advocacy of hatred that (i) constitutes ethnic incitement, vilification of others or incitement to cause harm; or (ii) is based on any ground of discrimination specified or contemplated in Article 27 (4)*." To the extent that the CoK provision excludes protection from vilification on the grounds of disability, it is not a bad thing. But the CoK provision risks narrowing protection of expression too far, when it does not limit exclusion to calls to violence. Obviously, this is

49 Final Report of the Committee of Experts on Constitutional Review (Nairobi: Committee of Experts, 2010) 111.

50 Ibid. Foreword at 11.

51 S v. *Makwanyane* (1995) 3 SA 391. In the longer term, such a decision is not out of the question. See, e.g., *Republic* v. *John Kimita Mwaniki* [2011] eKLR. But this held that art. 26(3) of the Constitution, which provides for the death penalty is inconsistent with art. 26(1) on the right to life, a judicial technique normally reckoned impermissible.

somewhat controversial. The CoK muddies the waters further by also excluding hate speech. But what is hate speech if it is not that advocacy of hatred in the clause italicized a few lines earlier? This reflects an apparent enthusiasm to include the phrase "hate speech" (it came into the CoE's second draft, and stayed).

10.5. STRUCTURE AND FUNCTIONING OF GOVERNMENT

Human rights of course also affect the functioning of government, but here we are looking at particularly the structures and, to a lesser extent, procedures of government, including the judiciary.

10.5.1. *Public Participation*

Public participation is a national value under the CoK. The CSA enshrines the principle not as an explicit value but in various other ways: legislatures may "make rules and orders concerning its business, with due regard to representative and participatory democracy ... and public involvement,"[52] and "*must facilitate public involvement in the legislative and other processes.*"[53] The principles of public administration include "[p]eople's needs must be responded to, and the public must be encouraged to participate in policy-making,"[54] legislation must provide for "the participation of people other than judicial officers in court decisions."[55]

The PSC wanted to delete provisions similar to that italicized in the preceding paragraph, but the CoE reinstated it.[56] The CoK also includes provisions about public participation in policy making (similar to that in the CSA) and in public finance decisions.[57]

This is an area in which South African decisions have been often cited. For Kenya, the idea that a law might be unconstitutional because of inadequate participation was totally novel, and South Africa, as the source for the main provisions, was an obvious place to look. Most often cited has been the *Doctors for Life* case.[58] The importance of that case is shown by the extraordinary

[52] Constitution of the Republic of South Africa 1996, s. 57(1)(b) (National Assembly).

[53] E.g., ibid. s. 59(1)(a) (National Assembly).

[54] Ibid. s. 195(1)(c).

[55] Ibid. s. 180(c).

[56] CoK art. 118(1)(b) (National Assembly).

[57] CoK art. 201(a).

[58] *Doctors for Life International* v. *The Speaker National Assembly* (2006) 6 SA 416 (CC). A quick search of the main Kenyan online case database (www.Kenyalaw.org) (accessed date

extent of quotation from it in *Robert N. Gakuru & Others* v. *Governor Kiambu County & 3 others*[59] by Justice Odunga (not by any means a judge unable to express his own meaning in his own eloquent words). He held that a county Finance Act was unconstitutional for want of adequate participation. He also quoted from *Glenister*[60] and *Merafong*.[61] The Kenyan courts have also relied upon *New Clicks*.[62]

The Kenyan courts have not been as bold as those of South Africa in declaring national legislation invalid for lack of participation. In a challenge to rushed amendments to security laws, the High Court held that there had been enough opportunity for public consultation.[63] The court seems to have allowed itself to be convinced without real inquiry that there was urgency that precluded more consultation, and ignored the fact that invitations published in newspapers circulating mainly in Nairobi and giving a mere five days, around Christmas, for submissions on a Bill amending, repealing or inserting over hundred sections of twenty statutes necessarily gave only a small section of the country time to be involved. However, more recently the High Court held that one reason for declaring unconstitutional a provision of national law was that it was introduced as an amendment to a Bill, with no public participation.[64] The court quoted at length from *Doctors for Life*, *Merafong* and *Matatiele*.[65]

10.5.2. *Courts*

The principal aspect of the judiciary meriting comment is the creation of a new apex court, the Supreme Court. The experience of South Africa was important in this. While the latter felt the need to introduce a new court to counteract the attitudes of apartheid-era judges, Kenya was troubled by corruption and subservience to the executive among the judiciary. The Panel of Commonwealth

November 20, 2017) produced a list of 387 cases citing *Doctors for Life*. Obviously, there is some double counting in this result, but it does indicate frequent citation of the case.

59 [2014] eKLR (available at www.kenyalaw.org/caselaw/cases/view/97000/) (accessed date November 20, 2017).

60 *Glenister* v. *President of the Republic of South Africa* (2011) 3 SA 347 (CC).

61 *Merafong Demarcation Forum* v. *President of the Republic of South Africa* (2008) 5 SA 171 (CC).

62 *Minister of Health NO* v. *New Clicks South Africa (Pty) Ltd* (2006) 2 SA 311 (CC).

63 *Coalition for Reform and Democracy (CORD)* v. *Republic of Kenya* [2015] eKLR (available at www.kenyalaw.org/caselaw/cases/view/106083/) (accessed date November 20, 2017).

64 *Law Society of Kenya* v. *Attorney General & National Assembly* [2016] eKLR (available at www.kenyalaw.org/caselaw/cases/view/122379/) (accessed date November 20, 2017).

65 *Matatiele Municipality* v. *President of the Republic of South Africa* 2007 (1) BCLR 47 (CC).

Experts that advised on this topic included not only a South African (Justice Yvonne Mokgoro of the Constitutional Court), but also a Tanzanian, a Ugandan and two Canadians. The Panel wrote[66] that in their experience

> "a further level of appeal to a court of last resort" significantly strengthens the quality of decision-making in the lower courts. Supreme Court judges have the aptitude and the time necessary to give mature reflection to the most difficult legal issues confronting the country. Their judgments provide necessary guidance for the lower courts and serve to ensure that the law, especially the Constitution, evolves in the manner necessary to address the changing needs of society.

It recommended a new Supreme Court comprising "a small number of select jurists of unquestionable skill, judgment and integrity," but did not recommend, despite the South African approach, a Constitutional Court:

> While a specialized Constitutional Court was admirably suited to meet the particular needs of the new constitutional order of South Africa, we are not persuaded that it represents the best solution for Kenya.

However, the CoE originally proposed both a Supreme Court and a Constitutional Court. It explained that this was in part a response to the postelection violence of 2007–8 (that led to restarting of a constitution-making process).[67] The latter court would not have been a final court (except in election petition cases), but would have had exclusive jurisdiction over certain constitutional matters. It was removed by the PSC and the CoE accepted that decision, but noted:

> that the removal of the provisions for a Constitutional Court inhibited the development of a pool of judges specialized in constitutional matters. It was particularly concerned that the High Court would not be well suited to exercise the full mandate initially accorded to the Constitutional Court.[68]

Another difference between the two constitutions is that under the CSA no declaration of unconstitutionality of legislation has effect unless confirmed

66 *Report of The Advisory Panel of Eminent Commonwealth Judicial Experts* (May 17, 2002) (available at www.commonlii.org/ke/other/KECKRC/2002/8.html) (accessed date November 20, 2017).

67 Preliminary Report of The Committee of Experts on Constitutional Review: Issued on the Publication of the Harmonised Draft Constitution (November 17, 2009) (available at www.katibainstitute.org/Archives/images/17-11-2009_Preliminary_Report.pdf) (accessed date November 20, 2017).

68 *Final Report of The Committee of Experts on Constitutional Review* (October 11, 2010) s. 8.11.3 (available at www.katibainstitute.org/Archives/images/11-10-2010%20CoE%20Final%20Report.pdf) (accessed date November 20, 2017).

by the Constitutional Court.[69] In Kenya the High Courts can make such a determination,[70] and have done so on many occasions, but there is a risk of this going unnoticed. A recent report on the implementation of the CoK said, "it is recommended that the Constitution be amended to provide that all declarations of unconstitutionality by the High Court and the Court of Appeal cannot take effect until they have been confirmed by the Supreme Court. This approach draws lessons from the South African Constitution ..."[71] The mischief that this was intended to remedy was identified as mainly, "very few matters relating to the interpretation of the Constitution will reach the Supreme Court to enable it to pronounce itself definitively about the meaning of various provisions of the Constitution. The risk then is that contradictory decisions by different judges of the High Court and the Court of Appeal remain in the country's jurisprudence for long thus causing confusion and stilling jurisprudential growth."

10.5.3. *System of Government*

Kenyans were cynical about the then current system dubbed the "Imperial Presidency" by some including President Kibaki so long as he was not President. Most drafts therefore proposed a parliamentary system. But there was no enthusiasm for a South African type of system: this too much resembled the previous Kenyan system. Support for a parliamentary system with a largely ceremonial president waned with the coalition government (power shared between president and newly resurrected prime minister) in the years 2008–10. The PSC took the opportunity to do away with the parliamentary system (a move connected with individuals' assessments of their chances of electoral success under different systems). The system that emerged was closer to that in the United States than to any other.

Most of the other issues about government are related to the system of devolution. But one issue worth commenting on is that of assent to legislation. The Kenyan provision is derived from that of South Africa. The latter allows the President to refer back legislation only because of doubts about

[69] CSA s. 167(5). It is believed that the decision by the CoE was influenced by a Ugandan member who considered that a similar system in his country had worked well.

[70] CoK arts. 23(3)(d), 165(3)(d)(i).

[71] *Interim Report of the Working Group on Socio-Economic Audit of the Constitution of Kenya* 2010 (May 2015) (available at www.info.mzalendo.com/file_archive/audit_of_the_Constitution) (accessed date November 20, 2017). The final report (which invokes South Africa much less often) (available at www.kenao.go.ke/index.php/reports/cat_view/2-reports/72-special-audit-reports) (accessed date November 20, 2017).

constitutionality. The Kenyan provision is not so limited: the president may refer back on any grounds. But then the CSA says, "[i]f, after reconsideration, a Bill fully accommodates the President's reservations, the President must assent to and sign the Bill; if not, the President must either assent to and sign the Bill; or refer it to the Constitutional Court for a decision on its constitutionality." The Kenyan draft constitutions – like the CSA – always assumed only two options: parliament can accept the president's reservations, or not. This has created a serious problem (unlike the more limited South Africa provision): the president has several times referred back Bills suggesting significant changes. Parliament considers it must pass either a Bill that adopts the president's suggestions or one that does not (by a two-thirds majority). Since it cannot achieve the latter (the President almost inevitably having a majority), they tamely do the former: the president becomes the legislator. No-one seems to have thought about this at the constitution-drafting stage and considered what, for example, happens in the United States. There the veto is just that: the Bill dies. Whether a new one is passed accommodating the President's views or insisting on the Congress views, it is a fresh Bill that goes through all the stages; but if they are sticking to their guns, they can compel the President to accept their Bill only by passing it with a two-thirds majority. Many Bills just die.

A final, nondevolution, issue is that of procurement. This is a major source of money leakage in Kenya (in torrents rather than in dribbles). The very first draft included a provision based on that in the CSA about a system that is "fair, equitable, transparent, competitive and cost-effective." But in the spirit of plugging every hole, the Kenyan version includes not only the possibility of affirmative action for those "previously disadvantaged by unfair competition or discrimination" but of exclusion of contractors with records of defective performance and persons who have not paid tax, or have been guilty of corruption or bad employment practices.[72] It has not stemmed the flood.

10.5.4. *Electoral Matters*

The CSA provides little detail on the electoral system, save to say that the National Assembly comprises between 350 and no more than 400 members through an electoral system that "results, in general, in proportional representation,"[73] with a similar provision for provincial assemblies.[74] For municipal

[72] CoK art. 227.
[73] CSA s. 46.
[74] Ibid. a. 105.

bodies it is more specific: there must be party lists, though these could be combined with ward members, presumably on a mixed member proportional basis (or MMP).[75]

Kenyans were (still are) obsessed with electoral integrity or lack of it. So, there are many provisions designed to achieve that elusive integrity, including a whole chapter on Representation of the People. The first draft proposed an MMP system. This owed nothing to South Africa and more to Germany and New Zealand. But this disappeared in the NCC; it had few supporters, mainly because of attachment to the known, and because, perhaps, members had not been greatly bothered by the evidence of lack of proportionality. The only steps taken to address this were rather weak provisions on equality of electoral district size. There is a small element of what is called "proportionality" in the provisions about party lists: elections for the extra seats (gender, disability, etc.) in Parliament and county assemblies "shall be on the basis of proportional representation by use of party lists."[76] The allocation of these list seats is in proportion to seats won, not votes cast. It simply reinforces the existing balance of seat power. In fact, it tends to tilt it further in favor of the winners, because with a small number of seats to be allocated through lists and a large number of parties, the larger parties inevitably benefit disproportionately. This is a far cry from the CSA provision.

10.5.5. *Devolution-Related Issues*

Devolution was on the agenda even before the official process began. This had nothing to do with South Africa, and a lot to do with Kenya's history: at independence Kenya had a quasi-federal system with eight provinces, with legislative powers, and their own police. The system was adopted due to pressure by leaders of smaller tribes to ensure a share of state power. The system was done away with after one year, and the controversies that existed at that time still linger.

The similarities between the CSA and the CoK are not about the levels or units of devolution or the actual powers devolved. Debate about the latter in Kenya was very limited and, although there were debates about the number and levels of units, these were very different from those in South Africa. While South Africa was concerned not to emphasize ethnic differences, the underlying issues in Kenya in the 1960s were ethnic, and things were little different

75 Ibid. a. 157(2)–(3). For MMP see "Electoral Systems" (2005) *Ace Project* (available at www.aceproject.org/ace-en/topics/es/esd/esd03/esd03a/default) (accessed date November 20, 2017).

76 CoK art. 90(1).

in the 2000s. Indeed, the ethnicization of politics has strengthened in Kenya over those years. However, the objectives of devolution set out in the CoK have little to do with ethnicity, other than the empowerment of minorities and marginalized communities (art. 174). On the contrary, its primary objective is defined as the fostering of national unity by recognizing diversity. Another objective (not stated explicitly) was to use devolution to weaken the imperial presidency, bringing government and decision making much closer to the people.

Although there was some South African input into the early learning processes and decision making of the CKRC,[77] there were other influences, especially that of Professor Ron Watts, the Canadian expert on federalism.[78]

There were more major changes in the proposals on this topic through the process than on any other issue. Most of the debate was about the number of tiers, and the number and type of units.[79] The ultimate result on these issues was very different from South Africa. While the latter has nine provinces (average population about 5.8 million) and 278 municipalities (population between the very small and the 4.5 million of Johannesburg), Kenya has forty-seven counties with an average population of about one million, ranging from the 120,00 or so in Lamu to the four million in Nairobi.[80] Kenya has administrative levels below the counties, but these are not local government in the sense of being elected, and their powers are not set out in the Constitution.

But in various respects, the Kenyan provisions became increasingly South African in successive drafts. Kangu comments that "[a]fter very delicate negotiations, ... the plenary adopted a much-improved draft which borrowed

77 Notably the involvement of Christina Murray and Richard Simeon who had been writing on the South African system: see, e.g., R. Simeon and C. Murray, "Multi-sphere governance in South Africa: an interim assessment" (2001) 31(4) *Publius* 65–92. They attended a CKRC workshop in 2001: see "Workshop on Devolution of Power, Held at Safari Park Hotel on 13th December, 2001" Verbatim report in typescript form (available at www.katibainstitute.org/Archives/index.php/ckrc-process/seminars-workshop-presentations) (accessed date November 20, 2017).

78 Who was a speaker at the same workshop.

79 The authors have written about the process until the end of the NCC in "Constitutional transitions and territorial cleavages: the Kenyan case" in G. Anderson and S. Choudhry (eds.), *Constitutional Transitions and Territorial Cleavages* (forthcoming).

80 For South Africa, the figures are from Y. Fessha and J. de Visser, "Drawing non-racial, non-ethnic boundaries in South Africa" in N. Steytler and Y. P. Ghai (eds.), *Kenyan-South African Dialogue on Devolution* (Cape Town: Juta, 2015) 81–101. The Kenyan figures are extrapolated for 2014 from the 2009 census by the Kenya National Bureau of Statistics in County Statistical Abstracts available at https://www.knbs.or.ke/county-statistical-abstracts/) (accessed date November 20, 2017).

quite a number of features from the South African Constitution."[81] The areas in which the South African precedent is most noticeable are the nature of inter-governmental relationships, finance and the national Parliament's structure and role in terms of devolution.

10.5.6. *Nature of Inter-Governmental Relationships*

Even the CKRC draft had language that was reminiscent of cooperative federalism. It said that:

1. Governments, national and devolved, must cooperate with one another in mutual trust and good faith by:
   - i. fostering friendly relations;
   - ii. assisting and supporting one another;
   - iii. informing one another of, and consulting one another on, matters of common interest;
   - iv. coordinating their actions and legislation with one another;
   - v. adhering to agreed procedures; and
   - vi. avoiding legal proceedings against one another.

This language is directly based on s. 41(1)(h) of the CSA. This specific language no longer appears, but the general principles of cooperation remain, with the final versions saying "[t]he governments at the national and county levels are distinct and inter-dependent and shall conduct their mutual relations on the basis of consultation and cooperation" clearly reminiscent of s. 40(1) of the CSA[82] and other provisions about cooperative relations.

Specific issues of inter-governmental relations in which the debt to the CSA is clear include specific provisions about mediation before litigation and the need for legislation to set up inter-governmental institutions. Most striking, however, is the provision about when the national government can override county legislation in areas in which they both have power to pass law. Article 191 of the CoK is essentially the same in intention as s. 146 of the CSA. Unfortunately, it is less clear in practice because the scope of concurrent jurisdiction of the two levels of government is less clear in Kenya. While the CSA has a schedule (4) listing areas of concurrent jurisdiction, there is no equivalent in the CoK, leaving the matter, as Kangu comments, to "be determined through interpretation."[83]

[81] J. M. Kangu, *Constitutional Law of Kenya on Devolution* (Nairobi: Strathmore University Press, 2015) 89. Kangu was the CKRC Commissioner who spent time in South Africa.

[82] "[G]overnment is constituted as national, provincial and local spheres of government which are distinctive, interdependent and interrelated": CSA s40(1).

[83] Kangu, Constitutional Law of Kenya (n. 81) 193.

There is some similarity between the two constitutions on the power of the national government to step into a lower level. In South Africa, the national government may intervene in a province – if the latter's government fails to carry out an executive function – by issuing a directive to the provincial executive telling it what it needs to do, or even by "assuming responsibility for the relevant obligation in that province to the extent necessary to (i) maintain essential national standards or meet established minimum standards for the rendering of a service; (ii) maintain economic unity; (iii) maintain national security; or (iv) prevent that province from taking unreasonable action that is prejudicial to the interests of another province or to the country as a whole."[84] The National Council of Provinces supervises this process and may bring it to an end. This broadly resembles CoK Article 190 called "Support for county governments." However, there is no equivalent, for provinces, in the CSA to the Kenyan nuclear option, under which the national government may set up an inquiry into a county and suspend the entire county government, leading to a county election for governor and assembly unless the Senate terminates the suspension before ninety days have elapsed.[85] Kangu points out, however, that municipal governments in South Africa may be suspended.[86] Most Kenyan counties fall somewhere between the South African provinces and municipalities in terms of size and perhaps of propensity to need support or intervention.

10.5.7. *Finance*

The principal institution for ensuring that the counties in Kenya have the resources needed for their functions is the Commission on Revenue Allocation. A commission with responsibility for finance was a feature of all drafts. The precedents for such a body are not exclusively South African: the Indian Finance Commission is the best known and, of course, older. The CKRC draft included a Commission on Local Government Finance (the title of which also revealed the rather more modest conception of devolution than now prevails). Some debt to the CSA was already visible in the provision that "the Commission should aim at defining and enhancing the own revenue sources of devolved governments with the objectives of encouraging fiscal responsibility and moving the devolved governments over time toward financial self-sufficiency." But much was left to be decided by future legislation,

84 CSA s. 100.

85 CoK art. 192.

86 CSA s. 139, see Kangu, *Constitutional Law of Kenya*, 302.

and the CKRC envisaged a more prolonged, and carefully planned, transition to devolved government than in fact transpired.

So, when a CKRC Task Force, formed to sort out controversial issues, during the NCC process proposed a body based on the South African Finance and Fiscal Commission, this was not really very new.

The language of the Kenyan draft became more like that of the CSA during the CoE phase. By the end of the NCC process the contours of devolution, as it is now, were clear except for the question of the number and levels of units. Specifically, the Commission on Revenue Allocation was in place, with powers similar to those of the FFC of South Africa. The criteria for allocation of revenue between national and county governments (and among the latter) had had echoes of the CSA since the beginning, but by the end of the NCC they were very similar, with the odd difference (such as referring to the needs of not the "national government" as in the CSA[87] but of the "Government" throwing an interesting light perhaps on the perception of the nature of devolution). Perhaps more significant was the absence of the requirement that these needs must be "determined by objective criteria." The Constitution as adopted is identical to the CSA on these points.

The procedure for revenue allocation is also similar, but not identical. The Commission on Revenue Allocation comprises a chair nominated by the President, two members nominated by political parties represented in the National Assembly, five nominated by the political parties in the Senate and Principal Secretary to the Treasury. The South African FFC includes one person nominated by each province – not by political parties – and nine others (the Constitution does not specify how they are identified – another example of the Kenyan tendency to dot every i and cross every t, which partly accounts for the greater length of the CoK).

The CRA is to make recommendations on revenue sharing between the national and county government levels. The amount of revenue to be allocated to counties must not be less than 15 percent of the sum allocated in the last year in which the relevant government body's accounts were approved by the Auditor General. These proposals are compiled in a Division of Revenue Bill, and the CRA must comment on this. This Bill begins in the National Assembly but must also be considered by the Senate. The South African FFC must similarly comment on the legislation dividing revenue.

The CRA makes the initial recommendations on the basis of revenue sharing between counties. These are considered by the Senate, which must

87 Ibid. s. 214(2)(c).

also consult the county governors, the Cabinet Secretary for Finance and the organization of county governments, as well as by inviting public input. The Senate then passes a resolution that can be amended or rejected by the National Assembly, but only by a two-thirds majority. The ultimate division is by the County Allocation of Revenue Act, introduced in the Senate, but passed by both houses. In South Africa, the resolution by the second house of Parliament does not happen. In that country, there is only one Act of Parliament – passed by both houses. Kenya took the terminology from South African law but divided the Bills.

A significant departure from South African precedent is the Equalization Fund. This was inspired by Switzerland and Canada rather than by South Africa. It is a fixed percentage (0.5 percent) and is to be used to "provide basic services including water, roads, health facilities, and electricity to marginalized areas to the extent necessary to bring the quality of those services in those areas to the level generally enjoyed by the rest of the nation, so far as possible."

10.5.8. *Devolution in the National Parliament*

Both constitutions provide for a second house of parliament with particular responsibility to protect the system of provincial/county government. But while the CSA, drawing on German precedent, structures that house – the National Council of Provinces – as the voice of the provinces, but including the provincial premier and members of the provincial assemblies in the delegation– the Kenyan Senate is very different. The latter is composed mainly of Senators directly elected by the county voters. But the idea that voting in this second chamber is usually by delegations of devolved assemblies– rather than by individuals voting as such –is taken by Kenya from South Africa. Although in the CSA the NCOP votes on all Bills and in the CoK the Senate only votes on certain Bills, the concept of "bills affecting provinces" in the former appears in the latter as "bills concerning county government." The distinction affects whether the second house must approve (CSA) or has any vote at all (CoK). Another similarity is the mediation committee – to be used to resolve disagreements on legislation between the two houses.

In fact, the idea that the second house represents the governments of the lower level units – and not the people of each unit as such – appeared in the CKRC draft: the principal members were the "Chairpersons of the District Councils." The NCC draft stated that a principal member was "one member elected from each district by the district council of that district." The second draft of the CoE shifted to a directly elected representative of each county; the idea of the Senate representing the governments of the counties had quite gone.

10.6. AFTER THE CONSTITUTION OF KENYA

Kangu comments, "this study pays particular attention to South African jurisprudence, because the drafters of the Kenyan Constitution used many provisions from the South African Constitution particularly in the area of devolution."[88] His own book's index has twenty-eight references to the CSA, forty-seven to the Constitutional Court and four to the Supreme Court of Appeal. A quick Google search of the Kenya Law case database[89] for "South Africa" "constitutional court" produced 1,250 results (of course there will be some repetition in these entries). Early entries in the list give a flavor of the contribution of South African jurisprudence to the interpretation of Kenya's new document:

> May 13, 2013 ... As the Constitutional Court of South Africa observed in the case of Brummer v Minister for Social Development 2009 (II) BCLR 1075 (CC) ...[90]
>
> Sep 23, 2016 ... In this aspect, the Constitutional Court of South Africa in the case of Doctors for Life International v The Speaker National Assembly (supra) ...[91]
>
> Apr 11, 2013 ... Mr. Mutua also referred the court to the decision of the Constitutional Court of South Africa in Irene Grootboom and Others v The Government of ...[92]
>
> Feb 26, 2016 ... composition of the Constitutional Court of the Republic of South Africa is drawn from ... [49] For example, the Constitutional Court in Gcaba v.[93]
>
> Jun 11, 2015 ... On the question of what constitutes fair administrative action the Constitutional Court of South Africa in its decision in PRESIDENT OF THE ...[94]

88 Kangu, Constitutional Law of Kenya 46.

89 See, www.kenyalaw.org – under the auspices of the National Council for Law Reporting. (accessed date November 20, 2017).

90 *Nairobi Law Monthly Company Limited* v. *Kenya Electricity Generating Company* [2013] eKLR (available at www.kenyalaw.org/caselaw/cases/view/88569/) (accessed date November 20, 2017).

91 *Bumasutra Savings and Credit Co-operative Society Ltd* v. *County Government of Nakuru* [2016] eKLR Constitutional Petition 6 of 2016 (available at www.kenyalaw.org/caselaw/cases/view/127225/) (accessed date November 20, 2017) quoting *Nairobi Metropolitan PSV Sacco Union Limited* v. *County of Nairobi Government* [2013] eKLR.

92 *Mitu-Bell Welfare Society* v. *Attorney General* [2013] eKLR.

93 *Chris Munga N. Bichage* v. *Richard Nyagaka Tong'i* [2016] eKLR (on doctrine of precedent).

94 *Muslims for Human Rights (Muhuri)* v. *Inspector-General of Police* [2015] eKLR (available at www.kenyalaw.org/caselaw/cases/view/110659/) (accessed date November 20, 2017) citing *President of The Republic of South Africa* v. *South Africa Rugby Football Union & Others* (2000) 1 SA 1 (CC).

> Apr 24, 2015 … In South Africa, the Constitutional Court has held in National Coalition for Gay and Lesbian Equality v Minister of Justice 1999 (1) SA 6 that …[95]

Cases in the area of the right to housing and public participation are among those that are relied on most often, though the Kenyan courts have usually been less bold than their South African counterparts. Indeed, the Kenyan courts' concept of obligations under socio-economic rights has rarely gone beyond the negative obligation to respect (not positively to violate) the rights.

There have been a number of cases involving equality and freedom of religion that have drawn on South African precedent. The wearing of a hijab by Muslim students in schools with school uniforms has been one issue. Cases have cited a South African case holding that to refuse an exemption to a Tamil student to allow her to wear a nose-stud amounted to unfair discrimination.[96] But the Kenyan courts have often not embraced the spirit of that case where Justice Langa, for the majority, said: "[g]ranting exemptions will also have the added benefit of inducting the learners into a multi-cultural South Africa where vastly different cultures exist side-by-side."[97] At least two cases have concluded that allowing Muslim girls to wear the hijab is somehow unfair to Christian students.[98] However, a recent Court of Appeal decision – on appeal from the first case has been more inclusive in spirit, and quoted Langa CJ in *Pillay*: "a reasonable accommodation is most appropriate where, as in this case, discrimination arises from a rule or practice that is neutral on its face and is designed to serve a valuable purpose, but which nevertheless has a marginalizing effect on certain portions of society."[99]

Article 23(3) provides that "[i]n any proceedings brought under Article 22, a court may grant appropriate relief, including …", and there follows a long list of specific remedies. It is more technically framed than the CSA provision about just and equitable orders.[100] It is improbable that without South

[95] *Eric Gitari* v. *Non-Governmental Organisations Co-ordination Board* [2015] eKLR (available at www.kenyalaw.org/caselaw/cases/view/108412/) (accessed date November 20, 2017).

[96] *MEC for Education: Kwazulu-Natal* v. *Pillay* (2008) 1 SA 474 (CC).

[97] Ibid. para. 102.

[98] *Methodist Church (Suing through its Registered Trustees)* v. *Teachers Service Commission* [2015] eKLR (available at www.kenyalaw.org/caselaw/cases/view/107653/) (accessed date November 20, 2017); *Republic* v. *The Head Teacher, Kenya High School Ex-parte SMY (a Minor Suing Through Her Mother and Next Friend A B)* [2012] eKLR.

[99] *Mohamed Fugicha* v. *Methodist church in Kenya (suing through its registered trustees)* [2016] eKLR (available at www.kenyalaw.org/caselaw/cases/view/125558/) (accessed date November 20, 2017).

[100] CSA s. 172(1)(b).

African precedent the Kenyan courts would have issued as *dirigiste* orders to government as have been seen in some cases. For example, Justice Lenaola ordered the Minister for Education to promulgate regulations or issues directions prescribing the obligations of public schools to respect the rights of students under Article 32 of the Constitution namely "the right to freedom of conscience, religion, thought, belief and opinion."[101] In another,[102] Justice Mumbi Ngugi ordered the respondents (including the Attorney General and the National Land Commission) to provide the court within sixty days with "the current state policies and programmes on provision of shelter and access to housing for the marginalized groups such as residents of informal and slum settlements," to direct them to a certain nongovernmental organization (NGO), and to other agencies, not specified, and to engage with the petitioners, the NGO and other relevant state agencies and civil society organizations to identify an appropriate resolution to the petitioners' grievances about their eviction.

But the latter case received disappointing treatment in the Court of Appeal.[103] That court said, "[i]t is our considered view that under the political question doctrine, a court has no jurisdiction to make orders relating to policy formulation or give guidelines on who should participate in the formulation of government policy."[104] This case has been appealed to the Supreme Court.

Again, without South African precedent, would the Kenyan courts have adopted the useful device of suspended orders of invalidity? It is specifically recognized in the CSA,[105] but not in the CoK. It was used in the case that declared the Kenyan constituency development fund unconstitutional, but gave Parliament a year to deal with the problem because of ongoing projects under the scheme.[106] (The Court cited *Premier: Limpopo Province* v. *Speaker of the Limpopo Provincial Legislature*).[107]

Legislation has also drawn significantly on South African models, as a result of constitutional similarities. For example, the Fair Administrative Action Act, 2015, was based to a considerable extent on the Promotion of Administrative

[101] *Seventh Day Adventist Church (East Africa) Limited* v. *Minister for Education* [2014] eKLR (available at www.kenyalaw.org/caselaw/cases/view/93354/) (accessed date November 20, 2017).

[102] *Mitu-Bell Welfare Society* v. *Attorney General* [2013] eKLR (available at www.kenyalaw.org/caselaw/cases/view/87948/) (accessed date November 20, 2017).

[103] *Kenya Airports Authority* v. *Mitu-Bell Welfare Society* [2016] eKLR (available at www.kenyalaw.org/caselaw/cases/view/123600/) (accessed date November 20, 2017).

[104] Ibid. para. 112.

[105] CSA s. 172(1)(b)(ii).

[106] *Institute of Social Accountability* v. *National Assembly* [2015] eKLR.

[107] (2012) 4 SA 58 (CC).

Justice Act (PAJA), but with improvements, as weaknesses in the South African legislation had become apparent. The Access to Information also drew on the Promotion of Access to Information (PAIA), although to a lesser extent.

The similarities have led to a variety of intellectual exchanges. South Africa has always (since the end of apartheid) been attractive to students from other parts of Africa, and the commonalities between the constitutions have made this a very appropriate destination for law students, who have studied, for example, devolution and economic social and cultural rights through a comparative lens. To draw examples just from our own institution (Katiba Institute) we carried out a joint project with the University of the Western Cape that led to a conference and ultimately a book comparing various aspects of the two countries' systems through pairs of chapters by South African and Kenyan authors.[108] A program of judicial training involved speakers from South Africa (Professor Nico Steytler and Jaap de Visser) as well as from Canada, and also led to a book.[109] A current project on producing a guide for the public service on fair administration[110] has held a preliminary meeting at which a valuable contribution was made by Professor Cora Hoexter.

With the imminence of the retirement of Kenya's first chief justice under the new constitution, we turned to South Africans for guidance on qualities of a CJ as a yardstick for choosing his successor.

South Africans have been involved in vetting of Kenyan judges (Albie Sachs), in an orientation program for the new Supreme Court (Zak Yacoob) and in a judicial training program (e.g., Hugh Corder on administrative law). Mokgoro, Yacoob and Sachs have made many visits to Kenya for a variety of purposes.

10.7. CONCLUSIONS ON THE KENYAN DEBT TO SOUTH AFRICA

The CSA has had a very significant impact on Kenya and the process continues. The CoK, or earlier drafts, has been partially copied in various constitutions, including Zimbabwe and Somalia. The Tanzanian draft, so far not adopted, also drew quite a lot on the Kenyan constitution. In Solomon Islands

[108] N. Steytler and Y. P. Ghai (eds.), *Kenyan-South African Dialogue on Devolution* (Cape Town: Juta, 2015).

[109] C. M. Bosire and W. Gikonyo (eds.), *Animating Devolution in Kenya: The Role of the Judiciary* (Nairobi: International Development Law Organization, 2015) (available at www.idlo.int/publications/animating-devolution-kenya-role-judiciary) (accessed date November 20, 2017).

[110] Inspired by the *Judge Over Your Shoulder* produced for the UK public service. See: *Judge Over Your Shoulder*, 5th ed (Government Legal Department, July 18, 2016) (available at www.gov.uk/government/publications/judge-over-your-shoulder) (accessed date November 20, 2017).

a draft in about 2007 for a federal constitution drew heavily on the Kenyan CKRC draft, and as that country moves toward actually adopting a new document, what emerges will probably also contain provisions reminiscent of Kenya, and of South Africa. A draft of a constitution for Fiji prepared in 2012 also owed a good deal to the Kenyan document and experience, and also directly to South Africa. That draft was rejected by the Government of Fiji, but a new draft that was adopted still shows some of that legacy: notably in socio-economic rights provisions.[111]

So, the South African experience, through Kenya, and through these the contributions of Germany, India and Canada, continue to have an impact – and points to the increasing trade in constitutions.

10.8. WHAT AFTER THE CONSTITUTIONS?

In this Section, we turn at the invitation of the editors in the first chapter to reflect on constitutionalism in respect of new constitutions like those in South Africa and Kenya. However, we do not use the hypotheses or frameworks outlined by them, because we believe that they are too western/US oriented to be of much value in explaining the African experience. The CSA and CoK were negotiated and adopted after, and partly as a consequence of, the collapse of the Cold War. The West no longer needed to prop up dictatorial regimes in Africa. Instead, they began to support the demands, over a long time, of liberal groups for a democratic constitution. It is not surprising that these constitutions seek to bring in what is now often referred to as "transformation."

A detailed response to the editors' invitation would require many pages; here we provide a broad but brief picture. It is not easy to assess the success or otherwise of a constitution, particularly of the long and ambitious kinds, such as those of South Africa and Kenya. There are few constitutions that succeed in all their endeavors, and many that fail substantially. We thought that we could better understand the dynamics of a constitution if we could compare the record of the implementation of these two constitutions (given both their similarities and differences as well as the context of their enactment). Both the constitutions aim for major changes in the objectives and structure of the state, empower the people, and aim for social justice for all. They are both shields to protect the hard-fought rights of the people and weapons to

111 Again, personal involvement plays a part. In Fiji the authors (Yash Ghai as chair of the commission), Christina Murray, and Phill Knight were involved; in Solomon Islands Yash Ghai, Phil Knight, Jill Cottrell – and now Nico Steytler. But the 2007 SI draft seems to have come off the internet.

redress the many discriminations and exploitations of the disadvantaged. By acknowledging the people as sovereign, the constitutions seek to empower the people and to define their role, which goes well beyond choosing their representatives.

However, the comparison is not easy, since the CSA has been in operation over twenty years (twenty-three if we count the transitional period), while the CoK came into full effect only four years ago, when devolution and the new system of government applied after general elections (in March 2013). But, on the whole, the South African Constitution has been more successful than the Kenyan in the pursuit of its constitutional objectives and aspirations. In a short time it dismantled a complex array of states and territories under the system of apartheid and integrated numerous bits of territory into a cohesive state, established a new system of government, developed relatively good relations between opposing ethnic communities, held peaceful and fair elections on a new system of franchise, established a regime of human rights, and set up a constitutional court of eminent lawyers who quickly and effectively established a regime of the rule of law. There is no doubt that, at least at one level, the Constitution did bring about a political and social transformation. Ethnic tensions have eased, though they have by no means disappeared, and political parties now draw supporters from all communities. Judicial decisions continue to be respected, however unpalatable to state authorities. The Constitution has brought about the new political order that the people wanted. In the last few years the constitutional order has come under attack (primarily from the president, apparently in collusion with some business interests) but its fundamentals remain.

The CoK did not achieve half as much. This despite the fact that the draft was drawn over a long period, with extensive public participation, expert advice, and, in the end, with 68 percent public support in the national referendum. A special commission was established to oversee the implementation. The Constitution had built into it a scheme for its implementation, with severe penalties for parliamentarians or the executive for its breach. In addition we had the benefit of the experience of and advice from South Africans about what led to success and what threatened it.[112] At a superficial level, all the institutions were established, with clear mandates; the extensive Bill of Rights came into force; corrupt judges were removed and a competent and

[112] For a brief analysis of why the constitution has had little impact, see Y. Ghai, "Constitutions and constitutionalism: the fate of the 2010 constitution" in G. Murunga, D. Okello, and A. Sjögren (eds.), *Kenya: The Struggle for a New Constitutional Order* (London: Zed Books, 2014).

honest group of lawyers joined the judiciary, with considerable power to protect the constitution. In due course a fair number of powers were transferred to forty-seven new counties. Much new legislation was enacted (though not always in the spirit that the Constitution prescribed). Several new, and mostly independent, institutions were established, geared toward the protection of constitutional values. But often the form and formalities have overshadowed the spirit and objectives of the institutions, values and procedures. Political parties paid scant regard to constitutional rules governing their formation or functioning, particularly as regards the formation of national unity, relying instead on ethnicity. The executive has shown even greater resistance to the constitution, strengthened the ethnic basis of politics, and frequently disregarded court decisions against it. The prevalence and scale of corruption has greatly increased, as has violence by the police.

Why have the fortunes of the CSA and CoK, similar in their orientation, operating in somewhat similar milieux, been so different? The contexts of the adoption of the constitutions were similar – end of an era and the start of another – but greater change was envisaged in South Africa. In other words, how we do explain the success or failure of a constitution? A proper discussion of the success or failure of key provisions in the case of both countries will take many pages and much time. Instead, we will discuss the factors that determine success or failure, with reference to these two constitutions.

There are at least two factors that can influence the outcome of the constitution – one is internal to the constitution, the other is external to it. Internal refers to the objectives, structures, internal coherence, etc., of the constitution. Much attention has been paid to this aspect. Factors external to the constitution – the state, society, economy – are generally more important than the first.[113] The state is often the most important; indeed it is the heart of the Constitution itself. The history and impact of the state in Africa are significantly different from that in the West. In the latter, there has generally been a close relationship between the state and the constitutional order. The Constitution has reflected the state (objectives, power relationships, institutions, etc.). However, in Africa, after annexation by imperial powers, the state preceded the constitution; there was often no real relationship between the two. In the initial period, there was no real legal framework for the acquisition or domination of a colony. A powerful state was established, which appropriated land, moved people around, conscripted labor, set up and ran the army

[113] Yash Ghai has analyzed the impact of "external factors" in "Chimera of constitutionalism: state, economy and society in Africa" in S. Deva (ed.), *Law and (In)equalities: Contemporary Perspectives* (Lucknow: Eastern Book Company, 2010).

and police – and established a bureaucracy with wide powers, the exercise of which could not easily be challenged. The state, controlled by the colonial power, dominated all aspects of the colony and its administration. As the colony moved toward self-government, the underlying structure of the state was unaffected. The constitutions bestowed by the colonial power on independence were great instruments of liberalism – but in practice power remained with the bureaucrats (now being localized), sharing it gradually with the emerging political class. Between them they managed to negate restrictions on their power and their own accountability. Gradually a local bourgeoisie emerged, in partnership with them, through corruption and favoritism. The state has remained the agency of this cluster, regardless of any contrary provisions in the Constitution and law.

The second key area is the economy. The privatization of the economy and the resulting labor were the key to the character of the state, with increasing emphasis on rights of property, the sanctity of contract, impartial dispute settlement – all leading up to the rule of law. In the colonies, there was no rule of law, and few restrictions on what the bureaucracy and later the political class could do. Postcolonial economies have a more elaborate legal framework and are more integrated globally, but they are by no means free economies. Most postcolonial economies are best described as "administered economies." The control over the economy that is given to the state has in general the support of local business community, because, by their relationship to politicians and bureaucracy, they are able to secure good deals. The connection between the state and economy is corruption. Kenya has shown how hard it is to fight this corruption, despite extensive laws promoting integrity and outlawing corruption. A very large amount of business is criminalized. Trade unions, which often played a critical role in the struggle for freedom, have been marginalized, if not coopted by the state. As political alliances shift due to temporary conveniences, there is honor among thieves. Thus, politicians, torn by occasional conflicts, sometimes quite serious as in Kenya's postelection violence in 2008, are nevertheless united by a common interest in the plunder of the state and suppression of their obvious ways. So, the political class is formed, making the adoption of reform, or at least its implementation, extremely unlikely.

The third area is society; the relationship between it and the Constitution is complex and contradictory. Unlike in Europe, the introduction of the colonial state responded almost entirely to the concerns and powers of an outside force. Because the state did not reflect the values and structures of local society, it had to rely on the considerable use of coercion. Consequently, the state had a much greater impact on society than the other way round. Over the years, African society has become more differentiated, in different ways, sometimes competing, often collaborating. But the centrality of the state to political, economic and even social management has remained. Major divisions in society are not social or class but ethnic. Ethnicity has dominated political strategies, alliances, allegiances and discourse. Elites find it easy to mobilize ethnic support and in this way, to aim for the exclusion of the competitors from the state. The persistence and mobilization of ethnicity are facilitated by the vulnerabilities produced by both the state and economy. Politicians have no interest in reform of the state, which might jeopardize their favored access to it. This has a profound impact on social cohesion and the way that the people perceive the state. Competing ethnic claims hinder social solidarity. Instead, ethnicity leads to the abuse or subversion of artefacts of democracy built into the constitution.

It also leads to the political passivity of the people, so that, although they are not happy with the turn of politics, the divisions of ethnicity prevent the growth of a class consciousness. The trade union movement is weak and unfocussed. Civil society does play some role in criticism of public policies and practices, but relatively little in raising the peoples' awareness of politics and economy, and the roots of their exploitation.

10.9. KENYA AND SOUTH AFRICA: LESSONS IN CONSTITUTIONAL SUCCESS OR FAILURE?

A reader might well say that our analysis may be relevant to Kenya, and may indeed explain the failure of the Constitution, but how does it apply to South Africa, which has had considerable success in establishing an entirely new constitutional order? There are a number of differences in terms of history, diversity, economy and politics between the two countries that might explain the relative success of South Africa. Its civil society is more advanced than in Kenya. It has a clear ideology about unity and fairness. Its fight was not just for the removal of the rule of white people, but for a state committed to fairness for all communities and equal rights of all the people. It tended to avoid ethnicity as social or political criteria. The freedom movement was fought not just by black people; all races joined forces. The fight was ideological for a nonracial, nonethnic South Africa. That commitment does not seem to have wavered.

The quality of the political leadership of South Africa is infinitely better, with a clear vision of the kind of South Africa it wanted. When they assumed control of the state, they remained faithful to that vision, in complete contrast to Kenya's politicians. The first leader in Kenya after independence, Jomo Kenyatta, was a person without vision (other than about himself and family, and at best the Kikuyu community), in total contrast to Nelson Mandela. The general quality of leadership in South Africa has been much higher than in Kenya. There seems to be a better balance between the state and society, workers and even capitalists.

South Africa's economy is more developed than Kenya's, particularly its emphasis on mining and industry. Its trade union was and is infinitely better organized than Kenya's, and committed to clear economic and political objectives (now enshrined in the constitution). It has played and continues to play a critical role in politics. Political parties are for real in South Africa, with clear policies, Kenya has neither. Social forces are well organized and more numerous. One could say with confidence that South Africa is a democracy, with a robust system of political parties, based on clear policies and without ethnic or racial or regional bias. With equal confidence, one could say that Kenya is scarcely democratic. The South African government accepts, however reluctantly, decisions of courts and other independent authorities– unlike the Kenyan government. There is the rule of law in South Africa but scarcely in Kenya. The dominance of the state has been less pervasive than in Kenya, for these and other reasons.

Finally, we come to the mode of participation, negotiations and agreement on the constitutions. The idea that a constitution will flourish if the people have been consulted and atrophy if not may not always be true. The Kenya process, at least in the early phases, was very participatory (including providing civic education), with a careful analysis of all the recommendations made to the drafters. South Africa's was much less so, being dominated by two major parties, popular though they were. The South African Constitution has flourished, the Kenyan one is atrophying.

11

Multi-Stage Constitution-Making: From South Africa to Chile?

Joel Colón-Ríos

One of the main features of the formal process that led to the adoption of the South African Constitution was its multi-stage character. The Constitution was not adopted by a single body (e.g., a constituent assembly), but through a process that involved different institutions, each of them incapable of creating, by themselves, a new fundamental law. The multi-stage model of constitution-making has been praised by Andrew Arato, who identifies as one of its great advantages that within it, no entity or person can claim to embody the sovereign will of the people. Multi-stage constitution-making has yet to make its way to contemporary Latin America, where the dominance of the traditional one-stage model remains largely undisputed. However, in Chile, where the government recently announced a process to replace the Constitution of 1980, the traditional one-stage model seems to have lost some ground. In fact, the Chilean process shares important characteristics with the multi-stage model praised by Arato. After comparing the South African and the Chilean processes, this chapter will argue that there are good reasons to think that, in the end, Chile might not entirely succeed in escaping from the allegedly more problematic aspects of the traditional model (i.e., the sovereign constituent assembly). Nevertheless, the way in which the Chilean process has incorporated different aspects of the model that operated in South Africa may go a long way toward avoiding the risks associated with assemblies that can somehow claim to act *as if* they were the people.

11.1. CONSTITUTION-MAKING IN STAGES

Constitutions, at least formally, have until recently been created through a one-stage process: either a king, a legislature, or a constituent assembly is attributed with full constitution-making power and proceeds to adopt a new fundamental law. When kings acted as constitution-makers (when, e.g., Louis XIV attempted to limit the power of his heir, or when James II attempted to become an absolute monarch), the nature of their actions was clear: they were simply exercising a sovereign power they thought, rightly or wrongly, belonged to them.[1] As Rousseau knew very well, that an individual may hold such a power is a cause for concern: it means that a people could end up being subject to a constitutional order that protects the private interests of the few and not the interests of the whole.[2] The problem does not go away when legislatures and constituent assemblies are the ones with the task of creating or radically transforming an existing constitution. True, in such scenarios, the legislature or the constituent assembly is generally seen as acting not on its own behalf, but on behalf of the sovereign people. However, there seems to be no way of ensuring that a legislature or a constituent assembly will not merely replace the existing constitutional order with one that seeks to protect the interests of certain elites or groups. Despite this possibility, this is the way in which "democratic" constitution-making usually takes place. From the perspective of the critic of the one-stage model that is indeed a very dangerous game to play.

Of course, there are a number of informal and formal mechanisms that make the constitution-making power of a legislature or a constituent assembly less dangerous than that of a king. First, unlike kings, legislators and delegates to constituent assemblies are usually elected (although usually only the former are actually accountable to the electorate).[3] As a result, it is likely that their preferences are similar to those of the electors and, accordingly, that they will tend to create constitutions that protect the latter's interests. Second, legislatures and constituent assemblies (perhaps more than kings) are subject to the pressure of public opinion and, in extreme cases, to the possibility of popular resistance to a highly unjust constitutional order. Third, constitutions drafted by legislatures and constituent assemblies are sometimes subject to popular ratification before they become valid. Nevertheless, none

[1] The idea that monarchs, even those attributed with sovereign power, could create new constitutions was challenged very early in the history of constitutional thought. See, e.g., J. Bodin, *On Sovereignty: Four Chapters from the Six Books of the Commonwealth* (J. Franklin ed.) (Cambridge: Cambridge University Press, 1992), 13, 18; Marsilius of Padua, *The Defender of Peace* (A. Brett trans. ed.) (Cambridge: Cambridge University Press, 2005) 52; J. Althusius, *Politica* (F. S. Carney trans. ed.) (Indianapolis, IN: Liberty Fund, 1995) 93.

[2] J. Rousseau, *The Social Contract and the Discourses* (G. D. H. Cole trans.) (London: Everyman's Library, 1973).

[3] In the sense that, unlike delegates to a constituent assembly, they may be subject to re-election.

of these mechanisms, not even a referendum, can necessarily guarantee that the constitution-making power will be responsibly exercised (as critics or the "populist" processes that recently took place in Venezuela, Bolivia and Ecuador would be quick to point out). For example, in the case of constituent assemblies, the "responsible" exercise of constituent power would not only require the adoption of a "good" constitution, but that the assembly resist the temptation to invade the jurisdiction of the ordinary powers of government. The problem, it seems, arises from the very idea of attributing a single entity, be it a legislature or a constituent assembly, with the authority to act on behalf of the sovereign people.

It is not surprising that, as a response to those risks, some scholars have engaged in the study of possible constraints to constitutional replacement.[4] In that vein, David Landau and Rosalind Dixon have recently questioned the desirability of the "sharp distinction between constitutional amendment, which can properly be constrained in order to protect against manipulation, and constitutional replacement, which is supposedly an exercise of the sovereign power of the people outside of any legal restraints."[5] For them, just as the ordinary institutions of government acting through an amendment rule, a constituent assembly attributed with full power of constitutional change can undermine the democratic nature of a juridical order. Therefore, there might be value in subjecting constitutional replacement to different types of limits. The current Constitution of Bolivia, for example, imposes (*ex ante*) procedural limits on the power of a constituent assembly convened according to a replacement rule: the assembly is only authorized to approve a draft constitutional text by a two-thirds majority of those present.[6] However, the extent to which such a provision could effectively limit a future constituent assembly (particularly when the Constitution describes it as "originary" and "plenipotentiary") is unclear.[7] In Venezuela, the court attempted to impose (*ex post*) procedural limits on a constituent assembly, by arguing that constituent power could only be exercised through a process that expressed a "true popular will."[8] This attempt, Landau and Dixon maintain largely failed.

4 D. Landau and R. Dixon, "Constraining constitutional change" (2015) 50 *Wake Forest Law Review* 859.

5 Ibid. 860.

6 Constitution of Bolivia 2009, art. 411.

7 In fact, the constituent assembly that adopted the Constitution of 2009 was subject to similar procedural limits, and was unable to fully constrain the constitution-making body. For a discussion, see Landau and Dixon, "Constraining constitutional change" 880–1.

8 Ibid. 876–7.

Those failures (or potential failures), in a certain way, explain why multi-stage constitution-making is for some an attractive alternative. As conceived by Arato, multi-stage constitution-making (which he also sometimes refers to as the postsovereign, postrevolutionary, round-table led, or two-stage model)[9], can assume different forms, but generally speaking, it has three main features.[10] First, an interim Constitution (or functional equivalent, such as a set of principles) is drafted by a nonsovereign negotiating entity (e.g., a round table). Second, a nonsovereign constitution-making body (which could take the form of a legislature or a special assembly) that would be required to draft a constitution consistent with the conditions developed during the first stage is elected. Third, in some cases, the process involves a mechanism of substantive restraints on constitutional replacement: the intervention of a constitutional court in the last stage of the process as a means of ensuring the consistency of the final document with the conditions set by the negotiating forum.[11] Importantly, unlike in typical "sovereign constituent assembly" scenarios, the entire constitution-making episode is characterized by the absence of a legal rupture.[12] In a typical "legal rupture" scenario, best exemplified by the cases of Venezuela and Colombia, the sovereign constitution-making body is convened in violation of the previous constitution's amendment rule.[13] Despite their technical illegality, those entities have sometimes been sanctioned by courts on the basis of their alleged democratic legitimacy (i.e., they are usually authorized by referendums and convened in periods of popular mobilization for constitutional change).[14]

For Arato, "[t]he great advantage of post sovereign constitution making is that it de-dramatizes conceptions of the constituent power, linked to mythological and dangerous notions of total rupture and the full embodiment of the will

[9] A. Arato, *Post-Sovereign Constitution-Making: Learning and Legitimacy* (Oxford: Oxford University Press, 2016), 10.

[10] Ibid. 91–2.

[11] In fact, Landau and Dixon use the South African example as the main instance of substantive restrictions on constitutional replacement: see Landau and Dixon, "Constraining constitutional change."

[12] Arato, *Post-Sovereign Constitution-Making* 92. There could nevertheless be certain illegalities as long as "the crucial legal rule, the amendment rule, actually constrains and limits the mutual expectations and actions of actors": at 92.

[13] For a discussion, see J. Colón-Ríos, *Weak Constitutionalism: Democratic Legitimacy and the Question of Constituent Power* (London: Routledge, 2012).

[14] See, e.g., Opinion No. 17 of the Supreme Court of Justice of Venezuela (19 January 1999); Opinion No. 138 of the Supreme Court of Justice of Colombia (November 9, 1990). Also sociological or de facto legitimacy – Cf. *Madzimbamuto* v. *Lardner-Burke NO; Baron* v. *Ayre* 1968 (2) SA 284 (RAD).

of the people."[15] The new model is thus an alternative between reform and revolution, allowing for the creation of an entirely new constitutional order while neutralizing the possibility of abuses of power that always accompany sovereign constitution-making entities. It also increases, according to Arato, the opportunities for learning, allowing those involved in the second stage to reflect on the lessons learned in the first.[16] This model has been put into practice in different ways in a number of jurisdictions, including Spain, Poland and Hungary. But the paradigmatic case of the new model is the process followed in the adoption of the South African Constitution of 1996. Arato, for example, maintains that "the South African process has been the most complete and most consistent development" of the new model.[17] This process has been studied at length before, and my intention in the next section is only to provide a brief summary of its main features.[18] I will then consider some of the similarities between that process and the one that has just begun in Chile. I will argue that, despite those similarities, and while formally resembling the postsovereign model, the Chilean effort might nevertheless retain the fundamental premise of the one-stage paradigm: the insistence on an institution that can somehow be understood as a means for the exercise of the constituent power of the people.

11.2. POSTSOVEREIGN CONSTITUTION-MAKING

11.2.1. *South Africa*

During South Africa's transition to democracy, the main political actors defended different types of constitution-making mechanism. The African National Congress (ANC), for example, maintained that the new Constitution should be adopted by a sovereign, democratically elected, constituent assembly.[19] That is to say, the creation of a new constitution through the traditional

[15] Arato, *Post-Sovereign Constitution-Making* 91.

[16] Ibid. 104.

[17] Ibid. 106.

[18] See, e.g., M. Faure and J. Lane, *South Africa: Designing New Political Institutions* (London: Sage Publications, 1996); S. Gloppen, *South Africa: The Battle over the Constitution* (Aldershot: Ashgate, 1997); J. Sarkin, "The drafting of South Africa's final Constitution from a human-rights perspective" (1999) 47 *American Journal of Comparative Law* 67; F. Haysom, "Special features and mechanisms in negotiating the South African Constitution," in G. Hyden and D. Venter (eds.), *Constitution-Making and Democratization in Africa* (Pretoria: Africa Institute of South Africa Press, 2002); P. Andrews and S. Ellmann (eds.), *The Post-Apartheid Constitutions: Perspectives on South Africa's Basic Law* (Johannesburg: Witwatersrand University Press, 2001).

[19] H. Klug, "Participating in the design: Constitution-making in South Africa" (1996) 3 *Review of Constitutional Studies* 18, 32–3.

one-stage model, in which a constituent assembly directly elected by the people is attributed with full constitution-making powers. The ruling National Party opposed that plan, and preferred a long transition to democracy that would result in a constitution negotiated by the political parties. This approach, according to Heinz Klug, was a manifestation of the fact that "the National Party was determined not to relinquish control before securing effective safeguards against the future exercise of state power by the black majority."[20] A third political actor, the *Inkatha Freedom Party* (IFP), also rejected the ANC's calls for a democratically elected constituent assembly. For them, the role of a constitution was to protect minority rights and, therefore, the new Constitution should be created through a process that gave a salient role to experts and minority parties (which would then be sanctioned in a national referendum).[21] In 1993, the ANC and the National Party agreed to a system of executive power-sharing that brought together key elements of the previously described proposals. Under this system, there would be a government of national unity (i.e., a government that would include the National Party) and a process that would lead to the creation of a new constitution.

That process took place in two main stages. The first stage, which Arato would call the round table stage, was under the control of the negotiating parties and did not involve formal opportunities for citizen involvement.[22] That stage resulted in the adoption of an interim constitution, which included a set of principles with which the final Constitution had to comply. The interim Constitution was formally adopted by the last apartheid parliament according to the procedure established in the Constitution of 1983. It established a bicameral parliament, with a directly elected National Assembly and a Senate composed of ten senators from each province (nominated by the parties represented in provincial legislatures).[23] The "national unity" aspect of the interim Constitution was institutionally exemplified in a provision establishing that parties winning more than twenty seats in the National Assembly would be entitled to a number of seats in the cabinet (a number that would be proportionally determined).[24] Between the first and second stages, democratic

[20] Ibid. 36.

[21] Ibid. 38.

[22] Ibid. 49.

[23] Constitution of the Republic of South Africa Act 1993, ss. 40, 48.

[24] Ibid., s. 88(2):

> A party holding at least 20 seats in the National Assembly and which has decided to participate in the government of national unity, shall be entitled to be allocated one or more of the Cabinet portfolios in proportion to the number of seats held by it in the National Assembly relative to the number of seats held by the other participating parties

elections took place (in 1994) in accordance with the previously mentioned provisions. The second stage of the process was triggered by Section 68 of the interim Constitution, which provided for the calling of a "Constitutional Assembly" (formed by a joint sitting of the National Assembly and the Senate) and established that that entity "shall draft and adopt a new constitutional text in accordance with this Chapter."[25] That same section provided that the new Constitution was to be adopted within two years of the first sitting of the National Assembly.[26]

Unlike the first stage of the process (i.e., negotiations by a nonelected body), the second stage had significant participatory components.[27] That public involvement, Klug has noted, was not so much about "mass action or public demonstrations" but "towards a more individualistic, yet equally active, form of participation in the attendance of discussion-meetings and the making of formal submissions to the CA."[28] A final step in the process (which could be seen as a third stage) had the Constitutional Court at the center. As noted earlier, the interim Constitution contained a list of Constitutional Principles[29]

25 Ibid., s. 68. Section 73(2) of the interim constitution contains a general two-thirds majority requirement (subject to certain exceptions and a dead-lock breaking mechanism) for the adoption of the constitution by the Constitutional Assembly.

26 Ibid., s 73(1).

27 For a short summary, see Sarkin, 'The drafting of South Africa's final Constitution' 70–2.

28 Klug, "Participating in design" 57. Simone Chambers has also stressed the participatory character of the South African process, highlighting the level of consultation carried out by the Constitutional Assembly (S. Chambers, "Democracy, popular sovereignty, and constitutional legitimacy" (2004) 11 *Constellations* 153, 162). Nevertheless, both Chambers and others express doubts as to the extent to which the submissions and petitions received by the Constitutional Assembly actually impacted the final constitutional text (ibid. 163; Sarkin, "The drafting of South Africa's final Constitution" 71). Moreover, Larkin notes that after a draft constitutional text was published in November 1995 for public comment, a number of contentious issues were discussed behind closed doors (ibid. 71).

29 There were 34 principles in total. Just to provide an idea of their form and substance, here are some of them:

> I The Constitution of South Africa shall provide for the establishment of one sovereign state, a common South African citizenship and a democratic system of government committed to achieving equality between men and women and people of all races; II Everyone shall enjoy all universally accepted fundamental rights, freedoms and civil liberties, which shall be provided for and protected by entrenched and justiciable provisions in the Constitution, which shall be drafted after having given due consideration to inter alia the fundamental rights contained in Chapter 3 of this Constitution; III The Constitution shall prohibit racial, gender and all other forms of discrimination and shall promote racial and gender equality and national unity; IV The Constitution shall be the supreme law of the land. It shall be binding on all organs of state at all levels of government; XI The diversity of language and culture shall be acknowledged and protected, and conditions for their promotion shall be encouraged. XII Collective rights of

and its s. 71(3) established that "A decision of the Constitutional Court" shall certify "that the provisions of the new constitutional text comply" with them. Importantly, these principles were put out of the scope of the constitutional amending power regulated by s. 74 of the interim constitution. The necessary implication of that approach was that the Constitutional Assembly that would draft the final Constitution lacked an unlimited constitution-making power and was subject to judicially enforced restraints. Indeed, the Constitutional Court refused to certify the new Constitution after concluding that several of its articles were inconsistent with the aforementioned constitutional principles.[30] Conceptually, this suggests that the Constitutional Assembly never was a sovereign organ, that is, that it did not fully represent the "sovereign people" (or, alternatively, that the principles contained in the interim Constitution were binding on the people).

For Arato, the multi-stage nature of this process "allowed for a period of testing of the operation of the provisional constitution and learning from this experience."[31] As exemplified in South Africa, even though the postsovereign model rejects the idea of an entity authorized to act in the name of the people, it does not have a hostile attitude toward popular participation in constitution-making. In fact, a key aspect of the model is the emphasis on the connection between popular participation in constitution-making and the legitimacy of a constitution. However, his understanding of popular participation is "less inspired by the populist projects of the Andes than by contemporary experiments with institutionalizing popular inputs" seen in places like Ireland, British Columbia and Iceland.[32] In Chile, since the question of the legitimacy of the Constitution of 1980 is one of the triggers for the current process of constitutional change, it is not surprising that among its main features one

self-determination in forming, joining and maintaining organs of civil society, including linguistic, cultural and religious associations, shall, on the basis of non-discrimination and free association, be recognised and protected; XIII 1. The institution, status and role of traditional leadership, according to indigenous law, shall be recognised and protected in the Constitution. Indigenous law, like common law, shall be recognised and applied by the courts, subject to the fundamental rights contained in the Constitution and to legislation dealing specifically therewith …

30 *Certification of the Constitution of the Republic of South Africa* (1996) 4 SA 744 (CC) para. 482. The Constitution was finally certified on December 4, 1996 in a judgment that ended with the following order: [w]e certify that all provisions of the amended constitutional text, the Constitution of the Republic of South Africa, 1996, passed by the Constitutional Assembly on October 11, 1996, comply with the Constitutional Principles contained in schedule 4 to the Constitution of the Republic of South Africa, 1993 (*Certification of the Amended Text of the Constitution of the Republic of South Africa* 1997 (2) SA 97 (CC)).

31 Arato, *Post-Sovereign Constitution-Making* 105.

32 Ibid. 9.

finds different mechanisms of public involvement. Perhaps more important for our purposes here, those mechanisms operate in what appears to be a multi-stage constitution-making process which shares significant similarities with the South African one. There are also important differences, however, one of them being the context in which these processes operated (or will operate) and the problems they were designed to overcome. In what follows, I will describe in some detail the constitution-making process brought forward by the Chilean government, stressing the ways in which, at least superficially, it can be understood as a manifestation of the postsovereign model.

11.2.2. *Chile*

In South Africa, multi-stage constitution-making was an important part of the transition from apartheid to liberal democracy.[33] Since the system that existed in South Africa prior to the adoption of the interim Constitution in 1993 was not democratic, it was inevitable that the process that would lead to a democratic constitution would have to be designed by nonelected institutions. In contrast, while the Chilean Constitution of 1980 was by no means democratically adopted (it was approved by a Military Junta and ratified in a referendum of highly dubious democratic credentials), its subsequent reforms in 1989 and 2005 mean that, at least formally, Chile today has a reasonably democratic system of government.[34] Accordingly, unlike in South Africa, the design of a constitution-making process in Chile has long being in the hands

[33] In terms of the transition to democracy, the 1988–9 process in Chile would be a much better comparator, but this chapter is of course focused on the making of new constitutions in these two countries.

[34] Major reforms occurred in 1989 and 2005: *Ley de Reforma Constitucional* No. 18.825 (August 17, 1989); *Ley de Reforma Constitucional* No. 20.050 (August 26, 2005). The 1989 reforms (ratified in a referendum) included, for example: the repeal of a constitutional prohibition of parties promoting "totalitarian doctrines"; an increase in the number of elected senators; and abolished the presidential power of dissolving the lower house of the legislature. In 2005, the changes included the abolishment of the political faculties of the military (which allowed it to influence the composition of the Senate and the Constitutional Court), and provided for a fully elected senate. For a useful discussion of these reforms, see C. Fuentes, "Elites, Opinión Pública y Cambio Constitucional," in C. Fuentes (ed.), *En Nombre del Pueblo: Debate Sobre Cambio Constitucional en Chile* (Santiago: Universidad Diego Portales, 2010). It has been argued that none of those changes altered the real structures of power in the country, and only took place when they no longer negatively affected the interests of the conservative political forces. For a recent discussion, see F. M. León, "El Proceso Constituyente en Curso en Chile" (2015) 16 *Revista Argentina de Teoría Jurídica* 12–15. For an analysis of the democratic deficiencies that were not dealt with in 2005, see J. Couso and A. Coddou, "Las Asignaturas Pendientes de la Reforma Constitucional Chilena" in C. Fuentes (ed.), *En Nombre del Pueblo: Debate sobre Cambio Constitucional en Chile* (Santiago: Universidad Diego Portales, 2010); C. Heiss

of democratically elected governments. The specific form that such a process should take has been the subject of immense debate in Chile (a debate that began shortly after the Constitution of 1980 was adopted and its legitimacy began to be questioned). Among those who thought that the Constitution of 1980 was illegitimate, part of the debate reflected the old controversy about reform and revolution: should the Constitution of 1980 be replaced through extra-constitutional means (e.g., a sovereign constituent assembly convened in violation of the established rules of constitutional change) or should it be reformed in a way that respects those rules of change and at the same time removes "the authoritarian enclaves" that reflected the drafters" distrust of popular politics?[35] The latter possibility was complicated by the fact that the Constitution of 1980 is particularly difficult to change (its supermajority requirements mean that any major reform needs the agreement of conservative political forces – as happened, e.g., in 2005).[36] Not surprisingly, after the 2005 reforms, an interesting controversy arose as to whether those changes could be properly seen as amounting to a new constitution and therefore as solving the legitimacy problems of the Constitution of 1980.[37]

The movement toward the adoption of a new constitution reached an important point in 2008, when Senator Eduardo Frei stated that the Constitution of 1980 needed to be replaced and made constitutional change a key part of his (unsuccessful) campaign to become President for a second time.[38] Coming from a member of the establishment (and not from the traditional left who had long insisted on the need for a new constitution) that declaration acquired particular importance. And while there appeared to be strong (though not unanimous)[39] support for the adoption of a new

and P. Navia, "You win some, you lose some: Constitutional reforms in Chile's transition to democracy" (2007) 49(3) *Latin American Politics and Society* 163.

35 See Couso and Coddou, "Les Asignaturas Pendientes" 193.

36 The constitution includes a supermajority threshold unlikely to be met without the agreement of the conservative forces that oppose major constitutional change: Constitución de Chile (as amended), Chapter XV: "El proyecto de reforma necesitará para ser aprobado en cada Cámara el voto conforme de las tres quintas partes de los diputados y senadores en ejercicio. Si la reforma recayere sobre los capítulos I, III, VII, XI, XII o XV, necesitará, en cada cámara, la aprobación de las dos terceras partes de los diputados y senadores en ejercicio." This amendment rule was made somewhat more flexible in the 1989 reforms. On the limits to democratic constitutional change imposed by this rule, see F. Atria, *La Constitución Tramposa* (Santiago: LOM Ediciones, 2013).

37 That was the position of President Ricardo Lagos. See Fuentes, "Elites, Opinión Pública" 64–5.

38 Ibid. 66 (for a discussion).

39 Most notably, the current constitution is defended by the *Unión Democrática Independiente*, a political party founded by Jaime Guzmán (a key factor in the creation of the Constitution of 1980).

constitution, there was no consensus about what mechanism should be used to achieve that goal. Some (including Frei), excluded the convocation of a sovereign constituent assembly, echoing the traditional fears of attributing an entity with an unlimited constitution-making power (and instead pointed to alternative processes of reform in which the legislature and the executive played a salient role). Others, particularly those on the left, insisted that a constituent assembly was the appropriate and fully democratic mechanism for establishing a new constitutional order.[40] The problem with the latter option, like in Colombia and Venezuela some years earlier, was how to make such an assembly possible in light of the amendment rule of the Constitution of 1980. In October 2015, President Michelle Bachelet moved the debate to a new level by describing the Constitution of 1980 as being the product of a dictatorship and as lacking legitimacy and, more importantly, announcing the beginning of a "constituent process."

The process, which can be understood as an attempt to overcome the reform/revolution dichotomy, involves four main stages.[41] The first stage (which at the time of writing was underway) is focused on public consultation: it involves a process of "civic education" as well as a number of "citizen dialogues" (which would take place at the individual, communal, provincial and regional level) where ordinary citizens will have the opportunity of presenting their proposals about the new constitution. A "citizen council of observers" (appointed by the President)[42] would have the task of ensuring that the consultation takes place in a free and transparent manner. This first stage of the process will be completed by the submission to the President of a number of *bases ciudadanas* (a phrase that is difficult to translate into English but that roughly refers to a

[40] See Fuentes, "Elites, Opinión Pública" 66–72.

[41] The materials provided by the government refer to seven stages, and some commentators refer to eight (see, e.g., F. Muñoz, "El proceso constituyente en curso en Chile" 16 *Revista Argentina de Teoría Jurídica* (Diciembre de 2015) 16), but some of the stages are better merged for the purpose of analysis.

[42] Gobierno de Chile, *8 conceptos del proceso para la Nueva Constitución*, October 13, 2015 (available at www.gob.cl/2015/10/13/8-conceptos-del-proceso-para-la-nueva-constitucion/) (accessed date November 20, 2017). See also Consejo Ciudadano de Observadores, *Acuerdo No. 4: Sobre la Participación Ciudadana y Las Bases Ciudadanas para una Constitución Discutida en Democracia* (March 2016) (available at www.ccobservadores.cl/wp-content/uploads/2016/05/acuerdo_n4_sobre_metodologia_de_participacion.pdf) (accessed date November 20, 2017). In that document, members of the "citizen council of observers" seem to conceive the nature of public consultation in a way that incorporates some of the elements of the citizen assemblies that have operated in places like Ontario, British Columbia, and more recently, Iceland and Ireland. For a critical discussion of this type of process, see E. Carolan, "Ireland's constitutional convention: behind the hype about citizen-led constitutional change" (2015) 13 *International Journal of Constitutional Law* 733–48.

set of principles developed by citizens), which will form the basis of the new Constitution (it appears that those "bases" will be drafted by a "citizen council of observers").[43] In the second stage, the President of the Republic will prepare a "constitutional project" (*proyecto de constitución*) that, in addition to resting on the previously mentioned *bases ciudadanas*, will reflect "the best of the Chilean constitutional tradition and recognize Chile's legal obligations towards the world."[44] The President's constitutional project was supposed to have been be submitted to Congress in 2017. The third stage of the process consists of an amendment to the Constitution of 1980 that will make its replacement possible by a mechanism determined by the Congress to be elected in 2018.[45]

The documents published by the government maintain that the new Congress will have four options to choose from (which would by then presumably be listed in the Constitution as a result of the previously mentioned reform): (a) a joint sitting of Congress; (b) a "mixed" constitutional convention which would include citizens and members of parliament; (c) a constituent assembly elected specifically for the creation of a new constitution; and (d) a referendum in which Chileans will choose among the previous three alternatives. The fourth stage will consist of drafting the final Constitution by the chosen mechanism, a constitution that will become valid if ratified in a referendum. This process can be seen as containing the essential features of the new model: the *bases ciudadanas* which will likely be drafted by nonelected "council of observers" (equivalent to a set of principles created by a nonelected entity); and the election of the Congress that will reform the Constitution in order to legalize the prospect of constitutional replacement by a future Congress or special assembly (roughly equivalent to the free election of a nonsovereign constitution-making body). None of the entities involved in the process, it seems, could claim to hold full constituent power. For example, the "council of observers" only has the power to propose a set of principles, the first Congress can only reform the constitution, and the final

43 "Gobierno cede y encarga redacción de Bases Ciudadanas a observadores," *El Mercurio*, April 6, 2016 (available at www.economiaynegocios.cl/noticias/noticias.asp?id=240316) (accessed date November 20, 2017).

44 Gobierno de Chile, *Infografía: conoce las etapas des proceso constituyente*, October 13, 2015 (available at www.gob.cl/infografia-conoce-las-etapas-del-proceso-constituyente/) (accessed date November 20, 2017). It is not clear what the reference to "the best of the Chilean constitutional tradition and recognize Chile's legal obligations towards the world" means, nor what would happen if such tradition and obligations run contrary to the *bases ciudadanas*.

45 This, of course, means that in the end, conservative political forces would be able, if they decide to do so, to use the current amendment process to block the proposed process of constitutional change.

constitution-making body would operate according to the (revised) constitutional amendment rule.

11.3. THE LIMITS OF POSTSOVEREIGN CONSTITUTION-MAKING

There are, of course, important differences between the Chilean process and the way that the postsovereign model worked in South Africa. Here, I will only point toward four of them. First, unlike the South African interim constitution, the *bases ciudadanas* will not have immediate legal effect. This is the natural result of Chile having amended the Constitution of 1980 and already having an operational democratic system of government (in that respect, the amended Constitution of 1980 plays the role of an "interim constitution"). Second, while in South Africa the first stage was generally nonparticipatory and driven by elites, in Chile, that first stage seems to be (at least in theory) about citizens themselves developing the principles in which they want their Constitution to be based. Third, the Chilean constitution-making body, as the South African one, will be elected, but the specific form it takes will be determined by either Congress or the electorate in a referendum. Fourth, while in South Africa public consultation by the Constitutional Assembly was seen as a sufficient form of popular participation, in Chile the new Constitution will only become valid if ratified by the people in a referendum. These last two differences suggest a particular concern with the direct involvement of the electorate that goes beyond participation in free elections (which is not surprising in a jurisdiction where "free elections" routinely take place and are therefore insufficient to invest a new constitution with the required legitimacy) and public consultation.

Nonetheless, as suggested above, the current process has a major similarity with the postsovereign model that arguably overshadows all those differences: unlike in other recent Latin American constitution-making episodes, the process is characterized by an effort to create a new constitutional order without a legal rupture and in a way that avoids the attribution of sovereign powers to a single institution. In fact, this is a process that closely resembles Arato's recent proposal for Chile:

> I envisage the operation of a negotiated model through a focus on the amendment rule in place. If a new constitution making procedure was to be established this would require amending the amendment rule. Such legal revision of the revision, and the qualified majority it requires, not to speak of one immune to judicial intervention, is possible only if the parties know the basic structure of the eventual outcome. I think this would have

> to be informally negotiated, aiming at a series of constitutional principles a la South Africa. It is important not to go too far in such negotiations, and produce a merely "contractual constitution," but to go far enough to attain the necessary majorities. Hence the goal is drafting basic principles rather than a full constitution. Chile evidently does not need an interim constitution, since it already has one under which constitutional change, even replacement can occur. Participation in these negotiations should be broad, conceding the primacy of political parties in parliament, but including some without current parliamentary mandates, as long as they have had a significant share of the vote. Decision making should be by qualified majorities, of at least a level that would guarantee passage in the two chambers. Public scrutiny and input should be made possible, in order to generate input producing a truly 21st century constitution and to establish real citizen control over the process, as against fictitious ones as under populist leadership. Since a freely elected assembly could add a great deal of constitutional content based on the electoral self-expression of the citizens, the aim of "pre assembly" agreement would remain confined to principles and to the drafting of a new rule of replacement or total revision. The latter would aim at precisely the election of a constitutional assembly under the limits of the drafters, who could give the constitutional court the right and duty to enforce them, again as in South Africa.[46]

That last point regarding the Constitutional Court's role in enforcing the principles against the drafters of the Constitution is not explicit in the government's plan, but there are some indications that the court may be involved in the later stages of the process (although it remains unclear what, if any, its precise role would be).[47] However, the President's role in preparing a "constitutional project" that reflects the *bases ciudadanas* sits somewhat uneasily with the way in which the new model is conceived by Arato. It seems to be an unnecessary step (why not allow the chosen constitution-making body to prepare a draft constitution that is consistent with those principles?), but it may simply be an over-emphasized manifestation of the fact that, in a constitution-making

[46] A. Arato, "Beyond the alternative reform or revolution: post sovereign constitution making and Latin America" 50 *Wake Forest Law Review* (2015) 891.

[47] "Tribunal Constitucional dice que no participará en proceso constituyente para mantener neutralidad," *El Mostrador*, October 29, 2015 (available at www.elmostrador.cl/noticias/pais/2015/10/29/tribunal-constitucional-dice-que-no-participara-en-proceso-constituyente-para-mantener-la-neutralidad/) (accessed date November 20, 2017). It must be noted here that in Chile, the organization and attributions of the present Constitutional Court have been identified as one of the non-democratic elements of the current constitution. See Couso and Coddou, "Las Asignaturas Pendientes" 200–10.

process, it is not uncommon for the executive power to present a constitutional project of its own. Notwithstanding the above, the process is largely consistent with the postsovereign model or, at least, it has borrowed important features from it. It is nevertheless possible that in the end, the process may not be able to escape the specter of the sovereign constituent assembly.[48] Arato himself contemplates that possibility, and maintains that if the political actors are unable to agree on the relevant principles or on a new amendment rule, he would reluctantly accept that the government declares that the "so-called road of popular sovereignty based on a plebiscite" is followed.[49]

That seems like a sensible approach, but what I have in mind is something different. The very words "Constituent Assembly" carry a particular force in Latin America. Despite being elected in a way similar to an ordinary legislature, constituent assemblies are seen as somehow closer to the people than any ordinary institution of government. A constituent assembly, understood as a means of exercising the "unlimited constituent power of the people" is not surprisingly seen by many as a necessary component of a legitimate constitution-making process. In the Chilean case, this is exemplified by the fact that, despite the very sophisticated multi-stage process proposed by the government, it is very possible that in the end, a constituent assembly is chosen (either by Congress or by the people in a referendum) as the mechanism in charge of giving Chile a new constitution. The question is, would that assembly be "sovereign?" That is, would it be seen as a repository of the unlimited constituent power of the people, and therefore not be subject to any form of positive law? Would it be able to do things such as creating and repealing ordinary laws, suspending a Congress that is somehow perceived as interfering with the constitution-making process, or dismissing judges that insist on asserting their jurisdiction to limit the assembly's power? Those are definitely serious concerns, and it is clear that the Chilean process was designed to avoid the risk of an omnipotent constituent assembly.

Not only is the potential "constituent assembly" qualified by the words "elected specifically for the creation of a new constitution" (which suggests that it would lack the power to do anything else), but also the substance of the Constitution it creates would arguably be limited by the *bases ciudadanas* as well as by the "constitutional project" presented by the President. At the same time, since its powers would derive from the revised amendment rule, one

[48] Arato recognizes that a constitution-making process can begin to operate according to a particular model, but then move toward another (Arato, *Post-Sovereign Constitution-Making* 110).

[49] Arato, *Post-Sovereign Constitution-Making* 33.

could even argue that it is really a *constitutional* as opposed to a *constituent* assembly. But there are nevertheless some problems. First, unlike in South Africa, it is not clear whether the *bases ciudadanas* (and the President's constitutional project) would be legally enforceable against a constituent assembly. Second, while the binding character of those documents could be established in the revised amendment rule (together with the qualification that the sole role of the assembly would be to draft a constitution to be later approved by the people), it is not entirely obvious that such an amendment rule would be an effective limit on the assembly. That is to say, if in the third stage the Congress itself determines to convene a constituent assembly, it would not be that difficult to conceive it as an institution governed by the amendment rule that made it possible. However, if the assembly is triggered by the people in a referendum, its political authority would be considerably higher than that of Congress, and the idea of seeing it as resting on a popular decision, rather than in a constitutional provision, becomes more plausible. The legitimacy of any mechanism of restraint is arguably weakened by the extent of popular participation in the process that it seeks to limit.

As a result, an attempt by the courts or by the government to interfere with its functions, to limit the content of the future constitution, might be perceived as an illegitimate (even if technically legal) act (particularly when the people themselves will have the power to veto, in a referendum, a constitution that they see as having unacceptable content). To illustrate (and at the same time challenge) this idea, let's for a moment assume that this in fact happens: the result of the third stage is that Congress calls a referendum, and the electorate votes for the convocation of a constituent assembly. Let's also assume that given its origins (a popular vote in a referendum), the assembly is widely seen as equivalent to the sovereign constitution-making bodies that operated in Colombia, Bolivia, Venezuela and Ecuador. Does that necessarily mean that it would have the power to disregard the *bases ciudadanas* or a mandate to abstain from attempting to exercise the ordinary powers of government? I think the answer to that question is no. It is of course true that to the extent that a constitution-making body is understood as authorized to exercise unlimited power, it would be able, if it wishes, to carry out functions that are usually attributed to government. But even in the one-stage model, a constituent assembly does not need to be seen as enjoying such wide authorization. That is to say, there is no reason why constituent assemblies cannot be understood as *only* authorized to propose a constitution to the people (the exclusive bearer of the constituent power).

Indeed, the very fact that the constitutional drafts prepared by constituent assemblies in Ecuador, Venezuela and Bolivia would only came into force if ratified in a referendum, suggests that it was the people, and not the constituent assembly, who were sovereign. The problem in those cases, I think, was not the one-stage model, but the failure to ground the limits to the power of the constituent assembly not in the very constitutional order that was to be replaced, but in the people themselves. That is to say, there is no reason why the powers of a constituent assembly, even of an assembly described as "sovereign" could not be limited beforehand[50] through a set of conditions (which in the Chilean case could include the *bases ciudadanas*, the prohibition to exercise ordinary law-making powers, etc.) that could be part of the question put to the electorate when the referendum to convene the Constitutional Assembly takes place.[51] In this sense, despite the problems generally associated with referendums and their generally "passive"[52] nature (i.e., the fact that they only give the electorate a veto or ratifying power but not the power to make modifications to the proposed document), they can play an important role in a democratic constitution-making process. They would prevent an otherwise unlimited constitution-maker (which could still be described as "sovereign") from engaging in the adoption of ordinary laws.[53] The sovereign character of such an entity would refer to the fact that it is not bound by positive law, but not being bound by positive law is not the same as not being subject to any limits.

11.4. CONCLUSION

If the argument presented in the previous section is right, then it would seem that the one-stage model does not necessarily carry the risks that multi-stage constitution-making is designed to solve. While multi-stage constitution-making

[50] In *What is the Third Estate?*, Sieyès himself wrote that a body of extraordinary representatives does not have to be attributed with the "*plenitude* of the national will": E. Sieyès, "What is the third estate?" in M. Sonenscher (ed.), *Political Writings* (Indianapolis, IN: Hackett Publishing Company, 2003) 139.

[51] There is no reason why the referendum question itself could not authorize a constitutional court to enforce the limits contained in the amendment rule. In such a situation, the court would not be assuming its ordinary role of limiting the constituted powers, but commissioned by the constituent people to ensure that the entity that has been tasked with the preparation of the draft constitution does not deviate from that mandate. However, it could be argued that in Chile, any inconsistency between the new constitution and the *bases ciudadanas* should be decided by the people themselves in a referendum.

[52] See Arato, *Post-Sovereign Constitution-Making* 118, 123–4.

[53] In Arato's terminology (based on the historical practice of American and French constitution-making bodies), this approach would transform the constituent assembly into a convention (the latter having as one of its main features the inability to engage in ordinary law-making).

can be described as "post-sovereign" in the sense that it does not attribute constituent power to any institution, the one-stage model is better understood as only attributing constituent power to the people (a power that, as Rousseau insisted, could not be represented). But there is something of immense value in the model that was perfected in South Africa: a process in which opposing political forces can be assured that the future Constitution will be consistent with a number of principles to which they would have agreed beforehand. The price to pay for that kind of process is losing the radically open character of an act of constitutional creation: the idea of a constitution-making body being able to deliberate about the content of the new Constitution without being substantively bound. In some contexts, where there is an urgent need for national reconciliation and for the creation of a stable democratic constitutional order, that is probably a fair price to pay. In Chile, where such an order largely exists, binding a constitution-maker to a set of principles would only be a fair price to pay if they are not the product of negotiations between elites, but of public deliberation. To the extent that that is what is going on in Chile, the process designed by the government has the potential of inaugurating a more inclusive form of constitution-making in the Latin American region.

12

A Cure for Coups: The South African Influence on Fijian Constitutionalism

Coel Kirkby

Fiji, it seems, is not like South Africa. It is a small archipelago in the South Pacific. Its population is smaller than Soweto. There is no large white settler population; instead its two main ethnic groups are iTaukei (62 percent) and Indo-Fijian (31 percent).[1] Fijians were not independent until 1970 and have since endured three coups, two successful and one failed. Despite their many differences, however, these two countries share a key similarity forged over a century of colonial rule. The British imperial government and the successor white government in South Africa restructured both countries on fundamental principles of communalism, a form of racialized segregation and authoritarianism. While these principles took different forms in the vastly diverging contexts, they nevertheless formed the deep constitutional structure of both countries and in similar ways continue to bedevil experiments in liberal constitutionalism since the mid-1990s.

The author worked for both the Constitution Commission in 2012 and the Citizens' Constitutional Forum, a Fijian nongovernmental organization, in 2012 and 2013. The author would also like to thank Jill Cottrell Ghai, Yash Ghai and Anna Dziedzic for their insightful comments on an earlier draft.

1 Indo-Fijians were a small majority of the population, but they have slowly declined relative to the iTaukei population as successive waves emigrated after each coup. In 2016, the Fijian government estimated the ethnic population figures as 537 838 iTaukei, 273 744 Indo-Fijian and 61 628 'Other' (the last population census was carried out in 2007): Fiji Bureau of Statistics, *Table 1.2 – Population by Ethnicity* (2016) (available at www.statsfiji.gov.fj/latest-releases/key-stats) (accessed date November 20, 2017). The term "Fijian" is deeply contested in Fiji. I will use the term "iTaukei," now most often to describe "indigenous" Fijians and the term "Indo-Fijian" for indentured laborers from India and their descendants. The term "Others" was a catch-all for all other non-Europeans, a perverse consequence of the fundamental distinction between settler and native applied to Fijian realities. Throughout this chapter these terms refer to racialized communities created through colonial laws and not as ethnicities. As for the difficult term "Fijian," I will reserve it to refer to those subjects then citizens of Fiji.

This chapter examines and evaluates the South African influence on liberal constitutionalism in Fiji. It does so through a study of Fiji's four and a half constitutions since independence. In the last two decades, Fijian constitution-makers drew on global constitutional sources, but the South African experience proved especially important when considering how to cure their shared colonial legacies of communalism and authoritarianism. The 1996 and 2012 Fiji Constitution Commissions likewise hoped to transform these legacies through liberal constitutionalism. In particular, they made liberal recommendations regarding the constitution-making process, the composition and structure of government, rights and their protection, and the role of the military. Again, like South Africa, these liberal ideals were subject to political compromises necessary to reach a final document.

The chapter begins by sketching the history of Fijian communalism in parallel to South African segregation up to the early 1990s. The British and settler governments created a form of racialized communalism and centralized authority, and later sought to clothe these in liberal forms of government. Their respective failures provide the constitutional context for political crises that led to parallel experiments in liberal constitutionalism in the 1990s. The second section shows how Fijian constitution-makers borrowed from the South African Constitution, especially its underlying philosophy of transformative liberal constitutionalism. However, the chapter concludes on a pessimistic note. Despite its formal liberal features, the current 2013 Constitution imposed by the military government has eradicated the constitutional entrenchment of communalism by centralizing government and guaranteeing the military a role as the ultimate arbiter of the rule of law. In short, the cure for communalism has been the return of authoritarianism.

12.1. DEEP CONSTITUTIONAL STRUCTURE IN FIJI AND SOUTH AFRICA

Fiji and South Africa share a common colonial legacy that formed their deep constitutional structure.[2] While under imperial and settler rule, both countries were structured along a radical legal distinction between racialized communities. All legal rights flowed from one's legal status as settler or native. In Fiji and Natal there was also an important status of indentured (Indian) laborer – a middle category suspended between civil and customary legal regimes.

[2] Cf B. V. Lal, *Broken Waves: A History of the Fiji Islands in the 20th Century* (Honolulu: University of Hawai'i Press, 1992); H. Klug, *Constituting Democracy: Law, Globalism and South Africa's Political Reconstruction* (Cambridge: Cambridge University Press, 2000).

In South Africa, this distinction reached its apotheosis with apartheid, while in Fiji it took a different form of communalism. Since the 1990s, both postcolonies have tried in their own way to grapple with this legacy of division through the ideal of constitutionalism and the practice of constitution-making. This common legacy provides a historical framework for studying the contemporary influence of the South African Constitution on Fijian constitutionalism.

At the end of the nineteenth century, British rulers in the Cape Colony, Natal and Fiji began to implement a new legal system for their native subjects. The key change according to Mahmood Mamdani was the invention of "settler" and "native" as political identities.[3] This distinction was the ideological innovation that justified the creation of distinct forms of legal rule for each. While settlers would continue to be governed under the laws common to Britain and the settler colonies, native subjects would increasingly be governed under a system of indirect rule and customary law. Indirect rule involved the colonial administration of native subjects through the arbitrary power of traditional authorities (e.g., "chiefs"). Customary law involved the application of a particular set of customs unique to each native ethnicity (e.g., "Zulu custom"). By the mid-twentieth century, both Fiji and South Africa had been reconstituted along this form of bifurcated governance.

In Fiji, this took the form of distinct legal systems for European settlers, iTaukei "natives" and Indo-Fijian laborers. The small settler population enjoyed civil laws that were similar to those for European subjects throughout the British Empire. Indo-Fijians, a disparate class of immigrant laborers on plantations or small farms, were under civil laws but were burdened with several communally defined legal disabilities. The most important disability was their precarious access to land, which was mainly secured through long-term leases from the "traditional" iTaukei owners (though effectively imposed on the owners by the British officials). In contrast, all subjects defined as iTaukei were administered through a hierarchical system of chiefs with broad authority to determine and impose customary law on all iTaukei subjects.[4] Customary law was codified in regulations administered by *rokos* (a kind of subordinate chief), as well as native magistrates in special *tikina* courts.[5] An

[3] M. Mamdani, *Define and Rule: Native as Political Identity* (Cambridge, MA: Harvard University Press, 2012); M. Mamdani, *Citizen and Subject: Contemporary Africa and the Legacy of Late Colonialism* (Princeton, NJ: Princeton University Press, 1996).

[4] The iTaukei system was entrenched in a series of laws and regulations: (i) the Fijian Affairs Act, cap. 120; (ii) the Fijian Development Fund Act, cap. 142; (iii) the Native Lands Act, cap. 133; (iv) the Native Land Trust Act, cap. 134; (v) the Rotuma Act, cap. 122; (vi) the Rotuma Lands Act, cap. 138; (vii) the Agricultural Landlord and Tenant Act, cap. 270; (viii) the Banaban Land Act, cap. 124; and (ix) the Banaban Settlement Act, cap. 123.

[5] See, e.g., Fijian Affairs Act, cap. 120, ss. 16–18.

individual's rights were determined by their place within a rarefied system of clan relationships, which determined their chiefly status, communal property rights, inter-personal obligations and other personal rights. As in South Africa, all Fijian women had a distinct communally determined set of gendered laws regarding marriage, inheritance, property and other matters.[6]

In colonial Fiji, the iTaukei community was represented in two important institutions. The first body was the *Bose Levu Vakaturaga* ("Great Council of Chiefs," or "GCC") created in 1876. It was composed of hereditary chiefs who indirectly represented the interests of iTaukei subjects to the British Governor. It developed in parallel to the Legislative Council as the indirect representation the iTaukei community. The second body was the Fiji Military Forces ["FMF"], the colonial military force composed almost entirely of iTaukei men. Baledrokadroka argues that it perpetuated a precolonial iTaukei culture of warrior subservience to chiefly (and ultimately British) authority.[7] The relationship between the GCC and FMF remained close as leading hereditary chiefs were also important military figures at independence in 1970.

The deep division between racialized communities was perpetuated through a series of constitutional reforms from the turn of the century to Fijian independence in 1970 – and beyond. In 1904, the colony's Legislative Council was expanded to nineteen nominated members and for the first time included non-European members. It was composed of ten official members appointed by the Governor, six elected by and from European men, and two iTaukei men appointed by the Governor from nominations by the GCC. No Indo-Fijian was appointed until 1917. Two decades later the Council was reformed to include up to thirteen official members, six Europeans and three Indo-Fijians elected on a restricted male franchise, and three nominated iTaukei. In 1937, the Council was again reformed along the principle of racial parity with five members each for Europeans, Indo-Fijians (two nominated and three elected members), and iTaukei (five nominated from GCC recommendations). The principle of racial parity was translated into that of communal representation in 1963. The Council was then composed of nineteen official members with six members from each "community," two nominated and four elected from all literate subjects, including women. A few years later, the British government tried to moderate this principle by creating "communal" and "national" constituencies. Each community could vote for representatives

[6] Cf. H. J. Simons, *African Women: Their Legal Status in South Africa* (London: Hurst Publishers, 1968); Lal, Broken Waves.

[7] J. Baledrokadroka, "The super confederacy: the military in Fiji's politics" (2015) 104 *Round Table* 127–35 at 128–9.

to its "communal" seats (nine each for iTaukei and Indo-Fijians, and seven for "general electors" including Europeans and Others). Voters also had an additional vote for three "national" constituencies (of nine in total) open to all communities.

By the 1960s, both Fiji and South Africa had been constituted as racialized polities for a century or more. Every community in each country had a distinct system of law and different forms of communal representation purportedly suited to its traditions. Under the communal ideal, these communities were self-contained and self-determining under the overarching and impartial authority of the British and, in South Africa, settler governments.

12.1.1. *Dominant Communalism and the 1970 Constitution*

Fijian independence came late and unasked. Unlike in South Africa and elsewhere in the Commonwealth, there was no broad nationalist movement demanding self-government. The British government entrenched the deep structure of racialized communalism in the 1970 Constitution. In a sense, this was remarkably similar to the Bantu Homelands Citizenship Act passed the same year in South Africa.[8] This law unilaterally denied all Africans their (precarious) membership in the larger polity and assigned each to an ethnic community in a "Bantustan," a racialized sub-state. Fijians were likewise unilaterally excluded from the imperial polity and compelled to join an ethnic community with a distinct legal system under the 1970 Constitution. Fiji thus became something like a self-governing collective of three "homelands" (iTaukei, Indo-Fijian and Other) under a single Constitution. The parallels to South Africa were no coincidence since both the white government in South Africa and the British governors in Fiji had consciously constructed their states along the fundamental principle of communalism for a century.

Fiji's 1970 Constitution did include a Bill of Rights – restricted to civil and political rights – typical of the documents drafted by the Colonial Office in this period. However, rights like equality, nondiscrimination and property were trumped by communalism in two ways. The first communal trump was a bicameral legislature structured by the principle of communalism. The fifty-two-member House of Representatives was elected from three separate communal rolls and a national roll, with a complicated system of communal and cross-voting to elect twenty-two iTaukei and Indo-Fijian, and eight other members.[9] While the lower house ensured nominal parity between the two

[8] No. 26 of 1970.

[9] Fiji Independence Order 1970 and Constitution of Fiji, cap. 1, s. 32 ("Constitution of 1970").

major communities, the Senate had a permanent iTaukei majority despite their then smaller population relative to Indo-Fijians. The Governor appointed seven senators on advice from the prime minister and six on the advice of the leader of the opposition. But iTaukei dominance was ensured by an additional eight members nominated by the GCC (plus one more nominated by the Council of Rotuma). The second trump was the constitutional entrenchment of iTaukei (as well as Rotuman and Banaban) communal rights. This remarkable feature effectively prohibited the alteration of any of the nine enumerated acts that protected such rights. These acts could only be amended with the support of three-quarters of all members of the House and, if the amendment affected "Fijian land, customs or customary rights," the additional support of six of eight GCC-nominated senators.[10] Thus the principle of communalism was perpetuated and iTaukei domination entrenched.

12.1.2. *Super-Dominant Communalism and the 1990 Constitution*

The antagonistic constitutional balance lasted while iTaukei-dominated parties controlled the House. In some ways, the Fijian Constitution resembled a simplified version of South Africa's 1983 tricameral Constitution. However, it still allowed either the iTaukei or Indo-Fijian community the possibility of controlling the lower house (and most importantly did not entirely exclude the majority of the country's population). Indeed, it was the victory of an Indo-Fijian dominated party in 1987 that precipitated the first military coup. The coup leaders clearly targeted Indo-Fijians, but they also challenged the hegemony of iTaukei chiefly authority – a key colonial legacy of indirect rule. Lieutenant colonel Sitiveni Rabuka and his fellow conspirators not only were junior officers, but also had nonchiefly backgrounds. While they spoke of restoring iTaukei domination, they were also undermining the long-standing authority of iTaukei chiefs. The first coup began a process of slowly detaching communalism from traditional chiefly authority and reinventing it as a pillar of iTaukei nationalism embodied by the iTaukei-dominated military.

In 1990, the military government drafted a republican Constitution that explicitly entrenched even greater iTaukei domination, as well as immunity for the coup-makers. The Bill of Rights largely reproduced that of the 1970 Constitution, but included a new "affirmative actions" clause allowing the state to discriminate in favor of "disadvantaged individuals or groups."[11]

10 Constitution of 1970, ss. 68(1)–(2).

11 The characteristic of an individual or groups that permitted affirmative action included "race, sex, place of origin, political opinions, colour, religion or creed." Yet the intention was to allow state programs that discriminated in favor of iTaukei: Constitution of 1990, s. 18.

There was also a standalone chapter on the "protection and enhancement" of iTaukei and Rotoman communities. The government could also override the Bill of Rights in the name of "promoting and safeguarding the economic, social, educational, cultural, traditional and other interests" of these communities.[12] Communalism was now an even greater trump to civil and political rights.

The 1990 Constitution also increased iTaukei control of government institutions. The offices of President and Prime Minister, and over two-thirds of the Senate seats, were explicitly or effectively reserved for iTaukei.[13] Parliament was reconstituted without cross-voting from the national roll. Instead, the communal seats were redistributed and enlarged to guarantee a permanent iTaukei majority. The special iTaukei rights laws were also made even harder to change as any amendment now required the support of all House members and three-quarters of the GCC-nominated senators.[14] The lasting legacy of the 1990 Constitution was not so much in its text, but in its vindication of the military as the ultimate arbitrator of constitutional government in Fiji. It was no longer chiefs but the "commoners" in the military who would guarantee the continued preeminence of the iTaukei nation.

12.2. LIBERAL COMMUNALISM

The 1990 Constitution was obsolete at birth as the collapse of the Soviet Union precipitated a decade-long "third-wave" of liberal constitution-making across the globe.[15] While South Africa rode high at the crest of this wave's optimism, Fiji appeared plunged in pessimism with its communal Constitution increasingly anachronistic in a world reconstituting itself along liberal principles. Only five years later the Fijian government finally acceded to cross-communal support for an independent constitutional review commission to recommend a new Constitution consistent with the global turn to liberal constitutionalism.

12.2.1. *Consociational Communalism and the 1997 Constitution*

The Constitution Review Commission ("Reeves Commission") was composed of Sir Paul Reeves, a former New Zealand governor-general, as chair, and two Fijians, Tomasi Rayalu Vakatora and Brij Lal. The Commission's

[12] Constitution of 1970, s. 21(1).
[13] Ibid., ss. 31, 83(2).
[14] Ibid., s. 78(1).
[15] See S. P. Huntington, "Democracy's third wave" (1991) 2 *Journal of Democracy* 12–34.

terms of reference required a difficult balance between (i) considering internal principles and standards of individual and group rights, (ii) guaranteeing the protection and promotion of iTaukei and Rotuman rights and (iii) ensuring the "rights, interests and concerns of all ethnic groups in Fiji."[16] The commission also tapped into Commonwealth experience through visits to South Africa, Malaysia and Mauritius, as well as legal advice from Alison Quentin-Baxter, a New Zealand lawyer who had worked as a constitutional advisor for several Pacific states.[17] As we shall see, the South African visit seemed especially important for the commissioners.[18]

The commissioners' proposed solution was a move away from racialized communalism toward the liberal constitutionalism exemplified in the South African constitution-making process.[19] The commissioners did not draw directly on the text of the 1996 South African Constitution, promulgated on December 18 of that year, since their report was submitted a few months earlier on September 6. Yet in their memoires the commissioners all remarked on the impression made by their visit to South Africa.[20] The Commission report was full of references to and recommendations based on the South African constitution-making experience, as well as the interim 1993 Constitution. The Fijian Constitution would likewise be a transitional document to move away from communalism. For example, parliament would be composed mostly of representatives elected from a common roll with the exception only of a minority of House seats still elected by communities. While iTaukei rights were protected, affirmative action was reserved for those in economic need regardless of communal membership.

However, many of these recommendations were not adopted by the bipartisan Joint Parliamentary Select Committee appointed to review the Reeves Commission report. Ghai and Cottrell note that some of the Committee

16 P. Reeves, T. R. Vakatora and B. V. Lal, *Towards a United Future: Report of the Fiji Constitution Review Commission, 1996* (Suva: Fiji Constitution Review Commission, 1996) 2.

17 A. Quentin-Baxter, "Making constitutions, from the perspective of constitutional adviser" (2003) 33 *Victoria University Wellington Law Review*, 237–74.

18 There is no space to fully examine the South African influence on the Reeves Commission. However, its report constantly references the South African case and sometimes directly recommends borrowing from it (and more often makes recommendations that echo South African solutions). For the complete list of the South Africa luminaries the commissioners met with, see Reeves, Vakatora and Lal, *Towards a United Future* 783.

19 See Y. Ghai and J. Cottrell, "A tale of three Constitutions: ethnicity and politics in Fiji" (2007) 5 *International Journal of Constitutional Law* 639–69 at 654–6.

20 See, e.g., P. Reeves, "The Making of the Fiji Constitution" (1998) 107 *Journal of the Polynesian Society* 223–8; B. V. Lal, *Intersections: History, Memory, Discipline* (Acton, A.C.T.: ANU E Press, 2012) 25; T. R. Vakatora, *From the Mangrove Swamps*, 2nd edn (Suva: Institute of Pacific Studies, 1998).

members were comfortable with racialized politics, while others disapproved of the Commission's comparative approach on the grounds that Fiji was a unique case.[21] President Ratu Mara and Prime Minister Rabuka both stressed that all Fijians required and indeed desired communal protection. Even if the world seemed to be moving to liberal constitutionalism, the special circumstances of Fiji demanded exceptional measures.

The real difference between the Reeves Commission and the 1997 Constitution was in the structure of government. The 1997 Constitution enacted many of the Commission's proposals except those for removing or at least marginalizing the principle of communalism. The commissioners had recommended a lower house with forty-five members elected from an open roll while preserving fifteen communal seats. However, the communal seats would remain as a transitional measure until all seats were elected from open constituencies. They likewise recommended electing upper house members to represent the provinces rather than communities (though some seats would remain reserved for under-represented communities). The 1997 Constitution did not fully accept this recommendation. Instead it inverted the ratio of open to communal seats for the lower house (twenty-five to forty-six) and maintained iTaukei hegemony in the Senate.[22] Moreover, it introduced a consociational element into the executive by requiring the prime minister to represent proportionally all parliamentary parties in his or her cabinet.[23] This feature was modeled not on South Africa's 1996 Constitution, but its interim 1993 Constitution that provided for a "government of national unity" through a form of executive power-sharing to manage ethnic conflict during a transition period before the final Constitution was adopted.[24] Multi-party executive government was a major constitutional innovation for Fiji that tried to remedy the presumed fact that one of the two major communities would always be excluded from government. As we shall see, power-sharing would prove immediately unwieldy and ultimately impossible in Fiji.

The Bill of Rights largely reproduced those in the 1970 and 1990 constitutions. It also included the Commission's recommendations for three significant changes drawn from the South African experience, as well as directly

21 Ghai and Cottrell, "A tale of three constitutions" 656.

22 1997 Constitution, ss. 51(1) and 64(1).

23 1997 Constitution, s. 99.

24 The multi-party cabinet was not recommended by the Reeves Commission and only included later as a compromise between the military government and political parties. Compare Constitution of the Republic of South Africa Act 1993, s. 88(2); Reeves, Vakatora, and Lal, *Towards a United Future*, ch. 12. On the subsequent Fijian experience with a multi-party cabinet, see Ghai and Cottrell, "A tale of three constitutions" 661–3.

drawing on the text of the 1996 South African Constitution in several places.[25] First, the limitations on certain rights were restricted by directly borrowing the stronger South African limitation phrase: "reasonable and justifiable in a free and democratic society."[26] Second, there were two new rights regarding labor relations and, most interestingly, a socio-economic "right to basic education and to equal access to educational institutions."[27] The text of these rights provisions was almost directly copied from the 1996 South African Constitution.[28] For added protection of rights, the 1997 Constitution also created an independent human rights commission with powers limited to educating the public about their rights.[29] Thus the South African model provided the basis for strengthening, expanding and restructuring the new Fijian Bill of Rights.

In addition to the Bill of Rights there were two other rights-related chapters that resembled the difficult compromises in the South African constitutional process between individual and communal rights. First, the "Compact" chapter listed twelve nonjusticiable principles, including (the former right to) affirmative action. The "Social Justice" chapter required the state to take affirmative action to provide "disadvantaged" groups or individuals with equal access to (i) education, (ii) land and housing and (iii) commerce and civil service.[30] This was an important step away from the 1990 Constitution's entrenchment of affirmative action only for the iTaukei community. Yet it did not go as far as the Reeves Commission would have in removing the communal principle for determining citizens' rights. Regarding iTaukei communal rights, for instance, the Reeves Commission would have also applied the principles of equality and nondiscrimination to iTaukei community and customary laws.[31]

[25] See, e.g., Reeves, Vakatora and Lal, *Towards a United Future* 125–7 and 130.

[26] Certain rights in both the 1970 and 1990 constitutions contained a standard clause that prohibited any limitation "not to be reasonably justifiable in a democratic society," which the Reeves Commission recommended extending to more rights. The 1997 Constitution accepted this recommendation while also revising the phrase to adopt that of the general rights limitation provision in s. 36 of the 1996 South African Constitution".

[27] Constitution Amendment Act 1997, ss. 33–9 ("1997 Constitution").

[28] There were minor adjustments to fit the text with the structure of the 1997 Constitution. Compare with Constitution of the Republic of South Africa 1996, ss. 23, 29 ("1996 South African Constitution"). While the Reeves Commission recommended a labor relations right modeled on the South African Constitution, it does not mention the South African right to education. This indicates that it was added later, though the South African borrowing is still clear: see Reeves, Vakatora and Lal, *Towards a United Future* 188–9.

[29] 1997 Constitution, s. 42.

[30] 1997 Constitution, ss. 6–7.

[31] Reeves, Vakatora and Lal, *Towards a United Future* 609–10; 613–14. The Commission also recommended moving the Native Lands Commission into the Constitution instead of keeping it in the Native Lands Act: at 594.

The 1997 Constitution thus returned to the awkward compromise of the first Constitution by providing a bill of justiciable rights that could be trumped by iTaukei communal rights.

The 1997 Constitution introduced new features of contemporary liberal constitutions, especially socio-economic rights and a human rights commission. In the Fijian case, however, they were largely disconnected from the ends of liberal constitutionalism. In general, these rights were not transitional mechanisms to achieve the goal of an equal, nonracialized society.[32] Instead, they were limited shields to be taken up by individuals should one community assert its legislative and executive dominance over another. Communalism nevertheless remained a central constitutional principle even if it was increasingly restrained by human rights and independent institutions.

12.2.2. *Moderated Communalism and the 2012 "Ghai" Draft Constitution*

The awkward compromises in the 1997 Constitution failed to successfully mediate inter-communal tension (and, more importantly, undo communalism as the deep structure of the Fijian Constitution). A few years after South Africa began its first full decade of democratic politics, Fiji suffered two coups in short succession. In 1999, the first elections under the new Constitution returned an Indo-Fijian dominated party as the majority. Mahendra Chaudhry, the party leader, became Fiji's first Indo-Fijian prime minister. However, exactly a year after the election, a small group of armed iTaukei men attempted to overthrow the government with the tacit support of a large portion of the iTaukei community and a small faction of the army. The president first declared an emergency under the Constitution, and then dismissed the government (Chaudhry and most other MPs were still being held hostage), prorogued parliament and took over executive power. The military government under Frank Bainimarama soon abrogated the Constitution and formed an interim administration, though later that year the High Court ruled the Constitution was still in force.[33]

The 2000 coup and its aftermath show the complicated Fijian experience of constitutionalism and communalism. All of the main actors (the coup leaders excepted) framed their actions in constitutional terms. A year later, SDL ("United Fiji Party"), the new iTaukei nationalist party, won a majority of seats with only a quarter of all votes cast in an election to re-establish civilian

[32] The one exception was a mandated ten-year expiry date for any social justice or affirmative action program: 1997 Constitution, s. 44(7).

[33] *Prasad* v. *Republic of Fiji & Attorney-General (No 4)* [2000] 2 FLR 89.

government. They immediately pursued aggressive pro-iTaukei policies, while the deposed Indo-Fijian party refused to fully commit to their role in the multi-party cabinet. After several years of increasing animosity, Bainimarama executed Fiji's fourth coup and imposed an interim government with himself as prime minister.[34]

Bainimarama justified his coup on two main grounds. First, it would bring an end to corruption – especially the corrupt self-dealings of the SDL government. Second, it would protect the Indo-Fijian community from iTaukei domination. This reversed the past justifications for coups and elevated the (almost exclusively iTaukei) military as the sole guarantor of inter-communal peace. The military was no longer the champion of a single community, but the extra-constitutional guardian of all communities. Moreover, this coup also ensured that every Fijian citizen – or more accurately every community – had at one time benefited from the intervention of the military.

The military government set out its vision in the Peoples Charter of 2008.[35] Most importantly, the Charter renounced all forms of communalism in favor of a single nation under a liberal Constitution. The military government repeatedly promised an election to return to democratic government, but instead formally abrogated the Constitution in 2009 after a Court of Appeal ruled that the coup was illegal.[36] Three years later, the military government created an independent commission to draft a Constitution that met a set of "non-negotiable" principles based on the Peoples Charter.[37]

While this constitution-making process was imposed unilaterally, it did appear to address at least some of the concerns of its proposed chair, Yash Ghai. The commission would be composed of two international experts and three local representatives (while the process refused to concede anything to communalism, these three members were from the iTaukei, Indo-Fijian and Other communities, respectively). The "non-negotiable" principles included the typical elements of liberal constitutionalism, such as equal rights for all citizens and the separation of powers. More importantly, the principles sought

[34] See generally J. Fraenkel, S. Firth and B. V. Lal (eds.) *The 2006 Military Takeover in Fiji: A Coup to End All Coups?* (Canberra: ANU Press, 2006).

[35] National Council for Building a Better Fiji, *Peoples Charter for Change, Peace and Progress: Draft* (August 5, 2008).

[36] *Qarase* v. *Bainimarama* [2009] FJCA 67; *Qarase* v. *Bainimarama* [2009] FJCA 9.

[37] The principles set out were: (i) a common and equal citizenry; (ii) a secular state; (iii) the removal of systemic corruption; (iv) an independent judiciary; (v) elimination of discrimination; (vi) good and transparent governance; (vii) social justice; (viii) one person, one vote, one value; (ix) the elimination of ethnic voting; (x) proportional representation; and (xi) voting age of eighteen years: Fiji Constitutional Process (Constitution Commission) Decree, no. 57 of 2012, s. 3(e).

to eradicate communalism by forbidding communal representation and omitting any special protection for iTaukei rights. However, the Commission was also compelled to ensure that the new Constitution granted the military immunity for all past coups.[38]

The military government also set out a five-stage constitution-making process with an ambitious timeframe of less than a year. First, there was a four-month period of civic education to be carried out by nongovernmental bodies. Second, the Commission would start by a period of public consultation, soliciting and analyzing the views of the general public. Third, the Commission would draft and submit a Constitution and an accompanying "explanatory report" showing how it met the "non-negotiable" principles and the views of the public. Fourth, a constituent assembly would debate and revise the draft Constitution.[39] This assembly would not be elected but appointed to represent a broad spectrum of civil society – though it excluded both political parties and ethnic communities to avoid the return of communalism. Lastly, a tribunal of judges would review whether the text met the "non-negotiable" principles – and if not return it to the constituent assembly for a final revision.

The Commission was composed of Yash Ghai and Christina Murray, the two foreign experts, and the three Fijian commissioners, Taufa Vakatale, Satendra Nandan and Penelope Moore. Ghai and Murray had worked in different capacities in several constitution-making processes in divided societies, especially those in South Africa and Kenya. They had also developed a distinct academic voice of liberal constitutionalism informed by their own experiences in the global South. Ghai was the chairman of the Constitution of Kenya Review Commission (2000–4) and advised in a number of constitutional transitions from Nepal to Libya. Murray had served as an academic member of the Kenyan Committee of Experts (2009–10) for Kenya's 2010 Constitution and as one of the seven experts advising the South African Constitutional Assembly in drafting South Africa's 1996 Constitution. Both Ghai and Murray had also worked in many other post-conflict constitutional processes in Africa and the Asia-Pacific. The Commission was assisted by Phillip Knight, the principal constitutional drafter from Canada, who had also worked on the South African and Kenyan constitution-making processes. His "plain language" drafting style was influential in the language and structure of the constitutional texts in these countries and the final 2012 Draft Constitution of Fiji.

38 Ibid., s. 7(4).

39 Fiji Constitutional Process (Constitution Commission) Decree no. 58 of 2012.

The Commission only began its work in July 2012 after the commissioners were appointed. They made up for their delayed start by immediately holding public meetings across the country, from major urban centers to far-flung islands. In total the Commission received over 7100 submissions, though well less than one hundred were in-depth proposals for the constitutional text. Yet public consultation was neither an afterthought as in South Africa nor an integral element supported by all political parties like Kenya. The constitutional process decree required a period of public consultation that acknowledged its importance to a legitimate (or at least credible) process.[40] The Commission's intense period of consultations across the country was also a practical necessity to overcome public skepticism and apathy about a process perceived to be devised and controlled by the military government. Public meetings were intended to create a safe public space for deliberation on rights and interests under a Constitution, which was essential for the Commission to increase its own legitimacy and that of its draft text.[41]

Yet the Commission was perhaps too successful in changing public perceptions of its independence and the potential of the draft text. Before the drafting process began, the military government amended the constitution-making process to strip the Commission of most of its mandate to consult with the people of Fiji on its draft Constitution.[42] The Commission could no longer publish the draft Constitution, consult the people on the draft or collect their views on the draft in a report to be presented to the Constituent Assembly. It also could no longer review and amend existing decrees to make them consistent with the Commission's draft Constitution. In just over a month, the Commission completed its draft text and formally presented it to the President on 21 December. Three weeks later the military government once again substantially changed the constitution-making process.[43] Appearing on television, the President and Prime Minister stated that the government would not accept

[40] It appears that the Attorney-General had read Ghai and others on the importance of public consultation to a legitimate and credible constitution-making process: M. Brandt et al., *Constitution-Making and Reform: Options for the Process* (Geneva: United States Institute of Peace, 2011) 9.

[41] Both Ghai and Murray have argued for the (qualified) importance of public participation in constitution-making: Y. Ghai, "Redesigning the state for right development," in B. A. Andreassen and S. P. Marks (eds.), *Development As a Human Right: Legal, Political, and Economic Dimensions* (Cambridge, MA: Harvard University Press, 2006), 141–66; C. Kirkby and C. Murray, "Constitution-making in Anglophone-Africa: we the people?," in M. Ndulo and M. Gazibo (eds.), *Growing Democracy in Africa: Elections, Accountable Governance, and Political Economy* (Cambridge: Cambridge Scholars Publishing, 2016) 102–6.

[42] Fiji Constitutional Process (Constitution Commission) (Amendment) Decree no. 64 of 2012.

[43] Fiji Constitutional Process (Constituent Assembly and Adoption of Constitution) (Amendment) Decree no. 1 of 2013.

the Commission's draft Constitution, but instead would prepare its own draft Constitution for the Constituent Assembly. The Prime Minister promised that this new draft Constitution would be released and a Constituent Assembly appointed in February. In yet another change in the process, the government abolished the requirement that the Assembly submit the approved draft Constitution to the Chief Justice for consideration by a Tribunal on whether the Constitution complied with the nonnegotiable principles.

While the 2012 Draft Constitution was not adopted, it was an important influence on the 2013 Constitution both in what was included and in what was left out. The Ghai Commission aimed to address the constitutional principle of communalism without denying the reality of deep communal legacies from colonial period. Its text was also constrained by the "non-negotiable" principles (as well as the knowledge that the military government would not accept any draft that contradicted its interpretation of those principles). The 2012 Draft Constitution included several innovations that were first recommended by the Reeves Commission but not implemented in the 1997 Constitution. It also attempted to move away from the principle of communalism without denying the reality of distinct communities in Fiji.

The Ghai Commission proposed a novel solution to the problem of government structured on the principle of communalism. There were to be two bodies to represent the Fijian people. The first was an appointed National People's Assembly, an upper house that met once a year to consider issues of national importance, make nonbinding recommendations to government and elect the President. The real innovation was its method of representing the people not through elected representatives but representative appointees from Parliament, local government, independent constitutional bodies and other prominent citizens. Their members would be appointed by the Constitutional Offices Commission and the Electoral Commission. In this way, the 2012 Draft Constitution moved away from an upper house that either represented the people regionally, as the Reeve Commission had proposed, or preserved an iTaukei veto, as all earlier constitutions had provided.

The second body, an elected Parliament, owed something to the South African experience. It was composed of seventy-one members elected by a system of proportional representation. The sixty seats were allocated by a system of multi-member constituencies and the remaining eleven distributed to ensure overall proportional representation.[44] This system was modeled on

[44] 2012 Draft Constitution, s. 70.

the South African system of representation in its National Assembly.[45] This 400-seat body is composed of 200 members elected from nine multi-member regional districts and 200 elected from a single national district. This mixed system attempted to balance the competing desires for regional representation and a broad representation of the will of the people. In Fiji, a greater emphasis was put on regional representation, in part as a check on the threat of single-party domination.

The 2012 Draft Constitution also attempted to moderate the role of ethnic politics without denying its historical reality. On the one hand, it placed limits on political parties organized along ethnic lines.[46] On the other hand, it recognized the GCC as an iTaukei cultural institution, but restricted its role to strictly one of nonpartisan consultation.[47] Even this role was controversial because the military government had abolished the body in early 2012 on the grounds that it was archaic, elitist and promoted inter-communal tension.[48]

The 2012 Draft Constitution placed a new emphasis on independent institutions. It reflected the experiences of Ghai and Murray in devising institutional checks in the political context of a dominant single party in South Africa and ethnically constructed parties in Kenya. The Westminster model of the separation of powers had failed when a single community captured all the branches of government. While Ghai and Murray still had doubts about whether independent institutions could address the problem of communal hegemony, they chose to build on the existing bodies in the 1997 Constitution.[49] The 2012 draft Constitution included all existing commissions and offices, but provided for greater independence through appointment procedures, and more responsibilities and powers. For example, the Constitutional Offices Commission would be composed of two *ex officio* members, as well as two men and two

45 The South African system is largely created by legislation as the 1996 Constitution only required that the electoral system include a national roll and proportional representation: see 1996 South African Constitution, s. 46(1).

46 See 2012 Draft Constitution, ss. 58–61.

47 2012 Draft Constitution, s. 56.

48 iTaukei Land Trust (Amendment) Decree no. 20 of 2012; iTaukei Lands (Amendment) Decree no. 21 of 2012; iTaukei Affairs (Amendment) Decree no. 22, 2012; iTaukei Trust Fund (Amendment) Decree no. 23, 2012. See also M. Field, 'Fiji's great council of chiefs abolished' (March 14, 2012) *Stuff.co.nz* (available at www.stuff.co.nz/world/south-pacific/6573396/Fijis-Great-Council-of-Chiefs-abolished) (accessed date November 20, 2017).

49 C. Murray, "Human Rights Commission Et Al: what is the role of South Africa's Chapter 9 institutions?" (2006) 9 *Potchefstroom Electronic Law Journal* 122–47; see also D. Baranger and C. Murray, "Systems of Government," in M. Tushnet, T. Fleiner and C. Saunders (eds.), *Routledge Handbook of Constitutional Law* (Abingdon: Routledge, 2013) 88.

women appointed by the Prime Minister and Leader of the Opposition "acting jointly."[50] This is a significant change from the 1997 Constitution that only provided for two commissioners appointed by the President (and thus effectively by the Prime Minister acting alone).[51] The hope was that this and other independent bodies would have great authority to check one community's capture of the main branches of government.

The Ghai Commission had to deal with a different problem of immunity for past coups. The terms of reference required immunity for such acts and it was understood that the military government would not accept any draft text that did not provide such immunity. Moreover, the Fijian situation differed in important ways from South Africa. In 1995, the South African "government of national unity" established the Truth and Reconciliation Commission as part of a wider transitional and constitution-making process.[52] In certain cases, the Commission could grant amnesty for politically motivated crimes disclosed by perpetrators. Thus, conditional amnesty was one of many compromises necessary to achieve a final Constitution. Since the Fijian process was controlled and ultimately accountable to only one party – the military government – the commissioners faced a difficult and different question of how to provide for immunity for past actions without legitimizing coups. Their solution was to guarantee immunity on the condition that an office holder take an "oath of allegiance and reconciliation" to uphold "democracy and the rule of law," and the Constitution itself.[53] In a similar way to the South African solution, this would have forced public office holders (including many past coup-makers) to implicitly renounce their past illegal actions before they could hold office in the new constitutional order.

The Bill of Rights in the 2012 Draft Constitution borrowed a great deal of the structure and substance of the South African Constitution. The architecture of the rights bills were remarkably similar. Both began with an overarching provision stating the relationship between rights, democracy and the rule of law, the state's duty to "respect, protect, promote and fulfil" these rights, and the limitations of rights.[54] The specific civil, political, cultural and socio-economic rights were very similar in substance and language, though the 2012 draft Constitution often included the latest "best-practice" (in particular the language in the 2010 Kenyan Constitution). For instance, the right of access to

50 2012 Draft Constitution, s. 151.

51 1997 Constitution, s. 143(1).

52 Promotion of National Unity and Reconciliation Act 1995.

53 2012 Draft Constitution, sch. 3, pt C.

54 Cf 2012 Draft Constitution, s. 18; 1996 South African Constitution, s. 7.

information in the 2012 draft Constitution used almost identical language to the same right in the South African Constitution. However, it also included a new provision on the "correction or deletion of untrue or misleading information" that reflected the new importance of digital information for individuals. The limitations of rights also removed the in-built limitations for each right found in all earlier Fijian constitutions. Instead, the bill adopted the structure of specific application, interpretation and limitation clauses. This was modeled on the Kenyan (and ultimately South African) Bills of Rights.[55]

The explicit constitutional protection for the private and public rights of women was perhaps the Ghai Commission's most radical break with the Fijian constitutional tradition. In a difficult exercise in drafting, the Ghai Commission included stronger rights for women despite significant resistance from the Methodist church, the largest iTaukei congregation, and the military government committed to gender-less rights. The commissioners' experience in South Africa, Kenya and elsewhere had shown the limits of constitutional rights in transforming the status of women. The commissioners also had to address a specific Fijian context where the two main communities were patriarchies constructed historically through personal and customary laws governing the status of women. The most important provision was one on rights of "women, men and families," which granted women's rights by carefully framing them as rights for both women and men.[56] To take one example, "[w]omen and men have the right to be free from any law, culture, custom or tradition that undermines their dignity, health, welfare, interest or status." The insistence on the rights of men in particular came from the 2010 Kenyan Constitution.[57] By recognizing the respective rights of women *and* men, the Commission sought to balance a need to address gender inequality with the reality of Fiji's deep history of legally enforced patriarchy.

The protection of women's personal legal status in the Bill of Rights was complemented by the protection of their access to public office through several provisions that guaranteed their equal participation in government. Women had long been on the margins of Fijian politics and government. In this, Fiji resembled Kenya more than post-apartheid South Africa, where women had consistently held about one-third of seats in the National Assembly – mainly due to the African National Congress's commitment to zipped lists in the context of an electoral system of proportional representation. The

55 Cf 2012 Draft Constitution, ss. 44.7; 1996 South African Constitution, ss. 8, 36–7 and 39; Constitution of Kenya Amendment Act 2009, ss. 20, 24, 52 ("2010 Kenyan Constitution").

56 2012 Draft Constitution, s. 45.

57 See, e.g., 2010 Kenyan Constitution, s. 27(3).

commissioners thus borrowed Kenyan-style solutions to gender inequality in public bodies, such as a constitutional guarantee that women would hold at least one-third of all seats in elected bodies.[58] The 2012 draft Constitution provided that women in the National Assembly would include half the twenty members appointed by the Constitutional Offices Commission and half the seventy-two members appointed by the Electoral Commission. Women were also guaranteed over one-third of seats in Parliament through a closed-list system of proportional representation. Each party had to rank their candidates on a closed list by a formula that ensured the election of women candidates.[59] Women's public participation was also enhanced by two further measures. First, the independent commissions and offices had to include an equal number of women and men.[60] Second, women were guaranteed the right to participate in decisions made by all public bodies.[61] Taken as a whole, these measures guaranteed Fijian women a central place within and outside state institutions, which was a major break with Fijian constitutional and political culture.

The contentious question of iTaukei land rights was largely dealt with in a chapter entitled "Our Natural Heritage." It provided a framework of rights, principles and institutions for managing land, water and natural resources. A new National Consultative Land Forum, similar to a body first proposed by the Reeves Commission, would provide an inter-communal institution for resolving disputes about the administration of land. However, iTaukei land rights were still protected and could only be amended with (i) an absolute majority in Parliament if the proposed amendment was approved by all Forum stakeholder groups, or (ii) a two-thirds majority if one or more of the Forum stakeholders disapproved.[62] While this did not eradicate iTaukei communal land rights, it removed their effective constitutional entrenchment and created a forum for dialogue on land issues.

While the 2012 draft Constitution did offer some limited protection for iTaukei, Rotuman and Banaban communal land rights, it provided almost none for their systems of customary law. Instead, it introduced a framework for a local government structure that would apply equally to all citizens. This was

58 2012 Draft Constitution, s. 81(b).

59 The party list had to ensure that at least one of the first two candidates were women, two of the first five were women, three of the first eight were women, and thereafter one of every three candidates were women: 2012 Draft Constitution, ss. 6(2), 80(3).

60 2012 Draft Constitution, ss. 70(4) 71(2), 139(1)(c), 151(3)(c).

61 2012 Draft Constitution, ss. 55(2)(c), 142(4)(b).

62 2012 draft Constitution, s. 17(3), sch. 2.

directly modeled on the Kenyan and South African constitutions, including their distinctive principle of inter-governmental "co-operation."[63] As in South Africa and Kenya, autonomous local government served two key purposes: it provided a check on the legislative monopoly of Parliament and provided a body for local governance based on the principle of common citizenship rather than exclusive community. This would have abolished distinct communal legal systems, a key element of "indirect rule" that had been perpetuated in every post-independence constitution.

12.3. LIBERAL AUTHORITARIANISM

The 2012 draft Constitution was never to be debated by a Constituent Assembly. Early 2013 passed without the release of a draft Constitution. According its public statements, the military government was holding off on the appointment of the Constituent Assembly until political parties were registered under a new decree. However, on March 21, the Prime Minister announced yet another major change to the constitution-making process. The Constituent Assembly was abolished, and instead the government would produce and promulgate its own Constitution.[64] The drafting of the 2013 Constitution was an opaque process. The main author seemed to be Aiyaz Sayed-Khaiyum, the Attorney-General since 2007, but with much greater responsibilities within the military government. He held an LLB in Law from the University of New South Wales as well as an LLM in Human Rights from the University of Hong Kong. He was also a former student of Ghai at Hong Kong and was familiar with his approach to Fijian constitutionalism. Indeed, Sayed-Khaiyum had invited Ghai to chair the Constitution Commission and copied parts of the 2012 draft Constitution directly into the 2013 Constitution. Initially, the public had just over a week to give their views, but the government later extended the deadline for public comments and claimed to have received 1093 written submissions.[65] After several more months the President promulgated Fiji's fourth Constitution on September 6.

63 Cf 2012 draft Constitution, ch. 12; Constitution of South Africa, ch. 7. However, the 2012 draft Constitution did make a minor concession to allow the government to make provision for the application of customary law provided it was consistent with the bill of rights: 2012 draft Constitution, ss. 51(2), 119(4), 184(2).

64 Fiji Constitutional Process (Adoption of Constitution) Decree no. 12 of 2013.

65 Unlike the Constitution Commission, none of these submissions have been made public. This figure also appeared to include text messages.

12.3.1. *Post-Communalism and the 2013 Constitution*

The 2013 Constitution is largely based on the 1997 Constitution with parts taken from the 2012 draft Constitution, various post-2006 military decrees and a few new additions. However, it differed in several key respects from the two earlier constitutions, all of which shared an underlying goal of creating a secular, liberal democracy with a limited recognition of communal rights. Despite its many superficial similarities to these documents, the 2013 Constitution systematically ensures that all branches, independent bodies and rights are controlled by the office of the Prime Minister and his or her party in Parliament, and perpetuates the military's role as the extra-constitutional guarantor of social order in Fiji.

The 2013 Constitution creates a unicameral legislature with a fifty-member Parliament elected from a single national constituency through an open-list system of proportional representation.[66] There is no upper house, nor constitutional recognition of the GCC. Not only is legislative authority centralized in a single body, it also removes most of the checks on the exercise of this power by the majority party. The Leader of the Opposition, an important figure in inter-communal balancing of earlier constitutions, has no role other than to sit on and appoint a member to the Constitutional Offices Commission.[67] Unlike the 1997 Constitution and 2012 Draft Constitution, there is no constitutional entrenchment of a public accounts parliamentary committee chaired by an opposition MP.

The 2013 Constitution thus represents a move away from earlier attempts to restrain executive power. While the Prime Minister had always been a powerful constitutional office, past constitutions had moderated its power. Two important checks on concentrated executive power were the dual exercise with the Leader of the Opposition of appointments to constitutional offices, as well as the multi-party Cabinet in the 1996 Constitution. In contrast, the 2013 Constitution removes long-standing constitutional checks on Parliament and centralizes executive authority in the offices of the Prime Minster and to a lesser extent that of the Attorney General.

The most important change is that the Prime Minister now has a dominant role in appointing the members of the independent bodies. The Prime Minister directly appoints the majority of members in the Constitutional Offices Commission and indirectly controls (through her or his appointees)

[66] Constitution of the Republic of Fiji 2013, s. 58 ("2013 Constitution").

[67] 2013 Constitution, ss. 78, 132.

appointments to all other independent commissions and offices.[68] In another centralizing move, the Prime Minister also has increased control over the judiciary. The Prime Minister appoints the Chief Justice after consulting the Attorney General and all other appellate court judges are appointed by the Judicial Services Commission after consulting the Attorney General.[69] Finally, the Prime Minister also has greater control over the bureaucracy as the Public Service Commission can only appoint and remove permanent secretaries with the "agreement" of the Prime Minister.[70] In contrast, the 1997 Constitution and 2012 draft Constitution both left these appointments to the Constitutional Offices Commission, which was also appointed on a more bipartisan basis. Thus the 2013 Constitution reproduces the same structure of independent bodies, modeled on the South African and Kenyan Constitutions, but it effectively undermines that formal independence through the Prime Minister's direct and indirect control over the bodies' members.

The Bill of Rights is now the main check on concentrated legislative and executive power.[71] The bill is constructed largely from the structure and substance of the 1997 Constitution with additional socio-economic rights drawn from the 2012 draft Constitution, which in turn drew on the South African Constitution (including the "horizontal" application of rights) and ultimately the International Covenant on Economic, Social and Cultural Rights ("ICESCR"). In addition to the long-standing civil, political and administrative rights, the bill introduces two major new categories of socio-economic and land rights, as well as new specific and general limitations on rights. It also omits any reference to women or gender with the single exception of "gender" as a prohibited ground for discrimination.[72] This deliberate omission is consistent with the military government's commitment to their "non-negotiable" principles, which refused to make special, explicit provision for the rights of women.

68 2013 Constitution, s. 132(2). The Fiji Independent Commission Against Corruption, a new constitutional body, is given constitutional status but its appointment process is left to a legislative enactment. Under the current decree the Commissioner is appointed by the President, which in practice means the Prime Minister under Fijian constitutional conventions: Independent Commission against Corruption Promulgation, no. 11 of 2007, s. 6.

69 2013 Constitution, s. 106(1)–(2). Three of the five Judicial Services members are *ex officio* members, all of whom are appointed to their respective offices by the Prime Minister.

70 2013 Constitution, s. 126(1).

71 This analysis of the Bill of Rights draws on R. Kant, C. Kirkby and E. Patira, *Fiji in Transition: Towards a Sustainable Constitutional Democracy* (Suva: Citizen's Constitutional Forum, 2014) 41–62 (available at news.ccf.org.fj/wp-content/uploads/2014/12/Fiji-in-Transition1.pdf) (accessed date November 20, 2017).

72 2013 Constitution, s. 26(3)(a).

The first new category of rights comprise socio-economic rights, including rights taken directly from the 2012 Ghai draft Constitution.[73] The second new category of rights is found in a new section protecting iTaukei land rights. These rights were not included in the first text of the Constitution circulated by the military government in March 2013 and only added after an angry reaction by the iTaukei community. The Constitution no longer protects a set of special legislation. Instead it only protects a specific right of the "customary" iTaukei owners to land (and so no longer protects iTaukei "customary" law or "chiefly" institutions).[74] This is a much more radical step than the 1997 Constitution and 2012 draft Constitution, which like the 1996 South African Constitution recognized customary law but made its application conditional on conforming to a Bill of Rights – especially the right of equal treatment for women.[75]

The 2013 Constitution also introduces a two-stage limitation for rights. This is a major break with the 1997 Constitution and 2012 draft Constitution that adopted a general limitation test based on the 1996 South African Constitution. First, most rights include a sub-clause allowing Parliament to limit the right in question either "to the extent that it is necessary" in general or for enumerated (though very broad) reasons, or for any reason at all. Moreover, there is a general limitation clause that allows Parliament to limit *any* right if it is both (i) necessary and (ii) prescribed by an ordinary law (or an action taken under such a law).[76] This remarkable clause seems to allow a majority in Parliament to limit any right on the grounds that it is "necessary" to do so. It is not clear how the "necessary" qualification affects the limitation of rights by Parliament.[77] In the context of specific rights, "to the extent necessary" sometimes refers to the limitation of a right to achieve a specific goal. Without a specific qualification, however, it appears that the general limitation clause allows Parliament to limit any right with an ordinary law. The limitation clauses in the 2013 Constitution may thus allow Parliament greater authority to limit rights than any previous Fijian Constitution.

The unprecedented concentration of power in the office of the Prime Minister and the severely limited Bill of Rights have exacerbated what Firth

[73] 2013 Constitution, ss. 34–8.

[74] 2013 Constitution, s. 28.

[75] Cf 2012 draft Constitution, ss. 45(7), 51(2); 1996 South African Constitution, s. 211.

[76] 2013 Constitution, s. 6(5)(c).

[77] The term "necessary" seems to have come from s. 35(4) of the 1997 Constitution. This clause allowed the limitation of the right to religion and belief if it was "necessary" to either "protect (i) the rights or freedoms of other persons; or (ii) public safety, public order, public morality or public health," or "to prevent a public nuisance."

and Fraenkel call the "militarization" of the Fijian state since the 2006 coup.[78] Bainimarama and his fellow military officers not only control the main offices of government, but have extended their reach deep into the public administration of the state with key ministries run by officers seconded from the military. Both the public service and the military are ultimately responsible to a single individual, Bainimarama. Moreover, ten former military officers were elected to Parliament in 2014, and thus the Prime Minister and 20 percent of all MPs are former military figures.

The concern here is not so much with Bainimarama himself as with the fundamental restructuring, indeed militarization, of the state sanctioned by the 2013 Constitution. Whoever controls Parliament effectively control all branches of government as well as the independent bodies. The only significant check on one-party domination is the military. The 2013 Constitution affirmed and expanded the special role of the military in Fijian politics. The military was granted immunity for all its actions related to coups in an unamendable provision.[79] The military's constitutional responsibilities resembled the 1990 Constitution more than the limited role envisioned by the 1997 Constitution and 2012 draft Constitution. For example, the Prime Minister could declare a state of emergency on the recommendation of the military commander and commissioner of police, which would be renewable indefinitely if approved by a majority of MPs in a monthly vote.

The constitutional provisions reflected the military's own vision of its role expressed in its submission to the Ghai Commission in 2012, which stated that it was "the last bastion for law and order in Fiji' and was responsible for guiding "the governance of this country, ensuring that peace, prosperity and good governance is practiced and adhered to."[80] The Fijian military now have total immunity for past actions and a broad constitutional role.[81] It is only accountable to the majority in Parliament and, ultimately, its own vision of a constitutional order guaranteed by its inherent extra-constitutional and extra-communal authority as the protector of all Fijians. Moreover, the constitutional amendment structure suggests that *only* an extra-constitutional intervention can effect constitutional change. In one of the world's most onerous amendment procedures, any proposed amendment will require the support of

78 S. Firth and J. Fraenkel, "The Fiji military and ethno-nationalism: Analyzing the paradox" in F. Fraenkel and B. V. Lal (eds.), *The 2006 Military Takeover* (Canberra: ANU Press, 2006) 128–32.

79 2013 Constitution, ch. 10.

80 Republic of Fiji Military Forces, *Submission to the Constitutional Commission* (December 2012).

81 2013 Constitution, ch. 10.

both (i) three-quarters of the members of Parliament and (ii) three-quarters of all registered voters in a referendum.[82] Given these near impossible conditions it is difficult to see how even the most minor and consensual constitutional change can happen in the future without external intervention. It is difficult to see how any serious constitutional deadlock could be broken except through the intervention of the military.

12.3.2. *Liberal Constitutionalism or Liberal Authoritarianism?*

The 2013 Constitution is a curious document. It appears to meet the external criteria for success proposed by Ginsburg and Huq: "(1) generate legitimacy for the state; (2) channel political conflict through formal institutions rather than violence; (3) limit the agency costs of government; and (4) facilitate the production of public goods."[83] Yet a closer look into these criteria suggests that the Constitution's formal attributes are belied by its substantive entrenchment of authoritarian and militarized government.

The legitimacy of the 2013 Constitution seemed to be affirmed by the 2014 election. Almost two-thirds of the 84 percent of registered voters who cast ballots did so for FijiFirst, the multi-ethnic party led by Bainimarama.[84] FijiFirst also capitalized on the personal popularity of Bainimarama, who alone received 202,459 votes representing two of every five votes cast.[85] Moreover, the Multinational Observer Group found that the elections "broadly represented the will of the Fijian voters."[86] Yet it is difficult to conclude that the elections were a valid proxy for the internal or external legitimacy of the 2013 Constitution. Many of those who voted for FijiFirst, as Fraenkel suggests, were choosing a return to civilian government at whatever cost and not necessarily endorsing the imposed Constitution.[87] While the European Union did embed three delegates in the Multinational Observer Group, it has earlier declined to send its own observer mission due to the military government's restrictions

82 2013 Constitution, s. 160.

83 A. Huq and T. Ginsburg, "What can constitutions do? The Afghan case" (2014) 23 *Journal of Democracy* 116–30 at 120.

84 Fijian Elections Office, 2014 *Elections Results* (available at www.electionsfiji.gov.fj/2014-election-results) (accessed date November 20, 2017).

85 Ibid.

86 Multinational Observer Group, "2014 Fijian Elections: Final Report of the Multinational Observer Group" (2015) 4. Available at www.parliament.gov.fj/wp-content/uploads/2017/02/2014-General-Elections-Final-Report-of-the-Multinational-Observer-Group-1.pdf (accessed date November 20, 2017).

87 J. Fraenkel, "The remorseless power of incumbency in Fiji's September 2014 election" (2015) 104 *Round Table*, 151–64.

on external observers.[88] With only a few years to analyze, no definitive statement on the legitimacy of the new Constitution is possible from either an external or an internal perspective.

It is also too early to say whether the new Constitution has ended the coup culture. But something may still be said of the success of the 2013 Constitution in channeling political conflict into democratic institutions during the last few years. Three parties had members elected to Parliament in 2014: FijiFirst with thirty-two seats, the Social Democratic Liberal Party ("Sodelpa," formerly the SDL) with fifteen and the National Federation Party ("NFP") with three. Sodelpa received a majority of iTaukei votes, though a large minority of iTaukei voters (especially younger voters and those in the military) opted for FijiFirst.[89] Although there have been flashes of conflict in Parliament, all parties continue to pursue politics through the institutions provided for in the Constitution. Yet again this picture of success must be qualified. FijiFirst has increasingly clamped down on any meaningful critique of its policies. The most egregious example is the Public Accounts Committee, whose NFP chairman was recently replaced by a FijiFirst MP. Thus, the only serious parliamentary body to scrutinize the government has been significantly weakened, especially in the context of the 2013 Constitution that had removed this key committee's long-standing entrenched independence.[90] Most importantly, the military continues to be closely tied to FijiFirst, the party of government. One-third of FijiFirst MPs are former military figures and many key civil service posts continue to be held by former soldiers originally seconded from the military from 2006 to 2014. The military has also continued its dubious role as guarantor of social order. In late 2015, military forces assisted police in arresting several dozen iTaukei men on charges of sedition and inciting communal antagonism.[91] The arrests were a timely reminder of both the persistence of

[88] A. Jacobs, Delegation of the European Union for the Pacific, Statement by EU Ambassador Andrew Jacobs on the Inclusion of European Experts into the Multinational Observer Group for the 2014 Fiji Elections (Press Release, Suva, August 25, 2014) (available at http://eeas.europa.eu/delegations/fiji/press_corner/all_news/news/2014/20140825_1_en.htm) (accessed date November 20, 2017).

[89] Fraenkel notes that it is difficult to get a detailed picture of iTaukei voting patterns since there was no ethnically based statistics, and many iTaukei voters appeared to abstain or simply not register: J. Fraenkel, "An analysis of provincial, urban and ethnic loyalties in Fiji's 2014 election" (2015) 50 *Journal of Pacific History* 38–53 at 49–50.

[90] N. Swami, "Prasad voted out as public accounts committee chairman" (May 12, 2016) *Fiji Times* (available at http://fijitimes.com/story.aspx?id=353488) (accessed date November 20, 2017).

[91] C. Kirkby, "Analysis: Fiji Constitution" (2015) *Blog of the IACL* (available at https://iacl-aidc-blog.org/2015/09/14/analysis-constitution-of-fiji/) (accessed date November 20, 2017).

communalism and the military's understanding of its extra-constitutional role as the ultimate guardian of social order in Fiji.

The final two criteria of limiting government agency costs and facilitating the production of public goods likewise suggest a more pessimistic conclusion. This chapter cannot evaluate whether the Fijian government is now less corrupt and more efficient. However, it is possible to sketch the ability of the constitutional structure of government to achieve such ends. The problem of government agency costs can be illustrated through the electoral system of proportional representation in a national single constituency for elections to Parliament. As Fraenkel notes, the military government chose this system in part as a political calculation to maximize the vote tally of FijiFirst through the popularity of its leader, Bainimarama. The result was that the median number of votes to elect an MP was only 2,691 (0.50 percent) in 2014. In a Parliament of only fifty members, this is a striking figure. The effect of such a system (regardless of any political calculations) is to disconnect the accountability of most MPs from the citizens who elected them. Indeed, voters only have a direct connection to the handful of leading figures that received the vast majority of votes cast. Citizens do not engage with government through a locally elected member, but rather the leaders of the two main parties. In the context of a Constitution that has drastically centralized authority in the office of the Prime Minister, this electoral system exacerbates the identification of government with a single figure through whom all requests and all benefits must flow. Whether this is more efficient than previous Fijian governmental system is an empirical question, though this brief illustration suggests that it hold serious political dangers in a highly centralized constitutional system.

The greater production and more equitable distribution of public goods was a key justification for the 2006 coup and the 2013 Constitution. The military government under Bainimarama had long argued that a liberal Constitution purged of the principle of communalism would allow government goods and services to be distributed to the poorest Fijians regardless of their ethnicity. This promise is entrenched in the socio-economic rights provisions of the 2013 Constitution. As in its common formulation in the ICESCR, "the State must take reasonable measures within its available resources to achieve the progressive realisation" of such rights. However, as shown above, the 2013 Constitution also provides several mechanisms for a government to abdicate these duties. Again, as with government agency costs, only an empirical study can show whether governments produce more public goods under the current Constitution. But there are serious reasons to be skeptical of whether these rights can compel a government given the constitutional provision of an effective override of the Bill of Rights, including those imposing a duty on the state to provide certain public goods.

12.4. CONCLUSION

After a two-decade experiment with liberal constitutionalism, Fiji has ended up with the external appearance of a successful liberal constitutional democracy. Yet its practice might be more accurately described as liberal authoritarianism. The 2013 Constitution claims to transform the old entrenched "communities" into a single state of Fijian citizens. Its appearance is that of a liberal Constitution, including the separation of powers, a Bill of Rights and independent bodies. This chapter argues that it is indeed transformative, but not quite as billed. The leader of the majority party in Parliament has unprecedented control over all three branches of government, as well as the independent bodies and the civil service. The military also retains its extra-constitutional role as the ultimate guarantor of Fijian social order as it perceives it. Yet as Baledrokadroka reminds us, "the military remains overwhelmingly an indigenous Fijian institution with all its iTaukei shibboleths."[92] Thus the great irony of the 2013 Constitution is that it entrenches the formal aspects of liberal constitutionalism as a cure for communalism, but its ultimate guarantor is the threat of extra-constitutional intervention by an almost exclusively iTaukei institution.

This chapter's pessimistic assessment of the present state of Fijian constitutionalism suggests a complicated relationship with South African constitutionalism. The two independent Fijian Constitution Commissions both looked to South Africa for solutions to problems of communalism. The Reeves Commission borrowed several textual provisions, especially regarding their recommendations for new gender, labor, social and economic rights. Most importantly, South Africa served as a model of what was possible, which inspired at least Reeves and Lal to propose more radical solutions to the deep communal structure of past Fijian constitutions. The Ghai Commission also borrowed some discrete sections from the South African Constitution. But the main influence of the South African Constitution was Ghai and Murray's experiences with and analyses of its successes and failures in South Africa and other countries that had adopted its constitutional solutions over the past two decades.

92 Baledrokadroka, "The super confederacy" 132.

Yet the Reeves and Ghai commissions both failed to radically alter the particular practice of Fijian constitutionalism. In 1997, the Joint Parliamentary Select Committee adopted many of the Reeves Commission recommendations with the crucial exception of their solutions to communal representation and special rights. The result was an attempted coup followed by an ethno-nationalist government and then a military coup. The Ghai Commission also recommended novel solutions to the central problem of communalism. The radical reforms were again rejected, but this time a military government instead imposed its idea of a liberal Constitution. The result was liberal authoritarianism. Despite these apparent and real differences, Fijian constitutionalism shares an important similarity with its South African form. Both countries' Constitutions have succeeded in banishing their shared legacy of racialized communalism – at least in their formal structures. But this seemingly successful suppression has come at the cost of a return to authoritarian forms and practices of constitutional government. As the incumbent parties increasingly assert their will against remaining constitutional restraints, the specter of communalism waits in the wings with the promise of an alternative to the politics of liberal authoritarianism.

13

Policing Democracy: The Influence of South Africa's Postapartheid Security Arrangements on Police Oversight under Kenya's 2010 Constitution

Richard Stacey

13.1. INTRODUCTION

In December 2007, Kenya's presidential election was contested by two main candidates, incumbent Mwai Kibaki and Raila Odinga. After the polls closed and votes were tallied, the Electoral Commission was unable to declare with certainty who had won.[1] Both candidates claimed victory, but Kibaki moved to have himself sworn in as president. Following revelations of electoral manipulation and fraud, however, violent protests broke out in parts of the capital and soon spread north into the Rift Valley and across Kenya. By the end of February 2008, 1,133 people were confirmed to have been killed[2] while 663,921 had been displaced.[3]

The violence led to renewed pressure for constitutional reform, after the earlier attempt to adopt a new constitution had been stymied by court applications and referendum defeat in 2005.[4] In 2008, a Committee of Experts on Constitutional Review was established by legislation and mandated to prepare a new draft constitution.[5] Also during 2008 the official inquiry into electoral

[1] Human Rights Watch, *Ballots to bullets: organized political violence and Kenya's crisis of governance* (March 16, 2008) (available at www.hrw.org/sites/default/files/reports/kenya0308web.pdf) (accessed date November 20, 2017).

[2] Commission of Inquiry into Post-Election Violence, *Final Report* (October 15, 2008) 383 (*Waki Report*).

[3] Human Rights Watch, *"Turning pebbles": evading accountability for post-election violence in Kenya* (December 4, 2011) (available at www.hrw.org/sites/default/files/reports/kenya1211webwcover_0.pdf) (accessed date November 20, 2017).

[4] See, generally, M. Mutua, *Kenya's Quest for Democracy: Taming Leviathan* (Boulder, CO: Lynne Rienner, 2008) and R. Stacey, "Constituent power and Carl Schmitt's theory of constitution in Kenya's Constitution-making process" (2011) 9 *International Journal of Constitutional Law* 587–614.

[5] The Constitution of Kenya Review Act 2008 (Cap. 3A).

violence, chaired by Court of Appeal Judge Philip Waki, found damning evidence of police complicity and involvement in the murder of protestors and bystanders, highlighting the impunity with which the police in Kenya operated and the extent to which they were susceptible to the partisan objectives of political actors.[6] The National Task Force on Police Reform was in turn established to make recommendations on enhancing police accountability to nonpartisan, civilian and democratic institutions.[7] Police reform in Kenya is thus tied up with the broader constitutional transition that followed the 2007–8 electoral violence, and is aimed at moving away from a history of "regime policing" toward a future of "democratic policing."

The new Constitution of Kenya was eventually approved at referendum in 2010. This chapter examines how the democratic transition in South Africa, which involved a move from a heavily securitized police state during the apartheid years to a system of democratic policing, influenced the architects of Kenya's new domestic security arrangements. South Africa proved a natural jurisdiction to which Kenya could look for comparative experience, not only because of their shared history as postcolonial, Anglophone, African states but also because in both countries the police forces were deployed in support of partisan political objectives and played a key role in maintaining the privileged position of a political elite. In both countries, the transition to constitutional democracy had to face the challenge of transforming a partisan, politically manipulable police force into a democratic police service, subject to nonpartisan civilian control and scrutiny, and accountable to the people for its conduct.

The chapter begins by contrasting the concept of democratic policing against the history of regime policing in both Kenya and South Africa. The chapter then looks at the process of reform, examining the Waki Commission Report and the report of the national Task Force on Police Reform (the Ransley Report, after its chairman Philip Ransley) for evidence that the arrangements and experience in South Africa were in the minds of those involved in police reform in Kenya. It compares Kenya's post-2010 arrangements for police accountability and oversight with those in South Africa, with particular focus on the establishment of an independent police complaints directorate in each country. The chapter notes how the Waki Report and the Ransley Report benefitted from several years of South African experience, identifying flaws in

6 Commission of Inquiry into Post-Election Violence, *Waki Report*, pt 4. See also K. R. Hope, "In pursuit of democratic policing: An analytical review and assessment of police reforms in Kenya" (2015) 17 *International Journal of Police Science and Management* 91–7.

7 The National Task Force on Police Reforms was established by President Kibaki under the chairmanship of retired judge Philip Ransely. It delivered the *Report of the National Task Force on Police Reforms* in October 2009 (*Ransley Report*).

the South African model for police oversight and adapting it to avoid those mistakes in Kenya.

The chapter ends by noting that despite a new constitution and new institutions of oversight, designed with attentiveness to the strengths and weaknesses of the South African model, police violence continues in Kenya. Reports of torture, violence and targeted extra-judicial killings at the hands of the Kenyan police continue to roll in.[8] Although police violence in South Africa has by no means been eradicated – the massacre of thirty-four miners by police at Marikana in August 2012 stands as the most visible example – some analyses suggest that levels of police accountability have risen and the effectiveness of oversight has increased at the same time that the police's mandate to use force has been expanded by legislation and executive order, and indeed supported by popular opinion.[9] The transplant of South African mechanisms of police oversight have proven less effective in Kenya because of a failure to reform the institutional structure of the police service itself. The decision to retain two distinct police services in Kenya, the Kenya Police Service (KPS) and the Administration Police, and to allow the proliferation of specialized units and divisions within these services has made it extremely difficult for oversight bodies to scrutinize the work of the entire police force.

The chapter thus offers a cautionary tale, noting that the success of adopting – and adapting – a neighbor's institutional framework for security sector oversight and police accountability depends, in part, on the underlying structure of the security sector. More broadly, Kenya's experience suggests reasons to be wary of institutional transplants from one constitutional context to another. It

[8] See, e.g., Open Society Justice Initiative and Muslims for Human Rights, *"We're Tired of Taking You to the Court": Human Rights Abuses by Kenya's Anti-terrorism Police Unit* (New York, NY: Open Society Foundation, 2013); Human Rights Watch, *Kenya: killings, disappearances by anti-terror police* (August 18, 2014) (available at www.hrw.org/news/2014/08/18/kenya-killings-disappearances-anti-terror-police) (accessed date November 20, 2017); Independent Medico-Legal Unit, *Guns: our security, our dilemma* (June 26, 2014) (available at www.imlu.org/2011-06-30-23-44-4/2015-08-28-09-08-23/reports/finish/2-reports/51-guns-our-security-our-dilemma-2014/0.html) (accessed date November 20, 2017); Kenya National Commission on Human Rights, *The error of fighting terror with terror: preliminary report of KNCHR investigations on human rights abuses in the ongoing crackdown against terrorism* (September 2015) (available at www.knchr.org/Portals/0/CivilAndPoliticalReports/Final%20Disappearances%20report%20pdf) (accessed date November 20, 2017).

[9] J. Hornberger, "From General to Commissioner to General: on the popular state of policing in South Africa" (2013) 3 *Law & Social Inquiry* 598–614; J. Berg, "Civilian oversight of the police in South Africa: from the ICD to the IPID" (2013) 14 *Police Practice and Research* 144–54; J. Steinberg, "Policing, state power, and the transition from apartheid to democracy: a new perspective" (2014) 113 *African Affairs* 173–91; B. Dixon, "A violent legacy: policing insurrection in South Africa from Sharpeville to Marikana" (2015) 55 *British Journal of Criminology* 1131–48.

seems facile to point out that the capacity of institutional mechanisms to achieve certain objectives or uphold principles to which a political community commits depends on whether those mechanisms fit the circumstances and specific conditions of the political community. Nevertheless, different structural conditions may undermine the efficacy of transplanted constitutional arrangements even where, as in Kenya, the statutory framework for police oversight attempts to avoid some of the mistakes of the model from which it borrowed.

13.2. "REGIME POLICING" IN KENYA AND SOUTH AFRICA

The distinction between "democratic policing" and "regime policing" is not difficult to explain, although it remains difficult to establish. Key characteristics of democratic policing are the police's adherence to law in the performance of their duties, police accountability for their actions both to superiors and civilian government, and transparency that allows regular scrutiny and observation of police activities by civilian government, independent institutions and civil society. But more than these characteristics, democratic policing is distinguishable from regime policing by the fact that a democratic police service gives operational priority to the needs of citizens and society, rather than to the needs of the state or political office-holders.[10]

Both the KPF up until its reform in 2010 and the apartheid South African Police force (SAP) up until the early 1990s are more accurately described as engaged in regime policing. Both forces were dedicated primarily to the interests of the ruling party – or at least to a particular political faction – and to protecting their own vested interests rather than serving the public interest.[11] In Kenya, regime policing began with a colonial military unit, the King's African Rifles, whose primary domestic function was to silence dissidence and dominate intractable indigenous communities.[12]

[10] D. H. Bayley, *Patterns of Policing: A Comparative International Analysis* (New Brunswick, NJ: Rutgers University Press, 1985); D. H. Bayley, *Democratizing the Police Abroad: What to Do and How to Do It* (Washington, DC: US Dept of Justice, 2001) (available at www.ncjrs.gov/pdffiles1/nij/188742.pdf) (accessed date November 20, 2017).

[11] J. N. Auerbach, "Police accountability in Kenya" (2003) 3 *African Human Rights Journal* 275–313 at 277; J. M. Akech, "Public law values and the politics of criminal (in)justice: a democratic framework for policing in Kenya" (2005) 5 *Oxford University Commonwealth Law Journal* 225–56 at 235–6; G. Cawthra, *South Africa's Police: From Police State to Democratic Policing?* (London: Catholic Institute for International Relations, 1992); G. Cawthra, *Policing South Africa: The South African Police & the Transition from Apartheid* (Cape Town: David Philip 1993).

[12] J. Oloka-Onyango, "Police powers, human rights and the state in Kenya and Uganda: a comparative analysis" (1990) 9 *Third World Legal Studies* 1–36 at 3.

This pattern largely continued after independence in 1963. Both President Jomo Kenyatta and President Daniel Arap Moi – the only two presidents until Kibaki's election in 2002 – used the police as a tool to "bludgeon critics into submission."[13] The Akiwumi Commission of Inquiry into Tribal Clashes, investigating violence during the 1992 and 1997 presidential elections, found that the KPF and in particular the "Special Branch" had acted to "sustain the continued ascendancy of the political party in power" by, for example, refusing to investigate allegations of misconduct by government officials, arresting supporters of opposition parties on "trumped up charges," suppressing or refusing to act on information or reports of supporters of the government attacking or harassing opposition supporters (a "conspiracy of silence"), and taking action "deliberately calculated to assist" violence perpetrated against opposition political groups.[14] The pattern continued into the new millennium, with political rallies planned by the opposition parties prior to the 2002 elections blocked by police antiriot squads,[15] and journalists critical of the government routinely arrested and charged with criminal libel.[16]

The Special Branch was a particularly effective tool of the Kenyan government, in part because it was removed from the political control of the Commissioner of Police and made directly accountable to cabinet. Its activities thus became closely aligned to the agenda of the government.[17] By the late 1980s, Amnesty International and other analysts had formed the view that the Special Branch was responsible for widespread detentions and torture and that it operated largely outside the purview of the law and hidden from official and public oversight.[18] Alongside the Special Branch, the General Service Unit (GSU) is a paramilitary police unit armed with military-grade weapons,[19] which has been deployed in "situations affecting internal security"[20] such as

[13] M. Ruteere and M. Pommerolle, "Democratizing security of decentralizing repression? The ambiguities of community policing in Kenya" (2003) 102 *African Affairs* 587–604 at 592.

[14] Report of the Judicial Commission of Inquiry into Tribal Clashes in Kenya (Nairobi: August 19, 1999) paras. 36–62.

[15] Nation Team, "Police block NARC rally at Uhuru Park" (December 19, 2002) *Daily Nation* (available at www.nation.co.ke/news/1056-300090-lcbtpiz/index.html) (accessed date November 20, 2017).

[16] Akech, "A democratic framework for policing" 240–1.

[17] Oloka-Onyango, "Police Powers" 11–12; L. Leakey, *Defeating Mau* (London: Methuen, 1954) 112–13.

[18] Amnesty International, *Kenya: Torture, Political Detention and Unfair Trials* (New York, NY: Amnesty International, 1987); Oloka-Onyango, "Police Powers" 26.

[19] E. Nowrojee, "Kenya: political pluralism, government resistance and United States responses" (1992) 5 *Harvard Human Rights Journal* 149–62 at 152; I. Kaplan et al., *Area Handbook for Kenya*, 2nd ed. (Washington, DC: Government Printing Office, 1976), 380.

[20] Akech, "A democratic framework for policing" 233.

the Mau Rebellion in the 1950s and displays of political opposition or civil disobedience.[21] The GSU was even sent abroad to quell challenges to Kenya's political allies in Zanzibar.[22] It continues to operate today, although the Special Branch has been disbanded.

In South Africa, the SAP worked alongside the intelligence services and the military to operate a "securitized" state structure. Under the National Security Management System (NSMS) established in 1979, members of the military and the police were deployed to staff "security committees" and "economic and social affairs committees" in every local government entity in the country.[23] Moreover, the hierarchy of the NSMS was such that all of these committees reported ultimately to the State Security Council (SSC), a cluster of high-ranking members of the military, intelligence service and police established to advise the government on matters of domestic security. By the late 1980s, the SSC had become the "de facto cabinet."[24] No governance decision was taken anywhere in South Africa without the input of the security sector.

Aside from the role that members of the SAP came to play in high-level policy and in local government in South Africa, their primary function was the enforcement of the battery of racist laws, including those that sought to make political resistance to the apartheid state more difficult. The Police Act 1958 went so far as to identify "internal security" as the SAP's "functional priority." Fulfilling this mandate led to a diversification of the expertise of the SAP, and consequent mission creep. The Security Branch was established within the SAP in 1947, mandated to gather intelligence on insurgent activity and political opposition that fell afoul of the various pieces of security legislation enacted by the apartheid Parliament. In 1967, the SAP began training policemen in counter-insurgency tactics, and by the 1970s the members of these counter-insurgency units were engaged in significant operations to destabilize

21 D. M. Anderson, "The battle of Dandora Swamp: reconstructing the Mau Land Freedom Army" in E. S. Atieno and J. Lonsdale (eds.), *Mau and Nationhood: Authority and Narration* (Athens, OH: Ohio University Press, 2003), 155; J. M. Klopp, "'Ethnic Clashes' and winning elections: the case of Kenya's electoral despotism" (2001) 35 *Canadian Journal of African Studies* 473–517 at 502; and Nowrojee, "Political pluralism, government resistance."

22 Statement to the House of Commons by Hugh Fraser, Under-Secretary of State for the Colonies, *Hansard*, HC Deb June 5, 1961, vol. 641, § 648.

23 Cawthra, *Policing South Africa* 31–2.

24 L. Nathan, "The 1996 Defence White Paper: an agenda for state demilitarisation?" in J. Cock and P. McKenzie (eds.), *From Defence to Development: Redirecting Military Resources in South Africa* (Cape Town: David Philip, 1998) 39, 51; N. Stott, "From SADF to SANDF: safeguarding South Africa for a better life for all?" (2002) 7 *Violence and Transition Series* 6, 7; S. Ellis, "Review essay: Truth and Reconciliation Commission of South Africa report, volumes 1–5" (1998) 42 *Transformation* 57–72 at 62.

and undermine opposition movements outside South Africa.[25] The rise in civil disobedience inside South Africa in the 1980s led the police to establish and train special riot-control units, equipped with military hardware, and to recruit and hastily train young black men to serve as auxiliary police forces in the black townships.[26] These auxiliary police forces, or *kitskonstabels* (instant constables) as they came to be known, were initially under the administrative command of local municipal councils, although they were eventually incorporated into the SAP as distinct police units.[27]

In addition, the self-governing "homelands" established for specific black ethnic groups as part of the government's vision of "grand" apartheid established their own police units, leading to a situation in which the SAP, itself consisting of a number of different units, shared law-and-order powers with at least eleven separate police units.[28] As in Kenya, the fracturing of the police into a number of different units facilitated the government's deployment of various police units for partisan purposes, with little scrutiny from official or civilian quarters. Indeed, in the early 1990s, a commission of inquiry headed by Judge Richard Goldstone, later to sit on the bench of the Constitutional Court of South Africa, found that the apartheid government had worked with the KwaZulu homeland police force to destabilize political opposition by fomenting violence between the African National Congress (ANC) and the conservative ethnic Zulu political movement, Inkatha.[29]

13.3. OVERSIGHT OF DEMOCRATIC POLICING IN SOUTH AFRICA

It became clear to members of the apartheid security machine in the 1980s and early 1990s that the continued suppression of the ANC and other liberation movements by force was unsustainable. The decision to seek a negotiated settlement to the armed struggle was strongly supported by the apartheid security establishment.[30] Indeed, the first conversations about a negotiated solution occurred between ANC members in exile and members of the apartheid intelligence services.[31] In 1992, the ANC set out its negotiating position in a document entitled *Ready to Govern*. It included a range of principles for the reform

[25] A. Seegers, *The Military in the Making of Modern South Africa* (London: Tauris, 1996), 225–6.
[26] Cawthra, *Policing South Africa* 62.
[27] Ibid.
[28] J. Brewer, *Black and Blue: Policing in South Africa* (Oxford: Clarendon Press, 1994).
[29] Second Interim Report of the Commission of Inquiry Regarding the Prevention of Violence and Intimidation (Goldstone Commission), quoted by Cawthra, *Policing South Africa* 174.
[30] Seegers, *The Military in the Making* 249; Cawthra, *Policing South Africa* 36.
[31] A. Sparks, *Tomorrow is Another Country* (Chicago, IL: University of Chicago Press, 1996) 111.

of the security sector, including the requirements that the security services be nonpartisan, "bound by the principles of civil supremacy and subject to public scrutiny and open debate," "accountable and answerable to the public though a democratically elected parliament," and that the police in particular should be "structured as a non-militarised service function."[32]

These principles guided the design of the postapartheid police service. Effecting the transition from regime policing to democratic policing in South Africa involved both structural changes to the institutions, and the establishment of effective mechanisms of oversight and command. These changes were described in broad strokes in the interim Constitution[33] and the 1996 Constitution,[34] and more fully implemented in legislation. The South African Police Service Act 1995 (SAPS Act) established the new South African Police Service (SAPS). The various homeland police units were absorbed into the SAPS along with the auxiliary constables, while the Special Branch and the handful of covert paramilitary counter-insurgency units were disbanded. The numerous riot police units within each police precinct were reformed into a single specialized unit within the police.[35] Structural changes were accompanied by changes to the ethos of policing, reflected for example in the name change from a militarized police *force* to a community-oriented police *service*,[36] and in the replacement of the military ranks of the old SAP (e.g., general and brigadier) with civilian ranks (e.g., commissioner and director).[37]

32 *Ready to Govern: ANC Policy Guidelines for a Democratic South Africa* (1992) (available at www.anc.org.za/docs/pol/1992/readyto.html) (accessed date November 20, 2017), s. Q.

33 Constitution of the Republic of South Africa 1993, ch. 14, especially ss. 218(1)(a) and 221(2)(a).

34 Constitution of the Republic of South Africa 1996, ch. 11, especially ss. 199(5)–(8).

35 Seegers, *The Military in the Making* 275.

36 W. R. Pruitt, "The progress of democratic policing in post-apartheid South Africa" (2010) 4 *African Journal of Criminology and Justice Studies* 116–40 at 121; Berg, "Civilian oversight."

37 Hornberger, "From General to Commissioner." The SAPS returned to the apartheid-era militarized ranks in 2010. This has been explained as part of the government's response to the public's call for a more effective response to rising crime rates, and goes along with measures to expand the legitimate use of force by the police. For example, in 2002, the Constitutional Court declared unconstitutional the provision in the Criminal Procedure Act 1977 authorizing the use of lethal force by the police in effecting an arrest (S v. *Walters* (2002) 4 SA 613). However, the provision as revised in light of the judgment has since been amended again: s. 49(2) as it appeared in 2003, after the court judgment, authorized the use of lethal force only if an offence posing a threat to life or serious bodily harm was in the process of being committed. Deadly force was limited to the immediate need to protect life and bodily integrity. The provision as amended in 2012 allows the use of lethal force if the arrestor reasonably believes that a person has already committed an offence involving the threat of serious bodily harm and is in the process of evading arrest – but whose actions need not pose an immediate threat to life or bodily integrity (see Criminal Procedure Amendment Act 2012). Hornberger suggests that

The challenge of ensuring accountability and effective oversight of the police was directly confronted during the constitutional negotiations. The solution reached by the political parties in the interim Constitution was to require the establishment of an independent complaints directorate (ICD) to exercise oversight of the police and investigate specific instances or allegations of misconduct and malfeasance. Section 222 of the Interim Constitution accordingly provided:

> 222. Independent complaints mechanism
>
> There shall be established and regulated by an Act of Parliament an independent mechanism under civilian control, with the object of ensuring that complaints in respect of offences and misconduct allegedly committed by members of the Service are investigated in an effective and efficient manner.

The 1996 Constitution does not include a similar provision and does not explicitly require the establishment of a police ombudsman, although it does presuppose that such a body exists. Section 206(6) of the 1996 Constitution provides that "an independent police complaints body established by national legislation must investigate any alleged misconduct of, or offence committed by, a member of the police service."

The first iteration of this police ombudsman was the ICD, established in terms of Chapter 10 of the SAPS Act. Section 53 of the SAPS Act provided that the ICD had to investigate any deaths in police custody or resulting from police activity, but enjoyed discretion as to whether to investigate misconduct or offences other than those involving deaths. In the latter category, the ICD could choose to refer cases to the SAPS for investigation. The ICD could do no more than make recommendations to the police commissioner or the Minister of Safety and Security (section 53(6)(i) and (j)). This lack of enforcement power led to criticism that while the ICD was relatively successful in holding the police accountable for deaths in custody or at the hands of the police, it was largely a "watchdog without teeth" with respect to less serious police misconduct.[38] The independence of the complaints process was also called into question: that the ICD could refer complaints to the SAPS for investigation, and the provision that mandated the ICD to "obtain the necessary resources and logistical support or engage the services of experts" in

the name of the SAPS would have been changed back to the South African Police Force if the term "police service" was not used in the Constitution itself (at 600).

38 J. Burger, "A watchdog without teeth? The Independents Complaints Directorate" (2008) 24 SA *Crime Quarterly* 29–34.

fulfilling its mandate, suggested that the SAPS would be heavily involved in investigating complaints against the SAPS.[39]

Some of these structural problems were remedied in 2011, when Chapter 10 of the SAPS Act was repealed and the ICD replaced with the Independent Police Investigative Directorate (IPID). Importantly, IPID was established by a stand-alone piece of legislation; the IPID Act 2011. An important addition to the mandate of IPID is that it is compelled to investigate a range of offences in addition to deaths at the hands of the police or in police custody, including allegations of rape, torture or corruption by police officers and any complaint arising from the discharge of a firearm by a police officer (section 28(1)). As to enforcement, the national police commissioner and any provincial commissioners are obliged to initiate any disciplinary proceedings recommended by IPID at the conclusion of an investigation (section 30(a)).

13.4. KENYA'S POLICE REFORM

The impetus for police reform in Kenya stemmed from revelations of police misconduct during the electoral violence in 2007 and 2008. The Waki Commission Report details numerous offences of rape, murder, assault, torture, looting and dereliction of duty committed by Kenyan policemen during the violence, particularly members of the GSU.[40] Of the 1,133 people killed during the violence, the Commission found that 405 were killed by gunshot wounds and that no evidence suggested that these shots were fired by anyone other than police officers.[41] The Report notes in addition that no investigations into allegations of crimes and misconduct committed by policemen during the period were ever initiated.[42]

While the violence surrounding the 2007 election was exceptional, and the violent and criminal police response was at least in part due to the general lack of preparedness on the part of the police and other security agencies,[43] the Waki Commission Report points to the existing culture of impunity and the lack of accountability for police misconduct as a factor contributing to police misconduct during the violence. The Commission lamented the absence of an independent investigative body, and argued that an independent complaints

[39] Berg, "Civilian oversight" 146.
[40] Commission of Inquiry into Post-Election Violence, *Waki Report* 253–58, 396–405.
[41] Ibid. 384–85.
[42] Ibid. 404.
[43] Ibid. 358–76.

and investigations institution would both increase police accountability and free up police resources for other public safety functions.[44]

The Waki Report identifies five guiding principles for police reform, including legal and political accountability.[45] In recommending that independent accountability mechanisms be established as an immediate priority, the Report refers specifically to South Africa's ICD as a model. However, the attributes that the Commission saw as important for a police ombudsman are precisely those that were missing from the ICD, and which South Africa's Truth and Reconciliation Commission had itself recommended the police ombudsman should have. These attributes are: establishment by free-standing legislation independent of general police legislation; genuine independence of the police and sufficient resources to guarantee operational independence from the police; powers to compel the police to cooperate with investigations and recommendations; and an obligation to investigate police corruption.[46]

In the wake of the Waki Commission, the National Task Force on Police Reforms was established to make recommendations for the comprehensive reform of the police, in order to "enhance effectiveness, professionalism and accountability."[47] With respect to accountability, the Task Force considered whether oversight of the police should be folded into the role of a police service commission, exercised by a standing committee of the legislature, or exercised by a more general ombudsman like the Human Rights Commission. In its final report (the Ransley Report), the Task Force ultimately recommended, as had the Waki Commission, that an independent police oversight institution be established. It is worth noting that prior to the Waki Commission and the National Task Force, the idea of an independent oversight body did not have much traction. The draft constitutional text defeated at referendum in 2005, for example, did not provide for the establishment of an independent police oversight authority but would rather have created a Police Service Commission responsible not only for recruitment, promotion, salaries and standards within the police, but also for disciplinary measures for police misconduct.[48]

In this context, the National Task Force considered foreign examples of independent police oversight bodies, including those in South Africa, England

[44] Ibid. 413.

[45] Ibid. 434. The other four guiding principle the Commission identified are representativeness, impartiality, a single, integrated but regionally decentralized command structure, and respect for human rights.

[46] Ibid. 442.

[47] *Ransley Report* ii.

[48] "Proposed New Constitution of Kenya," *Kenya Gazette Supplement* No. 63 (August 22, 2005) s. 266 (the 2005 draft Constitution). See also *Ransley Report*, 27.

and Northern Ireland. The Ransley Report identifies two different models of external accountability institutions. In one approach, the oversight body investigates all allegations of misconduct against the police, while in the other – a hybrid model – it is responsible for investigating only certain offences while supervising the police's own investigations into other offences.[49] South Africa's ICD, the Ransley Report notes, took the latter approach, the advantage of which is that it recognizes the reality that police are often resistant to external oversight. The hybrid model affords the police service a degree of discretion within which to maintain oversight of its members without the intervention of external actors. These mechanisms of internal and external accountability, the Report concludes, reinforce each other in a "web of accountability in which it becomes increasingly difficult for police misconduct to take place without consequences."[50]

Like the Waki Commission, however, the Ransley Report was circumspect in the extent to which it relied on the South African model. The Report recommends that an oversight agency should have the statutory power to follow up recommendations to ensure that they are implemented,[51] perhaps having learned from the ICD's impotence and ineffectiveness in this regard. At the same time, the Report notes that one of the limitations of Kenya's existing Police Oversight Board was that, since it had been established by ministerial notice rather than legislation, it operated at the pleasure of the executive and had little effect in moving Kenya away from regime policing. The Ransley Report therefore recommended that the existence of a police oversight authority be entrenched in the Constitution, with its operational details set out in legislation.[52]

13.5. CONSTITUTIONAL AND STATUTORY ARRANGEMENTS FOR POLICE OVERSIGHT IN KENYA

The idea that the existence of an oversight institution be guaranteed by the Constitution, with its details left to subsequent determination in statute, strikes an important balance between constitutional entrenchment and adaptive efficacy. The replacement of the ICD in South African with IPID indicates that a constitutional framework may do well to leave room for flexibility. The original design may not work as hoped, for reasons not anticipated

[49] Ibid. 81–2.
[50] Ibid. 82–3.
[51] Ibid. 88.
[52] Ibid. 85–6, 90.

by the drafters, or may simply need to adapt to changing circumstances and conditions. In Kenya, the room for adaptive efficacy is particularly extensive, because despite the recommendations of both the Waki and Ransley Reports, the 2010 Constitution does not establish or explicitly require the establishment of an independent police oversight body.

This gap in the constitutional text may be explained by something as simple as timing: the Ransley Report was only released weeks before the Committee of Experts published a new draft constitution on November 17, 2009. Also relevant is that the Committee of Experts was mandated to deal with only "contentious" issues arising from the failed 2005 constitutional process.[53] The Committee never identified police reform as a contentious issue.[54] Accordingly, consistent with the 2005 draft Constitution, article 246 of the 2010 Constitution establishes a Police Service Commission mandated to "exercise disciplinary control over" police officers as well as to recruit and appoint police officers, and determine promotions and transfers within the service.

At the same time, article 244(a)–(b) of the 2010 Constitution requires the police service to "strive for the highest standards of professionalism and discipline" and to "prevent corruption and promote and practice transparency and accountability." Nothing in the Constitution suggests that the Police Service Commission enjoys exclusive power to ensure compliance with these principles, however. The Independent Policing Oversight Authority Act 2011 (Cap 88) seized this gap, establishing the Independent Policing Oversight Authority (IPOA) "to give effect to" article 244 of the 2010 Constitution, to "hold the Police accountable to the public," and "to ensure the independent oversight of the handling of complaints" by the police.[55] IPOA is empowered to investigate any complaints against the conduct of the police, to monitor the conduct of the police and investigate misconduct on its own motion, and to monitor, review and audit all internal disciplinary processes conducted by the police's Internal Affairs Unit (s. 6). In fulfilling its mandate, IPOA has broad powers of investigation including subpoena, deposition under oath, entry, search and seizure (s. 7).

Like South Africa's ICD, IPOA is obliged to itself investigate allegations of deaths and serious injury in police custody (s. 25), while monitoring the

[53] Constitution of Kenya Review Act 2008 (Cap. 3A), s. 23(b)–(h).

[54] See Committee of Experts of Constitutional Review, *Preliminary Report* (November 17, 2009) ch. 6 (accessible at http://katibainstitute.org/Archives/images/17-11-2009_Preliminary_Report.pdf) (accessed date November 20, 2017).

[55] Independent Policing Oversight Authority Act, ss. 5(a)–(c).

police's internal investigations into less serious cases of misconduct. In this regard, Kenya's IPOA follows the hybrid model of the ICD. But in establishing IPOA in a dedicated piece of legislation, rather than in terms of general police legislation, the IPOA Act is a departure from past practice in both Kenya and South Africa and takes a similar approach as South Africa subsequently did in establishing IPID in a dedicated statute. IPOA also enjoys broader powers of investigation and enforcement than did the ICD: the Act makes it an offence for any person to fail to comply with a subpoena, lawful order or direction of IPOA, to refuse to answer questions relating in an IPOA inquiry, or to interfere with or refuse to cooperate with IPOA (s. 31). The Act authorizes IPOA to recommend not only criminal charges and internal disciplinary action against police officers, but also structural or procedural reforms to the police service (s. 29(1)). The Act provides further that IPOA can apply to court for enforcement of any of its recommendations (s. 29(2)).

13.6. THE IMPACT OF POLICE REFORM: UNFULFILLED POTENTIAL

The experience of police oversight in Kenya since these reforms serves to indicate that transplanting institutional structures from other parts of the world – even where those structures are improved upon in doing so – will not necessarily yield positive results. The architects of police oversight in Kenya learned from the mistakes of South Africa's ICD, and indeed the reforms made in South Africa in replacing the ICD with IPID reflect a similar set of improvements. But Kenya's efforts to establish a police oversight mechanism have been undermined by the failure to reform the structure of the police service itself. The National Police Service as constituted by article 243 of the 2010 Constitution consists of both the KPS and the Administration Police Service. The latter police service was established during the colonial era, primarily to assist tribal chiefs in the exercise of their local governance duties (Administration Police Act 1958, Cap 85, section 8(c)). The Administration Police and the Kenya Police evolved as specialists in rural and urban policing, respectively, although since they both bore the general mandate to preserve public peace, the duplication of police forces "served no identifiable purpose other than to bolster the coercive strength of the political executive."[56]

While the Waki Commission recommended that these two police forces be integrated into a single national police service,[57] the Ransley Report

[56] Auerbach, "Police accountability in Kenya" 291.

[57] Commission of Inquiry into Post-Election Violence, *Waki Report* 434–46.

recommended that they remain distinct.[58] The 2010 Constitution fell in line with the latter suggestion, and maintains these two forces as distinct institutions. Their continued separation, as well as the numerous specialized units within each service, has led to complaints of police harassment and the duplication of police functions, or what might be thought of as over-policing. In an investigation into police antiterror operations in the Nairobi suburb of Eastleigh, IPOA noted:

> The monitoring exercise also established that there was no proper liaison or coordination between the various units of the NPS. For instance as noted in the observations, in the process of searching residential areas, a building would be searched several times by different groups of Police Officers, whether by the Administration Police Service (APS), the General Service Unit (GSU) or the Kenya Police Service (KPS), during the day or night. This certainly inconvenienced members of the public who were forced to wake up several times to open their doors and/or premises for inspection.[59]

While the GSU is a relic of the colonial style of regime policing that Kenya inherited from the British, it is worth highlighting that more recently established police units have been accused of similar abuses. The KPS Anti-Terrorism Investigation Unit (ATIU), established in 2003, is frequently accused of excessive force during counter-terrorism operations. A 2013 report by the Open Society Foundations and Muslims for Human Rights (MuHuRi) documented abuses by the ATIU in Mombasa in 2012 and 2013, including extra-judicial executions, detentions and disappearances.[60] In 2014, Human Rights Watch released a report documenting ten cases of extra-judicial killing, ten cases of disappearances, and eleven cases of mistreatment, detention or torture at the hands of the ATIU and GSU in the eight months between November 2013 and June 2014.[61] A report released by the Kenya National Commission on Human Rights in September 2015 found evidence of twenty-five extra-judicial killings and eighty-one enforced disappearances as part of a pattern of human rights violations perpetrated by the ATIU, GSU and

[58] *Ransley Report* 42–3. A primary reason for this recommendation was a practical one: until such time as Kenya has a fully devolved system of government, the Administration Police was needed to assist the provincial administrations in the fulfillment of their duties.

[59] Independent Policing Oversight Authority (IPOA), *Monitoring Report on Operation Sanitization Eastleigh: Publically Known as "Usalama Watch"* (July 14, 2014) (available at www.rckkenya.org/v2/?media_dl=820) (accessed date November 20, 2017).

[60] Open Society Justice Initiative and Muslims for Human Rights, *"We're tired of taking you to the Court."*

[61] Human Rights Watch, *Kenya: killings*.

the Administration Police's Rapid Deployment Unit. These abuses, the report goes on, are "widespread, systematic and well-coordinated and include but are not limited to arbitrary arrests, extortion, illegal detention, torture, killings and disappearances."[62]

Commenting on the police response to terrorist attacks in the coastal town of Mpeketoni in June 2014, IPOA said:

> The Authority's enquiries indicate that discord between the units' command centers permeates even regular day-to-day operations of the police where there is widespread mistrust and rivalry. To some it seems the KPS and APS are in competition to outdo and sometimes undermine each other. This practice affects effective policing.[63]

The result is that it is difficult for IPOA to exercise effective oversight of the police where several police units are involved in the same police action, sometimes at odds with one another. The time it takes for IPOA to gather evidence and witness statements in relation to the conduct of more than one police unit, as well as the complexity of decoding the administrative and operational arrangements of several distinct organizations, undermines the efficacy of IPOA as an oversight body.

Finally, despite the Ransley Report's view that a hybrid oversight mechanism combining both internal and external accountability would promote acceptance of oversight by police officers, this has not been the case. In August 2016, the Kenya National Commission on Human Rights issued a press statement describing how IPOA officers were threatened at gunpoint and later detained in the cells by a senior police officer under investigation by IPOA. The KNCHR statement goes on: "Refusal to cooperate with IPOA and intimidation of its officers by the police negates the spirit of the ongoing police reforms and in fact only serves to perpetuate the culture of impunity within the police service."[64] Part of the explanation for this culture of impunity may be that the "vetting" of police officers required by s. 7(2) of the National Police Service Act, 2011 (Cap 85) has not progressed very far. By October 2015, after

62 Kenya National Commission on Human Rights, *The error of fighting terror with terror* at 6.

63 Independent Policing Oversight Authority (IPOA), *Report Following the Mpeketoni Attacks (June 15 and 16, 2014): Redacted version* (2014) (available at http://reliefweb.int/report/kenya/ipoa-report-following-mpeketoni-attacks-15-and-16-june-2014-redacted-version) (accessed date November 20, 2017).

64 Kenya National Commission on Human Rights, *Press Statement: Harassment and Arrest of Officers of the Independent Policing Oversight Authority* (August 4, 2016) (available at www.knchr.org/Newsroom/PressStatements.aspx) (accessed date November 20, 2017).

two years of work, the National Police Service Commission had vetted only 1,364 of about 35,000 police officers.[65]

13.7. CONCLUSION

It has become common for the designers of a new constitutional system for a country going through transition to learn what they can from the experiences of their global neighbors and peers, to identify the mistakes of other countries' constitutional transitions, and to look to the historical record to assess the effectiveness of different constitutional and institutional arrangements. Police reform in Kenya, particularly with respect to establishing effective oversight mechanisms, has relied on the experience of police oversight in South Africa and learned from its failures. The model of the ICD was not borrowed root and branch, with no appreciation of its shortcomings. Indeed, the changes Kenyan legislation made to the model were themselves adopted in South Africa, when the ICD gave way to IPID.

However, these new arrangements for police oversight have not reduced police misconduct or enhanced police accountability to government. On the contrary, the Kenyan police continue to be accused of serious crimes, with IPOA largely unable to hold police officers accountable for misconduct. These failures of Kenya's model of police oversight do not mean that the model itself, as it is now operating in South Africa, is fundamentally flawed. Some accounts explain police violence in South Africa not as a result of the police acting with impunity, outside the limits of their legitimate power and out of reach of civilian oversight, but rather as a result of the steady, statutory expansion of the legitimate scope of police violence.[66] Where the police have acted beyond the scope of these expanded powers, such as at Marikana, IPID has been quick to hold errant police officers to account.[67] The paradoxical result in South Africa is that civilian oversight and control of the police has been strengthened even as the police have been empowered to use greater force in combatting crime. The latter move, without the former, raises real concerns of a return to regime policing; but as long as oversight mechanisms are capable of holding the police to account for unauthorized uses of force or

[65] F. Mukinda, "63 Senior officers sacked over graft," *Daily Nation*, October 15, 2015 (available at www.nation.co.ke/news/63-police-bosses-sacked-over-graft/-/1056/2914516/-/11vor2hz/-/index.html) (accessed date November 20, 2017).

[66] S. Adelman, "The Marikana Massacre, the rule of law and South Africa's violent democracy" (2015) 7 *Hague Journal of the Rule of Law* 243–62 at 252.

[67] Berg, "Civilian oversight" 152–3.

other illegal conduct, there is some hope that even a militarized police force can be kept within the boundaries of democratic policing.

It is also important that the South African model of police oversight allows for adaptation and change. The 1996 Constitution entrenches the principle of police accountability and presumes the existence of institutions and mechanisms to fulfil that principle, but does not set in constitutional stone the details of measures to fulfil this principle. Rather, by leaving these details to legislation the Constitution ensures that changes can be made, as necessary, to continually increase the efficacy of police oversight. The replacement of the largely powerless ICD with the more effective IPID in 2011 speaks to the value of this flexibility.

Kenya's 2010 Constitution does not explicitly require the establishment of a police oversight body, but it does commit to the principles of police accountability and transparency that oversight serves. Like South Africa, Kenya enjoys the flexibility to adapt the statutory framework for police oversight to best serve these constitutional principles. In Kenya, however, the biggest challenge to effective oversight has not been the structure or power of oversight agencies, but the existence of two distinct police forces and the numerous divisions and units within each force. The transplant of South Africa's model of police oversight, adapted as it was, has been undermined by the opacity and complexity that this over-policing breeds. Unfortunately, the existence of both the KPS and the Administration Police is entrenched in the 2010 Constitution. IPOA's capacity to effectively scrutinize the police and hold them to account will continue to be undermined by this constitutional arrangement, regardless of the adaptive flexibility that exists in the institutions for police oversight in Kenya.

Both Kenya's 2010 Constitution and South Africa's 1996 Constitution commit to principles of transparency and accountability in policing. As a practice in constitutional design, the borrowing of constitutional principles should ideally be accompanied by careful consideration of the institutional arrangements that will best fulfil those principles under local conditions. It is not the function of this chapter to suggest what the best institutional arrangements for police oversight in Kenya might be, but rather to make the more general point that the transplant of South Africa's institutional arrangements for oversight without sufficient consideration of how Kenya's differently structured police services affects the efficacy of those arrangements, has left in place a police force that operates with impunity and undermines the constitutional commitment to principles of accountability and transparency.

14

The Diffusion of South African–Style Institutions? A Study in Comparative Constitutionalism

Charles Fombad

14.1. INTRODUCTION

The 1996 South African Constitution is the first on the continent to entrench what it refers to as "State Institutions Supporting Constitutional Democracy," or what are popularly known as the chapter 9 institutions.[1] Although models of similar institutions have emerged globally in the last few decades,[2] it may be argued that the South African Constitution was the first on the continent not only to constitutionally entrench these institutions of accountability but also to design them in such a manner that they are now being increasingly recognized and accepted as one of the core elements of modern constitutionalism.[3]

[1] This essay builds on and extends the theme developed in C. M. Fombad, "Role of emerging hybrid institutions of accountability in the separation of powers scheme in Africa" in C.M. Fombad (ed.), *Separation of Powers in African Constitutionalism* (Oxford: Oxford University Press, 2016) 325–44.

[2] F. Vibert, *The Rise of the Unelected: Democracy and the New Separation of Powers* (Cambridge: Cambridge University Press, 2007); A. Schedler, L. J. Diamond and M. F. Plattner (eds.), *The Self-Restraining State: Power and Accountability in New Democracies* (Boulder, CO: Lynne Rienner, 1999); C. Kenney, "Reflections on horizontal accountability: democratic legitimacy, majority parties and democratic stability in Latin America" (Paper prepared for the Conference on Institutions, Accountability, and Democratic Governance in Latin America, Kellogg Institute for International Studies, University of Notre Dame, 2000) 8–9, [5.2000] (available at https://kellogg.nd.edu/faculty/research/pdfs/Kenney.pdf) (accessed date November 20, 2017); K. J. Ackerman, "Independent accountability agencies and democracy: a new separation of powers?" (Paper presented at the Workshop on Comparative Administrative Law, Yale University, May 8–9, 2009) (available at www.law.yale.edu/documents/pdf/CompAdminLaw/John_Ackerman_CompAdLaw_paper.pdf) (accessed date November 20, 2017); A. S. Przeworski, S.C. Stokes and B. Manin (eds.), *Democracy, Accountability, and Representation* (Cambridge: Cambridge University Press, 1999).

[3] C. M. Fombad, "Post-1990 constitutional reforms in Africa: a preliminary assessment of the prospects for constitutional governance and constitutionalism" in A. Nhema and P.T. Zeleza (eds.), *The Resolution of African Conflicts* (Addis Ababa: OSSREA, 2008) 179–99.

As "watchdog" institutions whose powers and functions sometimes overlap with the oversight role associated with the traditional triad of government – the executive, legislature and judiciary – they raise a number of interesting theoretical and practical questions. However, it is the fact that these chapter 9 institutions have now been widely replicated in some recent African constitutions that raises a number of important issues for constitutionalism on the continent.

It is not often that legal principles, practices or institutions migrate from one African country to another. The chapter 9 model is perhaps one of the rare instances of an intra-African cross-fertilization of ideas. Given the enormous challenges that the continent has faced and continues to face with dictatorship, corruption and mismanagement of state resources and diverse forms of lack of accountability, are we beginning to see the emergence of a possible fourth branch of government that will enhance the prospects for constitutionalism, good governance and respect for the rule of law? Can these institutions make up for the increasing inability of the traditional checks and balances associated with the separation of powers to ensure that African governments operate in an open, transparent, accountable and responsive manner regarding the needs of their people? How transplantable are these institutions from South Africa to other African countries? This chapter does not intend to provide a comprehensive account of how these independent institutions are operating. Its more modest goal is to assess their design and ascertain its effectiveness in promoting and deepening constitutionalism, good governance and respect for the rule of law on the continent.

Section 14.2 provides an overview of the chapter 9 institutions. It is shown that, although they have distinct mandates, their primary goal is that of promoting accountability in government. This is followed in Section 14.3 by an examination of how these institutions have spread into Africa. It is shown that whilst there are countries that have arguably improved on the chapter 9 model, there are others that have only consciously or unconsciously adopted aspects of it. In Section 14.4, the prospects for using these institutions to sustain Africa's fragile constitutionalism trajectory are considered. The weaknesses of the present design, ways in which some of these weaknesses can be overcome and the importance of these institutions are analyzed. In the concluding remarks, it is shown that in spite of the commitment by most African governments to constitutionalism in the last two decades, the continuous expansion of presidential powers combined with the steady rise of dominant parties have reduced the effectiveness of the checks and balances associated with the three branches of government. The slow emergence of independent institutions such as South

Africa's chapter 9 institutions, if well designed, provides considerable scope for countering the numerous threats posed by majoritarian abuses and can also protect ordinary citizens from the consequences of their own naïveté, ignorance and impetuosity.

14.2. AN OVERVIEW OF SOUTH AFRICA'S CHAPTER 9 INDEPENDENT INSTITUTIONS

A wide variety of terms have been used in the literature to refer to the various nonelected and nonrepresentative institutions, bodies or organizations that have been created over the centuries to perform one or more of the functions usually vested in the legislature, executive or judiciary. The trend toward their constitutional entrenchment in Africa may be new, but many of the chapter 9 institutions have a fairly long history.[4] In spite of this, the nature and role of these institutions has remained a regular subject of academic debate and controversy, both in terms of their theoretical foundations in constitutional law and practice and in terms of their practical necessity and even legitimacy. The next section briefly looks at the nature and basic features of the chapter 9 institutions and considers what sets them apart.

14.2.1. *Basic Nature and Features of the Chapter 9 Independent Institutions*

The chapter 9 institutions are provided for in s. 181(1) of the South African Constitution. They are described as state institutions specifically established to "strengthen constitutional democracy" and consist of the Public Protector; the South African Human Rights Commission; the Commission for the Promotion and Protection of the Rights of Cultural, Religious and Linguistic Communities; the Commission for Gender Equality; the Auditor-General; and the Electoral Commission.[5] A number of similar institutions that discharge accountability functions are dispersed in several other provisions in

[4] C. M. Fombad, "The enhancement of good governance in Botswana: a critical assessment of the Ombudsman Act, 1995" (2001) 27 *Journal of Southern African Studies* 57–77; Fombad, "Role of emerging hybrid institutions"; C. Murray, "The Human Rights Commission et al: what is the role of South Africa's Chapter 9 institutions?" (2006) 9 *Potchefstroom Electronic Law Journal* 122–47.

[5] There is a seventh institution mentioned in this chapter, the Independent Broadcasting Authority, but unlike the other six, its basic framework has been established by ordinary legislation.

the Constitution.[6] The chapter 9 institutions are considered so critical to "supporting constitutional democracy" that they are specially protected by a number of constitutional principles. Three important features of these institutions are worth noting.

First, although, as can be seen from ss. 182–92 of the Constitution, they have distinct roles and responsibilities, they share a common role of checking government and in this way support and strengthen the country's constitutional democracy. An elaborate discussion of how each of these institutions discharges this accountability role is beyond the scope of this chapter. The focus here is on whether the framework provided is sufficiently robust to enable them to perform their functions.

A second point relates to the nature of these institutions. Generally, in the literature, some of these independent institutions have been referred to as "independent accountability agencies," "independent regulatory commissions," "independent agencies," "non-majoritarian institutions," "unelected bodies," and more frequently as the "fourth branch of government."[7] Although the South African Constitution refers to them simply as "State Institutions Supporting Constitutional Democracy," the idea of them acting as a fourth branch of government has become very popular. Whilst these institutions do occasionally discharge some of the legislative, executive and judicial responsibilities associated with the traditional three branches of government, they do not govern.

A third feature is that these institutions are of a highly specialized nature, dealing primarily with certain specific aspects of accountability, and most of them operate outside the three branches of government. There are also other accountability institutions that are provided for in the South African Constitution but they are not entirely independent, at least in the sense that they are located within or linked to one or more of the three branches of government: for example, the Public Service Commission and the Judicial Service Commission.[8]

Institutions similar to many of the chapter 9 institutions have at one stage or another been established in many African countries. What makes the South African institutions so special that they have been copied in one form or another by other African countries?

[6] See, e.g., the Judicial Service Commission (in s. 178); the Public Service Commission (s. 196); the National Prosecuting Authority (ss. 179–80); the Financial and Fiscal Commission (ss. 220–2); and the South African National Reserve Bank (ss. 223–5).

[7] Fombad, "Role of emerging hybrid institutions" 326–7.

[8] See ss. 196 and 178 of the South African Constitution, respectively.

14.2.2. *Distinctive Features of the South African Chapter 9 Independent Institutions*

Although institutions similar to the chapter 9 institutions have been around for more than a century, there is no standard form that they take and they often differ in terms of their legal status, location within or outside the three branches of government and mandate. In many countries, their constitutionality and democratic legitimacy has been questioned.[9] Perhaps one of the most important factors in assessing these institutions is their actual or potential effectiveness in achieving the goals for which they are created. There are two critical factors which, it is submitted, distinguish the chapter 9 institutions from similar institutions that had been set up in many African countries before 1996.[10] One is the aspect of constitutional entrenchment and the other concerns the special measures introduced to protect them from manipulation by the other branches of government.

First, entrenching the chapter 9 institutions in the Constitution instead of leaving them to be regulated by ordinary legislation (as was and is still the case in many African countries) offers two important advantages. The first is that once the basic framework for each of these institutions is clearly defined and protected in the Constitution, the fundamental principle of constitutional supremacy protects this framework from arbitrary changes by transient majorities or opportunistic leaders trying to promote their own selfish political agendas.[11] There can be no debate over the fact that constitutionally entrenched accountability institutions whose prime target is to hold the three branches accountable for their actions or lack of action are more likely to last longer and be more effective than any institutions established through ordinary legislation, because the structure and powers of the latter can be changed at any time by a transient majority in parliament to suit their political agenda.

The second advantage results from s. 2 of the Constitution which provides *inter alia* that "the obligations imposed by it must be fulfilled." It can be argued that unlike in most African countries where governments have often only implemented provisions of the constitutions at their convenience, the

9 M. Thatcher and A. Sweet, "Theory and practice of delegation to non-majoritarian institutions" (2002) 25 *West European Politics* 1–22.

10 A. Mukoro, The ombudsman phenomenon in African states public services (available at http://unpan1.un.org/intradoc/groups/public/documents/AAPAM/UNPAN029881.pdf) (accessed date November 20, 2017); J. P. Gashumba, Anti-corruption agencies in Africa: a comparative analysis of Rwanda, Sierra Leone and Malawi (Research paper, October 2010) (available at http://etd.uwc.ac.za/xmlui/handle/11394/1599) (accessed date November 20, 2017).

11 C. M. Fombad, "Some perspectives on durability and change under modern African constitutions" (2013) 11 *International Journal of Constitutional Law* 382–413.

implementation of the chapter 9 obligations is not left to the discretion of the government. The effect of this is to render the duty on the executive and legislature to establish these institutions in the exact manner contemplated by the Constitution: obligatory, legally enforceable and not discretionary. The manner in which the provision is phrased opens the way for an action for violation of the Constitution where the alleged "violation" consists of a failure to fulfil a constitutional obligation or, as the South African cases discussed below show, the improper fulfilment of such a constitutional obligation.

The other and quite clearly the main innovation of the South African Constitution insofar as these independent institutions are concerned is the four "establishment and governing principles," provided for under s. 181. Although, as pointed out earlier, many African constitutions, both pre- and post-1990, provide for the establishment of some of these institutions, especially the ombudsman, public service commissions and judicial service commissions, they have hardly been able to operate effectively because they are regularly exposed to political interference in one form or another. The four guiding principles designed to ensure that these institutions are independent and not just political charades of symbolic value are stated in s. 181 as follows:

i. These institutions are independent and subject only to the constitution and the law, and they must be impartial and must exercise their powers and perform their functions without fear, favour or prejudice.
ii. Other organs of state, through legislative and other measures, must assist and protect these institutions, to ensure the independence, impartiality, dignity and effectiveness of these institutions.
iii. No person or organ of state may interfere with the functioning of these institutions.
iv. These institutions are accountable to the National Assembly, and must report on their activities and the performance of their functions to the Assembly at least once a year.

The significance of these principles was underscored by the Constitutional Court when in certifying the 1996 Constitution, it pointed out that these institutions "perform sensitive functions which require their independence and impartiality to be beyond question, and to be protected by stringent provisions in the Constitution."[12]

[12] See *Ex Parte Chairperson of the Constitutional Assembly: In Re Certification of the Amended Text of the Constitution of the Republic of South Africa, 1996* (1996) 4 SA 744 (CC).

In a number of cases, the importance of these principles in acting as a powerful bulwark against the persistent problem of political manipulation of accountability institutions has been underlined. In *Independent Electoral Commission* v. *Langeberg Municipality*,[13] the Constitutional Court pointed out that as a result of the constitutional guarantees of the independence and impartiality of the Independent Electoral Commission (IEC), Parliament had a duty in making the legislation regulating its activities to ensure its manifest independence and impartiality and that such legislation was justiciable for conformity to the Constitution. The issue of independence was again underscored in *New National Party of South Africa* v. *Government of the Republic of South Africa*.[14] In this case, questions were raised about the independence of the IEC and the possibility of governmental interference with its proper functioning. The Constitutional Court, although concluding that the allegations had not been proven by the facts, nevertheless pointed out that the IEC as one of the chapter 9 institutions, is a product of a "new constitutionalism"[15] whose independence had to be jealously preserved by the courts. The Court pointed out that the principles in s. 181 imposed obligations that must "be scrupulously observed."[16]

The issue of institutional independence came up again in *Glenister* v. *President of the Republic of South Africa*,[17] although the institution concerned, the special corruptions fighting unit, the Directorate for Priority Crime Investigation (also known as the Hawks) is not one of the chapter 9 institutions. The constitutionality of the bill setting up this unit was challenged. Although there was no specific provision in the Constitution specifying that the unit must be independent, the Constitutional Court by a majority of five to four held that the constitutional obligation to set up an independent unit could be inferred from the duty imposed by s. 7(2) of the Constitution to "respect, protect and fulfil" the rights in the Bill of Rights. The Constitutional Court clearly established the principle that the constitutional duty to create a corruption-fighting unit was not discharged by creating one that will be ineffective because it was placed under the control of the very politicians whom it is required to investigate. The crux of institutional independence was not insulation from political accountability but rather a degree of autonomous management that enables these institutions to discharge their functions without fear, favor or prejudice.

[13] (2001) 3 SA 925 (CC).

[14] (1999) 3 SA 191 (CC).

[15] Ibid. para. 78 (Langa DP).

[16] Ibid. para. 162.

[17] (2011) 3 SA 347 (CC).

Finally, in what must be considered as a locus classicus, *the Constitutional Court, in Economic Freedom Fighters* v. *Speaker of the National Assembly & Others*, and *Democratic Alliance* v. *Speaker of the National Assembly*[18] held that the failure of the President to comply with the remedial action taken against him by the Public Protector was a violation of his duty under s. 181(3) to assist and protect the office of the Public Protector to ensure its independence, impartiality, dignity and effectiveness. It also held that the failure of the National Assembly to hold the President accountable and ensure that he complied with the remedial action taken against him was also in violation of their constitutional duty under s. 181(3). This is undoubtedly one of the most important cases demonstrating not only the importance of the establishment and governing principles but also the status of these chapter 9 institutions.

If, as has been posited above, it is the special constitutional status as well as the "establishment and governing principles," that make the chapter 9 institutions truly innovative and unique, to what extent can it be said that this has influenced developments in other African countries? It is worthwhile considering the extent to which they have been copied before assessing whether it was prudent to emulate the South African model.

14.3. THE SOUTH AFRICAN MODEL ABROAD

The diffusion, migration or transplantation of legal concepts, practices and institutions is commonplace today.[19] This takes place when one legal order, system or tradition influences another one in a significant way. Nearly all accounts of such diffusion in the literature focus on and concern instances where legal phenomena originating in a former colonial power are imposed on, imported into, or adapted by a former colony. Inter-African diffusion is so rare that even the prospects of this have scarcely been the subject of serious academic discussion.[20] This explains why the adoption of the South African-style independent institutions is of great interest. Is this the start of greater

[18] (2016) 3 SA 580 (CC) (*EFF* Case).

[19] All three terms will be used interchangeably. However, as Twining points out, diffusion is the broadest of the three terms and diffusion law includes reception, transplants, spread, expansion, transfer, exports and imports, imposition, circulation, transmigration, transposition and transfrontier mobility of law: W. Twining, "Diffusion of law: a global perspective" (2004) 49 *Journal of Legal Pluralism* 4–45.

[20] Nevertheless, the potential importance of an intra-African legal dialogue has been underscored in C. M. Fombad, "Africanisation of legal education programmes: the need for comparative African legal studies" (2014) 49 *Journal of Asian and African Studies* 383–98.

systemic cross-fertilization of legal concepts, practices and institutions within Africa's diverse inherited legal traditions?

An overview of the design of independent constitutional institutions in African constitutions that were adopted after the 1996 final Constitution of South Africa indicates the level of influence of its model. This influence ranges from full-scale to partial and then to small-scale superficial transplantation. Examples of these three levels of diffusion are examined briefly, but attention is focused on the full-scale transplantation category.

The first approach, a casual resemblance at worst or a superficial transplantation at best, describes the manner in which most civilian-style constitutions (Francophone, Lusophone and Hispanophone Africa) and Arabophone African constitutions have entrenched some aspects of the chapter 9 institutions. The Burundi Constitution of 2005, in arts. 161–6, established a number of "national councils," some of which may play a role in enhancing accountability and promoting constitutionalism. The 2010 Angolan Constitution in s. IV (arts. 192–7) provided for what is referred to as "essential justice institutions," made up of two institutions: an ombudsman and another, referred to as "legal practice." Other recent constitutional bodies that bear some resemblance to the independent institutions under discussion appear in the 2011 Constitution of Morocco (arts. 161–6) and the 2014 Constitution of Tunisia (arts. 126, 128 and 130). Apart from the fact that some of those associated with the drafting of the South African Constitution played a limited role in drafting some of these constitutions, such as the Angolan and Tunisian Constitutions, it is not very obvious that there was a conscious attempt to emulate the South African model.

The other two forms, the full-scale and partial transplantation approaches, are reflected in some (mainly post-1996) Anglophone constitutions. Two recent examples are the 2014 draft Tanzanian Constitution and the 2016 Constitution of Zambia. The draft Tanzanian Constitution, under Chapter 13 dealing with "responsible institutions," provides for three commissions – the Commission for Leadership and Accountability Ethics, the Commission for Human Rights and the Controller and Auditor-General of the United Republic (arts. 108–205). Other commissions are dispersed in several provisions in the Constitution (arts. 20, 204–6 and 217–23). By contrast, the 2016 Zambian Constitution provides for eighteen commissions and two independent offices. Whilst two of the three Tanzanian commissions bear some resemblance to the South African independent institutions, the Commission for Leadership and Accountability Ethics is a novelty whose nature and functions are rather obscure. As regards Zambia, only a few of its commissions (arts. 229–35), but both independent offices (arts. 242–52), are similar to their South

African cousins. It is, however, rather surprising that, for two constitutions that were only recently drafted, what they come up with is a caricature of the South African institutions. Their weaknesses are so numerous and profound that it suffices just to make two general observations. First, the wording of the relevant provisions in both constitutions is so loose, sloppy and confusing that it is not exactly clear what was in the minds of the drafters. In spite of the benefit of experience gained from the South African approach and the practice under it for more than two decades, the constitutional entrenchment of these independent institutions in both the Tanzanian and Zambian Constitutions offers little advantage over pre-1996 practices because the powers, functions, independence and financing of the institutions are all made to depend on ordinary legislation that can be changed at any time to suit the convenience of the party in power. A second point is that the institutions provided for are weak and most unlikely to be independent and effective in promoting transparent and accountable government.[21]

To a very large extent, the 2010 Kenyan and 2013 Zimbabwean Constitutions are the only examples of full-scale attempts at transplantation of the South African model. What approximates to South Africa's chapter 9 institutions is contained in Chapter 15 of the Kenyan Constitution, which has as its title, "Commissions and Independent Offices." This chapter contains general principles that regulate ten commissions[22] and two independent offices, which are dispersed in different parts of the Constitution. Surprisingly, one of the most innovative features of the Kenyan Constitution, the Commission for the

[21] In order to deal with one of the most serious problems of governance in Africa, art. 249 of the Tanzanian Constitution simply authorizes Parliament to enact a law to establish an organ to prevent and combat corruption. Furthermore, members of the commissions contemplated by the Constitution can be removed on vague grounds such as "violating the ethics of public leadership," "lack of professionalism" and "lack of discipline" (arts. 240 (1) and 247(1)). The Zambian Constitution displays similar weaknesses. In dealing with corruption and related offences, all the Constitution does is to provide for the establishment of three investigative commissions (the Anti-Corruption Commission, the Drug Enforcement Commission and the Anti-Financial and Economic Crimes Commission). No detail on their structure, powers and composition is provided. Perhaps the only slight improvement on the chapter 9 institutions are some clauses in art. 244 of the Zambian Constitution, which appear to indicate that the decisions of the Public Protector are legally binding, but these are couched in fairly obscure language.

[22] The Commissions are the Kenya National Human Rights and Equality Commission (art. 59); the National Land Commission (art. 69); the Independent Electoral and Boundaries Commission (art. 88); the Parliamentary Service Commission (art. 127); the Judicial Service Commission (arts. 171–3); the Commission on Revenue Allocation (art. 215); the Public Service Commission (arts. 233–6); the Salaries and Remuneration Commission (art. 230); the Teachers Service Commission (art. 237); and the National Police Service Commission (art. 246). The independent offices consist of the Auditor-General (art. 229) and the Controller of Budget (art. 228).

Implementation of the Constitution, although given a lifespan of only five years,[23] is not brought within the ambit of Chapter 15. What is certainly a major weakness with this attempt to "secure the observance by all State organs of democratic values and principles," and "promote constitutionalism,"[24] is the absence of any credible constitutional framework for combating corruption (art. 249(1) (b) and (c)). Article 79 merely gives parliament the power to enact legislation to establish an independent ethics and anticorruption commission, which is supposed to have the same status and powers as the Chapter 15 commissions. There is no obvious reason why the basic framework for such an important commission was not provided for in the Constitution itself.

Other weaknesses are that the independence of these commissions is not adequately protected nor is a duty imposed on the other branches of government to assist them in carrying out their tasks. A slightly more improved adaptation of the chapter 9 institutions appears in Zimbabwe's 2013 Constitution. Like the South African approach, it provides for "independent commissions supporting democracy," in Chapter 12,[25] "institutions to combat corruption and crime" in Chapter 13,[26] and a number of other commissions dispersed in different parts of the Constitution.[27] The Zimbabwean commissions, besides promoting constitutionalism, transparency and accountability in public institutions, are also required to "secure the observance of democratic values and principles by the state and all institutions and agencies of government, and government-controlled entities."[28] Unlike the South African and even Kenyan models, the Zimbabwean Constitution provides for two very critical, reasonably strong and independent specialized institutions: the Zimbabwe Anticorruption Commission and the National Prosecuting Authority.[29]

[23] See the Sixth Schedule to the Constitution, s. 5.

[24] See art. 249(1)(b) and (c).

[25] These consist of the Zimbabwe Electoral Commission (ss. 238–41); the Zimbabwe Human Rights Commission (ss. 242–4); the Zimbabwe Gender Commission (ss. 245–7); the Zimbabwe Media Commission (ss. 248–50); and the National Peace and Reconciliation Commission (ss. 251–3).

[26] These consist of the Zimbabwe Anti-Corruption Commission (ss. 254–7) and the National Prosecuting Authority (ss. 258–63).

[27] Other commissions dispersed in different parts of the Constitution are the Judicial Service Commission (ss. 189–91); the Civil Service Commission (s. 202); the Defence Forces Service Commission (ss. 217–18); the Police Service Commission (ss. 222–3); and the Correctional Service Commission (ss. 231). There is also the Auditor-General, provided for in ss. 309–14 who, although not brought within the general provisions regulating commissions in ss. 318–23, also plays an important part in promoting accountability.

[28] See s. 233 of the Constitution.

[29] Although s. 179 of the South African Constitution and art. 157 of the Kenyan Constitution provide for similar institutions, they do not have the same degree of independence and authority.

It is thus clear that the South African-style chapter 9 institutions have been consciously or unconsciously copied in different ways. However, what is important is not how close the imitation of the South African model has been but rather whether it is well designed to enable these institutions to accomplish their goals of, *inter alia*, promoting good governance and constitutionalism.

14.4. INDEPENDENT INSTITUTIONS AND THE PROMOTION OF CONSTITUTIONALISM

If we consider constitutionalism in its broadest sense as encompassing a system of limited government in which citizens are not only protected from arbitrary government but also able to effectively compel the government to operate within its constitutional limitations, then the potential significance of these independent institutions in promoting and sustaining constitutionalism and constitutional democracy becomes clear. As noted earlier, these independent institutions can now be considered among the core elements of modern constitutionalism. That being the case, the question then becomes whether the manner in which these institutions have operated in South Africa in the last two decades has proven their actual or potential effectiveness and justifies their adoption by other countries. Have those countries that have copied them fairly extensively, like Kenya and Zimbabwe, shown that there is something worth emulating in these institutions? As pointed out earlier, a comprehensive analysis of the operation of any or all of these institutions is beyond the scope of this discussion. The main objective here is to ascertain whether, from the design of these institutions and their mandate, they offer some prospects for enhancing constitutionalism in Africa at a time when it is under threat. Three main issues are addressed here: first, a brief overview of the challenges faced by the independent institutions in accomplishing their mission; second, their potential to make a difference; and third, the measures that need to be taken to strengthen these institutions.

14.4.1. *General Overview of the Performance of These Independent Institutions*

In a recent survey carried out by Good Governance Africa, one of the findings was that "less than 15 percent of participants regard the South African government as completely accountable, while close on 80 percent perceive the government to be "incompetent and corrupt."[30] One commentator recently

[30] G. Van Onselen, "Most South Africans have given up hope," *Sunday Times*, February 21, 2016, 4.

remarked that "when the history of South Africa is written a special chapter will be dedicated to the collapse of its institutions of accountability."[31] The newspapers are replete with accounts of corruption and gross mismanagement of public funds by senior government officials, often resulting in nondelivery of services. The frequency of service delivery protests has led some analysts, with perhaps a touch of exaggeration, to suggest that South Africa has become the protest capital of the world.[32] This is not surprising because in a 2006 paper Christina Murray, in painting a pessimistic picture, summarized the general press coverage of the South African chapter 9 institutions as portraying a dismal picture of "institutions lurching from one crisis to another."[33]

The only chapter 9 institution that has distinguished itself has been the Public Protector (the South African ombudsman). This has mainly been due to the fact that the incumbent head of this institution, Advocate Thuli Madonsela, has gained worldwide admiration for her courage and tenacity in fighting against maladministration, especially corruption in high places, including her now famous Nkandla report about the misuse of public funds in renovating the private residence of President Jacob Zuma under the pretext of carrying out security upgrades to protect the President and his family (Public Protector). In their short lives, the Kenyan and Zimbabwean institutions have also encountered numerous challenges. In a 2013 review, Ben Sihanya suggests that the Kenyan commissions have not been as effective as they could and should have been due to the persistence of "tribal colonization and tyranny ... in elections, appointments, tenders, contracts, service delivery and manipulation and intimidation especially in [the] public service."[34] The situation in Zimbabwe is not much different.[35] This relative underperformance of the institutions can be attributed to a number of factors, the critical one being the issue of design.

31 J. Malala, "President or mob boss? Cross no 1 at your peril. You might just end up 'sleeping with the fishes'," *The Times*, May 30, 2015.

32 "Is SA the protest capital of the world?" (October 29, 2015) *News24* (available at www.news24.com/MyNews24/IS-SA-the-protest-capital-of-the-world-20151029) (accessed date November 20, 2017).

33 Murray, "The Human Rights Commission et al" 124.

34 B. Sihanya, "Constitutional Commission in Kenya: experiences, challenges and lessons," (Paper presented at Conference on State Implementation of the Constitution since 2010, Laico Regency, November 20, 2013) (available at www.fes-kenya.org/media/publications/Constitutional%20Commissions%20-%20Prof.%20Ben%20Sihanya.pdf) (accessed date November 20, 2017); M. Laibuta, 'Money, politics and the rise of the "fourth branch of government" in Kenya' *Voices from the Field, ConstitutionNet* (July 12, 2013) (available at www.constitutionnet.org/news/money-politics-and-rise-fourth-branch-government-kenya) (accessed date November 20, 2017).

35 Zimbabwe Democracy Institute (ZDI), Zimbabwe Independent Commissions supporting democracy. Perceptions toward Zimbabwe Electoral Commissions and Zimbabwe Human

Although considerable thought went into designing these institutions, some of the flaws that rendered most of the pre-1996 institutions ineffectual, survived. A fairly serious one has been the failure to ensure that those who run these institutions are sufficiently independent to resist capture and manipulation by the executive. The mere use of the label "independent," or locating an institution outside any of the branches of government, will not shield it from political interference and manipulation. The politicization of the appointment process has often ensured that even where the appointments are made by the President acting alone or with the intervention of parliament, only political loyalists who are unlikely to threaten the *status quo* are appointed. Most studies of South Africa's chapter 9 institutions show that the ANC government has always ensured that it appoints only its sympathizers to head these institutions under its avowed policy of "cadre deployment," even if some of them, such as the present Public Protector, in contrast to her predecessor, have taken a firmly independent line.[36] The same is true of Kenya and Zimbabwe.

The legal framework for dealing with corruption, which is one of the continent's biggest challenges, is inexplicably weak in all three constitutions. In South Africa, although the Public Protector has investigated many complaints of corruption, embezzlement and misuse of public funds,[37] the specialized agencies that deal with this are created and regulated by ordinary legislation rather than by the Constitution. As noted earlier, cases have been brought to challenge the limited independence this legislation grants to the anticorruption fighting bodies. Although the Constitutional Court has intervened to insist on the adoption of legislation that ensures that the anticorruption institution is genuinely independent, the resulting legislation barely does this.[38] In Kenya, the Ethics and Anti-corruption Commission, as noted

Rights Commission. A snap survey report (June 2015) (available at www.zdi.org.zw/en/images/ZhrcResearchReport.pdf) (accessed date November 20, 2017).

36 B. Mbanjwa, "ANC won't scrap cadre deployment" (July 17, 2014) *IOL News* (available at www.iol.co.za/news/politics/anc-won-t-scrap-cadre-deployment-1.1721447#.VCvPd_mSyVM) (accessed date November 20, 2017).

37 It was only in the Public Protector Amendment Act 1998, that the Public Protector was given the powers to investigate complaints of unlawful enrichment and corruption.

38 After the South African government reviewed the South African Police Services Amendment Act in response the Constitutional Court judgment of 2012, Glenister once again challenged the constitutionality of the new legislation, arguing that the changes introduced did not grant the institution sufficient institutional and operational independence. His appeal to the Constitutional Court against a High Court order rejecting it was itself rejected because the court felt that the separation of powers prevented it from becoming too prescriptive as to what precise legislative measures the state needs to adopt to combat corruption. See Sapa, "Hugh Glenister loses in Hawks case" (November 27, 2014) *The Citizen* (available at http://citizen.co.za/282486/hugh-glenister-loses-hawks-case/) (accessed date November 20, 2017).

earlier, is given the status of a Chapter 15 commission under article 79 but regulated by ordinary legislation. The Anti-Corruption and Economic Crimes Act intended to deal with corruption is very weak and critics describe it as designed to protect members of parliament and their friends.[39] In Zimbabwe, although a specialized anticorruption agency, the Zimbabwe Anti-Corruption Commission, is constitutionally entrenched, its potential effectiveness is limited by the powers given to the President to appoint its chairperson when compared with similar positions for the other commissions.[40]

The perennial problem with African accountability institutions has been the fact that they have often acted as toothless bulldogs that raise a storm when dealing with petty offenders but leave the rich, powerful and well-connected undisturbed.[41] This has sometimes had to do with doubts about the nature and effect of the decisions or recommendations made by these independent institutions. The Nkandla scandal in South Africa illustrates not only what happens when the corruption involves high-ranking state officials, in this case the President, but also how difficult it is to enforce the decisions.

The Nkandla saga involving President Zuma has been the subject of public controversy regarding the use of public funds for private purposes by public office holders since the Public Protector's report was published in March 2014. The Department of Public Works carried out significant improvements on Zuma's personal residence costing over R246 million. An investigation carried out by the Public Protector at the request of some members of the public and the main opposition Democratic Alliance Party (DA) concluded that some of the fairly significant improvements carried out were not related to ensuring the security of the property and that Zuma had unduly benefited from these improvements.[42] It also concluded that Zuma had acted in violation of the ministerial handbook that guided such upgrades and was liable to repay some of the costs of improvements.

When the Public Protector's report came before Parliament, it appointed an ANC-dominated *ad hoc* committee to study it and make recommendations.

39 Sihanya, "Constitutional Commission in Kenya."

40 See s. 254(1)(a) which requires him to consult only with the Committee on Standing Rules and Orders, an essentially political body compared to the other commissions where in most cases he has to consult this committee as well as the Judicial Service Commission (see, e.g., s. 242(1)(a) dealing with the appointment of the chairperson of the Zimbabwe Human Rights Commission).

41 C. N. Fombad, "Curbing corruption in Africa: some lessons from Botswana's experience" (1999) 51 *International Social Science Journal* 241–54.

42 The non-security-related upgrades that Zuma was being asked to pay for included a large visitor's center, a cattle kraal, a chicken run, a large swimming pool, a culvert and an amphitheatre.

In August 2015, the ANC, with its 249 members in a Parliament of 400 members, easily adopted the report of the *ad hoc* committee that exonerated Zuma from paying for nonsecurity features in Nkandla. One of the opposition parties, the Economic Freedom Fighters (EFF), subsequently joined by the Democratic Alliance (DA) and the Public Protector, filed an action before the Constitutional Court. As noted in discussing the *EFF* Case earlier, the Court held that both the President in failing to comply with the remedial action and Parliament in acting on the report had violated the Constitution. The Constitutional Court's decision in this case in many respects conclusively settled the issue of the status of decisions or recommendations made by these institutions.

There might well be some merit in the argument that the role of these institutions should lie in "influence, not in formal power," and in "influence rather than enforcement."[43] This certainly cannot be enough. First, it would be absurd to create institutions like these and give them the power to spend large amounts of taxpayers' money to carry out investigations if the results of these investigations are simply ignored for political reasons by Africa's parliaments, most of which are controlled by dominant parties and imperial presidents. The reaction of the South African Parliament to the Public Protector's recommendations on the Nkandla scandal was therefore predictable.[44] The decisions, findings and recommendations must be fully implemented because any persons against whom adverse findings are made, especially since most of the processes are not adversarial, have a right, in accordance with the ordinary rules of natural justice, to challenge an outcome that is perceived as perverse and unreasonable through a process of judicial review. In other words, the

[43] Murray, "The Human Rights Commission et al." 132–3.

[44] Chief Justice Mogoeng Mogoeng in the *EFF* Case, in pointing out that the Constitution could not have intended the effect of the findings of the chapter 9 institutions to have no effect said:

> I hasten to say that this would not ordinarily be required of an institution whose powers or decisions are by constitutional design always supposed to be ineffectual. Whether it is impartial or not would be irrelevant if the implementation of the decisions it takes is at the mercy of those against whom they are made. It is also doubtful whether the fairly handsome budget, offices and staff all over the country and the time and energy expended on investigations, findings and remedial actions taken, would ever make any sense if the Public Protector's powers or decisions were meant to be inconsequential. The constitutional safeguards in section 181 would also be meaningless if institutions purportedly established to strengthen our constitutional democracy lacked even the remotest possibility to do so: (2016) 3 SA 580 (CC) para. 49. He added at para. 67 that: "The Public Protector would arguably have no dignity and be ineffective if her directives could be ignored willy-nilly."

outcome of the investigation can only be ignored where it has been judicially reviewed and reversed. Second, as the Constitutional Court rightly pointed out, the legal effects of any remedial measures proposed by these independent institutions will often depend on the nature of the issues investigated, the findings made and the general context.[45] Many of the investigations may result not merely in findings of simple acts of maladministration but also of criminal activity. In the Nkandla matter, there was overwhelming evidence of abuse of office and other criminal activities involving the President (who had taken an oath to "uphold, defend and respect the Constitution." To allow him to get away with such a flagrant violation of the law on the pretext that the Public Protector's recommendations were not binding on him not only is a violation of the oath of office but also allows him to place himself above the law and the Constitution. On the other hand, there may be situations where the appropriate remedial action may merely consist of a recommendation for mediation, conciliation, negotiation or a referral of the matter to another relevant public authority (e.g., to the prosecuting authority).

Another persistent problem has been the inadequacy of funds allocated to sustain the multiplicity of independent institutions. In both Kenya and Zimbabwe, extra precautions appear to have been taken to secure the financial autonomy of these institutions.[46] An under-resourced and understaffed institution will become easy prey to those who want to avoid exposure. Besides, restricting the resources available to these institutions could easily be used to frustrate or punish them. The Constitutional Court in South Africa relied on the "establishment and governing principles" in s. 181 of the Constitution rather than on any specific provisions dealing with financial matters, to state that the chapter 9 institutions have financial autonomy and should be afforded an adequate opportunity to defend their budgetary requirements before parliament and its relevant bodies.[47] This does not seem to be adequate protection against the use of funding to blackmail these institutions. For example, there is a growing feeling that the South African government backed by its majority

[45] See *EFF* Case para. 69.

[46] Article 249(3) of the Kenyan Constitution states that "Parliament shall allocate adequate funds to enable each commission and independent office to perform its functions and the budget of each commission and independent office shall be a separate vote." Section 325 of the Zimbabwean Constitution, in even more elaborate terms, requires not only that the institutions be given "adequate funds" but also that they be given "a reasonable opportunity to make representations to a parliamentary committee as to the funds to be allocated to them each financial year."

[47] See *New National Party of South Africa* v. *Government of the Republic of South Africa* (1999) 3 SA 191 (CC), 231.

in parliament is steadily undermining the position of the Public Protector by limiting the funds made available to it and thus forcing it to make drastic cuts in its services.[48] Nevertheless, the cost of keeping so many institutions operating is a huge burden on the exchequer and there is certainly reason to doubt whether there is a need for so many such institutions.[49] The Kenyans, for good reasons, have been debating the issue of reducing the number of these institutions.[50]

The proliferation of multiple niche area institutions has also posed questions of legitimacy as well as created the risks of duplication, overlaps and wastage. One of the main and persistent criticisms, especially from US scholars, is that the independent institutions possess and exercise important powers and authority normally conferred on one or other of the three branches of government, without being either directly elected by the people or directly managed by elected officials. This is what is usually referred to as the nonmajoritarian argument.[51] This criticism is closely linked to that made by some other opponents of these institutions, who argue that by blending the functions of the three branches of government these institutions violate the principles of separation of powers.[52]

It is submitted that these criticisms are of limited relevance, if at all, under Africa's written constitutions. First, there is nothing inherently inconsistent with the doctrine of separation of powers in requiring any of these institutions to perform a function that is normally associated with one of the branches of government. Far from violating the doctrine, by creating these institutions, they do nothing more than fragment and limit power in order to prevent

48 There have been several newspaper reports of staff leaving the Public Protector's office due to their heavy workload and incommensurate remuneration. At the end of 2015, five regional offices were closed because of financial constraints. See *Legalbrief Today*, Friday November 13, 2015, No. 3879. Also see, "Another resignation at cash-strapped Public Protector" (September 11, 2014) *SA Breaking News* (available at www.sabreakingnews.co.za/2014/09/11/another-resignation-at-cash-strapped-public-protector/) (accessed date November 20, 2017), where it was reported that a number of senior officials in the Public Protector's office had resigned because the salaries they were paid were lower than those for comparible positions in the public service.

49 Fombad, "Role of emerging hybrid institutions"' 333; Murray "The Human Rights Commission et al." 137.

50 L. Aluanga-Delvaux, "It's mixed reaction to proposals to cut down on commissioners" (March 15, 2014) *Standard Digital* (available at www.standardmedia.co.ke/sports/article/2000106892/it-s-mixed-reactions-to-proposals-to-cut-down-on-commissioners) (accessed date November 20, 2017).

51 Thatcher and Sweet, "Theory and practice of delegation."

52 S. B. Foote, "Independent agencies under attack: a sceptical view of the importance of the debate" (1988) 27 *Duke Law Journal* 223–37.

tyranny, which is the very raison d'être of the doctrine. Second, the so-called nonmajoritarian argument has no application where a matter is expressly provided for under a constitution. One reason is that these institutions are created by the very constitutions that provided for elected officials. Arguably, on balance of constitutional and democratic legitimacy, the institutions can claim more legitimacy than elected officials. Their existence is based on a constitution that was approved by the people. This contrasts with elected officials, whose legitimacy is at best transient, because it is based on their election by a section of the people. They are elected to promote the policies of a political party at a given time. Such elected officials can be voted out and their policies changed whilst the constitutional goals, objectives and values espoused by the institutions endure regardless of who has been elected.

A more serious criticism that easily reflects African realities is the suspicion that these institutions may end up as a convenient smokescreen for, rather than as means to counter, abuse of powers. In South Africa, the institutions were quickly set up and made operational. In Kenya, in spite of a specific and specialized institution, the Commission for the Implementation of the Constitution that was set up to facilitate the implementation of the Constitution, there were considerable delays in the establishment and operationalization of the constitution.[53] There were similar delays in Zimbabwe caused by the nonappointment of commissioners to some of the commissions, in spite of the fundamental constitutional principle in s. 324 that "all constitutional obligations must be performed diligently and without delay." It raises the important question of whether these institutions are really critical for the entrenchment and sustenance of constitutionalism and respect for the rule of law in Africa.

14.4.2. *The Place of Independent Institutions in Promoting Constitutionalism in Africa*

Do African constitutional designers need to adopt the South African-style chapter 9 institutions, as Kenya and Zimbabwe have done so extensively and other countries to a rather limited extent? Is there anything that they offer which justifies overlooking some of the disadvantages highlighted above? The

[53] E. Opiyo, "Limits on state power: examining the role of independent commissions and offices under Constitution of Kenya, 2010" (Paper presented at International Conference on Constitution Building in Africa, University of Western Capetown, September 6, 2013) 24–5 (available at: www.academia.edu/5742872/LIMITS_ON_STATE_POWER_EXAMINING_THE_ROLE_OF_INDEPENDENT_COMMISSIONS_AND_OFFICES_UNDER_CONSTITUTION_OF_KENYA_2010?auto=download) (accessed date November 20, 2017).

operation of these independent institutions in the last two decades suggests that they have an important role to play in supporting and sustaining the transition to constitutional democracy in Africa.

First, the traditional checks and balances associated with the separation of power principles which most post-1990 constitutional reforms entrenched in one form or another has been steadily compromised by several factors. Although its contemporary efficacy has been questioned, its perceived weaknesses have been exacerbated in Africa.[54] A major cause of this are the exorbitant powers conferred on the executive, particularly the President. These imperial presidents also control the dominant parties, which in most cases operate like pre-1990 single parties. As the Nkandla saga in South Africa shows, the country's modern liberal constitutional framework has not prevented parliament from being captured and becoming a puppet of the executive and therefore incapable of performing its constitutional duty to check and hold government accountable. Whilst the three branches retain and remain the primary medium for checking each other, it is now clear that the independent institutions have become a critical means not only to act as secondary mechanisms of checks and balances that complements them but often also to act where they fail, either because they are unwilling to act or because they are ineffective in their action.

What makes these institutions unique and of critical importance to Africa's democratic project is that they are often more effective through their easier accessibility, especially to the most vulnerable and indigent members of society, and their ability to be both reactive and proactive. For example, the Human Rights Commissions, which are decentralized and accessible at no cost to a complainant, will not only investigate complaints of human rights abuse and provide appropriate redress (quasi-judicial functions) but often also provide advice.[55] In many instances, these institutions act as intermediaries between the ordinary citizen and the three branches of government and give them an opportunity to address problems that none of the other branches would deal with. For instance, if the Public Protector did not intervene to investigate the improper use of public funds to renovate the private residence of President Zuma, it is most unlikely that any of the other institutions, especially parliament, controlled as it is by the ruling party, would ever have investigated the matter. These institutions therefore clearly complement rather than supplement the *trias politica* and in so doing promote accountability, responsiveness

[54] Fombad, "Role of emerging hybrid institutions."

[55] See, e.g., the broad mandate of the Zimbabwe Human Rights Commission in s. 243 of the Constitution.

and openness in a manner that the latter are incapable of doing. In most instances, the intervention of the independent institutions makes the accountability role of the *trias politica* easier to enforce. The Nkandla scandal reached parliament and eventually the courts because of the preliminary work of the Public Protector. The importance of the preliminary investigations carried out by a similar institution, the Gender Commission, was also acknowledged in the South African case of *S* v. *Jordan*.[56]

A second important feature of the independent institutions is the manner in which their mandates have been defined. They all have a general mandate to support and promote constitutionalism, constitutional governance and respect for the rule of law.[57] Each of the institutions has been given specific powers to deal with a particular matter. Taken as a whole, both the general and specific powers are over issues which either were previously given to one of the three branches of government or are now shared. There appears to be some risk of duplication and conflict over jurisdiction. Nevertheless, these independent institutions are likely to be more efficient in discharging these functions, because they are more independent and, as a result of specializing in one particular area, more efficient. It must now be recognized, and the Nkandla saga remains a classic example, that there are certain issues that can best be dealt with by one or the other of the three branches of government and others where the independent institutions are better placed to deal with them. If we look at what could be considered to be the four most pernicious evils that are threatening to derail Africa's budding constitutional democratic transition – maladministration, human rights violations, corruption and electoral fraud – these are matters over which the ordinary courts have not been very successful. The chances of success now look better when these independent institutions are involved. It is therefore not surprising that the reasons given by many Kenyans for favoring the establishment of many commissions was the generalized feeling by the public that they could not trust any of the three branches of government.[58]

56 (2002) 6 SA 642 (CC) para. 70.

57 In the case of South Africa, this appears in the title of chapter 9 itself. In Kenya, this is slightly more elaborately spelt out in art. 249(1) and in the Zimbabwe Constitution, s. 233 is even more elaborate. It states that the independent commissions have the following general objectives in addition to those given to them individually: "(a) to support and entrench human rights and democracy; (b) to protect the sovereignty and interests of the people; (c) to promote constitutionalism; (d) to promote transparency and accountability in public institutions; (e) to secure the observance of democratic values and principles by the state and all institutions and agencies of government, and government-controlled entities; and (f) to ensure that injustices are remedied."

58 Aluanga-Delvaux, "'It's mixed reaction to proposals."

Although the importance of the independent institutions cannot be gainsaid, the numerous challenges they face suggests that all is not well. How can they be made more effective?

14.4.3. *Enhancing the Effectiveness of the Independent Institutions*

The steadily rising level of corruption and maladministration in South Africa, as is evident from the survey of citizens" dissatisfaction with the delivery of services and the challenges that some of the independent institutions such as the Public Protector encounter, clearly suggests that all is not well. Similar problems have been encountered by the more recent independent institutions established under the Kenyan and Zimbabwean Constitutions.[59] The experiences of the last two decades suggest that the South African constitutional framework, although well-conceived and designed, is not as robust as it appeared to be. Two innovative aspects of its design need to be revisited.

The first is the idea of constitutional entrenchment. Constitutionalizing the chapter 9 institutions provided them with greater institutional durability and certainty and to a large extent shielded them from the arbitrariness and unpredictability that come with institutions created by ordinary legislation which can be changed at any time by opportunistic and transient majorities in parliament. Constitutions are not self-implementing documents and as we noted above, in both Kenya and Zimbabwe there was considerable delay in setting up the institutions provided for in the constitutions. This is, however, ironic, because both constitutions contain provisions that strive to enhance their implementation. In the case of Kenya, this was done by the creation of the Commission for the Implementation of the Constitution. In the case of Zimbabwe, s. 324 creates a potentially enforceable duty to implement the constitution "diligently and without delay." It can be argued that constitutionally entrenched independent institutions coupled with a mandatory duty to implement the Constitution and an institution to oversee and supervise the proper and effective implementation will ensure that these institutions are set up promptly in the manner contemplated.

The second innovation comprises the guiding principles in s. 181 of the South African Constitution. It is clear that these have not prevented the political interference and manipulation that has in the past rendered similar institutions toothless bulldogs established to impress investors and foreign donors. From the South African experience, two main things appear to have

[59] Ibid.; Laibuta, "Money, politics"; Sihanya, "Constitutional Commission in Kenya"; Zimbabwe Democracy Institute, Zimbabwe Independent Commissions.

gone wrong: one, the failure to ensure that those appointed to the institutions are genuinely independent and not subject to control and manipulation by the appointing authority and, second, ensuring the effectiveness of the institution's intervention. These weaknesses have only emerged in the course of the last twenty years of the operation of the South African legal framework. Nevertheless, the Kenyan and Zimbabwean Constitutions did nothing to remedy these defects and probably made them worse!

The effectiveness of independent institutions very much depends on their capacity to act independently, and this, to a large extent, depends on the method by which senior officials and members are appointed. Appointments must be made in such a way that the appointees do not feel beholden to those who appoint them. Section 193 of the South African Constitution goes to some lengths to prevent this by providing that the Public Protector and Auditor-General, although appointed by the President, must be chosen from persons recommended by at least 60 percent of the members of parliament and by requiring approval by a simple parliamentary majority for members of the other institutions. However, because the ruling ANC government has been able to maintain a parliamentary majority of at least 64 percent since the end of apartheid in 1994, it has been able to appoint its sympathizers or close associates to these institutions.[60] The fact that the Public Protector, Advocate Thuli Madonsela, turned out to be so independent that her report on Nkandla substantially undermined the authority and credibility of President Zuma was purely fortuitous, especially with the ANC's controversial policy of cadre deployment.[61]

Apart from the Auditor-General who has often come out with critical reports, cadre deployment has ensured that the other independent institutions are more restrained in their criticisms of government. Perhaps the most effective

[60] See "Zuma appoints former special adviser as IEC chairperson" (October 15, 2015) *eNews Channel Africa* (available at www.enca.com/south-africa/zuma-appoints-former-special-advisor-mashinini-new-iec-chairman) (accessed date November 20, 2017), which reports that in October 2015, President Zuma appointed a person who had previously acted as his special adviser to the very important position of chairperson of the IEC. See also, G. Budlender, "20 years of democracy: the state of human rights in South Africa" (2014) 25 *Stellenbosch Law Review* 439–50, who in commenting about South Africa's institutions says: "A disturbing feature of recent years has been the weakening and undermining of those institutions. We have had too many appointments in which a key qualification for appointment seems to be a willingness to protect those in power, or loyalty to a particular faction."

[61] The general assumption with the systematic placement of party loyalist through this policy is that they will put the interest of the party first before anything else. However, as in Advocate Madonsela's case, it may ultimately depend on the character of the person appointed. Such an appointee because of the party's trust and support may be more confident to act independently and resist partisan pressure than a person with little political clout.

strategy that the present South African government has used to get rid of heads of independent institutions that become too independent-minded is to make their working conditions so unfavorable that they are happy to resign with generous golden handshakes at the taxpayers' expense.[62] However, since somebody, most often the President, must appoint these officials, the challenge is that of designing a system of appointment that prevents the political party that controls the executive and legislature, as is usually the case, having the sole discretion of determining who ultimately is to be appointed. The system must ensure that appointments to these institutions are based mainly on merit and not political affiliation, and must also limit the scope for political interference.

Granted that presidential appointments are unavoidable, three safeguards are necessary to prevent those appointed becoming the lapdog of the President. First, it is important that persons appointed to these institutions are nonpolitical or, if political, should not have been actively involved in politics in the preceding five years. Second, all senior positions must be widely advertised, and members of the public should be encouraged to propose suitable persons. This should be followed by public interviews conducted by a Special Parliamentary Committee on Governance and Accountability, which should prepare a short list of appropriate nominees for appointment and submit this to the President. After completion of the interviews, at least two and not more than three nominees for each vacant position should be made, with the necessary motivation for each nomination. The President should make the final appointments from the list of nominees. The independence of the institution would be enhanced if the Special Parliamentary Committee on Governance and Accountability were constituted in a manner that ensures that the ruling party, regardless of its majority, does not have a voting majority in the committee.[63]

Constitutional entrenchment of independent institutions should ensure not only that the right persons are appointed but also that once appointed, they are able to perform their jobs without being subject to arbitrary removal.

62 T. Gqirana, "Govt pays out millions in golden handshakes" (July 6, 2015) *Mail and Guardian Online* (available at http://mg.co.za/article/2015-07-06-govt-pays-out-millions-in-golden-handshakes) (accessed date November 20, 2017).

63 At present, there is no Special Parliamentary Committee on Governance and Accountability in any modern African Constitution but it is a necessary complement to the independent institutions. This committee should receive quarterly reports from all the independent institutions, monitor their activities and ensure accountability. The Constitution should expressly state that it should be constituted in a manner that ensures an equal number of representatives from the ruling party and from the opposition parties and be chaired by a member from the opposition parties. It should have the powers to subpoena anybody to appear before it and should be able to co-opt such experts as it might need to assist it discharge its functions.

In this regard, the South African Constitution, particularly with respect to the removal of the Public Protector and the Auditor-General, makes the removal process very onerous by requiring the intervention of parliament and the President at different stages of the removal process.[64] The conditions for removal are even stiffer under both the Kenyan and Zimbabwean Constitutions.[65]

The credibility of independent institutions depends very much on the impact of the results of their investigations. These often take the form of recommendations, conclusions and findings which in most cases are not binding. In the light of the controversy surrounding the status of the Public Protector's report in the Nkandla case, it is perhaps desirable to put the matter beyond doubt by indicating very clearly the effect of the conclusions and recommendations arrived at. Nevertheless, where the investigations show that the law has been violated, it must be assumed that those against whom the conclusions have been drawn must comply with this. If the scourge of corruption, which often lies at the heart of abuse of power, is to be brought under control, then prosecution of corrupt activities must be mandatory.[66] Besides this, the possibility of alternative dispute resolution (ADR) techniques of conciliation, mediation and negotiation should always be provided to enable these institutions to play a more effective role in the nonjudicial settlement of disputes.[67] Reconciliatory and restorative justice approaches through ADR are potentially the most significant contribution that these independent institutions can offer as an alternative to the often protracted, expensive and acrimonious proceedings that characterize judicial proceedings.[68] The use of ADR by independent institutions can have the effect of grass-roots democratization, since by resolving individual disputes at a local level it encourages self-governance and

[64] See s. 194 of the Constitution.

[65] See art. 251 of the Kenyan Constitution and ss. 187 and 237(2) of the Zimbabwean Constitution.

[66] An example of a robust approach to this is s. 255(3) of the Zimbabwean Constitution which states: "The Government must ensure, through legislative and other means, that the Zimbabwe Anti-Corruption Commission has power to recommend the arrest and secure the prosecution of persons reasonably suspected of corruption, abuse of power and other improper conduct which falls within the Commission's jurisdiction." Legislation that falls short of this high standard can be challenged on grounds of unconstitutionality and, more specifically, falling foul of a diligent performance of a constitutional obligation as required by s. 324.

[67] See, e.g., art. 252(1)(b) of the Kenyan Constitution, which grants each of the independent offices the "powers necessary for conciliation, mediation and negotiation."'

[68] F. Mahomed, "South Africa's fourth branch: the relationship between Chapter Nine institutions and the judiciary and its implications for the doctrine of separation of powers" (Paper presented at the Round Table of the International Association of Constitutional Law on "The 'new' separation of powers: Can the doctrine evolve to meet the 21st-century context?," Johannesburg, May 28–29, 2015) 17–22.

accountability.[69] This helps not merely to enforce justice as the courts do but also to promote justice.

Notwithstanding their advantages, the creation of a multiplicity of independent institutions has its drawbacks. This not only entails huge financial costs but also often creates the risks of duplication, conflicts between the institutions and inefficiency due to cases falling between the cracks as a result of turf wars. The problem of too many independent institutions could be addressed by providing for permanent and *ad hoc* commissions, depending on the issues to be dealt with. From recent trends, it would seem that independent institutions of a permanent nature located outside any of the three branches of government are better equipped to deal with issues such as maladministration, corruption and misuse of public funds, human rights violations, elections management and minority rights issues.

Special attention needs to be paid to the design of anticorruption and national prosecution institutions. These two institutions are of critical importance if the endemic corruption that is slowly and progressively undermining all efforts to entrench constitutional governance is to be brought under control. On the other hand, other issues of accountability within the public, judicial, security, military and police services are better dealt with by independent institutions of a temporary or *ad hoc* nature, with part-time members who should meet if and when necessary. Nevertheless, both types of institutions should be regulated by the same constitutional principles that protect them from political interference and manipulation. In all cases, the need for an institution to deal with a particular matter and its mandate must be dictated by the specificity of the problem that it is designed to deal with.[70]

Ultimately, constitutional entrenchment of these institutions can at most provide only the basic legal framework. Detailed operational and structural issues are usually dealt with in ordinary legislation and there is often the risk that such legislation may undermine the ability of the institution to operate effectively and independently. To reinforce the whole idea behind the

69 M. Schoeny and W. Warfield, "Reconnecting systems maintenance with social justice: A critical role for conflict resolution" (2000) 16 *Negotiation Journal* 253–68.

70 For example, establishment of the Salaries and Remuneration Commission under the Kenyan Constitution was clearly a response to historical abuses by Kenyan parliaments which have regularly raised their salaries without regard to the economic and social conditions prevailing in the country, to a point where they have earned the dubious reputation of being some of the highest-paid parliamentarians in the world in spite of the country's low Gross Domestic Product. In spite of this, resources could have been saved and the goal of curbing parliamentary abuses in this matter could still be better served by providing for an *ad hoc* commission made up of part-time members who should meet when necessary. See, further, Laibuta, "Money, politics."

constitutional entrenchment of these independent institutions there is a need for a specific principle that requires that any legislation, action, measure or mechanism introduced (by law or otherwise) that threatens to undermine or compromise the general and specific mandate of any of the institutions must be declared null and void at the behest of any concerned individual. In this way, a piece of legislation that threatens to erode the independence of an institution can be declared void. This is very much in line with the principle that emerges from the *Glenister* and *New National Party of South Africa* cases discussed earlier. It is, however, necessary to expressly state this principle in the Constitution, rather than leave it for the courts to infer.

14.5. CONCLUSION

The consolidation of constitutional democracy is not a straight-line trajectory but rather like a spiraling gyre in which advances are bound to be followed by reversals in some cases with no certainty as to the ultimate direction. If the experiences of the immediate postindependence period are anything to go by, it would seem that there is a good chance of many countries on the continent slipping back into autocracy rather than becoming established democracies. This uncertainty in the governance trajectory, it can be argued, in the case of South Africa, has been mitigated to a large extent by its 1996 liberal Constitution. In the midst of the crisis of governance provoked by the Nkandla and other incidents, the chapter 9 institutions appear to have showed clear signs that they are capable of weathering the storm of bad governance. It is therefore not without good reasons that various African countries have copied the idea, consciously or unconsciously, or partially or fully.

Unlike in the past where the transplantation of foreign constitutional concepts and institutions came by way of foreign imposition rather than voluntary and conscious adoption, the chapter 9 institutions are evidence of intra-African borrowing, which at present is mainly intra-systemic within the Anglophone countries but is slowly becoming cross-systemic by breaking into the civilian legal traditions on the continent. Generally, unlike most other legal transplants based on concepts and institutions from the former colonial powers, the idea of independent constitutional institutions is not peculiar to any particular legal or constitutional tradition. The similarity of the experiences that African countries have gone through, from colonialism and its aftermath, to the challenges of dealing with ethnic, cultural and religious diversity, compounded by the problems of governance, such as corruption, human rights violations and nonrespect for the rule of law, means that they can learn from each other's experiences.

The prospects for entrenching constitutionalism opened by the 1996 Constitution raised high expectations that South Africa would lead the continent on the difficult path toward good governance and consequently economic recovery and growth. Two decades into its constitutional democracy under a black government, South Africa appeared in the last few years to be heading down the well-trodden path that led many African countries a few years after independence into political instability, repression, economic stagnation and generalized poverty. With a dominant and increasingly arrogant ANC whose control over parliament had limited its ability to hold government accountable, the specter of dictatorship was real.[71] Two developments it can be argued appear to have stopped any signs of creeping dictatorship in its tracks. First, the Public Protector's fearless investigation of the Nkandla scandal involving the President reinforced by the bold decision made by the Constitutional Court that both the President and the National Assembly by ignoring the recommendations contained in the report, had violated the Constitution. This judgment underscored the point that nobody is above the law. Second, and perhaps more significantly was the results of the August 2016 local government elections organized by one of the chapter 9 institutions, the IEC. With the heavy losses suffered by the ANC and the realization that they are not doomed to rule "until Jesus Christ returns,"[72] the years of complacency are likely over.[73] And this is where the chapter 9 institutions can make a big difference.

Whilst it is clear that these institutions, much like the other branches of government, have not worked perfectly and will probably never do so, they have nevertheless become an integral part of its modern institutions of governance. Their role can no longer be ignored. For example, the South African Public Protector receives about 40 000 complaints each year. What would

[71] See Budlender, "20 years of democracy." He accurately captures the mood when he points out that South Africa is in the midst of a struggle about whether to remain a genuine constitutional democracy or not because key institutions of state have been undermined and weakened and attempts are continuously being made to capture and use state institutions for anti-constitutional purposes. He adds that besides the serious problem of corruption, Parliament is failing to perform its constitutional function of oversight of the executive, and instead prefers to protect those in power.

[72] President Jacob Zuma has on numerous occasions since 2008 repeatedly said that the ANC is destined to rule until Jesus returns. See, K. Ngoepe, "ANC will rule until Jesus comes, Zuma says again" (July 5, 2016) *News24* (available at www.news24.com/elections/news/anc-will-rule-until-jesus-comes-zuma-says-again-20160705) (accessed date November 20, 2017).

[73] Unlike in 2011 when the ANC won with 61.95 percent and won control of seven of the eight metropolitan councils in South Africa, in the 2016 elections, its majority slipped to 53.9 percent and it lost control over four of the eight metropolitan councils in the country including those in Pretoria (the capital city) and Johannesburg (the economic center of the country).

have happened if it was not there? The Nkandla scandal and many other similar abuses of power that have been investigated by the Public Protector would probably never have been brought to light. The ANC would probably have done what is regularly done by electoral management bodies: intimidate the IEC to alter the election results in its favor.

The gradual emergence of independent institutions to complement the checks and balances provided by the traditional three branches of government reflects the peculiar needs, governance deficit and risks of today. Although, in substantially adopting the South African model, Kenya and Zimbabwe in some limited ways tried to improve on it, this chapter has pointed out certain loopholes that need to be closed. In most cases, the ordinary African voter is naïve: he or she often votes for purely sentimental and emotional reasons (blind ethnic, tribal or religious loyalty) or deeply felt but often misguided prejudices (in South Africa, all failings are due to apartheid and nothing else, and the alternative to the ANC is perceived to be apartheid). They pay scant attention to the record of the party or the individual being voted for. It is argued that if the independent institutions are well conceived and designed they will not only be capable of countering the numerous threats to undermine the fragile attempts to entrench constitutionalism and the rule of law by transient majorities, but also protect the ordinary masses against the consequences of their own naïveté, ignorance and impetuosity. These so-called "fourth branch institutions" are good exports to other African countries and much-needed bulwarks against the looming resurgence of authoritarianism.

15

Constitutionalism, Legitimacy, and Public Order: A South African Case Study

Aziz Z. Huq

Why do constitutions, or the broader political orders that coalesce around them, persist? One way to answer this question is to look at the institutional choices embedded in the text of the relevant organic document to see whether their designers were far-sighted or not.[1] Another approach is to ask whether they command the respect and loyalty of their citizenry.[2] Few constitutions persevere through sheer force of arms, violence, or terror. As Max Weber (2009 [1922]) explained, the state – and hence the constitution upon which it rests – commonly relies on a reservoir of popular support for its basic institutions.[3] In the absence of positive dispositions on the part of at least some substantial tranche of the people for some substantial part of the time, a state must make large expenditures on coercion, surveillance, and control. Political scientists, legal scholars, and social theorists operationalize this idea in terms of "legitimacy."[4] To be sure, the term "legitimacy" has been challenged for its vagueness and opacity.[5] And it is always important to distinguish "sociological legitimacy" (my focus here) from moral and legal variants.[6] But legitimacy remains a valuable tool for thinking about the preconditions of constitutional persistence.

The central role of "sociological" legitimacy in the maintenance of a constitution as a going concern raises a host of normative and empirical questions.

1 For example, Z. Elkins, T. Ginsburg, and J. Melton, *The Endurance of National Constitutions* (Cambridge: Cambridge University Press, 2009).
2 T. Ginsburg and A. Huq, "What can constitutions do? The Afghan case" (2014) 25 *Journal of Democracy* 116–30.
3 M. Weber, *From Max Weber: Essays in Sociology* (London: Routledge, 2009).
4 B. Gilley, "The determinants of state legitimacy: results for 72 countries" (2006) 27 *International Political Science Review* 47–71.
5 X. Marquez, "The Irrelevance of Legitimacy" (2016) 64 *Political Studies* 19–34. It is also an open question whether surveillance technology will ultimately render legitimacy an outmoded technology of state consolidation.
6 R. H. Fallon, "Legitimacy and the constitution" (2005) 118 *Harvard Law Review* 1787–853.

What is the range of strategies for building reserves of popular support for a constitution – understood as both the specific document and the political order to which it is affiliated?[7] How do the specific conditions and circumstances of a given nation at a particular moment in time cabin the range of potential legitimating strategies? Constitutional legitimacy, that is, might be a highly contextual and path-dependent matter. An obvious pathway is mediated by a claim to democratic credentials. Alternatively, societies or political orders might be characterized by legitimation pathways that hinge on historical or religious predicates (or, as in the United States, some confabulation of the two). Yet others – consider here recent experience of China under communist rule after 1980 – might endorse a relentlessly consequentialist and welfarist criterion of legitimacy that is grounded on the promise of anticipated economic growth for most (if not all). Among these diverse strategies, empirical questions arise about how different pathways might interact to reinforce or undermine each other. And normative questions might arise as to whether certain strategies of legitimacy are preferable to others. It might be argued, for example, that a legitimating strategy that hinged on economic welfare while stifling democracy was intrinsically inferior to one that relied on free and fair elections. The opposite argument in favor of the post-Deng Xiaoping China model, of course, is also possible.

This chapter considers an important, but rarely considered, question about constitutional legitimation: How might experiences with a particular kind of street-level bureaucrat[8] influence the legitimacy of a constitutional regime?[9] The post-apartheid experience of South Africa usefully illuminates the possibility that public experiences with policing – or rather the want of sufficient, effectual, and noncorrupt policing – can undermine trust in a government newly constituted under a constitution. Police are important precisely because they are dispersed, numerous, and localized representatives of the state. Members of the public are more likely to encounter police than judges, elected officials, or other state officials. Their view of the state as a whole, in consequence, may well be mediated by the behavior of police. As a correlative, there is some evidence to suggest that experiences with the police provide important signals of relative standing, recognition, and dignitary worth to individuals.[10]

7 B. Gilley, *The Right to Rule: How States Win and Lose Legitimacy* (New York, NY: Columbia University Press, 2013) 5.

8 M. Lipsky, *Street-Level Bureaucracy, 30th Ann. Ed.: Dilemmas of the Individual in Public Service* (New York, NY: Russell Sage Foundation, 2010).

9 There is a good deal of scholarship on the relationship between administration and constitutional regimes. My focus here, however, is on the discrete and different question of policing.

10 B. Bradford et al., “Officers as mirrors: policing, procedural justice and the (re)production of social identity” (2014) 54 *British Journal of Criminology* 527–50.

The functions of police in conveying information about the competence and integrity of the state on the one hand, and in setting the terms of identification with the state on the other hand, suggest that scholars of constitutional legitimacy should attend closely not solely to *macro* pathways of constitutional legitimation, but also *micro*-level or retail dynamics. The persuasive hold of a constitution, that is, might depend not just on high-profile questions of national policy. It might also turn on the behavior of highly dispersed officials, pursuing a range of state policies with high levels of discretion, and connected into the larger network of state institutions through loose and imperfectly articulated sets of intrastate networks. This presents a significant question for constitutional designers: perhaps the harvest from their labors depends not on their choices, but the dispersed and hard-to-supervise decisions of a vast cadre of public officials at the front lines of contact with the public. Although a constitution can include some tools for regulating many-level bureaucracies, it seems likely that this control will be partial. As a result, a constitution will rise or fall on the integrity of state institutions with only incomplete linkages to the document and the main institutions of government created thereby.

South Africa provides a useful lens to study this question. As I explain below in Section 15.1, policing received careful attention in both the interim and permanent constitutions of the mid-1990s. The assumptions animating these interventions, though, are at least up for debate. In Section 15.2, I explore in some detail how policing and the production of public order have remained a pressing, even intractable, problem for South Africans of all stripes. The realization of the ambitions of the 1996 Constitution thus proved elusive, at least in regard to policing. Moreover, recent empirical studies suggest that this failure of the *police* to maintain public order is undermining the trust in the *state*. Micro encounters with police hence seemed to have macro effects in terms of judgments about the state as a whole. Section 15.3 then steps back and considers the possible consequences of this dynamic for constitutional design, given the effort by the South African constitutional drafters to influence the post-enactment path of policing.

15.1. POLICING AND THE 1996 CONSTITUTION

Criminality and private violence have presented tremendous policy challenges in South Africa under its 1996 Constitution. The Constitution itself speaks both to the organization and the practice of policing, albeit in inchoate and arguably ineffectual ways. Subsequent experience under the 1996 Constitution suggests that the mechanisms included in that document, in addition to subsequent statutes, have not oriented policing on the ground toward public-regarding ends. It is useful to begin, though, by attending to the text itself.

South Africa is one of a handful of states to have had a system of racial hierarchy embodied in law – the apartheid regime established in 1948 and finally and definitively repudiated by the election of Nelson Mandela as president in 1994.[11] The ensuing Constitution of 1996 was adopted in the context of a transition from apartheid rule that was accomplished without large defections from the police or other security services.[12] Some changes to the national policing regime predated the Constitution. Until 1994, the South African Police Force had been organized into eleven homelands and tasked with maintaining a segregated polity.[13] Police forces were further internally segregated, with ill-trained black officers called *kitskonstabels* tasked with policing townships.[14] In 1995, the police force was centralized, the use of military ranks for officers was eliminated, and the "Force" was renamed a "Service." The Internal Security Act was also amended to constrain the police use of deadly force.[15]

In the context of these sustained efforts to shift the role of security forces away from the promotion of racial stratification, it is hardly surprising that both the interim and the permanent Constitutions of the mid-1990s would address the pathologies of Apartheid-era police regulation. To begin with, the interim Constitution provided explicitly for community policing.[16] Article 221 of that document envisaged "community-police forums" that would promote the "accountability of the Service to local communities and cooperation of communities with the Service" and evaluate "the provision of visible police services, including ... the provision, siting and staffing of police stations [and] ... the reception and processing of complaints and charges."[17] Further, art. 222 stipulated an "independent" complaints body that would operate under some form of "civilian" control.[18] These shifts might be understood as efforts to

[11] W. Beinart, *Twentieth-Century South Africa* (New York, NY: Oxford University Press, 2001).

[12] R. W. Johnson, *South Africa's Brave New World: The Beloved Country Since the End of Apartheid* (London: Penguin Books, 2010).

[13] W. R. Pruitt, "The progress of democratic policing in post-apartheid South Africa" (2010) 4 *African Journal of Criminology & Justice Studies* 116–40; M. Shaw, "Crime, police and public in transitional societies" (2002) 49 *Transformation: Critical Perspectives on Southern Africa* 1–24; M. Brogden, "Reforming police powers in South Africa" (1994) 17 *Police Studies* 25–44.

[14] Pruitt, "The progress of democratic policing."

[15] Ibid.; Brogden "Reforming police powers."

[16] M. Marks, C. Shearing, and J. Wood, "Who should the police be? Finding a new narrative for community policing in South Africa" (2009) 10 *Police Practice and Research* 145–55.

[17] Constitution of the Republic of South Africa 1993, s. 221.

[18] Ibid. s. 222.

make policing not only less racially segmented, but also as levers to dislodge inherited policing patterns of physical abuse and malign neglect.

Both of these design choices reflect then-contemporary trends in policing. The former provisions reflect the influence of an international movement toward community-oriented policing that was emerging in Europe, America, and Australia in the 1980s and 1990s as a reaction against the more technocratic style of policing that had dominated since the 1950s.[19] The core insight of community policing strategies is that police and communities are "coproducers" of security against crime; this basic intuition can be executed in a wide range of different kinds of police–community interactions.[20] At the same time that community policing was coming into vogue, various forms of "independent" review authorities were being adopted, such as civilian complaint review processes and auditors.[21]

Both design choices, furthermore, entailed literal transplantations of concepts and institutional forms from other national contexts in ways that are open to question. For example, the English scholar Michael Brogden has forcefully argued that the "community policing" model rests on assumptions about social structure and governance capacity that simply do not hold in contexts such as South Africa's, where the level of available bureaucratic capacity may not have equaled that of Britain or the United States.[22] Similarly, it is far from clear that "independent" review authorities are a panacea for police wrongdoing. Although internal investigatory processes can suffer from pro-police bias, they might also benefit from better access to information to determine when potential wrongdoing occurs, and what, in fact, happened. By contrast, independent bodies often depend on police for this information. Further, whereas internal processes are often staffed by police officers with experience with forensics and investigative techniques, there is no guarantee that such expertise can be recruited for an external agency. The choice between internal and external accountability mechanisms in the policing context, in short, presents a difficult trade-off between information and impartiality. Depending on the

19 W. G. Skogan and S. M. Hartnett, *Community Policing, Chicago Style* (New York, NY: Oxford University Press, 1997); H. Goldstein, "Toward community-oriented policing: potential, basic requirements, and threshold questions" (1987) 33 *Crime & Delinquency* 6–30.

20 J. H. Skolnick and D. H. Bayley, "Theme and variation in community policing" (1988) 10 *Crime and Justice* 1–37.

21 S. E. Walker and V. W. Bumphus, "The effectiveness of civilian review: observations on recent trends and new issues regarding the civilian review of the police" (1992) 11 *American Journal of Police* 1–24.

22 M. Brogden, "Implanting community policing in South Africa: a failure of history, of context, and of theory" (2004) 24 *Liverpool Law Review* 157–79.

context and the available resources, the trade-off may be best resolved in quite different ways.

The 1996 Constitution, like its interim precursors, speaks directly to the core aims and the structural organization of policing. In comparison to its interim precursor, it retreats from the community-focused understanding of policing, but preserves the idea of an independent police review power. As in the interim Constitution, there is a specific section solely focused on policing. In section 205 of the 1996 Constitution, the "objects of the police service" are characterized in anodyne and general terms: "to prevent, combat and investigate crime, to maintain public order, to protect and secure the inhabitants of the Republic and their property, and to uphold and enforce the law." Unlike section 221 of the interim Constitution, these general terms provide no direction as to the nature of the relationship between the police and the public, or any obligations in respect to procedural justice, community policing, or distributional equity. Indeed, it is possible to read the 1996 Constitution's Article 205 as a *volte-face* from interim iteration's section 221: where the latter stressed the organic relationship between the police and the population they serve, the former identifies abstract, technocratic objectives that sound in a more authoritarian "law and order" register than their precursors.

Yet the commitment to community-oriented policing did not vanish. In a 1998 White Paper published by the Ministry of Safety and Security, the new government identified the creation of a "legitimate police service" as a central goal of organizational and legal changes to policing.[23] That paper envisaged "a partnership between the police and communities" to deliver effective security.[24] That is, what had previously been installed at a constitutional level was sublimated into sub-legislative governmental policy. This shift, it should be noted, raises the interesting question as to whether street-level policing might have been rendered more effective by a constitutional commitment to community policing. In the absence of more evidence, testing this counterfactual is difficult.

Like the interim Constitution, the 1996 Constitution also speaks to questions of institutional structure and accountability within the police force. In section 206, political responsibility for a national policing strategy is shared between a cabinet-level official and provincial governments. It is striking that

[23] Shaw, "Crime, police and public in transitional societies" at 29.

[24] Quoted in A. Minnaar, "Community policing in a high crime transitional state: the case of South Africa since democratization in 1994" in D. Wisler and I. D. Onwidiwe (eds.), *Community Policing: International Patterns and Comparative Perspectives* (London: CRC Press, 2009) 28. For details of the White Paper's context, see A. Minnaar, "The Changing Face of 'Community Policing' in South African post-1994" (2010) 2 *Acta Criminologica* 189–210.

the most substantive constraint upon policing policy reflects a concern with provincial power, rather than individual or community-level interests, insofar as national policy must account for "the policing needs and priorities of the provinces as determined by the provincial executives."[25] Section 207 envisages a national police commissioner with a level of managerial responsibility for implementing the national policing strategy. The constitutional text is not clear as to whether this official is supposed to have supervisory and corrective responsibility for lapses in the legality or efficacy of policing. Nor is it clear that the office is vested with power to remedy such lapses.

Further, section 206(7) states that an "independent police complaints body established by national legislation must investigate any alleged misconduct of, or offence committed by, a member of the police service in the province." In addition to reflecting international trends in police reform, installation of an independent police review could be usefully understood in light of the rise of constitutionalized ombudsman institutions in the 1990s and 2000s focused on human rights or corruption matters.[26] Like an ombudsman, an independent police review authority at least seems to promise a neutral (if not necessarily well-informed) perspective on governmental malfeasance. It is yet another effort to create a neutral, legalistic space within the state for realization of rights free from short-term political hydraulics.

Finally, although not explicitly tethered to policing, elements of the Bill of Rights further speak to how police are envisaged as operating. Section 12 contains a commitment to the "free[dom] from all forms of violence from either public or private sources." Section 14 protects privacy from searches and seizures in absolute terms, but is modified by the general limitations language of section 36. The latter permits constraints that are "reasonable and justifiable in an open and democratic society based on human dignity, equality and freedom, taking into account all relevant factors elsewhere in the Constitution." The parallelism with (and divergence from) the US Fourth Amendment is striking. Like its South African counterpart, the US provision does not protect against all searches and seizures, but only those that are "unreasonable." Unlike the South African document, the US Constitution directs its energies at the margin to the regulation not of executive-branch officers, but of judges. It imposes constraints on when and how (presumptively judicial) warrants for searches and arrests can be issued. In practical effect, the US Supreme Court has often exploited the ambiguous term "unreasonable" as a means to

[25] Constitution of the Republic of South Africa 1996, s. 206.

[26] Linda C. Reif, "Transplantation and Adaptation: The Evolution of the Human Rights Ombudsman" (2011) 31 *Boston College Third World Law Journal* 269–310.

facilitate police discretion, but rarely as a way to account for "human dignity, equality and freedom."[27]

Calibrating the measure of appropriate police force in general terms presents a difficult problem. Police routinely exercise force in order to limit or restrain private violence. The more effective police are in this task, studies suggest, the less likely citizens are to endorse the extralegal use of force.[28] Hence, there is a trade-off in some instances between the police's use of force and the quantum of private violence. By lumping these two kinds of violence together, section 12 leaves it unclear how the trade-off will be resolved. It is not clear if the generic language of section 36 provides more precise guidance. Just like the vaguer language of the US Constitution, the South African approach thus leaves crucial questions unresolved, even at a fairly general level of abstraction.

15.2. POLICING AND PUBLIC ORDER IN THE POST-APARTHEID STATE

15.2.1. *Crime and Policing under the 1996 Constitution*

The aspirations of the 1996 Constitution in respect to policing and crime have not been vindicated. South Africa remains deeply afflicted by crime. Recorded crime rose after the establishment of democratic government, and, despite a reduction in some categories of violent crime over the last decade, other forms of offending have increased. House robbery, for example, almost doubled between 2002–3 and 2009–10, while business robbery increased 2.6 times over the same period. In 2011, in a nation of about forty-nine million inhabitants approximately fifty murders, 100 rapes, 400 armed burglaries and 500 violent assaults were reported *each day*.[29] To put this in perspective, South Africa's murder rate in 2011 was about 7.9 times that of the United States. Even as crime, violence, and insecurity have become pervasive features of post-apartheid life, neither the African National Congress's (ANC) efforts to maintain social order against crime nor its efforts to reorient the South African Police Service (SAPS) prevailed. Rather, policing has continued to be pervasively shaped by the historical legacy and contemporaneous effects of racial, economic, and

27 A. Z. Huq, "Judicial independence and the rationing of constitutional remedies" (2015) 65 *Duke Law Journal* 1–80.

28 J. Jackson et al., "Monopolizing force? Police legitimacy and public attitudes toward the acceptability of violence" (2013) 19 *Psychology, Public Policy, and Law* 479–97.

29 "Kill and be killed" (August 27, 2011) *The Economist* (available at www.economist.com/node/21526932) (accessed date November 20, 2017).

geographic stratification.[30] It has both reflected and shaped sharp economic and racial divides. Whether or not a different constitutional design might have yielded different outcomes, therefore, it is clear that the constitutional design of post-apartheid policing actually adopted resulted in national-level policy failure.

Violent crime became a major national issue for the ANC in the late 1990s as the flush of transformative change started to recede.[31] A very early government response took the form of a National Crime Prevention Strategy. This proved to be "stillborn" and hence ineffectual.[32] Post-apartheid governments instead instigated organizational change policies that have purported to aim toward a generally pro-active, community policing model.[33] For example, the police were rechristened the South African Police Service. This organization folded together the police, and the police forces of the former homeland – seemingly to be focused on a community-oriented form of security.

But the reality has been quite different. Government and police have uniformly over-promised and under-performed in regard to what can be "delivered."[34] The SAPS has been continuously presented as the answer to crime, and there have been repeated attempts to import the latest crime control models from Anglo-American police departments and academics.[35] "Crime-talk"[36] remains pervasive in the public sphere, revolving perennially around the failure of police and the state to protect citizens from violent crime. In response, the state promoted its own effectiveness in combating crime throughout the post-Apartheid period. This discourse persisted even as overall crime rates rose and has continued as those rates have fallen. This discourse ultimately led to the re-emergence of paramilitary style policing around the year 2000 that culminated in 2009 with President Zuma insisting the police were a "force," not

30 T. Leggett, "Performance measures for the South African police service: setting the benchmarks for service delivery" (2002) 49 *Transformation: Critical Perspectives on Southern Africa* 55–85.

31 J. Steinberg, "Security and disappointment: policing, freedom and xenophobia in South Africa" (2011) 51 *British Journal of Criminology* 1–16; J. Steinberg, "Crime prevention goes abroad: policy transfer and policing in post-apartheid South Africa" (2011) 15 *Theoretical Criminology* 349–64; A. M. Singh, *Policing and Crime Control in Post-Apartheid South Africa* (Aldershot: Ashgate, 2008); Leggett "Performance measures."

32 Steinberg, "Security and disappointment" 5.

33 Ibid.; J. Steinberg "Establishing police authority and civilian compliance in post-apartheid Johannesburg: an argument from the work of Egon Bittner" (2012) 22 *Policing and Society* 481–95.

34 Leggett, "Performance measures."

35 Steinberg, "Crime prevention goes abroad"; D. H. Baylay, *Changing the Guard: Developing Democratic Police Abroad* (New York, NY: Oxford University Press, 2006).

36 T. Sassoon, *Crime Talk: How Citizens Construct a Social Problem* (New York, NY: Aldine de Gruyter: 1995).

a "service,"[37] a shift in language justified by an alleged need to communicate to criminals that the state was not soft on crime.

Through this period, police increasingly relied upon apartheid-era policing modalities in townships, in particular "high density, high mobility, paramilitary policing."[38] As Mark Shaw rightly emphasizes, it is those who are poor and black who are most likely to be victims of this approach.[39] In contrast, the policing of urban business districts has been aimed at preserving the exclusion of black township residents from those areas.[40] The bifurcation of policing strategies has exacerbated geographic segregation by race and income.

As a result of the durability of an "old" policing culture, police relations with black urban populations in particular have remained characterized by the same "strong mutual defiance" that had been observed during the late apartheid era.[41] Police efficacy has suffered as a result. Police morale also remains fragile. Using a narrative form, Jonny Steinberg vividly recounts the fragility of police command of space in township areas, and the weakness of the formal institutions of policing.[42] Within the SAPS, he shows, morale remains low. This is perhaps not surprising, since South Africa has one of the highest rates of police deaths in the world.[43]

Many people in South Africa report difficult relationships with the police. These negative views seem to result from extremely negative experiences of police activity. In particular, the police's relations with young men from the townships are often tense.[44] So, too, is their relationship with immigrants and particularly undocumented foreigners,[45] or rape victims and other vulnerable

37 Leggett, "Performance measures"; J. Steinberg *Thin Blue* (Cape Town: Jonathan Ball Publishers, 2008); Steinberg "Crime prevention."

38 Steinberg, "Security and disappointment" 9.

39 Shaw, "Crime, police and public in transitional societies"14–15.

40 T. R. Samara, "Order and security in the city: producing race and policing neoliberal spaces in South Africa" (2010) 33 *Ethnic and Racial Studies* 637–55.

41 L. Fourchard, "The politics of mobilization for security in South African township" (2011) 110 *African Affairs* 246–68 at 252; Steinberg, "Security and disappointment"; Steinberg, "Crime prevention goes abroad"; Steinberg, *Thin Blue*.

42 Steinberg, *Thin Blue*.

43 D. Singh "Violators and victims: a historical review of policing in South Africa after a decade of democracy" (2004) 17 *Acta Criminologica* 86–98.

44 M. Marks, *Transforming the Robocops: Changing Police in South Africa* (Durban: University of KwaZulu-Natal Press, 2005).

45 A. Mosselson, "'There is no difference between citizens and non-citizens anymore': Violent xenophobia, citizenship and the politics of belonging in post-apartheid South Africa" (2010) 36 *Journal of Southern African Studies* 641–55; M. Neocosmos, "The politics of fear and the fear of politics: reflections on xenophobic violence in South Africa" (2008) 43 *Journal of Asian and African Studies* 586–94.

groups.[46] As in any policing context, if people feel unfairly targeted, or that they are not receiving the level of service they deserve when they report a crime, then the legitimacy of the police will likely suffer. In contrast to this evidence, Kynoch reports perceptions that SAPS officers are more approachable and respectful than their apartheid predecessors and that people expect the police to serve all citizens rather than narrow sectional interests.[47] That study is probably best read to suggest that South Africans may at least be open to positive experiences of encounters with police given the marginal improvement in policing since the early 1990s.

These problems are compounded by a long-standing problem of corruption. The latter undermines attempts at legitimating the South African police. Police malpractice has been a major concern in recent years as high-profile scandals reached the very top of the SAPS, including the suspension, replacement, and conviction of former national commissioner Jackie Selebi due to alleged involvement in organized crime, and the suspension of his successor, Bheki Cele, in October 2011 based on corruption allegations. These problems appear to reach right down through the organization.[48] It is no surprise that there is an entrenched public perception that the SAPS is corrupt.

Policing does not merely reflect South Africa's internal conflicts. It also reproduces and deepens them. Efforts to make the SAPS more diverse and inclusive have faltered, leading to limited changes to police-community relations. In a 2008 ethnography of the Durban police, Monique Marks found that "despite affirmative action and equity legislation and programs, Durban['s police force] was still plagued by deep racial and gender divisions."[49] Women and blacks, rather than being welcomed, were marginalized by "police managers who are steeped in old ways." Even to the limited extent that the police have become more racially diverse, police recruited from townships quickly cease to be identified as in-group members by those they police. As Steinberg explains, upwardly mobile police officers move to suburbs, "diving into a very

46 R. Morrell et al., "Hegemonic masculinity/masculinities in South Africa: culture, power, and gender politics" (2012) 15 *Men and Masculinities* 11–30; L. Vetten, "Paradox and policy: addressing rape in post-apartheid South Africa" in N. Westmarland and G. Gangoli (eds.), *International Approaches to Rape* (Bristol: The Policy Press, 2011).

47 G. Kynoch, "Apartheid nostalgia: personal security concerns in South African townships" (2003) 5 *South African Crime Quarterly* 7–10.

48 J. Burger, "To protect and serve: restoring public confidence in the SAPS" (2011) 36 *South African Crime Quarterly* 13–22.

49 M. Marks, "Looking different, acting different: struggles for equality within the South African police service" (2008) 86 *Public Administration* 643–58 at 646.

deep pool of expensive private services and a lifetime of debt" scorned by the subjects of their policing.[50]

Relatedly, the salience of crime as an issue in South Africa and the social divisions fostered by extreme inequality and the legacy of apartheid have, along with other factors, catalyzed alarming displays of xenophobia. "Foreigners," usually immigrants from other Sub-Saharan African countries, but also internal migrants, are blamed by some for many social ills, including crime.[51] The legitimacy of the police may, again, be caught up in the social strain that produces and is reproduced by this xenophobia.[52] Yet the effect of rising xenophobia on public judgments about the police is likely to be complex. Steinberg notes that anger toward immigrant groups was encouraged by state practices as the government attempted to maintain its bond with the poor. But their negative views are often motivated by anger at the perceived failure of the police to deal with immigrants' purported criminality.[53]

The failure of policing reform cannot be explained without attending to the deep, and widening, socio-economic rifts within South African society. South Africa is characterized by high economic inequality in comparison to other countries. According to the United Nations Development Program, it has a Gini coefficient of 57.8.[54] Alongside Brazil, this makes it one of the most economically unequal societies in the world. Economic inequality, moreover, tracks racial divisions. Apartheid policies ensured that racial divides would translate into economic inequalities. Apartheid "systematically and brutally" entrenched economic inequality along racial lines.[55] Unsurprisingly, by the fall of apartheid, income, employment, and education were distributed in a sharply uneven fashion between South Africa's generally recognized racial groups (blacks, whites, colored, and Indians).[56] Racial and economic divisions in South Africa also have a geographic dimension that influences how police are deployed. Samara,[57] has argued that urban centers, and in particular, business improvement districts, have been developed in ways that preserve the

50 Steinberg, "Security and disappointment" 352.

51 Steinberg, "Security and disappointment."

52 Mosselson, "There is no difference."

53 Steinberg, "Security and disappointment" 354–6.

54 United Nations Development Program, Human Development Report 2010 – 20th Anniversary Edition: The Real Wealth of Nations: Pathways to Human Development (Geneva: United Nations, 2010).

55 J. Seeking and N. Nattras, *Class, Race, and Inequality in South Africa* (New Haven, CT: Yale University Press, 2005) 2.

56 L. Thompson, *A History of South Africa* (New Haven, CT: Yale University Press: 2001) 299–30.

57 Samara, "Order and security in the city"; T. R. Samara, "Policing development: urban renewal as neo-liberal security strategy" (2008) 47 *Urban Studies* 197–214.

segregation of black townships from highly developed white urban areas. In his study of policing in Cape Town, he emphasizes how private and public security is deployed to prevent the "spillover of violence" from the largely poor black townships of Cape Flats into the highly developed urban center.[58]

A collateral effect of economic inequality is the temptation for the wealthy to "opt out" of the state system of social order maintenance through the purchase of private security and for the impoverished to turn to vigilante organizations.[59] The private security sector has grown rapidly since the 1990s, fed in part by defections from the post-apartheid SAPS.[60] Private and public policing functions, however, are not cleanly separated, but characterized by a "growing interpenetration and overlap."[61] Indeed, Marks and Wood present evidence that private security can interact directly with community policing initiatives and thereby serve as a "more responsive and reliable" substitute for the SAPS.[62] As a result of these trends, the provision of security is no longer exclusively (or even centrally) associated with the state as opposed to private networks defined by solidarity group, residence, or economic class.[63] Samara has demonstrated that the resulting proliferation of geographically sorted private policing produces a racial social ordering that tightly restricts the mobility of the urban black poor.[64]

In contrast, some less wealthy South Africans have turned to vigilante organizations to replace absent policing.[65] Again, the resulting structures are not always easy to cleanly separate from official state structures. Fourchard argues that grassroots vigilante organizations are hard to separate from formal structures established through community policing initiatives from the late 1990s onward.[66]

58 Samara, "Policing development" 204.

59 M. Marks and J. Wood, "South African policing at a crossroads: the case for a 'minimal' and 'minimalist' public police" (2010) 14 *Theoretical Criminology* 311–29; Samara, "Order and security in the city"; Shaw, "Crime, police and public in transitional societies"; B. Baker, "Living with non-state policing in South Africa: the issues and dilemmas" (2002) 40 *Journal of Modern African Studies* 29–53.

60 Pruitt, "The progress of democratic policing."

61 Baker, "Living with non-state policing"33.

62 Marks and Wood, "South African policing" 318.

63 Singh, "Policing and Crime Control."

64 Samara, "Order and security in the city."

65 B. Bearak, "Constant Fear and Mob Rule in South African Slum," *The New York Times* (30 June 2009); R. Abrahamson and M. C. Williams, "Public/private, global/local: the changing contours of Africa's security governance" (2008) 35 *Review of African Political Economy* 547–53.

66 Fourchard, "The politics of mobilization." See also, Steinberg, "Security and disappointment"; Samara, "Policing development."

The experience of poor South Africans with the SAPS, finally, cannot be untangled from the difficulties encountered by the post-Apartheid state. Failure to address backlogs in the provision and maintenance of basic services may further erode police legitimacy. Put bluntly, when people do not have running water, or are forced to use unenclosed "street toilets," their sense that *any* state agency can legitimately represent their interests may be undermined. There have been large protests in recent years due to dissatisfaction with household service provision, access, and quality. The police – especially Public Order Police (POP) units – have played a key role in monitoring and quelling these mass actions, and there have been a number of instances of police brutality, the most notable being the killing of Andries Tatane, a protester in Ficksburg in Free State province in early 2011. Such events may have strengthened the public's perception of an association between policing and failures in service provision.

15.2.2. *The Failure of Policing and Constitutional Legitimacy*

The 1996 Constitution implied a promise of sound policing. The post-apartheid state has thus far failed to deliver on that promise. But has this had any effect on the Constitution's legitimacy? Some evidence to that effect derives from a 2013 study conducted by a group of four criminal-justice researchers (including myself).[67] That study drew on data from the 2010 South African Social Attitudes Survey (SASAS), an annual national survey of 3,183 South African adults aged sixteen years and over conducted annually by the Human Sciences Research Council (HSRC). As relevant here, the survey focused on how experiences with the police – in particular perceptions of the police's efficacy and fairness – influenced normative judgments about not only the police, but also the state more generally. Our study did not ask about the Constitution. Nevertheless, it is plausible to think that our findings about normative judgments about the post-apartheid state have some correlation with normative judgments about the post-apartheid constitution.

A core finding of this study was that the legitimacy of the *state* was strongly correlated with the polity's experience of the *police*. Micro-level negative interactions with specific officers, in other words, translated into a macro-level effect of state delegitimation. Citizens attended not only to the effectiveness of the police when forming their legitimacy judgments in regard to the state, but also to the fairness of their actions (e.g., whether they acted with respect and

[67] B. Bradford et al., "What price fairness when security is at stake? Police legitimacy in South Africa" (2013) 8 *Regulation and Governance* 246–68.

impartiality and allowed individuals to voice their perspective). Consistent with a body of research that shows the importance of "procedural justice" in policing,[68] the results suggested that citizen's concerns about crime should not be acted on at the expense of efforts to improve the more affective aspects of the relationship between police and public. Correlatively, the study also found evidence that perceptions of broader state failure influenced judgments about the police. That is, when the government's trustworthiness and performance is in doubt, the legitimacy of the police also suffers. Perceptions of the policing function and of the state writ large were entangled. Police legitimacy is a vital element of the wider legitimacy of any democratic state, and the failure of a police force to deliver security in an efficient and fair manner can undermine the broader normative mandate of the state.

Experiences with police might have powerful effects on normative judgments of state's legitimacy for a number of reasons. Two are worth highlighting here. First, the police are at the front line of contact with the public. Police are especially likely to be present (or conspicuously absent) in stressful and emotionally charged situations such as the Marikana massacre of late September 2012. Hence, it is likely that judgments about the overall competence and fairness of the state writ large will be often inferred from experience with the state writ small, i.e., the police. Second, although relatedly, experiences with the police, and in particular perceptions of how the police treats the citizen, help form a sense of shared social identity and, correlatively, a sense of the citizen's relative standing as a citizen. As a result, policing has an "expressive" effect.[69]

As the criminologist Ben Bradford has argued based on studies of the United Kingdom and Australia, experiences of fairness at the hands of authority figures, such as police officers, tend to have positive effects on trust, legitimacy and people's compliance-related behaviors, because such experiences strengthen their connections to the social groups those authorities represent, promoting allegiance to group norms and values.[70] Bradford suggests that

[68] T. R. Tyler "Legitimacy and legitimating" (2006) 57 *Annual Review of Psychology* 375–400; T. R. Tyler, *Why People Obey the Law* (Princeton, NJ: Princeton University Press: 2006); T. R. Tyler, "Policing in black and white: ethnic group differences in trust and confidence in the police" (2005) 8 *Policing Quarterly* 322–24.

[69] J. Jackson, and B. Bradford, "Crime, policing and social order: On the expressive nature of public confidence in policing" (2009) 60 *British Journal of Sociology* 493–52. See also, J. Jackson and J. Sunshine, "Public confidence in policing: a neo-Durkheimian perspective" (2007) 47 *British Journal of Criminology* 214–33.

[70] B. Bradford, "Policing and social identity: procedural justice, inclusion, and cooperation between police and public" (2012) 24 *Policing and Society* 22–43. See also, Bradford et al., "Officers as mirrors."

people are sensitive to signs and symbols that communicate information about their status and position within a group, and that police treatment has an especially powerful communicative effect in this regard. His research finds that people evaluate police behavior in terms of its identity-relevant content, in particular, the message it conveys about membership in the nation. Policing – whether the failure to provide security or the unwillingness to treat individuals with dignity and respect – sends a strong message that an individual is not a coequal member of the polity. For the wealthy, it signals that the state is unable to supply your basic needs. Such messages, in turn, seem to have consequences for the legitimacy of the state. By extension, it is quite plausible to think that deterioration of moral support influences public views on the Constitution too.

In sum, there is good reason to think that micro-level interactions with police have an effect on macro-level normative beliefs about the state and the Constitution. A person whose daily experience of the state is its failure to provide basic security against crime and violence, who then finds the police to be corrupt and violent themselves, is not likely to have a positive view of other state institutions. The leap of inference I am offering here – one that ought to be treated as a hypothesis warranting further research rather than a solid conclusion – is to claim that this distrust of the state will leak into judgments about the Constitution upon which the state rests as a matter of law. In this way, the Constitution can be undermined as a legitimate instrument of government by the dispersed and only partially controlled actions of its street-level agents.

15.3. THEORIZING THE ROLE OF PUBLIC ORDER IN CONSTITUTIONAL LEGITIMATION

The South African experience suggests that policing and the problem of public order can play a role in the legitimation or delegitimation of a new constitutional order. This dynamic illustrates the possibility of linkages between the micro-level experiences of the state and macro-level effects of legitimacy and stability. It thus illuminates one of the pathways that may connect the mass of the public with relatively abstract constitutional dynamics. In this regard, it illuminates one modality of what might be called popular constitutionalism,[71] albeit not only consciously or directly focused on the text or substance of the constitution itself. This Part steps back by developing a tentative account of

[71] L. Kramer, *The People Themselves: Popular Constitutionalism and Judicial Review* (New York, NY: Oxford University Press, 2004).

when and how such popular constitutional effects might be observed, and what the implications are for constitutional survival.

As a threshold matter, it is important to point out that state legitimation effects are not contingent on a constitutional reference to policing. Even if the 1996 South African Constitution had said not a word about policing or public order, the efficacy and fairness of individual officers could still have had an effect upon state and constitutional legitimacy. A constitution might thus founder due to omissions, or because it speaks to policing and public order in a suboptimal fashion. Similar effects have been found in a wide range of other national contexts, from the United States[72] to Ghana,[73] without regard to constitutional commitments to public order. The promise of maintaining an effectual monopoly on violence, per Weber, may well be so ingrained in understandings of *what a state is* that constituting documents do not need to spell this out in order to create public expectations.

At the same time, the South African experience shows that a state's failure to supply public order may not prove fatal (in the sense of precipitating constitutional change) or even debilitating to the continued operation of a constitutional order. A state may rely on plural sources of legitimation. These might include a historical claim to be an authentic voice of the "people." This may be a claim with special potency in South Africa, for blacks at least. Until recently, the ANC had an effectual monopoly on political power. In August 2016, however, the party experienced an unprecedented string of electoral defeats at the municipal level, including in important cities such as Pretoria, where blacks make up three-quarters of the population.[74] A large question for the future stability of the South African constitutional order, therefore, may be whether a new class of political leaders can identify alternative pathways to state legitimacy even as the institutional apparatus of the state (including the police) are likely to remain highly corrupt and incompetent, so as to limit the delivery of effectual services. Different political parties have taken different positions in respect to this question, with the Democratic Alliance striving most clearly to position itself as the party of delivery rather than the custodian of a national democratic revolution. Other states with similarly deficient systems for service delivery have resorted to quite different legitimation strategies, and continue to survive (if not prosper in any conventional way) by focusing

[72] Tyler, "Legitimacy and legitimating."

[73] J. Tankebe, "Self-Help, policing, and procedural justice: Ghanian vigilantism and the rule of law" (2009) 43 *Law & Society Review* 245–68.

[74] N. Onishi, "A.N.C. Loses Pretoria, South Africa's Capital, as Setbacks Mount," *The New York Times* (August 6, 2016).

on the promise of external threats. The current North Korean and Iranian regimes provide useful examples in this regard.

A selective failure to supply public order, moreover, may be unjust but also remarkably stable. In the United States, for example, local and state police have a long history of both withholding effectual protection and also imposing supernumerary coercion on racial minorities. One consequence is that for racial minorities in the United States today, contact of any form with the criminal justice system tends to be politically enervating in the sense that it is associated with lower levels of political and civil engagement; this effect on an individual that is likely to worsen with time.[75] The result is a stable negative feedback loop: negative encounters with police reinforce the minorities' sense that they are not coequal citizens, which in turn leads them to give up on voting and other forms of civic engagement. Their disengagement in turn diminishes the chances of meaningful reform of policing emerging from the political process. A stable constitutional order, the American experience shows, can coexist with persistent racial (or social) stratification of a deeply iniquitous sort.

15.4. CONCLUSION

The post-apartheid state's failure to deliver on constitutional promises of public order and effectual security is an important determinant of state and constitutional legitimacy, even if it does not fatally undermine the prospects for the 1996 Constitution's continued survival. On a more general, theoretical level, the dynamics illuminated here illustrate the connection between macro-level dynamics of constitutional legitimacy with micro-level interactions occurring between individual citizens and street-level agents of the state. This micro/macro connection suggests that constitutional survival should be conceptualized as a problem of ordinary politics and administration, as much as a question of high theory and normative principle.

[75] A. E. Lerman and V. M. Weaver, *Arresting Citizenship: The Democratic Consequences of American Crime Control* (Chicago, IL: University of Chicago Press, 2014).

16

South African Social Rights Jurisprudence and the Global Canon: A Revisionist View

David Landau

The social rights jurisprudence of the South African Constitutional Court has become part of the global canon. Cases like *Grootboom*,[1] *TAC*,[2] and *Soobramoney*[3] are included in casebooks and discussed in a large volume of international scholarly literature. One question that has been too rarely asked is why the jurisprudence of the South African Court is canonical in a comparative perspective, and whether it deserves that status. This chapter seeks to answer those questions. It concludes in the end that the South African jurisprudence should be part of the canon, but in a more complex way, and with more of a shared status, than is commonly assumed.

Part of the fame of the South African cases stems from the Court's distinctive approach. The Court combines a set of features that, to my knowledge, is found in no other court around the world. It has eschewed simple forms of enforcement, like direct provision of benefits for more complex remedies, it has adopted a deferential approach to both the interpretation and enforcement of social rights, and it has focused its jurisprudence almost entirely on the poorest members of society. To some international commentators, these aspects of the Court's jurisprudence (especially early cases such as *Grootboom*) made it something like the ideal answer to a theoretical puzzle: how to square the enforcement of social rights with the particularly heavy strain that those rights put on judicial legitimacy and capacity. But this take, I argue, is based on asking a question that is not quite the right question. It is one derived from constitutional theorists focused on the United States and similar contexts, rather than the experiences of enforcement in the global south.

1 *Government of the Republic of South Africa* v. *Grootboom* (2001) 1 SA 46 (CC) (*Grootboom*).
2 *Minister of Health* v. *Treatment Action Campaign No 2* (2002) 5 SA 721 (CC).
3 *Soobramoney* v. *Minister of Health* (1998) 1 SA 765 (CC) (*Soobramoney*).

A second take has emerged to some degree as a reaction to this early literature. This revisionist view focuses on legal and political context: the jurisprudence of the South African Constitutional Court should be viewed not as a universalist solution to a theoretical problem, but as a response of a high-capacity court working in a formalist legal context, with a limited constitutional text, and most importantly in a dominant-party system. I argue that this second take is much closer to the mark than the first, but that it is still incomplete in some ways. It overemphasizes the inevitability of political and legal context and downplays the extent to which courts enforcing social rights are engaged in a common enterprise with common normative concerns.

Thus, this chapter argues that the jurisprudence can usefully be viewed in a third way: as neither the universalist answer to a theoretical question, nor a merely contextual response, but instead as part of a dialogue with other courts around the world that are seriously engaged in the enforcement of social rights. Such a dialogue suggests a common core task: courts must prod recalcitrant or low-capacity bureaucracies into action, both through their own actions and those of supportive groups. It suggests a broadened set of potential tools for the scholarly and judicial imagination, of which the creative jurisprudence of the South African Constitutional Court makes up a significant part. And at some stage, after further empirical work, it may allow the field to reach firmer conclusions about the kinds of approaches that may be most effective in tackling different problems in different contexts.

The rest of this chapter is organized as follows: Section 16.1 briefly defines the core elements of the South African model and explains why that model is so distinctive in a comparative perspective. Section 16.2 explores and rejects two existing takes on the South African jurisprudence: one as the universalist solution to the supposed heightened tension between social rights and judicial capacity and legitimacy, and the other as a mainly contextual response to a specific legal and political context. Section 16.3 lays out an alternative approach that views the South African Court as engaged in a common enterprise with courts elsewhere in the global south, and seeks to leverage that dialogue for insights into the best approaches in different contexts. Section 16.4 concludes.

16.1. DEFINING THE SOUTH AFRICAN MODEL

In a comparative perspective, the South African model of social rights enforcement is distinctive. In brief, its defining characteristic is that it combines complexity – the South African Constitutional Court has generally rejected individual remedies in favor of complex ones – with deference – the Court has been very conscious of overstepping its role. Furthermore, the Court's approach has been strongly pro-poor; it has avoided targeting relief toward middle-class or wealthier groups, unlike other courts around the world.

16.1.1. *Complex and Experimental*

Since its early decisions, the South African Constitutional Court has tended to reject an entitlement to direct individual relief from plaintiffs. In *Soobramoney*, for example, a plaintiff suffering from chronic kidney failure requested access to dialysis that would have prolonged his life but not cured him.[4] The state declined to provide the treatment because of resource constraints, and the South African Constitutional Court upheld that decision. The Court found that the state's decision to deny treatment to those in the plaintiff's position was reasonable given resource constraints. Moreover, the Court emphasized the impact of generalizing treatment given to the petitioner to all other individuals who were similarly in need of dialysis or other expensive treatments: "the health budget would have to be dramatically increased to the prejudice of other needs which the state has to meet."[5]

In *Grootboom*, similarly, the Court declined to issue an individual remedy to the petitioner, who was forced out of existing housing in an informal settlement without being given any other housing. The Court again rejected a claim for housing "upon demand," in light of resource constraints.[6] It instead famously issued a more general order requiring that the state establish a plan for those in the same position of the petitioner – that is those who had dire short-term needs for housing.[7]

The Court's approach in *Soobramoney* and *Grootboom* is in this sense consistent with its general approach in later cases. The Court has usually been reluctant to issue direct remedies either to individuals or to groups of plaintiffs. Instead, it has preferred to issue remedies that incentivize the state to make broader policy changes. The early attempt in *Grootboom* was to require the state to adopt a plan, without, however, establishing either timeframes or detailed requirements for that plan, or maintaining jurisdiction over the case.

4 *Soobramoney* para. 1.
5 Ibid. para. 28.
6 *Grootboom* para. 95.
7 The order required the state to develop a plan that took "reasonable measures such as, but not necessarily limited to, those contemplated in the Accelerated Managed Land Settlement Programme, to provide relief for people who have no access to land, no roof over their heads, and who are living in intolerable conditions or crisis situations." See ibid. para. 99.

Many later cases, particularly involving housing, have fallen under the label of engagement. The typical engagement case involves a threatened eviction from informal housing, like the *Grootboom* case – the engagement order does not require that the state adopt any particular policy with respect to the eviction or substitute housing for the petitioner, but rather demands that the state undertake structured talks with groups representing affected parties.[8] As Brian Ray has recounted in detail, over time the Court has tended to add additional procedural or substantive requirements to this process.[9] These later cases look different from *Grootboom* in terms of the form of the dialogue and its recipient: *Grootboom* is primarily about defining the outer bounds of the substance of the right to housing, and attempts to dialogue with the legislature; later cases chiefly seek to control the process by which evictions and similar acts take place, and dialogue mainly with local executive officials.[10] For our purposes, though, the key is that these various cases share a complex approach.

There are also other cases where the Court has adopted approaches that do not fit neatly into these boxes, but are still complex. In *Modderklip*, for example, where a private landowner sought eviction of informal settlements on his land, the Court refused to order the eviction but instead ordered the state to compensate the landowner for the occupation until adequate alternative housing could be arranged.[11] Such a remedy arguably acted to pressure the state into realizing the right. In *Joseph*, the Court extended something a bit like the engagement framework to a different context – the provision of electricity – by holding that the constitution encompassed the right to receive essential public services and therefore that the renters at issue (in this case victimized by the conduct of their landlord) had procedural entitlements before their electricity was cut off.[12] The overall approach can perhaps best be described as experimental; the Court has searched around for a number of different approaches to the enforcement of social rights.[13] Some of these, like engagement in eviction cases, have been returned to repeatedly; others have been used only once or several times and then abandoned.

8 *Occupiers of 51 Olivia Road* v. *City of Johannesburg* (2008) 3 SA 208 (CC); *Residents of Joe Slovo Community* v. *Thubelisha Homes* (2010) 3 SA 454 (CC).

9 B. Ray, "Evictions, aspirations, and avoidance" (2013) 5 *Constitutional Court Review* 173–232 at 224–30.

10 B. Ray, *Engaging with Social Rights: Procedure, Participation, and Democracy in South Africa's Second Wave* (Cambridge: Cambridge University Press, 2016) 192–9.

11 *President of the Republic of South Africa* v. *Modderklip Boerdery (Pty) Ltd* (2005) 5 SA 3 (CC).

12 *Joseph* v. *City of Johannesburg* (2010) 4 SA 55 (CC).

13 S. Woolman, *The Selfless Constitution: Experimentalism and Flourishing as Foundations of South Africa's Basic Law* (Cape Town: Juta, 2013) 318.

The Court's preference for more complex remedies is fairly distinctive in a comparative perspective. Case studies from other jurisdictions have shown that courts active in enforcing social rights often give individual relief to plaintiffs, particularly involving the right to health. For example, courts in Brazil, Colombia and several other Latin American jurisdictions routinely order state or nonstate actors to provide individual plaintiffs with medicines or treatments, when the denial of those medicines or treatments is linked to rights like the right to life and human dignity.[14] Individualized approaches therefore appear to be fairly common in the enforcement of socioeconomic rights in comparative constitutional law.

The South African Constitutional Court's avoidance of individual remedies in favor of complex ones seems to respond in part to a belief in equity, as made explicit by the Court in *Soobramoney* where it refers to the need for a "holistic approach" rather than one fixated on "the specific needs of particular individuals within society."[15] A court that gives individual remedies may reserve benefits only for those who actually bring suit. The effects of individual orders on broader government policies are ambiguous. In some cases, government actors or private providers may respond to an avalanche of individual orders by changing practices. In other cases, however, they may keep illegal practices intact and in fact make bringing suit a condition precedent to receiving benefits. In such cases, individual litigation may not improve outcomes overall, but simply shift the distribution of who receives a limited pool of benefits, a phenomenon sometimes called queue-jumping. This may be particularly problematic if, as supported by data from some contexts, those who sue tend to be relatively wealthy compared to those who do not but need benefits.[16]

Beyond that, it may also reflect a reluctance to issue direct relief that is rooted in ideas about deference explored in more detail below, as well as (perhaps) to the inherent difficulties involved in the enforcement of social rights. For example, the Court's engagement cases have at times been critiqued on something like the grounds with which scholars have critiqued direct individual remedies – they only benefit the groups involved in those cases, without

[14] F. Hoffmann and F. R. M. Bentes, "Accountability for social and economic rights in Brazil," in V. Gauri and D. M. Brinks (eds.), *Courting Social Justice: Judicial Enforcement of Social and Economic Rights in the Developing World* (Cambridge: Cambridge University Press, 2008) 100, 126; D. Landau, "The reality of social rights enforcement" (2012) 53 *Harvard International Law Journal* 189–247 at 209–11.

[15] *Soobramoney* para. 31.

[16] O. Ferraz, "Harming the poor through social rights litigation: lessons from Brazil" (2011) 89 *Texas Law Review* 1643–68 at 1660–2; Landau, "The reality of social rights enforcement" 214.

generalizing to other populations.[17] Some of the Court's engagement remedies have avoided expounding on the substance of the constitutional rights involved; these remedies seem to deemphasize broader rights enforcement in favor of resolving the case at issue. These types of remedies seem partially motivated by a sense of the limits on judicial role; the Court is willing to pressure the state into resolving a problem, but conscious of overstepping its bounds by doing too much to make a policy. The same may be true of cases like *Modderklip*, where the Court attempted to incentivize state compliance without directly ordering it.

16.1.2. *Pro-Poor*

The South African Constitutional Court's social rights jurisprudence has also been heavily targeted at the most marginalized members of society, rather than other groups like the middle-class. The beneficiaries of its major interventions have been groups like evictees from informal settlements, permanent residents excluded from welfare benefits, and pregnant women who lack the resources to take a drug needed to prevent mother–child HIV transmission. The focus on the poor is consistent with the prevailing scholarly image of the South African constitution as a "transformational" text aimed at overcoming entrenched racial and socioeconomic inequality.[18] It is also consistent with the major focus of the transnational literature on socioeconomic rights, which is that their fundamental purpose is to carry out social transformation by aiding the most impoverished members of society.[19]

But in a comparative perspective, this almost exclusive focus on the poor is also distinctive. In many countries, an important critique of social rights adjudication is that some forms of it benefit more affluent groups such as civil servants or the formal-sector middle class, rather than the very poor.[20] Courts may, for example, reverse or limit cuts to the benefits enjoyed by public-sector workers or those in the formal sector. A growing body of research also suggests

[17] Ray, "Evictions, aspirations, and avoidance" 222.

[18] K. E. Klare, "Legal culture and transformative constitutionalism" (1998) 14 *South African Journal on Human Rights* 146–87.

[19] S. Gloppen, "Courts and social transformation: an analytical framework," in R. Gargarella, P. Domingo and T. Roux (eds.), *Courts and Social Transformation in New Democracies: An Institutional Voice for the Poor?* (Aldershot: Ashgate, 2006) 35–59.

[20] Ferraz, "Harming the poor through social rights litigation"; Landau, "Reality of social rights enforcement" 200; A. Sajo, "Social rights as middle class entitlements in Hungary: the role of the Constitutional Court" in R. Gargarella, P. Domingo and T. Roux (eds.), *Courts and Social Transformation in New Democracies: An Institutional Voice for the Poor?* (Aldershot: Ashgate, 2006) 83.

that individual forms of relief, such as those reviewed above, may tend to be biased toward more affluent citizens, who are more likely to know their rights and to have the resources to bring suit. Thus, social rights enforcement is not automatically "transformational" in the sense assumed by the literature, and the South African jurisprudence is better placed on one end of a spectrum.

The pro-poor focus of the Court's jurisprudence again seems best explained by a combination of factors. It likely has something to do, as already noted, with the transformational "mission" of the South African constitutional text and the Court, the country's racial context, and surrounding political movements.[21] It may also have something to do with the kinds of rights enforced by the Court. In most of its cases, the Court has protected the right to housing by managing processes of eviction from informal settlement, as in *Grootboom* and the later engagement cases. Although a limited right, this is one that is likely to have a strongly pro-poor bias, as compared to certain other rights like the right to health. Finally, the way in which the Court has enforced these rights may be significant: simple remedies require that individual plaintiffs, who are more likely to be middle class, seek out the Court, while complex remedies may be more likely to reach poor plaintiffs who are less likely to sue individually.[22]

16.1.3. *Deferential*

Finally, and as noted by many commentators, the South African Court's approach has been marked by a relatively high level of deference toward the political branches.[23] This deference shows up both in judicial interpretation of social rights and in the crafting of remedies for their violations.

From an interpretive perspective, the Constitutional Court has consistently declined to establish a "minimum core" entitlement to social rights, despite guidance at the international level finding that such a core does exist as is a key part of the enforcement of these rights. In *Grootboom*, for example, the Court declined to set a minimum core entitlement to housing and instead rested its decision on the grounds that the existing lack of a short-term policy for those in the plaintiff's position was unreasonable.[24] In a more recent case

21 Klare, "Legal culture and transformative constitutionalism."

22 D. M. Brinks and V. Gauri, "The law's majestic equality? The distributive impact of judicializing social and economic rights" (2014) 12 *Perspectives on Politics* 375–93 at 387.

23 Ray, "Evictions, aspirations, and avoidance" 174; D. Bilchitz, *Poverty and Fundamental Rights: The Justification and Enforcement of Socio-Economic Rights* (Oxford: Oxford University Press, 2007) 176–7.

24 *Grootboom* paras. 32–3.

involving the right to water, *Mazibuko*, the Court reiterated and strengthened this point, again stating that it would exercise a reasonableness approach rather than defining a minimum core entitlement of a right to water for human consumption.[25] Despite being presented with international guidance from various organizations on the quantity of water needed for different levels of enjoyment of the right, the Court held that it lacked both the capacity and democratic legitimacy needed to define the minimum core. Commentators have also noted an interpretative preference in the Court's work for "avoidance" – it often resolves cases on sub-constitutional grounds, or by invoking procedural remedies such as "engagement," rather than defining and expounding on the substance of the rights at issue.[26]

Deference has also characterized the Court's approach to remedies. Many scholars have held up *Grootboom* as a paradigm case of a weak-form remedy – the Court there held the current plan unconstitutional and that a new plan must be devised that took better account of those in the petitioner's situation, but it did not order that the parliament act within a certain timeframe, nor did it place detailed restraints on the shape of any new plan.[27] In many respects, the more recent engagement remedies are similarly marked by deference. Rather than directly imposing a policy, the Court orders the state and affected parties to negotiate seriously in light of constitutional standards, in the hope that they reach an agreement. In contrast, the Court has generally declined to exercise supervisory jurisdiction or to issue structural injunctions in this area.[28]

None of this is to say that the Court's approach has been uniform.[29] The engagement remedy, for example, has experienced great variation over time, as the Court has utilized or declined to set additional procedural or substantive requirements. In some cases, the Court has also issued more direct orders. In some cases, the Court has also issued more direct orders. In the TAC case, for example, where cost was much less of an issue because the drug company had promised to provide a medicine preventing HIV transmission from mother to baby free of charge, the Court directly ordered the program to be expanded immediately to clinics and hospitals with existing capacity throughout the

25 *Mazibuko* v. *City of Johannesburg* (2010) 4 SA 1 (CC) paras. 55–61.

26 Ray, "Evictions, aspirations, and avoidance" 175.

27 M. Tushnet, *Weak Courts, Strong Rights* (Princeton, NJ: Princeton University Press, 2008) 242–4; T. Roux, "Understanding Grootboom – a response to Cass R. Sunstein" (2001) 12 *Constitutional Forum* 41–51.

28 S. Liebenberg, *Socio-Economic Rights: Adjudication Under a Transformative Constitution* (Cape Town: Juta, 2010) 438.

29 K. G. Young, *Constituting Economic and Social Rights* (Oxford: Oxford University Press, 2012) 174.

country, and for the state to take reasonable measures to expand the program elsewhere.[30] Even in cases where remedies have proven costly, the Court has occasionally issued direct relief: in *Khosa*, of example, it required that a costly welfare program be expanded to include permanent resident noncitizens.[31]

The Court's interpretive deference could also be overstated. Over time, the Court has given some substance, for example, to the right to housing, even as it has remained unwilling to define a minimum core. The Court has built toward a position where evictions cannot occur unless temporary adequate alternative housing exists, thus defining a partial minimum right to housing.[32] It has also developed *Grootboom's* mandate that some plan must exist for those with immediate and dire need for housing. In *Blue Moonlight*, the Court held that this encompassed informal settlements on both private and public land, and thus a municipality's failure to provide any budgetary allotments for alternative housing for informal settlements on private land was unreasonable.[33] As in *Grootboom*, though, the Court did not suggest how far a government actor would need to go, beyond providing some plan or provision for petitioners in such a position.

The point is not, then, that the Court's approach has been invariant over time. It is that in comparative terms, it has been relatively deferential toward the political branches. There are, of course, many countries where social rights are held completely or nearly completely nonjusticiable. But among those courts where social rights are actively enforced, the South African Constitutional's Court's approach is again distinctive. It merges a strong commitment to the enforceability of social rights with an equally strong concern about the limits of its institutional role.

16.2. TWO APPROXIMATIONS OF THE SOUTH AFRICAN APPROACH

This section considers two ways in which the work of the South African Court has been framed in comparative scholarship. In the first approach, which tracks the traditional international response, the jurisprudence of the Court is framed as the universalist answer to questions posed by constitutional theory. In the second, a kind of revisionist story to the first, the Court's work is reframed as a primarily contextual response to a particularly difficult political

30 Ibid. 155–7.

31 *Khosa* v. *Minister of Social Development* (2004) 6 SA 505 (CC).

32 Ray, *Engaging with Social Rights* 239.

33 *City of Johannesburg Metropolitan Municipality* v. *Blue Moonlight Properties 39 (Pty) Ltd* (2012) 2 SA 104 (CC).

and legal context. I will argue here that neither approximation is quite right, and search for a third possibility in the next part.

16.2.1. *The South African Jurisprudence as Universal Answer*

The Court's early decisions, especially *Grootboom*, had an extraordinary impact on the international scholarly community. Indeed, *Grootboom* is perhaps the single best-known social rights case in comparative constitutional law.

A major reason is because the case seemed to represent a distinctive model of judicial review, one shared by tendencies in other areas. Both Tushnet and Sunstein argued that the case reconciled the central tension in judicial review: between the need to enforce socioeconomic rights, and the limitations of judicial capacity and democratic legitimacy.[34] Both scholars, trained in the US tradition where social rights are oddities, argued that socioeconomic rights raise an especially strong form of the counter-majoritarian difficulty and related challenges. Tushnet, for example, draws on work by Frank Cross to argue that the enforcement of social rights differs from the enforcement of classical civil and political rights in degree if not in kind.[35] They tend to involve especially substantial budgetary expenditures, for example. Furthermore, they may possess a particularly strong form of "raging indeterminacy" – the sheer range of policy choices facing a court enforcing the right to housing or healthcare may tax their capacity and put them in a position to replace the proper role of the political branches.[36]

Sunstein, likewise, was initially against the inclusion of social rights in the constitutions of Eastern Europe, because he feared they would either freeze social programs and prevent the dismantling of communist-era welfare states, or stand as a set of unrealistic promises for the alleviation of poverty and advancement of social justice.[37] In the former case, where courts very actively enforced social rights to block reductions in social safety nets, they would infringe on policy choices and transitions that the newly democratic political regimes would need to undertake. In the latter case, where courts proved unable or unwilling to make social rights strongly justiciable, citizens would become disenchanted with these promises, undermining the legitimacy of the constitution.

[34] Tushnet, *Weak Courts, Strong Rights*; C. R. Sunstein, *Designing Democracy: What Constitutions Do* (Oxford: Oxford University Press, 2001) 224.

[35] F. B. Cross, "The Error of Positive Rights" (2000) 48 *UCLA Law Review* 857–924.

[36] F. Michelman, "The Constitution, social rights, and liberal political justification" (2003) 1 *International Journal of Constitutional Law* 13–34 at 31.

[37] C. R. Sunstein, "Against positive rights" (1993) 3 *East European Constitutional Review* 35–39.

Both of these scholars, and others, saw *Grootboom* as the approach best able to reconcile social rights with the challenges of judicial review. Because social rights raised particularly serious challenges for the capacity and legitimacy of courts, weak-form review would allow courts to enforce them without overstepping their bounds. *Grootboom* in essence allowed the judiciary to remind courts of their obligations by holding that there was a constitutional violation, while leaving the policy choice up to the political branches, which are better suited to making those choices. Sunstein argues that the remedy in *Grootboom* had the virtue of "promoting a certain kind of deliberation" in the political sphere without "placing undue strain on judicial capacities."[38] Tushnet likewise argues that weak-form review answers many of the practical critiques of the enforcement of social and economic rights, while acknowledging that it may be insufficient to actually realize progress on those rights in some cases, and even that the model may prove unstable as litigants and judges grow frustrated with the slow pace of change.[39]

Tushnet's last point, however, highlights the peculiar nature of this international read of the South African jurisprudence. First, it is incomplete – it tends to focus on a small handful of early cases (*Grootboom* particularly, but also *TAC*, *Khosa* and *Soobramoney*), while paying less attention to the Court's so-called "second wave" social rights cases, especially its engagement cases.[40] Second, the literature by domestic scholars and experts on the country regarding the South African Constitutional Court's early social rights jurisprudence has been much more critical. A number of these scholars have argued that progress on the realization of rights has been insufficient. They have criticized, for example, the Court's persistent refusal to define and use the minimum core, its refusal to issue stronger remedies such as structural injunctions, and its avoidance of constitutional interpretation in favor of narrower resolutions and sub-constitutional issues, even while acknowledging progress within the particular political and social context.[41] The general tenor of these critiques is that the Court could have achieved more if it was willing to give more substantive content to social rights, interpret them in ways that are harder edged and give the state less discretion to avoid their compliance, and adopt stronger remedies that would push the state toward greater and faster compliance with these norms.

[38] Sunstein, *Designing Democracy* 235–37.

[39] Tushnet, *Weak Courts, Strong Rights* 242–4, 254.

[40] Ray, *Engaging with Social Rights* 4.

[41] Bilchitz, *Poverty and Fundamental Rights*; Liebenberg, *Socio-Economic Rights* 173; D. M. Davis, "Adjudicating the socio-economic rights in the South African Constitution: Towards 'deference lite'?" (2006) 2 *South African Journal on Human Rights* 301–27.

A final key point is that the South African approach has not been widely copied by other courts. Many courts in Europe, Asia and Latin America, for example, have a robust tradition of enforcing social rights that has been almost completely untouched by *Grootboom* and that utilize very different devices to those noted above, such as enforcing individual rights to a service, blocking budgetary changes that reduce funding for pension or other benefits, or issuing and monitoring structural injunctions.[42] That is, the academic impact of the early South African jurisprudence has exceeded its impact on judiciaries around the world. This might again suggest that the South African approach is not a general response to a common problem, but something more particular.

This "curious divergence" between these different receptions of *Grootboom* suggests perhaps that the international scholarship does not have the question framed quite right.[43] Both Tushnet and Sunstein, for example, are writing from the tradition of US constitutional theory. The literature that they are responding to (1) views the counter-majoritarian difficulty, or the tension between judicial review and democracy, as the central question of constitutional theory and (2) views social rights as especially problematic, and thus as needing special justification and care.[44] Both of these frames push courts toward special levels of deference in the enforcement of social rights. In a comparative perspective, however, neither of these framings are self-evident. The tension between judicial review and democracy is a relevant issue in most countries where judicial review exists, but the intensity of these debates seems to vary from place to place, and is particularly high among the academic community in the United States.[45] The problematic or exceptional character of social rights is also a view that varies from place to place, and is often viewed as an off-shoot of American exceptionalism (although most constitutions of United States contain those rights).[46] Most new constitutions include social rights[47] and many courts around the world now enforce them in some form.

All of this suggests that some of the external scholarship on *Grootboom* is using it to answer the wrong question, or at least not the only question.

42 Landau, "The reality of social rights enforcement" 196–201.

43 T. Roux, *The Politics of Principle: The First South African Constitutional Court, 1995–2005* (Cambridge: Cambridge University Press, 2013) 262.

44 Tushnet, *Weak Courts, Strong Rights* 231–7; Sunstein, *Designing Democracy* 223.

45 S. Issacharoff, *Fragile Democracies: Contested Power in the Era of Constitutional Courts* (Cambridge: Cambridge University Press, 2015) 157, 279.

46 M. Versteeg and E. Zackin, "American Constitutional Exceptionalism Revisited" (2014) 81 *The University of Chicago Law Review* 1641–707 at 1681.

47 Although not all rights are equally common, the right to education is particularly widespread. C. Jung, R. Hirschl and E. Rosevear, "Economic and social rights in national constitutions" (2014) 62 *American Journal of Comparative Law* 1043–98.

From a certain perspective, for example, it may misstate the core challenge in enforcing social rights, which is effectiveness rather than the separation of powers. The question then would be: Which approach to enforcing social rights is most likely to succeed in carrying out social change? This change, of course, is a complex task in part because of limitations on judicial capacity and legitimacy. A court will likely need to play a "catalytic" role and gain the support of actors like civil society, rather than relying solely on the force of its own decisions.[48] But in this view the constraints of the separation of powers are flexible ones in the service of constitutional realization, rather than the primary challenge faced by enforcers of social rights. One need not accept the entirety "global south" critique of social rights wholesale to see that the meaning of the South African social rights jurisprudence may have been distorted to some degree by the projects of the US constitutional theorists who promoted it.[49]

16.2.2. *The South African Model as a Contextual Response*

A sharp alternative to the international narrative that grew up around the *Grootboom* case is to instead view the Court's work as a product of its particular social and political context. This story emerged as something of a revision to the initial international reception. Remedial complexity, for example, could be explained through the high capacity of the South African judiciary. Other courts that have relied heavily on complex remedies, such as India and Colombia, similarly seem to have been staffed by high-capacity judges. The pro-poor focus of the Court could be explained either through the identity of the judges on the Court or through the "transformative" vision of the South African constitution and the historical context from which it sprang.

Several contextual factors may also explain the deference of the South African Court. The first is constitutional text – the Constitution includes social rights to housing and healthcare but then qualifies them by stating that the main obligation is for the state to take "reasonable legislative and other measures, within its available resources, to achieve the progressive realisation" of each right.[50] The second is political context – the South African one-party state constrains the Court, preventing it from taking more aggressive action

48 Young, *Constituting Economic and Social Rights* 174–5.

49 D. B. Maldonado, "Introduction: towards a constitutionalism of the global south" in D. B. Maldonado (ed.), *Constitutionalism of the Global South: The Activist Tribunals of India, South Africa, and Colombia* (Cambridge: Cambridge University Press, 2013) 1.

50 Constitution of the Republic of South Africa 1996, arts. 26–27.

for the enforcement of social rights as in other areas.[51] Finally, the nature of the legal culture, which created a sharp divide between law and politics, may have made the Court more receptive to arguments based on the separation of powers than some other courts, and less willing to undertake aggressive interventions.[52]

This highly contextual story may also help to explain the lack of direct influence of the South African model on other courts. The South African approach may require a combination of factors that is unlikely to occur very often in comparative constitutional law: a high-capacity and innovative, yet somewhat formalistic, court working in a highly constrained political environment.

Many other courts active in enforcing social rights involve high-capacity institutions working in much less constrained political environments, where political fragmentation or other factors allow for a higher degree of judicial activism, and where judicial role conceptions are less formalistic. Colombia and India are notable examples.[53] In other cases, an unconstrained court (whether or not of a high capacity) may lack the innovative conception of judicial role displayed by the South African Court: the Brazilian Supreme Federal Tribunal, which has actively enforced social rights but focused on simpler remedies like simply ordering a treatment provided to an individual petitioner, is an example.[54] The Brazilian Tribunal in contrast has largely shied away from issuing complex remedies, and it may be that to such a court weak-form enforcement would not look much like judicial review at all.[55] Finally, a third, very common set of courts is both low capacity and highly constrained. Examples abound of courts operating in dominant-party systems that potentially lack the capacity and creativity to design innovative remedies – take Venezuela and Ecuador in Latin America, or many examples throughout Africa.

At the same time, the contextual story of the South African Court itself seems to be incomplete in some respects. The story about text, for example, is much weaker than it at first appears. The textual framing of the rights in the South African constitution is fairly distinctive by comparative standards. But

[51] T. Roux, "Principle and pragmatism on the Constitutional Court of South Africa" (2009) 7 *International Journal of Constitutional Law* 106–38 at 107; S. Choudhry, "'He had a mandate': The South African Constitutional Court and the African National Congress in a dominant party democracy" (2010) 2 *Constitutional Court Review* 1–86.

[52] Roux, *The Politics of Principle* 230–1.

[53] N. Robinson, "Expanding judiciaries: India and the rise of the good governance court" (2009) 8 *Washington University Global Studies Law Review* 1–69; D. Landau, "Political institutions and judicial role in comparative constitutional law" (2010) 51 *Harvard International Law Journal* 321–77.

[54] Hoffmann and Bentes, "Accountability for social and economic rights in Brazil" 131.

[55] Ibid. 133.

it is very close to matching the framing of obligations in international law, particularly in the International Covenant on Economic, Social and Cultural Rights. And it was the Committee in charge of interpreting this treaty that articulated the minimum core as a key part of obligations under it, along with other ideas like progressive realization and nonretrogression.[56] Thus the South African Court's rejection of the minimum core cannot easily be explained by text.[57] Moreover, the argument ignores the fact that even in some countries where the text has rendered social rights expressly nonjusticiable, courts have developed ways to enforce these rights, for instance by linking them to textually enforceable rights like the rights to life and human dignity. India's robust social rights jurisprudence is a good example.[58]

The story based on legal culture also seems in some respects incomplete. The combination of a high-capacity and yet formalistic court may indeed be fairly distinctive. However, an overly contextual analysis risks the ignoring of commonalities between the South African case and other cases. Legal formalism, for example, is common around much of the world. Nor should these characteristics be treated as immutable characteristics. Scholars have called for a contestation of South African legal culture, although the extent to which that contestation has actually occurred may be fairly limited.[59] A line of scholarship has argued, for example, that the new South African constitution required a sea-change in legal culture, away from a formalistic conception and toward a more transformational conception that will work social and political change.[60] Thus, essentializing the role of legal culture in South African jurisprudence threatens to deemphasize the amount of potential contestation within that culture. And as in many other contexts, enforcement of social rights seems to necessitate some shifts in conceptions of judicial role.

The political context argument is obviously the strongest of these three arguments; without question the ANC's dominant position has constrained

56 UN Committee on Economic, Social and Cultural Rights (CESCR), *General Comment No. 3: The Nature of States Parties' Obligations* (5th session, 1990) U.N. Doc. E/1991/23.

57 In *Grootboom* para. 28, the Court noted some modest differences between the textual formulation of the Covenant and the South African Constitution: "(a) The Covenant provides for a *right to adequate housing* while section 26 provides for the *right of access* to adequate housing. (b) The Covenant obliges states parties to take *appropriate* steps which must include legislation while the Constitution obliges the South African state to take *reasonable* legislative and other measures."

58 R. Sudarshan, "Courts and social transformation in India," in R. Gargarella, P. Domingo and T. Roux (eds.), *Courts and Social Transformation in New Democracies: An Institutional Voice for the Poor?* (Aldershot: Ashgate, 2006) 153 at 157–8.

59 Roux, *Politics of Principle* 192.

60 Klare, "Legal culture and transformative constitutionalism."

the Court. But as Roux has pointed out, these constraints are not absolute – they leave room for strategy and agency.[61] The ANC's commitment to the transformative constitution has in the past given the Court room to push the party on achievement of the social rights contained in the text.[62] The Court certainly has had more room to act on these issues than, for example, in advancing the rights of political minorities where it has been highly constrained.[63] The Court has chosen a particular set of approaches to achieve these goals. It has hewed close to the ANC in doing so, at times, for example, using social rights to legitimate the projects of the ruling party that might otherwise be suspect as discriminatory or as violating property rights. At other times, it has exploited divisions within the ANC, and popular support, to issue rulings where it receives support from some significant sectors of the party – Roux notes the TAC case as an example.[64] This means that the Court has chosen a set of jurisprudential approaches and strategies from a much broader set of possibilities.

Moreover, political context, like legal culture, may change over time. Very recently, the ANC has begun losing some of its dominance (especially at the local level) because of concerns over corruption and other issues. And as the political system fragments, this may open up new spaces for the Court. Thus, rather than treating the Court's approach as a fixed response to context, it may be sensible to ask how alternative approaches might have worked differently in that context.

16.3. AN ALTERNATIVE VIEW OF THE SIGNIFICANCE OF THE SOUTH AFRICAN JURISPRUDENCE

This leads to a third – and I think better – way to conceptualize the importance of the social rights jurisprudence of the South African Constitutional Court. This path rejects the view that the Court has found the universalist answer to the enforcement of these rights, drawn from broader tenets of constitutional theory. It likewise seeks a different perspective from one that views the Court's work as primarily of interest as a response to a particular political and legal context. Instead, it is worth drawing out the Court's work as an example of a judiciary that has been seriously engaged both with the project of enforcing social rights and with the difficulties derived therefrom. In that light, one

61 Roux, "Principle and pragmatism on the Constitutional Court of South Africa" 108.
62 Roux, *Politics of Principle* 388.
63 Ibid. 335.
64 Roux, "Principle and pragmatism" 125.

productive thing to do is to put the collective experiences of those courts seriously involved in the project of enforcing social rights – mostly found in the global south – in dialogue. Such an enterprise – urgently needed – has not been done, at least not to the rigorous degree that would be necessary.

The first element of such a task would be to recognize commonalities among different contexts, even while acknowledging their differences. There are many features of the South African context that are similar to what has been found elsewhere, particularly in the global south. For example, the arc of South African jurisprudence helps to explain some of the difficulties confronted by courts working in such contexts who seek dialogical forms of judicial review. The Court's initial approach in *Grootboom* fit the classical model of "weak-form" review: it pointed out a constitutional deficiency and invited the legislature to fix that deficiency. But subsequent attempts have not fit the paradigm as well. Instead of inviting legislative responses, the Court has adopted a more "managerial" model, seeking to place procedural (and to some extent substantive) constraints on eviction processes in an effort to protect vulnerable populations.[65]

At least within a global south context, this shift responds to familiar pressures: the risk that political institutions will prove either unresponsive or insufficiently responsive to a judicial invitation for dialogue. At times, this may drive the Court to place more substantive or procedural teeth on the review process. It may also drive shifts in the form and nature of dialogue, for example, away from legislative institutions and toward bureaucracies. The full sweep of the South African jurisprudence thus suggests that dialogical forms of judicial review may not make as much sense in global south contexts. They are, as Dixon argues, insufficiently attentive to the "blind spots" and "inertia" that afflict legislatures and other government actors, particularly in these contexts.[66] By making the main partner in dialogue the legislature, they also underplay gaps between law on the books and law in action, which are commonly seen as particularly pervasive in those contexts.

Perhaps the key task of social rights enforcement is thus to improve the performance of recalcitrant or dysfunctional bureaucracies. Those courts that have wrestled most seriously with the enforcement of social rights have all placed this problem close to the center of their models of enforcement. As three examples, not of the enforcement of social rights more generally but of those courts whose enforcement might be seen as canonical, we could mention

65 Ray, *Engaging with Social Rights* 209–11.

66 R. Dixon, "Creating dialogue about socioeconomic rights: strong-form versus weak-form judicial review revisited" (2007) 5 *International Journal of Constitutional Law* 391–418.

the Indian and Colombian high courts in addition to the South African. The three approaches have been quite different, but share some similarities. The Colombian and Indian courts have been more willing than the South African Court to use strong forms of review. The best-known example of social rights enforcement in each country is a structural injunction, on displaced persons in Colombia and the right to food litigation in India.[67] These are approaches that the South African Constitutional Court has generally been less willing to undertake.

At the same time, these various approaches share some commonalities. All rely at least in significant part on complex forms of review, suggesting that interventions reaching beyond a single individual are often needed to create bureaucratic change. Courts in all three cases also seem to be balancing several different concerns. First, the courts recognize that they cannot directly impose the details of policy, but must preserve space for governmental actors to do so. Second, the role of the courts is to prod the bureaucracy into effective action for the realization of social rights. Young calls this the "catalytic" function of judicial review, although it is not simply a question of incentivizing bureaucracies to pay attention to issues that they may have overlooked, but often also of building bureaucratic capacity on constitutional issues.[68] That is, noncompliance is often not caused in large part by a hostile bureaucracy, but by an incompetent, understaffed, or underfunded one. Finally, across all of these systems courts have tried to draft in help from nonjudicial actors – the process of prodding the bureaucracy toward compliance inevitably seems to require ample assistance from nonjudicial actors, such as civil society, private parties, or other state actors such as control organs.

There may be a number of different ways to aim at these goals. The structural injunctions in Colombia and India, like engagement and other remedies found in South Africa, are in this sense dialogical in nature. They seek to prod bureaucracies into changing practices or resolving problems, without directly setting the details of policy.[69] The differences are ones of degree, not of kind. The structural approach perhaps seeks to place more pressure on bureaucratic

[67] S. Shankar, "The embedded negotiators: India's higher judiciary and socioeconomic rights," in D. Bonilla Maldonado (ed.), *Constitutionalism of the Global South: The Activist Tribunals of India, South Africa, and Colombia* (Cambridge: Cambridge University Press, 2013) 95 at 120–1; C. Rodriguez-Garavito and D. Rodriguez-Franco, *Radical Deprivation on Trial: The Impact of Judicial Activism on Socioeconomic Rights in the Global South* (Cambridge: Cambridge University Press, 2015).

[68] Young, *Constituting Economic and Social Rights* 174.

[69] D. Landau, "Aggressive weak-form remedies" (2013) 5 *Constitutional Court Review* 244–64 at 247–50.

actors; it may also require that courts make more substantive decisions about the scope of a given right and its implementation. But one can envision these different approaches as lying along a spectrum, or perhaps more helpfully as constituting different tools in a toolkit.[70]

One value of the rich South African social rights jurisprudence is in contributing to the range of tools that can be used to enforce social rights. Approaches like engagement are unusual in comparative constitutional law at least for the enforcement of socioeconomic rights.[71] Moreover, the range of South African cases suggests that it is a flexible tool: administrative actors can be given relatively stringent procedural and substantive guidance, or relatively little. The South African Court's other "experimental" jurisprudence, such as the innovative damages remedy in *Modderklip*, also suggest creative ways in which courts can incentivize governmental actors to develop or improve policies and programs.

To date, and despite the extensive literature on South Africa, the scholarly imagination has only partially internalized the value of this jurisprudence. It has focused disproportionately on early cases like *Grootboom*, while not paying enough attention to the more varied and experimental subsequent jurisprudence.[72] More importantly, framing this jurisprudence as either the universalist answer to the enforcement of social rights or a merely contextual product has lessened the scholarly and judicial interchange that could be occurring with methods of enforcement.

One can identify several different approaches to the enforcement of social rights that are distinctive in comparative constitutional law for the enforcement of social rights: (1) weak-form review, as in *Grootboom*, where the Court seeks to prod the legislature into developing new programs or legislation to tackle important problems; (2) engagement, where the Court seeks to put governmental actors together with those affected by an eviction or other action, in order to incentivize them to reach agreement; and (3) private remedies, such as in *Modderklip*, where the Court forces the state to pay damages to private actors that it has incidentally damaged because of its failure to realize

[70] Ibid. 248.

[71] An analogous form of enforcement, however, does exist in some countries and under international law where state authorities are required to undertake processes of consultation with indigenous groups affected by projects on their lands. Convention (No. 169) concerning Indigenous and Tribal Peoples in Independent Countries, International Labour Organization, June 27, 1989, art. 6. For examples of the Colombian jurisprudence on this issue, see D. Landau and M. José Cepeda Espinosa, *Colombian Constitutional Law: Leading Cases* (Oxford: Oxford University Press, 2017).

[72] Ray, *Engaging with Social Rights* 4.

social rights.[73] Fundamentally, each of these tools is flexible; they can be given increasing or decreasing levels of judicial oversight depending on the circumstance. Comparative experience, as well as variation within the South African case, suggests ways in which this could be done. Deadlines, regulation of process or substance, continuing judicial oversight and follow-up orders, commissions of state actors or other groups, public hearings by the Court, and reporting requirements by the government or by state control institutions are some of the devices that have been used inside and outside of South Africa for this purpose.

A striking feature of all three of the South African Court's approaches mentioned above is that they rely heavily on external actors, aside from the Court and the government. For classical weak-form review to work, civil society groups will likely need to pressure the legislature into compliance. Engagement and the damages model likewise rely on nonstate actors to incentivize state compliance. When choosing between models, therefore, one of the things a court must consider is the distribution of external support in a given area. The Court has shown some sensitivity to this distribution – for example, it adopted a stronger remedy in *TAC*, a case that was brought by a robust civil society movement and was backed by significant public support.[74] At the same time, the remedial and interpretative approaches chosen by the Court can themselves have an effect on the strength and shape of this support.[75]

Here perhaps is where engagement with comparative approaches could be most beneficial. By changing the contexts within which engagement was deployed or the participants in the process, courts could draw in more civil society support. The South African Constitutional Court has primarily used engagement as a way to manage the process of eviction. It could be used more broadly, as Ray has recently argued, to shape policymaking.[76] For example, engagement could be required during certain legislative or administrative processes. Courts could also invite in a broader range of actors, beyond those, for example, who are involved in a given eviction process. Broadening the sphere of involved actors may help to broaden the impact of a given process. Other instruments, such as civil society commissions charged with monitoring compliance and formulating policy proposals, public hearings in which state

73 For a broader discussion, consult Liebenberg, *Socio-economic Rights Adjudication* 438–47.

74 Young, *Constituting Economic and Social Rights* 258–62; Roux, "Principle and pragmatism" 125.

75 Landau, "Aggressive weak-form remedies" 264.

76 Ray, *Engaging with Social Rights* 274.

actors are held to account by civil society groups, and charges to other state control institutions to monitor and report on government compliance, may also help a court to draw in allies that will help push bureaucrats toward compliance and improve governmental performance over time.[77]

The overarching point here is that the South African Court's jurisprudence can usefully be understood as a significant participant to a global dialogue on how to enforce social rights, one which must be refined through creativity, experience and careful attention to context. Advancing this dialogue of course requires that we adopt an approach that is rigorously empirical: it requires that we study, with great care, the effects of different approaches in their political and legal contexts. Some of this work has been carried out, both inside and outside South Africa, but much remains to be done. Comparative constitutional law at this stage can at least suggest some empirical questions that should be asked based on South Africa's jurisprudence, and elsewhere.

For example, how has the series of engagement remedies impacted the behavior of local bureaucracies through time? How has the Court's jurisprudence affected the rights consciousness of citizens toward social rights, or the nature of the country's constitutional culture? Has the jurisprudence of the Court had an impact on the strength and orientation of civil society working on related issues? How has the rigorously pro-poor approach of the Court impacted its patterns of support from the public and other groups? If we can answer these questions not just for South Africa but also for other jurisdictions, we can move beyond a merely classificatory literature and begin to answer questions about which kinds of approaches work in different contexts. The distinctive character of the South African Court's jurisprudence – its complex and creative but deferential nature, and its pro-poor emphasis – make it an ideal place in which to gain insight into some of those answers.

16.4. CONCLUSION

The social rights jurisprudence of the South African Constitutional Court is now firmly established as part of the canon of comparative constitutional law. This chapter has not sought to knock it out of the canon, but it has sought to reframe its significance. Rather than viewing the work of the Court as the model for other jurisdictions, it has argued that its distinctive approach – complex, deferential and pro-poor – is most usefully placed in dialogue with other courts, particularly in the global south, as part of a search for common

77 Landau, "Aggressive weak-form remedies" 260–1.

concerns and solutions, albeit ones informed by the nuances of political and legal context. The creative approaches of the Court have added to the repertoire of tools possessed by judges seeking to enforce social rights, and the Court's rich and experimental jurisprudence offers an empirical testing ground for key questions in the field. How much influence the South African jurisprudence is likely to have, of course, is likely to depend in large part on contextual factors. At least in the short run, for example, the Court is likely to matter more in Anglophone parts of Africa than in the very different interpretive and enforcement traditions of Latin America. And it may be that some aspects of the Court's approach are most useful in other countries with similar kinds of political constraint. But despite its contextual specificity, it is still possible and useful to view the South African Constitutional Court's social rights jurisprudence as part of a common struggle toward better answers to the difficult questions raised by the enforcement of these rights.

Index

For EU product safety concerns, contact us at Calle de José Abascal, 56–1°, 28003 Madrid, Spain or eugpsr@cambridge.org.

www.ingramcontent.com/pod-product-compliance
Lightning Source LLC
LaVergne TN
LVHW052020200926
848481LV00005B/1538